The First Prejudice

EARLY AMERICAN STUDIES

SERIES EDITORS
Daniel K. Richter, Kathleen M. Brown, and David Waldstreicher

Exploring neglected aspects of our colonial, revolutionary, and early national history and culture, Early American Studies reinterprets familiar themes and events in fresh ways. Interdisciplinary in character, and with a special emphasis on the period from about 1600 to 1850, the series is published in partnership with the McNeil Center for Early American Studies.

A complete list of books in the series is available from the publisher.

The First Prejudice

Religious Tolerance and Intolerance in Early America

EDITED BY

Chris Beneke and Christopher S. Grenda

PENN

UNIVERSITY OF PENNSYLVANIA PRESS

PHILADELPHIA · OXFORD

Copyright © 2011 University of Pennsylvania Press

All rights reserved. Except for brief quotations used for purposes of review or scholarly citation, none of this book may be reproduced in any form by any means without written permission from the publisher.

Published by
University of Pennsylvania Press
Philadelphia, Pennsylvania 19104-4112
www.upenn.edu/pennpress

Printed in the United States of America on acid-free paper
10 9 8 7 6 5 4 3 2 1

Library of Congress Cataloging-in-Publication Data
The first prejudice : religious tolerance and intolerance in early America / edited by Chris Beneke and Christopher S. Grenda.
    p. cm.— (Early American studies)
  Includes bibliographical references (p.) and index.
  ISBN 978-0-8122-4270-6 (hardcover : alk. paper)
    1. United States—Church history—17th century.
2. United States—Church history—18th century.
3. United States—Religion—To 1800.   4. Religious tolerance—United States.   I. Beneke, Chris (Christopher J.)   II. Grenda, Christopher S.
  BR517.F55 2011
  277.3'07—dc22
                                          2010015803

Contents

Introduction   1
    CHRIS BENEKE AND CHRISTOPHER S. GRENDA

PART I
Ideologies of Tolerance and Intolerance in Early America

Chapter 1. Faith, Reason, and Enlightenment:
The Cultural Sources of Toleration in Early America   23
    CHRISTOPHER S. GRENDA

Chapter 2. Amalek and the Rhetoric of Extermination   53
    JOHN CORRIGAN

PART II
Practices of Tolerance and Intolerance in Colonial British America

Chapter 3. The Episcopate, the British Union, and the Failure of Religious Settlement in Colonial British America   75
    NED LANDSMAN

Chapter 4. Practicing Toleration in Dutch New Netherland   98
    JOYCE D. GOODFRIEND

Chapter 5. Heretics, Blasphemers, and Sabbath Breakers:
The Prosecution of Religious Crime in Early America   123
    SUSAN JUSTER

Chapter 6. Persecuting Quakers? Liberty and Toleration in Early Pennsylvania   143
    Andrew R. Murphy

PART III
The Boundaries of Tolerance and Intolerance in Early America

Chapter 7. Native Freedom? Indians and Religious Tolerance in Early America   169
    Richard W. Pointer

Chapter 8. Slaves to Intolerance: African American Christianity and Religious Freedom in Early America   195
    Jon Sensbach

Chapter 9. Catholics, Protestants, and the Clash of Civilizations in Early America   218
    Owen Stanwood

Chapter 10. Anti-Semitism, Toleration, and Appreciation: The Changing Relations of Jews and Gentiles in Early America   241
    William Pencak

PART IV
The Persistence of Tolerance and Intolerance in the New Nation

Chapter 11. The "Catholic Spirit Prevailing in Our Country": America's Moderate Religious Revolution   265
    Chris Beneke

Chapter 12. The Boundaries of Toleration and Tolerance: Religious Infidelity in the Early American Republic   286
    Christopher Grasso

Notes   303

List of Contributors   385

Index   389

Introduction

CHRIS BENEKE AND CHRISTOPHER S. GRENDA

In colonial British America, religion distinguished outsiders from insiders. It furnished many of the categories through which people were classified, separating the saved from the damned, Christians from heathens, Protestants from Catholics, and conformists from dissenters. Like other means of social sorting before and since, religious distinctions offered seventeenth- and eighteenth-century communities a rich trove of justifications for discrimination. Yet in some places and in some times in early America, as in early modern Europe, diversity in religious belief and practice served markedly different functions, presenting occasions for both cross-cultural cooperation and earnest pleas for liberty. To the degree that the people inhabiting this place and time shared our modern understandings of intolerance and tolerance, they did so in the domain of religion. In the multiple ways that the following chapters illustrate, religion was the United States' first prejudice—an early and frequently inveterate source of bigotry, and the locus of the first sustained efforts to mitigate bigotry's effects.

The importance of early American religion is well established. For decades, surveys of colonial, early national, and antebellum U.S. history have abounded with ministers, theologies, revivals, and vague spiritual influences. Pre–Civil War histories have, Jon Butler observes, "long featured religion at almost every critical interpretative point."[1] Since the late 1980s, religion's historiographical weight has held steady. However, the field has changed in ways that reflect larger shifts in the study of American history, and that carry important implications for scholarship on religious tolerance and intolerance.[2] To begin, there has been a noticeable drift in emphasis from intellectual toward social and cultural history, from formal theology toward the "lived" experience of everyday practices and beliefs, and from denominational and church histories toward dynamic interactions within and between groups. Reflecting the broader disciplinary turn to cultural history, the language of encounters, negotiation, and discourse have entrenched themselves within the lexicon of religious historians; categories of analysis such as race and gender have reframed the outlines of research and argument; and, new objects of study such as material goods, sexual practices, and camp meetings have emerged as fertile domains of inquiry. Recent historians of early American religion have proven especially adept at uncovering and highlighting new forms of religious diversity as well as narrating the cross-confessional play of ritual and belief among Native Americans, African Americans, and European Americans. Compared to the state of the field just a few decades ago, we now possess a robust understanding of particular ethnic religious groups and specific religious traditions, from the subtleties of Native American spiritual syncretism to the mobilizing political discourse of Christian republicanism.[3] But despite the attention paid to the variety of early American faiths and the multifaceted range of borrowing and exchange that took place between them, leading religious historians have largely ceded the study of toleration and church-state relations to legal and constitutional scholars.[4]

For their part, historians of toleration and church and state have been mostly unswayed by the shifting currents of American religious history, including its recent turn to cultural and social study. Instead, they have continued to argue within a relatively autonomous and voluminous body of literature which focuses on the colonial origins of "original intent" and derives its substance from legislative enactments, constitutional maneuvering, and the intentions of leading founders. To be sure, many scholars in this field have provided nuanced accounts of the colonial, state, and national political and legal conditions that shaped the nation's new church-state frameworks. They have also placed interpretations of early state and federal constitutions within long traditions of ideological development.[5] Taken as a whole, however, the literature on church-state relations in early America has not accounted for the breadth of religious diversity in colonial British America and the early national United States nor the manifold ways in which tolerance and intolerance were justified and practiced.[6]

The First Prejudice uses the insights of religious history and church-state scholarship to illuminate the knotted contours of religious difference in early America. It considers religion as a source of legal repression, political conflict, group attachment, cultural transcendence, and individual freedom in the area that became the United States. The authors of the following chapters depart from both recent scholarship on the history of religious culture and the venerable study of church-state relations by their willingness to relate changes in law and rhetoric to the social experience of religious differences across British America and the early United States. They gaze broadly across the vast expanse of tolerance and intolerance in America, at the many varieties of persecution and the various manifestations of toleration, at the groups that were immediately affected by constitutional guarantees of religious liberty, and those that were not. In short, the essays in this volume should help both scholars and students develop common interpretive schemes and identify intersection points where the tangle of regulations, rhetoric, and customs that governed relations between early American faiths can be addressed without reflexively defaulting to the languages of toleration, religious freedom, or church and state.[7]

The constitutional events most closely associated with the history of toleration in early America—notably, the English Toleration Act of 1689, the Virginia Statute for Religious Freedom of 1786, and the ratification of the First Amendment in 1791—play a vital but not determinative role in the interpretations advanced in this volume. Neither are larger concatenations of events, such as the American Revolution, simply presumed to have wrought great or universal change. Although one author (Chris Beneke) does make the case that the Revolutionary era marked a widespread and durable transformation, others (such as William Pencak) discern less remarkable signs of change. And several contributors detect high levels of continuity across the seventeenth and eighteenth centuries, especially in the religious provisions that applied to enslaved people and Native Americans (Jon Sensbach and Richard W. Pointer), the structures of ideological justification (John Corrigan and Christopher S. Grenda), and the fraught relationship between the imperatives of civil order and the limitations on dissent (Susan Juster and Christopher Grasso).

Gauging how much tolerance or intolerance there was at any given place in early America, and whether it waxed or waned over time, presumes that we possess a stable sense of what tolerance and intolerance meant in the seventeenth, eighteenth, and early nineteenth centuries. But before we can appreciate the degree of change that took place in early America, we need to concede that almost no North America British colony would have warranted the term "tolerance" as it is used today. Well into the eighteenth century (and in some cases beyond), a belief in God, Christ, and sometimes both books of Christian scripture served as a legal prerequisite for enjoying full civil privileges. Religious bigotry made its way into countless interstices within the culture. Non-Christian faiths were bereft of formal legal protections and their African and Native American adherents were objects of forceful and repeated rounds of proselytization. Roman Catholics endured especially severe laws in this largely Protestant region (Connecticut threatened priests with banishment on their first appearance in the colony and death on the second).[8] Sunday Sabbath laws were enforced in many places and printed on the statute books everywhere. Dissenting practices were often forbidden and, if permitted, mostly kept from public view. Even colonies that served as havens for religious minorities imposed burdens that would be regarded as examples of religious intolerance today. Pennsylvania required an affirmation of Christian belief, "banned blasphemy, forbade Sunday labor, and urged settlers to attend church."[9] Rhode Island permitted only Christians to vote. Other colonies were considerably less accommodating to religious dissenters. The majority of the free colonial population lived under religious establishments, either Congregationalist (Massachusetts, Connecticut, and New Hampshire) or Anglican (Maryland, Virginia, North Carolina, South Carolina, and Georgia). In those colonies, as in most of Europe, government financial support was directed exclusively to state-sanctioned churches. Dissenting creeds, liturgical practices, and speech were all curtailed. There was literally little space for religious nonconformity—where they existed, established churches dominated the political, social, and physical landscape.

Of course, decreeing uniformity was one thing; achieving it was another. As the chapters by Susan Juster, Joyce Goodfriend, and Andrew Murphy illustrate, colonial regimes (even more than their contemporary European counterparts) rarely possessed the means to enforce a single system of doctrine, let alone determine what individuals actually believed. They might have succeeded at shaping the public religious environment, but that was not the same thing as squelching dissent. In fact, historians have already documented how vigorous networks of popular "superstition" and unorthodox Christian practices lingered stubbornly across early modern Europe and America.[10] Despite unfriendly legal environments, for instance, African Americans continued to practice traditional burying rites and consult faith healers; meanwhile, as Richard Pointer notes in this volume, more than a few English Protestants adopted aspects of Native American healing rituals. The majority of American colonies remained somewhat effective at confining religious dissent to private homes and nondescript churches, and refusing to recognize publicly any faith other than the established one. They were also, as Juster details, often scrupulous about punishing blasphemous and irreverent speech, as well as Sabbath violations and nonpayment of ecclesiastical taxes. Less conspicuous forms of nonconformity, however, went mostly undisturbed. When it came to religion among free people in colonial America, totalizing forms of indoctrination were impossible and severe physical punishments for private dissent were rare; but humiliating and routinized forms of discrimination were common.

The complex backdrop of ethnic groups, faiths, and charter obligations in colonial British America also makes it difficult to render simple judgments about the trajectory of religious and constitutional change over time. Each British American colony featured its own set of distinctive laws and social characteristics that gave interreligious interactions a peculiar stamp. Religion in the Americas, as the historian Carla Gardina Pestana puts it, "sorted people into migration streams, so that Protestants generally went to the colonies of specific countries, Catholics mainly to others."[11] A similar sorting process took place among the white Protestant groups who settled within Britain's mainland North American colonies. English Congregationalists planted settlements in New England, Quakers in Pennsylvania, and Anglicans in the southern colonies of Georgia, Maryland, Virginia, and North and South Carolina. Beginning in the late seventeenth century, forms of religious belief and practice multiplied rapidly as several hundred thousand Africans entered the colonies and European immigration patterns diversified. Methodists, Baptists, and Presbyterians made headway in the South; German Lutherans and Calvinists and Scots-Irish Presbyterians pushed across Pennsylvania; while Baptists and separate Congregationalists disrupted the religious uniformity of which early New Englanders had once prided themselves. As enslaved Africans and embattled Native Americans adapted elements of Christian belief and practice, still more varieties of Protestant Christianity sprouted across the colonies. Smaller groups of Catholic and Jewish immigrants added to the increasingly heterogeneous array of eighteenth-century faiths.

Ironically, growing internal religious diversity made the British mainland colonies more alike—as did an increasingly systematized and expansive system of British imperial law.[12] Subtle and comprehensive political and legal changes were also taking place across Britain's North American mainland colonies during the latter part of the seventeenth and the early part of the eighteenth centuries that gave colonial experiences a more consistent character. By the 1730s, property restrictions on dissenting churches had eased across the British Empire and a relatively wide range of free colonists were permitted to use tax monies to support their own churches. An expanding supply of newspapers, pamphlets, and books addressing an increasingly diverse public both opened new avenues of expression for dissenters and loosened the ideological grip of the dominant faiths. The interdenominational mixing that occurred as a result of continual migration, a vibrant market economy, and imperial conflict worked to unravel the constitutive elements of religious inequality.[13] It also made it harder to align religious identity and tax collection with geographical location. As William Tennent put it in his 1777 argument against a nonpreferential establishment in South Carolina: "as people of different sentiments live intermingled, . . . there could be no possible distinction of parishes, so as to accommodate different denominations."[14] The more geographic places and religious identities were disentangled, the more religious lines were blurred, the more difficult it became to maintain exclusive establishments and degrading forms of spiritual regulation. (Whether there was more or less personal bigotry may prove impossible for historians to measure.) An assembly could easily enact a law that constrained the activity of groups that were not Anglican or Congregational. But what about the evangelical "separates" who started their own congregational churches or the Methodists who maintained their affiliation with the Anglican church but attacked its defining features? By the latter decades of the eighteenth century, the conditions were in place for the acceptance of a more formal and encompassing kind of religious tolerance

These changes represented the work of experience. Logic had its own imperatives. As intellectual historians and historians of church and state have made clear, Revolutionary- and Founding-era provisions for "religious liberty" were undergirded by two related principles: the essential interiority of belief and the inevitability of religious differences. Inspired by the liberal theology of the Enlightenment, conscience-centered traditions within Reformed Protestantism, and secular arguments against doctrinal coercion, the educated officials, ministers, and printers who molded opinion in the middle decades of the eighteenth century tended toward the conclusion that authentic faith was the product of personal experience and reflection. The dignity of the soul and the integrity of the mind required that individuals could only be persuaded, not compelled, to adopt new beliefs. Even if the resulting diversity was not intrinsically appealing to contemporaries, they now understood that the varieties of human experiences and perspectives made the pursuit of uniformity as impractical as it was dangerous.[15]

While principled justifications for religious protections were becoming the norm in Europe and North America, a third idea emerged as an integral component of what people understood as religious liberty: the necessity of public practice. Late eighteenth-century commentary on the subject was informed by the usually unstated conviction that protecting the inviolability of conscience meant protecting its expression. After all, what was a system of belief without a church to embody its ideas and a congregation to perform its rituals? And what was a church that could not own property or accept donations? While polemical and philosophical tracts continued to emphasize liberty of conscience, contemporary legislation signaled a firmer commitment to guaranteeing "free exercise" as a fundamental right. The new states in post-independence America embraced forms of liberty that secured religious minorities the liberty to articulate their beliefs in public, worship openly, and, in a growing number of cases, to place their churches on an equal legal footing.

One common area of concern for the authors in this volume is the shifting line between public and private belief and action, as well as the difference between civil and religious matters. Beginning as early as the mid-sixteenth century, religious dissenters had been able to escape direct persecution so long as they did not pose a perceptible political threat and so long as they kept their unorthodox views and practices to themselves.[16] They did have to be both law-abiding and discreet. With the advent of more expansive protections for liberty of conscience, church property, rituals, and speech acts were transformed into inalienable rights that were substantially less constrained by civil law and social convention. At the same time, religious belief was detached from its association with worldly harm. Thomas Jefferson is well known for his insouciant remark in the *Notes on the State of Virginia* that nothing his neighbor believed, or failed to believe, would cause real injury. But Jefferson had already made the point about the proper limits between civil government and religion more fully and with more direct legal consequences. His Virginia Statute for Establishing Religious Freedom stated that the magistrate had no rightful authority "to restrain the profession or propagation of principles, on the supposition of their ill tendency." The text continued: "that it is time enough for the rightful purposes of civil government, for its officers to interfere when principles break out into overt acts against peace and good order." In other words, beliefs were no more than opinions and rulers had no business speculating on their potential effects. Religious freedom required civil restraint and civil patience.[17] The underlying foundation of Jefferson's statute—the inviolability of conscience—was forcefully stated, yet relatively uncontroversial. But the corollaries that Jefferson drew, particularly the notion that belief (or nonbelief) possessed no intrinsic connection to civil law or political stability, did not claim broad fealty. There were still many, as Christopher Grasso's chapter on the treatment of freethought and skepticism in the new nation exhibits, who were wary of tolerating the slightest intimation of unbelief. The orthodox feared, as the orthodox had always feared, that dangerous religious (or irreligious) convictions would undermine civil society. The not inconsequential difference between the seventeenth and eighteenth centuries was that a smaller proportion of convictions qualified as dangerous, provisions for religious liberty protected dissidents, and punishments for flagrant acts of dissent were generally much less severe.

Narratives of tolerance and intolerance that move in a linear fashion from persecution to toleration have their skeptics, especially among historians of early modern Europe. Scholars such as Willem Frijhoff, Benjamin Kaplan, and Alexandra Walsham emphasize the frequency with which tolerant practices in western Europe coincided with persecutory laws.[18] They call this state of affairs "coexistence," which Frijhoff defines as "the ecumenism of everyday relations."[19] As employed by historians, coexistence can exist either with or without a legal system that protects rights of religious belief and practice. Simply put, coexistence amounts to a non-principled form of peaceful religious interaction.[20] Where it manifested itself in the seventeenth- and eighteenth-century world, coexistence was often the product of demographic inter-layerings, abrupt policy shifts, or regime changes that deposited fragments of everyday ecumenism on otherwise intolerant legal and social terrain. Where let-live policies were too convenient to forgo, too ingrained to eliminate, or too lucrative to abandon, coexistence prevailed.

The British American colonies featured at least some examples of non-state-sanctioned religious coexistence.[21] Joyce Goodfriend's chapter in this volume provides striking examples drawn from seventeenth-century New Netherland. There, she argues, Jews and Lutherans managed to practice their faiths and live prosperous lives despite their second-class legal status. Colonial Maryland offers another compelling example of "coexistence." The fortunes of Maryland's Catholics and Protestants shifted markedly during the second half of the seventeenth century because of political tumult in England. The resulting compromises between official intolerance and everyday ecumenism laid the groundwork for an un-official, inequitable, and long-lasting truce. Similarly, during the first decades of the eighteenth century, all of the major colonial port towns, like their European counterparts, supplied illustrations of Jews and Christians, as well as the members of different Protestant denominations, living together in relative harmony. A more formalized kind of inter-denominational peace prevailed in some legislative halls: by the beginning of the eighteenth century, dissenting Protestant groups were penetrating the political assemblies in colonies with established churches such as the Carolinas; and by the middle of the eighteenth century, political parties with strong denominational affiliation competed for power in the legislatures of Pennsylvania and New York.

The coexistence model of religious interaction reverses the temporal relationship between rhetoric and practice that has long held sway among students of colonial and early national U.S. history. Over the last several decades, early American historians have advanced arguments that give ideas causal and chronological priority over behavior and depict idealistic principles yielding mixed practices, or gross exceptions, that tragically handicap the principles themselves. Among the more popular subjects in this genre is Thomas Jefferson, whose lofty proclamations on human equality are frequently contrasted with his slaveholding and his later written ruminations on race. It is hard to argue with the conclusion that Jefferson was a deeply flawed proponent of universal natural rights. But the popular habit of historical unmasking that indicts him as a hypocrite also carries the potential to simplify the complex ways in which law, rhetoric, and social conventions interact with one another. Something similar happens when scholars dwell on the Revolutionary eruptions of religious liberty or, alternatively, on their self-limiting failures. Coexistence historians may be better able to avoid this pitfall by giving priority to contingency and the entrenched habits that frame everyday interactions and stressing that tolerant practices often preceded their rhetorical justification and legal sanction. They attend to the intricacy of community relations, political compromises, and arbitrary social arrangements as much as they do the injunctions of elite rhetoric or the formal obligations of the law.

Whether the coexistence framework will apply as well to early America remains to be seen.[22] Post-independence America may present a special challenge for this line of interpretation because in this period we find, as Chris Beneke maintains in his chapter, a series of unidirectional changes in law and practice favoring religious liberty and civility. There were undoubtedly many more instances of robust religious coexistence in the late eighteenth and early nineteenth centuries than there had been decades before. But the Founding era also ushered in a substantive measure of legal equality for free people in every state, especially those free people who were white and male. This transformation did not simply substitute one confessional regime with another (Congregationalists did not dislodge Anglicans; Catholics did not dislodge Protestants), or mark a temporary halt in the practice of religious intolerance.[23] Instead, republican and egalitarian regimes replaced monarchical and hierarchical regimes. Moreover, the subsequent mixing of people from different ethnic and religious traditions took place within a legal environment that protected the formal rights of religious minorities, rather than simply tolerating their existence. There was religious peace in the early republic and there was an abundance of amiable inter-confessional interaction; but there was also an emergent tradition of procedural equality in public rhetoric and state constitutions across the new nation that transcended interreligious arrangements at the local level and that were not easily reversed or offset by new forms of religious oppression. The apparently linear and durable quality of the American bias against state intervention in religious affairs (as Landsman sees it) and the post-Revolutionary religious settlement in favor of a broad and robust form of religious liberty (as Beneke sees it) sits uneasily with conclusions that might be drawn from a coexistence model of religious differences.

At present, we know little about what made coexistence possible or how much of it there was in early America. Nonetheless, the coexistence framework does provide a useful, albeit imperfect, model for charting the manifold ways in which laws, rhetoric, and practice intersected across early America. If this volume can bring mainstream religious history and its focus on identity and practice into a fuller dialogue with the traditional concerns of church-state history and its focus on ideology and law, it may become possible for teachers and scholars to communicate more confidently about the history of tolerance and intolerance in early America. There is hard work ahead. To understand how religious differences were lived in early America, we may need to resuscitate a long neglected tradition in American religious historiography: town and parish studies.[24] That would mean renewed attention to local records, not unlike what Susan Juster achieves in this volume on a broader canvas. It would also entail investigations of the many sites where inter-religious interaction took place, including the unlikely places that recent cultural and social history has equipped us to probe such as homes, shops, taverns, and the streets.

It is too early to say whether coexistence models, which emphasize the non-linear character of historical change, will serve students of early America better than more familiar intellectual and church-state narratives, which chart something referred to as "the rise of toleration." Nonetheless, by prompting us to reflect on the effects of legislation and published thought, as well as their enactment and articulation; by prodding us to consider the everyday encounters of different kinds of believers; and by raising fundamental questions about changes in the treatment of dissent and the relations between different religious groups, this framework provides us with ample ways to think anew about religious tolerance and intolerance in the colonial and early national United States.

The following chapters offer a broad overview of tolerance and intolerance in early America. They encompass a wide gamut of groups and regions from Savannah Jews and enslaved Carolinians to Pennsylvania Indians and New York Calvinists. They also address a large swath of time from the early seventeenth century to the first decades of the nineteenth century. Not every region or significant event receives sustained attention. For instance, readers may notice the absence of a familiar milestone in early American religious history: the mid-eighteenth-century evangelical revivals known as the first "Great Awakening." No conscious effort was made to exclude the Awakening, nor slight its transformative impact on Protestant Christianity. The new levels of religious commitment these revivals inspired and the individual autonomy they fostered had a profound effect on the interaction of religious groups throughout the Atlantic world. Nonetheless, *The First Prejudice* raises the possibility that early American religious historiography might be guided by an additional series of geographical and chronological markers that denote, for example, sites of coexistence, the segregation and integration of different religious groups, and turning points in the treatments of religious differences and religious dissenters. By relating practice, rhetoric, and law, the essays in this volume should sharpen scholarly and popular dialogue on the history of religion, as well as the history of church and state. They should also contribute to a more illuminating and useful conversation about religious differences in colonial British America and the early United States.

The contributors' shared interest in religious diversity does not mean that they have composed a portrait of unbounded complexity. Indisputable patterns emerge over the course of this volume. It is clear, for instance, that tolerance and intolerance in British America were shaped by streams of ideology and law that cut deep grooves into the culture and placed severe constraints on the use of language and practice. As Christopher S. Grenda explains in "Faith, Reason, and Enlightenment: The Cultural Sources of Toleration in Early America," colonial Americans had little new to say about toleration. The flow of seventeenth- and early eighteenth-century arguments in favor of toleration moved essentially one way: from Europe to the colonies. For Grenda, sacred reasoning with concepts and passages drawn directly from the Bible best accounts for both the expansion and the peculiar contours of arguments on behalf of religious tolerance in early America. Such reasoning was, he argues, the chief means by which (nonconformist) sectarians advanced their influential case for toleration across the Anglo-American world. As a chief source of early modern ideas, the Bible and the Christian theology derived from it were deeply implicated in justifying intolerance as well. John Corrigan's account of the oft-cited Old Testament trope of the Amalekites ("Amalek and the Rhetoric of Extermination") and its American career illustrates how effectively European-born forms of biblical reasoning could justify colonial and early national persecution. The example of the unfortunate Amalekites provided a scriptural model of ethnic and religious violence, whereby the persecutors ascribed treachery, secrecy, and cowardice to the persecuted. Their story played a crucial role in structuring thinking about interreligious interaction in early America by supplying a sacred vocabulary through which the destruction of Native American villages and the harassment of European religious outsiders could be justified. There were many other models to be culled from the Bible, as well as almost two millennia of Christian thought and practice. When they persecuted, as when they tolerated, early Americans worked within the sometimes narrow confines of western European tradition.

More than just ideas about toleration made the cultural migration from Europe to America. Laws, institutions, and practices made the voyage as well. In "The Episcopate, the British Union, and the Failure of Religious Settlement in Colonial British America," Ned Landsman reconstructs the multitiered legal arrangements that molded both religious establishments and religious liberty within a large and complex imperial system. By accommodating competing establishments, this transatlantic legal pluralism created spaces for a relatively wide range of European faith and practice. In contrast to Grenda who sees more continuity than change in the development of early American understandings of religious tolerance, Landsman maintains that opposition to proposals for a colonial episcopate were essential to carving out a distinctive form of religious liberty that gave priority to "the freedom of the church from the state."

And yet there was often a conspicuous gap between early modern theories of tolerance and intolerance, colonial and imperial law, and the actual treatment of dissenters as both Joyce Goodfriend and Susan Juster make clear. Goodfriend's "Practicing Toleration in Dutch New Netherland" provides a vivid illustration of this historical disconnect. Her account of seventeenth-century New Netherland reveals how limited the legal rights of dissenters were in the presence of an established church and a unsympathetic state—the Dutch reputation for protecting liberty of conscience notwithstanding. Director-General Petrus Stuyvesant made repeated efforts to halt the preaching, stop the private meetings, and generally harass the colony's nonconforming Lutherans, Jews, and Quakers. Nonetheless, these three groups managed to worship in relative freedom, cultivate their communal religious identities, and flourish economically. As in the eighteenth-century colonial world described by Landsman, imperial officials on both sides of the Atlantic helped make this particular form of coexistence possible. Juster takes a broader geographical approach, but her conclusion supports Goodfriend's conclusions, as well as the work of coexistence scholars: the willingness and ability of dissenters to worship in private often made the difference between informal tolerance and direct persecution. She demonstrates how severe penalties for religious crime in British North America were more often legislated than executed, highlighting how law and practice did not always converge. Those Euro-American dissenters who were neither vocal blasphemers, conspicuous Sabbath violators, nor general disturbers of the peace were usually able to avoid corporal punishment. Their beliefs might have been abhorrent to colonial authorities and explicitly proscribed in law, but dissenters could avoid the harshest legal consequences so long as they were circumspect in their practice.

In "Persecuting Quakers?" Andrew Murphy uncovers a comparable set of limitations on the public articulation of dissent in William Penn's famously tolerant province of Pennsylvania. Despite the generosity of Pennsylvania's protections for heterodoxy, an unusually scrupulous early Quaker emigrant named George Keith managed to bump up against their limits. Above all, Keith could not abide what he perceived as egregious ignorance and unforgivable departures from orthodoxy among his Quaker neighbors. It was, as Murphy explains, the unambiguously non-private character of Keith's dissent that provoked their wrath. The ease with which religious dissent became a civil infraction in a place accurately portrayed as a haven for the persecuted both qualifies our understanding of how libertarian regimes treated dissent and underscores the finding that colonial religious crime often contained a discernible civil component, just as it usually involved a form of conspicuous behavior. That did not mean that colonial Pennsylvania was indistinguishable from Massachusetts or Virginia. Penn's holy experiment guaranteed protections for religious minorities that far exceeded those maintained in most other colonies. But it does mean that dissent, especially when expressed publicly, could be restricted despite such constitutional safeguards.

Neither Europeans nor white colonials gave much thought to religious liberty for Native Americans or African Americans, and historians have long followed their lead. Within the Euro-American imaginary, Richard W. Pointer observes in his groundbreaking chapter "Native Freedom?" Indians were regarded as heathens rather than heretics. Anglo-American authorities rarely legislated either intolerance or tolerance toward Native faiths. As a result, seventeenth- and eighteenth-century Indians encountered varying degrees of interference with their faiths. Many lived beyond the jurisdiction of Anglo-American political authority. Others carved out a degree of legal autonomy within it. Still others were able to practice traditional faiths because of the imposing logistical challenges and appreciable expense entailed by proselytizing Native Americans. There was nonetheless a special danger for Indians whose rituals tended to be more integral to their religions than their beliefs. As several authors in this volume indicate, early American civil authorities were slow to punish discretely held beliefs but quick to punish conspicuous practices of non-orthodox, or non-Protestant Christian, faith.

The institution of slavery presents still greater challenges for the traditional narrative of toleration and church-state relations. "Toleration," Jon Sensbach writes, "emerged in America at the same time that racial slavery became embedded in the social, legal, and religious structures of colonial American life." American slavery was so thoroughly coercive that public displays of faith were nearly impossible. Enslaved African Americans endured such unremitting control in their everyday lives that their spiritual constraints functioned as mere appendages of a larger disciplinary apparatus. Where religious freedoms for enslaved people did exist, they tended to be unsystematic and temporary. Sensbach notes how the same (1664) regime change in New Netherland from Dutch authority to English authority that (as Goodfriend shows) bestowed formal toleration on its free white inhabitants closed the door on the "half-freedom" that had allowed blacks a modicum of social and spiritual liberty. By contrast, on the slave plantations of colonial British America, there was rarely anything like half-freedom. Traditional African faiths were discouraged, literacy was prohibited, and unauthorized religious meetings were forbidden.

Despite persistently derogatory rhetoric and unfavorable laws, pre-Revolutionary Jews and Catholics did not confront the level of legal oppression and ethnic prejudice facing enslaved blacks and Indians. In fact, during the colonial period, these two religious minorities managed to create enough social space to worship in private and carry on peaceful everyday relations with their neighbors. As William Pencak shows in his "Anti-Semitism, Toleration, and Appreciation," the modest size of the Jewish population (approximately two thousand at the time of the Revolution) combined with their economic and political prominence within the domain of the British empire made Jews easy targets of political and economic scapegoating in the late eighteenth century. Anti-Semitism always simmered in the colonies and occasionally erupted in violence against Jewish people and Jewish symbols. This particular prejudice was more pronounced among ordinary Euro-Americans, or those who were socially marginal themselves, Pencak maintains, than it was among high-ranking colonials. Nonetheless, the unobtrusive quality of their religious practices, the value of their local economic contributions, and the rather consistent record of Jewish support for the Revolutionary cause helped ease their integration into the new nation. Just as importantly was widespread Founding-era enthusiasm for religious liberty and the efforts of Jewish leaders to make sure that it applied to those of their faith as well.

Anti-Catholic rhetoric proved as nimble and ubiquitous in Protestant America as anti-Semitism. Like Pencak in his analysis of colonial anti-Semitism, Owen Stanwood is struck by how much anti-Catholicism there was in the colonies given how few Roman Catholic adherents there were. From where—if the Catholic presence was small and principally confined to Maryland—did such antipathy arise? Searching for answers, Stanwood's "Catholics, Protestants, and the Clash of Civilizations in Early America" points beyond the oft-cited anti-Catholic print references to the broader geopolitical contest between Catholic and Protestant powers. If one looked past the borders of the thirteen colonies toward New France and New Spain, he argues, Catholics appeared to present real existential threats to Protestant America. Indeed, Stanwood observes, many Americans interpreted their history as a continuing struggle between Catholics and Protestants for control of the continent. Whether it originated from actual dangers or imagined threats, anti-Catholicism fundamentally shaped the religious landscape of this predominantly Protestant region.

But what could bring an end to, or at least mitigate, such a deeply entrenched and useful tradition of intolerance? Recent scholarly treatments of late eighteenth-century America have been quick to note that the Founding-era elimination of church establishments and penalties for dissent had much to do with the contingencies of war and the fickleness of alliances—and to downplay provisions for religious freedom as temporary expedients. By contrast, Chris Beneke's "The 'Catholic Spirit Prevailing in Our Country'" makes the case that a fundamental cultural shift was already underway by the American Revolution, softening the edges of religious difference, severing civic and religious identities, and promoting the public virtue of "nonsectarianism." In the history of religious minorities, particularly Roman Catholics, Beneke finds a decidedly "Whiggish" tale of progress. Whereas Christopher Grenda argues that ideological principles that undergirded the new state and federal constitutions of the post-independence period amounted to mere reformulations of seventeenth-century traditions, Beneke insists upon a broad and durable shift toward religious equality in the late eighteenth century.

Christopher Grasso's "The Boundaries of Toleration and Tolerance: Religious Infidelity in the Early American Republic" qualifies Beneke's Whiggish narrative with a less sanguine history of those who fell outside the lines of conventional monotheism or rejected it altogether. For the radically unorthodox, Grasso argues, the Revolutionary era did not mark an unambiguous break with the past. In fact, well into the nineteenth century, those who could not swear a Christian oath or affirm their faith in God and the afterlife were barred from office and from court. Meanwhile, blasphemy statutes, and other laws designed to uphold "piety" and "morality," transformed criticism of orthodox Christianity into alleged assaults on civil society. The sometimes precarious position of freethinkers and skeptics in the new nation highlights a recurring motif in the history of early American religion: the priority of maintaining civil order over the achievement of religious uniformity. Some of the founders (like Jefferson) tried to separate religious dissent from civil matters—but the longstanding tension between them could not yet be severed.[25] Still, punishments meted out during the early nineteenth century were proportionally less common and substantially milder than they had been in the seventeenth, and those indicted for such crimes were now avowed freethinkers, skeptics, and nonbelievers, rather than the members of dissenting sects. Although freethinkers and skeptics generally lost in court, the support for their challenges to blasphemy laws and religious prerequisites for civic participation received testifies to a newfound willingness in the population to recognize previously unappreciated forms of prejudice and to reconstitute freedom on broader grounds.[26]

The essays in this volume represent a broad, exploratory investigation of religious differences in early America, using the tools of both mainstream religious history and church-state history. The answers to many relevant and important questions remain largely unknown. For instance, we do not know to what degree religious tolerance and religious inclusion were the products of religious indifference. Church membership rates were famously low during the Revolutionary and Founding eras. Some scholars have argued that as few as one in five free people formally belonged to a church. Did religious liberty expand because people simply cared less about their faiths and their neighbors' faiths?[27] What if the chronic orthodox worriers were correct and skeptics, on the verge of outright infidelity, did actually abound? (A related interpretive possibility, that skepticism about conventional religion inspired libertarian policies during the Revolutionary era, has been more thoroughly investigated.)[28] Historians will need to learn more about the churchgoing habits of early Americans and their reasons for attendance and nonattendance before these questions can be answered satisfactorily. Given the coincidence of more regular ecumenical statements with the low church membership rates, the possibility has to be seriously considered.

Measuring the tolerance and intolerance in early America depends partly on our historical accounting methods. How much weight do we give to isolated acts of unofficial popular violence? What about endemic popular violence? The new nation spawned a host of new religious groups, some homegrown and some imported. What do we make of the fact that these groups were not always treated with the courtesy, or even the legal equality, reserved for better established and less radical groups? As historians, should we emphasize acts of popular violence and elite bigotry toward them, or the legal policies, economic opportunities, and cultural environment that allowed for their appearance in the first place? And how do we deal with the markedly different social spaces in which tolerance and intolerance manifested themselves? We know, for instance, that American port cities featured more religious diversity along organized, confessional lines and that the local elite was often accommodating toward dissenters because of their economic value. But can these towns be described as more religiously tolerant places than, say, frontier villages? Perhaps. Yet one of the better-known characteristics of farming populations in early frontier areas was their willingness to flock to any preacher with a good voice and a Bible.

Additional questions arise when we consider those whose freedoms were curtailed in other ways. Thanks to the contributions of Jon Sensbach and Richard Pointer, we have a much better understanding of what religious liberty did and did not mean for African Americans and Native Americans. But how do we conceptualize toleration within the family? Does it require a completely distinctive mode of analysis? There are empirical problems before us here as well. Despite the abundance of recent work on the religious experience of early American women, the religious liberty enjoyed by free married white women remains a matter of speculation. No one has systematically measured the extent to which women could dissent from their husbands and fathers (nor do we know much about the freedoms servants enjoyed at a time when the "family" extended well beyond the nuclear family).[29] How far could their beliefs and practices diverge? Were the conditions available in early America for women to attend their own churches? Interestingly, Maryland and Pennsylvania's seventeenth-century toleration acts provided for the protection of "his or her Religion/faith," while late eighteenth-century statutes only used male pronouns and possessive forms. Did such changes in constitutional language make a difference? It does not help us in this regard that early Americans had so little to say, at least publicly, about the religious rights of women.

Fortunately, we are not wholly without guidance when it comes to matters of religious freedoms in the household. Susan Juster has highlighted the sexual egalitarianism that prevailed among pre-Revolutionary evangelicals in New England and its revocation in the first decades of the new nation; while Catherine Brekus and Christine Leigh Heyrman have detailed the exoduses that wives and mothers often led from orthodox faith toward exciting new forms of evangelical worship, and the charismatic male preachers who inspired it.[30] Evidence of intermarriage might also indicate a relatively wide scope of domestic liberty for white women, and there is some of that as well. William Warner has found very high rates of intermarriage among Maryland's elite Protestant and Catholic families in the eighteenth century.[31] At the same time, Huguenots married non-Huguenots and, as early as the nineteenth century, Jews married non-Jews.[32] It is likely that still higher rates of intra-Protestant exogamy occurred among mainline Protestant churches such as Congregationalists, Presbyterians, and Anglicans. As with slavery, the larger context of female legal subordination may have trumped whatever religious liberties women were allowed, while high rates of intermarriage may only point to the strength of the emerging ideal of companionate marriage. And yet, if religious differences did not pose major obstacles to the fulfillment of that ideal, it is significant for our understanding of early American tolerance and intolerance.

It is unlikely that any of these questions will be answered definitively, at least in the near future. Like other fields of scholarship, the story of tolerance and intolerance in early America is destined to remain a provisional work, ever in need of revision. This volume is a step toward an overarching history of tolerance and intolerance in early America. That should make it a useful starting point. If the tradition of religious tolerance teaches us anything, it is the urgency of continuing our conversations.

A Note on the Use of Terms

"Tolerance" and "intolerance" are used in the following pages to describe state policies, social practices, and moral virtues.[33] Contributors have generally employed the term "toleration" in its seventeenth- and eighteenth-century sense as a state policy of "indulgence" for dissenting religious groups—as a revocable liberation from existing penalties. However, because tolerance lacks a verb form, the term "tolerate" will be used more liberally; and because "toleration" has no necessary English antonym (Thomas Paine did use the term "*in*toleration" at least once, but it was not employed on a regular basis in the late eighteenth century), "intolerance" and "persecution" will be used in its stead.[34] If all of this were not confusing enough, we should point out that an early modern term used concurrently with "toleration" was "liberty of conscience." Perhaps the most durable term applied to the protection of religious dissent from the seventeenth century to the early nineteenth century, "liberty of conscience" tended to refer to the sanctity of individual belief and the interiority of religious commitment (it was often used synonymously with yet another term, the "divine right of private judgment"). Liberty of conscience did not always entail the free exercise of religion, as did another term, "religious liberty," which came into widespread use in the United States during the second half of the eighteenth century.[35] "Religious liberty" (and its modernized equivalent, "religious freedom") entailed protections for both private conscience and public displays of faith. Numerous late eighteenth-century commentators were keen to distinguish "religious liberty" from "mere toleration," that is, the begrudging indulgence of dissenting faiths. Others, however, used the term "toleration" as a synonym for what their contemporaries called "religious liberty." Even the most stable of these terms, "liberty of conscience" and the "divine right of private judgment," were neither static concepts nor inert liberties. This Babel of terms and significations testifies to the vibrancy of the discussion of religious differences in the seventeenth and eighteenth centuries—and today.

PART I

Ideologies of Tolerance and Intolerance in Early America

Chapter 1

Faith, Reason, and Enlightenment

The Cultural Sources of Toleration in Early America

CHRISTOPHER S. GRENDA

The issue of religious toleration in early America is enormously complex. The essays in this volume highlight that complexity by revealing the range of ideas, social practices, and legal norms that determined the extent of toleration in early American society, both before and after the American Revolution. Yet even while considering this range, as well as the intolerance that preceded and survived the Revolution, one thing is clear: The idea of religious toleration was increasingly discussed in the burgeoning public sphere of the seventeenth- and eighteenth-century North Atlantic world of early America relative to earlier periods. The sheer volume of philosophical treatises, political pamphlets, and newspaper articles addressing toleration was far weightier in the seventeenth and eighteenth centuries than before. The defense and practice of religious intolerance certainly survived. At times, intolerance even thrived. Yet the impact of the discussions about religious toleration was felt in important ways. Apologists of intolerance increasingly found themselves on the defensive and sought to justify their views as never before. Thus by the mid-eighteenth century it was nearly impossible to write a comprehensive treatise of moral philosophy, the queen of the eighteenth-century social sciences, without addressing the issue of religious toleration, usually with approval. The discussion of the subject had simply become too prevalent for most commentators to avoid.

Although the discussions about religious toleration in the North Atlantic world of early America varied by time and place, they reflected persistent forms of reasoning across generations and boundaries. Thus even as contributors in various times and places addressed different contexts, their discussions contained patterned structures and processes of argumentation that were flexible and nuanced enough to fit those contexts and, as such, persisted over time, considerably forming the understandings and degrees of toleration throughout the period. Three such structures or forms of reasoning predominated. The first was a sacred form of reasoning. It started with biblical text and reasoned from key biblical concepts and passages to the conclusion that religious toleration was a divine directive and thus a requirement of the Christian faith. The second was a secular form of reasoning. It started with principles of utility and reasoned from the safety concerns of state or political society to the conclusion that toleration was necessary for the peace and stability of the polity. The third was an Enlightenment form of reasoning. It started with epistemology and reasoned most often from an empirical theory of knowledge to the conclusion that toleration was required by the nature of the human understanding.

None of these three forms of reasoning circumscribed the traditions of which they were a part. Biblical, reason-of-state, and Enlightenment thinking were all diverse phenomena comprised of various and often competing strains. These forms of reasoning, moreover, overlapped as few early modern writers, to cite one example, conceived of the state in strictly a-religious terms. Yet the three forms of reasoning were nonetheless distinct and informed the discussions about religious toleration in the seventeenth- and eighteenth-century North Atlantic world of early America. Whether contributors viewed biblical, reason-of-state, or Enlightenment reasoning as compatible or not, each privileged one form over the other and, very often, showed an awareness of doing so. The seventeenth-century English advocate of toleration Ralph Wallis, for example, privileged the sacred form of reasoning by redefining the safety concerns of secular writers in terms of biblical precept: "let's all submit to Christ / Our Prophet, Priest, and King / It's this t' our Countrey, State and selves / In the end will safety bring."[1] The eighteenth-century Scottish sponsor of toleration David Hume, in turn, used epistemological terms to dismiss such religious argumentation as "altogether unaccountable, and seeming quite beyond the reach of our ordinary faculties."[2]

Examining the reasoning processes of the early modern North Atlantic discussions about religious toleration is important for three reasons. First, it will reveal different and shifting understandings of toleration throughout the period, nuances not always appreciated in the historical literature and often masked by contemporaries' use of ambiguous terms such as the word "toleration" itself and corollaries such as "liberty of conscience" and "natural rights." Second, the examination will raise the following question about the American Revolution and Founding: To what extent were discussions of religious toleration and religious liberty at the Founding derivative discussions, dependent upon inherited forms of reasoning, and to what extent were they original discussions, generating original conceptions of religious liberty? This question—one of continuity and change—approaches the issue of religious toleration as a window through which to measure how transformative the American Revolution really was. It thus provides a fruitful point of scholarly comparison with other essays in this volume. Chris Beneke, in particular, sees the Revolution as fundamentally progressive in creating uniquely durable and universal forms of religious liberty, benefiting not just traditional Protestants, but Catholics, Jews, and upstart Protestant sects as much as others. Yet Christopher Grasso and Owen Stanwood are not so sure. They see more continuity than change in late eighteenth-century America in terms of a limited or inadequate toleration of non-Protestants and religious skeptics.

The examination of the early modern discussions of religious toleration sheds some light on this scholarly debate by suggesting a significant degree of continuity in late eighteenth-century America; the Revolutionary generation inherited the largely Protestant-derived arguments about religious toleration and religious liberty that they employed. Yet the examination also suggests important elements of change; the Revolutionary generation began a process approaching Beneke's vision of a distinct turn toward religious liberty by implementing the inherited arguments in public policy to a degree previously unknown. The result was a distinct development in the codification of old ideas. Thus even as Revolutionary Americans added little substantive novelty to the debate about religious toleration and religious liberty, they nonetheless added the all-important procedural novelty of codification itself. As several authors in this volume wrestle with this question of continuity and change surrounding the American Revolution, it bears considering how their analyses relate to the larger interpretive question of identifying when American culture accommodated the rights of individualism and the pursuit of individual fulfillment as a basis for the American civil order. Analyses indicating significant religious change during the Revolution suggest locating that accommodation earlier in American history, namely the late eighteenth century, than analyses emphasizing religious continuity on either side of the Founding.[3]

Finally, the examination will address a theoretical issue regarding religion, providing a second point of scholarly comparison. This issue is the role of religiously informed social thought in the processes by which a culture transitions from religiously less tolerant to religiously more tolerant attitudes and habits. Despite continued intolerance, such a transition was certainly occurring in this period. The boundaries of religious toleration were wider at the close of the American Revolution than at the opening of the seventeenth century. Significantly, during this process, the sacred form of reasoning grounded in biblical text often provided the most robust understandings of religious toleration and a primary impetus for the move from religious toleration to religious liberty. The influence of religiously informed social thought—as the influence of all forms of social thought, sacred or secular—was not, of course, one-dimensional. As both Jon Corrigan and Susan Juster indicate in this volume, religious argumentation continued to inform theories and practices of religious intolerance throughout the period. And as many scholars have noted elsewhere, secular and Enlightenment forms of reasoning were no doubt important in the development of religious toleration. These facts constitute important features of the early modern era. Absorbing them, however, should not distort the equally compelling reality that many early modern sectarians immersed in and armed with religious argumentation were often at the forefront of the discussions concerning religious toleration and religious liberty, not only in terms of their numbers, but also in terms of their theoretical contributions. Parts of this story have been told before, as in William McLoughlin's magisterial work on late eighteenth-century New England Baptists.[4] Yet a wider geographical and chronological perspective is needed. And this *longue durée* curiously suggests that transitions to broader religious toleration and developments in religious liberty can be compatible with the extensive engagement of religion and public culture in an increasingly open and accessible public sphere.

The Seventeenth Century

The seventeenth-century North Atlantic world was rife with religious intolerance. National laws of religious uniformity, state-sanctioned persecutions for religious dissent, and acts of religiously inspired violence littered the century's cultural landscape. Religious conflicts fueled Europe's Thirty Years' War (1618–48) between Catholics and Protestants, and the English civil wars

(1642–49) among Protestant sects. Such intolerance and conflict inspired the western world's first sustained discussions of religious toleration. The most vocal proponents of toleration in the early century period were sectarians who, in dissenting from state churches, founded Baptist congregations in Amsterdam and secret Baptist gatherings in London. They included John Smyth, Thomas Helwys, Leonard Busher, and John Murton.[5] Such Baptists found early seventeenth-century England inhospitable because the English state made dissent from the Protestant Episcopal Church of England illegal; required subjects to pay religious taxes to support the national or established church; and required membership in its Episcopal Church as a prerequisite for holding public office. State and church leaders also tightly controlled the press and the formation of public opinion through a strict licensing system for publications.

In this context of religious intolerance—persecuting dissenters from an established church, religiously taxing them, and restricting their access to public office and publication—Thomas Helwys wrote *A Short Declaration of the Mistery of Iniquity* (1612) and forwarded a copy to the king of England, James Stuart.[6] Helwys opposed such intolerance by quoting 2 Corinthians 10:4 in which the Apostle Paul explained, "the weapons of our warfare are not worldly but have divine power to destroy strongholds." Many sectarians dissenting from state or established churches viewed this biblical text as a foundation for the "two swords" and "two kingdoms" doctrines from which they reasoned for religious toleration. According to these doctrines, God had created an earthly kingdom with a carnal sword, which was the state's penal power to punish criminal offenders. The state thus possessed jurisdiction over the "outward things" of the subjects' bodies, goods, and behavior. God had also, according to these doctrines, created a heavenly kingdom with a spiritual sword, which was the power of God's Word in the act of persuasion. This power possessed jurisdiction over the "inward things" of the subjects' understandings, wills, and consciences. As Helwys explained, "God hath given unto the K[ing] an earthly kingdome"[7] with "all worldly power which tendeth to all the goods and bodies of his servants."[8] Yet "the God of Gods, and lord of Lords . . . hath reserved to himself a heavenly kingdome . . . & that with this [heavenly] kindgome, our lord the King hath nothing to do (by his kingly power) but as a subject himself: and that Christ is King alone."[9] The objects of Christ's kingdom were the inward things of the human mind,[10] which were subject only to the persuasion or illumination of the "spiritual swerd of the Lambe, which is the word of God."[11] Upon these sectarian principles, Helwys built a broad theory of religious toleration, which included Christians and non-Christians: "Let them be heretikes, Turks, Jewes, or whatsoever, it appertaynes not to the earthly power to punish them in the least measure."[12] He also included Catholics[13] because, as he noted, "men should chuse their religion themselves."[14]

Helwys's understanding of those who would qualify for religious toleration—the scope of his proposed toleration—was quite broad. Yet his understanding of what religious toleration meant—his theory of toleration—was relatively narrow. Helwys believed that Protestant sectarians, heretics, Turks, Jews, Catholics, and others should have the right to worship without suffering legal penalty by the state's carnal sword.[15] Penalties for religious dissent assumed many forms in the seventeenth century such as fines, arrest, confiscation of property, or banishment. Other forms of legal penalty for religion included religious taxation to support an established church, religious tests for public office, and exclusion from the public sphere. Because Helwys did not address these other forms of penalty, his discussion of toleration focused on the right to worship without the persecution of fines, arrest, confiscation, or banishment. In this, he offered a broad toleration, which included many groups, but a theoretically narrow toleration, which only sought the right to worship, not freedom from established churches, from religious taxes, or from religious restrictions on public office and the public sphere.[16]

Helwys's sectarian colleague Leonard Busher developed sacred reasoning into a more expansive theory of religious toleration in *A Plea for Liberty of Conscience* (1614), presented "to King *James*, and the High Court of Parliament then sitting."[17] Busher repeated Helwys's proposal for a broad toleration—"Christians; yea, Jews, Turks, and pagans"[18]—by also citing 2 Corinthians 10:4. He then added Hebrews 4:12, wherein the Apostle states, "the word of God is lively . . . and sharper than any two-edged sword . . . [as] a discerner of the thoughts and intents of the heart." Quoting these passages, Busher characterized the "religion of the gospel" as requiring the spiritual sword only—"the word preached only"—and described penal laws for religion as "antichristian."[19] Yet he not only requested freedom from fines, arrest, property confiscation, and banishment, but also sought freedom from religious taxation or tithes: "neither should any relics of the ceremonial law, as tithes and offerings, &c., be any longer in use."[20]

Busher also demanded a more open and accessible public sphere based upon 1 John 4:1, which instructs believers, "do not believe every spirit, but test the spirits to see whether they are of God." Busher often returned to this passage and understood it to require greater freedom in public discourse to "test the spirits" of authors than allowed by the church-state licensing systems for public print then common in Europe. He thus exhorted "all men, to prove and *try the spirits whether they are of God*; which they cannot do, except they hear and read other men's doctrines." Yet "neither can they if they would," Busher lamented, "so long as the bishops have power from the king and state to silence."[21] Busher then proposed several rules for printed exchange. Mindful of the secular concerns of state,[22] he introduced his rules with the heading, "permission of conscience, and freedom and liberty of the gospel, will no way be dangerous to the king or state, if such like rules as these be observed." Among them, he included, "that it be lawful for every person or persons, yea, Jews and papists, to write, dispute, confer and reason, print and publish any matter touching religion, either for or against whomsoever."[23]

Busher's understanding of religious toleration was thus theoretically more expansive than Helwys's because it included not only the right of worship, but also the ending of religious taxation and a more open public sphere. Yet Busher did not address religious tests for public office or religious establishments. Such issues were left for the next generation of sectarians to address, namely Levellers and English émigrés to Rhode Island.

The Levellers were a political movement of sectarians and soldiers in the English civil wars of the 1640s who affirmed earlier sacred arguments for religious toleration. Echoing Busher, the puritan Leveller William Walwyn used the two-swords doctrine to advocate a freer public sphere, explaining "the word of God is express for toleration" and thus "schism and heresy (when they appear to be such) are to be rooted out by reason and debate: the sword of the spirit, not of the flesh; arguments, not blows." This requires "giving liberty to every man to speak his mind and produce his reasons and arguments."[24] The Baptist Leveller Richard Overton similarly noted the two-kingdoms doctrine and advocated liberty in preaching, writing, and printing.[25] He explained how this biblical doctrine required a broad toleration of Christians and non-Christians because "the Kingdome of heaven or Christs Government over the whole world doth strictly charge his servants, the Kings and Rulers of the Earth (for by him Kings raigne) to suffer tares; Turckes, Jewes, Pagans, and Infidels, as wel as Christians to grow or live together in the Field of the World."[26]

Levellers also advanced the discussions about religious toleration in *An Agreement of the Free People of England* (1649). After advocating the right of worship[27] and ending religious taxation,[28] they sought to abolish religious tests for public office, excepting Catholics for their supposed foreign loyalties. As they explained, "They [i.e., Representatives in Parliament] shall not disable any person from bearing any office in the commonwealth for any opinion or practice in religion, excepting such as maintain the pope's (or other foreign) supremacy."[29] In criticizing most religious tests, Levellers attempted to move the discussions about religious toleration beyond merely a right to worship and toward what can be viewed as a preliminary understanding of religious liberty.

One important distinction between religious toleration and religious liberty is that toleration primarily concerns private endeavors whereas liberty possesses important public dimensions. Tolerated individuals or groups worship without suffering persecution, but may still be limited in their participation in the public sphere or excluded from public offices or other public dimensions of the polity. In contrast, liberty indicates participation in the polity's public arenas—its offices, discussions, and spaces. Such liberty prevents the state from supervising the formation of public opinion and culture or controlling access to its offices on religious grounds. Thus Busher's earlier attempt to develop a more open and competitive public sphere contained an element of religious liberty while the Levellers' qualified attempt to prohibit religious tests for public office added another element still. Yet by the time Levellers published the *Agreement*, their political fortunes had waned. A new Council of State had executed King Charles and arrested leading Levellers who signed the *Agreement* as "prisoners in the Tower of London." The new regime of Oliver Cromwell then instituted limited religious toleration. It replaced the established Episcopal Church with an established Calvinist church, which tolerated Christian sectarians in principle, and, to an extent, Anglicans and Catholics in practice.[30]

Because the seventeenth century was an era of overseas expansion, the discussions about religious toleration gradually developed into a larger transatlantic phenomenon. Two pioneers in expanding the geography of the discussion were John Clark and Roger Williams, sectarian émigrés to Rhode Island who advanced the theoretical dimensions of the discussions in the period of England's civil wars. Both Clark and Williams reaffirmed key biblical concepts and passages of sacred reasoning as when Clark advised English readers in *Ill Newes from New-England* (1652) to "consider the words spoken by the Apostle *Paul*, who would have us to know (as he declares it, 2 Corinthians 10:4) that the weapons of his warfare were not carnall." "The Sword and power of the Magistrate," Clark explained in reasoning for toleration, "was never appointed by Christ to inform and rectifie the minds and consciences of men."[31] Upon this biblical foundation, Clark grafted a secular-utility argument,[32] claiming that persecution "cannot well stand with the prosperity and safety of a State, or Nation, upon a politick ground or consideration." His theoretical contribution in this context was to analyze the failure of intolerance in terms of the relationship between religious parties and political authority. It "best suits with policy," he explained, "1. To engage not only one party or sect alone, but all parties therein to the present power, and to the supporting thereof. 2. To do this not by giving away any part of the power to any party or sect to oppress or inforce others." From this, Clark drew an equal-protection conclusion as he exhorted leaders of state "to afford its protection equall to all without respect onto any."[33] In making this argument, Clark anticipated what eighteenth-century writers termed the "science of politics," which analyzed society's interests groups and factions in relation to the state and the making of public policy.[34] Yet despite this contribution, Clark was unclear regarding the policy implications of his analysis. He condemned persecution, but did not address religious tests or taxes. His sectarian colleague Roger Williams did.

Williams was the founder of the colony of Rhode Island (1644) who twice returned to England to advocate toleration. In *The Bloody Tenent Yet More Bloody* (1652), he criticized religious tests for public office[35] and denounced religious establishments by alluding to two popular sectarian biblical texts, 2 Corinthians 10:4 and Hebrews 4:12. "Christ Jesus abolished his own national and state-church," Williams explained, "that the two-edged sword of the word of the Lord in the mouths of his true messengers, might alone be brandished and magnified."[36] Or, as Williams asserted repeatedly, "a national church is not of Christ Jesus."[37] Following these sectarian ideas, Rhode Island never created a religious establishment and avoided religious tests for public office during Williams's lifetime.[38]

By the mid-seventeenth century, then, practitioners of sacred reasoning had contributed five elements to the discussions about religious toleration and had advanced those discussions toward religious liberty. They demanded toleration in worship and freedom from religious taxation. They advanced toward liberty by seeking to open the public sphere, abolish religious tests for public office, and end religious establishments. Yet the implementation of these ideas about toleration and liberty was thwarted in the early 1660s when the English monarchy was restored and an intolerant Episcopal Church of

England reestablished. Thereafter, the discussions about religious toleration continued, but narrowed in scope and theory. This narrowing reflected a shift in the discourse as sacred arguments waned, secular arguments waxed, and early Enlightenment arguments emerged.

The shift in the discussions was evident in Peter Pett's *A Discourse concerning Liberty of Conscience* (1661), wherein Pett explained, "Nor shall I at all in these papers consider what Liberty to the Consciences of others' Religion, but purely what political interest prompts us to give."[39] After Europe's Thirty Years' War and the English civil wars, concerns about state interest, national welfare, and political expediency assumed greater prominence in the discussions about religion. Concern with expediency was, of course, not unknown to earlier generations, as was evident in Clark's analysis, and sacred reasoning certainly did not disappear. Yet a shift in emphasis was discernible as late-century authors tended toward principles of political utility in their reasoning. Pett defined his work in these political terms, as "Proposals about what Liberty in this kind is now Politically Expedient to be given, and severall Reasons to shew how much the peace and Welfare of the Nation is concern'd therein." The religious toleration resulting from such a secular emphasis on political utility tended to be narrow in scope and theory. The point was less to exegete biblical text than "to prove how much a due liberty," in Pett's words, "will conduce to the peace and safety of the Nation."[40] For Pett, the "due liberty" consistent with England's national interest was the toleration of Protestant sectarian worship[41] balanced by a national or established church funded by religious taxation.[42] His version of "liberty of conscience" considered neither non-Christians nor issues of religious liberty.

Late-century secular reasoning was also evident in the writings of the English Quaker William Penn. Penn advanced elements of religious liberty by conspicuously omitting references to an established church or religious taxation in "The Frame of Government" for the province of Pennsylvania founded in 1682.[43] He also criticized religious tests for public office in England.[44] Yet most of his writings for an English audience were relatively modest and reflected the shift in emphasis of the late-century period. He employed the conceptual distinctions of earlier sectarians,[45] but in *England's Present Interest Considered, with Honour to the Prince, and Safety to the People* (1675), he framed the question of religious toleration in terms of state interest: "What is most Fit, Easy and Safe at this Juncture of Affairs to be done, for the quieting of Differences, allaying the Heat of contrary Interests, and making them subservient to the Interest of the Government?" For Penn, the government's interest was to repeal penal laws for religion.[46] He suggested that intolerance had resulted in the wars and instability of recent generations and thus highlighted the state's interest in adopting religious toleration. Similar to Pett, he viewed toleration as the right of Protestant sectarian worship—"by Law [to] establish the free exercise of their Worship"[47]—but in his English writings he did not address religious taxation and specifically consented to an established church in England.[48]

The instability and wars to which Penn referred were not confined to England, but had engulfed much of Europe in the Thirty Years' War. As a result, the shift in emphasis toward secular concerns with stability in discussing religious toleration pervaded European culture. The German Samuel Pufendorf employed such reasoning while also sharing important perspectives with the early Enlightenment thinkers Pierre Bayle of France and John Locke of England. All three wrote in response to the Revocation of the Edict of Nantes (1685), which heightened religious persecution in France.[49] Locke authored *A Letter concerning Toleration* (1685),[50] Bayle *A Philosophical Commentary* (1686–87), and Pufendorf *Of the Nature and Qualification of Religion in Reference to Civil Society* (1687).[51] All three affirmed the conclusion of the two-kingdoms doctrine—state jurisdiction over outward behavior—without detailing the doctrine's informing theology.[52] They also sought to establish boundaries between civil government and religion[53] based on the respective purpose of each institution.[54] And they were all concerned with late-century geopolitics in which Protestant states led by Prussia and England faced Catholic alliances led by France.

Yet Pufendorf's writings expressed the state-interest concerns of secular reasoning more than the epistemological concerns of the Enlightenment. He sought a philosophical framework for international peace among nation states[55] and counseled an established church for each: "where there is not any Publick Form of Religion established in a Commonwealth, it is the Sovereign's care, that one may be composed." He suggested intolerance toward atheism, an increasing philosophical concern, and the banishment of religious dissenters in the interest of public safety.[56] However, Pufendorf also recommended religious toleration. He offered secular reasons for a form of toleration that was limited in scope and theory. Pufendorf worried that excessive banishment of dissenters might prejudice the state, explaining that sovereigns may "tolerate such of their Subjects as are of a different Opinion from the Established Religion. For, it may so happen, that the number of the Dissenters is so great, as not to be expelled without great Prejudice to the State."[57]

By "dissenters," Pufendorf primarily meant Christians or even just Protestants.[58] He did not address the issue of non-Christians, religious taxation, religious tests for public office, or access to the public sphere. His secular reasoning seemingly could not accommodate such people or issues.

Bayle and Locke were early Enlightenment figures whose rationales and understandings of religious toleration were closely linked with their respective epistemologies.[59] Bayle was an epistemological skeptic in religion.[60] He denied the ability to know objective criteria that could distinguish orthodoxy from heresy: "Faith affords us no other Criterion of Orthodoxy than the inward Sentiment and Conviction of Conscience, a Criterion common to all, even the most heretical Souls."[61] Yet Bayle was not a skeptic regarding all knowledge. As a rationalist, he distinguished primary from secondary qualities of objects. For him, primary qualities such as shape and size were numerical because they could be measured, weighed, and demonstrated mathematically. They possessed a real or objective existence. Secondary qualities such as color or taste were not real, but subjective and merely reflected how the mind experienced an object. For Bayle, religious beliefs were like secondary qualities: "the Truths of Religion in particular, [are] not of the Propertys of Numbers, or the first Principles of Metaphysicks, or Geometrical Demonstrations"; they "are not Entitys distinct from the Mind."[62]

From this epistemological perspective, Bayle advanced what he called "the Rights of an erroneous conscience" by which he meant that sincerity of belief, not objective criteria, established the believer's right to toleration.[63] Bayle hoped this focus on sincerity, which was subjective, would replace traditional battles over orthodoxy with acknowledgments of diverse religious viewpoints. He thus told the "orthodox" that "Impietys and Profanations" appear as they do "if you define things by your Notions of 'em, but not if you consider 'em according to the Definitions of the [other] Sect; for they pretend, that the Impietys and Profanations are all of your side."[64] Bayle again emphasized the plurality of perspectives by noting how every church or "Party believes it self the Orthodox" or "looks on it self as the only true Religion."[65] He hoped recognition of such plurality would advance toleration of sectarian worship by ending legal penalties for religion such as fines, arrest, imprisonment, and banishment. He repeatedly identified such penalties as the focal point of *Philosophical Commentary*.[66]

Locke also addressed religious plurality—"every Church is Orthodox to it self"[67]—but from a different epistemological perspective. Locke was an empiricist, not a rationalist. He rested his case for toleration on the idea that the mind receives information passively through the senses and then uses that information to formulate ideas and beliefs. Locke viewed the initial reception of information as passive because the process of sensory intake was not willed, but involuntary. Since this involuntary process yielded the information subsequently developed into ideas and beliefs, Locke maintained that individuals receive more than they choose their own religious beliefs—"belief being not in their own power."[68] He stressed this notion of the involuntary nature of the understanding as a basis for religious toleration as early as his 1667 "Essay on Toleration."[69] Therein, he linked it to inalienability, suggesting that if religious beliefs are involuntary—not in one's power to determine—one cannot alienate that power to another, including the magistrate. "No man can give another man power," Locke explained, "over that over which he has no power himself. Now that a man cannot command his own understanding, or positively determine today what opinion he will be of tomorrow, is evident from experience and the nature of the understanding, which can no more apprehend things otherwise than they appear to it."[70]

The involuntary nature of the understanding also informed Locke's *Letter concerning Toleration*.[71] In the *Letter*, Locke denounced attempts "to introduce any thing into Religion, by the means of Laws and Penalties."[72] His main point was that legal penalties for religion were ineffective because the understanding was involuntary, its ideas and beliefs were not subject to the compelled choice that legal penalties entail. Religious beliefs, he affirmed as before, were "not in mens power" and thus could not be changed under penalty of law: "such is the nature of the Understanding, that it cannot be compell'd to the belief of any thing by outward force."[73] Locke repeated this point many times:[74] "Penalties in this case are absolutely impertinent; because they are not proper to convince the mind"; "Penalties are no ways capable to produce Belief."[75]

Because both Bayle and Locke sought to repeal legal penalties for religion, their respective understandings of such penalties defined the scope and theory of their toleration. Significantly, they both understood legal penalty to mean fines, property confiscation, arrest, corporal suffering, or banishment. Bayle criticized "Fines, Imprisonment, and Banishment," and explained that "neither Banishment, nor Prisons, nor Fines, are of any service in this respect." "There's no ground then," he concluded, "for maintaining that Banishment, Prisons, Confiscations of Goods, and such-like Penaltys" are effective.[76] Locke similarly denounced "Confiscation of Estate, Imprisonment, Torments," and other "corporal Sufferings" in which dissenters are "punished either in Body or Goods."[77] While focused on corporal penalties, neither Locke nor Bayle addressed the penalties of religious taxation or religious restrictions on public office. They were also reticent on religious establishments.[78] Their early Enlightenment theories of religious toleration were thus narrower than the sacred-reasoning theories of Busher, the Levellers, Clark, and Williams, all of whom addressed additional forms of legal penalty and advanced the discussions toward religious liberty.

Although Locke's and Bayle's toleration were theoretically narrower than sacred versions, they applied to a broader range of believers than secular arguments. Similar to Pufendorf, Locke advocated intolerance of atheists and Catholics;[79] Bayle was ambivalent about atheists and partially tolerant of Catholics.[80] Yet unlike Pufendorf, Locke and Bayle explicitly tolerated non-Christians. As Locke explained, "neither Pagan, nor Mahumetan, nor Jew, ought to be excluded from the Civil Rights of the Commonwealth, because of his Religion."[81] Given Locke's reticence on the theoretical issues many sectarians addressed, his inclusion of a broad range of believers indicates he understood "Civil Rights" in religion to mean freedom from corporal penalties, not relief from religious taxes, establishments, or tests for public office. In fact, Locke maintained membership in the established Church of England all his life[82] and endorsed England's so-called Toleration Act of 1689.[83] That act addressed religious penalties such as fines, property confiscation, arrest, and corporal punishment, but only exempted orthodox Protestants from such penalties. It thus resembled secular arguments for toleration in focusing on Protestants and was, as Locke noted, "Not perhaps so wide in scope as might be wished for."[84] Yet even as Locke addressed the act's narrow scope in protecting only Protestants, he omitted its theoretical limitations. The act maintained England's religious establishment, religious taxes, and religious tests for most public offices.[85] Lockean rights simply did not define such practices as forms of legal penalty. To the extent that such practices were part of seventeenth-century discussions, openly analyzed and explicitly criticized, they were primarily addressed by practitioners of sacred reasoning who moved those discussions toward religious liberty.

The Eighteenth Century

Religious intolerance was still widespread during the early decades of the eighteenth century. Wars driven by religious identities resumed in the imperial conflicts between Protestant Britain and Catholic France. Social acts of religiously inspired violence against churches and property remained. And state persecutions for religious dissent persisted through the century into the American Revolutionary era.[86] Yet religious intolerance was less severe and more transitory in the eighteenth-century North Atlantic world of early America than before. The worst forms of corporal punishment such as beating and execution became rare, as did the most extensive forms of banishment and arrest for religion. Even fines and confiscations of property abated. And imperial England's Anglican establishment was milder and less intolerant than before. Moreover, the British colonies of Rhode Island, Pennsylvania, and New Jersey solidified policies of no religious establishments and no religious taxation while even the Congregational establishments in Massachusetts and Connecticut exempted dissenting Protestant groups from religious taxes.[87] This assortment of experiences and policies meant that discussions about religious toleration and religious liberty continued through the eighteenth century. Those discussions were largely derivative in nature, less innovative than imitative of the sacred, secular, and Enlightenment arguments of previous generations.

The derivative nature of the discussions remained evident in the American Revolutionary era as late-century Americans debated issues of religious toleration and religious liberty in terms generally inherited from the Protestant past. A significant degree of continuity with that past thus ran through the Revolutionary discussions about religion, making the event of the Revolution more conventional than transformative on the level of intellectual and discursive development. Yet in important ways the Revolution still marked a turning point in the discussions regarding religion. Those discussions grew uniquely intense in the era of Independence and Founding, compressing decades' and even centuries' worth of ideas and ardor into a short period of revolutionary change. This intensity reflected the fact that the Revolution created a sense of increased possibilities of converting the discussions from discourse to public policy, from pamphlets and treatises to legal codification. Such Revolutionary codification, when it occurred, was still largely understood in Protestant terms and thus did not immediately inaugurate an era of equal and inclusive religious liberty for all.[88] Yet such codification did establish the principle and encouraged the rhetoric of legal impartiality, which provided a foundation for the expansion of religious-rights claims and, eventually, religious liberty in subsequent generations.

An important early eighteenth-century contribution to the discussions about religious toleration was Anthony Ashley Cooper's *Characteristicks of Men, Manners, Opinions, Times* (1711). Cooper was the third Earl of Shaftesbury and Locke's childhood tutor. His *Characteristicks* was important because, excepting Locke's *Second Treatise of Government* (1689), it "was the most reprinted book in English" in the eighteenth century.[89] It was also a foundation for the moral-sense theory that influenced the culture and higher education of early America both before and after the American Revolution.[90] As became more common in the eighteenth century, Shaftesbury denounced penal laws in religion, those "*petty* Inquisitors [who] threatened with *Punishment*, or *penal Laws*." He presented himself as "asserting thus zealously the Notion of a *religious liberty*, and *mutual Toleration*." Yet Shaftesbury simultaneously affirmed the virtues of a tolerant religious establishment, what he called an "*establish'd Faith* under a tolerating, mild, and gentle Government."[91] As he explained, "'tis necessary a people shou'd have a *Publick Leading* in Religion. For to deny the Magistrate a Worship, or take away a National Church, is," Shaftesbury avowed, "mere Enthusiasm."[92]

Shaftesbury's reasoning on religious toleration was secular. His primary purpose was to ensure social peace and political stability. He supported his reasoning with the enlightened values of *belles lettres* to produce a theoretically narrow high-brow understanding of religious toleration that called for the toleration of Protestant sectarians while characterizing them as overheated religious enthusiasts.[93] He viewed sectarians, or dissenters from state churches, as having prompted authorities to use penal laws which, in turn, led to much of the "Bloodshed, Wars, Persecutions, and Devastations in the World."[94] To avoid such conflict and instability, Shaftesbury proposed that ridicule and raillery replace persecution and penal laws as a peaceful and stable means of counteracting sectarian influence. "We tolerating *English* Men," he explained, "not contended to deny these prophesying Enthusiasts the Honour of a Persecution, we have deliver'd 'em over to the . . . Puppet-Show at *Bart'lemy*-Fair. There, doubtless," Shaftesbury continued, "their strange Voices and involuntary Agitations are admirably well acted, by the Motion of Wires, and Inspiration of Pipes." Shaftesbury hoped such puppet-show ridicule of sectarians would render their persecution unnecessary and thereby render social institutions secure: "And whiles *Bart'lemy*-Fair is in possession of this Privilege, I dare stand Security to our National Church, that no Sect of Enthusiasts, no new Venders of Prophecy or Miracles, shall ever get the start, or put her to the trouble of trying her Strength with 'em."[95] Having thus extolled the substitution of ridicule for persecution, Shaftesbury praised "our Doctrine of *Indulgence*."[96] To him, this doctrine forbade the use of penal laws by enlightened establishments, but permitted, through an omission of proscriptions, religious taxation and religious tests for public office.

A similar understanding of religious toleration influenced two authors who addressed religious taxes and religious tests in the generation following Shaftesbury, the British pamphleteers John Trenchard and Thomas Gordon. Trenchard and Gordon were two of the most widely read British authors of the eighteenth-century's second quarter as they promoted natural rights, free speech, free trade, and limited government.[97] Parts of their most significant work, *Cato's Letters* (1720–23), were reprinted in Boston, Philadelphia, New York, and Charleston,[98] and their *Independent Whig* (1720–21) enjoyed two complete American editions by 1750 and more thereafter.[99]

Trenchard and Gordon employed both secular and Enlightenment reasoning, but emphasized the latter as partisans of Locke's empiricism. They too viewed the mind as receiving information passively and thus endorsed the involuntary nature of the understanding, the view that individuals receive more than they choose their own ideas and beliefs. As a result, they maintained that such beliefs are not subject to an individual's power or will: "men's thoughts are not subject to their own jurisdiction"; an individual's beliefs "must be confessed to be out of his power";[100] "Our Actions are in our Power, but our Thoughts are not."[101] Trenchard and Gordon described religion in similar terms, as "independent upon all human directions." They reasoned that individuals do not control their own religious beliefs and thus cannot alienate them to another: "Religion therefore, which can never be subject to the jurisdiction of another, can never be alienated to another, or put in his power." Since religion was unalienable and "utterly excludes all force, power, or government," Trenchard and Gordon advocated the toleration of sectarian worship. They denounced corporal persecutions such as fines, arrest, or banishment[102] and declared the mind free, "uncontrollable by external force, which cannot reach the free faculties of the mind, or inform the understanding."[103]

Having stated their epistemological grounds for the inalienability of religious belief, Trenchard and Gordon advanced a theoretically narrow understanding of religious toleration. The connection between their epistemology and their toleration concerned irrationality. For them, the inalienability of religious belief made penal laws and persecution ineffective and thus irrational as public policy, as Locke had maintained. Yet such inalienability did not preclude enlightened establishments, religious taxes, and religious tests. These latter policies were unrelated to epistemology and therefore not inherently ineffective. As such, they were not irrational. Trenchard and Gordon thus condemned what they considered irrational penal laws and persecution, but defended what they viewed as rational or enlightened religious establishments supported by religious taxes and religious tests for public office. Their views reflected not only their empirical understanding of knowledge, but also their empirical understanding of human development. They viewed human character as malleable, formed by its environment, and sought to construct a social environment conducive to human virtue.[104] Such an environment included an establishment[105] of publicly funding ministers who cultivated virtue in their listeners.[106] They tolerated sectarians or dissenters who worshipped outside the establishment, "without the Consent of any Bishop," but viewed sectarian pastors as unqualified to receive taxes or tithes because they did not teach the established opinions of the state: "every religious intelligent Man is . . . entitled to be a Pastor, in the Scripture Sense of the Word, tho' not to receive the *legal Wages* of a Pastor. He may preach and pray, and deliver the Sacrament, when Temporal Laws do not restrain him; but cannot take Tithes, which are annexed to certain Conditions and Opinions established by the State."[107] Trenchard and Gordon also viewed public office as tied to the state's religion. They dismissed objections to England's "Test Law" restricting most public offices to Anglicans by noting with approval that it "excludes dissenters from offices." They characterized objections to this exclusion as "a dispute only about a non-entity: for it is certain, that no one dissenter in England would be in any office of value, if that law was repealed."[108] Trenchard and Gordon thus defended natural rights in religion,[109] but defined such rights as freedom from corporal penalties, not from religious establishments, taxes, or tests.

Trenchard and Gordon's and Shaftesbury's contributions highlight the ambiguity of key concepts in the discussions regarding religion. Shaftesbury proposed "mutual toleration" and "religious liberty," and Trenchard and Gordon defended the inalienability of religion as a natural right grounded "in the state of nature."[110] Yet these writers defined the concepts of liberty and rights in ways that appear theoretically narrow from later-day perspectives, and even from some contemporary perspectives, because they combined such concepts with support for religious establishments, religious taxes, and religious tests for public office. Such ambiguity, far from an anomaly in the eighteenth-century discussions, formed an essential part of their character as contemporaries competed to define terms and concepts in ways suitable to their particular goals.

In this context of competing definitions, the British-American Jonathan Dickinson made significant contributions to the discussions regarding religion. Dickinson was a Presbyterian minister from New Jersey, which, founded in 1664, had developed without legal penalties for religion and without religious establishments and religious taxes.[111] The colony also possessed broader access to public office than England, requiring in 1683 that officeholders be Christian before narrowing such access to Protestants.[112] In the 1720s and 1730s, Dickinson engaged in extended pamphlet debates with English Whigs from Connecticut and New York. These Whigs, Samuel Johnson and James Wetmore among others, represented the political and constitutional ideas of England's Hanoverian regime. With these adversaries, Dickinson focused on public policy regarding religion not in the colonies, but in England and criticized the religious establishment, taxes, and tests of the Whig state governing the British Empire. Although this focus limited the potential implications of his thought, his contributions were important because he employed sacred reasoning in writing from a sectarian or dissenting perspective. In the process, he used key concepts such as "natural Right" or "civil Rights" in ways that broadened their meaning and thereby helped move the discussions about religion toleration toward religious liberty.[113]

Dickinson's sectarian or dissenting perspective was evident in the titles of his works such as *The Vanity of Human Institutions in the Worship of God* (1736) and *The Reasonableness of Nonconformity* (1738). Even before these works, however, in his most important one, Dickinson had indicated the trajectory of his thought when he impugned religious establishment tax funding by critically remarking how "established Clergy . . . *every where* exact their *Salary*, from those of other Persuasions, where they can legally do it."[114] In *Vanity of Human Institutions*, he expressed a core component of his thought by employing the sacred reasoning of the two-kingdoms doctrine, explaining that "God is the only Lord of Conscience. He has left no Authority upon Earth to make any Laws for his Subjects in the immediate Affairs of his Kingdom." Dickinson expounded this doctrine as precluding Trenchard and Gordon's notion of the state establishing religious opinions or principles by law. He wanted "no particular Profession or Principles established by Law." Dickinson then expounded further by denouncing the idea of religious establishments, declaring "Legal Establishment has no place among us."[115]

Having denounced religious establishments and their systems of tax funding, Dickinson addressed the public-office issue in a sequel to *Vanity of Human Institutions* and in *Reasonableness of Nonconformity*. The limitations of his thought were most obvious in this context as he did not address the Protestant tests for public office in New Jersey, but focused on the more prescriptive Anglican tests in England. Referring to England's Test Law, he denounced "those very Rites, on Account of which so many excellent Men in our Nation are not only refused all Privileges in the Church, but all Offices in the State."[116] Using the first-person plural to speak for dissenters to Whig leaders in Hanover England, he explained, "Are not the Stumbling Blocks of your Rites and Ceremonies thrown in our Way? Must we not comply with these to every Punctilio of a Ceremony (tho' never so much against our Consciences) or be rejected, excommunicated, refused all Christian Priviledges; and in *England* be rendered uncapable of any temporal Honours and Dignities, in the State?"[117] In criticizing Anglican tests for public office, Dickinson neither explained whether "Christian Privileges" included Catholics nor did he consider the legal status of non-Christians. In this, he actually narrowed the conclusions that some seventeenth-century proponents of sacred reasoning had drawn from biblical precept, namely the toleration of Christians and non-Christians alike. Yet in denouncing religious establishments and religious taxes, and at least critically addressing the religious-test issue, Dickinson sought to move the eighteenth-century discussions about religious toleration toward the broader theoretical issues of religious liberty.

The types of debates between Dickinson and English Whigs were not a one-generation phenomenon in British America, but continued after Dickinson's death at mid-century. These debates included various issues of concern to colonists from English dissenting communities, which were the majority of the colonial population. Such issues ranged from the increase of Anglican proselytizing in the colonies to the creation of a colonial Anglican bishop,[118] which was never achieved, to the establishment of a colonial Anglican college, accomplished in 1754. It was this latter endeavor that encouraged the New York lawyer William Livingston to enter the discussions regarding religion. Similar to Dickinson, Livingston engaged English Whigs in extended pamphlet and newspaper debates about the nature of religious toleration. And like Dickinson, Livingston was a Presbyterian. However, Livingston was not an orthodox Calvinist like the New Jersey minister had been.[119] Rather, "rejecting all orthodoxy as irrational," according to one biographer, Livingston was a proponent of "liberal" Christianity, valuing religion for its ethical content, but adverse to revivals, doctrinal adherence, and ritualism.[120]

With these rational views and in opposition to Anglican plans for a college in New York at mid-century, Livingston became the lead author of a weekly periodical entitled *The Independent Reflector* (1753–54). For this endeavor, Livingston drew on British sources such as Joseph Addison and Richard Steele's *Spectator*[121] as well as Trenchard and Gordon's *Independent Whig*, especially when addressing the founding of the College of New York (1754). Although the college possessed a religiously diverse board of trustees and guaranteed liberty of conscience, its charter required an Anglican president, an Anglican moral philosopher, and Anglican liturgy in the college chapel.[122] In response, Livingston declared "the Liturgy . . . which is by the said Charter to be established in the said College is not established in this Province of New York."[123] He was largely correct. Although New York's royal governors directed taxes from the province's lower counties to the local Church of England, other New York towns used taxes to support other Protestant churches.[124] Livingston did not oppose religious taxes or their use by many churches—what scholars call a "system of multiple establishments"[125]—but he did object to legal privileges for one sect over others, as in the Anglican plans for the college.

Livingston expressed his objections by using secular and Enlightenment reasoning, particularly the former. His secular reasoning was evident in the priority he accorded to utility and his emphasis on the state's interest in domestic peace and stability. He favored "every Thing promoted that bears the Stamp of general Utility" and opposed the college's charter because "that general Utility can never be expected from a Scheme so precarious and liable to abuse."[126] The college charter, he continued, would disturb social peace and tranquility, leading to "a general Discontent and Tumult, which, afflicting all Ranks of People, will naturally tend to disturb the Tranquility and Peace of the Province." Livingston even suggested the instability of sectarian war—"a perpetual religious War"—as the consequence of college policy.[127]

Livingston also alluded to corporal penalties. Although the college's charter suggested neither the enforcement of doctrinal beliefs nor the use of legal penalties, Livingston denounced "forcing the conscience by *Pains and Penalties*" and, following the epistemological logic of Trenchard and Gordon, referenced the irrationality of "punish[ing] Men by penal Laws, for not believing right."[128] His major contribution to the discussions about religious toleration inhered in such references and allusions. He did not advance the theory of religious toleration, nor broaden the number of people to whom it applied, but evinced a heightened sensitivity to the coercion inherent in the law's privileging of one denomination over others. By equating an Anglican president and moral philosopher and Anglican liturgy at the college with the religious violence and legal penalties of the past, he indicated that the earlier vigilance against pain and punishment for religion was equally valid against denominational privilege in relatively tolerant mid-century New York.[129]

Although advancing neither the theory nor scope of religious toleration, Livingston's heightened sensitivity to denominational privilege resonated with other writers in the mid- to late eighteenth-century period. Similar to Livingston, religious dissenters in England known as "rational dissenters" also combined secular and enlightened perspectives to denounce denominational privilege.[130] James Burgh, Richard Price, and Joseph Priestley, all of whom enjoyed a healthy American readership through the American Revolution, criticized Anglican privilege in England. Burgh initiated such criticisms in *Crito, or Essays on Various Subjects* (1766–67). Therein, he denounced Anglican tests for military office: "Build an impenetrable wall of *separation* between things *sacred* and *civil*. Do not send a *graceless* officer, reeking from the arms of his *trull*, to the performance of a *holy* rite of *religion*, as a test for his holding the command of a regiment."[131] Because previous enlightened and secular authors had omitted or endorsed religious tests, Burgh's criticism represented an advance in such circles in the late-century period. Yet Burgh's "impenetrable wall of separation" was not, as some suggest, an advocacy for the modern notion of the "separation of church and state."[132] He defined "separation" as ending the denominational privilege of Anglican tests, not as prohibiting cultural and financial contact between civil and religious institutions. Similar to Livingston, he objected not to religious taxes per se, but to denominational inequality in their distribution.

The tendency to conflate eighteenth-century arguments against denominational privilege with modern notions of the separation of church and state is not uncommon. This tendency reflects an inclination in some historical literature to be insufficiently attentive to the nuances and terms of debate in the early modern discussions about religious toleration. In *The Evidence for a Future Period of Improvement in the State of Mankind* (1787), for example, Price praised the American Federal Constitution's "total separation of religion from civil policy."[133] One historian thus describes Price as a "staunch defender of the separation of Church and State."[134] Yet Price wrote *Evidence* in 1787, more than a decade before the phrase "separation of church and state" entered the American lexicon[135] and when America's "total separation" was the prohibition on religious tests for federal office in Article VI of the un-amended Federal Constitution. Price praised Article VI because it prohibited in America what he sought to abolish in England, namely, in his words, denominational "Test Laws" restricting "eligibility to civil and military offices."[136] His understanding of "separation" was thus ending denominational privilege, not prohibiting institutional and financial contact between religious and civil institutions. This understanding was apparent in the combined publication of Price's *Observations on the Nature of Civil Liberty* (1776) and his *Additional Observations on the Nature and Value of Civil Liberty* (1777). Separately, these works were reprinted in Boston, Philadelphia, New York, and Charleston.[137] Together, they were published as *Two Tracts on Civil Liberty* in London, Dublin, and Philadelphia (1778).[138] Therein, Price similarly praised the denominational equality in Pennsylvania and Massachusetts, notwithstanding Massachusetts' policy of religious taxation, which he understood to be channeled according to the denominational wishes of each individual:

> In Pennsylvania (one of the happiest countries under heaven before we [the English government] carried into it desolation and carnage) all sects of Christians have been always perfectly on a level, the legislature taking no part with any one sect against others but protecting all equally as far as they are peaceable. The state of the colonies north of Pennsylvania is much the same and in the province of Massachusetts Bay, in particular, civil authority interposes no further in religion than by imposing a tax for supporting public worship, leaving all the power of applying the tax to the support of that mode of public worship which they like best.[139]

As discussed below, Baptists in Revolutionary Massachusetts were considerably less sanguine about their situation and employed sacred reasoning to object to this purported policy of impartial religious taxation.

The rational dissenters thus promoted denominational equality, which meant no denominational privileges in public office or public funding. In this, they advanced discussions toward religious liberty in the enlightened and secular circles of the late eighteenth century. The tendency to conflate denominational equality with modern notions of the separation of church and state obfuscates their argument[140] and reflects the unstated assumption that only two policy options exist for the relationship between religion and civil government, the complete separation or the close union of church and state. Yet numerous gradations exist between the opposite poles of separation and union, and one such gradation was the rational dissenters' ideal of denominational equality.[141] That such equality was their ideal was clear. In *Observations on the Importance of the American Revolution* (1784), which Thomas Jefferson praised,[142] Price criticized "a civil establishment of a particular mode of religion, that is, where a predominant sect enjoys exclusive advantages."[143] In *Essay on the First Principles of Government* (1771), Priestley also criticized the inequality of exclusive advantages and sought equality by ending denominational tests for public office and by channeling religious taxes to the denomination of one's choosing. "Whether he choose to conform to the established religion or not," Priestley proclaimed in reference to public office, "let every man, who has sufficient abilities, be deemed qualified to serve his country in any civil capacity." On the channeling of religious taxes, Priestley continued: "The most unexceptionable establishment of religion that I have yet heard of is that of some of our North-American colonies, in which all the inhabitants are obliged to pay a tax for the support of some form of the christian religion, but every man's contribution is faithfully applied to the use of whatever church, or society, he himself shall choose. To such an ecclesiastical establishment as this, few persons, I believe, in the present state of things would have much objection."[144]

Priestley was correct that relatively few persons in his generation objected to an ecclesiastical establishment based upon denominational equality in the distribution of public funds. Yet some did object. And, significantly, the most widespread objection to such an establishment during the American Revolutionary period was voiced by sectarians or dissenters employing sacred reasoning. Scholars call Price and Priestley's notion of channeling one's religious taxes to one's denomination a "multi-establishment" because it allowed multiple sects to receive public funding. The most common arguments for such multiple establishments during the American Revolution were products of Enlightenment and secular reasoning. This fact was obvious in England in the writings of Price and Priestley, and apparent in America in the debates concerning religion and civil policy in Massachusetts and Virginia. By contrast, the most influential objections to such multi-establishments during the American Revolutionary period were products of sacred arguments derived from sectarian experiences.

The Enlightenment and secular rationales for a multi-establishment in Massachusetts appeared in Article III of the Declaration of Rights of the Massachusetts Constitution of 1780. The article's secular reasoning affirmed the state's interest in financially supporting religion because religion helped maintain "the good order and preservation of civil government," a theme permeating the article's logic:

> As the happiness of a people, and the good order and preservation of a civil government, essentially depend upon piety, religion, and morality; and as these cannot be generally diffused through a community, but by the institution of the public worship of God, and of public instruction in piety, religion, and morality,—therefore to promote their happiness, and to secure the good order and preservation of their government, the people of this commonwealth have a right to invest their legislature with power to authorize and require . . . the several Towns, Parishes, precincts and other bodies politic, or religious societies, to make suitable provision, at their own Expence for the institution and the Public worship of GOD, and for the support and maintenance of public Protestant teachers of piety, religion, and morality, in all causes which provision shall not be made Voluntarily.[145]

The Enlightenment reasoning informing this article was less explicit, but no less important. The article assumed an empirical epistemology. It assumed that human character was formed empirically through experience and that good character and morals could be shaped through the proper engineering of the social environment—in this case publicly funded religious institutions and instruction. Such engineering would, in turn, purportedly lead to stability in state and society.

The same secular and Enlightenment rationales for a multi-establishment were prominent in Revolutionary Virginia. In 1785, the *Virginia Gazette* published "On the Importance and Necessity of Religion to Civil Society." The anonymous author argued from the secular premise of religion's importance to social stability to the conclusion that religious taxation for public worship was "necessary for the support of government [and] the very being of society."[146] The tax in question was a general assessment bill in the Virginia Assembly which imposed a religious levy that individuals could direct to their own denomination. The bill's supporters included George Washington and John Marshall, future president and chief justice respectively.[147] The bill paralleled Article III of the Massachusetts Declaration of Rights in emphasizing that ministers served society's interest through moral instruction. It explained that public provision for religion is compatible with the liberal principle of denominational equality: "it is judged that such provision may be made by the Legislature, without counteracting the liberal principle heretofore adopted and intended to be preserved by abolishing all distinctions of preeminence amongst the different societies or communities of Christians." The bill then highlighted the state's interest in ensuring such funding by linking religion to the preservation of society: "religion hath a natural tendency to correct the morals of men, restrain their vices, and preserve the peace of society, which cannot be effected without a competent provision for learned teachers, who may be thereby enabled to devote their time and attention to the duty of instructing such citizens."[148]

Unlike in Massachusetts where a similar measure became Article III, enlightened and sectarian opponents defeated Virginia's general assessment bill. In recounting this defeat in Virginia, historians often emphasize the roles of James Madison and Thomas Jefferson. Yet sacred arguments were the most prevalent and popular arguments opposing such multi-establishments in the era of the American Revolution. In Massachusetts, for example, the evangelical Baptist Isaac Backus opposed all forms of religious taxation in his *Appeal to the Public for Religious Liberty* (1773). Therein, he proclaimed, "where is the officer that will dare to come in the name of the Lord to demand, and forcibly to take, a tax which was imposed by the civil state!"[149] In *An Appeal to the People of the Massachusetts State, Against Arbitrary Power* (1780), Backus directly attacked Article III with the proscriptions of revelation. "The third article," he objected, "asserts a right in the people of this State, to make and execute laws about the worship of God; directly contrary to the truth, which assures us that we have but ONE LAWGIVER in such affairs. Isai. 33.22, James 4.12."[150]

In Virginia too, where Madison and Jefferson played important roles, sacred arguments were by far the most widespread and influential force opposing a multi-establishment and promoting disestablishment. Presbyterians from Prince Edward County, dissenters in Anglican-dominated Virginia, petitioned the Virginia Assembly as early as 1776: "we do most earnestly request and expect that you would go on to complete what is so nobly begun; raise religious as well as civil Liberty to the zenith of Glory, and . . . pull down all Church Establishments."[151] That same year, members of the Hanover Presbytery, organized and led by religious leaders of the evangelical College of New Jersey, similarly requested disestablishment by referencing the time-honored sacred argument concerning the spiritual weapons of 2 Corinthians 10:4. "When our blessed Saviour declares his kingdom is not of this world, he renounces all dependence upon State power," they explained, "as his weapons are spiritual, and were only designed to have influence on the judgment and heart of man." "Therefore," they concluded, "we ask no ecclesiastical establishments."[152] The following year, the same Presbytery explained the situation in Virginia: "the propriety of a general assessment . . . for the maintenance of the ministers of the gospel . . . is deferred by our Legislature to the discussion and final determination of a future Assembly." Petitioning the Assembly again, the Presbytery objected to such an assessment by declaring in reference to the two-kingdoms doctrine that "every good Christian believes that Christ has ordained a complete system of laws for the government of his kingdom."[153] A few years later, a larger group of lay Presbyterians petitioned the Assembly yet again. They directly attacked the general assessment bill by proclaiming that "Jesus Christ hath given sufficient authority to his church, for every lawful purpose: and it is forsaking his authority and direction, for that of fallible men, to expect or to grant the sanctions of civil law to authorize the regulation of any Christian society."[154] Baptists from Powhatan County also petitioning the Assembly were similarly aggressive in affirming "Jesus Christ [as] the sole Head and Lawgiver" in religious affairs. The Powhatan petitioners explained to Virginia legislators that lay Baptists "are of opinion that the principle on which the [assessment] bill is founded is utterly repugnant to, and inconsistent with the original genius and simplicity of the Christian Church." Assessment, they continued, is "wholly of human invention and directly contrary to that plan on which the gospel manifests it [the Church] to have been constituted by Christ and his Apostles."[155]

Amid such sacred arguments, Madison certainly deserves credit for opposing the assessment bill in the Virginia Assembly and for authoring his own petition, a "Memorial and Remonstrance Against Religious Assessments" (1785). Although some have read the modern notion of the separation of church and state back into "Memorial,"[156] Madison's petition was the product of the eighteenth-century Anglo-American world, not the twentieth-century United States. As one leading legal scholar observes, Madison's "argument has a definite 'sectarian' quality."[157] Rather than temper religious duty with the Enlightenment language of virtue and benevolence, as was customary in contemporary high-brow circles,[158] and rather than emphasize secular interests and the claims of society, Madison affirmed the priority of a religious duty in which the good of society was not immediately at stake. As he explained, "duty is precedent, both in order of time and in degree of obligation, to the claims of Civil Society."[159] Despite the popularity of Madison's "Memorial," however, it was not even the most influential disestablishment petition of 1785, which was an anonymous petition from Goochland County dated November 2. This petition received the greatest subscription and served as a blueprint for several others. Its expressed goal was to remove obstacles hindering the spread of the gospel as the petitioners advocated disestablishment because they were concerned with the best "means of prospering the gospel" so adherents can "manifest to the world that they are inwardly moved by the Holy Ghost."[160] Given the prevalence of such arguments in Revolutionary Virginia, it is not surprising that Madison's "Memorial" employed similar language. After reviewing the pernicious effects of past "ecclesiastical establishments," Madison argued that religious taxation hindered the diffusion of the "light of revelation." As he explained, "the policy of the [assessment] Bill is adverse to the diffusion of the light of Christianity. The first wish of those who enjoy this precious gift ought to be that it may be imparted to the whole race of mankind." Yet, Madison continued, the bill "discourages those who are strangers to the light of revelation from coming into the Region of it; and countenances by example the nations who continue in darkness, in shutting out those who might convey it to them."[161]

Such petitions supported the Assembly's passage of Thomas Jefferson's Bill for Establishing Religious Freedom in 1786. This bill's passage is noteworthy because it prohibited religious taxes for single and multiple establishments,[162] and proscribed religious tests for public office,[163] thereby achieving disestablishment. The bill also broadened eighteenth-century discourse on religion by not referring to any religious groups, implying that its proscriptions on religious tests opened access to public office without significant qualification. Yet notwithstanding these noteworthy features, Jefferson's bill contained few if any novel ideas. Attributions of great meaning and influence depend more on scholarly conjectures about Jefferson's subjective motives than on the bill's actual text because the latter was derivative in logic and argument.[164] Denunciations of religious establishments, religious taxes, and religious tests were not novel, but possessed a long historical pedigree usually grounded in sacred argument as well as a contemporary prevalence in the petitions of religious dissenters in the American Revolutionary period.

The derivative nature of Jefferson's bill reflected the inherited character of the American Revolutionary discussions about religious toleration and religious liberty more generally. Whether it was Enlightenment and secular rationales for establishments, petitions and pamphlets of dissenters employing sacred reasoning, or ambiguous use of concepts such as "rights" and "liberty of conscience," Revolutionary Americans debated religious toleration and religious liberty in terms less innovative than imitative, rendering the Revolution in this context more conventional than transformative in the realm of ideas. The Revolution, simply stated, included significant continuity with the past. Yet the Revolution was not wholly conventional in its treatment of religion. Jefferson's bill may not have represented an advance in substantive argument, but it did represent an advance in legal procedure. It was codified as law. Although the bill's passage depended upon the grassroots petition campaign of religious dissenters who had flooded into Anglican Virginia in the decades before the Revolution and inundated the Virginia Assembly with their demands for religious liberty in the 1770s and 1780s, the bill nonetheless was not a petition or pamphlet, but proposed legislation passed into law. As such, it marked an important point in the historical development of religious liberty. That point remained largely grounded in a Protestant context and it did not usher in an era of impartial religious liberty. Yet it built upon the heightened sense of possibility opened up by the Revolution and helped establish the ideal of legal impartiality as a foundation for later claims and debates. It was, in short, a law unlike any other.

Conclusion

The sacred, secular, and Enlightenment forms of reasoning of the seventeenth and eighteenth centuries reflected the cultural processes by which the societies of the British North Atlantic transitioned from religiously less tolerant to religiously more tolerant ideas and practices. The fact that religious intolerance continued through this period and beyond does not indicate that an important transition was not underway. It rather highlights that such cultural transitions are enormously difficult, usually sporadic, often circuitous, and certainly prolonged in their development. This was true for the early modern English-speaking North Atlantic as for any culture undergoing such remarkable change in its attitudes and habits.

Unfortunately, an integral part of this important change in the early modern British North Atlantic is clouded today by attempts to historicize the current debates and legal formulations of church-state jurisprudence and constitutional thought. Obscured is the fact that much of the energy moving early modern society and culture toward greater religious toleration and religious liberty was sectarian in nature, rooted in the religious commitments and experiences within sectarian cultures, reasoned through in sacred thought processes, and often expressed in sacred idioms. Thus contrary to much legal-minded scholarship today, usually informed by modern-day legal issues, concepts, and language,[165] the transition to more tolerant ideas and practices in the early modern period was not primarily about segregating religion from politics, secularism, or the separation of church and state. Nor was it simply about the proliferation of sects, though such proliferation was important as James Madison noted in *Federalist* 51 how security "for religious rights" increased with "the multiplicity of sects."[166] Rather, the transition to more tolerant ideas and practices was largely about how various sectarians understood and drew on their religious traditions as a cultural resource for engaging the public sphere and discussing the interplay of religion, law, and society. Undoubtedly, different understandings of those or similar religious traditions also provided resources for intolerant ideas and practices, as other essays in this volume reveal and as cultural traditions almost always do, whether sacred or secular. The point is not that the role of religion in early modern cultural change was one-dimensional, but that it was multi-dimensional and that flattened understandings of this complex picture distort the dynamic roles of religious commitments and sacred arguments in the formative development of American culture and politics. Indeed, even valid references to a "Godless Constitution" and a "secular state" miss this rich and multilayered way in which religious perspectives constructively engaged American public culture by contributing to public discourse on the structural relationships between the state, law, and society.[167]

Chapter 2

Amalek and the Rhetoric of Extermination

JOHN CORRIGAN

> The Bible is true.
> —Andrew Jackson

The definitive nineteenth-century biography of the nation's seventh president concluded with its author observing: "It does not appear that he ever repented of anything, ever thought that he had been in the wrong in anything, or ever forgave an enemy as a specific individual."[1] But as William Graham Sumner and a throng of other biographers since have noted, the General gave signs of embracing the good book, especially late in life, when he doled out morsels of its wisdom, wrapped in words of tender affection, to his family and friends during his final June, in 1845. In assessing his life and representing it to others, and in communicating his aspirations for his adopted son and grandchildren, he deployed the language of biblical faith that they all shared and recognized as the linguistic vehicle best suited to deathbed farewells. For Jackson and his circle, and for many other Americans as well, the Bible was true in all kinds of ways, from the literal veracity of its words to its beautiful consolations and intuitively appealing provocations and its status as iconic artifact, a book that could be held, smelled, and felt.

From the colonial era through the antebellum decades, the Bible profoundly informed the lives of many Americans. The Old Testament, in particular, furnished a living archive of images of leaders, brigands, prophets, warmakers, and slaves, their trials and triumphs, devotions and doubts. The literature of the early Republic itself was saturated with references to the Old

Testament. Americans habitually imagined themselves into the stories about the Israelites, seeing their own causes joined with those of Moses, Abraham, Saul, and Ruth. Christians and Jews, and the unchurched as well, fashioned complex self-understandings, individual and collective, from those inspiring stories. It did not matter that the patterns of interpretation and application that they wove were often byzantine in their architecture, or paradoxical, or entirely contradictory. Americans banked on the appropriateness of biblical themes, characters, and plots in sorting out the meanings of things in the Republic. The American experience in the colonial setting and the early Republic unfolded within the narrative of the Old Testament just as much as it was ruled by the various legacies of the Enlightenment, the ethos of democracy, the market, and the blight of slavery. As the Harvard historian Perry Miller observed a century later, "The Old Testament is truly so omnipresent in the American culture of 1800 or 1820 that historians have as much difficulty taking cognizance of it as of the air people breathed."[2] The influence of the Old Testament, at least in as much as it furnished controlling imagery for thought, constituted an important part of what another twentieth-century writer, Pierre Bourdieu, might have called a *doxa*, "the ensemble of fundamental beliefs which do not even need to affirm themselves in the guise of an explicit dogma, conscious of itself."[3] Included in that doxa was an understanding of the nature of religious conflict. The fact of biblical literacy among readers meant that writers could shorthand their arguments without losing texture by invoking a proper name or geographic feature or string of words in place of an otherwise longer prose elucidation. Such shorthand was especially expedient in cases where authors were intent on drawing sharp distinctions between social groups. In figuring difference, they might juxtapose the Mosaic community of believers to the cruel Egyptians who enslaved them, or congratulate Esther on outing the evil Haman, or simply reference the story of Cain and Abel. Polemicists whose claims required the master stereotype of an acutely blameworthy group conjured the story of the Amalekites.

The Amalekites, descended from Esau, appear in several places in the Old Testament. Or more properly, they disappear, for their fate at the hands of God is to serve as fodder for a massacre that, when recalled by the Israelites over time, will instruct the faithful in the importance of obeying God's commands. The Amalekites were a wandering tribe that trailed the Hebrews during their flight from Egypt, falling upon the sick and weak in the rear, killing them and claiming their possessions.[4] Moses presided over a miracle in the desert in which the Jews defeated the Amalekites, but did not entirely destroy them. A few centuries later the prophet Samuel informed Saul, Israel's first king, that God wished the Amalekites annihilated: "Thus says the Lord of hosts: 'I will punish Amalek for what he did to Israel, how he ambushed him on the way, when he came up from Egypt. Now go and attack Amalek, and utterly destroy all that they have, and do not spare them. But kill both man and woman, infant and nursing child, ox and sheep, camel and donkey.'"[5] Saul, however, spared the life of Agag, the Amalekite king, as well as the livestock, which he intended to sacrifice formally to God. Consequently Samuel reprimanded Saul that "to obey is better than sacrifice," put Agag to the sword, and abandoned the king to his regrets for his disobedience.

With regard to the larger theme of religious tolerance and intolerance, Old Testament references to the Amalekites are important less for their lesson in obedience to God than for their illustration of the theme of genocide.[6] Even before the successful campaign of Saul, God had promised to "blot out" the Amalekites, and, more specifically, to "blot out the remembrance" of them, as he spoke to Moses: "I will utterly blot out the remembrance of Amalek from under heaven."[7] In Deuteronomy, the extermination of the Amalekites is specifically linked to God's awarding possession of the land to the Hebrews, and to the underhandedness of the Amalekites: "Remember what Amalek did to you on the way as you were coming out of Egypt, how he met you on the way and attacked your rear ranks, all the stragglers at your rear, when you were tired and weary; and he did not fear God. Therefore it shall be, when the Lord your God has given you rest from your enemies all around, in the land which the Lord your God is giving you to possess as an inheritance, that you will blot out the remembrance of Amalek from under heaven. You shall not forget."[8] Crucial to the meaning of this excerpt is the final line stressing to the Israelites, prior to Saul's victory, the necessity of remembering the evil done by the Amalekites, at the same time that God vows to erase all memory of them. This association of remembering with forgetting is essential to appreciating the complex logic informing religiously driven campaigns to exterminate one's opponents. Such campaigns are undertaken not only to blot out the existence of an enemy, but to bury the memory of that enemy as well, the act of violence issuing from hatred being itself an enactment of a simultaneous urge to forget. At the same time, however, crusades to exterminate the other are contrived to remember that the other has been erased from memory. So the scriptural recounting of the act of annihilation of the Amalekites and God's promise to purge from collective memory all traces of them is itself a testimony, a remembering. It is this ambivalence, a choppy movement between hatred and forgetting, that has been historically central to relations between religious opponents. That ambivalence, moreover, reaches more broadly into confrontations between religions, framing the self-understandings of groups in conflict. In many encounters we find the oppressors constructing the oppressed as the mirror of certain negative characteristics of themselves, that is, as a doppelganger of the Amalek within the oppressor. American Protestant groups that perceived Catholics as a threat, for example, met secretly in order to condemn the "secrecy" and "predilection to violence" of Catholics and to lay plans for their extermination. Their plans adopted the language of genocide, the "blotting out" of one's opponents along with memory of them, and the identification of underhanded and conspiratorial enemies as Amalekites.

English Backgrounds

In his groundbreaking studies of nativism and hate groups in nineteenth-century America, David Brion Davis argued that social movements practicing violent intolerance were descended from European precursors. The genetics were especially vivid in the case of religious intolerance, Davis writing that "there was a general continuity between such movements and the traditional European response to radical religious sects and secular brotherhoods; anti-Catholicism, of course, was as old as the Reformation, and its principle arguments and accusations changed very little over the centuries."[9] The means of transmission of this prejudice were many, and included the example of physical violence as well as the modeling of rhetorical strategies. In rhetorical skirmishes about religious differences, Amalek sometimes made a most dramatic appearance, and this was especially so in England in the years surrounding the Puritan revolution. As the early twentieth-century *Cambridge History of English and American Literature* pointed out, "The publication of the *Authorised Version* of the Bible in 1611 had set men thinking of the treasure that had fallen into their hands, and very many now read persistently the one book upon which they looked as the guide to salvation . . . ; and men learned to identify themselves with the conquering, exterminating children of Israel, and to look upon all who opposed them in politics or church doctrine as men of Belial, Moabites, Amalekites and other adversaries of Israel and of God."[10]

Partaking of the early seventeenth-century tendency to conjure Amalek, Thomas Taylor, who often preached at St. Paul's Cross in London and authored a voluminous body of theological and devotional works, undertook in 1624 to explain to his auditors the urgency of resistance to Catholicism by preaching *An everlasting record of the utter ruine of Romish Amalek*. Taking as his text Exodus 17:14, cited above, Taylor professed that "in our way to heaven we must make account of many Amalekites." Observing that God historically had delivered the faithful from the clutches of the Amalekites who had risen against them, he asked his audience why it was necessary that God destroy the Amalekites *and* the memory of them. Taylor explained that it was their "fraud" and their "underhand practices" that were "crafty and cowardly done" that sealed their fate before God, but above all it was their disregard of their affiliation with Israel, their neglect of their "neere relation," that doomed them. Taylor observed that "it was unnaturall, for Amalek was of the same blood and neere kinred with Israel . . . so as they forgetting bloud and kinred, nourish an unnaturall wrath" against Israel, and were destroyed because of that.[11] Catholics, whose security in England had eroded steadily for a century, were for Taylor and some other Puritan leaders the epitome of faith-traitors, and therefore evil in the same ways as the Amalekites. For Taylor, the "Romish Amalekites," who, "of all Religious," are the most cruel and "smiting," hide in "the vaults of caves of black darkness" hatching "their plots for seduction and destruction." Because of these "plots and projects," but especially because they "forget all naturall bonds," just as did the Amalekites, the "Romish Amalekites" are "written by God for destruction." As Christians who had underhandedly subverted the true faith, twisting it into malignant priestcraft and empty ritual, Roman Catholics reenacted the drama of Amalekites who turned on their kinsmen fleeing Egypt, ambushing the weakest of the refugees in cowardly fashion. As affiliates, by virtue of their Christianity, to English Protestants, they were especially dangerous. Accordingly, for Taylor, it was Christian "dutie . . . to fight with God in blotting out their remembrance," to "utterly destroy the kingdom and the memory of Amalek," that is, Catholics.[12]

In the following decades, Puritan writers continued to develop the theme of the Romish Amalek. During the summer of 1641, when Parliament was advancing its campaign that would eventually require all men above the age of seventeen to pledge to champion the Protestant Church of England against popery, supporters of that campaign cast the program in Old Testament terms. John Geree, in *Iudah's ioy at the oath* (1641), told his congregation in Tewkesbury that the oath would serve as a "touchstone to discover . . . who be of us, who against us, who of Israel, who of Amalek."[13] Anti-Catholicism after the restoration of the monarchy retained the focus on Amalek and began to broaden it by demonstrating more directly the relation of religion to political enmity. John Flavel, who found himself out of a job as minister in Dartmouth following the Restorationist Act of Uniformity in 1662, applied his highly regarded abilities for phrase-turning to a condemnation of Catholic influences in England. The opening sections of *Tydings from Rome or England's alarm* (1667) articulate the depth of Protestant anxieties about English Catholics. "Abhor Popery and be eminent in your zeal against it," preached Flavel. "Rome is that Amalek with whom God will never make peace; neither should we."[14]

Demonstrating the increasing tendency of anti-Catholic writers to allow their condemnation of popery to bleed over into a blanket sentence upon Catholic nations, Flavel observed that "It was Queen Elizabeth's Motto, No peace with Spain and it should be ours; no peace with Rome." Warning his audience that Catholics were "FALSE: BLOODY: BLASPHEMOUS," Flavel reminded them of the Gunpowder Plot hatched by Guy Fawkes and others in 1605. Fawkes and his co-conspirators had planned to blow up the Houses of Parliament during the State Opening, counting on the likelihood that James I and his family, together with a critical mass of Protestant leaders, would be killed in the explosion. Found out in the nick of time, the plot was foiled. Protestants led prayers of gratitude for divine providence, "the goodness of God in that deliverance," for escaping "the Powder Plot, that Catholic Villany."[15] Protestant reflection on the plot from the beginning had seen some measure of class and regional politics in the central religious conflict. Not surprisingly, as rhetoric like Flavel's filtered down into the streets from the outdoor pulpit behind St. Paul's and from other preaching venues, the English Protestant imagination pulled appraisals of political difference even more closely into orbit around core religious issues. In the process, the stain of Catholic treachery, and the requirement of crusading zeal against it, was more precisely transmitted to political enemies. It might be suggested, as a footnote to Flavel's anti-Catholicism, that the idea of Catholic collusion to subvert the order of government was something that Flavel intuitively came to understand from his own experience as a pastor exiled from his church by the government. Meeting secretly for services with former members of his congregation in a nearby town, he accumulated over the course of a decade some firsthand experience of subversive behavior that mirrored what he saw in his Catholic foes.

By the 1620s, as the literary historian Arthur F. Marotti observes, Puritan writers such as Thomas Scott had already taken steps toward entertaining a "conspiracy-theory approach to contemporary politics" fueled by their reflection on religious difference.[16] By 1677, English anti-Catholicism and condemnation of other nations and peoples thought to be treacherous had been rhetorically joined under the umbrella of several interlocking themes, including plots, conspiracies, and betrayals by kindred. Andrew Marvell's *An Account of the Growth of Popery, and Arbitrary Government in England* (1677) exemplified this pattern of thinking in its claim to be an unmasking of a broad conspiracy against English government and religion. "What is thus true in regard to the state holds as well in reference to our Religion," declared Marvell, who in this *Account* and in other works, stressed the need for a well-managed army and navy, and a muscular policy toward anti-English schemes arising on the continent. Illustrating his arguments with reference to various incidences of ostensible Catholic perfidy, Marvell asserted that at "the very bottom of their hellish conspiracy, there was yet one step more; that of religion."[17] The "conspirators" against England were plotting "to bring all back to Rome."[18] English historian Jonathan Scott has detailed the complex relations between political contestations and religious differences in England during this period, pointing out that from the 1620s through the civil war, "religious and political fears remained closely intertwined." For Scott, "it was, however, religious perceptions" that ordered thinking about political conflict, "and it was religious belief that was primarily responsible in England for driving participants in what became the civil war to take sides."[19]

Marvell linked the survival of English liberties, what American revolutionaries later referred to as the "antient rights of Englishmen," to the defense of Protestantism with its rights of conscience that were thought to be one of its distinguishing features vis-à-vis Catholicism. The phrase "liberty of conscience" recurs in Marvell's writing, and the writing of his contemporaries.[20] During this time of incessant anxieties about popish plots English writers significantly enriched a Protestant historiography grounded in the trust that liberty of conscience was of Protestant provenance.[21] That line of interpretation, so cultivated, widened the field for application of conspiracy theory to all sorts of political debates, while at the same time upholding the basic assumption that religion was at the root of the problem. Protestants' posturing as the defenders of liberty of conscience against Catholic plots to subvert it also provides historians opportunity for viewing something of the complexity of relations between persecutors and victims. Catholics, said Marvell, instead of counseling men to abide by their consciences, "seem'd to place all the business of Christianity in persecuting men for their consciences." Keeping in mind that those who picture themselves as the victims of conspiracy and persecution (in this case Protestants) oftentimes reflect in their own behavior the crimes that they condemn in their persecutors (here, Catholics), we navigate a little further into the mental worlds of the seventeenth-century actors. How did Protestants of the late 1670s and early 1680s, thinking themselves victims, make sense of the spectacle of the hanging and drawing and quartering of the two dozen or more Catholics who in their agonies insisted on their innocence?[22] It might have been the case that in such public performances of hatred, extermination of the other proceeded apace with a cleansing of memory, so that seeing was in fact forgetting, or at least an alteration of memory. That is, persecutors could forget that their own behaviors mirrored those attributed to their enemies by engaging in acts of hatred that destroyed their enemies and, hatred being a pathway to forgetting, simultaneously removed them from memory.

In 1678, in the year following the publication of Marvell's *Account*, Parliament heard Titus Oates's deposition about his uncovering a Catholic plot against James II. Later discovered to be a patchwork fantasy of lies and half-truths—Oates was imprisoned, but not before his testimony sent several men to their executions—*A True Narrative of the Horrid Plot and Conspiracy of the Popish Party* (1679) catalogued an assortment of political entities and religious opponents whose covert activities threatened England. In one way or another, Oates connected France, Denmark, the Netherlands, Ireland, Rome, Jesuits, Benedictines, Dominicans, and Carmelites, among others, with an anti-English/anti-Protestant conspiracy. For Oates, Marvell, and other writers of the time, the political upheavals and the human suffering that came with the Thirty Years' War (1618–48) kindled a watchfulness of England's relations with other nations alongside an impulse to ferret out domestic intrigues. These inclinations led to storytelling that found its way into print as revelations about discovered plots abroad and at home. A booklet published in London in 1696 purported to be "A true history of the horrid conspiracy to assassinate his Sacred majesty, King William" and to foment rebellion against Protestantism in general, with help from French invaders. Another book that same year observed the recent military affairs of the British Isles, Flanders, and some other areas of Europe "with a particular relation of all the plots and conspiracies against the life of King William and his government" and promised "especially a large account of the late horrid conspiracy" to assassinate the king "and bring in a French power." Sir Richard Blackmore's contribution to explaining the role of "Popish Bigots . . . to attempt the subversion of the present Government," appeared early in the next century in the form of an expose entitled *A True and Impartial History of the Conspiracy Against the Person and Government of King William III*.[23]

The development of the "popish plot" literature, which spanned virtually the entire seventeenth century in England, spilled over into the eighteenth century and in so doing took some new directions. One elaboration was the assignment of Old Testament correspondences to English military heroes. The enemies of England—especially the French—were cast in these dramas as opponents of biblical proportion. As William Perse explained in his thanksgiving sermon for the victory of the Duke of Marlborough over the French in Flanders in 1706, the French, in "harrassing all our neighboring territories" had behaved in the same way as the biblical Amalekites who had set upon the weak fringes of the Jewish body that had wandered in the desert. The Duke of Marlborough played Moses, "as in the case of Amalek." Perse reminded his audience of "the promise of God to blot out the remembrance of that cursed race of Amalek," and upheld the English victory as a step in that direction, as a solution to "the French Power, which was insulting all our Neighbours round about."[24]

The imagery of Amalek as it was developed by English writers and ministers from the early seventeenth century to the late eighteenth century crossed the Atlantic. It did so with some dispatch, beginning with John Flavel's *Tydings from Rome*, which was published in Cambridge, Massachusetts, in 1668, the year after it had been published in London. Oral transmission of these representations came by way of English visitors such as George Whitefield, who informed a Philadelphia audience in 1746 how Duke William rescued England from "popish cruelty" in the form of Jacobites, whom he defeated at Culloden that year, "that Amalek might not prevail."[25] As late as the antebellum period, Amalek was a standard image in American reflections on English history. Political periodicals such as the *American Whig Review* and the *United States Democratic Review*, which frequently referenced English political history and theories of government and republished English writings on those subjects, could comfortably describe for their American audiences a Cromwell who regarded papists as Amalekites. That included airing the theory that Cromwell slaughtered the Irish in deliberate reenactment of Old Testament justice: "Cromwell smote the Irish, as the children of Israel did the Moabites and Amalekites, with the edge of the sword, under the sanction of a divine mission, and in the full faith that he was fighting the battles of the 'Lord of Hosts.' "[26]

Although Americans acquired a familiarity with the rhetoric of Amalek from English writers and preachers, their appropriation of the story would be conditioned by the peculiarities of culture and politics in the United States. Some Americans, such as John Greenleaf Whittier, would continue to remind their countrymen of an English past in which Presbyterians and Puritans shot down "rank after rank of the men of Amalek."[27] Others would adapt the story to fit the situation in North America. Political differences would always matter and would remain entwined with religious debates. Most important, however, would be the growing frictions between traditionally Christian Americans and the new religion, Mormonism; the ongoing Euro-American contestation with Native Americans for space and place; an American version of anxiety over Catholics; and resurgent fears of Jewish conspiracies, alongside an assortment of other sporadic American battles involving religious groups.

Amalek in America

American religious leaders in New England and elsewhere, through the nineteenth century, were familiar with the story of Amalek, as would be any Christian minister, and especially a Protestant one, whose sermonizing required knowledge of the Bible. Protestant leaders, from the beginning of the settlement of New England, invoked Amalek in making points about Christianity in the New World. John Winthrop, in his well-known "covenant" speech aboard the Arbella just prior to the Puritans' arrival in Massachusetts Bay in 1630, drew his auditors into a consideration of the core meaning of covenant by raising the specter of the Amalekites. He compared the importance of obedience to God in the work of building a Christian community in New England to God's commission to Saul "to destroy Amalek."[28]

The imagery deployed by Winthrop informed generations of Anglophone literature about North America. The colonial theologian Jonathan Edwards, in *A History of the Work of Redemption* (1739), a project that he intended before his untimely death to be his great work of divinity, his mature theology, made more precise application of Amalek to the unfolding of history. "The dangers that the saints must meet with in their course through the world," he wrote, "were represented by the fiery flying serpents which the children of Israel met with in the wilderness. The conflicts the church has with her enemies, were represented by the battle with the Amalekites, and others they met with there."[29] In reflecting on the enemies of the church in his *Systematic Theology* (1846), the nineteenth-century revivalist and abolitionist Charles Grandison Finney argued that justice toward them was an aspect of love, but tough love, to be sure. The "prayers for the punishment of the wicked" that "abounded" in the Old Testament, were, Finney warned, "no vindication of the spirit of fanaticism and denunciation that so often have taken shelter under them. As well might fanatics burn cities and lay waste countries, and seek to justify themselves by an appeal to the destruction of the old world by flood, and the destruction of the cities of the plain by fire and brimstone." But Samuel's hewing the Amalekite leader Agag in pieces, and King David's "strongly developed" inclination toward annihilation of the wicked, were models of right action because "those sinners deserved to die."[30]

Other Americans adapted the narrative to do different kinds of argumentative work. Alexander Campbell, founder of the Disciples of Christ, wondered about the morality of capital punishment. He asked in the title of one lecture, "Is capital punishment sanctified by divine authority?" Answering in the affirmative, he observed, "And what shall we say of the father of the faithful [Moses], returning from the slaughter of the confederate kings? . . . of Samuel, the pure and pious Samuel, hewing to pieces with his own hand the king of Amalek?" Such were cardinal instances in which "God has made the purest, the holiest and the best of men, as well as angels, the executioners of his justice."[31] The Adventist prophetess Ellen Gould White referenced Amalek in pointing out how the hand of God could cause unexpected reversals in the course of events. In more than one instance, she demonstrated her familiarity with a line of interpretation that had emerged in the late seventeenth century and that made gradual gains in popularity into the nineteenth century. White, in referring to the Amalekites in 1870, observed: "God marked their boastful words against him, and appointed them to be utterly destroyed by the very people they had despised." Such thinking about reversal was continuous with the view of Mary White Rowlandson, who, in narrating her captivity in 1682, remarked on her predicament: "Another thing that

I would observe is the strange providence of God in turning things about when the Indians at the highest and the English at the lowest." The Indians, "thinking surely, Agag-like, 'the bitterness of death is past,'" the Lord opened the gates of hell and "hurled themselves into it" just at the time that the Christians that they persecuted had nearly abandoned hope.[32] Such a sense of reversal was part of a larger complex of ideas that coalesced around the Amalek story. Reversal was ideationally linked to imagined inversions and to the mirroring of parties affiliated through hatred.

Colonial New England minister Cotton Mather, never one to miss a chance to publicly bless the New England Puritan cause or to foretell its destiny, summoned Amalek to rally colonial forces to a "just war" against the Indians in 1689. "Turn not back till they are consumed," urged Mather. "Tho' they Cry; Let there be none to Save them; But beat them small as the Dust before the Wind." We pray, he said, for "vengeance upon our murderers . . . against the Amalek that is now annoying this Israel in the Wilderness." In this sermon we glimpse as well an early stage in the developing intersection of seventeenth-century Puritan rhetoric about papal plots and the call for extermination of the Indian. Mather made note of Catholic association with the Indians in tones meant to indicate its meaningfulness. "The Papists," he declared, "contribute what help they can" to the Indians, "and say Mass with them (as of Late) after their Little Victories." Which, in the broader scheme of things should not dispirit or confuse the soldiers, "but the rather from thence prognosticate their Approaching Ruine."[33] This joining of anti-Catholic polemics to condemnation of Native Americans was an important stage in the American rendering of the Amalek story, vesting it in richer detail and interlocking themes that suited it eventually to wholesale reapplication to American Catholics, Mormons, Jews, Jehovah's Witnesses, and others. All of this took place, moreover, alongside development of other tropes, as Christopher S. Grenda notes in this volume, that represented toleration as a desideratum of colonial and early national political culture.[34]

War Against Native Americans

Native Americans were considered heathen by the Christians who colonized the Americas and, as such, were judged culturally and religiously inferior. The missionary enterprise, particularly in the case of the Catholic nations of Spain and France, was grounded in a policy of saving souls, and, among the

Spanish especially, inculturating American indigenes. Europeans distinguished themselves from Native Americans by referring to themselves as Christians, signaling in that way that religion was bound up inextricably with other cultural differences that were manifest in European encounters with Indians. Violent religious rhetoric was everywhere deployed against Indians when those encounters turned sour. The unconverted and culturally unrepentant were envisioned as enemies, and in the worst situations, when colonists imagined Indians as kindred who had turned against them, as Amalekites.

While English colonists believed that Indians were contrary and inferior in many ways, they also recognized them as kindred. Crucial to the English construction of the Native American was a belief that Indians, whatever their differences with Europeans, shared a bond with the English that lay buried deep in the religious history of both groups. New Englanders especially arranged the image of the Indian in accordance with theologically grounded historical patternings of people and place that were familiar to them through preaching and religious literature. Participants in the Virginia Company's colonization of North America, as Alden T. Vaughan and Karen Kupperman have shown, had imagined Indians as the English themselves had lived at an earlier point in time. That is, they envisioned Native Americans as "Britons," England's Saxon ancestors, heathens all until the Romans forced Christianity upon them. English reports about Native Americans in this vein were, in Kupperman's words, "mirrors in which English readers could see their own virtues and vices reflected."[35]

More importantly, and specifically, the English quickly came to regard Native Americans as the descendants of the Ten Lost Tribes of Israel. Western writing about the fate of the twelve Jewish tribes of the Old Testament had long ago concluded that in the aftermath of social and political pressures upon the Jews, two tribes had remained in Judah and the other ten had been "lost" (meaning that they had been dispersed). Beginning with the Spanish and French, European explorers and missionaries in the Americas had developed detailed theories that identified Indians as lapsed Jews, and even lapsed Christians. The renowned Dominican missionary Bartolomé de las Casas, for example, considered the possibility of the Indians being descended from the Jews. Historian Sabine MacCormack, in her analysis of the manner in which the Spanish came to see Andean peoples as descendants of the Ten Lost Tribes, explains how Spanish writers such as Garcilaso de la Vega, Pedro Cieza de León, and José de Acosta, in their histories of the Incas and other writings, found linkages between Indian mythologies and material cultures and the Jewish and Christian religions. Indians, according to these writers, had gradually "forgotten" the Jewish revelation. Moreover, as the Spanish compared what they saw in Indian culture to what they read in their New Testaments, they began to argue that traces of Christian preaching were discernible in the vestigial subtleties of Indian life. Some Spanish accordingly concluded that Indians had fallen away from Christianity over time, and that Amerindian religion in general and Inca religion in particular were, as MacCormack observes, viewed as *praeparatio evangelica*, that is, preparation for the gospel. French missionaries came to some of the same conclusions as the Spanish. As historian Luca Condignola has remarked, the writing of missionaries such as the Capuchin Pacifique de Provins expressed the view that the role of the missionary was to recover the faith, to reawaken it, in Amerindians. In his words, the missionary labored to "bring these savage people *back* to the knowledge of the true God we adore." The abbé Bobé in 1719 likewise explained how "Israelites under the dispersion by Salmanasar passed into North America," and he linked them specifically with the Sioux.[36]

Among New Englanders, the paradigm of the Lost Tribes was, as Alden T. Vaughan has written, "optimistic in that, like the Old Britons model, it assumed the Indians to be ripe for conversion."[37] The Puritan missionary John Eliot embraced the theory and helped popularize it in the mid-seventeenth century. His cause was joined in Amsterdam by the Jewish Rabbi Menasseh ben Israel whose *Hope of Israel* (1650) proclaimed "*that the first inhabitants of America were the ten tribes of the Israelites,*" and in Norfolk, England, by Presbyterian clergyman Thomas Thorowgood, author of *Iews in America; or Probabilities that the Americans are of that Race* (1650).[38] Other writers in England and the Americas lent their voices to support the theory from the earliest settlement of the colonies. Cotton Mather, in *The Mystery of Israel's salvation opened*, declared that the time was coming "when all Israel will be saved, and then will converting work go on gloriously . . . even among the Indian." Planting his analysis firmly in the soil of Puritan theology, Mather argued that "they are broken off from that covenant and church relation which once they stood in. This is true concerning the Israelites or ten tribes. . . . But there is a day coming, when God will receive them into favour again." Other well-known advocates of the theory were Roger Williams, William Penn, Samuel Sewall, and Jonathan Edwards. Edwards, in *History of the Work of Redemption*, argued that the Indians were led from Canaan by the devil, who by degrees was able to persuade them from their worship of God to worship of himself.³⁹ Charles Crawford's essay *Upon the Propagation of the Gospel*, published in Philadelphia in 1799, carried the theory into the eighteenth century, as did James Adair's *History of the American Indians* (1775), which was largely about "observations, and arguments, in proof of the American Indians' being descended from the Jews." Adair offered detailed explanation for residual Jewish culture in everything from Indian manner of counting time, to healing, burial, religious rituals, language, theocratic ideas, naming, and numerous other topics. William Apess, a Pequot, published his own version of the story in 1831 as *The Indians: The Ten Lost Tribes*.⁴⁰

Not all Americans rushed to embrace the theory that the American Indians were of the Ten Lost Tribes. Anne Bradstreet raised questions about it as did Cotton Mather, at least when he composed his seminal book, *Magnalia Christi Americana* (1702).⁴¹ Those who found it appealing, however, were drawn to it not only because of some interest in the human history of the American continents, but because of a view of history that included the belief that the Jews were to be converted before the return of Christ to the world. In New England, the notion that Indians were descendants of the Jews offered an exhilarating challenge to Christians who looked expectantly to the glorious end of time. Ministry to Indians was not merely an undertaking to convert heathen. It was activity that fell squarely in the center of a theologically driven agenda of history, and of human participation in the events that would lead to the culmination of history in Christ. Puritans knew from their Bibles that the Jews were to be converted before the dawn of the millennium. The Indians were considered ripe for conversion because their evangelicization was a way to bring them back to the revelation of God originally given to them as Jews. It is unlikely that any New Englander who had encountered Indians believed that they would suddenly convert in droves to the Christian faith. In fact, their conversions were not impressive either in terms of numbers or longevity. But missionaries approached the Indians with a sense of their own participation in the unfolding of a divine plan. They fully expected Indians to become Christian, to remember that they were children of God who had lapsed from the revelation given them centuries earlier. Christians who believed that Indians were the remnant of the Lost Tribes approached them as kindred souls, expecting Indians to respond by professing belief in Christian monotheism. Accordingly, as David Lovejoy has written, "missionaries loved the notion, for Christianizing pagans who were also descendents of Jews fitted the Bible's prediction for the millennium and would fulfill, in fact, one of its preparatory demands." When Richard W. Pointer observes (in a chapter in this volume) that John Long and David Brainerd glimpsed something worthy in the religiosity of Indians—and that a "countercultural strain" of tolerance was mixed in with intolerance of Native American religion—we can see how the Euro-American fantasy of the kinship of Indians and Christians could affect attitudes in different and sometimes opposed ways.[42]

For colonists, battles with Indians tended to be local affairs, or at least contextualized within a fairly narrow regional geography. Calls for the annihilation of one's enemies in such a setting were limited to a project steeped in the experience of immediacy and proximity arising from regular social contact. In the nineteenth century, Americans who drew upon the Amalek story in characterizing their opponents often envisioned a more extensive field of battle than colonial writers. Native Americans, for example, by the first decade of the century were largely considered a continental problem, and so were Mormons in later decades, particularly after their trek to Utah. As Anglo-American settlement proceeded westward, and as notions of manifest destiny acquired a grander scale in American self-understanding, the conceptualization of the "land" upon which conflict was played out began to change. Americans came to view themselves more confidently as bearers of a superior civilization, moving inexorably and by virtue of divine commission to claim their rights to continental—and eventually global—hegemony. Amalek was more than a local opponent. In the continental scale of encounter, references to Amalek increasingly denoted a broad class of opponent whose right to exist anywhere was in question. In such fashion, a report of a U.S. commissioner of Indian affairs in 1863 observed that "there is a deeply rooted antipathy between the habits, religion, and customs of a savage race, and the pursuits and teachings of civilization."[43]

New England thinking about elimination of the Indian from the land in the seventeenth century drew upon the Amalek narrative in casting Indians as evil and the English colonial warriors who battled them as martyrs or prophets. So, for example, the New England Confederation, in typical fashion, declared war on the Narragansett tribe in 1675 by observing of the "Narrohigansetts and their confederates": "So Sathan may combine and stir up many of his instruments" in the same way that "Amalek and the Philistines did confederate against Israel."[44] At other key moments in the English conquest of the northeastern tribes, sermons and speeches focused on the battlefield leadership of specific persons, much in the same way that English rhetoricians had placed figures such as the Duke of Marlborough at the center of their narratives. During the eighteenth century, as filiopietistic New England chroniclers were canonizing the heroes of the first generation and bestowing laurels upon the heads of contemporary defenders of the New England way, they also commended Indian fighters in eulogies and remembrances. Their memories of such persons were of Moses-like or Joshua-like heroes who prevailed over evil Amalekites. And in cases where colonial soldiers died in battle against Native Americans, they were celebrated as martyrs, and in a few instances even though the circumstances of their sacrifice did not immediately suggest heroism, or even competence, in the face of the enemy. Thus in relating details of the "fight at Piggwacket" in 1725, Thomas Symmes sermonized that Captain John Lovewell, who lost his life, the battle, and a majority of his force bounty-hunting Indian scalps, resembled Joshua, Moses's "Renowned general, in his wars with the Aborigines of Canaan," the Amalekites.[45] Just how far the colonial imagination had come in picturing the collective future of Native Americans as empty of promise, as already on course to be blotted out, is redolent in Symmes's preaching. Offered by Symmes as "a very Celebratory Elegy," the sermon is grounded in a trust that extermination of the Indian was only a matter of time.[46] That was the faith likewise of Captain Samuel Appleton, who wrote to a friend regarding his role as commander of the colonial forces arrayed against the Narragansett tribe in 1675: "By the prayers of God's people, our Israel in his time may prevail over this cursed Amalek; against whom I believe the Lord will have war forever until he have destroyed him."[47]

Some nineteenth-century American writers, looking back on the colonial period, wrote forthrightly about New Englanders' belief that Native Americans were Amalekites deserving of utter annihilation. In so doing, they read back into the colonial period a nineteenth-century story about conflict between Indians and whites as a far-reaching crusade informed by a cosmic view of good versus evil. That story had its roots in colonial America, but was amplified and refined during the first part of the nineteenth century. So, the Confederate veteran Robert Lewis Dabney, whose polemical goals were complicated, defended the honor of the South post–Civil War by raising the issue of slavery in the North, that is, "the enslaving of the Indians. The pious 'Puritan fathers' found it convenient to assume that they were God's chosen Israel, and the pagans about them were Amalek and Amorites. They hence deduced their righteous title to exterminate or enslave the Indians."[48] Dabney, in his eulogy for General Thomas "Stonewall" Jackson in 1862, on the other hand, apparently had no difficulty in identifying Jackson himself as the hammer of the Amalekites, this time in the form of the Union.[49] *Putnam's Magazine* observed in 1857 that Christians in colonial North American treated Indians "as the Amalekites and Canaanites had been treated by the Hebrews." George Bancroft, in his monumental *History of the United States*, discerned that New Englanders assumed that they had "a right to treat the Indians on the footing of Canaanites or Amalekites." The *North American Review*, remarking on seventeenth-century English encounters with Indians in the northeast, concluded: "Heathen they were in the eyes of the good people of Plymouth Colony, but nations of heathen, without question, as truly were the Amalekites." Edward Eggleston looked back in 1883 on the "scenes of savage cruelty" at Mystic in 1637, when a colonial force that had trapped Pequot women and children systematically shot and burned them, a genocide, Eggleston added, that ministers rhetorically justified through "citation of Joshua's destruction of the Canaanites." The *Living Age* likewise observed of the event, "As the Israelites slew the Amalekites, so did the Pilgrims slay the Pequot." Bostonian Frederick D. Huntington, who eventually became a bishop of the Protestant Episcopal Church, commented in 1859 that the military exercises against Native Americans in New England were led by men who were "evidently of an energetic spirit and quite an Old Testament cast of mind."[50]

New England Puritans, building on the foundation provided them by English writers, condemned Indians as Amalekites, wrote and preached excitedly about blotting them out, and rhetorically presented the Indian-fighter in the figure of a biblical hero. Before the middle of the nineteenth century, a crucial linkage had formed among several component ideas, namely, the Indian as both distant other and as religious kindred, the desirability of exterminating one's enemies, of destroying their traces in collective memory, and of justifying such actions through appeal to a well-known, even ingrained, biblical narrative. That complex of ideas evolved partly through the ongoing influence in America, during the eighteenth century, of English anti-Catholic writings, which themselves had proffered a similarly multifaceted understanding of religious enemies. In America, thinking about Amalek in the eighteenth century also was refined through the coalescence of an ideology of America as a "redeemer nation" called to defeat evil wherever it threatened Christianity. And the transition from colonial status to new nation lent a particularly urgent and pointed tone to the Amalek rhetoric, as Americans made efforts to explore the continent, draw and defend boundaries, and situate themselves as the dominant power in North America. In short, then, ideas about kindred betrayal and extermination developed through incidences of contact between Native Americans and persons who had migrated to the Americas from Europe. The colonial understanding of religious opponents was grounded in the distinction that early English colonists made, like French and Spanish before them, between Christian and heathen. It is also important to bear in mind the influence of the theory that Indians were of the Ten Lost Tribes. Indians were the religious other at the same time that they were religious collaborators—distant brethren, but brethren nevertheless. In terms suggested by Roy Harvey Pearce, they were complexly idealized as both noble savages and heathen in need of conversion.[51] The European encounter with Native Americans did not spontaneously generate the inflammatory rhetoric we have examined, whatever the circumstances of those encounters. New Englanders adapted the anti-Catholic rhetoric of English polemicists to their work in constructing the Indian as enemy. In so doing, they brought to the fore the notions of extermination and of blotting out memory. They also began to shape an understanding of enemies as inherently secretive, as seeming allies or friends who in fact conspired to destroy them. The seeds of this were present from the beginning, inherited from English anti-Catholic rhetoric. Most importantly, Americans who commented on relations with Indians in these terms fully expected that their readers and auditors grasped the Old Testament framework for these ideas. As that rhetoric developed over the course of the nineteenth century, it gradually shifted its primary reference from the story of Amalek per se to a more precise focus on the modus operandi of the other, to the secrecy, conspiracy, and cowardice of Catholics, Mormons, Jews, Native Americans, and others. Those who sought to stir up hatred still made explicit reference to Amalek in their discussion of Indians and, increasingly, in complaints about Catholics and Mormons. But the emphasis was moving to certain characteristics of the religious other, to the other as a traitor and a coward and a conspirator in secret schemes against "real" Americans. All of these character traits were rooted in American renderings of Amalek and the Amalekites. As Richard Slotkin observed, writers exploited the image of Indians first as demons and then as humans—cunning, malignant, savage people—in service of inventing themselves as Christians in the new land. For Slotkin, and more pointedly for historian Jill Lepore, that process of invention was always haunted—and driven—by a fear of savagism at the same time that it drew upon a sense of kinship with Indians in the fashioning of an identity that was "American" as opposed to European.[52]

The French and Indian War (1755–63), which pitted Protestant New Englanders against "papist" French and their Indian allies, featured lively denunciations of Catholicism that characterized Catholics as Amalekites. As James West Davidson has shown, the logic of the millennial thought of New Englanders included an English willingness to see French Catholics as hopelessly corrupt and therefore fit to be annihilated during the approach of the eschaton.[53] In this frame of mind, Nathan Stone preached a sermon following English victories in Canada in 1760 that cast the defeated French adversaries as "Amalektish enemies," and reminded his auditors that the Bible taught that "Thou shalt blot out the remembrance of the Amalekites from under heaven."[54] Such language was progressively reinforced through the incorporation of other texts into the Old Testament core of stories about the Amalekites. For example, the application of texts drawn from the *Revelation to John*, an apocalyptic book of the New Testament, had been standard in Protestant writing about Catholics since the Reformation, and it continued in America. It was in this tradition of inter-testamental patterns of interpretation that the *Christian Monitor* reminded its readers in 1809 that "the ten-horned beast therefore represents the Romish church," a conclusion drawn throughout the century by many other Protestant exegetes of the text, as they engaged *The Revelation to John* alongside Old Testament condemnations of the enemies of God. Such interpretation added muscle to the other biblically framed calls to arms against Amalekites and built momentum for intolerance of Catholics. In more general terms, combinations of Old and New Testament justifications for annihilation of the other were interwoven so thoroughly by the nineteenth century that a writer for the *Boston Investigator* had no trouble in 1844 making sense of the meaning of a Jonesboro, Tennessee, *Whig* editorial that declared, "Our opinion is, that there is to be no peace in this country, till the Mormons and Catholics are exterminated." The editorial, said the *Boston Investigator*, was about "blotting out Amalek," that is, Mormons and Catholics, and doing so in anticipation of the coming "millennium."[55] By bringing an end to the existence of their enemies, some Christians expected to bring an end to time itself, the final resolution of the struggle against Amalek being the end of history, a forgetting on a mass and absolute scale.

PART II

Practices of Tolerance and Intolerance in Colonial British America

Chapter 3

The Episcopate, the British Union, and the Failure of Religious Settlement in Colonial British America

NED LANDSMAN

The exceedingly long controversy over the project of bringing an Anglican bishop to colonial British America has never been an easy matter for American historians to explain. Originating in intermittent plans introduced during the seventeenth century, the Anglican effort to obtain a bishop recurred enough times a century later to form an almost continual point of contention. The most puzzling aspect of that effort is probably its persistence, in the face of general indifference if not outright hostility from much of the Anglican populace in North America, vocal opposition from rival churches, and a consistent lack of support from the British government at home. It culminated, moreover, in the concerted campaign by a group of middle-colony Anglican Churchmen to bring the project to fruition during the 1760s, amid a colonial resistance movement that was challenging existing forms of imperial authority and that showed no inclination to accept additional impositions. It seems, in retrospect, to have been a fool's errand, put forward in the face of prevailing values of civil and religious liberty and the reality of a remarkably heterogeneous and religiously fragmented American society.

To Whig historians the explanation for the persistence of the Anglican proposals was not hard to find: the pursuit of the bishop was an integral part of an insistent British imperialism, an effort to impose greater control on the colonies from the center whenever and wherever that could be accomplished. A settled Episcopate would both establish English control over an often independent colonial Anglican Church and help to stifle the wayward spirit of colonial dissent. Thus Carl Bridenbaugh, in the most aggressive formulation of that position, contended that Anglican efforts reflected a "lust for dominion" and "aimed at nothing less than the complete reordering of American Society."[1] One major difficulty with that line of argument, however, is the general lack of support those efforts received from imperial authorities. Indeed, the push for an Anglican bishop came predominantly from *American* clergy. Much of their effort was devoted not to combating the opposition in the colonies, but rather to consistently unsuccessful attempts to persuade the imperial government to act.

The lack of support from home was partly a matter of policy—the fear that the effort would produce a larger outcry from American opponents than it was worth—at least from the perspective of secular authorities concerned with other issues. In 1750, Horatio Walpole noted as much, contending that the introduction of bishops would provoke dissatisfaction among dissenters, who were otherwise well affected toward the government.[2] Moreover, American opponents had strong connections and important allies on the issue among interest groups in London, especially English dissenters, as well as with the Church of Scotland.[3] Still, the Whig viewpoint fails to explain why those clergy in North America who supported the appointment of a bishop were as insistent about the cause as they were. It would be difficult to attribute their support to metropolitan imperialism. In fact, one of the criticisms against which promoters of the American bishop had to contend was the suggestion that the creation of such an official was designed to increase American independence from metropolitan control.[4]

Recent scholars have taken Anglican arguments more seriously. For those who favored a colonial bishop, it had little to do with imposing English or British authority upon independent-minded colonists. Rather, it was integral to Anglicanism itself. The Church of England was an apostolic church: the authority to appoint ministers, it was believed, was handed down from the Apostles in an unbroken succession. Those who lacked ordination from officials who received their own appointments in proper fashion could never be true ministers of Christ. That authority was vested in the Church and in England was inextricably interwoven with the state. Ministers appointed in any other way necessarily stood outside of that succession. Bishops were needed, moreover, to impose discipline and bolster clerical authority; even in those colonies in which the Church was established, the clergy had lost considerable influence to an increasingly assertive laity.[5]

By the end of the colonial period, advocates for a bishop were willing to trim the particulars of their request severely in an effort to overcome widespread opposition. Their specific request would be to appoint a bishop who would have no authority at all over those outside of the Church of England or even over lay members of that body. Their sole motive, they suggested, was to complete the structure of their church as all other denominations were permitted to do. Invoking the policy of toleration, Anglicans claimed that it was their church, and not those of their opponents, that suffered persecution.

Given the persistence of the Anglican effort, the question we must address is why no resolution to the bishop controversy could ever be reached. That is all the more striking because in the quarter century after the "Glorious Revolution," both England and Scotland achieved religious settlements that persisted in their essentials for the rest of the century, based upon secure national churches with substantial toleration for dissenters. The church structures of the two nations differed, and it took the high-handed action of a Tory parliament in 1712 to gain toleration for Scottish Episcopalians, but the core components of those settlements were never again seriously challenged. The primary struggles thereafter either took place within those churches or concerned the removal of the disabilities that dissenters confronted. That they would remain dissenters was hardly in doubt.

In North America, no comparable religious settlement was ever attained. Instead, the situation varied from colony to colony and over time, with some of the basic ground rules of ecclesiastical order frequently at issue. The Church of England obtained a legal establishment in most of the southern colonies, but the question of toleration there long remained unsettled. New England maintained working Congregational establishments in Massachusetts and Connecticut, but they would be rigorously contested by local Anglicans who claimed that the legitimate legal establishment belonged to their Church. In the mid-Atlantic, Pennsylvania maintained a high degree of spiritual freedom, but New Yorkers jousted over whether the Church of England had a valid establishment in the lower counties around New York City. In the rest of the colony it certainly did not, nor did it in New Jersey, although both Anglicans and Presbyterians in that colony at various times sought to make it their ecclesiastical headquarters.[6]

That a full religious settlement in North America would have faced substantial difficulties is obvious. The historical antagonism between the Church of England and English dissenters, the religious diversity of British North America, and the entrenched position of the New England churches were formidable obstacles. Yet similarly strong hostilities of even longer standing had not prevented solutions in Britain. Diversity by itself did not preclude a settlement based upon toleration and even the indulgence of distinct regional churches, even if in Scotland that resolution had to be imposed from above. There remains the very real question as to why resistance to such a settlement in North America was as successful as it was, especially in the face of the very strong countervailing trends toward consolidation and uniformity that emerged in Britain's eighteenth-century empire.[7]

Paradoxically, what precluded a settlement in North America was the very solution that was achieved in Britain. In eighteenth-century America, the principal points of contention were never simply those of establishment or toleration in the abstract, but rather the status of churches within Britain's overseas empire. In 1707, the Act of Union united England and Scotland under a single government, but with separate legal, educational, and ecclesiastical establishments, creating a multinational and, in important respects, multicentered British state. In securing the positions of the Churches of both England and Scotland, the authors of the union unwittingly disestablished the imperial Church but provided no coherent alternative in its place. Instead, they left Britain with two national churches, one of which was intimately interconnected with the state, and one that was decidedly not.

American historians have rarely devoted much attention to the union, assuming that the transition from an English to a British empire little affected its colonial dependencies. As a result, they have failed to examine the development of church-state relations or provincial understandings of religious liberty against the background of the particular characteristics of the British imperial state. They have simply not appreciated the extent to which the union disrupted and decentered existing lines of authority between metropolis and colony. In areas ranging from religion and intellectual life to politics to trade, the union provided Americans with new sets of imperial connections and alternative cultural authorities.[8] By securing multiple ecclesiastical establishments within the newly united kingdom, the union left colonial Anglicans the problematic task of reestablishing the place of an English national church in a British American empire, while creating space for those in the Reformed Churches, who had previously been dissenters, to lodge significant claims of cultural and ecclesiastical autonomy and equality.

The long Episcopate controversy was an expression of the ongoing uncertainty over the imperial status of the English church in British America. It brought to the fore previously separable questions of the relationship of church and state, of national churches within a multinational state, and of church and empire. In response to continuing Anglican efforts to secure substance for their status as a national church, their opponents used the implications of the union to redefine church and state in the imperial context. Drawing upon older Reformed traditions that allowed their churches a measure of ecclesiastical independence without disavowing state support, opponents would move toward a position that emphasized the freedom of the church from the state, of the community from any church with state entanglements, and of provincial churches from imperial establishments. Those would become essential elements in the new understanding of religious liberty that emerged in Revolutionary America.

In early 1707, the traveling Irish Presbyterian minister Francis Makemie was arrested in New York at the instigation of that colony's Anglican governor, Lord Cornbury, on charges of preaching without a license. Makemie's initial plea rested on England's Act of Toleration, under which he claimed the privileges of a Protestant dissenter. The governor, according to the minister's account, disputed that claim. The toleration was an act of the English Parliament, and in Corbury's view applied only to England and not to the colonies, which were governed according to their charters and whatever instructions the queen saw fit to issue. Dissenters might apply for leave to preach, and Cornbury, who was both an active proponent of the establishment and a firm supporter of toleration, was not averse to granting it. He merely denied that those outside the Church of England had any inherent right to preach.[9]

Even as Makemie and Cornbury debated, the constitutional ground was shifting under them. On May 1 of that year, while the minister was still awaiting trial, England and Scotland completed their Parliamentary union. When Makemie reappeared in court he altered the grounds for his plea. He now agreed that the toleration did not extend beyond the bounds of England. Toleration implied a religious establishment, and Britain, unlike England, did not have one. Or rather it had two: an Anglican church south of the border, and a Presbyterian establishment in Scotland. Thus Makemie belonged to a church "as nighly related and annexed unto the Crown of England, as the Church of England themselves."[10] Religious establishments within the new United Kingdom were therefore local or national rather than British or imperial, extending only to the territories over which their authority had explicitly been settled. Makemie won the case, the potential significance of which for colonial dissenters was recognized by Cotton Mather, who praised "that brave man, Mr. Makemie. . . . Without permitting the Matter to come so far as to Pleading the *Act of Toleration*, he has compelled an acknowledgment that those Lawes aforesd are but Local ones, and have nothing to do with the Plantations."[11]

As Mather recognized, the union and the Makemie verdict had undermined some basic assumptions about the imperial establishment, by which those outside of the Church of England were entitled to nothing more than the limited toleration that Cornbury was prepared to offer. Hardly anyone seems to have realized this beforehand. The union had been negotiated wholly to settle the relationship between England and Scotland. The latter nation, far smaller and weaker than its neighbor, had seen its interests slighted by their joint monarch, while the former was concerned about the strategic dangers that would result if Scotland should choose a separate monarch to succeed the childless Anne, as they were threatening to do. The only way that North America entered into the discussion at all was in regard to the commercial benefits the opening of England's overseas empire would provide to the Scottish economy. If it had occurred to anyone that the union might have ramifications for the empire itself, he or she does not seem to have recorded it.[12]

Makemie may have provoked the situation deliberately. He does seem to have fancied himself an attorney as well as a preacher; he signed his narrative of the event "A Learner of Law, and Lover of Liberty." He set up his arguments about the union quite carefully. He first accepted the previously offered contention of the governor's side that the Toleration Act did not extend to North America, in order to maintain that the Act of Uniformity could not apply there either. Still, his approach was cautious. Before the minister himself raised his arguments about the union, he first allowed his attorneys to reassert earlier contentions that he was protected as well by the toleration.

The significance of the union for North America came from measures included to protect the Church in Scotland, thereby ensuring that the new United Kingdom would have multiple national churches. With many fewer members in the new British Parliament, Scotland risked the possibility that an English majority would overturn its Presbyterian religious settlement and institute Episcopal government in the Scottish Church. Thus along with the Act of Union, the Scottish Parliament passed an "Act for Securing the Protestant Religion and Presbyterian Church Government," providing that the

"True Protestant Religion contained in the . . . Confession of Faith with the form and purity of Worship presently in use within this Church and its Presbyterian Church Government and Discipline . . . shall Remain and Continue unalterable." Moreover, every Sovereign succeeding to the throne was to swear to "inviolably maintain and preserve the foresaid settlement," and these conditions were "expressly Declared to be a fundamentall and essentiall Condition of the said Treaty or Union in all time coming."[13] The English Parliament, with less urgency, adopted a similar, albeit differently worded, measure for the security of the English Church.

On the surface, the union would seem to have created two coequal religious settlements. In fact there were significant asymmetries. One was a product of the respective size of the nations and their consequent representations in Parliament. England possessed approximately five times the population of Scotland, and its parliamentary contingent similarly outnumbered that of their northern partners. Could the English majority disrupt the Scottish settlement? While the union was being debated, Daniel Defoe traveled to Edinburgh on behalf of the government to argue that the security of the Scottish Church would be fundamental to the union itself and thus unalterable, and language suggesting exactly that was incorporated into the security act.[14] Still, many skeptics wondered whether such a limitation was possible within a system that recognized no established bounds to what a Parliament could do.

Scots Presbyterians would soon have reason to regret their accommodation. In 1712, a new Tory Parliament set out to clip the wings of the Presbyterian Church through a set of measures including the restoration of ecclesiastical patronage and toleration for Scottish Episcopalians. Presbyterians objected to all of those measures as violations of the union, but there was little they could do but protest in the face of a determined Parliament.[15] Still, there were obvious limits to the danger the Church confronted, as no one seemed prepared to attack the basic Presbyterianism of the Scottish Church.

The imbalance in Parliament was of little consequence in North America because there was no Presbyterian establishment to threaten. The union created a second asymmetry, however, that would pose greater difficulties for Americans: the divergent relationships of the two national churches to the new British state. In the case of the Church of England, church and state were thoroughly intertwined. The monarch remained head of the English Church, its position reinforced by the act of security of the English Parliament, which required kings and queens to uphold the place of the church. Bishops sat in the House of Lords, where they voted on measures affecting not only England but Scotland and the Scottish Church. Moreover, the connection to the state was an essential component of Anglican principles. The result would be significant ambiguities about the relative status of those two churches within imperial Britain. Where Makemie had contended successfully that the union had erased any inherent imperial establishment, the precise rights and privileges that other churches possessed were called into question by the continuing integration of the English Church with the British state.

The importance of the union for the American churches was largely because it came at a time when the Anglican Church was working toward securing its supremacy in most of the colonies. Its ascendance was rooted in the Restoration, as part of the general design to integrate the coastal mainland of North America under English (and monarchical) control. Yet James's Catholicism, as well as a general reluctance on the part of the Stuarts to create an ecclesiastical rival to monarchical authority, precluded a push for Protestant uniformity or full Anglican establishment. Thus while New Englanders were forced to accept an Episcopal presence in their region as a counter to their Puritan establishments, aspirations for Anglican hegemony elsewhere were thwarted by the enlarged influence of Quakers, Catholics, and Dutch Reformed churches, all of which James encouraged.[16]

Those monarchical restraints disappeared with the Glorious Revolution, and supporters of the Church of England began an aggressive effort to secure their place as the imperial church by extending their establishments across the colonies. In New York, the legislature in 1693 passed a Ministry Act intended to bolster religion in the lower four counties. The act was ambiguous, providing for the funding in each town of a "good sufficient Protestant minister," but a succession of Tory governors interpreted the law as requiring that only Anglican ministers receive public support, even where the towns intended otherwise. In 1702, the new governor, Lord Cornbury, ordered the removal of the Presbyterian minister from the church and manse in the town of Jamaica and his replacement by an Anglican clergyman, despite the fact that the predominantly Presbyterian population there had paid for the buildings.[17]

In the southern colonies the promotion of the Church was less inhibited. In 1706 the Church of England was established in Carolina. Before that, the Bishop of London appointed powerful commissaries for that colony and for Virginia and Maryland. The Virginia commissary, James Blair would serve as the most powerful churchman in Virginia until the middle years of the eighteenth century, while his Maryland counterpart Thomas Bray was instrumental in the creation of two powerful organizations, the Society for the Promoting Christian Knowledge (SPCK) and the Society for the Propagation of the Gospel (SPG), the latter explicitly working to strengthen the Church in North America.[18]

The union and the Makemie verdict did not immediately end Anglican efforts to attain a supremacy. Instead, Anglicans and Presbyterians, the two churches secured by the union, spent much of the next two decades wrangling over its implications. A particular concern of Anglicans seemed to be the appearance of "Scotch Presbyterian" clergymen who, like Makemie, were not accustomed to accepting mere dissenting status. In 1710, Carolina's new Anglican commissary complained that newly arrived Scottish ministers were stirring up "faction and sedition" in the colony. He suggested to his superiors that henceforth, in spite of the toleration, the only dissenting preachers allowed in Carolina should be those sent by English churches, "it being an English colony originally before the Union act." The commissary went on to explain that English Presbyterians had long accepted their status as dissenters and would thus cause less trouble than their Scottish counterparts.[19]

Anglicans were equally aggressive in the Middle Colonies. In 1712, the New Jersey minister John Talbot secured property in Burlington, New Jersey, to stand as the residence for the American bishop he hoped would follow.[20] And in 1716, the Presbyterians of New York City, fearing that Anglican governors would seek to seize their property as they had done elsewhere, petitioned the council for a charter that would secure their title to the church they had built. At the behest of the Anglican clergy the council refused. For half a century the New York congregation continued to press its request, and the council continued to deny it.[21]

If the union did not curtail Anglican attempts to establish supremacy, it did provide opponents with an effective counterweight. Accordingly, in 1724, New York Presbyterians, still lacking a charter for their church, hit upon a novel scheme: the church session vested its buildings first in the ministers of the Church of Scotland and subsequently in the Scottish Church itself. Because the position of that church was secured by the union, their title could not easily be challenged.[22]

Others recognized that the guarantees the union provided to the Church of Scotland created a safe haven in the American Presbyterian Church. Thus in the second decade of the eighteenth century, nearly all of the Congregationalist churches located outside of New England, and beyond the protection of its legal establishments, joined the new Presbyterian synod. In 1707 that newly formed Presbytery had only about seven ministers in a similar number of congregations. A decade later it had grown to nearly twenty ministers and perhaps two dozen churches under the first American synod.[23] The year 1717 also witnessed the beginning of a vast migration of Presbyterians from Ulster to North America. There were of course a variety of reasons for that migration, including a severe decline in the linen trade. Religion also played a part, as Ulster Presbyterians suffered disabilities in Ireland from which the newly secured status of the Presbyterian Church in North America would protect them. That communion soon became the fastest growing in the colonies.[24]

Presbyterians increasingly relied upon Makemie's argument that the union had opened up North America to their efforts. In 1710, the Scots Presbyterian minister James Anderson of New York addressed an appeal to the Church of Scotland for missionaries to the colony. Although the governor objected, Anderson noted that "the Church of Scotland is established in Great Britain as well as that of England, and no doubt have liberty of sending forth missionaries." That applied especially to those colonies where no Anglican establishment had specifically been created, "to these places especially within the dominions of Great Brittain, where the Church of England is no more established than the Church of Scotland."[25] The union thus provided those who had been dissenters with the opportunity to claim ecclesiastical equality, secured largely through their association with the Scottish Church.

For nearly two decades, North American Anglicans did their best to ignore the implications of the union, but events in the year 1725 pushed it to the center of ecclesiastical debate. In that year, the Congregationalist clergy of Massachusetts petitioned their government to allow them to hold a synod to address internal matters of their churches. Two Anglican ministers in the colony opposed the motion, contending (among other things) that Anglican officials—in this case the Bishop of London—had long exercised authority over the American Church. To them, this signified that "the Colonies in America are annex'd to the Diocese of London" and therefore the synod should not be conducted without the Bishop of London's approval. The claim was surely a stretch; a Royal Commission subsequently affirmed the bishop's jurisdiction in the American colonies, but with authority confined to visiting only such churches "in which Divine Service according to the

Rites and Liturgy of the Church of England shall have been celebrated." The bishop could summon and discipline its ecclesiastical officers "and no person else."[26]

The decision reaffirmed Makemie's contention that the union had placed the colonies beyond the reach of England's Act of Uniformity. The colonies therefore lacked legal establishments unless they had specifically been created, as they had been in the southern colonies. Anglicans could no longer maintain that the English Church automatically followed an English imperial domain. Nonetheless, the ruling denied that the New England colonies possessed legitimate established churches either, or the authority to create them on their own, whatever local practices they might maintain. The result would be a new debate about the relationship between church and state in the imperial constitution. The implications of the union stood at the center of that argument.

Having failed in their effort to ignore the union, Anglicans in North America of necessity now decided to embrace it, while turning its legal implications on their heads. Thus the Bishop of London argued that if the Act of Uniformity did not establish Anglican supremacy in the region, the union did. By the Act of Security, every monarch at his or her coronation was required to subscribe an oath pledging to maintain the Church of England in England, Ireland, Wales, and "the territories thereto belonging." The bishop drew the implication that the union thus secured the dominant position of the Anglican Church in North America.[27]

The immediate debate turned on the meaning of the word "territories." As the language employed predated England's colonial acquisitions, the opponents undoubtedly had the better of the argument in contending that the phrase was never meant to include the American colonies. The more important question that emerged concerned the second asymmetry that had developed out of the union settlement. While the union secured the national churches of both England and Scotland, only the Church of England was intertwined with the British government. The monarch remained head of the Church of England; bishops still sat in Parliament. The Scots Church, being Presbyterian, in its very nature had no comparable involvement. The question thus arose: could the Church of England in fact be merely an English Church if it was so closely connected to the British state?

The Anglican response was negative. If the king was head of the Church, then the Church he headed was unquestionably the national church of the kingdom, which he was sworn to uphold. Anglicans conceded that the union had secured the Scottish Church as well, but only within Scotland itself. Scotland had its own religious settlement, and Anglicans had no desire to challenge it. But that, in their view, was simply an indulgence granted to Scotland as the price of union, with few implications beyond its bounds.

That argument had its most direct ramifications in New England. Until the second quarter of the eighteenth century, nearly everyone had taken for granted the reality of Congregationalist establishments in the principal colonies of Massachusetts and Connecticut. The Restoration government had forced New Englanders to accept an Anglican chapel, and the Church of England had sought and obtained toleration for itself under the new Massachusetts charter negotiated as part of the Revolution settlement of 1691. Still, they remained predominantly Puritan colonies in which church and state were closely linked.

Congregational predominance was called into question in 1722 when Yale's rector, Timothy Cutler, shocked hearers at the college's commencement ceremony by finishing his prayer with the distinctly Anglican call, "and let all the people say, amen." He later affirmed that he and three other members of the Yale community were planning to take orders in the Anglican Church. They started out as dissenters from the local Congregational churches, but before long they were promoting the argument that they, rather than the legally privileged Congregationalists, represented the true Connecticut establishment.[28]

Among those who argued the case was one of the new converts, Samuel Johnson, then of Stratford, Connecticut. In a series of three letters to his Congregationalist neighbors, whom he called his "Dissenting Parishioners," Johnson contended that the Congregationalist majority around him had erred by separating from the Church of England, a true Apostolic church. They had replaced it with a church of their own making. He further denied that Congregationalists were in fact established in Connecticut, citing the Lords Justices' letter of 1725 that under the union no such creation could represent a valid establishment. But what would become the most important argument thereafter was his contention that Connecticut Anglicans derived their authority not from mere local law but from the authority of the Bishop of London, to whom that authority was granted by "the supreme authority of our nation."[29]

Johnson's position was developed into an extended argument by James Wetmore of Rye, New York, another member of the Yale group who had converted to the Anglican communion. Wetmore laid out the basic case for the primacy of the Anglican Church in America. As early as 1728, he had requested that the Bishop of London endeavor to have all of the Acts of Parliament applying to the English Church extended to North America, allowing for a full establishment and the appointment of bishops. Soon thereafter, Wetmore also published a letter "to his Dissenting Parishioners"—again meaning those who belonged to the Connecticut's state-supported Congregationalist churches—arguing that there were dangerous consequences in separating from what he called "the established Episcopal Church." The people of Connecticut were, he contended, "Parts of the Nation" and "bound to pay obedience to the National Laws."[30]

Wetmore subsequently amplified the Bishop of London's earlier contention that the union itself had secured the place of the Church in the colonies. While the minister conceded that the Act of Union had inviolably established Presbyterianism in Scotland, he suggested that that same act had limited its reach to the nation north of the Tweed. The act for securing the English Church had placed it in England, Wales, and the territories belonging thereto. By contrast, the act for securing the Scottish Church referred only to Scotland.[31]

Implicit in Wetmore's argument was a larger interpretation of the union as something other than an alliance of equal partners, owing to the Anglican connection to the state. Thus he referred to the Church of England as "the National Establishment, the Religion of our Mother Country, and the Nation whose King, is the King of *Connecticut*."[32] Moreover, his view of England was expansive as well as imperial, dominating the state not only through numbers but through the position of its church, which was thoroughly entangled with the state. Scotland, by contrast, was a mere province, with separate laws and institutions that applied only to itself and whose reach did not extend beyond Scotland's bounds.

Wetmore's contentions provoked a long dispute with the Reverend Noah Hobart of Fairfield, which focused much of what had been in dispute over the previous years.

Hobart attempted to turn the tables on his adversary, addressing those he referred to as "members of the Episcopal separation in New-England," contending that they and not those in New England's Congregationalist churches were the true schismatics. He tried to counter Wetmore on every point. He denied the scriptural and historical basis for either Episcopacy or the Apostolic succession. He defended the legitimacy of the New England Congregationalist establishments. He questioned the authority of the Bishop of London within the American colonies. And, most telling of all, he debated the meaning of the terms that Wetmore had employed: the established church, the nation, and the national laws.[33]

Hobart's position began with Makemie's argument and then went beyond it. England, he contended, was no longer a separate kingdom, but part of the new kingdom of Great Britain. That kingdom had "two different ecclesiastical establishments." "If therefore the *one* of them may claim our Subjection . . . the *other* has an *equal* Claim to it." That led Hobart to a claim not only of ecclesiastical equality for rival churches, as Makemie had, but for their independence. "To be *equally obliged* to conform to both [establishments], is, in Reality, to be not obliged to conform to either."[34] Moreover, the supremacy of the state church would lead to "an unnecessary and hurtful State of Dependance." More than once he criticized Wetmore's reference to "colonies depending on the Crown of England," and "Territories belonging to the Kingdom of England." Hobart conceded that the colonies depended on the mother country politically, while noting that that country was Britain and not England. Ecclesiastical dependence was another matter, in his view, one that the union had precluded.[35]

The ultimate point of dispute was over the implications of the connection between church, nation, and empire. Wetmore continually invoked the idea that the Church of England was the church of an English nation, integrated with the state, and to which the colonies were necessarily subordinate. He therefore unwittingly confirmed Hobart's contention that Anglican claims made ecclesiastical dependence an issue. Hobart denied that the Anglican Church was the church of the United Kingdom, referring to it instead as the ecclesiastical establishment of "South Britain." Where Wetmore referred repeatedly to the existence of a national establishment, Hobart refuted its imperial implications, declaring a national church to be, in its very nature, "a *local* Thing." It necessarily had "Bounds and Limits." Hobart's principal concern was local autonomy and independence from the claims of what he considered a false imperial church. His concerns were not so much for the liberties of individuals as those of churches, even those of New England, which claimed a privileged legal position for themselves.[36]

For all of the arguments over the status of the New England churches, imperial authorities showed no inclination to take any overt action on the matter, and the debate eventually subsided. Instead, leading Churchmen in that region returned to their earlier quest to obtain an American bishop as the surest way to secure their position as the Church of England in America. In so doing, they restored the church-state question to the center of ecclesiastical controversy for years to come, affecting both ecclesiastical alignments and the shape of religious contention. In that effort, they were joined increasingly by clergymen from the mid-Atlantic colonies, including Samuel Johnson's younger acquaintance Thomas Bradbury Chandler of Elizabethtown, New Jersey. He and an associated group of clergymen from New York and New Jersey soon became the leaders of the movement.

For a number of years, middle-colony Churchmen corresponded about the best means to advance the prospects for a colonial Anglican bishop, but it was an issue that few dared to raise because of the violent opposition it aroused. Finally, in 1767, Chandler put forth a detailed, albeit muted, proposal. To overcome objections from those outside of the Church, his proposal disavowed any secular authority for bishops through ecclesiastical courts. In fact, it denied them any authority at all over non-Anglicans. It limited their work to those colonies where Anglicans already had a substantial presence. And to quell objections from lay Anglicans unaccustomed to excessive clerical authority or rule from afar, Chandler would have granted the bishops disciplinary powers over no one other than the clergy.[37]

To Chandler, that should have been an uncontroversial request. He contended that he was asking only that Anglicans be granted the same liberty as other denominations to maintain their full ecclesiastical structure. That, as Chandler observed, was something that even toleration should have allowed. Chandler was asking more for the shell of an establishment rather than for a real one, one that was compelled to cede at the outset any authority over those who did not voluntarily join. Chandler elsewhere admitted that the proposal did not aim at the full Episcopacy he really desired or that he thought could have been expected in a "Christian country." But in a society that maintained a substantive commitment to toleration, he did not see how there could be objections to the request.[38]

Nonetheless, the proposal inspired a flurry of publications from opponents in several denominations, who doubted, with reason, that any bishop established by Parliament could ever be effectively restrained. In that sense, dissenter objections to an American bishop paralleled Whig suspicions of the Stamp Act or Townshend duties: the bishop, like the taxes, might perhaps have been tolerated if objectors had been confident that the matter would end there, but they doubted that either the Church or Parliament, neither of whom recognized definitive limits on its authority, could ever be confined by mere promises.

Part of the difficulty with Chandler's proposal was that he retained most of the language of establishment even as he ceded much of the content. He refused to view the Anglican Church in any other light than that of first among equals. While claiming to offer full liberty to his religious opponents, he insisted upon calling them "dissenters." He continued to call the Anglican Church the "national Religion," a religion that stood, as he said, "in a peculiar Connection with, and Relation to, the national body." "If any one Denomination is intitled to a Superiority above others," he insisted, "then, the Claim of the Church of England to this Preference, is not to be disputed."[39]

Chandler's language reflected his larger ambition. The principle at issue was always more than mere competition among rival churches, or even state preferences; it could hardly have been the latter, with the union settlement protecting both national churches. It was instead about a church intertwined with the state, as the Church of England was. Its adversaries were concerned not only with the respective positions of the churches, but the privileged roles its leaders would hold in society, in addition to the state of dependency this would all entail.

The essential point for Chandler was that the Church of England had a "peculiar Connection" to the nation, even though the nation in question was now the "British nation." He could hardly have done otherwise; episcopal practice and the theory of apostolic succession required the Church to retain its intimate relation with the state. The English Church was "so happily connected and interwoven with the Civil Constitution, that each mutually supports and is supported by the other." That extended, moreover, to the imperial domain; the Church in America was "inseparably connected with the Church at Home," and was "so essentially the same with it, that it must ever subsist or perish, by the same Means."[40]

The bishop was designed to have a leadership role in that society, even if dissenters were fully tolerated. Chandler could never imagine that the leaders of the Anglican Church could be anything but leaders of society as well. Thus while his proposal specified that the bishop was not to possess any form of civil authority at the outset, he conceded that in the future such powers might be added. But he denied that his opponents would have any grounds for objection if that were to happen. "All that the Happiness and Safety of the Public require," Chandler wrote, "is, that the legislative and executive Power be placed in the Hands of such Persons, as are possessed of the greatest

Abilities, Integrity and Prudence: and it is hoped that our Bishops will always be thought to deserve this Character." He simply did not understand the extent to which his adversaries regarded the possession of civil authority by a church official as itself a threat to their civil and religious liberties. The Church was a part of the state, and its leaders were entitled to respect from everyone.[41]

Chandler was similarly insensitive to his opponents' antipathy to paying to support bishops they did not want. While Chandler's plan did not for the time request tithes to provide for the bishop's support, he could perceive no danger there either. For "should a general Tax be laid upon the Country . . . such a Tax would not amount to more than Four Pence in One Hundred Pounds." Any who would object to so small a sum, he contended, "deserves not to be considered in the Light of a good Subject, or Member of Society." Chandler offered this argument the year after the repeal of the Stamp Act, to which Americans objected on precisely the grounds that, whatever the amount, they demanded a voice in its creation and its use![42]

In a rejoinder to Chandler, Charles Chauncy of Boston objected to the presumed connection between the Anglican Church and the imperial state. Like others who attacked the plan, Chauncy denied opposing the mere existence of Episcopal bishops or of harboring any desire to persecute the Church. If Anglicans in America wanted to appoint their own bishops, there was nothing stopping them from doing so. The problem came because their authority would derive from Parliament and from what Chauncy called a "State-Establishment," a church that owed its position to its involvement with the state.[43] To a Reformed minister such as Chauncy, the union had undermined all such special claims. Those clergymen were seeking not toleration but ecclesiastical equality.

Chauncy further questioned Chandler's equation of his church with the English establishment. The question was whether there could really be an Anglican Church, rather than just an Episcopal Church, within the colonies at all. Chauncy doubted it. He recognized a Church of England, a Church of Scotland, and a Church of Ireland, but Chauncy insisted that a "Church of England in America" was a phrase he did not understand.[44] The American Church after 1707 was an anomaly. The Church of Ireland was the Irish Episcopal Church; it was not the Church of England in Ireland. The Episcopal Church in Scotland was a dissenting communion. An Anglican Church in America would be a state-sanctioned imperial institution, controlled from afar, in contradiction to the equality of churches the union implied.

A similar set of responses to Chandler's proposal came from a trio of Delaware Valley Presbyterians writing as the "Centinel" in the *Pennsylvania Journal and Weekly Advertiser*: Francis Alison, John Dickinson, and George Bryan. Like the Bostonian Chauncy, they contended that the issue was not bishops per se, but rather their introduction by act of Parliament. They objected to the equation of the Church with the state. How, they wondered, could others be safe in the face of the appointment of a bishop from a church that considered itself "intwined with the Interests of the Nation," and not only England but the whole "British Nation." To that Church alone went all "Natural Right to any degree of Civil and Military Power."[45]

Like Chauncy, the Centinel writers denied the existence of such a thing as the "Church of England in America." The failure to counter Anglican claims would lead to ever-greater dangers from the Church. Chandler had claimed one million adherents to the Church, an assertion far removed from the American reality. But Chandler, by virtue of the Church's alliance with the state, was counting everyone not adhering to one of the other churches as "*virtual* Churchmen," who as such would be made subject to the authority of bishops and to taxation for their support.[46] There was, then, a general agreement that the crux of the dispute was about the interconnection between the Church and the state. How, the Centinel asked, could any group of clergy "which thinks itself peculiarly entitled to National Favour, and asserts itself to be so essentially connected with the State [would] if once established ever give Ease or Peace to other Churches in America, whom they now treat as Dissenters?"[47]

It was not only those outside of the Anglican Church who opposed Chandler's proposal. So also did much of the Anglican laity, who were troubled by the Church's attempt to restore the colonial churches to a state of dependence upon bishops, especially those appointed from England. That was especially pronounced in Virginia, where the Church had been shaped by the long presence of the Scottish Episcopalian, James Blair. Under Blair, the Church appointed large numbers of Scots ministers. It also developed an ecclesiastical form centered on a division of authority between the ministry and a vestry of prominent laymen. Those developments led Blair's enemies to accuse him both of Scotticizing the Church and of Presbyterianizing its structure. The vestry in Virginia and elsewhere had little desire to see their influence reduced in favor of a bishop who would increase the authority of the clergy, the English Church, and the British state. Dependence was as much an issue for lay Anglicans as for northern dissenters.[48]

The controversy over bishops, and over the status of the imperial Anglican Church, did much to shape the ecclesiastical landscape of British America. First, it helped determine the principal alignment in ecclesiastical controversy. During the 1740s, the evangelical revival movement known as the Great Awakening had ruptured denominations such as the Presbyterians and Congregationalists, often aligning the anti-revivalist Old Side and Old Lights with the equally skeptical leaders of the Anglican Church. That was especially evident in Pennsylvania, where Old Side Presbyterians in the divided denomination joined with Anglicans in forming the new College of Philadelphia, in part as a counter to the New Side Presbyterian College of New Jersey. The college was led by the Anglican William Smith of Pennsylvania, while the Presbyterian Francis Alison served as deputy provost.[49]

The alliance did not last. Smith and Alison had a falling out, partly over Smith's advocacy of the Episcopal cause, and Alison was soon working to heal the division in the Presbyterian Church. That project was completed with the Presbyterian reunion of 1758, and Old Side and New subsequently worked together in the Jersey College, which Alison hoped would serve as a bulwark against Anglican advances. Alison remained a vocal opponent of Anglican expansion and the Episcopate, emerging as a leading contributor to the Centinel essays. A similar realignment occurred in the joint opposition to the bishop voiced by prominent anti-revivalists in New England such as Charles Chauncy and by New Light Congregationalists. Anglican claims to primacy brought religious liberals, conservatives, and evangelicals together in opposition.[50]

The Episcopate controversy and the debate about the imperial church proved to be unifying and empowering for its opponents. It led to considerable cooperation across denominational lines, linking not only Presbyterians with Congregationalists, but also members of the Dutch Reformed Church in New York and New Jersey. Together those groups established several distinct organizations of opposition, including a Society of Dissenters in New York and an effort at denominational union formulated by Ezra Stiles of Rhode Island. The latter was designed to include not only North Americans but an alliance with the national Church of Scotland, as were several other efforts at unity in opposition to Anglican claims.[51] In addition, Congregationalists and Presbyterians became increasingly comfortable with applying the name "Presbyterian" in referring to both denominations. Presbyterians in that sense were not just members of the Presbyterian Church, but all of those who believed in ecclesiastical government by presbyters—ministers and lay elders—rather than bishops, and who opposed the subordination to and integration of the church with the state. Uniting together those groups would provide the northern colonies with an aggressive counterestablishment.

The long contest over the imperial church also shaped the way that members of the principal Reformed denominations came to talk about religious liberty. Although they consistently opposed Anglican claims of supremacy, they rarely advocated the separation of church and state. The Church of Scotland and the New England congregations were, after all, state-supported churches. Rather, their primary concern was the independence of the church *from* the state, a long-standing concern in Reformed Churches. They did not oppose church links to the state, per se, but rather the integration of civil and ecclesiastical authority upon which the Anglican Church depended. From this position, opponents of a colonial bishop denied that the churches of the New England provinces were in fact state establishments. They were churches assisted by the state but independent of it. They were neither intertwined with nor subordinate to state authority.[52] Religious liberty was only threatened by full state establishments, wherein the church was part of the state, which in turn elevated the position of the Church and Churchmen in society.[53]

Such a view of church and state was well illustrated in the controversy that had developed over the creation of an Anglican college in New York during the 1750s. The decade before, in the aftermath of religious revival, evangelical Presbyterians sought a charter for a Presbyterian college in New Jersey. The appeal was granted with little opposition. By contrast, in the following decade, when Episcopalians in New York sought a charter for an Anglican college in that colony, they met with a very different reception. There, the offer of an institution linked to Trinity Church provoked strident opposition and turned into a full-fledged newspaper war over the merits of establishing what opponents called a "Party-College."[54]

Much of the rhetoric employed in the college controversy mirrored that in the contest over an imperial church. Thus an Anglican letter-writer in the *New-York Mercury* asserted the right of the Church of England as the "established" church in an "English" colony to control the college, a position that by this time had been rejected even by the attorney general in Britain. The Presbyterian William Livingston, writing in the *Independent Reflector*, disputed the claim, quoting from Hobart at length in maintaining that the union, in securing two separate ecclesiastical establishments, had effectively left the New York colony independent of any establishment not specifically made for it. Livingston's publisher followed with a reprint of Francis Makemie's *Narrative*.[55]

As would be the case with Chandler's bishop proposal, opponents succeeded in limiting the most aggressive Anglican claims. Presbyterian attacks on the college forced Anglicans to defend their initiative as one intended only to provide their church with the same kind of institution that Presbyterians already had in New Jersey and that Congregationalists possessed in New England. And while they denied any intention to interfere with the rights of non-Anglicans, they still assumed that Anglican officeholders would be natural leaders of society. As Benjamin Nicoll wrote in response to Livingston, the Anglican clergy in the province claimed "no Power . . . but such as their good Conduct and Behaviour, gave them a Right to Claim." The proposals of the trustees, he contended, would have no greater effect than the likelihood that a Church of England man would be selected as president of the college. He did not perceive that many outside the Church of England were coming to see its integration with civil institutions as antithetical to their liberties, their progress, and their prosperity.[56]

That was just the point of opposition that William Livingston expressed toward the college in the *Independent Reflector*. While he disavowed the idea of any church controlling the college, he displayed far greater concern about an Anglican-led college than he had for the state-supported Presbyterian College of New Jersey. A "Party-College," as he called it, would result in excessive influence for church leaders. So far would they control the college that "the civil and religious Principles of the Trustees, will become universally established, [and] Liberty and Happiness will be driven without our Borders." He did not seem to fear the same danger from the New Jersey College, which the state did not control, but where state support was freely granted and freely accepted. If the college were built on "the Plan of a general Toleration" and a "free Constitution," both the college and the community would prosper and make the people "great and happy."[57]

The link between Episcopacy and the imperial state hardly enhanced its popularity in North America in the years before independence. The Episcopate proposal failed not only because of vocal opposition and the reluctance of imperial officials to add another issue to colonial grievances, but also because the union had torn a hole in the imperial constitution. Across the Atlantic the ambiguities it created were little remarked because, with the Hanoverian succession and the end of the Tory attack upon the privileges of the Church of Scotland, the de facto contours of the ecclesiastical settlement were established. In North America they remained subject to persisting uncertainties about the nature of the imperial churches and about colonial dependency.

If the source of the continuing Episcopate controversy was imperial union, it took imperial disunion—in the form of the separation of thirteen colonies of British America from British rule—to resolve it. The Episcopal Church in an independent America could no longer claim allegiance to a Church of England headed by a British king and interwoven with the British state. The Church in fact was divided by the war, with the most vocal of those who favored an imperial bishop siding with Britain and Loyalism, and often removing themselves from the scene. By contrast, many of the southern gentry who dominated the vestry rebelled against British rule and a British head of their Church.[58]

Instead, the Episcopal Church after the war separated from the state even without disavowing state support. The result in effect confirmed the outcome Charles Chauncy had articulated: there would be no longer a Church of England in America, but only an American Episcopal Church. The power of the vestry was upheld, creating new episcopal structures with bishops that were subordinate neither to the king nor the English Church. They were not in fact creatures of the state at all, and the first American bishop, Samuel Seabury, had to travel to Scotland, where the remaining Episcopal bishops were Jacobites, in order to obtain an ordination that did not require the taking of an oath of loyalty to royal authority. And while the new American religious settlement did not immediately require the full disestablishment of the churches, it was apparent that they could argue for state support only so long as they remained separate from the new governments. Americans had not yet settled on the separation of church and state in the founding of their nation, but the freedom of the church from the state was an essential principle in the new republic.[59]

That many Americans defined religious liberty in that manner had much to do with the long experience of religion and empire. In securing multiple national churches, the union left the relationship of those churches to Britain's imperial space permanently unsettled. For nearly three-quarters of a century, the Anglican Church in America was obliged to defend its connection to the state even as it failed in repeated efforts to cement its place as the imperial church. The uncertainty resulting from the transition to a British empire left room for the emergence of substantial ecclesiastical assertiveness among North Americans and, combined with other new intellectual connections, a considerable measure of spiritual and cultural autonomy.

The long eighteenth-century campaign for the liberties of churches in America would do much to shape religious alignments and keep the church-state question very much in the fore. In an environment of near-universal support for the concept, if not always the practice, of toleration, the independence of the church from the state would become a baseline for religious liberty in the new American governments. That would ultimately buttress the larger movement for still greater forms of religious liberty, even if many of the participants in the debate had not sought those ends along the way.[60] The principal debate thereafter was between proponents of continuing state support for those newly restricted churches and advocates of a total disestablishment.

Chapter 4

Practicing Toleration in Dutch New Netherland

JOYCE D. GOODFRIEND

For centuries, the Dutch Republic has been hailed for leading the march toward religious toleration in seventeenth-century Europe. Among the many achievements of this geographically compact but economically mighty nation, its role as sanctuary for people fleeing religious persecution from across Europe has ranked high. Yet the intricate maneuvering that underlay this roseate picture went largely unnoticed until scholars began to probe the ambiguous relations between church and state in the seventeenth-century United Provinces. This recent scholarship has revealed that the vaunted religious toleration of the Netherlands rested neither on ideology nor policy, but instead on a series of ad-hoc compromises negotiated between urban magistrates and Calvinist *predikanten* (ministers).[1] In short, religious toleration, far from being universally subscribed to in the seventeenth-century Netherlands, was persistently contested.

The fragility of the scaffolding for the edifice of toleration in the seventeenth-century Netherlands became apparent every time a dispute arose between the *predikanten* and the magistrates over the proper treatment of non-Calvinists. The singular tactic of looking the other way, or connivance, was central to the fabrication of a safety net of toleration. Adherents of religions technically barred from holding worship services in public could do so behind closed doors in hidden churches or *schuilkerken*.[2] What amounted to street-level coexistence of people of different religions became a fact of life in the seventeenth-century Netherlands, but it was not buttressed by ideological justifications nor was it overtly endorsed by the government. Magistrates continually shied away from codifying their concessions to various groups or adopting a consistent policy of toleration. The result was a tenuous patchwork system that required periodic recalibration. Its equilibrium could never be taken for granted.

This nuanced interpretation of the practice of toleration in the seventeenth-century Netherlands is the template against which the seemingly antithetical story of intolerance in New Netherland, the Dutch West India Company's colony in the mid-Atlantic region of North America, during the long administration of Petrus Stuyvesant (1647–64) must be measured. Historians of New Netherland have already modified the popular impression of Director-General Stuyvesant as a bigot who unilaterally persecuted Lutherans, Jews, and Quakers by attributing his policies to the depth of his attachment to Dutch Calvinism. In contrast to his predecessor, Willem Kieft, who granted considerable latitude to adherents of non-Reformed churches, Stuyvesant nourished the hope that a religiously uniform society could be created in the colony. If, as research has shown, Stuyvesant's posture as an authoritarian ruler was belied by his obligation to take heed of the opinions of his council as well as New Amsterdam's Burgomasters, still it was his agenda that fundamentally shaped the course of events in New Netherland.[3] Notwithstanding improved knowledge of Stuyvesant, a fine-grained analysis of the role of the putative victims of Stuyvesant's policy in establishing patterns of religious coexistence in the colony is much needed. Conceiving of the Lutherans, Jews, and Quakers not as the prey of a determined persecutor but as politically savvy groups capable of contriving ways to resist Stuyvesant's decrees enables us to tease out what might be called the alternative vision of society at the root of their struggles for recognition in the Dutch colony. These religious dissidents may not have fabricated a blueprint for an ideal social order, but, wittingly or not, they helped make toleration feasible in seventeenth-century America.

Reimagining the New Netherland toleration drama in a more capacious way hinges on drawing a more textured picture of the confrontations between authorities and the critics of Stuyvesant's policy. Such an approach may reveal that there were as many shades of opinion on toleration in New Netherland as there were in the United Provinces. Given the Dutch colony's instability, it may be best to describe it as a laboratory for coexistence where unplanned experiments in accommodating diverse groups were conducted. Although the nectar of toleration was occasionally sampled in New Netherland, it was only under the new English governors starting in 1664 that it became available to all persons of European descent. In the seventeen years prior to its conquest by England, New Netherland was under the dominion of Petrus Stuyvesant, the son of a Reformed *predikant*.[4] As a man who believed the ideal society was one in which Protestant values infused every aspect of life, Stuyvesant developed policies for the colony based on a vision shared by Calvinists in the Netherlands, as well as in the neighboring Puritan colonies of New England. Those who controlled the state were obliged to direct people in ways set forth in the Bible. As Stuyvesant labored to create a well-ordered Calvinist domain, he had to deal with both religious backsliders and religious competitors. It was, he explained, "necessary that common and public sins such as drunkenness, profanation of the Lord's name and Sabbath, the public and common cursing even by children along the streets, the gatherings of sectarians and other disorderly groups, be countered and promptly prosecuted by the renewal of good regulations and laws."[5] Along with dictating morality and imposing rigorous Sabbath regulations went upholding religious uniformity, since Stuyvesant feared that the open practice of faiths other than the Reformed would not only disrupt society but also incur God's displeasure.[6]

Appreciating the inner logic of Stuyvesant's vision as well as its appeal to influential constituencies in the seventeenth-century Atlantic world—most notably Calvinist clergy and their devoted followers—is vital for understanding the history of toleration in New Netherland. Equally important is recognizing the multiple sites on which the director-general's plan for a Calvinist society was challenged, by whom, and for what reasons. Imagining the fledgling society as the scene of overlapping contests between strict Calvinists and those who, for reasons of their own, supported a more inclusive society allows us to trace the fitful course of toleration in the colony of New Netherland.

Preventing rival religions from gaining a foothold in New Amsterdam entailed either co-opting or excluding those intent on challenging the Reformed church's monopoly on public worship. Lutherans were prime candidates for inclusion in Stuyvesant's Calvinist community since it was only their allegiance to the Augsburg Confession (1530) that distinguished them from Reformed Protestants. Present in New Netherland since at least 1639, Lutheran immigrants—Germans, Danes, Frisians, Norwegians, Swedes, Poles,[7] and people from the United Provinces—began to multiply after 1648, when the end of the Thirty Years' War in Europe (and the peace with Spain) propelled many to the Dutch North American colony.[8] "Yearly, by the ships arriving here," the Lutherans noted in 1653, "we are being strengthened by people of our faith."[9] Immigrants were a valuable commodity in New Netherland and therefore no obstacles were placed in the way of the material advancement or civic participation of the Lutheran newcomers who settled in Manhattan and Beverwijck.[10] Stuyvesant and his clerical allies hoped to fold these Lutherans into the Reformed community rather than to expel them, as he attempted to do with the Jews and the Quakers who were considered incapable of adopting Calvinist values.

"Adherents of the unaltered Augsburg confession," as the colony's Lutherans called themselves, aroused Stuyvesant's ire not because they failed to live up to Reformed morality, but because they rejected Reformed doctrines and wished to practice their own faith in public. As a Calvinist, Stuyvesant regarded Lutheran beliefs as erroneous, but he could not assail Lutherans on doctrinal grounds because he was obliged to adhere to the principle of liberty of conscience enshrined by the Dutch in the 1579 Union of Utrecht. Only when they appeared to threaten the religious unity that was central to his social vision did Stuyvesant find reason to act against them. "If the Lutherans should be indulged in the exercise of public worship," New Amsterdam's ministers explained, "the Papist, Mennonites and others, would soon make similar claims. Thus we would soon become a Babel of confusion, instead of remaining a united and peaceful people."[11]

Although the Dutch principle of liberty of conscience guaranteed Lutherans the right to observe their religious faith in the privacy of their homes and families, Stuyvesant and the *predikanten* were not content to stand by as city dwellers disassociated themselves from the Reformed church. Because the Dutch Reformed church was New Amsterdam's one public church, the Lutherans, as Protestant Christians, reluctantly attended worship on occasion and brought their children there to be baptized by Reformed clergymen and educated by Reformed schoolmasters. The ministers counted on this immersion in a Reformed environment, convincing Lutheran auditors to alter their religious confession. "For as long as no other religion than the Reformed has been publicly allowed, all who wish to engage in public worship come to our service. By this means it has happened that several, among whom are some of the principal Lutherans, have made a profession of religion, and united with us in the Lord's Supper."[12] Conceding that "some of our people, not persevering in the faith, who undoubtedly had the largest means, withdrew," Lutherans bristled at the deliberate efforts of New Amsterdam authorities to win over their children.[13] The Lutheran minister who arrived from Europe in 1657 explicitly condemned the Reformed clergy's "plan and intention, in time, by sweet whistling, to convert to their religion the children who have been baptized by them."[14]

The prospect of ever more Lutherans abandoning their faith was alarming to local Lutheran leaders who lamented that "owing to the lack of free exercise of our religion so many of us have struck out on other paths, which they never knew before, whether they were fit to walk on or not."[15] Unwilling to renounce their beliefs, they made plans in 1653 "so that no more persons would forsake the faith."[16] Not only did they request Stuyvesant's "permission to call a Lutheran minister out of Holland, and also to organize separately and publicly a congregation and church" but they "addressed letters to . . . [the] States of Holland, and to the Directors of the West India Company."[17] These efforts failed to bear fruit as company directors, under pressure from New Netherland's clergy and from the Amsterdam Classis, denied their request.[18] Nevertheless, the city's Lutherans elected to "assemble secretly for the observance of [their] religion, to edify [themselves] mutually with the reading of some sermons, and to strengthen [themselves] in the faith."[19]

These clandestine services came to the attention of Stuyvesant and his Council and, on February 1, 1656, they issued an ordinance banning conventicles, which put a stop to the private assemblies of New Amsterdam's Lutherans. This carefully worded law stated that the authorities did not intend "any constraint of conscience . . . nor to prohibit the reading of God's holy word, family prayers and worship, each in his household," but were interdicting "all public and private conventicles and meetings, whether in public or private houses, differing from the . . . customary and ordained reformed religion."[20] By making a distinction between family worship and private gatherings, Stuyvesant was, in effect, ruling out any sort of communal worship, however discreetly conducted. Compelled to obey the law, which carried heavy fines for participants, the Lutherans petitioned Stuyvesant to make an exception for them "that henceforth we may not be hindered in our services. These with God's blessing we intend to celebrate, with prayer, reading and singing."[21]

The directors of the West India Company condemned Stuyvesant's approach to the Lutheran problem in New Netherland, apprising him that "we would . . . have been better pleased, if you had not published the placat against the Lutherans, a copy of which you sent us, and committed them to prison, for it has always been our intention, to treat them quietly and leniently."[22] In their view, dissenters from Reformed orthodoxy, though not entitled to worship openly, should be allowed to gather in private for religious purposes. For Stuyvesant, who put the narrowest of constructions on liberty of conscience, any form of toleration was anathema.

Backed by the Reformed clergy and sustained by his own beliefs, Stuyvesant did not falter in his vision of a unitary Calvinist community, despite criticism from above and agitation by New Amsterdam's Lutherans, who implicitly endorsed a conception of community at variance with that of Stuyvesant. Without challenging the privileged position of the Reformed church in the colony, they called attention to the Dutch precedent of connivance, through which Amsterdam's Lutherans practiced their faith, contending that it legitimated their setting up a separate church.[23] New Netherland's Lutherans had never forsaken their quest for a local pastor and when Rev. Johannes Gutwasser [Goetwater] arrived to serve them in July 1657, Stuyvesant and his clerical allies marshaled their resources to prevent the Lutherans from initiating public worship in New Amsterdam. To win popular support, Reformed ministers Megapolensis and Drisius drafted a petition to the *Burgomasters* and *Schepens*, the city's magistrates, in which they methodically outlined six reasons for opposing the Lutheran plan and emphasized that the public exercise of the Lutheran religion in New Amsterdam would be "injurious to the political as well as to the religious interests of this place."[24] The Burgomasters' response, framed in a report to the director-general and council, no doubt pleased defenders of Calvinist orthodoxy. Having summoned Goetwater and examined him, they recalled that they had "bound ourselves under oath to help maintain the true Reformed Religion, and to suffer no other religion or sects," then "charged the said Goetwater, not to hold public or private exercise in this city." Adding that this was a matter that concerned the whole province, they requested that "measures be found, by which the true Reformed Religion will be maintained, and all other sects excluded."[25] With this endorsement of their policy by the city magistrates, Stuyvesant and his council set in motion measures that effectively prevented the Lutherans from practicing their religion. Holding services was out of the question when, as Gutwasser reported, the penalty was "100 pounds Flemish in general, or 25 pounds for each person who is found to be present."[26]

Stuyvesant's punitive measures, in combination with the reluctance of the Dutch West India Company and the States-General to guarantee New Amsterdam's Lutherans the same freedom of worship enjoyed by Lutherans in Amsterdam, effectively suppressed the city's embryonic Lutheran congregation. After Gutwasser had been deported, Dominies Megapolensis and Drisius exulted that the Lutherans "again go to [the Reformed] church, as they were formerly accustomed to do" and "one of their principal men . . . is now one of the most punctual attendants, and has his pew near to the pulpit."[27] Concessions that the company ordered Stuyvesant and the Reformed ministers to make regarding objectionable phrases in the formula of baptism were instrumental in this outcome, but Stuyvesant's strictures against assembling for worship in private homes must have steered many local Lutherans to the Reformed church.[28]

The pall that had settled over New Amsterdam's Lutherans by the early 1660s was palpable to a Dutch Lutheran recently arrived from Leyden. Sword cutler Hendrick Bosch had found "a large congregation adhering to our Christian Unaltered Augsburg Confession" in New Amsterdam. "Although hope among us has not lessened," he explained, "the fact is, alas, that many of the congregation begin to stray like sheep and that they dare not come together here to offer any sign of devotion, much less trust themselves jointly to sign a petition to your honors [Amsterdam Consistory] for fear of being betrayed."[29] Stuyvesant's heavy-handed tactics had, at the least, neutralized the threat of the Lutherans to organize a competing denomination in New Amsterdam and, at most, had swayed some adherents of the Augsburg Confession to switch their allegiance to the Reformed church.

Though Stuyvesant might have indulged in the belief that he had forestalled the emergence of a Lutheran church in New Amsterdam, a Lutheran community had nevertheless coalesced. That it failed to receive official sanction is less significant than that it remained relatively intact despite the concerted efforts of Stuyvesant and his clerical allies to destroy it. In their struggle for formal recognition, believers in the Augsburg Confession had cemented bonds with each other and developed a sense of common purpose. Corresponding with the Consistory of Amsterdam's Lutheran church, signing petitions to local and metropolitan authorities, pledging financial support for a minister, and concealing and protecting the beleaguered Rev. Gutwasser during his harrowing stay in the city all strengthened their collective ties. Perhaps symbolic of the unity forged in crisis is the fact that Lutherans from a variety of cultural backgrounds in Europe were able to transcend ethnic differences and agree on Dutch as the language of worship in their new home.[30] Though some succumbed to the pressures exerted by Stuyvesant and drifted away, a substantial nucleus estimated at 100 in December 1664 remained to gather for public worship in English New York City, a place notably more tolerant than Stuyvesant's New Amsterdam.[31]

Lutheran settlers posed the greatest threat to New Netherland's Reformed church and their resistance played a decisive role in checking Stuyvesant's ambition to create a religiously uniform society. It was the Lutherans' determination not to surrender their religious identity—a resolve that did not falter even when their coreligionists in Amsterdam admitted that they lacked the power to protect them—that prevented their merger with the Reformed. Although the Lutherans' bold move to bring a minister to the colony and initiate public worship was repelled, the presence of a covert Lutheran community in New Amsterdam anticipated the emergence of a more tolerant society.

During his battle with the Lutherans over the legitimacy of setting up an independent congregation, Stuyvesant was confronted by a small number of Jews, most of them exiles from the recently overtaken Dutch colony of Brazil, who demanded a place in New Amsterdam.[32] Not doubting that these Jews would subvert his planned Calvinist community, Stuyvesant sought the approval of the Dutch West India Company's directors to deport them. By way of justification, he assailed the Jews for "their customary usury and deceitful trading with the Christians" and denounced them as "the deceitful race—such hateful enemies and blasphemers of the name of Christ."[33] Dominie Johannes Megapolensis also was quick to demonize the Jews as "people [who] have no other God than the unrighteous Mammon, and no other aim than to get possession of christian property, and to win all other merchants by drawing all trade toward themselves." Characterizing the Jews as "godless rascals, who are of no benefit to the country, but look at everything for their own profit" and noting that "we have had to spend several hundred guilders for their support," he asked the Classis of Amsterdam to persuade the company directors to authorize the removal of the Jews from New Amsterdam.[34]

However intense his anti-Semitism, Stuyvesant rested his decision to banish the Jews on a more fundamental premise. Because Jews could never be candidates for inclusion in a community of Reformed Christians Stuyvesant sought to expel them. New Amsterdam's Burgomasters and Schepens assented when the director-general and his council had "resolved that the Jews, who came last year from the West Indies and now from the Fatherland, must prepare to depart forthwith."[35] Seeking to block Stuyvesant from ousting them, the Jewish newcomers mobilized the support of Jewish leaders in Amsterdam, who petitioned the directors of the Dutch West India Company to "grant the Jewish nation passage to and residence in that country." Sensitive to the political influence of Amsterdam's Portuguese Jews and mindful of the colony's need for settlers, the directors ordered that "these people may travel and trade to and in New Netherland and live and remain there, provided the poor among them shall not become a burden to the company or to the community, but be supported by their own nation."[36] Prevented by the company directors from sealing off New Amsterdam from Jews, Stuyvesant resorted to limiting their participation in the city's economic and civic life and devising ways to extract money from them.

Orders from overseas secured Jews a place in the Dutch colonial city, but the Jewish immigrants themselves worked in manifold ways to counteract Stuyvesant's impositions. In virtually every instance, the director-general attempted to thwart their initiatives, but more often than not he had to concede the validity of their arguments. New Amsterdam's Burgomasters were more ambivalent about the entry of Jews into the city, not hesitating to treat them inequitably in taxation, but giving them a fair hearing in judicial proceedings. City residents followed suit, rarely befriending the Jewish newcomers, occasionally insulting them, and commonly engaging in business dealings with them. For their part, the Jews pressed for the same privileges in the economic and civic spheres as their fellows possessed in Amsterdam as well as the freedom to practice their religion, but never demanded to be included in New Amsterdam's social or religious communities.

Once it became clear that they would not be expelled, the Jews set about establishing themselves in New Amsterdam's economy. They began trading with other colonists, engaging in petty exchanges involving items such as shoes as well as larger-scale transactions in commodities such as tobacco. Although the company directors specifically ordered that New Amsterdam's Jews "not be allowed to have open retail shops," one of the items proposed for deliberation by municipal authorities in January 1657 was "keeping open store and selling by retail practiced to the present time both by Jews and all foreigners."[37] If Jews initially participated in New Amsterdam's retail trade, the denial of Jacob Cohen Henricques's request "to bake and sell bread within this City, as other bakers, but with closed door" in April 1657 suggests that the latitude initially allowed Jews in the New Amsterdam marketplace was curtailed.[38]

Jewish merchants encountered resistance from Stuyvesant when they endeavored to extend their trade beyond the city to Fort Orange and the South River in 1655, but the council opened a loophole through which traders could proceed with cargoes they had already shipped.[39] When a subsequent petition in 1656 reintroduced the issue, the request was not specifically denied.[40] By 1658, Asser Levy was actively trading in Fort Orange. In one transaction, he sold three ankers of brandy to Hans Vosch.[41] Levy appeared as a plaintiff in the Fort Orange court several times in the next few years, attempting to obtain payment for debts from at least seven different men. In most of these cases, the defendants admitted their debts and the court ruled in Levy's favor.[42]

Although Jews were able to accumulate capital through trade, they encountered obstacles in how they could spend it. When they sought to purchase real estate, signifying they intended to remain in the community, Stuyvesant blocked them. In 1655, Teunis Craay put up for sale at auction the house that Salvador Dandrada, a Jewish merchant, had been renting. Cray was ready to accept Dandrada's high bid of 1860 guilders and convey the house to him, but was prevented by Stuyvesant and the council.[43] New Amsterdam's Jews contended that this policy contravened practice in the Netherlands, where, according to the directors of the Dutch West India Company, "the purchase of real estate" was "allowed [Jews] . . . without any difficulty."[44] The willingness of local residents to act in defiance of Stuyvesant's policy appears to have nullified his efforts. By 1662, Asser Levy was buying real estate in New Amsterdam.[45]

The economic success of the Jews in New Amsterdam came at a price. When the Burgomasters mandated subscriptions for the city's defenses in 1655, five of the seven Jewish men listed were burdened with assessments of fl.100, a sum equal to the tax on the city's most prominent burghers.[46] Defenseless against this discriminatory exaction, they attempted to make political capital out of their sizeable contributions to the city's finances by requesting Stuyvesant in March 1656 to reconsider decisions adverse to the Jews and to grant them the right to "travel and trade to and upon the South River, Fort Orange and other places [in] New Netherland" as well as the right to purchase real estate. Pointedly reminding him that the city magistrates had recently demanded from each of the five petitioners "one hundred guilders towards the payment of the works of this city, amounting alone [for them] to . . . f500, aside from what others of their nation have been ordered to contribute," they spelled out their argument. "If, like other burghers they must and shall contribute," they should be permitted to "enjoy the same liberty allowed to other burghers." Well aware of the rights enjoyed by their coreligionists in Amsterdam, they enjoined Stuyvesant to comply with the February 15, 1655, company directive "whereby permission and consent was given them, with other inhabitants, to travel, live and traffic here and to enjoy the same liberty."[47]

For the immigrant Jews, being treated in the same way as other free inhabitants of New Amsterdam meant participating in civic life. On April 11, 1657, Asser Levy requested to be admitted as a burgher of New Amsterdam, "claim[ing] that such ought not be refused him, as he keeps watch and ward (*tocht and wacht*) like other Burghers." To strengthen his case, he showed "a Burgher certificate from the City of Amsterdam, that the Jew is Burgher there."[48] The Burgomasters turned down his request, referring him to Stuyvesant and the council. Ten days later, Salvador Dandrada, Jacob Cohen Henricques, Abraham DeLucena, and Joseph D'Acosta, more prominent Jews, took up the cause, noting that "one of our Nation" had been refused a burgher certificate by the Burgomasters. Again citing the company directors' directive of February 15, 1655, that "we should enjoy here the same freedom as other inhabitants of New Netherland enjoy," these men sought to persuade Stuyvesant and the council "to please not exclude nor shut us out from the Burgher right" but "to give us the customary Burgher certificate." In their argument, they rehearsed the two important facts that "our Nation enjoys in the City of Amsterdam in Holland the Burgher right" and that "our Nation, as long as they have been here, have, with others, borne and paid, and still bear, all Burgher burdens."[49]

Jews may have forced Stuyvesant to admit them as citizens of the city, but they could not bring him to include Jews in the militia. Compounding the injury, Jews were assessed 65 stivers per month "for the . . . freedom of being relieved of general militia duties."[50] When Asser Levy and Jacob Barsimson, who identified themselves as men who "must earn their living by manual labor," requested "to be permitted to keep guard with other burghers" in lieu of paying "the tax which others of their nation must pay," Stuyvesant refused, adding sarcastically that they were free to "depart whenever and wherever it may please them."[51]

Although barred from New Amsterdam's militia and weighed down with excessive taxes, Jews received evenhanded treatment in the municipal court, where they appeared as both defendants and plaintiffs. Significantly, Christians with grievances against individual Jews did not resort to violence or intimidation, but used established legal procedures to resolve them. Moreover, Christians were willing to appear in court to answer complaints from Jews. In all of these cases, the Burgomasters followed the rules of Dutch jurisprudence. After weighing the evidence, they issued rulings both in favor of and against Jews. At times, rulings that benefited Jews were appealed to the director-general, who often overturned them. An unfavorable judgment in a suit brought by Jacob Barsimson in 1656 prompted Allard Anthony to appeal, winning reversal on January 30, 1657.[52] Three years later, a similar ruling provoked an appeal from Warnaer Wessels, who complained that "he finds himself greatly injured . . . in the judgment handed down by the honorable court of this city, dated 29 January [1659] between him and Jacob Barsimson, Jew."[53]

Despite the fact that rulings in the municipal court were subject to reversal by Stuyvesant, Jews placed their trust in the Burgomasters' proceedings and did not hesitate to take legal action against Christians. In 1656, Jacob Barsimson lodged a complaint against Maryn Luyckersen, whom he had entrusted with twelve pairs of shoes to trade for him at the North. Luyckersen failed to obtain butter or wheat for Barsimson and had not repaid him adequately for the shoes. The court decided in favor of Barsimson and Luyckersen complied with the court's order. In this and other cases, the court showed no bias against Jews and a Christian burgher acknowledged a legitimate obligation to a Jew.[54]

Even more compelling evidence of the Burgomasters' impartiality comes from decisions demonstrating their respect for the sacredness of the Jewish Sabbath and other central features of Judaism. When Jacob Barsimson failed to appear in court as a defendant on Saturday, June 3, 1658, the court decided that "Though deft. Is absent, yet no default is entered against him, as he was summoned on his Sabbath."[55] The Burgomasters also made concessions to Jews by modifying customary practices for them. When Asser Levy and Moses Lucena were accepted as sworn butchers in 1660, the Burgomasters granted Asser Levy's request "to be excused from killing hogs, as his religion does not allow him to do it." Levy and Lucena were also permitted to take "the oath which the Jews are accustomed to take."[56]

For the most part, New Amsterdam's Christians took their cue from the Burgomasters and dealt with the Jews in a civil fashion. Residents rented them dwelling places interspersed among the houses in which Christians lived. Joseph D'Acosta, for example, leased "a certain house . . . within this city of Amsterdam in New Netherland, next to the house in which the lessor [Michiel de Carreman] dwells at present and the house of Jacob Wolphertsen van Couwenhoven, at present occupied by his late wife's mother."[57] Notary Salomon Lachaire did not object when Asser Levy employed him to draw two notes on May 2, 1662. On June 5, 1662, he "went with Assar Levy over to the Ferry and there drew up a notarial obligation against Auke Jans" and "wrote another obligation for [him] against Evert Direxe van Nas." On September 1, 1662, Lachaire again served as Asser Levy's scribe, writing "four letters to Patria each two pages" and "4 invoices."[58] Christians cooperated with the immigrant Jews on numerous occasions, but remained wary of them. Negative stereotypes of Jews remained potent on both sides of the Atlantic in the mid-seventeenth century as immigrant Jews personified a religious culture seen as antithetical to Protestant Christianity. The fact that most spoke to each other in Spanish or Portuguese made them seem all that much more foreign.

At a minimum, Europeans who dwelt in New Amsterdam expected Jews to accommodate themselves to the mores of a Christian society. Authorities acted swiftly when a Jew attempted to conduct business on the Christian Sabbath. Schout Cornelis Van Tienhoven charged that Abram De la Sina "has kept his store open during the Sermon, and sold by retail, as proved by affidavit." He concluded that "deft. Shall be deprived of his trade, and condemned in a fine of six hundred guilders."[59] Yet just how strong ordinary citizens' distaste for Jews was remains in question. Both Stuyvesant and Dominie Megapolensis tried to implicate New Amsterdam's residents in their anti-Semitism. Stuyvesant made known "the aversion and disaffection of [the city's] militia to be fellow soldiers of [the Jewish] nation, and to mount guard in the same guardhouse," offering as evidence a 1655 petition of the captains and officers of New Amsterdam's militia asking "whether the Jewish nation resident in this city should mount the guard under their militia banners."[60] Earlier, the director-general claimed that he had learned that the Jews were "very repugnant to the inferior magistrates, as also to the people having the most affection for you [the directors of the Dutch West India Company]."[61] Megapolensis played on the anxieties of his flock, broadcasting an alleged report from newly arrived Jews from Holland that "a great many of that lot would yet follow and then build here their synagogue." The reaction was predictable: "This causes among the congregation here a great deal of complaint and murmuring."[62] Yet evidence of overt prejudice by individuals is sparse. In a 1661 document prepared for submission to the Burgomasters and Schepens in a complex case in which Asser Levy was involved, Frans Jans van Hooghte referred to an agreement as "capable of better proof than a Jew's testimony."[63] In August 1658, Josep d'Acosta asserted that "Joannes Verveelen said to him, "You are a Jew, you are all cheats together," but Verveelen, a well-to-do merchant, denied saying it.[64]

With their long history of exclusion and persecution, the Jewish newcomers were not inclined to mix with the larger society. In this new setting, their paramount goal was to reaffirm their identity as a distinctive people. Although united by their faith, the Jews who arrived in New Amsterdam between 1654 and 1657 had to knit the fabric of community out of disparate materials. Most had been uprooted from the Dutch colony of Brazil, recently recaptured by the Portuguese. Others came directly from Amsterdam. The majority were Sephardic Jews, but at least a few were Ashkenazic. Although most did speak Spanish and/or Portuguese, some knew Dutch.

To validate the nascent community and strengthen the bonds between its various members, the Jews desired to worship in public as their brethren did in Amsterdam. On June 10, 1656, Stuyvesant informed the company directors that the Jews "have many times requested of us the free and public exercise of their abominable religion, but this cannot yet be accorded them."[65] On the issue of establishing a synagogue in New Amsterdam, the directors agreed, ordering that the Jews may "exercise in all quietness their religion within their houses, for which end they must without doubt endeavor to build their houses close together in a convenient place on one or the other side of New Amsterdam—at their own choice—as they have done here."[66]

Although New Amsterdam's Jews resided amid the city's Christian dwellers and not just in one district, they probably assembled at one person's house for worship. With the requisite number of men and "a Sepher Thora [Torah scrolls] of parchment with its green veil and cloak and band of India damask of dark purple," which the Parnassim of Amsterdam had given Abraham de Lucena to take to New Amsterdam, they presumably gathered on their Sabbath for services in the Sephardic tradition.[67] Perhaps the Jewish community's religious leader was one of the three men—Abraham de Lucena, Salvador Dandrada, and Jacob Cohen—who successfully petitioned "on behalf of the others" to be allowed to "purchase a burial place for their people."[68] Not only were the Jews' determined to bury their fellows in ground made sacred according to their own traditions, but they also insisted on abiding by their dietary laws [kashrut]. Although it was not until 1660 that Asser Levy and Moses Lucena were sworn in as what amounts to Kosher butchers, it is likely that they were slaughtering cattle in the customary manner before this date.

At least some Jewish immigrants may have seen New Amsterdam merely as a way station. In 1662, for instance, Abraham Lucena appeared before the

Burgomasters and "reports that he has been asked to pay three beavers for the Burgherright. He says, he does no business here and has only come on his way to Holland, but if he remains he will pay."[69] By the time Dutch rule ended in 1664, virtually all of New Amsterdam's Jews had moved on to Amsterdam or elsewhere in the Atlantic world where they might have had connections. The dissolution of New Amsterdam's short-lived Jewish community was symbolized by the return of the Torah scrolls to Amsterdam prior to 1663. Only Asser Levy persisted in the city, residing there until his death in 1682. He was not Sephardic and therefore could not expect greater opportunities among Amsterdam's Portuguese Jews.[70] Moreover, as a Dutch speaker, he stood a greater chance of integration into local society than his coreligionists. Levy rapidly carved out a place for himself in New Netherland's commercial life and was so bold as to hire a Christian's daughter as a maid servant.[71]

New Amsterdam was far from an ideal environment in which to nurture Jewish life in America. Yet since the city was under the control of a Dutch trading company, Jewish immigrants, familiar with practices in the Netherlands, speculated that it might be a place where they could gain those privileges that had been conceded to Amsterdam's Jews. In Petrus Stuyvesant, they encountered a formidable foe. Though he was forced by the Dutch West India Company directors to admit Jews to New Netherland and not to interfere in their religious life, his adversarial stance hastened their decision to venture elsewhere.

With the voluntary departure of most of the Jewish immigrants, Stuyvesant virtually attained his goal of ridding New Amsterdam of Jews, but not before having to tolerate them for several years. Yet the score of Jews who had carved out a place for themselves in this small urban society challenged Stuyvesant's constricted vision of a community predicated on religious exclusions and made a case for the viability of religious coexistence. They never pressed to be integrated with the dominant Protestants. Fully in agreement with the contemporary Dutch practice of treating Jews as a separate "nation," they maintained their collective identity throughout their sojourn in the colony, in the process demonstrating the practicability of a plural society composed of Christians and Jews.[72]

Jews and Lutherans were not the only religious groups that challenged Stuyvesant's plan for a Calvinist New Netherland. Baptists and Quakers also sought a place in the colony. In 1655, Dominie Megapolensis informed the

Amsterdam Classis that "we have here Papists, Mennonites and Lutherans among the Dutch."[73] Although individual Catholics intermittently stopped in the colony, Protestant sectarians known as Baptists in England and Mennonists in the Netherlands posed a more tangible threat to New Netherland's religious orthodoxy.[74]

Heightened suspicion of New Netherland's English residents in the wake of the First Anglo-Dutch war (1652–54) made the prospect of entertaining religious deviants such as Baptists and Quakers unnerving. In 1652, "Anna Smits [Smith], an Anabaptist" offended Dominie Megapolensis by "using slanderous and calumniating expressions against God's word and his servants."[75] Perhaps she had ties to Gravesend, a Long Island town whose inhabitants were followers of Lady Deborah Moody, who had left Massachusetts Bay because of her Anabaptist beliefs.[76] In November 1656, Baptist William Wickenden, "a cobbler from Rhode Island . . . [who said] he had a commission from Christ . . . began to preach at Vlissingen [Flushing] on Long Island and then went with the people into the river and baptized them."[77] William Hallett, the town's sheriff, was punished severely for "allowing (Baptist) conventicles in his house, contrary to law" and Wickenden was sentenced to a heavy fine and banished, though a few days later, the fine was remitted because "nothing can be got from him."[78]

The severity of Stuyvesant's treatment of Baptist preacher William Wickenden and the sheriff who had permitted Baptist meetings in his house foreshadowed the extreme reaction of New Netherland authorities to the Quakers who reached New Amsterdam in August 1657. Mary Weatherhead and Dorothy Waugh, women in their twenties, "declared in the streets" of New Amsterdam, as Quaker chronicler Humphrey Norton put it.[79] More details of the event came from the Dutch ministers. The "two strong young women . . . began to quake and go into a frenzy, and cry out loudly in the middle of the street, that men should repent, for the day of judgment was at hand. Our people not knowing what was the matter, ran to and fro, while one cried 'Fire,' and another something else. The Fiscal, with an accompanying officer, seized them both by the head, and led them to prison. On their way to jail, they continued to cry out and pray according to their manner, and continued to do the same when in prison."[80]

Though observers were probably just confused, Dominies Megapolensis and Drisius, fearful that Weatherhead and Waugh's strange behavior might inspire townspeople to question authority, alerted their superiors in Amsterdam that the women had "labored to create excitement and tumult among the people."[81] The Quakers' contempt for worldly authority marked them as subversives. The *Woodhouse*, the Quakers' ship, had "no flag flying from the topmast," "fired no salute before the fort, as is usual with ships on their arrival [and] [w]hen the Fiscal went on board, they tendered him no honor or respect." Worst of all, "When the master of the ship came on shore and appeared before the Director-General, he rendered him no respect, but stood still with his hat firm on his head, as if a goat."[82]

Theological grounds for condemning the newcomers were also evident to Dominies Megapolensis and Drisius, who informed the Classis that "Last year there also arrived at Boston, in New England, several of these Quakers, but they were immediately put in prison and then sent back in the same ship."[83] Surely heartened by the stance of their Puritan neighbors, the Dutch ministers declared that these radical sectarians were part of Satan's international army. "The same instruments which he [the devil] uses to disturb the churches in Europe, he employs here in America."[84] Stuyvesant was equally sure of the perils posed by Quakers, whom he viewed as an "abominable Heresy," and he gave New Amsterdam's residents dramatic evidence of the lengths to which he would go to prevent the dissemination of Quaker ideas in New Netherland.[85]

Not long after Mary Weatherhead and Dorothy Waugh (who had been held in "miery dungeons . . . where was much Vermine" for eight days) were marched with "their arms tyed, and rods made fast to them, and two Negroes going with them" put on a boat sailing for Rhode Island, Stuyvesant staged a horrific display of power against another of the recently arrived missionaries, Robert Hodgson, who had gone to Long Island to spread the Quaker message.[86] Arrested in Hempstead and brought to New Amsterdam for judgment, Hodgson was subjected to brutal treatment, much of it in public. Stuyvesant's intention was clear. He wanted the city's residents to absorb the lesson that the promotion of alternative forms of religious expression would not be tolerated in the Calvinist state that he was erecting in New Netherland. Megapolensis and Drisius selectively documented the proceedings, noting that "after he had kept him in confinement for several days, [the magistrate] adjudged that he should either pay one hundred guilders or work at the wheelbarrow (Kruywagen) with the negroes. This he obstinately refused to do, though whipped on his back. After two or three days he was whipped in private on his bare back, with threats that the whipping would be repeated again after two or three days, if he should refuse to labor."[87] Like the Massachusetts magistrates described in Susan Juster's chapter in this volume, Director-General Stuyvesant was prepared to use the force of the state to secure religious orthodoxy.

Robert Hodgson's personal testimony of the punishments and deprivations he endured in the name of his faith mirrored the stories of countless early Quakers on both sides of the Atlantic who refused to submit to the demands of orthodox officials. By taking this uncompromising stance and embracing suffering, the young Quaker put into question the validity of Stuyvesant's religious truths, thereby emboldening others to make independent decisions on religious issues. Hodgson's narrative makes clear that not all New Netherlanders condoned physical coercion in religious matters. Stirred to action by the gruesome sight of the Quaker's body after undergoing repeated whippings, witnesses sought to alleviate his torment. Hodgson recounted that "A Woman came to me, and washed my stripes . . . and went home to her husband, and letting him know how it was with me, he proffered the Sheriff a fat Ox if he would suffer me to come to his house." Affected not only by the severity of the punishments meted out to the youthful missionary but by his stoicism, onlookers wished to intercede for this man whom Stuyvesant had branded as an enemy of the state. "There were many friendly (both Dutch and English) that would have paid [the fine]" that would have gained him his freedom. Hodgson refused their generosity.[88]

Empathy for the brutalized Quaker led two people of high status to exert pressure on Director-General Stuyvesant to desist. At the time Hodgson was being whipped, a person of stature, most likely an Englishman, tried to sway Stuyvesant from carrying out his punishment of the Quaker. According to New Amsterdam's ministers, "A letter was brought by an unknown messenger from a person unknown to the Director-General. The import of this, (written in English), was Think, my Lord-Director, whether it be not best to send him to Rhode Island, as his labor is hardly worth the cost."[89] This diplomatic entreaty was matched by a more personal one from Petrus Stuyvesant's sister Anna. As Quaker George Bishop told it, "The Governour's Sister was Instrumental in his [Hodgson's] liberty, who his sufferings took deep upon; and she being very sad, the Goverrnour asked the cause, which she told him, and he set him free."[90]

The Hodgson episode did not resolve the question of toleration for Quakers in New Netherland. They continued to hold meetings and gather converts in Long Island's English towns, while Stuyvesant consistently worked to prevent these assemblies. Following Henry Townsend's conviction, fining, and imprisonment for violating the law against conventicles, his fellow

Flushing townsmen, not Quakers themselves, protested the treatment of Quakers to Stuyvesant. In a petition subsequently known as the Flushing Remonstrance, they questioned the authority of New Netherland's government to prohibit people from practicing their faith in light of the Dutch ideal of liberty of conscience. They specifically referred to "the law of love, peace and liberty in the [Dutch] states extending to Jews, Turks, and Egyptians, as they are considered the sonnes of Adam, which is the glory of the outward state of Holland."[91] The Flushing petitioners had raised the debate over toleration in New Netherland to an ideological plane.

Stuyvesant's response was draconian. He rounded up the petitioners and singled out Flushing's Schout, Tobias Feake, for harsh punishment. Feake's sentence distilled Stuyvesant's thinking on Quakers and on toleration. Characterizing the Flushing remonstrance as "a seditious, mutinous and detestable letter of defiance," he assailed the writers for "justify[ing] and uphold[ing] the abominable sect of Quakers, who vilify both the political authorities and the Ministers of the Gospel, and undermine the State and God's service, and absolutely demand[ing], that all sects, especially the said abominable and heretical sect of Quakers shall and must be tolerated and admitted."[92] To broadcast his views, Stuyvesant issued a "proclamation of a day of Prayer which was read from the City Hall after the usual ringing of the bell" on January 21, 1658. In it, he denounced this "new, unheard of, abominable Heresy, called QUAKERS; seeking to seduce many, yea, were it possible, even the true believers."[93]

Pronouncements and punishments did little to quench enthusiasm for Quaker teachings on Long Island.[94] "The raving Quakers have not settled down," Dominies Megapolensis and Drisius reported in September 1658, "but continue to disturb the people of the province by their wanderings and outcries. For although our government has issued orders against these fanatics, nevertheless they do not fail to pour forth their venom."[95] Resolved to prevent the Quakers from securing a place in New Netherland, Stuyvesant redoubled his efforts to curtail the spread of Quaker ideas. In August 1662 he seized on a report from the magistrates of Rustdorp [Jamaica] that "the majority of the inhabitants of their village were adherents and followers of the abominable sect called Quakers, and that a large meeting was held at the house of John Bound [Bowne] in Vlissingen [Flushing] every Sunday" to initiate new legislation.[96] With information that "seditious & erroneous boecks writings & letters are brought in and dispersed among the Common people" Stuyvesant and the council prohibited "not only the importation of such printed or unprinted books, writings or letters, but also the communicating or dispersing, receaving, hiding of the same." In the same ordinance of September 21, 1662, they also banned Conventicles or meetings whether "in houses, barnes, ships, barkes, nor in the Woods nor fields."[97]

As a man of substance in his community, John Bowne was a perfect target for Stuyvesant, who decided to make an example of this Quaker convert, described in 1656 as "a verri jintiele young man, of gud abilliti, of a louli future, and gud behafior."[98] Bowne recollected that he was brought before the director-general and council in New Amsterdam and told that "I had broken there law." Unwilling to admit that the "Servants of the Lord" with whom he had held meetings were what Stuyvesant termed "hereticks deceuers [deceivers] seducers," Bowne was condemned and sentenced to pay "a hundrd and fifty gilders and charges."[99] He refused and was remanded to jail, where he remained for three months as efforts were made to get him to pay the fine or alternatively to leave the colony with his family. Bowne's recalcitrance ultimately convinced the director-general to send Bowne "out of the province by . . . ship, in the hope that others might thereby be discouraged." If this method failed, then Stuyvesant was prepared "to proceed against such persons in a more severe manner."[100] After Bowne was deported, Stuyvesant indeed enacted a new ordinance in May 1663 commanding "all Skippers, Sloop captains . . . not to convey or bring, much less to land within this government, any . . . Vagabonds, Quakers and other Fugitives, whether men or women."[101]

Bowne's own account of his imprisonment in New Amsterdam does not mention encountering any hostility from the city's Dutch residents, many of whom likely had witnessed the brutal punishment of Robert Hodgson five years earlier. Only once did his Quaker identity provoke a reaction. After a meeting with Stuyvesant was cancelled because he was unwilling to "put of my hatt and stand bare headed," as the director-general insisted, Bowne recalled that "the solgers did breke out in lafter at itt."[102] The Dutch West India Company soldiers may have regarded Bowne as eccentric, but notary Salomon Lachaire translated the "judgment of the Supreme Council" into English for him and "widdow wesels" allowed him to store his belongings in her house.[103] Most significantly, merchants Govert Loockermans and Cornelis Steenwyck acted as intermediaries for Bowne in his communications with Stuyvesant.[104] Bowne's ability to blend in with New Amsterdam's mercantile community is evident in his notation that after returning to Manhattan from a furlough in Flushing he "went amongst the marchants by the weay house and Stinwicke went with mee to his house."[105] Men with an eye toward the metropolis and the expansion of New Netherland's trade were dubious of Stuyvesant's claim that Quakers imperiled the colony. Winnowing out potential commercial partners on religious grounds did not serve their interests or those of the workers whose livings depended on their enterprises.

The same utilitarian calculus that drove New Amsterdam's merchants lay at the root of the company directors' decision to allow Bowne to return from Amsterdam to New Netherland as a man free to carry on his business. Stuyvesant was reprimanded by his superiors in the company for deporting Bowne and instructed to "shut your eyes, at least not force people's consciences, but allow every one to have his own belief, as long as he behaves quietly and legally, gives no offence to his neighbors and does not oppose the government."[106] With this directive the Quakers gained a de facto place in New Netherland. Stuyvesant had tried unsuccessfully to halt Quaker proselytizing in his territory, convinced that the dissemination of such radical teachings would do irreparable harm to the colony. But his efforts were stymied by the receptivity of English Long Islanders to Quaker preaching, the amenability of New Amsterdam's merchants, and possibly burghers in general, toward dealing with Quaker converts such as John Bowne, and the refusal of the company directors in Amsterdam to prosecute Bowne as the dangerous heretic Stuyvesant claimed he was.

The Quakers were more concerned about making converts than establishing toleration. Lacking a significant base of support in the Netherlands, the Long Island Quakers depended on at least the tacit support of other English colonists to overcome the obstacles placed in their way by Stuyvesant's continuing crusade against them. Whatever its ideological import, the Flushing Remonstrance, in which Calvinists stood up for the right of their newly converted neighbors to practice the Quaker faith, made plain that English Long Islanders could abide religious diversity. When John Bowne returned home to Long Island in 1664, he found English towns that tolerated Quakers.

Quakers on Long Island, two dozen Jews in New Amsterdam for several years, and persistent underground Lutheran communities in New Amsterdam and Beverwijck after the deportation of the Lutheran minister all suggest that, despite Stuyvesant's concerted efforts, non-Reformed groups gained a foothold in New Netherland during the 1650s and 1660s. Nevertheless, the semblance of religious coexistence evident in the Dutch colony in no way matched the far more inclusive religious arrangements in Amsterdam, where both Lutherans and Jews were allowed to worship openly by the mid-seventeenth century and Quakers never became the objects of coordinated persecution orchestrated by the state or subjected to public brutalization.[107]

The generous practice of toleration in mid-seventeenth-century Amsterdam is traceable to the urban elite that dominated municipal affairs. Magistrates whose paramount concern was the city's economic fortunes placed a premium on peaceful relations among its diverse residents. Granting otherwise orderly dissenting religious groups the opportunity to worship unmolested seemed a small price to pay for the harmony that was seen as underpinning prosperity. Reformed ministers championed orthodoxy but were at a disadvantage in their contests with the city's rulers, who spurned ideological debates on religious toleration. Though energetically pressing their demands on multiple occasions, clergymen usually gained little more than rhetorical support for the primacy of Reformed doctrine. Nevertheless, these symbolic victories confirmed the continuing influence of Reformed church leaders in seventeenth-century Dutch society, ensuring that the practice of toleration in Amsterdam remained contingent, rather than guaranteed by law.

Despite the fact that New Netherland was the possession of a commercial company that welcomed the contributions of diverse immigrants, the religious toleration exhibited in the colony was a pale facsimile of that found in Amsterdam. Toleration was stunted in New Netherland due to the distribution of power under the colonial system of governance. In the Netherlands, where power was decentralized, provincial and municipal authorities held the largest shares in government, but in New Netherland, authority was centered in the director and his council. With power essentially vested in one individual (though council members could disagree with him), the religious views of the man who filled the director's office counted disproportionately in determining the degree of toleration present in the colony. When Petrus Stuyvesant, a man of extreme Calvinist views, took over the reins of government in 1647, the prospects for religious toleration diminished. Under the administration of his predecessor, Willem Kieft, a relatively robust form of toleration had existed. "No religion is publicly exercised but the Calvinist, and orders are to admit none but Calvinists, but this is not observed," wrote Father Isaac Jogues, a Catholic priest who visited Manhattan in 1646, "for besides the Calvinists there are in the colony Catholics, English Puritans, Lutherans, Anabaptists, here called Mnistes [Mennonites], etc."[108] Kieft's laissez-faire religious policy was thrust aside by Stuyvesant, who insisted on Reformed orthodoxy.

More than a few New Netherlanders may have harbored reservations about the wisdom of Stuyvesant's use of the power of the state to achieve religious uniformity, but prudence dictated that they express their objections in private. One Reformed minister, J. T. Polhemus of Midwout, Long Island, did question the coercive measures applied to the Quakers, writing in 1664 that "The Quakers . . . are compelled to go before the court, and be put under oath; but such compulsion is displeasing to God."[109] But New Amsterdam's Burgomasters failed to block Stuyvesant's moves against religious dissidents. Only recently empowered, they were not in a position to emulate Amsterdam's magistrates in shielding alternative forms of worship in the city. The need to be circumspect must have led to their acquiescence in Stuyvesant's expulsion of the Lutheran preacher. However, their initial endorsement of Stuyvesant's anti-Jewish policy was later tempered by a series of court decisions involving individual Jews that were notable for their impartiality. Silent on Stuyvesant's anti-Quaker initiatives since Quaker intrusions into the city were rare, the Burgomasters likely approved of the stance of their fellow Cornelis Steenwyck, who had no compunction about assisting Quaker John Bowne. If their views were attuned to those of most burghers (and this is suggested by their articulation of the communal consensus against Stuyvesant's strict Sabbath regulations), then we can postulate that Stuyvesant's opposition to religious toleration was not widely endorsed by New Netherlanders.[110]

The limited measure of toleration that did surface in New Netherland was in large part the product of the Dutch West India Company directors' interventions in the colony's religious affairs. Pragmatic politicians committed to preventing religious conflict in the colony and thereby facilitating the flow of profits overseas, the directors remained subject to pressures from constituencies on both sides of the Atlantic. Well aware that aggrieved groups in New Netherland could tap their contacts in the homeland, they walked a tightrope as they hammered out a policy on toleration. Wary of provoking the Lutherans, they cautioned Stuyvesant in 1659 to rein in New Amsterdam's ministers by having them avoid "precise forms and offensive expressions." This was crucial "especially when we consider the difficulties, liable to arise, which might result in the permission to conduct a separate divine service there; for the Lutherans would very easily obtain the consent of the authorities here upon a complaint and we would have no means of preventing it."[111]

This frank acknowledgment by the company directors that governmental authorities in the Netherlands had the power to overrule them when it came to allowing minority religions to worship openly illustrates the delicate balancing of interests that underlay the practice of toleration in the Netherlandic world of the seventeenth century. Repeatedly, the directors endorsed moderation as a means of keeping religious peace in New Netherland, holding up as a model for Stuyvesant the government of Amsterdam, which "has always practised this maxim of moderation and consequently has often had a considerable influx of people."[112]

Reproving Stuyvesant and the local clergy for carrying Reformed orthodoxy to the extreme was not equivalent to sanctioning toleration. The directors' advocacy of moderation in dealing with religious dissidents at most prevented Stuyvesant from using coercion to forestall the dissemination of religious truths at odds with Calvinist ideas in New Netherland. Whatever steps were taken toward validating the notion of a tolerant society came from colonists outside the Reformed orbit who, with the cooperation of neighbors, presented living proof that people of different faiths could dwell side by side in New Netherland. Lutherans, Jews, and Quakers, while not offering a principled defense of toleration, all challenged the religious exclusiveness that was the foundation of Stuyvesant's imagined Calvinist society, with varying results. The Lutherans lost their battle for public worship but resisted absorption into the Reformed majority. The Jews disbanded their religious community but not before proving that Jews and Christians could coexist in New Amsterdam. The Quakers, by dint of their inroads in the English towns on Long Island, made credible the possibility that a religiously diverse society could flourish in New Netherland.

New Netherland's record on toleration is at best mixed. Petrus Stuyvesant's determination to maintain the dominance of the Reformed church, in both its Dutch and English incarnations, in the colony he governed constrained those who perceived the advantages of religious toleration. Stuyvesant's quashing of the Lutherans' attempts to exercise their religion openly surely holds as much significance as the concessions his superiors in Amsterdam forced him to make to Jews and Quakers. Still, the tableau of religions on New Netherland's stage, however ephemeral, was not irrelevant to the form of religious coexistence that emerged under English rule. The Duke of York may have implemented religious toleration in his new domain to further his own ends, but his decision to guarantee the right of all European settlers to practice their faith unmolested by the state gained substance from the history of struggle on the part of Lutherans, Jews, and Quakers (as well as sympathetic Reformed believers) to subvert New Netherland's policy of religious uniformity.

With the Reformed church no longer in a privileged position and the groups that had pushed for toleration under the Dutch now granted legal standing, a crucial step had been taken toward imagining a principled form of toleration. That step entailed, first and foremost, the lived coexistence from which examples of toleration could be drawn. As the contours of a religiously plural society took shape in eighteenth-century New York, the potential for peaceful interaction between people of different faiths that had remained latent under Dutch rule was gradually realized.

Chapter 5

Heretics, Blasphemers, and Sabbath Breakers
The Prosecution of Religious Crime in Early America

SUSAN JUSTER

Charles Arabella could not help himself. Having accidentally spilled "some scalding pitch upon one of his feet," he swore "by God." Though his "blasphemous words" were clearly "spoken in a great passion," Arabella nonetheless found himself convicted of the crime of blasphemy, a capital offense in most British colonies. The court mercifully ordered him to be "bored through his tongue and fined £20 sterling" instead of sentencing him to death; one report claims his tongue was bored "three times." Unable to come up with the fine, Arabella remained in prison for six months before successfully petitioning the Council of Trade and Plantations for his release.[1]

A tale seemingly straight out of the collected works of Nathaniel Hawthorne, whose persecuting Puritans stalk the popular history of religion in early America, there are some surprises in this story. Arabella was not, in fact, a victim of Puritan bigotry. He was a resident of the colony of Maryland and his unfortunate verbal lapse occurred in 1701, long after the Act of Toleration of 1689 had presumably ushered in a new era of moderation in Britain and its overseas possessions. Yet rather than moving to decriminalize religious crimes such as blasphemy in the wake of that landmark legislation, the colony of Maryland revised its "Act Against Blasphemy" in 1715 to toughen its provisions. As the governor of Maryland explained, "The Act for punishment of Blasphemy, prophane swearing, cursing and drunkenness . . . not being thought sufficiently to provide against those enormous offenses, was reenacted, more severe penaltys inflicted and the execution of them more severely enjoyned."[2] While there is no evidence that the act was more strenuously applied after 1715 than before, its ringing endorsement of "severe penaltys" for crimes against God sounds a discordant note within our conventional histories of the American colonies as beneficiaries—indeed, as harbingers—of a more enlightened attitude toward religious heterodoxy and the expression of dissent. Scholars have long argued that, though hardly islands of religious liberty, the American colonies, including the Puritan commonwealths, were relatively free of the kind of bigotry and persecutory fervor that marked the darkest years of Europe's confessional wars. Even Catholics—the favorite whipping boy of rabid Protestants everywhere in Anglo-America—were largely spared the physical assaults and collective degradations inflicted upon them in the Reformed states on the European continent, despite the persistent strain of vicious anti-Catholic rhetoric that characterized public discourse in the colonies as Owen Stanwood documents in this volume. Stephen Foster notes in surveying New England's laws against heresy that "the list of victims is mercifully short, and the punishments meted out, with several appalling exceptions, were not very severe."[3] We're all familiar with the "appalling exceptions" he's referring to—the four Quaker missionaries who went bravely to their deaths in 1659 and 1661, and the handful of Baptists and Quakers who were whipped, maimed, and exiled for their faith in the decades leading up to the Restoration. Yet most historians accept the general premise that colonial Americans enjoyed a degree of religious toleration uncommon in the western world before the democratic revolutions of the late eighteenth century made "liberty" a theoretical as well as practical achievement.

This chapter does not dispute the larger consensus that legal prosecutions for religious crimes were an occasional rather than regular feature of the colonial court system, but rather surveys the legal records over the first century of English settlement to see just how often Anglo-Americans found themselves on trial for their religious beliefs or behaviors.[4] All together, the published records of New Hampshire, Massachusetts, Plymouth, Rhode Island, New Haven, Connecticut, New York, New Jersey, Pennsylvania, Maryland, Virginia, and North Carolina over the period 1620 to 1700 yield just over one hundred cases of religious crimes—a figure large enough to dispel an overly optimistic view of the British colonies as happily heterodox yet small enough to confirm the general absence of a large-scale campaign against dissent. This is by no means a comprehensive survey. County-level records are not included, nor the files of justices of the peace or other local officials. Certain crimes—notably profanity and blasphemy—were more likely to be heard at the local than the provincial level, though others (e.g., heresy) are fairly well represented in these records. Comprising no more than a fraction of the total legal activity taking place in colonial courts, these cases nonetheless reveal that magistrates were not averse to using the strong arm of the state to compel conformity and punish dissent.

The most common religious crimes included Sabbath-breaking, heresy, blasphemy, contempt of church and slander of church officials, and abuse of church property.[5] Such crimes occupied the ill-defined margins of the various colonial legal structures. In the absence of formal ecclesiastical courts, colonial magistrates had only two options to police religious behavior: the secular courts and the churches. Neither was equipped to manage the problem of religious nonconformity effectively. Civil courts were burdened with adjudicating the social and economic conflicts endemic to frontier communities and the churches had jurisdiction only over their own members. What came before colonial juries and magistrates were thus only the most flagrant, most pressing, or most remediable offenses.

Enforcement focused primarily on two kinds of offences: sacrilegious speech (blasphemy, profanity, slander) and contempt of the Sabbath. For reasons that are still unclear, dissenters were generally untroubled by colonial magistrates except when their heterodox beliefs were voiced in an offensive manner or when they refused to honor minimal expectations of religious conformity such as attending church on the Sabbath (or at least not visibly engaging in other activities), granting due deference to ministers and other church officers, and paying their ecclesiastical taxes. Fully one-third of the offenders faced corporal punishment in the form of whipping or maiming, or incarceration in the stocks. If not quite Hawthorne's dens of bigotry, the British colonies were no Eden of religious liberty either.

A common thread runs through all the cases discussed below: the symbiotic relationship between religious and political order on the margins of empire. The fragility of authority in the remote Atlantic provinces was the universal plight of all who aspired to rule in the first century of settlement—governors, magistrates, ministers, masters, ship captains, fathers. Complaining about unruly dependents was the lingua franca of Anglo-American colonialism, linking the multiple projects that together constituted the British Empire (an "accidental empire," in the view of many historians). As events in England would shortly prove, harnessing the spiritual and commercial energies of a discontented and articulate people to the interests of an expansionist state was a fraught enterprise in the first decades of the seventeenth century. Rebellion against God and king became a reality in 1642, but well before Englishmen took up arms against their religious and political masters the specter of a coordinated attack on church and state haunted the architects of Britain's overseas empire. Their fears may seem exaggerated from our vantage point, but they were an accurate reflection of the prevailing presumption that authority was unitary and indivisible. The close affiliation of heresy with sedition in English criminal law was but one indication that, to the English, God and crown were allied powers.

Both law and rhetoric in some early colonies, which in the case of New England hearkened back to Mosaic norms, portended severe treatment for dissenters in their new settlements. The colonies of New Haven, Connecticut, Massachusetts, and Maryland were the most vigorous in adopting criminal codes against heresy, blasphemy, and other religious offenses in the first half of the seventeenth century. Declaring that "the worde of God shall be the onely rule to be attended unto in ordering the affayres of gouernment in this plantation," the New Haven magistrates explicitly modeled their law code on the Old Testament: "Itt was ordered that the juridical lawes of God, as they were delivered to Moses ... shall be accounted of morrall equity, and gen'rlly binde all offenders, and be a rule to all the courts in this jurisdiction."[6] The other New England colonies also adopted Mosaic law, including a 1634 injunction, at the behest of Roger Williams, that women wear veils when in public.[7] Citing the biblical injunction to not suffer unbelievers to live, the Massachusetts code mandated death for heresy, which was defined so broadly as to include all nonconformists. This was a significant departure from English jurisprudence. The reformation of England's ecclesiastical laws that had been underway since the 1530s had stopped well short of imposing the death penalty for heresy, except, possibly, in the case of "obstinate heretics" who resisted all entreaties to recant and whose obstinacy was regarded as a form of spiritual madness. Even during the Interregnum, when Puritans ruled with an iron fist at home, first offenders were punished by fines, imprisonment, and public rituals of abjuration rather than execution.[8] The unprecedented harshness of the Massachusetts laws against heresy drew a sharp rebuke from the crown's Solicitor-General Francis Winningham in 1677, who singled out "putting to death for matters in religion and otherwise" as one of his main objections to the charter, along with fining and whipping people for not attending church and "[having] forbid, under a penalty, the observation of Christmas Day, and other festivals of the Church."[9] The New

England colonies' first law codes did not survive the demise of their original charters after the Restoration in 1660 when the crown moved swiftly to curb the troublesome autonomy of its overseas possessions. With the issuing of a new charter for Massachusetts in 1691, the Puritan commonwealth's bold experiment in Mosaic law came to an end.

Close scrutiny from Whitehall and the shifting political fortunes of England's dissenting sects meant that colonial laws regarding nonconformity were frequently revised, though not always in the direction of greater toleration. Maryland's code, which originally afforded the Roman Catholic church full liberty ("the Holy Church within this Province shall have and enjoy all her Rights, liberties, and Franchises wholly and without Blemish," 1640), was revised under the Protectorate to strip Catholic residents of this protection: "none who profess and Exercise the Popish Religion Commonly called by the Name of the Roman Catholick Religion can be protected in this Province by the Lawes of England" (1654).[10] The colony of Connecticut, which issued a spate of new laws against heresy in the wake of the Quaker invasion of the 1650s, revised its ecclesiastical laws no less than seven times between 1656 and 1721. Freedom of conscience for all whose beliefs were "orthodox and sownd in the fundamentals of Christian religion" was secured in 1669, though by 1676 the Assembly found it necessary to strengthen the laws against Sabbath-breaking. Further exhortations to exercise "a spirit of courage" in executing the laws against profaning the Sabbath "with such severity that others may heare and feare" followed in 1686, 1709, 1714 (the "Act to Suppress Prophaneness and Immorality"), and 1721 (yet another "Act for the more effectual preventing of prophanation of the Lord's Day"). In this "Land of Steady Habits," as nineteenth-century historians lauded the province of Connecticut, irregular church behavior, profanity, and general contempt of religion were endemic problems throughout the colonial period.[11]

Maryland stands out in a number of ways in the legal history of early America, including the unusual specificity of the punishments mandated for certain crimes. No other colony prescribed the exact form of execution in capital crimes. Those convicted of treason were to be "punished by drawing hanging and quartering of a man [or] by drawing and burning of a Woman"; those guilty of lesser felonies such as homicide, polygamy, sodomy, and rape were to be hanged; and the worst offenders—those who committed sorcery, blasphemy, or idolatry—were to be burned alive. As in England, social rank determined the manner of death: noblemen who committed treason were to be accorded the privilege of beheading instead of drawing and hanging, while any felon who "can read Clerk like in the judgment of the Court" was to "lose his hand or be burned in the hand or forehead with a hot iron" rather than face death.[12] Even the famous 1649 Act Concerning Religion, one of the earliest affirmations of the right of free exercise of religion in American history ("noe person or persons . . . shall from henceforth bee any waies troubled, Molested or discountenanced for in respect of his or her religion nor in the free exercise thereof"), laid out a series of harsh penalties for certain crimes against God. Any Christian who blasphemed God, "that is Curse him, or deny our Saviour Jesus Christ to bee the sonne of God," was to be put to death, and those who "shall use or utter any reproachful Speeches concerning the blessed Virgin Mary" were to be "publiquely whipt and bee imprisoned." Those who "prophaned" the Sabbath "by frequent swearing, drunkenness, or by any uncivill or disorderly recreation" faced fines, and repeat offenders were whipped in public. Ever sensitive to the potential for unruly speech to turn against the colony's leaders, the magistrates showed special vindictiveness in dealing with "mutinous or sedicioues speeches" against Lord Baltimore, ordering a graduated series of punishments ranging from fines to "boaring of the Tongue, slitting the nose, cutting of[f] one or both Eares, whipping, branding with a red hot Iron in the hand or forehead, [or] any one or more of these as the Provinciall Court shall think fitt."[13]

The unsettling juxtaposition of general liberty of conscience with some of the bloodiest punishments for sacrilegious and blasphemous speech on record in the Maryland code neatly summarizes the ambivalence of most colonial Americans toward the thorny dilemma of maintaining orthodoxy in the New World. Keenly aware of the political and social costs of unrestrained religious conflicts from the still-fresh memories of the English Civil War, in which many had found themselves on the wrong side of the law, Anglo-Americans sought a middle ground between coercion and pragmatic toleration. In Christopher Grenda's typology, most colonial lawmakers combined secular and biblical forms of reasoning in which political utility, backed by scriptural precedent, were paramount in arguing for a limited degree of religious liberty.[14] The New Jersey Assembly and Council disagreed over the need for a more stringent bill for "the better observacon and keeping holy the first day of the week or Lords day" in 1682, with the council arguing for greater tolerance. The new law "enforces people by paynes & penaltyes to worship whether their worship be true or false," the council argued. "[I]f false, better none than any, Better to bee silent than to offer the sacrefice of fooles," they concluded. "The worship of the wicked is Abomination of the wholly [holy] God."[15] Maryland's defense of liberty of conscience was likewise not an assertion of principle but a reluctant concession to the realities of religious difference: the preamble to the clause explained that "the inforceing of the conscience in Matters of Religion hath frequently fallen out to be of dangerous Consequence in those commonwealths where it hath been practiced." Most dangerous of all was the spirit of disputation, which in England had led to uncivil war, and the colony's leaders made sure such name-calling would not be tolerated in their province: all who lobbed the epithets "heretick, Scismatick, Idolator, puritan, Independent, Presbiterian, popish prest, Jesuited papist, Lutheran, Calvenist, Anabaptist, Brownist, Antinomian, Barrowist, Roundhead, Separatist, or any other name or terme in a reproachfull manner relating to matter of Religion" at a fellow (Christian) colonist forfeited ten shillings or faced a public whipping. Liberty of conscience, then, yes; but not liberty of expression. The distinction mattered to a people who prided themselves on the vaunted "liberties" they enjoyed as free-born English subjects but knew firsthand the political and social evils of unrestrained sectarianism.

For all the harshness of its law code, Maryland in fact executed no one under the provisions against blasphemy, sorcery, or idolatry. In this, the colony was entirely unexceptional. Colonial statutes were among the most unforgiving in the Anglophone Atlantic, but executions were rare, reserved for the most incorrigible heretics and almost always resorted to only after multiple attempts at reclamation had failed. The four Quaker "martyrs" hanged on Boston Commons between 1659 and 1661—Marmaduke Stevenson, Mary Dyer, William Robinson, and William Leddra—are the exceptions that prove the rule: all were banished repeatedly and put to death only after they defiantly returned to Boston to preach in what many at the time considered an act of sacred suicide. The gap between the mandated and the applied punishment in capital crimes was a common feature of Anglo-American jurisprudence in the early modern era, especially when juries were involved. Juries were reluctant to condemn neighbors to death in the absence of overwhelming direct testimony and generally preferred to stigmatize rather than hang or burn religious nonconformists, no matter how provocative or offensive their ways of worship. The last Englishman burned for heresy was Edward Wightman, who went to the stake in 1611. No colonist faced such a dreadful fate, though hundreds of Indians were burned alive in the Pequot War of 1637 in what one Puritan minister called a "divine slaughter."[16]

The scarcity of mortal penalties, however, did not mean that dissenters escaped physically unscathed. Corporal punishment was liberally applied and extended from whipping to branding, mutilation, and dismemberment. Quakers suffered the most. Dozens of Friends, both men and women, were whipped, some on more than one occasion, and a handful were dismembered or mutilated during the high-water mark of Puritan repression in Massachusetts in the 1650s.[17] Humphrey Norton was "severely whipt and burnt in the hand with the Letter H for spreading his Heretical Opinions," while John Copeland, Christopher Holder, and John Rouse were sentenced to *"have your right ears cut off by the Hangman."*[18] Even the restoration of Charles II in 1660 did not stop the violence. The infamous 1658 law under which Dyer and company were executed was superseded by the "Cart and Whip Act" of 1661, which ordered all "vagabond Quakers" to be "stripped naked from the middle upwards and be tied to a cart's tail and whipped" from town to town until they were driven out of the jurisdiction. Repeat offenders were to be branded on the left shoulder with the letter R and again whipped out of the colony.[19] Under these provisions some of the more disturbing persecutions of the colonial era occurred, including the whipping of seven women in the 1660s and 1670s who, in a typically provocative Quaker gesture, had appeared partially nude and in sackcloth as a public "sign" to the Puritans of their sins. Lydia Wardel was whipped for appearing "as a naked sign"; Deborah Wilson, along with her mother and sister, was whipped through the streets of Salem while her husband "followed after, clapping his hat sometimes between the whip and her back"; Margaret Brewster, with ashes smeared on her head and her face black with soot, was whipped from the Old South Church through the town of Boston in 1677; and, most notoriously, Elizabeth Hooten, an elderly Quaker minister whose sufferings had already received extensive sympathetic coverage in Britain, received 10 lashes on her bare back in at least 14 different locales during the mid-1660s.

By the end of the seventeenth century, sanctions for religious crimes, as for other felonies, shifted away from corporal punishment and public shaming to imprisonment and fines. In 1638, Thomas Dewey and James Davis were ordered by a Virginia county court to "sitt by the heeles in the stockes the next Sabboth following in tyme of devyne service" for "disordering and abuseing themselves upon the Sabboth day." Nearly one hundred years later, their fellow Virginians Richard Cornelius and Thomas Grimston were merely bound for good behavior for their similar "rude and disorderly behavior" at the parish church.[20] In Connecticut, Peter Bassaker was "seuerely whipt" in

1648 for his "filthy and prophane expressions (viz. that hee hoped to meete some of the members of the Church in hell err long)," whereas John Hall was only fined for a similar contemptuous outburst against the church (he called his minister, Mr. Stow, "a pestilent person, a plague to the place") in 1757.[21] As late as 1711, however, as illustrated by the story of the impetuous Charles Arabella, a blasphemous outburst could bring swift and violent retribution.

While the manner of punishment shifted over the course of the seventeenth century, the kinds of offenses that most bothered colonial magistrates remained remarkably consistent: sacrilegious speech (50 of 147, or 33 percent) and contempt of the Sabbath (77 of 147, or 55 percent). The distribution of 147 prosecutions for religious crimes from 1620 to 1700 in the court records consulted was as follows: heresy, 5; blasphemy, 20; profanity/swearing, 30; sabbath breaking, 45; profaning the sabbath/contempt of sabbath, 32; miscellaneous, 15.[22]

The profile of prosecutions for religious crimes resembled that for other types of crimes in colonial British America, where disorderly speech and contempt of institutions always rankled magistrates unsure of their social standing or political authority on the far fringes of empire. Slander, in particular, was a perennial sore spot, accounting for a plurality of legal actions in the Puritan commonwealths and Virginia over the course of the seventeenth century.[23] The conventional portrait of early America as filled with sharp-tongued colonists and sharp-eared magistrates has a lot of truth to it. And given the centrality of the Word to reformed Protestantism, especially on the "hotter" variety that flourished in colonial America, sacrilegious speech—whether directed at fellow saints, the minister, the church, or God himself—was unavoidable in such a word-centered religious culture. Indeed, it was inevitable. What better way to mock the church than to speak "prophanely" about its leaders? What more effective way to indicate one's disaffection with the theological or liturgical practices of the church than to disrupt worship or—as one clever, if drunken, Anglican minister did in North Carolina—baptize a bear?[24] The forms of resistance to the church turned the foundational principles of reformed religion on their head: that the Word was a source of truth and salvation, that the institution of the church and the ministers who served it was the visible gathering of God's saints on earth, that religious authority flowed from God and not from man. God was not to be mocked. But his human representatives were fair game.

Sacrilegious Speech

Profanity was a catch-all term that covered a multitude of verbal sins, from playful jabs to full-throated swearing that verged on the blasphemous.[25] Given that most Anglo-American oaths were derivatives of sacrilegious phrases ("God's wounds," "by the blood of God," "God damn"), all profanity was irreligious in one sense or another, making the differentiation of religious from nonreligious speech crimes difficult. In its frequent invocation of the injured and rent body of Christ—"by God's arms, "by God's bones"—swearing in the Christian tradition can be seen as "tantamount to a ritual re-crucifixion," a verbal mockery of the miracle of incarnation.[26] When the Puritans came to power in England in the 1640s they lumped profanity with theater-going, gambling, and other acts of public sacrilege as part and parcel of their aggressive campaign to reform manners. Under Oliver Cromwell, swearing in the militia—the traditional prerogative of masculine profanity—was swiftly and severely punished by boring and, in one case, branding of the tongue.

British colonists in the first century of settlement were prosecuted for singing "profane songs" (one Bamfield, "severely whipped" in 1645), "sw[earing] before God" (Goody Gregory, stocked for 3 hours in 1641), "scoffing at Religion in a Turbulent Spirit" (Henry Sherlot, a French dancing master, 1681), "sw[earing] by the bloud of god" (Robert Shorthose, "tongue put into a cleft stick," 1636), calling "the Church of Boston a whoare, a strumpet" (Francis Hutchinson, banished upon pain of death, 1641), "Diabolically Cursing" (Beleiffe Gridley, 1664), and using "passionate and unadvised words" (Arthur Mason, 1671). And this was in Massachusetts alone. Altogether, some thirty colonists found themselves before the bar for using words in a way that was deemed an affront to God or the church.

Ministers came in for their fair share of abuse, especially in the southern colonies where the established Church of England struggled to maintain its foothold among the desperate young men who arrived by the boatloads as indentured servants in the seventeenth century. One poor parson in Virginia appeared repeatedly in court in the 1620s to protest the insults his parishioners threw at him—"stoned priest and piurde man," "blockheded parsone," "base baudie fellow," "foole, dunce, base fellow"—to no avail. The Protestant ministers of St. Mary's County, Maryland, complained that they "doe daily suffer" from the abusive speeches of one William Lewis, "who saith that our Ministers are the Ministers of the divell; and that our books are made by the instruments of the divell." In his defense Lewis charged the ministers with preaching anti-popery, "vizt that the Pope was Antichrist, and the Jesuits, the Antixian [Antichristian] ministers." Because "these his offensive speeches, & other his unseasonable disputations in point of religion tended to the disturbance of the publique peace & quiet of the colony," the court fined Lewis 500 pounds of tobacco and ordered him to remain in the custody of the sheriff until he could post bond for good behavior.[27]

Colonial statutes clearly differentiated the lesser forms of sacrilegious speech such as profanity and swearing from more serious ones like blasphemy, and reserved the ultimate penalty—death—for the latter. But in practice, magistrates found it difficult to distinguish garden-variety swearing from more deliberate mockery of God. In the secular and ecclesiastical courts of Anglo-America, the statutory line between profanity and blasphemy was deliberately porous. How, for example, should we classify the following case? Richard Smoolt, a servant, was charged by his mistress with "sundry grosse miscariadges," including "scoffing at the word of God which was preached by Mr. Cheevers" and "other rebellious carriadges in the famylye." Denied the use of a cooking pot, Smoolt "bid the Divell goe with it" and turned abusive. "When his Mrs. Came to correct him for a lye, he turned againe and did wringe her by the arme. . . . He asked her daughter Rebecca if she were not with child and therein slaundered her."[28] In this one brief record are at least six different offenses: contempt of church ("scoffing at the word of God"), blasphemy ("the Devil goe with it"), slander, lying, disobedience, and physical assault. Not surprisingly, the court ordered the unrepentant Smoolt to be "seuearly whipped."

Thomas Thornhill of Barbados was charged with "blasphemous language" in 1684 because, according to several witnesses, he "had used at a christening some vain and inconsiderate expressions." The magistrate ultimately concluded that "the whole company was so far gone in drink that none could remember what was said," and dismissed the charges.[29] A Massachusetts jury had a harder time deciding whether to convict Benjamin Sawser, a soldier, for blasphemy in July 1654. While the evidence was clear that Sawser, "being in drinke," had "spoken profainely & Ignorantly Blasfemus words in say[ing] Jehova is the Devel & knew noe god but his sworde and that should save him," the grand jury, trial jury, and Court of Assistants all diverged on the crucial question of whether these words warranted the death penalty. The grand jury indicted Sawser for blasphemy, but the trial jury ("the jury of life and death") acquitted him "on point of ignorance"; in their review of the verdict, the higher court "did finde the prisoner guilty of speaking that which we apprehended amounteth in substance to what the lawe expresseth so farr as to make the offence capital." Poor Sawser languished "in chains" in prison while the courts hashed out his fate, but managed to escape before the issue could be resolved.[30] Even the stern magistrates of New Haven, who rarely showed leniency in matters of religion, agreed that George King should be whipped rather than mutilated for swearing "by God." "The Govern'r told him that when the son of an Egiptian blaspheamed the name of God it was not borne. It's the piercing through the name of God in passion, which is a high provokation of God . . . & by a mans words he may loose his life. It was hoped it was only a rash & sinful oath, some have bin boared through the tongue, others have bin in the stocks & their tongues in a cloven stick. But hopeing it was not dispitfully don, the centance of the court was, that he should be whipped."[31] A small mercy, perhaps, but a mercy nonetheless.

The special urgency with which Puritan authorities viewed sacrilegious speech was part of a longer process of "rediscovering" blasphemy, in Leonard Levy's words, that the Reformation had spurred across continental Europe.[32] The enshrinement of *sola scriptura* at the heart of the Reformation made language the key battleground for God's latter-day saints: as David Lawton puts it, "Where God is Word, the Devil is anti-Word—not merely, *pace* Augustine, the absence of Word, but its perversion." The status of blasphemy as the original sin flowed logically from the importance of Scripture.[33] "Of every class of sins no one is more horrifying than the crime of blasphemy," concluded a parliamentary commission to review the ecclesiastical laws in 1552. Citing with approval the biblical precedent of public stoning for blasphemers, the commission proposed applying the same penalties with which the "persistent insanity of heretics is punished," or death, in other words.[34] A landmark case in 1676 declared blasphemy to be a crime against the state as much as a crime against God and brought it under the jurisdiction of common law for the first time. John Taylor's confused but clearly sacrilegious pronouncements that "Christ is a whoremaster" and "I am a younger brother to Christ, an angel of God" so scandalized the House of Lords that they ordered Taylor confined to Bedlam and referred the case to the highest court in the land. Lord Chief Justice Matthew Hale sentenced Taylor to stand in the pillory in three different places, wearing a paper saying "for blasphemous words, tending to the subversion of all government," and—crucially for the history of English jurisprudence—stated that "injuries to God" are punishable in the criminal courts because "the Christian religion is part of the law itself."³⁵ Despite the sweeping implications of Hale's opinion, very few executions followed, though one poor Scottish lad, eighteen-year-old Thomas Aikenhead, was hanged in 1695 for his antitrinitarian views at the insistence of Edinburgh's ministers.

One of the interesting features of blasphemy cases is that they afford an opportunity for the orthodox to, in effect, "unsay" the sacrilegious speech by reporting verbatim the offending words; the 1650 Parliamentary act against the Ranters offers a particularly vivid example with its detailed recitation of the blasphemies being condemned.³⁶ The colonial records are, alas, less helpful in this regard. In most cases, the blasphemous words that landed malcontents in trouble went unrecorded. Katherine Aines was sentenced to be "publickly whipt he[re] att Plymouth, and afterwards att Taunton, on a publicke training day, and to were [wear] a Roman B cut out of ridd [red] cloth and sowed to her upper garment on her right arme" for her "blasphemos words," but we don't know what Plymouth's own Hester Prynne, with her scarlet B, said that so angered the magistrates.³⁷ Nathaniel Silvester, a Quaker from New Haven, wrote a "slanderous & blasphemous" letter to the General Court in May 1660 that, "together with some information of sundry calumnious and opprobrious speeches uttered at Southold against ye court & magistrates of New England," led to court to seize a hefty £100 of Silvester's property.³⁸ Another Quaker, Solomon Eccles, was ordered by the governor of Barbados to "stand in the pillory in the Open Markett on St. Michaels town one day from 12 till one of the clock at noon with these Words, For Blasphemy over his head & on his back and breast in Capitall Letters" in 1681.³⁹ Sometimes the offenders themselves were ignorant of what they had done to deserve their punishment. John Rogers, a Baptist resident of New Haven, was "accused of blasphemy, I know not by who, and judged by a Court of Assistants to sitt on the gallows with a halter about my neck, and from thence to return to prison, and there to continue till I paid £5 for reproaching the Ministers." Rogers's ordeal was not over after the mock hanging; he complained that he was "cruelly scourged," whipped a second time when he refused to ask for mercy, and returned to prison "where I was chained to the sill, without bed or covering, and neither meat nor drink offer'd me in the space of three days, where I lay six weeks in this perishing manner . . . I know not for what; in which prison I was kept three years after."⁴⁰

In a handful of cases, we are fortunate to have the blasphemous words that landed offenders before the bar. Phillip Read of Concord, a "Chirurgeon or practitioner in Phisick," was accused of having "Blaspheme[d] the holy name of christ & also on a motion then & there made to pray to God for his wife then sick blasphemously Cursed hiding the divill take yow & yor prayer."[41] Jacob Lumbrozo, a Jewish resident of St. Mary's County, Maryland, was charged with blasphemy in 1658 after a conversation with his neighbor John Fossett turned to theological matters. Fossett deposed that he and Lumbruzo, "falling into discourse concerning Our B[lesse]d Sauior Christ his Resurrection," exchanged sharp words over the question of Christ's divinity. Fossett's avowal that Christ "was more then man, as did appear by his Resurrection" provoked Lumbruzo to reply "That his Disciples stole him away" after his death. Pressed to explain the miracles performed by Christ, Lumbruzo answered, "That such works might be done by Negromancy, or sorcery, or words to tht purpose. And this Depont replyed to the sd Lumbrozo, that hee supposed, tht the sd Lumbrozo answer tooke Christ to be a Negromancer. To wch the sd Lumbrozo answered nothing byt laughed." Another neighbor Josias Cole testified that "the Jew Doctor, knowne by the name of Jacob Lumbrozo," when asked "what hee was that was Crucifyed att Jerusalem," answered, "hee was a Man. Then the sd Cole asked him how hee did doe all his miracles? And the sd Lumbrozo answered hee did them by the Art of Magick." Unfortunately, we don't know the final disposition of the case. Court records indicate only that Lumbrozo was ordered to remain in the sheriff's custody until the next Provincial Court.[42]

The Lumbrozo case is unique in that it pitted Christian against Jew, but it highlights the important role that blasphemy charges played in sectarian conflicts in the British colonies. The battle between Quakers and Puritans was in large part a war of words, and the criminal statutes against sacrilegious speech were one of the most potent weapons in the arsenal of the colonial authorities. All but five of the blasphemy cases in these records involved Quakers, whose verbal pyrogenics were legendary on both sides of the Atlantic in the 1650s. When the constables came to the home of Richard Crabb and his wife on May 31, 1658, "to demand the Quakers books," they were met with a volley of venom from Goody Crabb. "The vengeance of God hangs ouer your heads at Stamford for takeing away o[ur] land without commission & wronging of them," she spit, "& then she fell a railing o the ministers & said they were priests & preached for hire & called them Baalls preists, & she would not heare them, & said we was shedders of bloud, ye bloud of the s[ain]ts of God." Her husband stood idly by and "did not so much as rebuke her," the court noted in disgust. Goody Crabb continued her tirade for "almost a houre together," pausing only to call "for a drink to refresh her, wch . . . she did to strengthen her to goe on in those wicked speeches."[43] Joseph Gatchell was ordered to stand in the pillory "& to have his toung drawne forth out of his mouth & peirct through with a hott Iron" for his avowal of the Quaker principle of universal salvation at the home of his kinsman Jeremiah Gatchell. When challenged by his cousin who asserted that "whosever Repents & believes shall be saved," Gatchelle "Answered if it be so, he [Christ] was an Imperfect savior & a foole."[44]

At least the Quakers disputed their fellow Protestants on recognizably Christian grounds. Other colonists went much further, disregarding Christianity and even revealed religion altogether. William King "uttered & declared i.e. that he was the Eternal son of God & yt he was holy & pure as God himself," for which he was "severly whipt with Twenty Stripes."[45] Captain William Mitchell of Maryland did "most prophanely in publick discourse profess himself of no Religion at all."[46] In a rare case of crosscultural prosecution, Pawquash, a Quillipiock Indian, was brought up on charges in New Haven in 1646 for having "blasphemously sa[id] that Jesus Christ was mattamoy & naught, & his bones rotten, & spake of an Indian in Manitoieses plantation assended into heaven." The court sentenced him to be "seaverly whipt for thus scorning at our worshipping God & blaspheame the name of our Lord Jesus, & informed him that if he should doe soe hereafter or now, it had bin against the light he now has, it would hazard his life."[47]

Blasphemy charges could serve blatantly political as well as sectarian and conversionary ends. John Coode, the former Anglican priest turned rebel, was accused of blasphemy in the 1690s after he fled Maryland seeking refuge across the border in Virginia. Depositions filed in 1696 claimed that Coode, "though holding priest's orders in the Church of England, said amongst other things that religion was but policy, and that all religion was to be found in *Tully's Offices*." For these and other inflammatory statements, the "deformed, club-footed" Coode, with a "face resembling that of a baboon," was outlawed for "horrid impious blasphemy and contriving rebellion" by Governor Nicholson.[48]

There was a natural logic behind the coupling of blasphemy and rebellion in the case of Coode, and the threat of political disorder lay behind many of the blasphemy cases heard in colonial courts, most obviously in the case of the Quakers, but in less overt ways in other cases as well. Arthur Smith's (unrecorded) blasphemous words threatened to "ouerthrow the order & gouerment God hath established in church & commonwealth," the New Haven court concluded in 1659, though they refrained from condemning Smith to death in the hopes that he "hath spoken p[ro]phainely" rather than "blasphemously."[49] The line between religious and political disorder was a porous one in the post-Reformation era, and certain crimes such as heresy and witchcraft came to be defined more as acts of sedition than of sacrilege in the seventeenth and eighteenth centuries. Blasphemy was no exception to this trend.

Contempt of Church

For all the attention paid to sacrilegious speech by colonial magistrates, the majority of prosecutions for religious crimes in the seventeenth century concerned contempt of church: Sabbath-breaking (performing unauthorized activities on the Sabbath), disruption of worship, challenging the authority of ministers or other church officers, refusal to pay ecclesiastical taxes, or deliberate nonattendance at services. Because these offenses were so commonplace, they are among the least detailed in the court records, often denoted by the umbrella phrase "breaking the Sabbath."

The violence implicit in the phrase "breaking the Sabbath" itself rarely surfaced, but on occasion contempt did take physical form such as hauling pew cushions out of the church, smashing altars (a deliberate if less theatrical version of European iconoclasm), and spitting at ministers.[50] One of the most disturbing incidents occurred in New York City on a cold winter night in February 1714, when some "wicked and Sacrilegious" persons broke into Trinity Church, the temporal and spiritual home of the Church of England in the colonies, and left the sanctuary in shambles. Having "broke into ye North Window of the Steeple," the vandals "broke down the window of the Vestry room did cut or tare off the Sleve of one of the Surplices that was in the said Room, and did Rent and Tare another to pieces and not being contented with that did carry the same Surplice with several common prayer books and Psalm books into ye Church Yard and having spread the Surplice on the Ground and put the common prayer books and Psalm books round it left their Ordure on the Sacred Vestments as the greatest outrage and most Villanous indignity they could offer to the Church of England Her Holy Priesthood and in defiance of God and all Religion."[51] In another celebrated incident that received widespread coverage abroad as well as at home, the residents of Boston attacked the Anglican church during New England's own version of the Glorious Revolution in 1689, when they sent the royal governor, Sir Edmund Andros, packing. As a contemporary explained, "The Church itself had great difficulty to withstand their fury, receiving the marks of their indignation and scorn, by having their Windows broke to pieces, and the Doors and Walls daubed and defiled with dung, and other filth, in the rudest and basest manner imaginable."[52] Quaker Thomas Maule corroborated this account, accusing his fellow Bostonians of "breaking the Church Windows, tearing the service Book, making Crosses of Mans Dung on the Doors, and filling the Key-holes with the same."[53]

Elsewhere, less orchestrated attacks occurred as Protestant sects squared off over the spoils of establishment. Anglicans and Presbyterians engaged in an unseemly tug-of-war over the pew cushions in a meeting house in Jamaica, Long Island, in 1707. "We had a shameful disturbance, Hauling and Tugging of Seats; shoving one the other off, carrying them out and returning again for more," wrote a disgusted John Bartow to the Society for the Propagation of the Gospel in Foreign Parts.[54] His neighbor Thomas Haliday complained that, in his parish, the dissenters "most contemptuously carryed away all the Goods of the Church and at the same time told me to be gone that I was a knave and a villain."[55] The most pointed attack by dissenters on an Anglican chapel was recorded by Charles Woodmason in the Carolina backcountry. "At the Congaree Chapel, a pack of vile, leveling common wealth Presbyterians in whom the Republican Spirit of 41 yet dwells . . . enter'd and partly tore down the Pulpit." The following Sunday "after the Communion was ended, they got into the Church and left their Excrements on the Communion Table."[56]

It is not surprising that most of these incidents date from the early eighteenth century. Not until the constitutional settlements of the 1690s did the Anglican Church emerge as a powerful political force in the British colonies capable of eliciting such violence from dissenters long accustomed to a certain degree of official latitude. The seventeenth-century record is both less dramatic and more forthcoming when it comes to cases of contempt of church. Rather than attacking the physical edifice of the church, malcontents staged more discrete acts of irreverence. Sometimes these were simple cases of (mostly) young men misbehaving in church: Joseph Leonard was guilty of "sporting and laughing in Sermon tyme," William Bromfield earned himself a stint in the stocks for "prophaining the Lords day and stealing wine from his Ma[ste]r wch he drunk and gave to others," Samuel Terry was discovered "standing with his face to the meeting house wall . . . chafing his yard to provoak lust," and Zebadiah Williams was fined ten shillings for "his unseemly and prophane carriage on a Sabbath in the meeting house at Northampton in the tyme of Publike ordinances Laughing and Juttung others that sat by him to their disturbance thereby Rendering the ordinance unprofitable to himself and others."[57]

In other cases, the disrespect aimed at the institution of the Sabbath was far more pointed. Alexander Colman (or Calman) received fifteen stripes "on ye naked body well laid on" for "endeavoring to make disturbance of the people in time of publick worship on the last Lords day in the 3d meeting house in Boston by Going in wth only a dirty frock of canvice all bloody & no other cloaths."[58] The Baptist John Russell was imprisoned for "renouncing Communion wth the church of Christ" at Charlestown, and "Joyning himself wth the schismattical church of Annabaptists."[59] Philip Ratliffe was sentenced to be "whipped have his eares cut of fyned 40 & banished out of ye lymitts of this Jurisdiccon" for "uttering mallitious & scandalous speeches against the governm't & the church of Salem."[60] There is good reason to think such behavior is seriously undercounted in the legal records. Ministers, Anglicans in particular, complained repeatedly that mockery of the church went unpunished in colonial America. "Scandals are both given and taken when the Ecclesiastical Sword is wanting," they complained. "We have none to Rule and Govern, no Eccl'ical Sword to punish the unruly, reduce the erring and cut off the obstinate heretique."[61] When some of "the looser sort at their Drunken Revellings and Caballs" interrupted a communion service in James Adams's church in Virginia, nothing was done; "such flagrant Crimes, notwithstanding of my Complaint to our Magistrates go unpunished and unregarded," he protested to the home secretary of the Society for the Propagation of the Gospel in Foreign Parts.[62] The lack of an American bishop was singled out by Anglican ministers as the most serious obstacle to their efforts to maintain orthodoxy in the colonies, but the reluctance of colonial juries to use the laws on the books to prosecute contempt against ecclesiastical institutions was probably more important. None of the assaults on churches uncovered in newspapers and the records of the Colonial Office came before the courts, including the widely publicized vandalism of Trinity Church in New York. The irregular enforcement of colonial statutes against religious dissent thus belied their much more robust presence in colonial law and rhetoric.

If we were to look only at the words of ministers and colonial governors, we would be forgiven for concluding that colonial America was "awash in a sea of profanity" (to paraphrase Jon Butler).[63] The pragmatic toleration that historians celebrate was, to men like the Rev. John Talbot, nothing more than a license for the worst kind of impiety. "Here's nothing established but such a Moderation to all that's good, and such a Tolleration of all that's evil, yea of the most damnable heresies which by the way is a damnable Tolleration, and worse than the worst persecution that ever was in the world, for that only destroys men's bodies but these destroy body and soul in hell for ever, which is damnable with a Vengeance and will make the last state of poor America worse than the first," he warned in 1709.[64] Most of his colleagues would have heartily agreed with this dire assessment of the state of organized religion on the far edges of empire. The indifference of the province's imperial masters was far more troubling to ministers on the ground than the impiety they confronted on a daily basis. Even when the "ecclesiastical sword" was available in the form of strict laws and severe penalties, colonial governors seemed unwilling to risk an imperial rebuke by vigorously enforcing the laws against dissenters and derelicts.

The legal records tell a somewhat different story. Heresy, blasphemy, and contempt of the Sabbath were serious crimes—capital ones in most jurisdictions—and magistrates made earnest if sporadic efforts to enforce these laws. When irreligious behavior threatened to rise to the level of a collective assault on the institutions and symbols of orthodoxy, as in the Quaker "invasion" of the 1650s, the law responded swiftly and brutally. Sacrilegious speech was prosecuted more vigorously than Sabbath-breaking, despite the greater incidence of the latter in the available records. Blasphemy elicited the most violent response: tongues were bored, bodies branded and whipped, though the ultimate punishment of death was never applied. Never amounting to more than a handful of cases in any one colonial jurisdiction, the prosecution of sacrilegious speech nonetheless reveals that magistrates did recognize the difference between the merely profane and the truly seditious, and did their best to crack down on speech that challenged the authority of God and his church. If blasphemy were not a capital crime, we would likely find many more cases pursued in the colonial courts. The presence of the maimed and branded in the towns and villages of colonial America, however few in number, was a stark reminder that the North American provinces were not so different after all from the persecuting society their residents had fled.

We all know how the story ends: with the enshrinement of freedom of religion on the national level as one of the bedrock principles of American democracy in the federal constitution, and the achievement of a voluntary system of denominationalism that made that freedom a practical reality as well as a legal right. True, the protections of the First Amendment did not extend to the states until the twentieth century, and a robust political culture of "christian republicanism" ensured that religion would continue to be enshrined in the public ceremonies and practices of American democracy for at least one hundred fifty years after the adoption of the Bill of Rights. But as a general rule, it is fair to say that historians have accepted the notion that religious freedom prevailed in 1791. Chris Beneke reminds us that genuine religious liberty, as opposed to grudging toleration, was a fragile and very recent thing in the early republic, barely a generation removed from the horrors of the confessional age; those Protestants, Catholics, and Jews who marched arm-in-arm through the streets of Philadelphia in 1788 were "not much further from the brutal persecution of dissenters than we are from the lynchings of African Americans."[65] It is an intriguing analogy. Religious prejudice functioned in the colonial era much like racial prejudice does in modern America, as an ever-present if not always publicly acknowledged force shaping the everyday life and civic culture of its residents. And, much like the vestiges of racial prejudice still present in our legal system, the persistence of statutes against blasphemy into our own day is a vivid artifact of a past we might prefer to forget.

Chapter 6

Persecuting Quakers?
Liberty and Toleration in Early Pennsylvania

ANDREW R. MURPHY

> Oh! Whither co you think these things will run? Will it not give people just cause to say, the Quakers are turned persecutors?

Pennsylvania has long been considered a singular success story in the history of Anglo-American religious liberty. In the standard narrative, William Penn's colony illustrates how adherents of diverse religious views can peacefully coexist, creating a vibrant public life bound together by civil interest and a commitment to the common good. As one historian explains, the "highly mobile society of laymen" who comprised Pennsylvania society was "drawn from all social classes and from many parts of the Old and New Worlds." Following Penn's long career of advocacy on behalf of his persecuted Quaker brethren across Europe, and his constant efforts to ensure liberty of conscience[1] for his colony's inhabitants, Pennsylvania's capital of Philadelphia grew from modest beginnings in the early 1680s into what another historian calls the "richest, fastest-growing, and most cultivated of American cities" by the middle of the next century.[2]

The successes of Penn's colony notwithstanding, the early years of Pennsylvania history also highlight the difficult realities that attend the founding of new societies and the challenges of securing social order in the face of strident dissent. The Keithian schism, which bitterly divided the Pennsylvania Quaker community during the early 1690s and resulted in the prosecution of religious dissenters in the colony's civil courts, provides an especially vivid example of what Susan Juster, in the preceding chapter, calls "the fragility of authority in the remote Atlantic provinces."[3] Indeed, the Keithian critique went beyond theology to raise other vital and equally contested issues in the colony's young life: the relationship between ministry and magistracy and thus the relationship between church and state, the Quaker peace testimony, and the role of Pennsylvania Quakerism within a larger British imperial system. In tying his critique so closely to prominent figures in Pennsylvania government and society, and in justifying his actions by referring to Quaker pioneers such as George Fox and Penn himself, Keith presented an extraordinary threat to the colony's ruling elite. This threat, highlighting how a religious schism was intricately tied to civil order and thus how church was linked with state even in the relatively tolerant environs of colonial Pennsylvania, forms a central part of the following narrative.

Despite the importance of the Keithian schism for understanding the development of religious tolerance in colonial Pennsylvania, it has received little scholarly attention over the years. In fact, the episode has rarely been identified as a locus of debate over religious toleration and figures hardly at all in the standard histories of American religion. Neither Keith nor the schism receives any mention in Thomas Curry's *The First Freedoms*, Edwin S. Gaustad's *Religious History of America*, or Winthrop Hudson's *Religion in America*. Most historians have echoed Edwin Bronner's description of the Keithian affair as a "quarrel" and the trials as "a credit to no one," emphasizing Keith's irascible temper and pugnacious demeanor.[4]

Yet the Keithian schism was of much greater importance than such historians have indicated. In questioning the link between religion and the civil order, the schism brought forth sharply differing understandings of conscience and conscience's liberty in a civil society. The schism thus forced Pennsylvanians to revisit and debate the politics demanded by the longstanding Quaker commitment to liberty of conscience, since the precise meaning of that commitment lay at the heart of this episode in early Pennsylvania history.

Exploring the divisive dynamics that the Keithian schism brought to the surface in the context of the relatively broad religious liberty that obtained in early Pennsylvania thus yields a more balanced and realistic understanding of America's "first prejudice" and its symbiotic relationship with the "first freedom." Appreciating the significance of both religious schism and religious liberty in early Pennsylvania requires a careful consideration of Penn's arguments for liberty of conscience and religious toleration, and the ways in which the founder sought to translate his tolerationist commitments into American political realities. It also requires that we acknowledge the young colony's fragility and the deep political anxieties that Keithians elicited from the Quaker elite who ruled during Penn's long absences from the colony. After exploring both the schism and the rhetoric in which it was couched by both sides, this chapter concludes by addressing some broad parallels between the Keithian schism and earlier episodes of religious dissent in early America, especially that of Anne Hutchinson and Roger Williams in New England, and by reflecting on its ramifications for the ongoing story of religion in America.

Penn's Tolerationism

William Penn was one of the best known and most prolific religious dissenters in Restoration England. His conversion to Quakerism as a young man during the mid-1660s represented a radical embrace, by a member of a prominent political family, of a sect more commonly associated with the uneducated and enthusiastic. The Restoration years saw the growth and transformation of the Quaker movement from a body emphasizing the experience of inner Light and Christ within into a far more ordered system of Monthly, Quarterly, and Yearly Meetings, complete with traveling clergy, oversight of members' writings, and ecclesiastical disciplinary structures. By the 1660s, what had been, according to one historian, "one of the most radical sects ... looking for the coming of the Kingdom of God on earth" in the wake of the English Civil Wars had developed into the more settled and organized "Religious Society of Friends" concerned with its own internal discipline and structure.[5] Penn played an important part in this process, emphasizing human reasonability alongside the inner spiritual experience so crucial to Quakerism and "plac[ing] a higher value on social order than most Quakers." One historian describes a Penn who "dressed suavely, spoke well, and almost always acted the aristocrat, even to the extent of being a bit of a dilettante."[6] His writings display a synthetic attempt to bring together the wide array of seventeenth-century tolerationist arguments and to place them in the service not only of oppressed Quakers, but of religious dissenters generally.

Politically speaking, Penn drew his tolerationist arguments from the particularities of English history and politics. Arguments based on the English "ancient constitution," for example, illustrate Penn's early Whig sympathies, emphasizing toleration as fully compatible with traditional English political practices and with the notion of a government balanced from antiquity between crown and Parliament. As early as 1670, Penn, in his mid-twenties, was already an aggressive advocate for liberty of conscience, describing it as one of "those freedoms, to which we are entitled by English birthright."[7] The Whig version of the ancient constitution understood Parliament to represent the English people, with a legitimate share in the realm's governance. It was a uniquely English argument aimed at an English audience and during the 1670s Penn placed a great deal of faith in a more enlightened Parliament's potential to provide toleration for Protestant dissenters. Writing in support of his friend Algernon Sidney for the House of Commons near the end of that decade, Penn returned to the idea that religious liberty was a matter of English birthright, emphasizing the principles of consent and property as foundational to the ancient constitution which itself predated both Protestantism and Catholicism.[8] Of course, Restoration Parliaments did not prove very receptive to calls for toleration and religiously repressive legislation was far more likely to come from Parliament than from the crown during these years. Even later in life, when Penn's youthful Whig sympathies had been replaced by a close personal relationship with the king and a defense of royal prerogative in pursuit of religious liberty—a nod to political exigencies that Penn considered a tactical, not a fundamental, shift in his position—he continued to cite the ancient constitution and to invoke toleration as an English birthright guaranteed by the most fundamental law of the land.[9]

In addition to these political arguments, Penn also offered epistemological or psychological justifications for religious toleration, namely that religious coercion does not work. Since belief is a faculty of the understanding and not the will (a point later made famously by John Locke, who called belief "the inward and full persuasion of the mind"[10]), it simply can not be produced by physical force: "the understanding can never be convinced by other arguments than what are adequate to her nature," and external penalties are unable to alter "faults purely intellectual."[11] In this sense, persecution was not only a category mistake, a fundamental misunderstanding of the reasons why people hold the conscientious beliefs that they do, but also doomed to fail on purely practical grounds. While persecution was incapable of ever accomplishing its desired end because of its epistemological weakness,

Penn maintained that toleration accorded with an adequate recognition of the way that the human intellect actually operated.[12]

Yet even Hobbesists and Penn's Anglican critics agreed with the epistemological arguments that human beings could not choose their beliefs. Rather, their political opposition to toleration leaned heavily on recent English history, when religious and political dissent had often gone hand-in-hand and Protestant dissenters had overseen the beheading of an Anglican king. But Penn pushed forward with the argument that dissenters ought to be able to *behave* and *worship* as their minds persuaded them; that liberty of conscience, if it were to mean anything, must include the liberty of religiously inspired conduct as well as mere belief. In 1670, he defined liberty of conscience as "the free and uninterrupted exercise of our consciences, in that way of worship, we are most clearly persuaded, God requires us to serve him in . . . which being, a matter of faith, we sin if we omit."[13] Pennsylvania would provide Penn with his greatest opportunity to put this position into practice, and he consistently attempted to secure the broadest possible worship rights for all religious groups within the colony's borders (often with less success than hoped given the hostility of many in the English government who retained ultimate authority over his colony's laws).

In addition to the political and epistemological justifications for toleration, there were also religious ones. Like many dissenters, Penn viewed religious toleration as a fundamental corollary of Protestantism and of true Christianity. Although he was famously close to the Roman Catholic King James II, and came under intense scrutiny after James's displacement in the Glorious Revolution, Penn shared widespread English suspicions of Roman Catholicism and bemoaned the tendency for claims of infallibility to lead to persecution. During the Popish Plot of the 1670s, Penn cautioned English Protestants to "flee Rome at home!" He had earlier dismissed coercion for conscience's sake as carrying "an evident claim of infallibility, which Protestants had been hitherto so jealous of owning."[14] Nonetheless, Penn was steadfast in his support for the worship rights of England's Roman Catholics, at least those Catholics willing to attest their political loyalty. Persecution was rooted, in Penn's view, as in Locke's, in spiritual pride and in fundamental misunderstandings of the nature of Jesus's ministry, which had nothing to do with the power of the sword and which was described by Christ himself as "not of this world." A proper understanding of the nature of Christ's kingdom, namely that since it was not of this world "what use can there be of worldly weapons to erect or maintain it?" would lead in turn to a proper understanding of earthly politics and to firm guarantees of religious liberty. Of course, worldly clergy might attempt to clothe their greed for power in Christian garb or associate religious dissent with political radicalism, but Penn located the model for noncoercive religion and liberty of conscience directly in the teachings of Jesus and the example of the early church.[15] Bringing together the epistemological and religious arguments, Penn described toleration as "natural, because it preserves nature from being made a sacrifice to the savage fury of fallible, yet proud, opinions . . . [and] Christian, since the contrary expressly contradicteth both the precept and example of Christ."[16]

All of these arguments—the epistemological, the political, the Scriptural—together formed the basis of Penn's view of England as a *civil commonwealth*, characterized by a balanced governing relationship between crown and Parliament and a generic Protestant public ethos. For Penn, the cement of civil society was civil interest and he stressed that "as Englishmen, we are . . . mutually interested in the inviolable conservation of each other's civil rights."[17] The fact that tolerating polities such as the Netherlands prospered economically did not escape Penn's notice either and his arguments emphasized the material advantages that would accrue to those nations that pursued a policy of toleration. Indeed, Pennsylvania's Quaker merchants played a significant role in a thriving transatlantic British economy.[18]

Like his contemporary John Locke, Penn did not advance a wholly novel or unprecedented "theory" of religious toleration. Rather, he brought together strands of argument that had been circulating in British religion and politics for much of the seventeenth century, and constructed a multifaceted defense of toleration for loyal religious dissenters. Though his career took many twists and turns over the course of his nearly five decades in British public life, he never retreated from the powerful argument that he sketched out in his 1670 treatise *The Great Case of Liberty of Conscience*: that religious toleration is natural, reasonable, and Christian, and reflects the practice of enlightened rulers throughout history.[19]

The "Holy Experiment" and the Keithian Schism

With the unrest of the Popish Plot at the end of the 1670s and the consequent fading of hopes for toleration in England, Penn turned his attention to America. Having some prior knowledge of the American settlements due to his role in settling a dispute among Friends in East and West Jersey, and with a hefty debt owed him by the crown, Penn sought land in America, telling his friend James Harrison of his hope "that there may be room there, though not here, for such an holy experiment" to secure liberty of conscience.[20] As envisioned by its founder, Pennsylvania would establish no church and require neither religious tests for officeholding nor the swearing of oaths in legal proceedings. J. William Frost has described Penn as aiming for a "noncoercive Quaker establishment" in his colony, in which the moral influence of Quaker principles and the presence of a large concentration of Friends in positions of influence would provide generalized social advantages, while avoiding the tendency of other establishments (e.g., England's and New England's) to persecute dissenters and aggrandize their own leaders.[21] In Edwin Bronner's words, Penn "expected the Light . . . to permeate every facet of life in his plantation, and particularly the government."[22] Penn received his charter from Charles in 1681 and journeyed to America the next year.

Due in large part to Penn's aggressive promotional efforts and his extensive network of Friends across Europe, the colony was religiously and ethnically diverse from the beginning.[23] Although a Quaker elite wielded a significant amount of power in the colony's political and economic affairs, many other religious, ethnic, and cultural groups from a variety of backgrounds—including Germans, Dutch, French, Swedes, Scots, and Irish; Anglicans, Presbyterians, Lutherans, Baptists—played important roles in the life of the colony during its first decade.[24] Just as the Keithian schism was beginning to rend the fabric of Philadelphia Quakerism, Francis Daniel Pastorius, the founder and leader of Pennsylvania's Germantown settlement, noted that "we [Germans in Germantown] live peaceably and contentedly."[25] At the same time, the dominance of Quakers in the political and economic life of the young colony, while it reflected the founder's vision, also aroused resentment among those outside the Quaker fold as well as those Quakers of more modest means or divergent religious views. Pennsylvania's Anglicans, for example, successfully petitioned for the establishment of an Anglican church in the colony in 1695, using Quaker hegemony as one of their chief arguments.[26] Anglicans' frequent complaints about their exclusion from power in the colony suggest that Pennsylvania's religious diversity did not always operate as harmoniously as the founder insisted. Still, compared to the meager religious guarantees enjoyed by dissenters in other colonies at the time, Pennsylvania stood out for the extent of its protections, which benefitted a wide range of religious groups.

Into this diverse, vibrant, and at times contentious mix of peoples came George Keith, described by E. Digby Baltzell as "the best educated man in Philadelphia of the first decade."[27] Prior to his arrival, Keith had played an important role in the spread of Quakerism in England, Scotland, and the colonies, traveling with Fox and Penn in Germany and the Netherlands during 1676. He had been in America since 1685, when he was appointed surveyor-general of East Jersey and had advocated on behalf of Friends throughout the colonies since his arrival. During a visit to Boston in June 1688, for example, Keith had harshly criticized the anti-Quaker writings of such Puritan divines as Cotton Mather and Samuel Willard, and had attempted to arrange a public debate with these representatives of New England Puritan orthodoxy. Though unsuccessful in that particular endeavor, Keith irked Mather enough to draw his scorn from the pulpit and in print.[28] Keith arrived in Philadelphia in 1689 to take up a position as schoolmaster.

Notwithstanding his defenses of Quakers against their Puritan persecutors, Keith was deeply troubled by what he found upon settling in Pennsylvania. In his travels around the countryside, Keith reported, he encountered Quakers who knew nothing of the basics of Christian doctrine and the creeds. According to Frost, Keith was "distressed at the ease with which one could become a Quaker in America," and he expressed alarm at what he perceived as Pennsylvania Quakers' excessive emphasis on "the Light within" at the expense of Scripture and doctrine.[29] For Keith, Quakerism was true Protestantism and all Friends needed to be conversant with the basics of Christian belief. As he had explained years earlier in 1679, it made no sense to "distinguish betwixt the Christian and the Quaker; whereas every true Christian is a Quaker, namely, one that trembles at the Word of God; and every true Quaker, is a Christian."[30] This level of religious ignorance and heterodoxy among everyday Quakers appalled him. Keith's efforts to shore up the theological and ecclesiastical foundations of Pennsylvania Quakerism, along with his disputatious temperament, which was long acknowledged even by his supporters and close associates, set him on a collision course with the colony's Quaker leadership.

In response to this religious laxity and doctrinal ignorance, Keith drafted a catechism for use in the instruction of the colony's Quaker youth, as well as a proposal for a system of elders and church government that he hoped to institute in the colony's Meetings. Keith presented his catechism as "designed not only for children, but such others come to age, who need, and are desirous to be instructed in the first principles and grounds of the Christian religion," and he concluded the catechism by noting that it would be "well that the great profit and use of the scriptures were more understood and valued by Christian professors in general."[31] The catechism emphasized the importance of Jesus's death as remedy for human sin and provided extensive Scriptural justification for its Christological argument that knowledge of Jesus Christ is "necessary matter of Christian faith, in order to eternal life and salvation."[32] Keith's system of elders and deacons to manage Quaker discipline was presented in "Gospel Order Improved," an unpublished document circulated in early 1690. That document also voiced support for a Quaker creed and recommends a more exacting set of requirements for admission to Meeting membership. The church government proposals were tabled by Pennsylvania's Public Friends, according to Jon Butler, largely because they "flew in the face of Quaker practice." Clearly Quaker elders hoped that the issues Keith raised would go away if they delayed consideration of his objections.[33] The proposal for a catechism was roundly rejected by the 1690 Yearly Meeting, although it received support from Rhode Island Quakers, who were at that time embroiled in a divisive schism of their own.[34]

The remainder of 1690 and 1691 saw rising tension between Keith and his supporters on the one hand and the main body of Pennsylvania's Quakers, including the colony's Public Friends (that is, Quaker clergy) on the other. A number of the most prominent Public Friends—Thomas Lloyd, Samuel Jennings, and Arthur Cook—also held high office in Pennsylvania's civil government.[35] Thus Keith's growing resentment of religious authority in the colony, which had frustrated him so when the Meeting refused to endorse his catechism and system of church government, easily crossed over into political and social contention. As Keith's criticisms of religious practice in Pennsylvania became more and more strident, his oppositional rhetoric inflamed the colony's public life more generally. Nor was the colony's religious and political elite about to take Keith's criticisms in stride. By the time of the September 1691 Yearly Meeting, Keith had been accused of heresy—specifically, of denying the sufficiency of the Light within, insisting that something beside the Light was necessary to salvation—by William Stockdale, another Public Friend. However, the Meeting declined to find either Keith or his accuser guilty of heresy, which only further angered Keith. One of them must be wrong, he argued, and anyone who accused a non-heretic of heresy must himself be a heretic. This confrontation was just the first of many between Keith and other Public Friends.

It is unclear whether Keith and his followers began meeting separately from the main body of Pennsylvania Quakers due to a precipitating incident or whether their separation grew gradually out of the increasingly rancorous disputes between Keith and Public Friends; but by spring 1692, Keithians were holding separate meetings and in June of that year the Public Friends Meeting disowned Keith. (In some places, apparently, Keithian meetings rivaled orthodox Meetings in numbers of adherents.)[36] Even at this point, however, the schism seemed less than total and a number of emissaries traveled between the groups advancing proposals aimed at reunification. Because each side's conditions for reconciliation involved the near-total recantation of criticisms made of the other, though, these efforts proved futile. The appearance of two visiting English Quakers, Thomas Wilson and James Dickenson, also failed to heal the breach, largely because of their view that Keith's separation, since it was based on doctrinal differences and not fundamentals of faith, was not justified.[37]

Keith's alliance with the printer William Bradford placed these disputes squarely in the legal and political realm.[38] In his account of *Some Reasons and Causes of the Late Separation* published in June 1692, Keith cast himself as the defender of Christian orthodoxy, decrying the manifold theological errors among Pennsylvania's Quakers and the worldly pretense of the Public Friends.[39] In October he published *An Appeal from the Twenty-Eight Judges to the Spirit of Truth and True Judgment*, his response to the Public Friends who had cast him out earlier that year. In the *Appeal*, Keith repeated his critiques of his fellow colonists' theological errors. He also took aim at the conduct of Public Friends, who "claim a superiority over . . . the Lord's heritage and people, as if ye were not capable nor qualified to judge them, but . . . on this pretended authority (too like the Roman-Hierarchy) they have sent their paper of judgment against us to you." The final of Keith's twelve points in the *Appeal* asked the Yearly Meeting to consider "whether there is any example or precedent [in] Scripture, or in all Christendom, that ministers should engross the worldly government, as they do here?" In Keith's view, Christ had forbidden his followers to wield the sword, and exercise of governmental power was inherently coercive and violated the Quaker peace testimony. *The Appeal* called on the upcoming Yearly Meeting to take up the issues behind the schism, including the dispute over heresy between Keith and Stockdale, and produce a definitive ruling on them.[40]

Keith's *Appeal* to the upcoming Yearly Meeting was clearly an appeal to lay Quakers to resist the overweening pretensions of their clergy, many of whom were also civil magistrates. But any observers who hoped for clarity to emerge from the 1692 Yearly Meeting were sorely disappointed. Several mutually contradictory accounts circulated, each offering a different version of events. Francis Makemie, a Pennsylvania Presbyterian minister and frequent critic of Quakers, claimed that the Meeting vindicated Keith and condemned Thomas Lloyd. Samuel Jennings, one of the magistrates with whom Keith had repeatedly clashed during the previous two years, stated that Keith was himself disowned after repeated attempts at reconciliation. The Yearly Meeting apparently received condemnations of the Keithians from a number of the surrounding Quarterly Meetings and drafted letters to local Meetings as well as Friends in England justifying their course of action toward Keith. At some point during the proceedings Keith and his followers exited, and two parallel Meetings were held simultaneously. Keith emerged from that Meeting or Meetings with roughly seventy adherents, or approximately one-fourth of the total. In the months that followed, condemnations of Keith and the Keithians came from Friends' Meetings as far away as Barbados and Maryland.[41]

But if the status of the Keithians vis-à-vis the Meeting remained unsettled early in fall 1692, the civil dimension of the Keithian schism was just coming to a head. The *Appeal*, after all, had not only addressed internal Quaker dynamics, but also raised another longstanding concern among Friends that went to the heart of public life in the young colony and its relationship with English authorities: the legitimacy of Quakers exercising civil magistracy.[42] Keith's actions in taking these disagreements outside of the Meeting in this way—publishing and distributing the *Appeal*—had represented a sharp departure from Quaker practice and further polarized Pennsylvania society. Bradford and John McComb, respectively the printer and distributor of the *Appeal*, were arrested and put in jail. In October 1692, a grand jury charged Keith and Thomas Budd with reviling civil magistrates, and Bradford and McComb with printing and distributing a seditious pamphlet. All of these charges grew out of the strident and increasingly vocal dissent offered by the Keithians against civil magistrates, especially Thomas Lloyd and Samuel Jennings.

What made the case so perplexing from a legal point of view was that these civil magistrates were also Quaker ministers. In their defense before the court, Keith and Budd claimed that their harsh words had not been directed at Jennings and Lloyd *qua* magistrates, but *qua* fellow church members, in the context of a religious meeting, and that thus Jennings and Lloyd should not have gone to law but should have pursued their controversies by way of "gospel order."⁴³ On this account, the prosecutions amounted to civil punishment for religious activities, the interposition of state power into a religious body's private affairs, and a fatal intermingling of ecclesiastical and political power that had long been anathema not only to Quakers but to Protestant dissenters more generally. Indeed, the very notion of conscience and Pennsylvania's commitment to liberty of conscience as a fundamental right were at stake in Keith's critique. Furthermore, Keith raised the specter of an appeal to England during his testimony, a threat that resonated with colonial elites all too familiar with the colony's tenuous legal status in the wake of William Penn's legal woes; indeed, the crown would strip Penn of the government of his colony, and appoint New York Governor Benjamin Fletcher to rule Pennsylvania in early 1693.

The results of the trial are difficult to interpret. Keith and Boss were convicted, though only of "speaking slightingly" of magistrates. Each was fined, though the fines seem never to have been collected. The jury did not reach a verdict on Bradford though the government kept his press and type for six months, an action with potentially severe consequences for his ability to make a living. Keith continued his attacks on the Pennsylvania Quaker elite, and the following months saw two Monthly Meetings in the city, each claiming to represent true Quaker principles. One particularly noteworthy episode described by Gary Nash involved the construction and subsequent demolition by the two competing factions of their opponents' preaching platforms in the same Philadelphia meetinghouse:

> The climax came in early 1693 at the largest meetinghouse in Philadelphia. On a Saturday night . . . partisans of Keith worked feverishly at one end of the meetinghouse to erect a gallery from which their leader might exhort the worshippers the next morning. Keith's opponents had long controlled the permanent gallery at the opposite end of the room and denied the apostate entrance to it. The next day, as Quakers filed into the meetinghouse for the weekly devotions, they found themselves caught in the cross fire of two groups of impassioned Friends. Accusations and counteraccusations filled the air. . . . But the verbal exchanges paled before the physical demonstration that followed. Axes appeared from nowhere as each group sought to destroy the other's gallery. Posts, railings, stairs, seats—all went down before the angry blows of the two opposed camps.⁴⁴

When Governor Fletcher arrived in April 1693, he found petitions from Keith and Bradford, seeking the new governor's assistance in clearing their names (Bradford sought the return of his printing press and type; Keith, a certificate of good behavior). Bradford obliged, and these events are generally considered the conclusion of the Keithian schism as an episode in the history of Pennsylvania. And yet the schism continued across the Atlantic. Later in 1693, Keith and Budd sailed for England to plead their case with English Quakers. Jennings and several companions made a similar trip to ensure that the 1694 London Yearly Meeting heard their side of the affair as well. That meeting declared that Keith ought not to have printed and published his criticisms of fellow Friends, and the following year's meeting disowned Keith for failing to withdraw his criticisms of Pennsylvania Quakers.[45]

Keith and the Rhetoric of Conscience and Persecution

Underlying the contentious exchanges between Keith and his interlocutors was a struggle over the very meaning of terms such as conscience (and thus liberty of conscience) and persecution. The competing accounts of the trials and conflicts of 1690–93 echoed longstanding debates in both England and New England. In the rhetorical justifications of their respective positions, each side strove to present itself as a faithful representative of Quaker and, more generally, Christian orthodoxy. Once we understand what the argument over the term "conscience" was about, we can better understand the various dimensions of the struggle between Keithians and the defenders of Pennsylvania Quakerism.

The orthodox Protestant view, derived via Calvin from Aquinas and Jerome, held that the conscience was a faculty that enabled an individual to know God's law, and thus the term inherently carried with it an objective standard of right and wrong.[46] Understood in this way, conscience implied a degree of *knowledge* (*con-scientia*) and not simply whim or opinion; accordingly, one might act sincerely, upon mistaken beliefs, and err in the process. In other words, one could not claim liberty of conscience to participate in manifestly ungodly behavior; and "erroneous conscience" was a standard term in the casuistic literature. Most early modern tolerationists similarly accepted the idea that conscience could err and did not deny the objective standard contained in the orthodox formulation.[47] At the same time, they emphasized another aspect of the term, a subjective element of the conscience, and argued that as a faculty of the understanding and not the will conscience could not be forced into assent to any particular proposition. Tolerationists also drew on Scriptural sources (including the parable of the wheat and the tares as well as Paul's injunction in Romans 14:5, that each believer should be "fully persuaded in his own mind," and Romans 14:23, that "whatsoever is not of faith is sin") to argue that one was compelled to follow the dictates of one's conscience, even if erroneous. To be precise, the difference was not over whether conscience could err, but over the appropriate political response to individuals with erring consciences. This increasing emphasis on the *subjective* aspect of conscience—not a denial that conscience could err, but a defense of the right to sincerely held error in the face of state power—represents one of the most significant contributions of the early modern tolerationist tradition.[48]

Such differing notions of conscience and the politics of conscience had long informed arguments over what constituted persecution, and were central to arguments on both sides of the Atlantic. Tolerationists had consistently advocated the rights of erring consciences, while defenders of orthodoxy tended to espouse the traditional definition that more heavily emphasized its objective aspects.[49] The Massachusetts magistrates' expulsion of Roger Williams during the 1630s did not constitute persecution, John Cotton claimed, which lay in "the affliction of another for righteousness' sake" (i.e., if an individual was not engaged in righteousness he could not be persecuted.)[50] When Cotton dismissively referred to "some point of doctrine which in conscience [Williams believes] to be the truth, or . . . some work which in conscience you believe to be a religious duty," Roger Williams responded that "to molest any person, Jew or Gentile, for either professing doctrine, or practicing worship merely religious or spiritual, it is to persecute him, and such a person (whatever his doctrine or practice be, true or false) suffereth persecution for conscience." Pushing these points to a logical conclusion, English dissenter William Walwyn argued in 1644 that "though the thing may be good in itself, yet if it do not appear to be so to my consideration, the practice thereof in me is sinful."[51]

Taken for granted in all these debates over the meaning of conscience was dissenters' "peaceful carriage" and humble demeanor. Cotton, as the spokesman for New England orthodoxy, maintained that errors in fundamentals kept discreetly to oneself, and nonfundamental errors held in a meek or humble manner, fell outside the civil magistrate's authority. But errors held "with a boisterous and arrogant spirit, to the disturbance of the civil peace" interfered with civil government's responsibility to preserve order. And the concern for order was never far from the minds of New England magistrates. Shortly after expelling Anne Hutchinson from Massachusetts Bay, the magistrates ordered that her sympathizers be disarmed: "There is just cause of suspicion, that they, as others in Germany, in former times [i.e., the Muenster commune], may, upon some revelation, make some sudden eruption upon those that differ from them in judgment."[52] Vocal leaders of organized dissenting forces such as Anne Hutchinson and Roger Williams felt the full force of orthodoxy in their expulsion from hearth and home, whereas their quieter supporters were often left more or less undisturbed.

Given the centrality of liberty of conscience to Penn's career and to the colony that he founded, it is not surprising that the participants in the Keithian conflict drew on the notions of rightly ordered and erroneous conscience in justifying their own actions and seeking to discredit the motives and arguments of others. Keith's accuser Samuel Jennings defined persecution as "a suffering inflicted upon the sufferers, for the discharge of their duty to God," a formulation that echoed Cotton's and that made the question of whether Keith was persecuted turn on whether or not he was, in fact, discharging his duty to God.[53] In other words, Jennings held that there was an external, objective standard for determining proper action and thus for determining whether one was legitimately forbidden from undertaking such action.

Keith took issue with Jennings's definition of persecution, drawing explicitly on the rights of erroneous conscience and describing Jennings's view as "far too narrow, as not including such suffering as is inflicted upon men, that may be in error, and hold erroneous doctrines and principles. . . . The true definition of persecution is a suffering inflicted upon the sufferers, not only for the discharge of their duty to God, but for all that a man thinks to be his duty to God."[54]

Thus Keith sought to open the door to a broader understanding of conscience and its prerogatives than either Jennings or Lloyd was willing to admit. As far as the Keithians were concerned, their prosecution before the civil magistrates was persecution plain and simple, since even if their beliefs were false they should have had the liberty to affirm them, in accordance with Friends' principles. Furthermore—and, rhetorically speaking, far more interesting—in support of his position, Keith claimed that his position faithfully represented the view of Quakers including Penn and Robert Barclay. (Recall that Keith had argued Quakers' affirmation of Christian doctrine in his defenses of them before New England divines.) Nor was Keith making this argument up out of whole cloth: Barclay's *Apology*, one of the touchstone texts of Quaker theology, affirmed the political sanctity of erroneous conscience, defining conscience as *"that persuasion of the mind which arises from the understanding being possessed with the belief of the truth or falsity of any thing*; which though it may be false or evil upon the matter, yet if a man should go against his persuasion or conscience, he would commit a sin; because what a man doth contrary to his faith, though his faith be wrong, is no ways acceptable to God."[55] Penn himself had acknowledged, in his 1681 *Brief Examination*, that "I do not intend, that any Person or Persons should be in the least harm'd for the External Exercise of their Dissenting Consciences in Worship to God, though *Erroneous*; for though their Consciences be blind, yet they are not to be forced; such Compulsion giveth no Sight, neither do Corporal Punishments produce Conviction."[56] Jane Calvert argues that "Keith was more in keeping with the Quakerism of the Friends' early years than most of his contemporaries."[57] Wrapping himself in the mantle of the proprietor and in the Quaker tradition more generally, Keith aggressively proclaimed his orthodoxy and attempted to turn the tables on his opponents by stressing the parallels between Philadelphia Quakers and New England Puritans.

Of course, beliefs were only part of the picture in all of these arguments over liberty of conscience. Defenders of orthodoxy were especially concerned to argue that claims to liberty of conscience must not be allowed to threaten civil society's very existence or to excuse individuals who refused to live peaceably with their neighbors. In Keith's analysis of the situation, Thomas Lloyd shared a characteristic of power-hungry rulers, in both church and state, the world over: the inability to countenance any dissent, and the eagerness to prosecute any who stand up and protest their grip on power. His citation of Penn and Barclay noted above was intended to defend himself from accusations of theological heterodoxy, but Keith also sought to link his cause to George Fox himself, in defending himself against charges of sedition and disrespect for magistrates. If contentious behavior was sufficient to justify civil actions against religious dissenters, Keith argued, it is difficult to see how Fox himself could have escaped jail in Lloyd's Pennsylvania: "at this rate, many Friends, and particularly G. F. is guilty of reviling magistracy, who more sharply and severely reproved pride and injustice in some justices of the peace . . . in England, than ever we did in Pennsylvania." Keith topped off this rhetorical flourish by citing two specific examples from Fox's *Journal*, in which the first Friend excoriated English magistrates as vicious oppressors; and the trials of a host of other eminent Friends including Penn himself.[58] Keith's defense of himself during and in the wake of the schism represented a clear attempt to ground his own cause firmly in the Quaker orthodoxy of Fox, Barclay, and Penn.

But Pennsylvania Quakers struck back, not surprisingly, and stressed the fragility of social order in a young colony: "In the infancy of the settlement of Pennsylvania," Samuel Jennings argued, "the legislators saw cause to make provision by a law, to secure the reputation of the magistrates from the contempt of others."[59] Taking care to distinguish persecution from prosecution, Jennings charged that Keith had slandered and traduced the magistrates, "pretending it was for matters purely religious," and had "endeavaour[ed] to raise sedition and subvert the government, and for that cause only, and not upon any religious account, were they prosecuted."[60] No claim of conscience could justify the sort of seditious behavior that the Keithians had engaged in, Jennings argued, which constituted a gross abuse of Christian liberty and a violation of the standards of civil and godly behavior on which Pennsylvania's collective good depended.

Ecclesiology, Politics, and Quaker Magistracy in an Imperial Context

Claims and counterclaims—of conscience and persecution—connect the judicial proceedings against Keithian dissenters with issues of religious liberty and toleration in early Pennsylvania. But there was always more at stake in these disputes than spiritual faculty or the internal workings of the Society of Friends. In addition to their theological objections to Pennsylvania Quaker practices, Keith and his followers decried the worldly pretensions of Public Friends as unworthy of true ministers of the Gospel, and questioned whether Quakers should exercise civil magistracy. In the various rhetorical moves made by Keith and his opponents, we find echoes of the seventeenth-century English approach to religious differences (where the armed conflicts of the Civil Wars yielded a beheaded king and a military regime)—what Susan Juster, in another chapter in this volume, calls "the symbiotic relationship between religious authority and political order on the margins of empire." Although prosecutions for religious crimes were relatively rare, Juster points out, one of the most frequently prosecuted offenses included the "slander of church officials." Surely Keith's distinction that he denounced his critics as fellow churchmen and not as magistrates, as we shall see, failed to convince many in Pennsylvania's elite. To explore these dynamics, we turn to issues of ecclesiology and political power.

Certainly Keith and the Public Friends had been on a collision course for some time. As we have seen, the rejection of his proposed catechism and system of church governance by the Yearly Meeting led Keith into an increasingly confrontational stance toward the prevailing structures of authority in the colony. Public Friends quickly coalesced against him and Keith's ally Thomas Budd bitterly denounced them for their practice of visiting Meetings around the region "clothed with their magistratical robes." When these Public Friends encountered opposition, Budd continued, they "call out for a constable, thereby endeavouring to trample us down by their magistratical power and authority."[61]

That Public Friends played such important roles in other domains—government, the economy—during Pennsylvania's early years only added to the ferocity of Keith's denunciations of the fatal intertwining of ministry and magistracy in the colony. During his trial, Keith insisted that the harsh critiques directed at Samuel Jennings and Thomas Lloyd were said by coreligionists to coreligionists—that is, in their roles as Public Friends and not as colonial magistrates—and thus fell far outside the legitimate sphere of the civil power. Calling Jennings ignorant and presumptuous, for example, "was not said of him, as he was a magistrate, but as he professed himself to be a Christian and a minister of Christ."[62] At trial, Bradford described the *Appeal* as "wholly relating to a religious difference."[63] At least two of Pennsylvania's non-Quaker judges apparently agreed. As Keith described in his account of his trial, "Lacy Cock a Lutheran, and John Holme a Baptist, declared their dissent from them in these proceedings, signifying, 'That the matter was a religious difference among themselves (viz. the Quakers) and did not relate to the government.'"[64] If church members could be brought before civil courts for things said to fellow church members in the context of a religious dispute, Keith and Budd argued, then Friends had indeed fallen far from their earlier commitments to egalitarianism and the Inner Light; and, Keith added with more than a hint of irony, it was hard to see how Pennsylvania's public life differed from "New England's spirit of persecution." Indeed, at least in New England clergy did not hold political office.

Keith thus combined a theological dedication to Christian orthodoxy with a more general Quaker anti-clericalism, which constituted one of the sect's most deeply rooted characteristics from its earliest days.⁶⁵ And for Keith, such a posture continued long after his departure from Pennsylvania, as he tangled with the London Yearly Meeting in 1694 and 1695. After his return to England in 1694, Keith denied that any Quaker Meeting could judge matters of conscience, calling such claims "downright popery."⁶⁶ And, after being disowned, Keith complained that the Second Day Meeting, which consisted of Public Friends, "may be fairly compared to the conclave of cardinals in Rome."⁶⁷ But Keith was not alone in making these critiques of clerical authority. Many Friends, including Fox and Penn, had long warned Public Friends about arrogating too much influence to themselves, and the Society of Friends itself had been born in a struggle against the commingling of church and state power in England. Penn knew firsthand Thomas Lloyd's penchant for aggrandizing power and, early in the dispute, wrote from England that he was willing to believe that "T[homas] L[loyd]'s height, has administered occasion for a difference in spirit between [Keith] and him from the first. For as to doctrines, they cannot but agree; though George's way of explaining Scripture phrases, may be a little too philosophical."⁶⁸

Of course, when designing the colony, Penn had hoped that Quakers could infuse public life with virtue without in any way endangering religious liberty. Keith's argument in the *Appeal* that no Christian and certainly no minister of the gospel ought to hold the office of civil magistrate since Christ had forbidden his followers to use the carnal sword was bound to further complicate these arguments. Taken seriously, it struck at both the theory and practice undergirding Pennsylvania society.⁶⁹

The transatlantic context, the ways in which Pennsylvania's domestic politics echoed across the Atlantic and intertwined with larger conflicts in England, added another wrinkle to these political, legal, and ecclesiastical disputes. The Keithian schism threatened to raise fundamental questions about Quaker civil authority and to provide ammunition to Penn's critics in England as well as America. The political problems implicit in such disputes were myriad, including the refusal of Quaker governors to require oaths in legal proceedings, as well as accusations charging Quaker magistrates with failing to administer justice impartially and to provide for the colony's defense against French and Indian attacks. Collectively, of course, such issues raised urgent questions about whether Penn and his coreligionists were fit to govern the colony.

The timing of Keith's dissent and the prosecutions could hardly have been worse for Penn, who now had to deal with reports of seditious and contentious behavior taking place in his colony. Penn had been away from Pennsylvania since 1684, when he embarked on what he thought would be a fairly limited voyage to defend his colonial boundaries at court against his neighbor Lord Baltimore's rival claims. Arriving in England, Penn was swept up in the efforts by his old friend James II to declare liberty of conscience for all Englishmen, including Roman Catholics. James had attempted to enact toleration for both Protestant and Catholic dissenters in England by issuing a Declaration of Indulgence, a strategy that worried many Protestants as setting a dangerous precedent of royal power at the expense of Parliament.[70] Penn became a frequent visitor at the court and a vocal supporter of the king's extralegal efforts at toleration. When the king fled before the advance of William III in 1688, Penn was left in a precarious position as well-known propagandist of a discredited regime. He was accused of treason, placed under house arrest, and even went into hiding for a time. Under William and Mary, Penn's hold on his colony became extremely tenuous. He turned over the deputy governorship to John Blackwell, a New England Puritan, in the late 1680s and lost control of his colony altogether in 1693 when, as we have seen, the crown appointed Fletcher to rule both colonies.

The issue of colonial defense was a central element of the attacks on Penn and closely related to the royal appointments of non-Quakers to rule the colony. It took aim at perhaps the most fundamental responsibility of government, the safeguarding of the population from external attacks. The Quaker peace testimony proved a substantial obstacle to any satisfactory resolution of the issue, as the Assembly resisted both Blackwell's and Fletcher's attempts to secure funding for military defense. Keith's attack on Quakers exercising magistracy in the *Appeal* raised just the wrong issue at just the wrong time. In a 1693 letter to Pennsylvania Friends, Penn reported that "the trial of [George Keith] has been industriously spread all about the nation. . . . [T]he advantage the disaffected among us make by it against. . . . Friends having power, against me, and you in particular are great and lamentable."[71] Shortly thereafter, Penn himself recommended that Quakers agree to provide for the colony's military defense, reluctantly going along with a plan to supply eighty militiamen as a condition of his regaining the colony in 1694 and advising the Provincial Council that "[w]e must creep where we cannot go and it is as necessary for us in the things of this life to be wise as to be innocent."[72] The Pennsylvania Quaker leadership was caught on the horns of a dilemma in this matter. Keith and his followers accused them of wielding an improper coercive power, while other critics accused them of not using enough coercion, of failing to employ the force necessary to defend the colony.

Or perhaps, others opined, Quakers were all too inclined to exercise worldly powers, but they did so in ways that redounded solely to their own benefit. Critics charged that although Quakers had protested loudly against persecution while a minority in England, "now, being got in the saddle of government, and being rulers themselves, they deny liberty of conscience to others."[73] Given how assiduously Quakers had cultivated their reputations as defenders of liberty of conscience, the Keithian schism and the prosecutions that went along with it threatened a public relations catastrophe of the first order. After all, when Keith titled his "transcript" of the trial *New England's spirit of persecution, transported to Pennsylvania*, the implication was clear. Quakers were no different than those persecuting New England Puritans. While a minority, they were defenders of liberty; when in charge, they became jealous of their power and persecuted dissenters within their borders. Anglicans in America repeated such charges and accused Pennsylvania Quakers of interfering with their freedom of religion as well as providing fellow Quakers preferential treatment in the distribution of public offices. Penn's correspondent Thomas Holme reported "grudges in some, that none are put in places of power, but Friends."[74]

Conclusion: The "First Prejudice" in Pennsylvania?

So was the Keithian schism an example of religious persecution, of America's "first prejudice"? Or was it merely a civil prosecution conducted to deal with a tumultuous faction that cloaked its seditious activities under the guise of religion? The answer to such questions depends, of course, upon how one defines persecution, liberty, and conscience. The Keithian schism began as a theological controversy within the Pennsylvania Quaker community and, because it touched on questions of authority, cohesion, and discipline within the community, quickly assumed ecclesiastical dimensions. These religious debates intertwined with preexisting social and political fault lines, and led finally to civil prosecutions of members of the dissenting faction on charges of social and political disruption and sedition. What made Keith so disruptive—as with Roger Williams nearly sixty years earlier in New England—was his unwillingness to compromise with the realities of institutional religious life, whether it was worshiping with the unregenerate (in Williams's case) or countenancing Quaker ministers exercising magistracy (in Keith's case).

Like Keith, Williams and Hutchinson initiated theological controversies from within their colony's dominant religious group, controversies that took on a life of their own and sharply divided their communities. Of course Hutchinson and Williams paid a far heavier price than Keith or any of his followers ever paid, namely banishment and expulsion from the colony. Keith's case did not present the explosive gender dynamics of the Hutchinsonian affair; nor did it lead to the founding of a new settlement like Williams's flight to Providence in 1636. Nonetheless, the vision articulated by each of these religious dissenters would have virtually annihilated their colonies' basic foundations as understood by those colonies' founders. Each was inspired by what I have elsewhere called a "perfectionist" strand, an impulse toward drawing more stringent boundaries between "church" and "world," and policing those boundaries more vigilantly.[75] Keith, Williams, and Hutchinson were unwilling to make the kinds of compromises with pragmatic realities that a broad and inclusive church required (such as worshiping with the unregenerate in Williams and Hutchinson's case or countenancing the exercise of magistracy by Quakers in a Quaker colony in Keith's case). For each of these dissenters, church purity and sound doctrine should be one's foremost task, regardless of the disruptive social effects of pursuing such purity. In assessing blame for such disruption, furthermore, Keith asserted, it is not separatists who should be condemned, but those who countenance heresy and thus bring on separation by orthodox believers, "as when the sun shines warm on a dung-hill, the dung-hill is to be blamed for the stink, not the sun." (Revealingly, Williams also used the imagery of the dung hill, in a letter to John Winthrop: "I beseech you do more seriously then ever, and abstract yourself with a holy violence from the dung heap of this earth."[76])

Civil magistrates in each case reacted to these religiously inspired episodes of social conflict by stressing their civil aspects, refusing to allow defenses based on "conscience" to justify disruptive behavior. Such reactions highlighted the ways religious dissent imperiled social order and civil peace. Similarly, the larger context of relations with a politically turbulent England set the stage for civil authorities in each of the colonies to move aggressively to suppress religious dissent in their midst.

If the Keithians' objections fueled the fire of anti-Quaker propaganda in England and America, their critique would continue to roil Pennsylvania's political waters. Edward J. Cody's claim that the schism "emerges as an important factor in the development of separation of church and state" seems rather overstated, to say the least; more to the point, Jon Butler and J. William Frost have argued persuasively that the Keithian affair did "hel[p] to ensure religious diversity" due to the fact that Keithians who did not rejoin the main body of Pennsylvania Quakers went on to strengthen other denominations including the Anglicans and Baptists.[77] In 1756, of course, when Friends "withdrew" from the colony's government, they did so based on the Quaker peace testimony, though not without a nod to Keith or his role in advancing such a position during the colony's early years. (Butler has pointed out that the "withdrawal" was far less total than we might think, but it was a significant reorientation in the relationship between Friends and Pennsylvania politics.)[78]

Some years after his trial, in 1701, an anonymous critic took note of "one wonder more, added to the seven wonders of the world": George Keith, whom this critic ridiculed as "once a Presbyterian, afterwards about thirty years a Quaker . . . and now an itinerant preacher (upon his good behaviour) in the Church of England, and all without variation (as himself says) in fundamentals."[79] For George Keith's contentious relationship with American Quakerism had not ended with his ultimately unsuccessful 1694 journey to England in search of vindication from the Society of Friends. After his ejection from the society by the 1695 Yearly Meeting, Keith took holy orders in the Church of England and returned to America as an emissary of the Anglican Church's Society for Propagating the Gospel in Foreign Parts in 1702. It may not be quite correct to say that Keith had come full circle—what circle joins the Presbyterian, the Quaker, and the Anglican?—but he certainly had come a long way since his contentious days in Philadelphia just a decade earlier.

PART III

The Boundaries of Tolerance
and Intolerance in Early America

Chapter 7

Native Freedom?

Indians and Religious Tolerance in Early America

RICHARD W. POINTER

"You, above all the Inhabitants of the Earth, ought to be zealous in establishing the generous Principles of religious Freedom." Otherwise your actions "may possibly be attended with Consequences that are fatal." Without religious liberty, "the temporal Interests of the Colonies" will be "obstructed," the "out-lying Parts of the British Settlements" will be "doomed to live in Ignorance and Error," and the "native Indians" will either "continue in their present deplorable State of Idolatry, Cruelty and Vice; or . . . become your most dangerous Enemies, by the Adoption of the Principles of Popery."[1]

With the fiery zeal of his nineteenth-century namesake, John Brown, Anglican vicar of Newcastle, England, thus sounded out a clarion call on behalf of the "Principles of Christian Liberty" to Britain's American colonists in April 1763. Brown was keenly aware that the recently agreed upon peace ending the long Seven Years' War heralded a new political and religious day for British North America. He rightly surmised that the colonies' future well-being depended heavily on the fate of her westernmost settlements and their relations with neighboring Indians. Under those circumstances, he exclaimed, a "genuine spirit of Christian Liberty" would be essential for the advancement of true Christianity and political security within the colonies. But why? How could "Christian liberty" be the key to the colonies' political and religious flourishing?

Brown formulated his answer chiefly by targeting the main enemy to combat. No greater threat loomed against British North America than "the

Dangers that may and must arise" from the "Popish Settlements which lie contiguous to [them]." Lurking in the woods were Catholic missionaries and "Papist Indians." With military victory secured, the French Catholic territories were now in British hands. But much more than that was needed to ensure permanent Protestant success. In fact, disaster would strike, Brown insisted to the colonists, "unless a true Spirit of Christian Liberty and Zeal unite[d] and animate[d]" them to the "effectual Civilization and Conversion" of their Native neighbors. Here was the only sure antidote to the ills that could spoil the colonies' future: winning Indian souls. And it required that Protestants put aside their parochial disputes and work together to gain Natives' political and religious allegiance. Religious liberty ("Christian liberty"), understood by Brown to mean mutual Protestant respect and a willingness to cooperate in beneficial interdenominational endeavors, would reverse past Protestant intolerance toward other Protestants that had produced debilitating sectarian disputes and as a result, puny efforts to evangelize Natives. For while they had been persecuting one another during the prior two hundred years, zealous Spanish Catholics had "converted one half of the vast southern Continent, and murdered the other." Even more ominously, nearby French Catholics, thanks to the generous terms of the peace accord, would still be in a position to "reason . . . persuade . . . cajole . . . [and] terrify the poor Indian Nations: and by every Means of Truth and Falsehood, draw them over to their Party."[2]

Ironically, Brown attributed Catholics' missionary effectiveness to their religious intolerance, which, he explained, arose from a "consistent Principle and Belief, that there is no Salvation beyond the pale of their Communion." That conviction, which he said no Protestant claimed about their own religious traditions, had fueled aggressive, pervasive missionary efforts that netted "Papist Indians [who] have catched the persecuting and intolerant Spirit of Popery." Among Protestants, he insisted, neither their religious nor their political principles could allow them now to respond in kind with persecution, let alone violent extirpation, of their Catholic rivals. Nor would church establishments be the right instrument for competing because "on the continent of British America, the Matter [of church-state relations] hath been quite otherwise" from European practice. Legal religious establishments had worked well enough in the Old World but the diversity of the colonies' Protestant faiths had made them impractical in the New. The only recourse for colonial Protestants, then, was to overcome their past "uncharitable Disunion and Dislike" among one another and instead seek to match Catholic zeal in spreading their faith to America's indigenous peoples. And what better way to do that than to support two Anglican-inspired but interdenominational Protestant colleges in Philadelphia and New York whose future graduates could constitute the "able and zealous Labourers" needed for "counterworking the Designs of Popery, and [bringing about] the Civilization and Conversion of the savage Indians"?[3]

Only in that way did John Brown, on the last page of his prefatory address, fully announce the real purpose of his pamphlet and sermon: to raise money in England and the colonies for these educational projects. What notice London or Philadelphia readers took at the time of Brown's words is hard to say, but those words are worth a second look now for what they reveal about Anglo-American perspectives on the relationship between religious liberty and Native Americans. In many respects, Brown's views on religious freedom were in keeping with the latest transatlantic thought on that subject in the 1760s. As he assessed the colonies' situation, he saw the need for a more complete religious liberty for all Protestant groups rather than mere toleration since many of them had had a long presence in America and all of them were roughly "on an Equality with Respect to Property and Power." However dubious the latter claim now seems, Brown used it to support his vision of a level ecclesiastical playing field in America for Protestants, and his desire that Protestant interrelations would be more ecumenical and less sectarian. He wanted colonial Protestants to realize how much they had to gain by forming a united front based on "the great and essential Principles of Christianity." Not surprisingly, given the long history of Anglo-American antipopery that Owen Stanwood traces elsewhere in this volume, Catholics fell outside the bounds of that front literally and figuratively for Brown as he conceptualized America in 1763; at most, he would begrudge them the toleration in former French lands promised them in the terms of surrender. As for Indians, they were even more peripheral to his vision when it came to religious freedom. In a tract and sermon dedicated to the theme of religious liberty in the colonies, Natives entered the equation only as threats to Protestant freedom, victims of Catholic intolerance, or proper objects of Protestant evangelism. Brown held out the hope that Indians could someday be the beneficiaries of Christian liberty but only in the sense of their escaping idolatry or popish superstition through receiving the true gospel from ecumenical Protestants. Otherwise, the notion of religious liberty seemed neither applicable nor appropriate for North America's original inhabitants. It was an idea that John Brown and most other Anglo-Americans simply did not associate with Indians.[4]

Understanding how and why Indians, like African Americans as Jon Sensbach shows, stood outside most discussions of religious tolerance and freedom among British North Americans is one purpose of this chapter. Yet surveying the content of Anglo-American rhetoric and ideology will hardly tell the whole story of Indians and religious liberty in early America. So this chapter will also explore a different set of issues that open up when the lived experience of Native Americans is considered. For example, what happened in practice to Indian religious ways amid the myriad encounters between Indians and Europeans? How did claims of English authority affect Native religious expression and ritual? What aspects of Indian "heathenism" were singled out by the English for suppression? Where and when were Indian religions of whatever sort tolerated and why? How were Protestant Christian Indian communities treated by colonial political officials and laws? And how did Native peoples choose to function religiously within and outside the bounds of British imperial authority? Examining such concrete questions, even in preliminary ways, promises to round out our understanding of Anglo-American thought and its relationship to legal action and social practice. It may also give a richer picture of the religious worlds of Natives and newcomers, and deepen our grasp of the breadth and limits of religious tolerance in early America.

Heathens not Heretics

By the time John Brown delivered the sermon *On Religious Liberty* at St. Paul's Cathedral in London in 1763 that became the basis for his pamphlet, western and central European Catholics and Protestants had been wrestling for two centuries with the implications of their respective Reformations for the religious rights and privileges of all living within their communities. From their medieval Christian forebears, leading defenders of these faiths in the sixteenth century had inherited the conviction that religious intolerance and persecution were not to be viewed "as evils but as necessary and salutary for the preservation of religious truth and orthodoxy and all that was believed to depend on them." In particular, there was widespread agreement at that time that those deemed heretics could be and should be weeded out and punished lest they be allowed to undermine the fabric of church and society. By definition, heretics were Christians who had betrayed their faith and now threatened to subvert God's work in the world.[5]

The splintering of western Christianity in the sixteenth century into multiple groups complicated these matters considerably for church and state officials. Catholic authorities proved more willing than their Protestant counterparts to pursue and prosecute heretics, but Protestants also possessed the capacity for persecuting Catholics, as well as one another. Predictably, early modern European states were deeply troubled by the nonconformists who resolutely insisted that they too were Christians. Discussions of religious tolerance, whether driven by political prudence or abstract principle, therefore were understandably focused primarily on the questions of whether Catholics should tolerate Protestants, whether Protestants should tolerate Catholics, and whether conforming Protestants should tolerate nonconforming Protestants.[6] A related question did receive some attention, especially in the Iberian peninsula: how should Christian governments and the church treat members of non-Christian religions? Spain and Portugal's large Jewish and Muslim populations had forced Iberian Christian authorities to wrestle with that issue repeatedly in the late medieval era. And even after Jews and Muslims were expelled, hard questions persisted regarding the treatment of the remaining *Conversos* (Jewish converts to Catholic Christianity) and *Moriscos* (Muslim converts to Catholic Christianity). The advent of overseas expansion and the creation of Spanish and Portuguese empires in the Americas in the late fifteenth and sixteenth centuries only gave new urgency to these matters as Iberian subjects encountered whole continents of previously unknown non-Christian peoples. Well-known debates followed among theologians, missionaries, the papacy, military commanders, and state officials over how to perceive and act toward Indians. Where did they fit into God's scheme of salvation? Did Natives have rights that needed to be respected, including the right to remain adherents of their ancestral religions? Was it ever justifiable to use force to combat idolatry or to bring about evangelism?[7]

Here, in brief, was the legal and cultural context of religious tolerance and intolerance when the English began to plant colonies in the Americas. Virulent anti-Spanish sentiment among the English persuaded them that their imperial rivals had committed untold atrocities in their treatment of indigenous peoples, including a long legacy of forced and therefore false conversions. The English wanted no part of that and as a result, had no trouble agreeing with Spanish missionary Bartolomé de las Casas's critique of his own nation's abuse of New World Natives. But beyond that conviction, there was no clear sense among the English of how to proceed in relation to Indians, either in terms of evangelistic strategy or state policy regarding religious differences. Virtually all Englishmen agreed that Natives needed Christian salvation but that concern usually seemed a long way from the confessional issues that had divided English society for the past three generations. Accustomed to highly specific controversies over the fine points of ecclesiastical structures, liturgical customs, and general questions of Protestant conformity, new English arrivals and their descendants in the New World were not predisposed to worry in the same ways about Native heathens. Only occasionally did arguments over the proper bounds of Indians' liberty of conscience arise, as in the exchanges between John Cotton and Roger Williams in New England in the 1640s, when Williams asserted that all persons, Natives included, should be free to believe as they wished with no consequences from the "civil sword."[8] Otherwise, as they encountered Indian and African varieties of "paganism" during the seventeenth and eighteenth centuries, the range of problems presented by these alien religions and their adherents from the Anglo-American perspective seemed entirely novel. Epic struggles over the exacting details of Christian theology and ecclesiology carried over to British North America, as many of the other chapters in this volume ably demonstrate. There they dominated colonial thought and action regarding religious toleration and liberty. Meanwhile, their confrontations with Native Americans and Africans entangled colonists in what they usually took to be a different type of spiritual warfare, one that often seemed far removed from considerations of toleration, let alone freedom.

And yet, in a variety of ways, conventional matters of religious tolerance were indeed relevant to colonial-Indian relations. To begin to understand how and why that was the case, it makes sense to start by reviewing how English newcomers generally assessed Indian religious beliefs and practices. It is tempting to suggest that explorers, traders, soldiers, and settlers, not to mention missionaries, universally and categorically dismissed Indian religions as devilish, idolatrous, superstitious, or wicked. Plenty of them did and for them, contact with Native religious ways served primarily to give sharper definition to what theretofore had typically been rather inchoate notions of whom or what a heathen was.[9] When circumstances warranted, it also made it easier for them, as John Corrigan demonstrates, to embrace extreme views of Indians as Amalekites or other evildoers. Native Americans incarnated heathenism for British colonists and gave it a mind, body, and spirit. When Jonathan Edwards described Indian religion in the 1750s as "the grossest ignorance, delusions, and most stupid paganism," he echoed what most colonials had been thinking and saying about Native beliefs all along.[10] Still, such a sweeping generalization does not begin to capture the full scope of European or British colonial responses. For one thing, some Europeans, especially in the sixteenth century, first had to be persuaded that the Americas' peoples had any religion at all. Certainly the Indians did not seem to have the sorts of systematized beliefs Christians associated with their own faith or with Judaism and to a lesser degree, Islam. And few Euro-Americans ever caught on to the fact that within most Native American religions, practice was emphasized at least as much as conviction. Nevertheless, over time, as the number of newcomer contacts with Natives rose exponentially, most early British colonists conceded that Indians had spiritual ways of their own. Even then, however, Euro-American cultural blindness and Indians' preference for keeping sacred matters hidden left most settlers across colonial history remarkably ill-informed about Native faiths.[11]

Much of what they did know, or thought they knew, of Indian religions shocked, appalled, or bewildered them. But not everything. In particular, many Euro-Americans in the English colonies had occasion to become familiar at some level with Indian medical cures and healing practices. Some settlers borrowed freely from Native remedies, especially in times when their confidence in their own physicians or medical techniques had wavered. For Native Americans, all their efforts to heal physical ailments had an essential spiritual component. Colonial Protestant and Catholic leaders were quick to dismiss (and sometimes to contest) the spiritual power of Indian healers even when they acknowledged the value of Indian treatment, but not all European immigrants or their offspring accepted that conclusion. Some were willing not only to try Native cures or preventative health methods such as sweat baths, but did so in the Indian fashion, with the appropriate rites and rituals. Prominent among those who experimented in that manner were traders, many of whom spent extended periods of time deep within Indian-controlled territory and gained a familiarity with Native ways few other Euro-Americans shared. Euro-Americans taken captive by Native warriors similarly spent much time in Indian communities. Known popularly as "white Indians," these men, women, and children were "Indianized" to varying degrees. Changes in religious values and beliefs usually took longer than other forms of assimilation, so by no means did all captives experience them. But within those who did, some type of intellectual and experiential "zone of tolerance" toward Indian religion opened up, not unlike what may have occurred among the far more numerous colonists who dabbled with Native cures. Whether motivated by curiosity, cunning, desperation, or disgruntlement, those Euro-Americans found cause to reconsider blanket rejections of Native faiths and to make room for elements of them within their mental worlds and cultural experience.[12]

Similar types of religious and cultural borrowing went on between English colonists and Indians living "behind the frontier," that is, among Indians living within the confines of British-controlled territory. More will be said about those Natives below. For now it is important to note that even in Puritan-dominated New England in the seventeenth and eighteenth centuries, a "shadowy world" of popular or folk religion existed in which some settlers and Indians shared common spiritual concerns and exchanged religious ideas and practices. For that type of English colonist, occasional or regular contact with Native Americans exposed them to an array of other ways of connecting with the supernatural among which they could pick and choose. Whenever they were willing to incorporate and fuse in some manner elements of Indian spirituality with what they employed of European faiths, they displayed an intellectual and spiritual openness—what could be called a tolerance—for Native religions. Those Indian religions themselves were dynamic, diverse sets of beliefs and practices that often borrowed freely from other ways, including European traditions. Anything but static or fixed, they presented provincials with an evolving mix of religious possibilities.[13]

Other colonists within British North America developed an ideological tolerance for certain Indian religious beliefs and practices without actually adopting any aspects of them. The rhetorical ridicule and intellectual indifference toward Native beliefs and values demonstrated by most of their colonial peers seemed an inadequate response to what these whites had personally heard and seen as they interacted with Indians. From their perspective, Native Americans had arrived at plenty of truths, and they were repeatedly struck by how close Native convictions were to central Christian teachings. As a result, a small group of colonials offered an alternative assessment of Native religious ideas that served to confirm the colonials' own faith in the universality of Christian truth but at the same time granted some legitimacy to Indian spirituality and morality. Take, for example, the reflections of English trader John Long. His travels among the Indians of the upper Great Lakes revealed to him the Natives' special awareness of God's providential care. Long's own brushes with danger had made him realize that whites were too prone to credit their "own sagacity and foresight" for escape or deliverance. Meanwhile, Indians thought "more properly," saying that "it is the Master of Life from whom we derive that presence of mind which has extricated [us] or procured us relief." Moreover, Natives asked God for their "daily support," attributed to him their military victories, and even thanked him for the courage to endure torture with composure and defiance. For Long, watching and listening to the faith of the Chippewas served to remind him of familiar Christian truths, ones he sought to pass on to his Euro-American readers.[14]

Figures even closer to the center of colonial Christianity such as missionary David Brainerd sometimes developed a more empathetic view of Indian religion as a result of contacts with Natives. In his case, that was perhaps never truer than amid his remarkable encounter with an Indian reformer on one of his visits to the Pennsylvania interior. This shaman was one of a number of leaders in the 1740s who stressed the need for pan-Indian cooperation and a return to ancient Native ways. Brainerd rehearsed how upon meeting this man "none appeared so frightful or so near akin to what is usually imagined of infernal powers; none ever excited such images of terror in my mind." Dressed in animal skins and a wooden mask, and dancing about with a rattle, he "came near me [and] I could not but shrink away from him." Brainerd proceeded to see the reformer's sacred space, "a house consecrated to religious uses, with divers images cut out upon several parts of it." A less experienced Brainerd would likely have ended the encounter there, with quick denunciations of the Indian's devilish idolatry. But by this point in his career Brainerd was accustomed to conversing with Natives and so he entered into an extended dialogue with him about their respective spiritual journeys and beliefs. Not surprisingly, both men disagreed with elements of the other's faith. But Brainerd's account of the incident placed more stress on the discovery that there was also much common ground, both experientially and theologically. Each man had gone through a heart change, a conversion, several years earlier, and then felt God's call to proclaim the truth they had found to needy souls. Both were disheartened when Indians failed to heed their message, both were perceived as "precise zealot[s] that made a noise about religious matters." Brainerd reported those parallels without feeling the need to pronounce who or what was right. Whether that silence constitutes "a tentative and partial recognition of native systems of belief," as one recent scholar has suggested, is debatable. But it surely shows a level of respect and tolerance for certain Indian ways that a younger, less native-wise Brainerd would never have demonstrated. So, as he reflected back on this powerful meeting, Brainerd was prompted to conclude that "there was something in his temper and disposition that looked more like true religion than anything I ever observed amongst other heathens."[15]

The experiences of John Long and David Brainerd, alongside those of other colonials who found themselves in positions to conclude that Native religions were worth a second look and might have something of value for them, should temper the impulse to imagine that Euro-Americans in all times and places in British North America uniformly held the same low opinion of Indian beliefs and observances. Certainly Long and Brainerd continued to believe that Indians needed Christian salvation but their experiences show that personal attitudes could change or be reshaped amid closer encounters with Natives. And they demonstrate that sometimes those changes moved in the direction of affording Indians' alien ways at least a modicum of respect and occasionally much more, even (for some) to the point of concluding that Indians were "well as they are" when it came to religion. How strong that countercultural strain was within British colonial America is difficult to gauge, but the evidence is growing that it was a good deal more substantial than previously thought.[16]

Nevertheless, there is still no doubt that the dominant cultural outlook on Indian religion (and more broadly, on Indian culture) within Anglo-America was highly negative. Whether labeled "Satanic witchcraft" or something nearly as derisive, it held little if any value in the average colonial's mind. As such, not surprisingly, it almost never got any consideration when British colonists or their political leaders discussed publicly the merits, or lack thereof, of broadening the religious rights of one or another colonial constituency. Neither the statutory nor the cultural revolutions regarding toleration and pluralism in early America that Chris Beneke has documented can be said to have extended to Native Americans; or, to be more precise, Native American adherents of traditional Native American religions. Again, as indicated above, colonials associated religious toleration, tolerance, and liberty overwhelmingly with the Protestant-Protestant and Protestant-Catholic divides. When some late eighteenth-century Americans moved beyond those bounds to consider others in relation to religious freedom, they still limited their discussion to Jews, deists, Universalists, and atheists. Indians as a group were heathens, and heathenism was not worthy of legal protection or intellectual respect.[17]

In fact, the problem of Native American "heathenism" seems to have declined in significance for colonials in the eighteenth century not so much because Natives were becoming Protestants (hopes for missionary success sometimes waxed but more often waned through the century) but because so many Natives had died. Widespread Indian de-population portended in some colonial minds the "disappearance" of Indians altogether. Under those circumstances, one hardly had to worry about potential threats posed by the Natives' pagan faiths, though many colonists saw fit to either maintain or actually intensify their denunciations of Indians as the century wore on. Growing racial prejudice and the belief that Native religions would go "the way of the flesh" along with their Indian adherents reinforced one another in plenty of Anglo-American minds. And if some Indians did manage to survive, they thought it would only be because Indians had chosen to give up their traditional ways and adopt Euro-American "civilization," including Christianity. In that scenario, Indian religions would once again die out. Either way, then, Indian heathenism was not long for this world.[18]

If such arguments sounded most often from those provincials anxious for the demise of all things Indian, more astute or sympathetic colonial observers of Native cultures had their own reasons for believing that by the mid-eighteenth century, Indian heathenism represented much less of a force to be reckoned with than it had for the first few generations of European newcomers. As they met with Indians to negotiate land deals, broker political settlements, and exchange trade goods, or encountered Indian religious reformers, they became more aware at roughly the same time as their own transatlantic Great Awakening was occurring that Native communities were experiencing their own "crises of faith" in the face of the pressures created by the ever-expanding European presence and the contest for empire in early America. Native confidence in the power and efficacy of their traditional religions had been tested ever since the Europeans' arrival, and had certainly been shaken by decades of disease, war, displacement, Christian evangelism, and death. As Indian communities devised strategies for maintaining themselves, internal divisions and disputes over religion were not uncommon. Attentive colonials could sense that Indian power, and by extension, Indian traditional religions, no longer presented as formidable a threat.[19]

The same could not be said of so-called "Papist Indians." They represented as grave a threat to British colonial fortunes in the years leading into the American Revolution as they had for most of the prior century. At least that is what many provincials in Britain's northern colonies believed. Overall, they had had a longer and bloodier history with Catholic Indians than their southern counterparts in the Chesapeake or Lower South. Anti-Catholicism may have played a role in provoking English attacks on Spanish mission villages in Florida in 1704 as part of Queen Anne's War. It surely played a role in fomenting the longstanding and bitter rivalry between New England and its eastern neighbors in Maine and beyond, the Wabanaki and their French Jesuit allies. In the wake of the terrifying raid on Deerfield, Massachusetts, in 1704, Cotton Mather railed against the evil force the duo had created: "The *French Papists* have made them [the Wabanakis], rather *twice more the Children of Hell*, (more averse to true *Christianity*,) than while they were meer *Pagans*." Subsequent captivity narratives reinforced the point, especially when some captives proved unredeemable: Catholic Indians, thanks to French evil designs, were a doubly dangerous foe capable of inflicting catastrophic losses upon Protestant communities. Dutch Reformed pastor Theodore Frelinghuysen (son of the famous revivalist) echoed those sentiments a few decades later to the representatives at the Albany Congress in 1754. After painting a grim picture of a possible French Catholic victory in North America, he proposed that both British Protestant colonists and their Native American neighbors would lament such an outcome. "Will not the very Savages, the Natives, the Aborigines of this Land, reproach us," Frelinghuysen warned, if the British failed to do their political, military, and religious duties in warding off French and Indian Catholic enemies. He could hear future Indians saying, "You [British] are gone, and we are Slaves! We are worse than Negroes, for their Masters take Care of them. . . . We are worse off than the very Brutes, than the wild Beasts, who, without a Soul, run in the Woods."[20]

Frelinghuysen's portrait of Indians as both allies of the French and victims of their rule could evoke both disdain and sympathy for Natives. Neither sentiment though was going to incline British colonists to think about Catholic Indians when they talked about religious tolerance. There may have been smatterings of Catholic Indians living within the confines of British mainland colonies in the eighteenth century but they had little impact on the dominant image that had long held sway of who and what such people were like in Anglo-American Protestant minds: Catholicized Natives, and especially those under the sway of zealous Jesuits, were an unfortunate but nevertheless diabolical lot who the British needed to save or be saved from.

Within British North American colonial perspectives, then, Indians and their religions were rarely on the intellectual map when it came to formal grants of religious toleration or liberty. More often conceived of as heathens than heretics, Natives usually did not fit into the categories of religionists who were gradually being redefined by one another as acceptable or at least tolerable citizens with religious rights in the early modern Anglo-American world. While Euro-American attitudes toward traditional Native beliefs and rituals were not as monolithically negative as has sometimes been portrayed, prevailing sentiments about what a Protestant Christian government and society should condone nevertheless dictated against any consideration of extending legal status or legitimacy to Indian ancestral faiths. And Catholic Indians surely did not fit the bill either. As the colonial era progressed, some observers such as Englishman John Brown remained persuaded that Indian heathenism, or worse yet, Catholicized Natives, represented a major threat to Anglo-America. Others were less worried, convinced that providence or fate or demographics were inexorably bringing Indians and their ways to an end. Whether persistent threat or dying breed, though, Native Americans and the beliefs that sustained them were typically outside the circle of what colonials contemplated when they debated the bounds of religious freedom.

Beyond the Pale and Behind the Frontier

Of course, rhetoric is one thing, practice is another. English colonists may have only rarely considered Indians (at least the non-Protestant ones) appropriate subjects for religious toleration but that in itself does not reveal everything, or even very much, about the actual experience of Native Americans. Within the fluid political and religious environments of early America, how much freedom did Indians have to worship as they pleased? How far did the English go in law and practice in trying to supervise or control Native religious expression? And where did the de facto boundaries of religious tolerance lie for Indians living within the broad expanse of British North America?

Answers to those questions had much to do with where Indian communities stood in relation to English authority. Or to put it another way, religious toleration in any legal or political sense could only be extended or denied by the English where English authority actually held sway. For much of colonial history, whatever spoken or written claims Englishmen made to the lands and peoples of North America, the practical reality was very often something different. Tiny, scattered English settlements gradually expanded over the course of the seventeenth and eighteenth centuries, and as they did, English assertions to holding real power took on more credence. But even by the time of the American Revolution, large chunks of the interior of Anglo-

America remained in Indian hands and under Native cultural dominance. Throughout early American history, within that Indian country, how much influence, let alone control, British colonial law or religious preference exercised varied from one community to the next. Whatever the case in those places, Natives there faced different circumstances from Indians living within territory under more direct colonial rule.

Provincials at the time and historians later on have noted those differences and attached various labels to Indians to capture the essence of their setting. "Neighbour-Indians," "remoter Indians," "settlement Indians," "wandering Indians," "friend Indians," and "praying Indians" are just some of the names used to portray where Natives found themselves literally and figuratively in relation to English authority. For present purposes, legal historian Yasuhide Kawashima's threefold categorization of Indians in Massachusetts as "independent tribes," "plantation Indians," and "individual Indians" provides a useful rubric for comparing the experiences of Natives within and outside of Indian country in relation to Euro-American religious authority.[21]

"Tribal Indians" were those Indian communities who retained much of their political autonomy and who remained comparatively "foreign Indians" in the minds of English colonials. How "foreign" they were depended largely on how much contact they had with settlers, traders, or agents of English rule. Because the border or frontier between Anglo-America and Indian country was constantly moving and not just in one direction (sometimes the English lost territory to Indians previously gained from them as was the case in King Philip's War), it is difficult to generalize about what Indian peoples belonged in this category at any one time. In broad terms, however, tribes situated to the west of English colonial settlements (typically in piedmont regions or beyond the mountains) fit the bill for longer portions of early American history than other Native groups. Within this Indian country, Native Americans were ostensibly free from English interference to practice their religions as they chose, though some had to deal with religious intrusions from other Europeans. British colonial legislation extending or limiting religious rights was irrelevant to them. Treaties held and agreements reached with English colonial diplomats rarely if ever touched directly on religious matters. And few Protestant missionaries ventured into their territory and when they did, they didn't stay very long, thanks to typically hostile receptions from local Indians.[22] Yet it would be a mistake to imagine that Indian religions, even among these "remoter" peoples, remained fully immune from the reach of English colonialism. As indicated earlier, the political, economic, cultural, and biological effects of the coming of the Europeans rippled across Indian villages near and far, presenting them and their traditional religions with unprecedented challenges. From Maine to Georgia, Natives on both sides of the frontier reaffirmed, re-crafted, or rejected their faiths alongside other core elements of their cultures and lifestyles to cope with the arresting changes brought by the European presence. By the mid-eighteenth century, those pressures gave rise to nothing less than an Indian Great Awakening in which religious reformers such as the Delaware Neolin typically called their people back to their ancient ways while also incorporating elements of Christian teaching. In practice, then, even where Anglo-Americans made very few direct attempts to interfere with Native American religious beliefs and observances, and lacked the authority to grant or deny religious liberty to indigenous groups, they still could provoke spiritual crises and contests over sacred power.[23]

"Plantation Indians" and "individual Indians" were those Natives "caught behind the westward-moving line of Anglo-American dominance." What distinguishes the two groups is with whom they lived; plantation Indians continued to live in Native enclaves whereas individual Indians lived in English towns. Plantation Natives' behind-the-frontier Indian villages spotted the maps of Britain's colonial holdings up and down the Atlantic seacoast.[24] Some of those enclaves predated the European presence; others arose in response to it as Indian refugees clustered together in search of mutual security. Whichever the case, the demands and pressures surrounding whites placed upon them made life for such Indian communities unsettling. Subject to colonial political authority and land hunger, they were often forced to move (in many cases more than once) to accommodate the whims and wishes of traders and settlers. Economically, they had to constantly adjust to the dictates of Euro-American markets. Culturally, they faced perpetual questions about how much of their traditional ways they should give up to survive in an English-dominated world. Amid this tumult, plantation and individual Indians contended with neighboring whites and provincial officials who generally resented their presence, disdained their cultures, and remained indifferent to their survival.

What of their religion? How did it fare while living in Anglo-America? Was there room for plantation Indians to worship as they pleased? Examples from the Lower South and New England provide some clues. Identifiable groups of plantation Indians or those called "Settlement Indians" by neighboring whites existed in the Carolinas by the first two decades of the eighteenth century. In the wake of military conflicts with enemy Indians and the British, as well as the devastating effects of disease, some Saponis, Pedees, and members of other Native tribes clustered near colonial settlements at Fort Christiana and Charleston.[25] By that point, the English in the Carolinas had had two generations to sort out their ideas and policies on religious freedom. The seventeenth-century founders of Carolina had hoped to attract an adequate supply of settlers by offering a modicum of religious liberty. Though never fully implemented, the Fundamental Constitutions issued by the Lords Proprietors and intended to be a kind of political blueprint for the colony contained liberal language about religious freedom that reflected the input of political theorist John Locke. Locke insisted that "neither pagan nor Mohometan nor Jew ought to be excluded from the civil rights of the commonwealth because of his religion." This framework was theoretically broad enough to include non-Christian Indians, and in fact, article 97 of the 1670 version of the Fundamental Constitutions stated that the Natives of Carolina were "utterly Strangers to Christianity" but their "Idolatry, Ignorance, or Mistake" gave the English "no right to expel them or use them ill." Moreover, in order for "heathens, Jews, and other dissenters from the purity of Christian Religion" to feel comfortable in the new colony, "any seven or more Persons agreeing in any Religion shall Constitute a Church or Profession." The Fundamental Constitutions thereby gave protections to Indian religious rights that few if any other colonial political frameworks offered in early America. Yet no matter how broad these terms of religious toleration are judged to have been (and they were tempered by other more restrictive laws), there are few signs that these provisions made much impression on the English colonists who settled in the colony, or that they shaped the practical realities of Indian lives there. As elsewhere, Anglo-American newcomers in Carolina conceived of religious toleration almost exclusively in relation to fellow Europeans. Some later statutes did address issues concerning religious toleration for African slaves, but no comparable legislative or conceptual attention appears to have been paid to Indians.[26]

For the Carolinas' plantation Indians in the early eighteenth century, then, the bounds of their religious freedom ended up having little to do with matters of written law or rhetoric and almost everything to do with their new, lived reality resulting from their near proximity to whites. Their choice to move closer to British settlements was a survival strategy but it came at a price: regular colonial interference with their everyday lives. Some white intrusions were comparatively benign, others such as sexual attacks on Native women much less so. Within the religious realm, this interference mostly took the form of periodic encounters with white Christian evangelists either in passing or in their villages. Usually they were confronted by Anglican missionaries of the Society for the Propagation of the Gospel sent to minister primarily to white settlers, and Africans and Indians as opportunity afforded. Letters home to the mission society in the 1710s and 1720s testify to the episodic rather than sustained efforts made by them to introduce nearby Natives to Christian doctrine and practice. Ministerial tactics included peppering the Indians with questions about their customs and cosmology, observing Native ceremonies whether invited or not, and investigating Indian burial places. Neither their words nor their actions communicated much respect for Native ways. No wonder these plantation Indians proved to be such hard ground in which to plant Christian seeds. They remained instead, in the words of one disgruntled pastor, "wholy addicted to their own barbarous and Sloathful Customs."[27]

Thus, in the case of Carolina's plantation Indians, religious pressure from whites constituted more of an occasional annoyance than a sustained attack. With no resident missionaries among them, Natives rather routinely warded off Christian advances or borrowed selectively from the new ideas presented to them. Either way, in matters of religion, they retained considerable discretion in a world that otherwise severely constrained their options. Such "freedom of worship" for Natives to remain "heathen" was hardly desirable in the eyes of some colonists (despite what the Fundamental Constitutions had originally affirmed) but neither church nor state in the Carolinas was prepared to do much about it.

Something similar seems to have prevailed in many other colonies, especially outside of New England. A kind of practical neglect or indifference toward plantation Indians' religious ways typified the responses of most provincials and their governments most of the time. And even when legislatures did act, they were not especially restrictive. In Virginia, for example, several laws were passed between 1619 and 1715 aimed at promoting strategies for Christianizing neighboring Indians but none of them placed explicit limits on Native beliefs or practices. In an even rarer move, New York in 1695 explicitly excluded "any Native or free Indian within this province not professing the Christian Religion" from having to abide by a new Sabbath-protection law.[28] That was hardly the approach of church and state in Massachusetts. Colony leaders there insisted from the very beginning that the charter granted to the Massachusetts Bay Company "gave them supreme authority over all the people—Indian and English—within their jurisdiction." Massachusetts authorities intended for Indians to understand that they were now "subjects unto the same king." Area Native peoples responded variously, some submitting, others violently resisting, still others looking for alternative seats of power among other Europeans and Indians to use as a counterbalance to Bay colony claims. Half a dozen Massachusett Indian sachems formally submitted to the colonial government in 1644, most likely in hopes of gaining protection against neighboring hostile Narragansett Indians. That action led the colony's General Court to launch a series of missionary initiatives that inspired the labors of John Eliot and the creation of fourteen "praying towns" over the next generation.[29] It also passed statutes in 1646 against blasphemy and idolatry aimed at "such pagan Indians as have submitted themselves to our government." Averring any intent to "compel them [the Indians] . . . to the Christian faith, either by force of arms or by penal laws," the legislature nevertheless established death as the appropriate sentence for blasphemers, white or Native, and fines up to ten pounds for Indians who would "powwow or perform outward worship to their false gods or to the devil."[30] Some historians have made much of these laws, suggesting that they coerced Massachusett men and women into a religious conformity with Puritan ways. But a more recent assessment argues that the laws had more bark than bite. Richard Cogley points out that the colony's records indicate that it "never indicted, much less convicted and executed, any native for blasphemy or fined a pagan Indian for idolatry." The purpose of the statutes, in his view, had less to do with coercing Indian obedience and more to do with placating God, who according to minister John Cotton, might judge the colony harshly if it explicitly tolerated pagan worship.[31]

Even so, the laws no doubt gave Indians pause for thought, as did the local legal codes drawn up by Eliot and other colleagues at the request of the General Court to regulate Native behavior in the praying towns. Used alongside other means to effect change in Indian ways such as economic incentives, diplomatic pressure, and theological suasion, those codes constitute perhaps the most direct statutory effort in seventeenth-and eighteenth-century British colonial America to place limits on Indian religious practice. Intent on both civilizing and Christianizing Indians gathered in the praying towns, the English confronted the question: What aspects of Native culture do we suppress or alter? More to the point, what religious practices need to be eradicated? Naturally, the English answered the latter question on the basis of what characteristics of Massachusett life and culture struck them as "religious" in character. They thus prohibited what they understood as conspicuous religious indiscretions such as powwowing and Sabbath-breaking.[32] In addition, because of the close fusion of things English and things Christian in the missionaries' minds and their conviction that Natives needed to adopt both, their codes also included statutes concerning the work routines, sexual relations, and personal appearance of Christian Indians and not-yet-Christian Indians. Some of those laws touched on other essential components of Massachusett spirituality without the English fully realizing it. For example, provisions aimed at ending Indian women's separation from the community during menstruation and others seeking to alter Native mourning rituals interfered with deeply sacred acts charged with spiritual power. In doing so, the praying town codes officially curtailed traditional Massachusett and neighboring Indian peoples' religions more fully than the English were even aware.[33]

Yet such legal proscriptions are only one side of what happened to Indian faiths in the Bay colony. They make clear that the English expected these plantation Indians to give up their heathen religions (and much of the rest of their aboriginal cultures) now that they lived within the bounds of Christian, civilized society. But how far the English were willing to go or how hard they were willing to work to make that happen is unclear. The lack of written records from these communities detailing enforcement makes it difficult to judge how constrained Natives felt or acted in their religious expression. Local political authority within the praying towns was left largely in Native hands. They may have had enough autonomy to let the members of their communities sort out their religious preferences amid the changes brought by colonialism in their own Native ways apart from the legal structures and codes introduced by the English. Powwowing, for example, certainly continued in the newer praying towns among the inland Nipmuck Indians in the mid-seventeenth century and may very well have done the same in the older praying towns closer to the coast. But it is also true that it now had to be done in a much more covert way and as such, likely lost much of its social clout within the community as a whole. Perhaps it is safest to say that within the praying towns' first generation (1640s–1670s), Indians, like their English counterparts in white settlements, operated within a highly prescriptive English legal, cultural, and religious framework but nevertheless retained enough freedom to diverge considerably among themselves in their levels of Christian devotion and practice, and in the extent to which they held onto elements of more ancestral religions.[34]

Similar patterns characterized the experience of plantation Indians in Massachusetts for the next hundred years, stretching from King Philip's War in 1675–1676 to the American Revolution. The former conflict and its aftermath brought many new restrictions upon praying town Indians amid growing animosity toward Indians of all types, Protestants included. Nevertheless, recent studies of Native communities suggest that some plantation Indians managed to adapt and persist, in part by making Christianity their own, much as black slaves were able to do. Though their populations were dwindling and the challenges posed by white land encroachment and economic marginality were mounting, they creatively managed to indigenize Christian faith so that it became a key element for them in the construction of new identities and communal networks as well as the retention of vital aboriginal ways.[35] Take, for example, the group of Mohicans living just across the Massachusetts border in Shekomeko, New York. Events surrounding the life of one of their community leaders, Shabash, epitomized their woes in the 1720s and 1730s. Besides losing multiple family members to epidemic disease, Shabash was repeatedly frustrated in his attempts to gain just payment for sales of his family's once substantial lands. Amid his distress, Shabash took to drink. During one drunken stupor in 1738, he had a powerful vision which included an image of intoxicated, naked Indians lying helpless as a wave of water was about to swallow them. Shabash awoke sobered by this horrific picture (perhaps a portrait of the effects of colonialism) and ready to look for new spiritual resources for himself and his people. Within a couple of years, he and other Mohicans began to find that power in Moravian Christianity and before long, they had made that faith their own, "both thoroughly Christian and thoroughly Mohican." For a few short years, Shabash (now Abraham) was able to oversee a revitalized community in Shekomeko thanks to the renewed energy and meaning infused by Moravian belief and practice. Before long, however, the dual forces of continued population loss and white political opposition forced almost all of its surviving members into exile in Pennsylvania where whole new challenges would face Native and white Moravians in the decades ahead.[36]

Even when Natives embraced Christianity, English suspicions remained. As had been true among past generations of Euro-American Christians going back to the Spanish in the early sixteenth century, white Christian leaders in Massachusetts and elsewhere in the late seventeenth and eighteenth centuries worried over what they feared were pagan remnants in the faith and practice of their fellow Indian believers. And so, predictably, they made occasional, generally unsuccessful, efforts to get Native Christians to weed them out. While noteworthy, those efforts took place within a larger pattern of allowing Protestant Indian churches across southern New England some freedom to find their own way in the 1700s. Though rarely afforded anything approaching full religious equality or an eager right hand of fellowship from the English, Native Protestants in some places and at some times were nonetheless able to carry on their worship services and other congregational activities as they saw fit, often under the leadership of an Indian pastor. Perhaps as a consequence, over time, a majority of plantation Indians in New England embraced some form of Protestantism. If that moved them closer to their white neighbors religiously and as a result, made them less susceptible to religious intolerance, it also subjected them to a rising tide of Anglo-American racism. That racism came to color all aspects of white-Indian relations. Now Natives had to contend with something worse than accusations of heathenism: repeated reminders from their Anglo neighbors that they were inferior beings with no hope of remedy.[37]

No groups of Indians confronted white racism more directly or regularly than the "individual Indians" who lived and worked in English towns. Typically no longer connected closely to an identifiable Indian enclave, their numbers were increasing in the eighteenth century as more Natives sought to survive economically by taking up jobs and living in English communities. Virtually all who made that choice came to occupy positions near the bottom of colonial society. Many became indentured servants within white households, a measure of Indian land loss and indebtedness. As servants, separated from Indian families and communities, they faced especially strong pressures to conform with all things English. Ancestral customs and languages were routinely ridiculed by whites and often, as a result, neglected by Natives. Indian dress, food, speech, and manners took on Anglo accents.[38]

What all of this meant for individual Indians' religious lives is difficult to discern. Most of these Indians were long hidden from historical view and are only now receiving scholarly attention. Since many of these folk in New England came from families that had been Christian for one or more generations, some maintained a link to a local Indian church; others migrated from their Indian congregations into English ones and there tried to make the adjustment to Anglo-American expressions of the faith. Nathan Hood and his extended family in Plymouth County, Massachusetts, nicely illustrate the challenges that accompanied some of those choices. In the late seventeenth and early eighteenth centuries, Hood's clan constituted an important set of interconnected Wampanoag Christian families at Manomet Ponds, an isolated Indian enclave outside of Plymouth Center. Hood's immediate family enjoyed relative prosperity as land-owning yeoman farmers. But then calamity struck them in the form of disease, medical debts, and shrinking landholdings. By 1722, Nathan had sold all his land and moved his family to "Plain Dealing," the farm of Josiah Cotton, a local judge and longtime lay missionary to the Indians of Plymouth County. Hood and Cotton became close associates over the next eighteen years. Throughout that time, Cotton preached from Hood's wigwam during the biweekly worship services among Plain Dealing's small number of Indian Christians. In return, Hood and his offspring received a place to live as tenants, steady employment, and occasional charity from Cotton and the New England Company that sponsored his mission work. Through such arrangements, Hood gained for his family a measure of economic stability, community solidarity, and perhaps spiritual sustenance. But he also gave up the economic autonomy and the greater degree of Native control over congregational life they had earlier enjoyed in Manomet Ponds. Meanwhile, Hood's kin in his former hometown struggled for much of the eighteenth century to hold onto control of their own church in the face of growing English settlement. By the 1730s, whites were numerous enough in the area to propose forming an integrated congregation with Natives that would meet in the Indian church building but be staffed by an English minister. Manomet Ponds' Indian Christians balked at that prospect and against the odds, managed to have Indian preachers serve their separate Native congregation into the 1760s.[39]

For those individual Indians who did become part of white churches, their treatment no doubt varied from one congregation to the next; but their low social status and Indian racial character presented considerable obstacles to equal treatment. In their favor, New England's growing freedom for a variety of Protestant denominations, and the greater number of them as a result of the Great Awakening, offered eighteenth-century Natives more choices of worship.[40] Evidence from the colony of New York, where Protestant pluralism had been of much longer standing than in New England, indicates that Natives took advantage of that type of opportunity when it was available. At the same time it must be noted that wherever Indians were bound to white families (and those who were, were typically younger), they could be subject to the religious preferences and demands of their owners. Yet even that constraint looked very different from one household to the next. For some, it meant regular exposure to the family's piety in the form of having to hear family prayers, attend their church, or even be catechized. For others, it apparently meant being largely left alone. Anglican minister James Wetmore in the 1720s complained that among the five-hundred-plus Indians attached to English households as servants and slaves in Suffolk County on Long Island, no efforts were being taken to win them over to Christianity. Even if Wetmore's report is partially dismissed as an effort to gain for him a new missionary post, it suggests at minimum a certain level of apathy on the part of English masters and mistresses about what their Indians believed and maybe even practiced.[41] Perhaps most surprisingly, living with or aside English families could sometimes mean being asked to share your knowledge of non-Christian Indian religion. Recent analysis of Wampanoags in southeastern Massachusetts reveals that many of them living within English towns embraced and practiced an eclectic, hybrid supernaturalism that drew upon a number of religious traditions, some Christian, some not. They were joined as "eclectic spiritual cobblers" by surprising numbers of their white neighbors who similarly adopted diverse spiritual resources to cope with the vicissitudes of this life and the uncertainties of the next. Much borrowing and exchanging went on from Indians to whites and back again as early American peoples of all races searched for a satisfying faith.[42] SPG missionary Isaac Browne indicated as much when he described the religion of the Indians in his Long Island parish in 1743 as a "Miraculous compound of Paganism and Methodism."[43]

Individual Indians thus faced varying and potentially dizzying blends of white racism, Christian evangelism, religious neglect, and spiritual reciprocity in English towns. There, like plantation Indians, they were sometimes subject to laws that aimed to eliminate overt opposition to Christian beliefs and morality.[44] But even in the absence of such laws, they felt daily pressure to Anglicize their lives. Yet despite the force that English political and cultural authority could exert, both types of behind-the-frontier Natives remained in command of their own religious ships. They exercised a liberty of conscience that navigated their choices of religious rites and beliefs to many points along a wide theological and spiritual spectrum. Anglo-American public culture was not prepared to condone, let alone endorse, heterodox or pagan elements of those personal faiths. But within that Anglo-American world's religious culture, there also existed more private spaces for whites and even for Native Americans to work out the shapes and contours of their religions according to the dictates of their own hearts, minds, and souls.

Tolerance and Intolerance

Twenty years or so after John Brown's pamphlet on religious liberty appeared a Massachusetts woman, Hannah Adams, published her own testament of sorts to religious freedom. Adams set out to provide an unbiased encyclopedic listing of all of the world's religions from the time of Christ forward as well as a description of the current state of religion on each continent. Appendix four was dedicated to the "Religions of America" and dutifully treated the new United States state by state before turning to British America (she had sections on Nova Scotia and Canada) and Spanish America. Readers would have been hard-pressed not to be impressed with the multiplicity of sects, admittedly mostly Christian, that coexisted, sometimes even on equal terms, within the new republic. America's thriving religious diversity, many likely concluded, was surely a sign of the ever-greater religious freedom being offered its peoples.

Would Indians be included in that freedom? Neither Adams nor very many in her audience likely posed that question and if they did, spent much time pondering it. But Adams did choose to include Indians and their non-Christian religions in her discussions of the United States and other parts of North America. And she presented their beliefs and practices in an even-handed manner alongside descriptions of the Euro-American religious bodies of those regions. No ethnographer, Adams relied on earlier published sources for her knowledge of Native faiths and in the process, passed along the accuracies and inaccuracies they contained. Yet in placing Indians' religions on a kind of equal plane with other faith traditions in her analysis, Adams imparted to the former an intellectual respect and respectability worthy of the label "tolerance." Her book's epigram from 1 Thessalonians 5:21, "Prove all things, hold fast that which is good," made clear that the Bible in her mind was the proper testing ground for religious truth. Adams was no proponent of religious relativism. But her inclusion of Natives' non-Christian cosmologies and her expressed desire to present them fairly displayed a tolerant spirit marked by respect for beliefs other than her own, an implied willingness to coexist with holders of other faiths, and an implicit endorsement of the right of others to believe as they wished.[45]

How many of her contemporaries or predecessors in early America shared that spirit is hard to say. Animosity toward Indians was, if anything, on the rise in the 1780s, leaving the average white American less, not more, inclined to tolerate Indians, their religions (of whatever sort), or anything else about them. In the decades that followed, Native Americans in the early Republic would, like their Euro-American counterparts, explore many different spiritual paths, initiating a host of new religious movements aimed at revitalizing their communities. Indian prophets such as Handsome Lake and Tenskwatawa stood alongside the likes of Joseph Smith and William Miller in an American religious milieu that at once afforded greater toleration but also witnessed escalating religious violence. In fact, a significant number of whites seemed to wish to be done with Natives altogether. This darker strain of Euro-American prejudice was hardly new. It had surfaced over and over again in British North America, particularly in times of military crisis when a spirit of intense suspicion and hatred toward Indians possessed many colonial minds. In those moments, religious intolerance toward Native Americans was usually subsumed by a deeper, darker racial prejudice that paid little heed to what god Indians prayed to. Thus, the colonial record includes the foul treatment of praying Indians in King Philip's War and the massacre of Moravian Indians at Gnadenhütten in the War of Independence. Still, religion justified (and may have also motivated) violence against Natives and it fostered a conviction that all Indians, regardless of what they claimed, were heathens needing to be purged of their paganism if not their lives.[46]

Combating Indians and their religions occupied Anglo-American energies intermittently throughout the colonial era. Sometimes that meant outright war, as with the Pequots in Connecticut in the 1630s. More often it meant using other forms of power to chip away at the edifice of Native heathenism. Anglo-American tools included everything from moral suasion and theological argument to legal statutes, economic incentives, and diplomatic agreements. Such tactics and the enflamed rhetoric that often accompanied them can leave the impression that colonials were united in their commitment and systematic in their actions to extirpate all vestiges of Indians' non-Christian faiths. But neither was the case. As a group, British colonists were not intellectually prepared to consider non-Christian Native peoples appropriate subjects for legally sanctioned religious toleration, and by and large, that was as true in the 1770s as it had been a century or two earlier. But neither were they of one mind when it came to assessing the value or validity of Indian religious ways. The English colonial "front" against Native religion was never so total or so powerful as to preclude wondering and borrowing on the part of some colonists. Those latter impulses mitigated the will to wipe out all remnants of such religion within the bounds of English authority, an authority which itself had limits, not only in Indian country but amid the quotidian realities of plantation Indian villages and English towns. Moreover, throughout colonial history, it was neither diplomatically wise nor ecclesiastically possible, given the limited human and material resources of colonial churches, to carry out any type of comprehensive assault on Indian religions. Thus, although constrained by the forces of colonialism, most Indians in the seventeenth and eighteenth centuries retained enough freedom to chart their own course when it came to keeping the faith—whichever one they embraced.

Chapter 8

Slaves to Intolerance

African American Christianity and Religious Freedom in Early America

Jon Sensbach

In summer 1774, as the American revolutionary movement intensified, the sun scalded the Virginia countryside. The ground withered and the corn was "roll'd up with the heat & Drouth." On a hot Sunday morning at the end of July, the man who wrote those words, Philip Vickers Fithian, a tutor on the plantation of Robert Carter in northern Virginia, emerged from his house. He saw one of Carter's 600 slaves, Thomas, more commonly known as Daddy Gumby, who was reputed to be ninety-four years old. A few days earlier, Fithian had helped Daddy Gumby draw up a list of his children and their ages, and as thanks the nonagenarian had offered him eggs and produce from his garden. This morning, as the tutor sleepily stepped outside in his dressing gown, Daddy Gumby approached him, saying:

> "Well Master you never call for no Eggs. I can now give you a *Water Melon*."
>
> "No, Thomas, with your Wife & family enjoy these things. I am well provided for."
>
> "Well, Master, I promised you Eggs, for writing you will think I never designed to pay you—God yonder in Heaven Master will burn *Lyars* with *Fire and Brimstone!*—I speak Truth I will not deceive you. Men are wicked, Master; look see the Grass is burnt: God burns it to punish us!"

"Is the ground dry, Dadda?
"O! All dry, all burnt—Pray, Pray, Master, do you go to Church?"
"No Dadda it is too hot."
"Too hot, Good God, too hot! I shall affront you, Master—Too hot to serve the Lord! Why I that am so old & worn out go on Foot."

Fithian, who was also a minister-in-training at the College of New Jersey, had been unmasked as a lazy cleric. As the nineteenth-century African American spiritual would later have it, he had been "'buked and scorned," and he had no answer. Confessing himself a "little non plus'd," he slunk away and skipped church.[1]

With startling candor, Daddy Gumby had taken the unwitting tutor directly to the heart of black culture in America. On the eve of the American Revolution, an increasing number of enslaved people called themselves Christian, and their religion, forged in the great evangelical revivals of the eighteenth century, had emerged as an apocalyptic judgment on the world. God's wrath would redeem the righteous, scorch the wicked. And who were the wicked? As Daddy Gumby saw it, they were all around. Hypocrites. Liars. Church-avoiders. And, unsaid but implied: Virginia slaveowners who cried out for liberty while chaining 100,000 people. A plantation overseer who once boasted to Fithian of his method to rid slaves of "Sullenness, Obstinacy, or Idleness": "Take a Negro, strip him, tie him fast to a post; take then a sharp Curry-Comb, and curry him severely til he is well scraped; & call a boy with some dry Hay, and make the Boy rub him down for several minutes, then salt him, then unlose him. He will attend to his Business (said the Inhuman Infidel) afterwards!"[2]

Like an Old Testament prophet, Daddy Gumby witnessed against the falseness devouring the world. Behind the sheltering camouflage of fire and brimstone, he chastised Fithian, saying in effect: "Hear this Truth, and hear it well. We are God's people—we are better Christians than you. If you think Virginia is hot, try Hell."

Almost nothing is known about Daddy Gumby, when he was born, where he was from (given his advanced age, he probably was from Africa) or the origins of his religious beliefs. He had perhaps survived the slave ship, had witnessed firsthand the rise of racial slavery in colonial Virginia, and had seen and felt the brutality with which it was enforced. In a kind of shorthand autobiographical revelation of this life, he left two vital clues about himself. By requesting Fithian's help in recording the names and ages of his children, he appears to have wanted to anchor himself in human genealogical time, to testify to a record of survival and family progression under slavery. And in condemning the tutor's laziness in terms that foretold the day of judgment, he rooted himself as well in apocalyptic time, when the last would be first and fire would cauterize the world. He jumped at the chance to use prophecy as a crowbar to pry open the hypocrisy of the tutor, upbraiding him in harsh language that, were it not couched in religious terms, might have been enough to earn himself severe punishment for scolding a white man. Daddy Gumby's short, sharp retort had unveiled what would become the essence of the emerging black evangelical church in America: its claim to a higher morality, a loftier standard of godly law that rebuked white people for their irreligion. Whereas whites had enslaved Africans because of their reputed barbarism and lack of religion, black Christians turned the formula completely upside down. White people were now the uncivilized pagans and Christianity was kept alive only by Africa's children.

It was much the same elsewhere in the colonies, where enslaved people protested bondage in religious terms more explicitly than Daddy Gumby. In Massachusetts in 1774 a group of slaves sent the following petition to the governor: "We have in common with all other men a natural right to our freedoms without Being deprived of them by our fellow men as we are a freeborn Pepel and have never forfeited this blessing by any compact or agreement whatever. There is a great number of sincere members of the Church of Christ, how can the master be said to bear my Burden when he bears me down with the chains of slavery?" The governor ignored the logic and the plea. In Virginia in 1777, a newspaper advertised for the recapture of a runaway slave, Jupiter, "a great Newlight Preacher," who had escaped after his master had whipped him for "stirring up the Negroes in insurrection."[3]

Just as the American Revolution left the great majority of 400,000 enslaved Americans still in bondage, black Christianity stayed on the margin of American religious and civic life. Most white Americans remained untouched and unmoved by African American moral appeals. The African American experience stood largely outside, if not in opposition to, the narrative of increasing religious toleration that defined Anglo-America from the late seventeenth century through American independence. In fact, toleration emerged in America at the same time that racial slavery became embedded in the social, legal, and religious structures of colonial American life. Because African American Christianity used divine prophecy to critique the Revolution's complacent whites-only republicanism, promising that the last should be first, it remained an object of contempt and suspicion for most white Americans. Did freedom of conscience apply to people who did not have freedom of their own bodies? Did it apply to the practice of African religions brought to America on the slave ships? Did Christianity encourage the enslaved to rebel against authority, as so many planters and colonial officials feared? Law, custom, and evolving practice pointed white colonists in conflicting directions on these questions, while enslaved people devised their own forms of worship, largely in stealth.

The word "toleration" lies at the heart of the matter because it conveys a relationship of power between the tolerator and the tolerated. Only those invested with legal, political, or social authority have the prerogative to tolerate or not tolerate their subjects' beliefs and practices. Of course, the decision to tolerate or not can involve negotiation that may not always be one-sided. Yet with less power than anyone else in early America, enslaved blacks fall outside of our conventional understandings of religious toleration. Indeed, with no other group of Americans was the question of spiritual freedom so intimately connected to legalized, corporeal un-freedom. Thus the question of African American spirituality far exceeded the issue of toleration for religious dissenters since it was bound up with white colonists' ideas about civilization and barbarism, the very foundation of racial slavery. More than any other demographic or social group, enslaved people of African origin challenge the way historians approach early modern treatments of religious dissent, because the rhetoric, laws, and practices that applied to European, and Euro-American religious minorities rarely if ever applied to them. As an attempt to address that challenge, the following chapter examines the contested emergence of African American Christianity during an age of legally entrenched racial slavery and slowly expanding religious liberties in early America.

Debates over toleration for enslaved Africans in America were waged chiefly in Protestant colonies, since the Catholic Church did not consider the admission of enslaved or subordinate people a question of either religious toleration or racial difference. Well before the appearance of enslaved Africans in Europe and in the Americas in the fifteenth and sixteenth centuries, the Church had made provision for incorporating slaves into its body spiritual. In lands under Catholic jurisdiction, all non-Christians, including slaves, were designated as *extra ecclesiam*, a status that conferred rights and obligations derived from a pastiche of "the rediscovered teachings of the ancients, the Bible, natural law, customary law, commentaries, canon-law precedents, theological treaties, and papal bulls." When non-Christians converted to the faith, those rights and obligations were redefined within orthodox Christian norms, to which converts were expected to adhere. As Spain and Portugal colonized the New World in the sixteenth century and imported enslaved Africans to America, their baptism and incorporation into the Church became a vital tool for social control by civil and ecclesiastical authorities. In the early sixteenth century, Spanish authorities were told to make sure converts understood that Christianity did not change their condition of enslavement, but the point was not always taken. Church membership conferred the right to official sanction for marriages and many Africans continued to view this recognition as a means to claim that "they are free and have obtained liberty," as a royal official complained.[4]

Thousands of those taken from Africa to America by Portuguese and Dutch slavers were, in fact, already Christian. Beginning in the late fifteenth century, Portugese and Italian missionaries had made significant inroads in the kingdoms of Angola and Kongo in west-central Africa, where Christianity became deeply indigenized. African Catholic captives taken in slaving wars and sent to America were readily incorporated into the Church in New Spain, Brazil, and New France. Though enslaved Africans did not necessarily find freedom in the Roman Catholic Church, many nonetheless gained a measure of spiritual protection there. The recognition of marriages and the ability to forge extended links of fictive spiritual kinship through baptism and godparenthood served as powerful mechanisms for strengthening bonds of family and community. Christianity thus played a central role in the lives of hundreds of thousands of enslaved Africans and their descendants in Catholic America.[5]

By contrast, Protestants colonizing the Americas a century after the Spanish and Portuguese had few clear precedents upon which to draw as they first enslaved Africans and then sought to define legal slavery and its relationship to Christianity. The connection between slavery and Christianity, rather than the issue of religious toleration per se, framed the discussion about the suitability of Christianity for enslaved people and decisions made in those early, unsettled years proved highly influential in later discussions of toleration for African Americans. Protestant leaders from Britain and the continent convening at the Synod of Dort in 1618, for example, could not agree on a unified policy concerning the desirability of baptizing slaves, but asserted that baptism improved the slave's lot. One Swiss theologian contended that baptized slaves should be "used as hired servants clearly according to the customs of other Christians."[6]

English and Dutch settlers cobbled together piecemeal slave codes in their seventeenth-century American colonies from a mélange of sources, none of which spelled out the role of the enslaved within the church family. Indeed, clarifying that role became central to the writing of laws governing slaves, which in time became customized in formal slave codes written in virtually all Protestant colonies. The English laws that began emerging in mainland North America and the Caribbean as early as the 1630s reveal the tangled connections between the origins of chattel slavery and the legal, religious, and social construction of race in colonial British America. As numerous scholars have shown, these laws were adapted from a combination of English common law, villeinage law, police law, social custom, and other colonies' codes, and they reflected local conditions, usually in response to enslaved Africans' efforts to gain freedom.[7]

Perhaps the most-scrutinized succession of these laws were drafted between the 1630s and 1670s by legislators in Virginia, Barbados, and Maryland who sought to remove the legal and social ambiguity that had characterized the status of the enslaved population during the first three decades of those colonies and to close religious loopholes through which a few Africans had managed to gain freedom. Since English common law prohibited the enslavement of Christians, some enslaved Africans had claimed, and been granted, liberty upon receiving baptism. These emancipated people contributed to the growth of a small but visible class of free blacks in a planter-dominated society that was striving to secure a stable labor source by equating blackness with perpetual servitude. Clearly, Christianity threatened the slave-labor system the emerging planting class envisioned.[8]

After the Restoration in 1660, imperial authorities sought to promote Christianity for slaves in America as a means of social control without threatening the emerging institution of slavery and without hindering planters' right to manage their own affairs. In 1661, the Council for Foreign Plantations issued a "Draft of an Act for the Baptizing and Better Ordering of Negroes and Infidels in the King of England's Plantations in America," encouraging the work of missionaries to baptize slaves, who would be "reduced in short time to great civillity." The council acknowledged, however, that the act would not "impead, restrain, or impair the Jurisdiction, power, Authority, liberty or priviledge" of governors, masters, or planters.[9]

Accordingly, colonial officials sought to resolve any lingering ambiguity about the connection between Christianity and African American freedom. In 1663 the Maryland legislature drew up "an act obligeing negros to serve *durante vita* . . . for the prevencion of the dammage Masters of such Slaves may susteyne by such Slaves pretending to be Christned And soe pleade the lawe of England." More succinctly, the Virginia General Assembly in 1666 passed a law that "the conferring of baptisme doth not alter the condition of the person as to his bondage or freedome." The Assembly claimed that the law would allow masters to "more carefully endeavour the propagation of Christianity," but such apparently innocuous language masked the radical intent behind the statute and the revolutionary result it brought.[10]

By defining "Negros" as slaves, these statutes severed the connection between people's spiritual and legal status under common law, excluding them from its protection. Slavery, as Winthrop Jordan pointed out years ago, "could survive *only* if the Negro were a man set apart; he simply had to be different if slavery was to exist at all." The new slave laws flaunted a raw display of power defining that difference. In 1682 the Virginia law was expanded to exclude Indians, Muslims, and other "pagans" from common law protection, explaining that any captives "whose parentage and native country are not christian at the time of their first purchase" were liable to lifetime enslavement. These marks of exclusion became enshrined in the formal Virginia slave code of 1705 and in every subsequent revised code of the colony and then the state. In the newly racialized formula, the Pauline divide between the body and the soul, which English common law had seemingly collapsed in its prohibition on enslaving Christians, was spectacularly resurrected in the colonial setting and applied to "pagan" others, even if they embraced Christianity.[11]

Other English colonies adopted similar laws at about the same time, though in a somewhat difference sequence. The Barbados slave code of 1661, the influential "Act for the Better Ordering and Governing of Negroes" (adopted more or less intact by Jamaica in 1664, South Carolina in 1696, and other colonies), made no direct mention of baptism for slaves. The Barbados Assembly, however, in 1681 declared its opposition to Christianity for enslaved Africans not on the basis that they would use it to claim freedom but on cultural grounds, arguing that Africans' "Savage Brutishness renders them wholly uncapable" of accepting Christianity. In this case religious intolerance reinforced both cultural disdain for Africans and the fear that baptism would spoil the slave workforce. The Jamaican code of 1664 had similarly contended that African slaves were a "heathenish brutish and an uncertaine and dangerous kind of people." But a new provision in the revised 1696 Jamaican code urged masters to instruct slaves in Christianity and "cause to be baptized all such as they can make sensible of a Deity and the Christian Faith," and stipulated that baptism would not bring freedom to slaves.[12]

By 1700 most English colonies had slave codes in place that sought to control their reputedly barbaric African populations. The issue of whether baptism conferred freedom had been legally resolved as English planters, colonial administrators, and churchmen reached consensus that it did not. Great ambivalence remained, however, about the role of Christianity in upholding the slave codes. One position, seemingly held by the majority of slaveholders, maintained that slavery was to be enforced through brute physical oppression and that Christianity was potentially harmful to the effort. Another held that Africans were incapable of understanding Christianity and that no effort should be expended trying to convert them. A third, embraced by a scant minority, held that slaves were, or might be, capable of adopting the Christian religion and that it might even help "civilize" them—indeed, that slavery itself offered captive workers a chance for spiritual redemption. But under no circumstances should enslaved people who sought out Christianity expect release from bondage. Most slaveowners nonetheless downplayed the links between Christianity and African American freedom, and few allowed slaves access to baptism.

The debate followed a similar course in seventeenth-century Dutch America. Unencumbered by English common law, the Dutch based their slave laws on Roman precedents. Like the English, however, they improvised, interpreting the law of Christianity and slavery as circumstances prompted them. Clearly baptism did not offer a direct legal aperture to freedom, but much else remained ambiguous. In the West Indian colony of Curacao, captured from the Portuguese in 1634, the Dutch West India Company enjoined Dutch Reformed ministers "to instruct the Portuguese, Spaniards, and their children in the fundamentals of the Christian religion, and also the blacks and Indians." Many masters, however, opposed the injunction, not wishing to consider Africans as brothers and sisters in Christ. As a result, few Africans were converted. In New Netherland, enslaved Africans began joining the Dutch Reformed Church as early as the 1620s and one church official even argued that if the slaves "want to submit themselves to the lovely yoke of our Lord Jesus Christ, Christian love requires that they be discharged from the yoke of human slavery." Perhaps because of such sentiments, rumors persisted that baptism would grant freedom to slave children, leading a Dutch minister to complain that blacks "wanted nothing else than to deliver their children from bodily slavery, without striving for piety and Christian virtues." Still, conversion to Christianity helped blacks expand their social mobility by forging a web of connections to white Dutch society. They sued in the courts, traded and owned property, acquiring a kind of fuzzy legal status known as "half-freedom" that occasionally led to full freedom. After the English conquest of New Netherland in 1664, a new set of "Duke's Laws" for New York eliminated much of this social flexibility and erased all ambiguity about the role of religion in fostering it, declaring that the new code "shall not extend to sett at Liberty Any Negroe of Indian Servant who shall turne Christian after he shall have been bought by Any Person."[13]

In the Danish Caribbean the situation was much the same, largely because the ruling class in Denmark's colonies (St. Thomas, colonized in 1670, St. John in 1716, and St. Croix in 1733) was comprised largely of Dutch planters, and Dutch Reformed was the principal denomination on the islands, along with some Danish Lutheranism. Though Reformed policy technically urged that "the poor and blind pagans be led to the knowledge of God and their salvation," the practice was minimal. "At one time," according to the eighteenth-century German missionary Christian Oldendorp, "it was customary in Danish and English islands alike that a baptized slave was given his freedom. And even though that practice was abandoned, it was still to be feared, according to the beliefs of those opposed to the practice, that converted slaves might become too clever, too similar to the Whites, and therefore more inclined to rebellion." As one planter told a missionary in 1733: "We must always keep the Negroes down, because we are only a handful of whites. If one said to the Negroes that all men are equal before God, their respect for the whites would be weakened." Echoing Barbadian and Jamaican planters, many slaveholders "were actually said to have believed that the blacks were a creation of the devil and were thus incapable of eternal salvation." By no means a universal view among whites, it was nonetheless common enough to hinder Africans' entry to Christianity.[14]

By the late seventeenth century in the Protestant Americas, therefore, Christian law was made to conform with civil law, specifically the demands of controlling a potentially rebellious population. No laws forbade slaves from adopting Christianity. No government or church document specified intolerance toward their baptism; official policy in the Anglican and Reformed churches in fact sanctioned and encouraged the baptism of slaves. In practice, however, most planters continued to regard black Christianity as an enemy of the slave codes and of discipline for a people whose barbarism was to be met with force, not Christian benevolence. Some planters still harbored doubts about whether baptism conferred freedom or other privileges to slaves the planters were unwilling to grant. Others feared the social leveling implicit in Christianity's promise of spiritual freedom. And still others brought their own interpretation of divine law to the discussion, arguing that Africans were beyond redemption altogether. Even as late as the 1760s the cantankerous Virginia planter Landon Carter, in one of his more exasperated moods, raged that blacks "are devils, and to make them otherwise than slaves will be to set devils free." Opposition toward African American Christianity was therefore less a product of official or popular religious intolerance toward dissenters than of cultural biases toward the enslaved and lingering fears among planters about the dangers of baptizing them. The economic power of the slaveholders overpowered civil and ecclesiastical policy that favored Christianity for unfree Africans.[15]

Because religion in the case of enslaved African Americans was so closely connected with legal status and race, the late seventeenth-century debates in England and the colonies about religious toleration and freedom of conscience applied very differently, or not at all, to them. Provisions for toleration in Restoration-era colonies such as New York, Carolina, and Pennsylvania and in England's Toleration Act of 1689 were designed to accommodate Protestant dissenters such as Quakers and Baptists from the British Isles and Europe, not the religions of non-white people pulled into the imperial orbit. The language of most of those colonial charters and of the Toleration Act was race-neutral, neither specifically forbidding nor allowing Christianity for people of African descent. That neutral language, however, masked a broader legal exclusion: African religions, including Islam, considered barbaric and uncivilized by many, were not even contemplated as objects of toleration by policy makers. One colony that did spell out racial difference with regard to religion was Carolina, where the Fundamental Constitution of 1682 extended toleration to Indians in an effort to gain their alliance. Although the "Natives . . . who will be concerned in our Plantation are utterly strangers to Christianity," their "Idolatry, Ignorance or Mistake gives us no right to expel or use them ill." The constitution expressed the hope that this "enlightened" policy would draw Indians into compact with the colony and eventually lead them to Christianity. The document did not prohibit enslaved Africans from practicing Christianity, but it stipulated that "Every Freeman of Carolina shall have absolute power and authority over

Negro slaves of what opinion or Religion whatever." This was toleration of a sharply circumscribed kind.[16]

Some outspoken churchmen condemned the planters' intolerance toward black Christianity, which they blamed on mistakenly low views of African culture and intelligence. Anglican Morgan Godwyn denounced planters for questioning the very humanity of enslaved Africans, an excuse he said enabled them to allow slaves to continue living in "Impiety" and "Barbarity." Africans, Godwyn insisted, were fully human and needed an equal chance to hear of Christ's redeeming grace.[17] In Massachusetts, similarly, proslavery minister Cotton Mather berated masters for leaving slaves in darkness on the "pretense" that they were too "dull" to understand Christianity. The "poor *Negro's* especially are kept Strangers to the *way of Life*," existing only to serve the master's "*Drudgeries*" though "their *Souls*, which are as white and good as those of other Nations, their *Souls* are not look'd after, but are *Destroyed for lack of Knowledge*. This is a desperate Wickedness. But are they *dull?* Then *instruct* them the *rather;* that is the Way to *sharpen* them."[18] Slaveowners, he charged further, leaned on the tired fear that baptism would emancipate slaves. "What Law is it, that sets the Baptized Slave at Liberty?" he asked in *The Negro Christianized* of 1706. His answer: none. By contrast, Mather's Massachusetts counterpart, Samuel Sewall, argued in his famous pamphlet *The Selling of Joseph* (1700) that slavery was wrong because "all Men, as they are the Sons of *Adam*, are Coheirs; and have equal Right unto Liberty," but he was not particularly sanguine about prospects for black conversion. Africans would never blend into Anglo society, he argued, and would "remain in our Body Politick as a kind of extravasat Blood."[19]

Confronted by such obstacles, and with no apparent benefits to be derived from the masters' religion, enslaved Africans in the Protestant Americas showed little but contempt and ridicule for Christianity. By the early eighteenth century, there were hundreds of thousands of black Christians in the New World, but only a small handful of them were Protestant, scattered throughout the English and Dutch colonies. Though a growing number of ministers supported the Christianization of slaves, missions by the Quakers in Barbados in the 1670s and by the Anglican Church's Society for the Propagation of the Gospel in South Carolina and Barbados in the early eighteenth century were stoutly opposed by planters and produced few converts. Many Africans clung to the beliefs and rituals that had made the transatlantic voyage with them, which Morgan Godwyn described as "*Heathen Rites* . . . barbarous behaviour and practice in *Worship* and *Ceremonies* of *Religion* . . .

their *Polygamy* . . . their *Idolatrous Dances,* and *Revels.*"[20] As disdainful and fearful of African religions as white colonists were, planters feared Christianity among their slaves even more, and so many tolerated African worship practices on their plantations. It was a pity, wrote Peter Kalm, the Swedish botanist who traveled in North America in 1748, "that the masters of these Negroes in most of the *English* colonies take little care of their spiritual welfare, and let them live on in their pagan darkness."[21] Such "toleration" of African religions represented much more a de facto accommodation to the spiritual needs of the enslaved workforce than a de jure recognition of dissenters' right to free worship.

Toleration for black Christianity by the planters would come only from sustained pressure by Africans and African Americans themselves to gain access to Christian teaching. In the 1720s and increasingly thereafter, disparate groups of enslaved people in multiple colonial settings began to make those overtures. An important factor was a growing Creole population of American-born blacks, with no firsthand memory of Africa, who were acquiring more familiarity with European languages and cultural ways than their parents and grandparents. Of course African religions and languages lived on in many slave quarters, but for some African Americans not only might Christianity be more comprehensible and less emotionally remote than for the first generation of African captives, but it might also fill a spiritual void among those with no direct connection to or affinity for African religious practices. Many no doubt believed that Christianity could offer access to the masters' culture, providing an extra element of respect and protection from abuse.[22]

And there was always the lingering hope that Christianity might still open a window to freedom, whether through baptism, the chance that an enlightened fellow Christian might one day emancipate his slaves, the identification with the Israelites' quest for deliverance, or the conviction that Jesus the emancipator would one day convert spiritual equality to bodily liberty. In 1723, an anonymous mixed-race slave in Virginia wrote to Edmund Gibson, bishop of London, whose see included Virginia, asking for freedom and the right to receive instruction in Christianity, requesting that "your honour will by the help of our . . . Lord King George and the rest of the Rullers will Releese us out of this Cruell Bondegg and this wee beg for Jesus Christs his Sake who has commanded us first to seeke the kingdom of god and all things shall be added un to us." Explicit in the petitioner's appeal was the link between slavery, the masters' ungodliness, and the desire for Christian instruction. "Wee are commandded to keep holey the Sabbath day and wee do hardly know when it comes for our task mastrs are as hard with us as Egypttions was with the Chilldann of Issarall god be marcifll unto us ... our desire is that godlines Shoulld aboundd amongs us and wee desire that our Childarn be putt to Scool and Larnd to read through the Bybel." Terrified of retribution, the writer kept his identity secret.[23]

Presumably nothing came of the appeal, but recognizing a growing desire for Christianity among an increasingly Creole population, Anglican ministers in the early 1720s pressed Virginia slaveholders to allow them to catechize and baptize slaves. They emphasized the benefits of inculcating docility among slaves, reiterating the by-now standard disclaimer that christening did not liberate anyone. A growing number of planters finally began to heed the appeal, apparently recognizing that religion could serve as an effective ideological support for the legal, punitive, and military superstructure enforcing slavery. One minister, Adam Dickie, observed in 1732 that planters had become "sensible of the advantage of having their Slaves made Christians for they who formerly were theives, lyars, Swearers, prophaners of the Sabbath, and neglecters of their business, from a Sense of Religion and of their Duty have left off all these things and make Conscience of everything they do." With planters granting the clergy greater access to their enslaved workforce, more and more slaves were baptized—from just a few by the early 1720s in one typical Virginia parish, St. Peter's in New Kent County, to thirty-four between 1725 and 1729, and eighty-one more between 1735 and 1740. Observing these developments with satisfaction, James Blair, a longtime advocate for slave baptism, reported in 1729: "The Negroes themselves in our neighbourhood are very desirous to become Christians; and in order to it come and give an account of the Lords prayer, and the Creed, and ten commandments, and so are baptized and frequent the church."[24]

The conditions by which slaveholders and the enslaved understood baptism remained contested. Planters continued to complain that baptism made slaves proud and that they sought Christianity only for perceived social benefits while disregarding its spiritual message. These fears were borne out in 1730 when hundreds of slaves in the Chesapeake region rose in rebellion after a rumor spread that the authorities had suppressed an edict from the king supposedly granting freedom to slaves who accepted Christianity. The rumored connections between Christianity and freedom would have likely resonated with the rebels, many of whom, as Kongolese or Angolans, were probably already Christian. In southeastern Virginia, some three hundred slaves escaped to the Dismal Swamp where they "did a great deal of Mischief in that Province before they were suppressed." Using Indian slave catchers to hunt down the maroons, authorities put down the revolt and executed its leaders, after which the governor ordered militiamen and overseers to bring weapons with them to church to prevent uprisings on Sunday. African Americans continued to be christened in Virginia, but they were not allowed communion, confirmation, or ordination, and baptism did not protect them and their common-law spouses from being sold apart.[25]

By the 1730s, transatlantic Protestant revivals produced a new surge in mission outreach among evangelicals eager to spread the news of God's redemptive grace to as many people as possible whatever their race, ethnicity, or legal status. Following this universalizing impulse, enthusiastic preachers ventured into southern and Caribbean plantation country proclaiming Christian love to enslaved Africans, sometimes naively unsuspecting of the trouble they were courting. Their spiritual egalitarianism and warm empathy, often expressed in powerful terms that favored emotion over formal doctrine, earned them favor among the enslaved but censure from slaveholders whose longstanding fears of Christian leveling were once again put on notice. Those masters, wrote Peter Kalm in 1748, "would be very ill pleased at, and would by all means hinder their Negroes from being instructed in the doctrines of Christianity, to this they are partly led by the conceit of its being shameful, to have a spiritual brother or sister among so despicable a people; partly by thinking that they should not be able to keep their Negroes so meanly afterwards; and partly through fear of the Negroes growing too proud, on seeing themselves upon a level with their masters in religious matters."[26] In many instances, slaves were punished and preachers persecuted for attending religious meetings together.

Despite this opposition, enslaved African Americans reached out to the evangelicals more eagerly than they ever had to the mainstream churches. Scattered examples from disparate colonies indicate that this experimentation was underway simultaneously in multiple places by the 1730s and 1740s. After the charismatic itinerant evangelist George Whitefield visited South Carolina in 1740, for example, one planter, Hugh Bryan, held religious meeting with his slaves and proclaimed "sundry enthusiastic Prophecies of the Destruction of Charles Town and Deliverance of the Negroes from servitude." A "Moorish slave woman on a plantation" was overheard "singing a spiritual at the water's edge." Bryan's slaves were said to be learning "a Parcel of Cant-Phrases, Trances, Dreams, Visions and revelations" and that they did "nothing but pray and sing and thereby neglect their work." Alarmed by these dangerous reports, the South Carolina legislature reprimanded Bryan and forced him to renounce his evangelical activity with the slaves. But they were too late. Enthusiastic Christianity had already taken root among them.[27]

One of the early centers of black Protestant Christianity lay outside mainland North America, on the Caribbean island of St. Thomas, a small Danish colony forty miles east of Puerto Rico. There German-speaking Moravian evangelists arrived in the early 1730s to preach among a fiercely oppressed population of enslaved Africans and Creoles. After initial apathy from the slaves and resistance from planters, they hit upon the technique of recruiting a few prominent leaders from within the slave community, whom they designated mission assistants or "helpers," and who then in turn recruited others from the quarters. These leaders provided an effective level of black leadership and organizing control in the mission. The Moravians were scarcely antislavery, but their emotional emphasis on the equalizing effect of Jesus's blood sacrifice, made more visceral through literacy lessons, appealed to many slaves and made the missionaries appear as allies and protectors. The Bible, some slaves said, came alive as a wisdom-giving magic book. Weathering violent attacks by planters, the small congregation grew to more than six hundred by the early 1740s, and when missionaries extended their outreach to the other Danish islands of St. John and St. Croix with equal success, the combined missions numbered some seven thousand black Christians by the 1770s. In this setting, therefore, Afro-Caribbean determination to seek out Christianity eventually outlasted the harsh opposition of planters, though Moravian missionaries strenuously assured the latter their message was pro-slavery. Other evangelicals, particularly the Methodists, paid careful attention to the Moravians' strategy and methods, many of which proved influential in their own mission fields slightly later in North America.[28]

On a more modest scale, a similar Christian revival led by Presbyterians flourished in Hanover County, Virginia, during the 1740s. Minister Samuel Davies settled in the county in 1749 determined to preach among the slaves, whom he described as "poor neglected negroes . . . whose souls none care for, as though immortality were not a privilege common to them with their masters." God was displeased, he wrote, that "Thousands of poor Slaves in a Christian Country, the Property of Christian Masters, as they will be called," remained "almost as ignorant of Christianity, as when they left the Wilds of Africa." Many slaves responded eagerly to his message of an emotional connection with Christ, some of whom admitted that they sought baptism as a means to "an *Equality* with their Masters," others out of a heartfelt desire for spiritual regeneration. Here, too, slaveholders expressed concern that Christianity would elevate the slaves' sense of self-worth and undermine the social order, but Davies responded that some black Christians "seem to have made greater progress in experimental Religion than many sincere Christians of a fairer colour."[29] New Light preachers such as Davies and others were heavily invested in northern Virginia in the 1750s and 1760s, and perhaps it was from one of them, at a revival meeting or in a church balcony reserved for slaves, that Daddy Gumby first heard his own call to witness.

As all of these examples demonstrate, African American Christianity still involved relatively small numbers of people by the mid-eighteenth century. Nonetheless, it had emerged as a popular movement throughout the enslaved population of the British mainland colonies and the Caribbean. As African Americans understood it, the syntax of Christian godliness turned on its head the very religious doctrine that was meant to enslave them, making it a creed of liberation instead. Identifying themselves with the Israelites and their tormenters with the Egyptians, as the anonymous Virginia petitioner had done in 1723, the enslaved saw themselves as the instruments of God's mighty hand. Jesus, the iconic "suffering servant," had given himself to save the outcast, the oppressed, the damned. If his mission was to purify the world of sin and redeem its victims, then who were better positioned to benefit from his justice and mercy than those in bondage? Once apprehended in these terms, Christianity became the slaves' way to declare moral superiority over their masters and no amount of legal oppression could stop them from seeking it out. In evangelical meetings and gatherings deep in the woods, through a Bible quietly changing hands or a hymn sung at the water's edge, in clandestine conversations after dark in slave villages, and guided by a new cadre of black spiritual leaders and preachers both male and female, African Americans probed the meaning and texture of Christian belief. As they did so, they made a key transition from thinking of Christianity as a legalistic avenue to freedom through baptism to internalizing its doctrines at the much deeper juncture of experience, intellect, and emotion. In 1754, an enslaved Congregationalist parishioner named Greenwich in Canterbury, Connecticut, claimed to "have ben instructed by the Lord" and used scriptures to contest his bondage. Challenging the hoary tale of Noah's curse on his grandson Canaan that white Christians had long repeated to justify African enslavement, Greenwich countered: "some say that we are the seed of Canaan and some say that we are the Tribe of Ham but Let_that be as it will Justise must Take Plase." It was written in the Bible, he continued, that "non[e] should impose upon another nation," and that it was ungodly to supply arms to combatants in a "continual war amongst themselves" and "when you have don this you will steel as many of them and bring them over Into your Contry to make slaves of them their soul and body." Greenwich's critique welled up from the deepest springs of biblical righteousness. This was what the slave masters had feared all along.[30]

African Americans' new turn to Christianity was not without its religious and psychological costs. Historian Jon Butler has proposed that the decline and eventual eradication of African religions in America constituted nothing less than an "African spiritual holocaust." "No other Old world peoples," he writes, "suffered such wholesale destruction of their traditional religions as did Africans enslaved in Britain's North American colonies." Similarly, Sylvester Johnson has contested what he calls scholars' "uncritical celebration of the Christianization of colonized peoples" that led to the "genocidal eradication of African religions." He doubts "that the historical study of the Atlantic world will ever take seriously the violence involved in the history of hatred against African religions; this Christianization process, instead, is easily lauded as a triumphal story of black progress, an enunciation of modernity." Richard Price has called the African American adoption of Christianity a "Faustian bargain, the willingness to sell their own souls" to a religion that sanctioned their own enslavement and required them to put away "heathenism." As these characterizations suggest, the decision to forego African practices in favor of Christianity was no simple matter of exchanging one religion for another but often involved a painful calculus of spiritual loss and perceived gain.[31]

Yet it is also worth remembering that, in the face of massive religious intolerance, it was not easy for enslaved people to gain access to Christianity either. In Protestant America, the enslaved were long denied Christianity except under rigorous strictures and those who sought it out were often met with violent reprisals. Still they persisted. This fortitude suggests that the transition to African American Christianity should be viewed not so much as part of a triumphalist narrative of Christian progress or even of African American progress toward modernity, but rather as an important chapter in the black freedom struggle. Whether African religions were destroyed in America, continued to thrive in places such as Brazil, Haiti, and New Orleans, or fused with various forms of Christianity to live on in altered guise elsewhere, Africans themselves were actively involved in these processes of spiritual reimagination and reinvention. They were under extraordinary duress, to be sure, but their choices reflected their best reckoning with the limited options open to them. And increasingly, people of African origin came to believe that Christianity offered a way out of slavery. As they did, it was they who modernized Christianity, not the other way around. African American voices became the conscience of modernity, insisting that slavery was incompatible with Christianity and with a western world testing the extent and limits of freedom. The intolerance black seekers confronted on this journey therefore provides an important measure not only of white colonists' bigotry, but also of African American determination.

This linkage of Christianity and freedom took many forms. As more African Americans absorbed Christianity, the culture of evangelicalism fostered a sense of spiritual equality and biracial fellowship that threatened to undermine the bedrock of racial separatism upon which slavery was grounded. As "New Light" Baptists, Presbyterians, Methodists, and Moravians fanned out through the mid-eighteenth-century South and embedded themselves in the heart of plantation country, they not only tolerated but welcomed enslaved black coreligionists. This embrace was no idle rhetorical gesture but a principle motif in the evangelicals' worldview. To make the world over in their regenerate image, they would accept anyone who embraced the New Birth, experienced conversion, enjoyed an emotional relationship with the Savior, and immersed themselves in the Christ's redemptive power. In prayer halls across the South, black and white worshipers were baptized together, sat side by side on church benches, exchanged such ancient rituals as the kiss of peace, the laying on of hands and the washing of feet, and addressed each other as "brother" and "sister." Evangelical preachers such as Devereux Jarratt, Freeborn Garretson, Samuel Davies, and others reported mass revival meetings attended by hundreds of black and white seekers "express[ing] their love for Jesus." Many congregations reported majorities of African Americans.[32]

These manifestations of biracial fellowship were imperfect, to be sure, as was to be expected in the midst of a slave society. Some churches maintained segregated seating, while social and spiritual parity was difficult to maintain in these microcosmic communities composed of both free and slave. Still, the lines between slavery and freedom could blur in these settings, where the blood of Jesus was said to wash away all spiritual distinctions between people. In the decades on either side of the American Revolution, enslaved congregants sometimes took their masters to church "court" to sue for more Christian treatment. More than a few guilt-stricken white evangelicals freed their slaves, and some Baptist and Methodist churches forbade white members from owning slaves. By no means did these gestures topple the racial hierarchy of slavery, but that did not stop planters and government officials from fearing that it might. Nor did it stop them from bemoaning the alarming trend of spiritual equality and religion-inspired manumissions. Such concerns were not without warrant. Evangelicals promoted the sense that black and white congregants were bound together in the larger Christian family by shared values and the experience of spiritual rebirth, thereby breaking down longstanding barriers to the toleration of African American Christianity. In this, as in other ways, the evangelical churches provided vital arenas for the larger late eighteenth-century revolutionary struggle to level social hierarchies and democratize civic life.[33]

To some white evangelicals, the logic of spiritual equality and Christian fellowship led inexorably toward emancipation. For others, however, it pointed in the opposite direction. Well before the Revolution, some prominent evangelicals had foreseen the problems of cultivating Christianity among the enslaved and they sought to mitigate, or wholly deny, the egalitarian implications of their mission. Aided by a growing number of sympathetic planters such as Jonathan Bryan in South Carolina and James Habersham in Georgia, ministers such as George Whitefield, Samuel Davies, and Joseph Ottolenghe emphasized the humanitarian imperative to bring African Americans into the "light" without undermining the institution of slavery. If they could not prevent the slaves from embracing Christianity, planters and ministers sought to regulate which version they heard. Slaves were to be encouraged to wrap themselves in Jesus's loving embrace, to feel the saving power of his grace and confide their cares in him. But they also were exhorted to follow his example of humility, to turn the other cheek, and to obey worldly authority. In this vision, Christianity was a religion of all-embracing comradeship and love, but unquestionably a proslavery one—a felicitous equation assigning the responsibility of generous care and Christian benevolence to the master and the duty of submission and Christian gratitude to the slave. Thus was born the paternalist compact between enslaver and enslaved as the masters understood it. On this understanding, slaveowners no longer stood between their slaves and Christianity; instead they merely exposed them to a selective reading of salubrious biblical texts. "Servants, obey your masters" and similar injunctions from a host of Pauline letters became standard refrains in plantation missions and racially integrated northern churches in the decades before the Revolution, the only path through which many masters allowed their slaves to approach Christianity.[34]

Whether the strategy worked is unclear at best. Missionaries and planters alike insisted that formerly intractable slaves were rendered meek and industrious by Christian teachings, and it is true that congregational order in many churches demanded a certain adherence to rules and hierarchies, which were by no means incompatible with slave society. The enforcement power of the planters was strong, but they could not control everything their slaves heard or thought. Some slaves could read the Bible and forge their own interpretations. Planters complained constantly about Christian slaves who ran away, about those who were "fond of singing hymns, and exhorting [their] brethren of the Ethiopian tribe," or those, like a slave woman named Hannah, who "pretend much to the religion the Negroes of late have practised." Despite the many indications that Christianity reinforced the ideology and practice of slaveholding, the evidence is at least as abundant that African Americans considered Christianity a creed of prophetic salvation, liberation, and even rebellion.[35]

As had been the case since the early seventeenth century, the age of the American Revolution reflected, and even revived, limitations on African American religious expression. The ethos of toleration that emerged through the eighteenth century and culminated with the First Amendment and the Virginia Statute for Religious Freedom did not apply to people whose bodies were not free. A Virginia toleration bill of 1772 extended to Protestant dissenters "the full and free Exercise of their Religion, without Molestation of Danger of incurring any Penalty whatsoever." African American Christians, however, were excluded from these provisions. Ministers who baptized slaves, admitted them to church membership without their master's consent, or encouraged them to disobey their owners "under Pretence of religious Worship" could be jailed for up to a year.[36] And the Virginia Statute of 1786, drafted by Thomas Jefferson, resolved that "no man shall be enforced, restrained, molested or burthened in his body or goods, nor shall otherwise suffer on account of his religious opinions or beliefs, but that all men shall be free to profess, and by argument to maintain, their opinions in matters of Religion." These freedoms, the statute declared, "are of the natural rights of mankind," and any attempt to repeal them would infringe those rights.[37] Yet neither the statute nor the Bill of Rights specifically included African Americans in their protection of religious and civil liberties, which was important because enslaved people were continually "enforced, restrained, molested,

[and] burthened" because of their beliefs. They were not free to profess their religious opinions and their natural rights were violated every day. In 1790 the Virginia Baptist preacher John Leland, a strong advocate of spreading Christianity among the enslaved population, complained that though slaves had the right "beyond contradiction" to liberty of conscience, many slave owners still punished them viciously for attending religious meetings.[38]

By the early nineteenth century, southern planters fully shifted their strategy in the struggle to control the spiritual lives of enslaved workers, now eagerly embracing the concept of the plantation mission. They had enthusiastic allies in white evangelicals, who were under pressure from planters to conform to the social order of a slave society and eager to show they were no longer subversive radicals. It was they who provided the preachers necessary for the drive to convert southern slaves to an acceptable form of Christianity. The figure of the white pastor extolling the virtues of lamb-like submission became a fixture on many plantations. Planters and ministers sought to maintain strict surveillance over black religious meetings, which was why so many gatherings ended up being held secretly in the woods.[39]

Just as importantly, as white racism intensified throughout the early republic, evangelicalism's challenge to slavery dissipated. Planters pressed their own congregations to drop provisions banning slaveholding members. Evangelical leaders distanced themselves from the distinctive biracial ritual practices that once signaled spiritual leveling within their churches. In a conservative backlash against the racial fluidity that characterized their congregations in the late eighteenth century, Baptists, Methodists, Moravians, Presbyterians, and others all erected new divisions between white and black worshipers in the early nineteenth century. In one church after another from Maryland and Virginia to Kentucky, the Carolinas, and Georgia, black congregants were moved into segregated seating, denied the primitive practices of footwashings and the laying on of hands, buried in separate graveyards, and in many cases eventually moved into separate churches altogether. African Americans were still welcomed into the Christian family, but it was now a racially segregated family. Black Christianity, with its assumption of spiritual and even social equality, could never be fully tolerated in a society predicated on slavery and racial inequality.[40]

Much the same took place in northern states, where, though slavery itself was on the wane after the Revolution, white Christians similarly recoiled from the egalitarianism once heralded by racially mixed congregations. In Methodist, Episcopal, and other churches in Philadelphia, Boston, New

York, and elsewhere, white congregants made it clear that in the spiritual as well as the civic realm, this was to be a white man's republic. Slave and free black members were roughed up, told to move to separate seating, and invited to leave. The invitation was accepted. Under the forceful leadership of free blacks such as Richard Allen and Absalom Jones, who had endured discrimination in their Methodist Episcopal congregation in Philadelphia during the 1790s, African Americans withdrew and formed their own African Methodist Episcopal churches, inaugurating the era of the independent black church as a refuge from the racism washing over the young nation. Free African Americans thus took advantage of new religious freedoms in the new nation to expand their sphere of religious and political expression. In the coming decades, independent black churches would be important bastions from which the struggle against slavery would be waged.[41]

The African American experience, then, helps us reevaluate the concepts of religious toleration and freedom of conscience in American history. Can the United States really claim to have forged a national identity in religious freedom? Many historians view the American Revolution as a watershed event for the advent of religious freedom in the new nation. Indeed, the transition from toleration to religious liberty and from establishment to disestablishment at the national level does represent both the culmination of several centuries of philosophical reasoning on religious freedom and one of the major advances in religious practice in the western world. At the same time, the idea of religious liberty, whether abstract or applied, could not be separated from the social practices in which it was embedded, as outsiders to the mainstream Anglo-American Protestant body politic were often reminded. Jews gained legal religious freedom but endured periodic popular intolerance. The generally widespread public acceptance Catholics received after the Revolution degenerated into anti-immigrant, anti-Catholic violence in the 1830s. Even more than those groups, Native Americans remained targets of hostility and violence from whites who associated native spiritualities with barbarism, as had been the case since the early colonial period. Free blacks enjoyed no guaranteed protection of religious practice, either, although their churches remained sacred sanctuaries in the face of continued intolerance.[42]

At the far end of the spectrum of religious freedoms denied, enslaved Americans stood alone. For them, the Revolution was not a watershed. Christianity was always about freedom for African Americans, and while slavery persisted they could never gain full recognition for practicing it—which was why they practiced it in the first place. The black prophetic tradition sought to redeem the promise of America. For more than two centuries, African American Christianity emerged in conjunction with, and in defiance of, efforts to prevent and control it. For free people of color in the young United States, freedom of worship was no longer an abstract concept, tantalizingly out of reach. But for the great majority of African Americans, toleration and religious freedom—those concepts so fundamental to the creation of the United States—never applied fully until 1865. As Langston Hughes would write many years later:

> There are words like *Freedom*
> Sweet and wonderful to say.
> On my heart-strings freedom sings
> All day everyday.
>
> There are words like *Liberty*
> That almost make me cry.
> If you had known what I knew
> You would know why.[43]

Chapter 9

Catholics, Protestants, and the Clash of Civilizations in Early America

OWEN STANWOOD

In 1774 the Continental Congress reached out to the inhabitants of Quebec. American colonists were engaged in a bitter struggle with Parliament over the rights of colonial subjects within an imperial system and they needed to present a united front against British tyranny. In particular, the Congress urged French Canadians to reject the Quebec Act, a recent act of Parliament that, among other things, provided for the establishment of the Roman Catholic Church and French-style civil law in Canada. This was a blueprint for tyranny, the Congress argued, challenging French Canadians to "take a noble chance for emerging from a humiliating subjection under Governors, Intendants, and Military Tyrants, into the firm rank and condition of English freemen." The French audience proved difficult to persuade. After all, inhabitants of British America had a long history of hating their French neighbors and they often targeted the Catholic religion as a pernicious faith incompatible with reason or good government. Only a few months earlier the same Continental Congress had referred to Catholicism as a force that had "dispersed impiety, bigotry, persecution, murder and rebellion through every part of the world." Canadians themselves, according to a Rhode Island newspaper, were "licensed slaves" and "children of popery," intended by the British as a sinister army to force the colonists to surrender their liberties. Not surprisingly, Canadians eventually decided to remain loyal to Great Britain, a circumstance that one New Englander blamed on their being "extremely ignorant and Bigoted" and under the sway of the priests. But it was hard to deny that the British colonists' own anti-Catholic inheritance limited the appeal of the patriot cause. Antipopery served as one cornerstone of a common identity, but at the same time it antagonized people who could have been allies, drawing new borders across North America that persist to this day.[1]

Historians, like French Canadians, have noticed early America's intense anti-Catholicism, but they have rarely known what to do with it. In fact, it appears to have been a prejudice directed at no one in particular. Very few Catholics lived in the British mainland colonies, yet Protestant Americans hated them obsessively and demonstrated this antipathy in everything from Pope's Day rituals to the illustrations in almanacs and the famous *New England Primer*. At the same time, observers of American religious development from Adam Smith to Jon Butler have stressed colonial religious diversity and relative toleration, making the vitriol against Catholics seem out of place and even un-American. While nineteenth-century anti-Catholicism—directed against Irish and continental immigrants and closely intertwined with nativism—has been easy to integrate into a more typical story of American ethnic animosity, scholars have barely even tried to decipher its seventeenth- and eighteenth-century antecedents. Those who have, often writing from a confessional Catholic perspective, have tended to define antipopery as an irrational holdover from European confessional struggles, a constant among Protestant people that need not be closely analyzed.[2]

For a number of reasons, this older interpretation of early American antipopery is no longer tenable. Over the past few decades, historians of early modern Britain have redefined fear of popery not as an irrational prejudice, but as a set of symbols and rhetorical tools that allowed early modern Protestants to define the fundamentals and limits of their own faith. In this body of scholarship, antipopery does not need actual Catholics to be effective; indeed, Protestants more often used the language of antipopery against members of their own community who appeared insufficiently Protestant. Moreover, antipopery was not a monolithic ideology: it had many tropes that various political interest groups could use at different times. Common fears of Catholics sometimes caused stark divisions within the English political nation and sometimes brought subjects together against external enemies. It could buttress the authority of kings or inspire revolutions against monarchy. This new, subtle reading of antipopery has allowed early modernists to rethink the relationship between religion and politics in Britain, and it could do the same for the interpretation of anti-Catholicism in the American colonies, where Protestants of various stripes used anti-Catholic rhetoric for often contradictory purposes.[3]

As important as this new scholarship is in rethinking early American antipopery, other recent movements within the colonial field further underscore the need to reconsider the subject. The field, as one scholar noted, has exploded. No longer content to focus on the traditional thirteen British colonies, colonial historians have turned in increasing numbers to non-English colonies and especially to the backcountry, redefining early American history as a contest between cultures and, especially during the eighteenth century, between empires. Few have noted that this enlarged perspective fundamentally reorients the religious history of North America. Rather than an insignificant minority, Roman Catholics were a formidable presence, dominating the colonies of Acadia, Canada, Louisiana, and Florida and maintaining a vast network of Indian missions. Moreover, the Protestant inhabitants of the eastern seaboard knew about this Catholic presence and inflated it in their minds. As a result, many British Americans viewed themselves as warriors in a religious contest for North America, a chapter in the centuries-long struggle between true Christianity and its enemies. For many Protestants—if less so for Catholics—the settlement of America became a holy cause, and this viewpoint remained strong enough to prevent the integration of Canada into the American republic and draw permanent international borders across the continent.[4]

Attention to this "clash of civilizations" helps to establish a new timeline of early American religious history: a timeline that stresses connections between North America and the rest of the Christian world while also attending to developments throughout the North American continent. The story begins with the settlement of Spanish Florida in 1565, an outpost built on the ashes of a previous French Protestant colony. For the next century Protestant pirates and settlers saw North America as a fitting place to challenge Spanish pretensions for universal dominion, and this goal helped to inspire the founding of English and Dutch colonies. The first major turning point occurred with England's "Glorious" Revolution of 1688-89, an event that turned antipopery into a state ideology and inaugurated a series of wars between Protestant Britain and Catholic France. The context changed again when Britain's victory in 1763 removed the French as a major external threat, allowing colonists to later redeploy anti-Catholic rhetoric against the British themselves. Throughout this long history, fear of Catholics remained a constant backdrop in the American Protestant consciousness. At the same time, antipopery had a history: its meanings and implications changed depending on the larger context. A fearful colonist in early Virginia acted very different from a fearful settler in the Pennsylvania backcountry in 1763, even though both would have used the same rhetoric to describe their fear.

In addition, the study of early American antipopery helps us understand the relationship between rhetoric, law, and practice in North America's religious development.[5] Early modern antipopery was above all a language, a rhetorical tool used by Protestants to impose order on a very complicated world. Of course, this rhetoric had direct consequences for people's lives: it inspired the creation of penal legislation that criminalized Catholic worship in many parts of the British world and enabled agents of the state and ordinary people to commit shocking acts of discrimination, both against Catholics and those people—Indians, Quakers, slaves, and many others—whom Protestants suspected of Catholic leanings. At the same time, however, the study of early American antipopery demonstrates that there was no necessary line between rhetorical vitriol, legal discrimination, and bad treatment. Not every Protestant jurisdiction imposed penal laws and many of those laws that were in place remained unenforced. Protestants who believed in the existence of diabolical popish conspiracies could still do business with Roman Catholics or even be friends with their Catholic neighbors. In other words, tolerance and intolerance were not mutually exclusive, and this is a contradiction that deserves more sustained investigation.[6]

In the Shadow of New Spain, 1556–1660

The first lasting European settlement in North America was born in an orgy of confessional violence. During the 1560s, French Huguenots attempted to settle the southeastern coast of the continent, the region known to the Spanish as La Florida. Funded by the Protestant Admiral Gaspard de Coligny, the new colony's founders intended to create a French Protestant bastion in the New World, one that would act as a counter to the established Spanish Catholic settlements to the south. Unfortunately for the Huguenots the powerful Spaniards were in no mood to surrender a territory they considered theirs by virtue of papal donation and previous exploration. In 1565 the Spanish king sent an expedition under Pedro Menéndez de Aviles to deal with the French interlopers.[7]

The result was a scene so violent that one historian has termed it "St.

Bartholomew in America," a reference to the Catholic massacres of Protestants in Paris in 1577. After landing on the feast day of St. Augustine and blessing the new settlement, Menéndez set out to defeat the "Lutheran" heretics. The Spanish troops stormed the town without challenge and killed several hundred, sparing only the women and children and those, like the colony's governor René Goulaine de Laudonnière, lucky enough to escape into the woods. Several days later Menéndez located another group of Frenchmen who had shipwrecked just south of St. Augustine at a place known since as Matanzas ("slaughter") Inlet. After the men surrendered without a fight, the Spanish commander decided to put them to death anyway, save the few Catholics among them, "because they were Lutherans and enemies of our Holy Catholic faith."[8]

The violent origins of Spanish Florida serve as a convenient place to begin the story of imperial competition for North America. From the very beginning, settlement of the continent reflected geopolitical rivalries with strong religious implications. For most of the sixteenth century, Spain and Portugal dominated the Americas, with their rivals scrambling to establish marginal bases, especially in strategic locations alongside the route of the "treasure fleet" that brought the wealth of the Indies back to Spain. In addition to being the world's foremost power, Habsburg Spain also took on the mantle as the defender of the Roman Catholic faith. Thus political rivalries between Spain and its challengers often took on a religious hue. In the Netherlands, for example, the Calvinist states of the north fought a bloody war against Habsburg domination, while England, after the accession of Elizabeth, engaged in a cold war against the Spanish that briefly became hot during the showdown with the armada in 1588.

This context of religiously informed imperial rivalries also affected the exploration and settlement of the New World, but not in uniform ways. The sixteenth century did not witness a simple struggle between Catholic states and Protestant states, since state involvement in overseas endeavors remained tepid at best. Instead, coalitions of Protestants mounted expeditions, usually with only the nominal approval of their monarchs, and collaborated with coreligionists of other nationalities to an extent that historians, focused on nationally defined colonization efforts, have rarely appreciated. In the 1550s and 1560s, French Huguenots led the Protestant cause in America with their short-lived settlements in Brazil and Carolina, but they always viewed themselves—at least the Protestants who formed the majority of the projects' backers—as members of a coalition that stretched beyond France. Jean Ribault, the leader of the first failed colony in Carolina who met his end at the Matanzas massacre, looked for aid in Elizabethan England. And so, it is not surprising that the colony's bloody denouement resounded in England and the Netherlands just as it did in France.[9]

Indeed, the founding of St. Augustine became one of the events that inspired an upsurge in Protestant colonial projects during the late 1500s. Protestants who escaped the massacre wrote about their experiences in both French and English, and these reports were joined with Bartolomé de las Casas's denunciation of Spanish cruelty toward the Indians and Dutch reports of the duke of Alva's actions in the Low Countries as planks in the "Black Legend" of Spanish Catholic cruelty. The colonization effort, therefore, became another way to resist Spanish plans for "universal monarchy." While the particular theology of antipopery—driven most of all in England by the apocalyptic writings of John Foxe and John Bale—impacted popular beliefs, the colonial projectors preferred a less theological and more political brand of anti-Catholic rhetoric. They stressed the practical benefits of colonization, including the economic rewards, but they almost always couched their rhetoric in a larger religious context.[10]

By the 1580s it was the English, rather than the French or Dutch, who became the most daring challengers of Spanish pretensions in North America. They did so as self-conscious members of an embattled Protestant coalition. Sir Humphrey Gilbert, a gentleman who led Elizabethan colonization efforts in both Ireland and America, promoted colonization as one way to "annoy the king of Spain," and made clear that the main justification for annoying him was that his "Catholic majesty" was in fact an agent of Antichrist. And even as he urged Elizabeth to take the lead in this effort, he also reminded her to "First . . . seeke the kingdome of heaven" by forging alliances with Protestant princes and challenging those who "are at open and professed warres with god himselfe," meaning the Spanish and their allies.[11]

It was the famous projector Richard Hakluyt, however, who explicitly defined English colonization as "a great bridle to the Indies of the kinge of Spaine." In his most explicit defense of English colonization, Hakluyt adopted the familiar binary language that inflected Protestant critiques of Catholicism, calling for a Protestant brand of colonialism that served as a perfect mirror of the Catholic Indies. The Spanish empire, Hakluyt claimed, pretended to be for the benefit of Christ, but that was just pretense; like the Roman Catholic Church, the Spanish aimed at "filthy lucre," and they used a combination of trickery and abject cruelty to keep the people of the Americas in "greate tyrannie." Following Las Casas, Hakluyt focused on cruelty toward the Indians: the Spaniards "teare them in peces, kill them, martir them, afflicte them, tormente them and destroye them by straunge sortes of cruelties." The hypothetical Reformed empire, on the other hand, would possess the highest of motives. Its chief aim would be "the gayninge of the soules of millions of those wretched people, the reducinge of them from darkness to lighte, from falshoodde to truthe, from dombe Idolls to the lyvinge god, from the depe pitt of hell to the highest heavens." Moreover, Protestants could expect to be greeted as liberators by the grateful natives; after all, the two peoples were partners in suffering, as Spanish cruelties in America perfectly matched those used by Catholics during the Marian persecutions in England and the Dutch Revolt. The "western discoverie" would help to spread the "gospele of Christe." If it also served to enrich the Queen of England and her subjects, and provide employment for the poor, that was all the better.[12]

As numerous historians have noted, the earliest English settlements in Virginia bore the stamp of Hakluyt's vision. The first governor of the failed colony at Roanoke, Ralph Lane, viewed the colony as a challenge to Spain, which he called "the swoorde of that Antychryste of Rome and hys sect." While settlers under Lane tried to build a permanent English presence in Virginia, sea dogs like Sir Francis Drake wreaked havoc on Spanish shipping and settlement throughout the Americas in a privateering campaign with significant religious implications. These became clear in Drake's 1584 sack of St. Augustine, the town built on the blood of the French martyrs two decades before. Drake's fleet learned they had captured the town when a French Protestant prisoner rowed out to the ship playing "the tune of the Prince of Orange his song" on a fife. Even thousands of miles across the ocean, the standard of Europe's Protestant hero, the martyred Dutch stadholder, bound coreligionists of different nationalities together against a common Catholic enemy.[13]

Seventeenth-century colonial projects retained much of the official rhetoric of the late 1500s. While England and Spain were at peace during the reign of James I, official justifications of the early settlement of North America abounded in apocalyptic, anti-Catholic language, which was newly resurgent after the Gunpowder Plot by Catholics to kill the king and blow up Parliament in 1605. As one historian has noted, a "militant internationalist Protestant ideology" served to justify colonial expansion in Virginia as well as New England and the Caribbean. According to a minister preaching to a group of Virginia Company investors in 1610, for instance, the purpose of the colony was not "present profit," which was likely to be scant anyway, but "the destruction of the devils kingdom, and the propagation of the gospel."[14]

From this perspective, the militant Protestantism of the founders of New England appears to be merely a continuation of earlier endeavors. True to form, the Puritans who settled the region justified their mission partly as a challenge to Spain. Some of their coreligionists aimed closer to the heart of the Spanish enterprise, establishing a plantation colony on Providence Island in the Western Caribbean off the coast of present-day Nicaragua. While the Puritans continued the anti-Catholic colonization efforts of their Huguenot, Virginian, and Dutch forbears, however, the English state abandoned the mission, adopting a new style of Protestant worship under Archbishop William Laud that took a much softer line against the Roman church. As a result, from the 1630s through the execution of Charles I in 1649, the most militant anti-Catholics in England as well as the colonies were often dissidents, using the language of antipopery against a church and king that seemed insufficiently Protestant.[15]

In a colonial context, perhaps the most alarming sign of the king's de facto toleration of popery appeared in the foundation of Maryland. In 1629 George Calvert, Lord Baltimore, received a royal patent to settle the region of Chesapeake Bay north of Virginia. The patent caused controversy not just because some settlers from Virginia already lived in the area, but also because Calvert, a former secretary of state, was a well-known Catholic and partly intended the colony as a place where English Catholics could avoid the strictures of England's penal laws criminalizing their faith. Though few actual Catholics ended up in the colony, it became a flashpoint for confessional conflict in North America during the mid-1600s and many of the fears that emerged there later reappeared in other parts of the continent.[16]

The first stirrings of trouble in Maryland occurred during the heat of England's mid-century Civil War. On two occasions, opponents of the Catholic proprietor—now Cecil Calvert, the original grantee's son—organized rebellions designed to place the colony in Protestant hands, often with the assistance of Virginians. They claimed that Baltimore intended to create a "receptacle for Papists, and Priests, and Jesuits," and that he even intended to bring 2,000 Irish to the colony who "would not leave a Bible in Maryland"—surely an alarming prospect only a decade after Catholics had risen up against Protestants in the Irish Rebellion of 1641. Colonial agent Leonard Strong was even more blunt when he described the series of events that led a cadre of Protestants to throw off the Lord's authority, claiming that Baltimore required subjects in Maryland to "countenance and uphold Antichrist," meaning the Catholic Church. Strong described Baltimore's willingness to use tyrannical force to ensure his enemies' submission, even to the extent of employing Indians. When proprietary forces faced off against Protestant dissidents in the "Battle of the Severn" in 1655, according to Strong, "the Indians were resolved in themselves, or set on by the popish faction, or rather both together to fall upon us: as indeed after the fight they did, besetting houses, killing one man, and taking another prisoner."[17]

While Baltimore managed, through clever strategizing, to regain his colony, religious tensions persisted. In the wake of Bacon's Rebellion in neighboring Virginia in 1676, opponents of the new Lord Baltimore, Charles Calvert, sent an appeal to England that expressed many of the fears that would become commonplace around the colonies in the next decade. The "Complaint from Heaven" represented Baltimore as a partner in a global Catholic design: "the platt form is, Pope Jesuit determined to over terne Engl[an]d with feyer, sword and distractions within themselves, and by the Maryland Papists, to drive us Protestants to Purgatory . . . with the help of French spirits from Canada." The petition used the Catholic plot to explain recent attacks by Susquehanna Indians, as well as the unwillingness of Baltimore and Virginia Governor Sir William Berkeley to meet the Indian threat. The complaint also described a plan by Jesuits to infiltrate the colonies by sending priests in disguise. "These blake spirits disperse themselves all over the Country in America," the writers claimed, and held secret correspondence with French Jesuits, plotting destruction for American Protestants. Within a decade these peculiar American fears—of a French and Indian plot to destroy Protestant America—had spread around the colonies and sparked a major political transformation.[18]

The French Threat, Indians, and Empire, 1675–1715

During the last years of the 1600s, early Americans experienced a great fear, a massive panic over a popish threat that transformed colonial politics. This fear originated in the rise of Louis XIV's France as a great power. In 1672 the Sun King's massive armies overran the Netherlands, once the vanguard of the international Protestant cause. At the same time, the king began to chip away at the liberties of France's Huguenot minority, culminating in the Revocation of the Edict of Nantes in 1685. Louis XIV's treatment of his neighbors and subjects proved especially distressing for English Protestants. In the eyes of critics, the Stuart King Charles II showed a predilection toward French-style absolutist government, and his brother and heir James, duke of York, was an open Catholic. By 1676, the Whig poet and politician Andrew Marvell warned the English nation of the ongoing plan "to change the lawfull Government of England into an absolute Tyranny, and to convert the established Protestant Religion into downright Popery." This international context made the rumors that circulated in 1678 especially worrisome. A former Jesuit novice named Titus Oates spread reports of a "horrid Popish Plot" to kill the king, burn the city of London, and force the city's inhabitants to convert to popery. While completely fictional, the plot struck a nerve among nervous Protestants and led to a period of political unrest that culminated in an unsuccessful attempt to exclude the Catholic duke of York from the line of succession.[19]

While confessional strife abounded in Europe, the American colonies experienced problems of a different sort. During the mid-1670s relations between natives and newcomers took a particularly violent turn. In addition to the skirmishes in Virginia that led to Bacon's Rebellion, a coalition of Algonquians under the leadership of the Wampanoag sachem King Philip challenged New England, leading to a bloody conflict that shattered the region's fragile racial balance. As early as 1676 some New Englanders had begun to blame their Indian troubles on "vagrant and Jesuitical priests" who had worked for years "to exasperate the Indians against the English, and to bring them into a confederacy, and that they were promised supplies from France, and other parts, to extirpate the English Nation out of the Continent of America." These fears connected local troubles on the frontier to the alarmist rumors coming in from Europe, right down to the involvement of the vanguard of the popish cause, the French king. By the time that the Dutch travelers Jasper Danckaerts and Peter Sluyter traveled the colonies in 1679–1680, they discovered similar fears from Maryland to Boston. In New York and the Chesapeake colonists expressed fear that Jesuits would inspire an "outbreak" among the Indians, while in Boston some inhabitants "declared we [Danckaerts and Sluyter] were French emissaries going through the land to spy it out" and refused to offer lodging to the travelers.[20]

In the colonies, as in England, fears of Catholic machinations contributed to political instability. Imperial officials were in the process of reforming the administration of the empire, attempting to bring the colonies under closer supervision. In such a highly charged atmosphere, some colonial subjects were prone to see popish plotting in even the mildest attempts at centralization. In New Hampshire, for instance, a new royal governor named Edward Cranfield feuded with the local assembly and called for a fast day to commemorate the execution of Charles I, convincing an assemblyman named Edward Gove that the governor "was a papist and intended to bring in popery." In this case, Gove attempted a half-baked armed insurrection against the governor and ended up in the Tower of London, but the rebel's views, if not his tactics, spread around New England during the 1680s. By the middle of the decade royal officials had escalated their campaign against colonial "liberties," and many Anglo-American subjects had become convinced that imperial reforms, like Indian attacks, were connected to the Catholic "plot to bring us low."[21]

The Protestant interest reached its nadir in 1685 when James II became king, floods of Huguenot and dissenting refugees arrived in the colonies, and the crown established the autocratic Dominion of New England in place of the old Massachusetts commonwealth. The forces of popery seemed to be waxing in America as well as Europe, prompting some ministers to preach about the duty to resist ungodly rulers. The stage was set for an unprecedented outburst of anti-Catholic energy around the colonies, but it took a combination of trouble in the backcountry and revolution in England to finally push matters to a crisis.[22]

The political crisis began with a series of violent episodes in western Massachusetts and Maine during summer 1688. Enemy Indians killed several English settlers and allied natives in an assault that resembled those of the past, but with one important difference. According to one witness, the perpetrators said that "we live in Canada" and "are going to fight by ordre off the Governr off Canida" in retaliation for attacks by the English-allied Iroquois League. The evidence appeared indisputable. The two planks of the larger plot—one European and orchestrated by the French, the other American and led by enemy Indians—had coalesced on the edges of New England. Frightened subjects demanded that their leaders act to protect them from the enemy and the new royal governor, an experienced military hand named Sir Edmund Andros, formed an expedition to meet the threat.[23]

The military expedition only served to make matters worse. The governor impressed hundreds of young men from Massachusetts towns, leaving them undefended and exposed, and the governor's men failed to locate a single enemy Indian. At the same time, soldiers on the front spread reports of bad treatment at the hands of their English commanders—some of whom were "papists"—as well as suspicious statements suggesting that the leaders of the Dominion of New England aimed to betray the country to a "foreign power." Finally, news circulated of the Catholic king's troubles at home and of a possible invasion by James II's daughter Mary and her Protestant husband William of Orange. By February, when colonists learned that James II had fled to France, they believed they understood the situation. The deposed king was using his representatives to deliver his former American colonies to his French protector, with the help of Indian and Irish shock troops.[24]

During spring 1689, virulent rumors of this nature circulated around the English colonies. In the town of Sudbury, Massachusetts, an Indian told his English neighbors that the governor had courted the Christian Indians to join a French and Irish army in attacking Boston, giving the Indians "a booke that was better than the bible" that contained pictures of the Virgin Mary and the twelve apostles. Andros claimed that "all that would not turn to the governor['s] reledgon and owne that booke should be destroyed." Further south in New York, a Dutch colonist repeated an almost identical story, charging Andros with employing Mohawk Indians to invade Manhattan, while settlers in the Potomac Valley accused Catholics in Maryland of contracting with "Canada Indians" to murder the region's Protestants. In all three regions, the rumors caused political uprisings. On April 18 thousands of Bostonians took to the streets and forced the governor to hand over authority to a "committee of safety," claiming that they acted to thwart a long-time popish plot against New England, while a month later a group of militia commanders took control of New York's fort to protect it from attack by papists. Finally, in July, the militia captain John Coode led a group of Marylanders in storming St. Mary's City, putting a final end to the Calvert family's experiment in Catholic rule.[25]

The uprisings of 1689 proved important milestones in the development of American anti-Catholicism. In the short term, they brought anti-Catholic zealots into power in three English colonies, leading to a period of intense legal discrimination against the region's few Roman Catholics. During the 1690s colonial legislatures enacted or renewed laws against the practice of Catholicism, while in some places, like Jacob Leisler's New York, officials persecuted and jailed even those Protestants who expressed sympathy or support for Catholics. Yet this spasm of repression was not the most lasting effect of the rebellions. The Glorious Revolution also suggested that antipopery could be a force for unity rather than division in the colonies, that it could bind the continent's diverse subjects into an imperial coalition led by the Protestant heroes William and Mary, and directed against Catholic France.[26]

The seeds of this newfound imperial cohesion appeared during the war between England and France—the War of the League of Augsburg, King William's War in North America—that lasted for much of the 1690s. In the face of a dire external threat, Anglo-Americans began to rethink their feelings about imperial centralization and they increasingly used the language of Catholic conspiracies to justify their newfound patriotism. A typical expression came from Silvanus Davis, a magistrate from Maine who spent several years as a prisoner in Quebec during the war's earlier years. His captivity made Davis a believer in the evils of popery. Through conversations with the French governor Louis Buade, comte de Frontenac, Davis became convinced that "there was a papist designe against the prodestan Intrest in New Engeland as in other parts of the world," and that the only way to defeat this design was for all good Protestants to band together against the common enemy.[27]

During the 1690s, this anti-Catholic nationalism took hold throughout the colonies, but especially in the Northeastern communities most exposed to French and Indian attacks. The most original expressions of this sentiment appeared in Indian captivity narratives, a new literary form that combined fears of religious and racial outsiders. The narratives vividly described a contest for North America between heroic Protestants and an Antichristian enemy composed of French Catholic demagogues and their violent Indian servants. The captives, meanwhile, overcame these hardships by holding fast to their faith. For instance, when Hannah Swarton's French captors entreated her to "turn *Papist*," she battled them with scripture, bringing up biblical passages that contradicted Roman Catholic beliefs and practices. Captives among the Indians resisted in different ways. Two women named Hannah Dustan and Mary Neff, for instance, killed and scalped their Indian captors on the way to New France, returning to a hero's welcome in Boston—and literary immortality at the hands of Cotton Mather.[28]

At the same time, some imperial officials began to use antipopery to fashion a new imperial political culture. One of the pioneers in the practice was Richard Coote, earl of Bellomont, an Irish peer who served as governor of Massachusetts, New York, and New Hampshire from 1697 to 1701. Bellomont believed the colonies to be targeted by a perfidious enemy and he identified Jesuit priests in the backcountry as the primary threat. While the Indians constituted "a cruel and perfidious enemy in their own nature," they had been "taught and encouraged to be more so by the Jesuits and other popish Missionaries from France," who instructed their proselytes to "kill your people treacherously," as he told New Hampshire legislators. Bellomont initiated a campaign to chase the Jesuits out of the backcountry, both by making their residence in his provinces illegal and by attempting to arrest some of the missionaries. At the same time, Bellomont stressed to colonial subjects the virtues of King William and the English empire as defenders of the faith. In one speech to the Massachusetts Assembly, Bellomont lauded the king as "the Glorious Instrument of Our Deliverance from the Pitious Fetters and Chains of Popery and Tyranny which had almost overwhelmed our Consciences, and Subverted all our Civil Rights." In an answer to one of Bellomont's speeches the Massachusetts representatives echoed his sentiments, calling William "our most Glorious Deliverer under GOD, from Popery and Slavery; Circumstances most intolerable and odious to true *Englishmen*, above any men in the World."[29]

The decades surrounding the Glorious Revolution witnessed a wholesale transformation of the political and religious landscape of early America. A patchwork of competing colonies loosely attached to a number of European nations had been reduced to a contest between the French and English empires, with Indian nations perched uncomfortably between the two. Moreover, people on the English side of the divide had begun to define the struggle as a religious one, a battle for the soul of the continent. This clash of civilizations would only become more intense during the first half of the next century, when the French emerged as a unifying enemy even as British Americans dealt with unprecedented religious diversity within the colonies.

Papists and Protestants in Provincial America

During the first sixty years of the eighteenth century, antipopery functioned as an ideological glue holding the Anglo-American empire together. During this period, as numerous historians have noted, the colonies became more self-consciously English than they had ever been before. Royal government and common law courts predominated in most colonies, while colonists became voracious consumers of English manufactured goods. In addition, communication networks across the Atlantic improved, allowing Americans to keep close track of European events. In addition to these legal and economic changes, the colonies developed a new political and religious culture, defined by a militant but ecumenical Protestantism and a robust provincial nationalism. This culture rested on opposition to Catholic France, but also developed a distinctly American wrinkle, as Protestant Americans increasingly used the language of antipopery to define people of other races, whether African slaves or native Americans, as inassimilable outsiders unable to become proper British subjects.[30]

The most prominent feature of provincial political culture was a love for the king and the empire that stretched from the elite to popular level in every colony. This monarchism, however, was explicitly based on the monarch's identity as the defender of the international Protestant cause. On the death of William III in 1702, for instance, one New England minister crafted an elegy linking love of the king to his role in the Glorious Revolution, when the colonies were "quite depriv'd of *Liberty* and *Property*," and "sinking under *Arbitrary Power* and *Tyranny*; almost overwhelm'd with *Popery* and *Slavery*." In that dire circumstance this "Illustrious and Noble Prince . . . came over the sea to help them," effectively turning New Englanders into royalists of a sort. This sentiment also prevailed following the Hanoverian succession in 1715, wherein George I and his progeny earned the throne because they, unlike nearly fifty more direct heirs, were not Catholic.[31]

The same Protestant-inflected monarchism became especially clear during moments of political crisis such as the Jacobite "risings" of 1715 and 1745. On both of those occasions, the heirs of the deposed Stuart dynasty attempted to regain the throne by mounting invasions of the Scottish Highlands. In neither case did the Jacobites—as loyalists to the old line were known—come close to triumphing, but they did provoke nervous displays of loyalty and anti-Catholic vitriol, which appeared in somewhat exaggerated form in the colonies. In New England, for instance, popular ministers such as Benjamin Colman railed against the plot to prop up "a popish Pretender," and underscored the region's "Zeal and Fidelity to the PROTESTANT SUCCESSION, the peaceful reign of the KING, and the true interests of the Nation as to their Civil and Religious Rights." Thirty years later, the evangelist George Whitfield struck a similar note, but with more menacing language, speculating that a Jacobite victory would have brought "whole swarms of monks, Dominicans and friars," who "like so many locusts, [would] have overspread and plagued the nation."[32]

While public figures expressed their loyalty in sermons and print, ordinary people established traditions of their own. The most famous ceremony of imperial belonging appeared in Boston and other colonial cities each November 5, the anniversary of Guy Fawkes's unsuccessful attempt to assassinate the king and members of Parliament in 1605. The date had served as an occasional holiday during the seventeenth century—especially among members of the Whig opposition during the 1680s—but increased in prominence after 1688, in part because William of Orange's landing also occurred on that date. In the colonies, and especially in urban centers, Pope's Day celebrations allowed ordinary people to express their love for the monarch, their antipathy toward the pope (and often the Pretender as well), and engage in some of the ritual inversion common among plebeian elements in early modern Europe. In Boston and other cities crowds of mechanics and laborers constructed effigies of the pope and the Pretender, paraded them around town, and burned them in effigy, sometimes accompanied by a giant, choreographed brawl. While historians have noted the subversive potential of the celebrations—which inverted authority in the same way that Carnival celebrations did in Catholic Europe—they also clearly supported imperial authority as ordinary people declared their allegiance to an empire that they believed would defend them from popish enemies.[33]

If antipopery served to make the colonies more English, it also made them Protestant, but in a different way than it had in the seventeenth century. Somewhat paradoxically, antipathy toward Catholicism actually furthered the growth of toleration and Protestant ecumenism in the colonies. This process can be detected in another sermon on the death of a king, this one preached by Cotton Mather on the occasion of Louis XIV's demise in 1715. Mather used the happy occasion not just to condemn the errors of popery, but specifically to condemn the late king's record as a persecutor. "The Jawes of the fiercest *Crocodile*," he spoke, "would have been full of *Tender Mercies*, in Comparison of his Merciless *Cruelties*." As a result, good Protestants needed to attempt to do the opposite, to be more lenient in overlooking theological differences, especially among Protestants. "This I am sure of," Mather concluded at the end of his sermon, "There is a Day coming, when the *Spirit of Persecution* shall be *shaken* out of the Church; and all *Parties* of *Christians*, even the *Uppermost*, as well as the rest everywhere, shall be ashamed of it: *Persecuting Laws*, and *Persecuting Tests*, will be no more known in the World."[34]

One of the key applications of this doctrine concerned the acceptance of Protestant refugees from the far corners of the world. During the first decades of the eighteenth century vast numbers of newcomers from around Europe arrived in the colonies, beginning with the Huguenot refugees who fled the

Sun King's persecution during the 1680s, and continuing with the Palatine migrants to New York in 1709 and the Salzburgers, expelled from their homes in dramatic fashion in 1735 and eventually welcomed in the new colony of Georgia. These migrants increased the level of religious and ethnic diversity in the colonies, and even beyond the places they settled—in Boston, for example—the same spirit of cooperation between Protestants led to a markedly different religious culture. By 1722, when John Bonner published a map of Boston, the old Puritan capital had four Congregational churches of varying degrees of orthodoxy, a French church, a Baptist one, an Anglican one, and a Quaker meeting house. The days of official persecution of Protestant dissenters were largely over—thanks in large part to the need to unite against the persecuting papists.[35]

If antipopery encouraged cohesion and ecumenism in the heart of English America, it operated as a far more destructive force on the margins. Indeed, colonial subjects and imperial overlords collaborated in creating new definitions of imperial identity that defined any number of groups—including actual Roman Catholics, ethnic outsiders, and especially Indians and slaves—as people who could never enjoy the liberties of British subjects. This violent side of provincial antipopery appeared most clearly on the northern and southern frontiers, but could easily travel to other regions during times of particular crisis. In essence, many Protestants believed that their freedom of conscience could only be preserved by violently confronting those who would destroy that liberty beyond its borders.

The southern borderlands between Spanish Florida and English South Carolina provided one flashpoint for conflict. As early as the 1690s Carolinians complained that the Spanish colony was a troublesome neighbor. Officials in Florida maintained a network of Franciscan Indian missions and also offered sanctuary to escaped slaves, who they hoped to convert to Catholicism. The peace between Spain and England forced English Carolinians to acquiesce until 1702, when the coming of the War of the Spanish Succession turned the region into a war zone. English and Yamasee expeditions destroyed the Catholic missions in the region, selling thousands of "Spanish Indians" into slavery. Despite their efforts, the slave defections only increased, especially after the foundation of the black town of St. Teresa de Mose north of St. Augustine in 1738. The town functioned as both a mission and a military outpost manned by former slaves, making it doubly intimidating to English observers in the mid-1700s.[36]

In summer 1739, fears escalated with the arrival of a stranger in the new town of Savannah, Georgia. The newcomer first claimed to be a Jew, then a German, but finally admitted he was "born in Old Spain." The man continued on his way, but events several months later in South Carolina led Georgians to rethink the encounter. A group of slaves near the Stono River had risen up against their masters, killing several and heading south toward Florida before being apprehended by the militia. In the new reading, the stranger must have been "corrupting the Negroes of Carolina" to rebellion—a relatively new adaptation of antipopery that claimed that blacks, like Indians, were naturally susceptible to the advances of papists. Another source of concern was the fact that many of the slaves came from Angola, where "the Jesuits have a Mission and School . . . and many Thousands of the Negroes there profess the Roman Catholic Religion." In fact, the slaves probably came from the Kingdom of Kongo, a part of Africa that had developed its own Catholic tradition, as well as military traditions that the Africans called on during their revolt. No one can know if the rebel slaves were actual Catholics, but frightened planters definitely *thought* they were. By the time Britain and Spain went to war in the War of Jenkins' Ear that year, Africans had joined the pantheon of "popish" enemies.[37]

These fears of a black fifth column spread to other parts of the colonies. In 1740 Georgia Governor James Oglethorpe circulated reports, ostensibly originating from Indians in the vicinity of St. Augustine, that "the Spaniards had employed emissaries to burn all the magazines and considerable towns in the English North America," and that priests in disguise—like the Jewish-German-Spaniard in Savannah—were lurking and insinuating into the good graces of weak-minded people around British America. Thus the alarm when a number of suspicious fires appeared around New York City in 1741 and some slaves were implicated in setting them. When rumors of a conspiracy surfaced, officials could not accept that "these silly unthinking creatures could of themselves have contrived and carried on so deep, so direful and destructive a scheme." They naturally assumed that Spanish papists were behind the design.[38]

In the legal proceedings that followed, paranoid fears of popery served as a prominent backdrop in one of the most disturbing episodes in early American history. Prosecutors located the conspiracy in the long history of popish intrigue during the trial of John Ury, a schoolteacher identified as a "popish priest" who encouraged slaves to rebel and claimed that "he could forgive sins." The trial recycled a number of standard anti-Catholic arguments. Roman Catholics, according to the prosecutor, "hold it not only lawful but meritorious to kill and destroy all that differ in opinion from them," and held a particular goal to destroy "the Northern heresy." Their first method was to trick the laity into serving the church through "juggling tricks," before moving on to easier targets such as slaves. Moreover, this latest plot was just one in a string of outrages, from the "tragical instances of popish cruelty" in the Piedmont during the 1600s, the massacres in Paris, "the horrible slaughters of the duke d'Alba" in the Netherlands, and in general "that ocean of foreign blood with which the scarlet whore hath made herself perpetually drunk." Protestants in New York added more blood to the ocean, executing thirty slaves and four whites, some of whom were burned at the stake.[39]

While Spaniards and slaves threatened the Southeast, French and Indians predominated in much of the rest of the continent, and the conflict grew particularly heated in the northeastern borderlands. From the Province of Maine to the old French colony of Acadia, "popish Indians," missionaries, and French habitants forged powerful alliances, occasionally attacking English communities in terrifying assaults that in turn spawned violent reprisals. The culture of violence in the region was supported by an ideological antipopery that called on Protestants to resist popish enemies and spread their faith abroad—by violence if necessary. An authority on many matters in eighteenth-century New England, Cotton Mather wrote the most about these "*Popish Heathens*," who used violence against innocents, and the "*Papists*," who finished the work by "debauch[ing] them into the *Delusions* and *Idolatries* of Popery." The struggle called for some predictable sacrifices: more Bible-reading among the laity; more missionary work by Protestants; and a new militancy among both ordinary people and the region's leaders.[40]

One key result of this militancy was the conquest of the French colony of Acadia in 1710, which became the province of Nova Scotia. The new colony provided a particular challenge to imperial administrators, as it retained a sizable population of French-speaking Catholics, Acadian "neutrals" guaranteed the freedom to stay and practice their faith by the Treaty of Utrecht of 1713. Their continued residence on the edge of the British Empire caused consternation for the colony's leaders. From the moment they took control, British officials worried that the neutral Acadians could act as spies for France. This concern was exacerbated by the presence of Mi'kmaq Indians and a number of Jesuit priests such as Jean Le Loutre, a man described in one instance as a "wicked monster" who was "more inhumane and Savage than the natural Savages."[41]

The three ethnic groups coexisted uneasily during the long peace between 1715 and 1744, but the renewal of war complicated relations. Nova Scotia's leaders encouraged emigration of dependable Protestants to the region, especially New Englanders with their "knowledge of cultivating new lands, well rooted allegiance, and fondness for the Protestant religion." At the same time, officials came closer to endorsing a plan that had been discussed for decades: the removal and dispersion of the province's French Catholics, whose religious and ethnic ties made them impossible to trust during wartime. The Acadians were "French Bigots," according to Massachusetts Governor William Shirley, who would "cut our own People's Throats whenever the Priest shall consecrate the Knife." In 1755, British officials finally decided to remove the Acadians, subsequently dispossessing 7,000 people and propelling them into a makeshift diaspora around the British colonies. Alongside the dead of New York and Stono, the migrants became some of the most visible casualties of early American antipopery—human reminders of the limits of toleration and ecumenism.[42]

The political and religious culture of provincial British America revolved to a great extent around the fear of Catholics—and particularly of the French empire and its Spanish, Indian, and African allies. This fear, shared by colonists from Maine to Georgia, helps explain some of the seeming paradoxes of colonial life. For instance, fears of popery inspired the acceptance of religious outsiders in many parts of North America, while also serving to justify the most vicious violence and discrimination. It bound the colonies more closely to the empire than ever before and inspired massive shows of loyalty, but also cultivated a suspicion of arbitrary power. The political culture of empire depended on the existence of a strong French empire, a behemoth just beyond the borders to remind colonials exactly what they were fighting against. In 1763, at the end of the Seven Years' War, Great Britain defeated France and acquired all of North America east of the Mississippi River. British victory over France brought the provincial era to a sudden close, and changed the nature of the imperial relationship. With the popish enemy gone, the empire itself faced an enemy that was, in part, of its own making.

Toward Revolution

The British victory in the Seven Years' War changed the face of North America. To New Englanders such as Reverend Jonathan Mayhew, it heralded the beginning of a new golden age on the continent. Had the French won, "we should doubtless have been deprived of the free enjoyments of the protestant religion; harrassed, persecuted and butchered, by such blind and furious zealots for the religion of Rome, under the direction of a priesthood and hierarchy." After the conquest of Quebec, the continent could now blossom, leading to "the exalting of these little provinces and colonies, as it were into many kingdoms," though still dependent on "the British empire in Europe." Put simply, colonial subjects hoped to benefit from the conquest. They were confident that the British victory would promote the spread of Protestantism and liberty throughout the continent.[43]

Almost as soon as the war ended, however, British imperial officials adopted a policy toward Catholics that marked a rapid departure from previous practices. The Treaty of Paris brought thousands of new subjects into the empire, not least the 60,000 French Catholics in Canada. Sheer numbers precluded their expulsion. As a result, the British changed their official policy toward Catholicism in the empire almost overnight, from one of active persecution to accommodation. By 1770, British officials were even encouraging Catholic migration from Europe to the colonies. In his ill-fated attempt to set up the colony of New Smyrna in East Florida, for instance, Andrew Turnbull recruited Catholic settlers from Minorca and then set out to acquire priests for them. While a minor colonial project, the irony is startling. Just after the British managed to conquer St. Augustine, that Catholic city built on the blood of the Huguenot martyrs, they invited Catholic settlers with priests in tow to resettle it. Clearly, something had changed in the British Empire.[44]

The formal indication of this new policy came in the Quebec Act of 1774. That parliamentary act came after long deliberations and aimed to stabilize governance in the recently conquered territory. The legislation granted two major concessions to French subjects: it allowed the continuance of civil law, rather than English common law in the province; and it established the Roman Catholic Church. The act displayed a pragmatic approach toward management of the empire, a recognition that different political and religious cultures required their own political constitutions. Ironically, the act came just as the same officials increasingly abandoned compromise with recalcitrant colonists to the south, who were waging their own struggle over the rights of colonists in an imperial system. Consequently, inhabitants of the older colonies interpreted the Quebec Act as a signal of British abandonment of the old ideals of Protestant liberty and Protestant imperialism.[45]

The Quebec Act did not cause the American Revolution. But by providing colonists with an occasion to rehabilitate the anti-Catholic arguments that had proven so critical for their self-understanding for centuries, it allowed American patriots to begin to transfer their old anti-French antipathies toward the British Parliament and ministers. In the eyes of many American Protestants, the Quebec Act operated to prop up both popery and arbitrary government. The governor and council in the new colony had the ability "to tax the colony as they please," to change criminal law, to imprison anyone without just cause. The tyranny of the civil law dovetailed with the spiritual slavery of the Roman Catholic Church. "From the same poisonous root," wrote one pamphleteer, "arises the most horrible religious tyranny, that my mind is capable of conceiving." The Continental Congress protested that "the Legislature of Great-Britain is not authorized by the constitution to establish a religion, fraught with sanguinary and impious tenets, or, to erect an arbitrary form of government, in any quarter of the globe." They feared a design to separate Canada from the colonies and populate it with "Catholic emigrants from Europe" so that it "might become formidable to us, and on occasion, be fit instruments in the hands of power, to reduce the ancient free Protestant Colonies to the same state of slavery with themselves."[46]

The establishment of popery and arbitrary rule in Quebec, therefore, allowed American revolutionaries to interpret their new contest as just a new chapter in the centuries-long Protestant struggle for America. During the sixteenth century, intrepid Protestants had ventured their lives and fortunes to wrest control of North America from Spanish papists, and they had succeeded against great odds. Then beginning in the late 1600s they faced a new enemy, a terrifying coalition of French and Indians, and after decades of struggle defeated them as well. Then just as peace and Protestantism should have prevailed on the continent, the old imperial overlords appeared as papists in disguise, determined to punish their American subjects "because they will not admit to be Slaves, and are alarmed at the Establishment of Popery and Arbitrary Power in one Half of their Country."[47]

But if the American Revolution allowed patriots to recycle their old anti-Catholic rhetoric, it also came with its share of ironies. By 1778, Americans found themselves allied with the old enemy: Catholic, absolutist France. As a result, Protestants had to alter their rhetoric. No longer could they portray the struggle as one against "popery and slavery," when their key ally was not just Catholic but the very enemy that had served as the blueprint for everything that Protestant Americans detested and feared. Some Americans, however, accepted this irony and attempted to justify it. Elbridge Gerry of

Massachusetts chronicled the "miraculous change in the political world" that led England to despotism and France to the defense of liberty. "The king of Britain [is] aiding the advancement of popery," Gerry wrote, "and the king of France endeavouring to free his people from ecclesiastical power." There was no hypocrisy here: for Gerry the real battle was not against the Catholic Church necessarily, but against any institution that attempted to usurp the throne of Christ by claiming "ecclesiastical power."[48]

The French alliance may not have spelled the end of American anti-popery, but it did change the nature of religious discourse in the new nation. Whatever their dislike of the Catholic faith in particular or centralized churches in general, Americans could no longer define themselves against a Catholic enemy that had not threatened them since the 1760s, and now even defended them from the attacks of a vengeful mother country. The old way of organizing British American political identity—as good Protestants fighting for the control of North America against popish rivals—no longer corresponded to reality, and the leaders of the republic grasped for new languages of political belonging. This was good news, of course, for the small number of Roman Catholic people who lived in the United States, and now enjoyed better treatment and more social recognition than their colonial counterparts could have imagined. Antipathy toward Catholics and Catholicism remained, however, and emerged with a vengeance fifty years later, when boatloads of poor Irish began to crowd into American cities.[49]

Chapter 10

Anti-Semitism, Toleration, and Appreciation

The Changing Relations of Jews and Gentiles in Early America

WILLIAM PENCAK

The status of the small number of Jews in early America from their first arrival in New Amsterdam in the early 1650s until the beginnings of a significant, largely German migration in the 1820s may be best expressed through three interacting concepts: anti-Semitism, toleration, and appreciation. These concepts overlapped in that early American Jews often experienced more than one at once and there was not necessarily a clear chronological progression from prejudice to appreciation. For example, in the colonial era, Jews were tolerated but experienced significant anti-Semitism, particularly from non-elites. They were allowed to live and practice their religion in peace despite popular antipathy toward them and their exclusion from voting or holding public office (except in New York, where imperial officials insisted on it). Yet toleration and popular anti-Semitism coexisted with an elite appreciation of Jews, or philo-Semitism, that developed, as in Europe, among those who worked and socialized with them more or less as equals.

American Jews' overlapping experiences of popular anti-Semitism, toleration, and appreciation continued as social and political contexts changed during the era of the Revolution. For the most part, American Jews were staunchly pro-Revolutionary, which aided their quest for political equality and social acceptance. That quest, coupled with Jewish patriotism, paid significant dividends as Jews acquired the suffrage and eligibility for public office in most states, as well as the public thanks of notable men including George Washington himself.

However, their participation came at a price. As Jews experienced these significant gains in political equality and social appreciation in Revolutionary America, they also suffered important losses, which, ironically, were related to their gains. As Jews acquired political influence, public prejudice against them became more acute. In some quarters, Jews were now perceived as a significant threat to the republic rather than merely an obnoxious yet inconsequential minority. These developments were related to the proliferation of print and a heightened political awareness in all ranks of society, as well as the increasingly democratic ethos of the Revolutionary period. The Revolution expanded the possibilities for lower- and middle-class men to challenge the governing elite with which upper-class Jews were identified. In sum, the seminal event in the founding of the American nation was not an altogether positive development for Jews.

This ambiguity in the Jewish experience continued into the decades of the early republic. The very political involvement Jews could engage in because of their political rights at times provoked the demagogues of an increasingly democratic age to label them a far more serious danger than they ever before been considered. With the extension of democratic rights to poorer citizens and the newly arrived western immigrants (mostly Germans and Scots-Irish), elite politicians could mobilize popular prejudices to hold Jews responsible for the political ills of the new nation, thereby creating a new form of prejudice that I term political anti-Semitism, which questioned the wisdom of allowing Jews to participate in civic life. In this context, political leaders did not hesitate to employ traditional but contradictory stereotypes of Jews—greedy and wealthy, on the one hand, poor and grasping on the other; religiously archaic on the one hand and irreligious on the other. Depending on whom the Jews themselves supported, both political parties, Federalists and anti-Federalists (and their Republican successors) made anti-Semitism an important part of their political rhetoric. With the overwhelming triumph of the Republicans and Thomas Jefferson in the election of 1800, anti-Semitism died out in the public debate for nearly a generation. Yet the traditional stereotypes remained, nursed primarily in Federalist New England. They would visibly reemerge in the 1820s as Jews developed a far more prominent presence in the United States.

Colonial Jews

New York City is the best place to begin tracing the interaction of popular anti-Semitism with elite toleration and appreciation of Jews. It possessed the longest colonial Jewish history, and only here did the Dutch and British imperial elites extend full political rights for Jews. They were allowed to vote and hold public office first because of pressure from powerful Jews in the Dutch West India Company, and then because New York's English proprietor James, the duke of York and future King James II, was a Roman Catholic who made toleration of minorities his general policy. These interventions from above could not end social prejudice, but they did establish an important colonial precedent for the toleration of Jews.

In 1654, the arrival of twenty-three refugees from Brazil in New Netherland led to a situation in which an intolerant local population was forced to acquiesce to toleration.[1] The Dutch West India Company, which ruled both colonies, had welcomed Jewish merchants and money to finance/manage their Brazilian enterprise, which came to an abrupt end at the hands of the Portuguese. Between a third and a half of the approximately 1,500 Europeans in Brazil were Jews, and the main street in Recife was actually named the "Street of the Jews" because so many Jewish merchants lived there.[2] Unlike old Amsterdam, which tolerated Jews, New Amsterdam was settled mostly by Dutch Reformed Calvinists from the rural provinces, whose intolerance was well represented by Governor Peter Stuyvesant. He wrote to the Dutch West India Company within three weeks of the Jews' arrival and demanded their expulsion. Otherwise, these "hateful enemies and blasphemers of the name of Christ," would soon practice "their customary usury and deceitful trading."[3] As Joyce Goodfriend shows in her chapter in this volume, Stuyvesant also had little use for Lutherans and Quakers who sought to practice their faith openly in a settlement whose precarious existence, he believed, required religious conformity.

The leading New Amsterdam Calvinist minister, Johannes Megapolensis, also found the toleration of Jews to be obnoxious. To him, the handful of Jewish merchants who preceded the refugees offered an equally compelling argument for expulsion. Megapolensis claimed that they would not support their impoverished coreligionists economically, as was customary with most churches in Europe and the New World. He lambasted the Jews as "godless rascals" who "have no other God than the mammon of unrighteousness, and no other aim than to get possession of Christian property and to overcome all other merchants by drawing all trade to themselves." Given New Amsterdam's tiny population, even three or four Jewish traders could have excited this fear.[4]

For the Dutch West India Company, however, toleration was an economic necessity. Influenced by Jewish stockholders, five of whom numbered among the major underwriters who had invested at least 30,000 guilders, the company ordered Stuyvesant to allow the Jews to stay. It stressed both the fact that "many of the Jewish nation are principal shareholders" and that the Jews of Brazil had "at all times been faithful and have striven to guard and maintain that place, risking for that purpose their possessions and their blood." As would later be true in the American Revolution, Jews were considered worthy of rights not simply because of equal merit, but because their exertion for the common good went beyond the ordinary.[5]

Yet in the same missive that the company ordered toleration, it also recognized anti-Semitism as the general national sentiment, which needed to be accommodated. In fact, the situation was even more complex, because the company decided to omit any favorable reference to the Jews in its instructions to New Amsterdam (possibly because it also had to placate the town's population and especially the anti-Semitic Stuyvesant, who was its first capable governor). While granting Jews the right to stay and do business, the company told Stuyvesant that "we would have liked to effectuate and fulfill your wishes and request that the new territories should not be allowed to be infected by people of the Jewish nation, for we foresee therefrom the same difficulties which you fear." Stuyvesant also won the concessions that the wealthy Jewish community of old Amsterdam would subsidize their impoverished brethren in the New World, and that the Jews would live together in New Amsterdam in an informal ghetto.[6]

We have scraps of evidence that Stuyvesant's and Megapolensis's anti-Semitism persisted, and that they were shared by the rank-and-file New York Dutch. When Jacob Leisler overthrew colonial governor Edmond Andros in 1689, one of Leisler's prominent followers, Jacob Melyan, equated "a Jew" with "a crook" and criticized Jews for keeping money in their own hands (Jews were often forced to do business among themselves because of anti-Semitic prejudices). And New York Chief Justice William Atwood considered New York Jews prominent enough to be grouped with "some Englishmen, French . . . and some few Dutch who all assumed the name of the English party" to oppose Leisler, whose followers were primarily Dutch. On the other hand, as Joyce Goodfriend shows, Dutch real estate owners and merchants, or members of the elite involved in an international trade, did business with Jews and in general treated them civilly. Under the proprietary rule of the Duke of York (after 1685 King James II) Jews had been tolerated as part of James's plan to woo non-Anglicans, in particular, to secure acceptance of his fellow Roman Catholics. Historian John Murrin has shown that it was primarily upper-class Dutch merchants and farmers who supported this initiative. It thus made sense that the Jews would oppose a government that overthrew one that had treated them well.[7]

Toleration of Jews resumed when Governor Henry Sloughter arrived in 1692 and executed Leisler. This marked the third time New York Jews received powers and privileges from the English that local inhabitants denied them.[8] Throughout the eighteenth century, New York Jews could vote and hold public office, although none were elected to prominent posts.[9] The New York State Constitution of 1777 merely institutionalized the status quo with respect to Jews when it became the first document in the western world formally to proclaim that "free Toleration be forever allowed in the state to all denominations of Christians without preference or distinction and to all Jews, Turks, and Infidels."[10]

Georgia was the only colony besides New York where a relatively large number of Jews suddenly arrived during the colony's infancy. There too, imperial leaders enforced toleration despite local prejudice. The colony's trustees planned Georgia as a utopian experiment that would put prisoners and the poor to work under the government's aegis, and solicited help from wealthy British Jews. This involvement proved unpopular with Gentiles and the invitation to Jews to apply to be settlers was revoked. The Jewish promoters, however, presented the colony with a fait accompli by sending over forty-two colonists on the *William and Sarah*, which arrived in July 1733. These Jews temporarily constituted about a quarter of the infant colony's population, and at once earned the favor of Governor James Oglethorpe when Samuel Nunes Ribiero—the former personal physician of the Grand Inquisitor of Portugal who had been forced to flee when his secret Judaism was discovered—single-handedly ended an epidemic that was decimating the colony through cool baths and homeopathic drinks.[11]

Georgia's trustees soon came to do more than tolerate the Jews: they relied on them as an element of stability amid an unruly population. In 1741 the head trustee, the earl of Egmont, commented that the Jews had "behaved so well as to their morals, peaceableness, and charity, that they were a reproach to the Christian inhabitants," who Oglethorpe termed a "diabolical people" filled with "pride, ignorance, malice, and rapaciousness."[12]

The Christian ministers of Georgia had the opposite reaction: their anti-Semitism grew as the Jews failed to convert. The young John Wesley, the Anglican minister, and Johann Boltzius, the Lutheran pastor who accompanied German immigrants from Salzburg, turned against the Jews when they mistook their initial friendliness for a desire to convert to Christianity. Boltzius, like many anti-Semites, did not trouble himself that his prejudices contradicted each other: he managed to blame the Jews for (among other perceived failings) their exclusivity by keeping Kosher—"they would rather starve than eat meat they do not slaughter themselves"—while at the same time being too willing to indulge in "drinking, gluttony, and dancing" with "people of all nations, races, and religions" at the tavern of the Jew Philip Minis. (Boltzius only mentioned in passing that the same behavior occurred at the two taverns owned by Gentiles.[13])

Unlike the convicts who came to Georgia at the expense of the trustees, Georgia's Jews had arrived with their own resources. They thereby ranked among Georgia's colonial elite from the very first. A similar position was held by Francis Salvador of South Carolina, a young Jew who came to that colony in 1774 to develop backcountry lands and was elected a member of the provincial convention for the Ninety-Sixth District, despite laws forbidding Jews to be elected to public office. As Susan Juster has shown in her chapter in this volume concerning prosecutions for religious crimes, enforcement of religious conformity was intermittent in the colonies and depended on people and circumstance. Where a man such as Salvador could win the favor of his community, his fellow inhabitants welcomed him without reservations. For a trusted and well-respected inhabitant—even a Jewish inhabitant in a mostly Christian colony—such restrictions could be waived.[14] Despite long-held anti-Semitic prejudice, at least a begrudging toleration of Jews prevailed in colonial Georgia, as it had in New York.

Imperial Jews

By the mid-eighteenth century, Jewish merchants had become important figures in the imperial system. But their very appreciation by, and connection to, British authorities led colonial Gentiles to make Jews into scapegoats when the military affairs and imperial relations turned sour. A good proportion of colonial Jews participated at high levels of the British Empire through trade and government service. Most notably, beginning in 1760 and until the American Revolution, the victualing, clothing, and arming of British troops in North America was entrusted to a London syndicate that included Moses Franks as one of its four members. Son of the wealthy merchant Jacob Franks of New York, he had been sent to London to learn commerce from his uncle. Franks then turned military provisioning into a family business. His brother David Franks and Gentile former mayor of Philadelphia William Plumsted took charge of the contracts in Pennsylvania. They in turn subcontracted their business on the frontier to the Jews Joseph Simon of Lancaster and his son-in-law Levy Andrew Levy, along with the Gentile William Trent, who collectively built the first store in Pittsburgh. In New York, Moses's father Jacob and two Gentiles, David's brother-in-law Oliver Delancey and John Watts, handled matters. Three of the four merchants who tended to the British army in Canada were also Jews. Britain entrusted the expansion and preservation of its newly acquired empire in America to Jewish merchants. They did a good job, or they would not have been retained until the American Revolution.[15]

The Jewish merchants' inescapable connections with Indian tribal leaders provoked accusations among the settlers on the Pennsylvania frontier that they were in fact betraying the inhabitants for monetary gain. In 1766, a writer in the German-language newspaper *Der Wochentlichte Philadelphische Staatsbote* attacked the "Jew landlords" as "terrible people who make false claims and purchase land for a small sum of pocket money," then "set upon German plantations" to the "ruin" of the families who lived there. The author thus implicitly compared Jewish landowners to hostile Indians, who had been setting upon the plantations and had only been defeated the previous year at the end of Pontiac's War. David McClure, the Scots-Irish Presbyterian minister at Lancaster, where the frontier trader and land developer Joseph Simon was the wealthiest inhabitant, chimed that while the Jews carefully observed their Sabbath, they "hesitate not to defraud" and "neglect the weightier matters of the Law, as judgment, mercy, and faith." In a perfect example of how elite philo-Semitists would counter popular anti-Semitism, Anglican minister Thomas Barton defended Simon as "worthy and honest," as did Lancaster rifle manufacturer William Henry, who termed him "a Wealthy Jew of High Character." Thus, two of the town's two most prestigious inhabitants, as well connected with the imperial system as Simon himself, took his side.[16]

In mid-eighteenth-century Newport, Rhode Island, the wealthiest inhabitant, Aaron Lopez, was also a Jew. He too fell afoul of popular sentiment while simultaneously garnering the support of tolerant members of the imperial system when he sought enfranchisement. In 1762 he applied for naturalization and the right to vote as a British citizen under a law passed by Parliament in 1740 to encourage emigration to the colonies. The Rhode Island assembly, representing the most democratic colony, where every officeholder was elected annually by all the voters, refused the request. When Lopez appealed to the colony's superior court, it sided with the assembly, stating the naturalization law was for "increasing the number of inhabitants in the plantations, but this colony being already so full of people that many of his majesty's good subjects . . . had removed," there was no need to naturalize more people. Opposition to Lopez may have been anti-Semitic, or it may simply have reflected the fact that the house was dominated by rural farmers and residents of democratic Providence, who would not have taken kindly to Lopez's votes with the more aristocratic merchants of Newport. But Lopez had no trouble gaining his naturalization in Massachusetts, where he owned property and could thus claim residence. There his petition was granted by a superior court that included Peter Oliver, Andrew Oliver, and Thomas Hutchinson, respectively the future chief justice, lieutenant governor, and governor of Massachusetts, all of whom became loyalists. In any event, when Newport's wealthy merchants proved reluctant to oppose British measures following Boston's lead to protest British policy in the mid-1760s, popular leader James Otis was quick to blame their recalcitrance on the city's Jews.[17]

In the 1760s, the potency of anti-Semitic stereotypes was evident among well-established colonial Jews themselves. To preserve their own respectability they were quick to use the features applied to Jews generally to newcomers who were poor and far more "Jewish" in appearance than the assimilated upper class. While not numbering more than a hundred, the new arrivals still doubled the size of the Pennsylvania Jewish community, which was mainly Ashkenazim of German or Eastern European origin. Unlike the elite Jews who were physically indistinguishable from their Gentile counterparts, they wore beards, always kept their heads covered, dressed in long shawls, and, in some cases, spoke only limited English. "We are plagued with a new parcel of Jews," Philadelphia's Mathias Bush wrote to Barnard Gratz while the latter was in England, "pray prevent, what is in your power to hinder, any more of that sort to come." Some of the newcomers were in fact scoundrels—like

Meyer Levy who appeared in Pennsylvania in 1760 to sell over two thousand pounds of goods he had stolen in New York, or Emmanuel Lyon, who persuaded Jews to give him money on the pretense he was a "great scholar and well versed in the Hebrew tongue."[18]

Because new and old Jews could not tolerate each other, Philadelphia and Charleston each hosted two separate Jewish congregations (Philadelphia by the late 1760s, and Charleston by the late 1780s). In New York, Shearith Israel somehow remained united, but there the quarrels were the worst of all. Old members mocked the length of the newcomers' prayer shawls during services, and then the two sides took their disputes outside where words turned to fisticuffs. Jewish merchants sued each other for absurd amounts of money (up to £10,000) based on accusations of cheating and damage to each others' reputations. They bickered over who had precedence in reading the Torah, physically removed women from the prestigious front bench of the upstairs women's gallery, and even set their quarrels before the provincial courts. In anticipation of the American Jewish community in the late nineteenth century, the parties to this dispute have sometimes been considered as Sephardic (assimilated, mostly Iberian) and Ashkenazi (Eastern European newcomers). In fact, while all the first congregations in each city in America followed the Sephardic ritual, most of their members had come from Germany or Eastern Europe.[19] In dealing with newcomers, established Jews, like their friends in the colonial elite in dealing with city artisans or frontier settlers, were unwilling to grant the opportunities they themselves had had years before. Elite Jews were tolerated by the Christian majority (though outside New York they did not have political rights) and did not wish to compromise their privileges by being identified with immigrants with whom they had little in common except their faith.[20]

Revolutionary Jews

The American Revolution enfranchised Jews in many states and led to a greater appreciation of their contributions by the people who worked with them in achieving independence. At the same time, the Revolution altered and intensifed the nature of anti-Semitism. Political rights expanded broadly, making it possible for politicians to appeal to anti-Semitic prejudices to gain office using a new breed of prejudice that can be called *political anti-Semitism*—attacks on the granting of civil and political rights for Jews in political debates. As Jews made important contributions to the new republic, they became more visible—and more closely associated with the Revolutionary elite that came under lower- and middle-class attack. Jews were no longer perceived as being merely greedy and immoral. Their very wealth and intelligence made them real threats to lead other alienated citizens, so their opponents charged, and imperiled what they hoped would be a Christian republic.[21]

Political anti-Semitism appeared first and most vividly in the refusal of Pennsylvania to enfranchise Jews in the Constitution of 1776, which has widely been regarded as the most democratic code of laws produced during the Revolution. Pennsylvania Jews unanimously supported the American Revolution, having previously shared a double victimization with the Philadelphia lower classes and people of the western counties in that they could not participate meaningfully in provincial as well as imperial politics. Yet when the "radicals" overthrew the conservative proprietary government that refused to endorse independence, they wrote into section ten of the constitution an oath of allegiance that disfranchised not only Jews, but also Quakers and all those who in conscience would not swear that both the Old and New Testaments were divinely inspired.[22]

The politician who suggested the Christian oath and built on popular anti-Semitism to ingratiate himself with the revolutionary authorities was Henry Melchior Muhlenberg, the leading Lutheran clergyman in America who was suspected (correctly, it later turned out) of loyalist sympathies. As many others had done before, and many have done since, a man whose own loyalty was doubtful attempted to divert attention from the accusations against him by projecting them onto minorities. Muhlenberg tried to persuade the other Philadelphia ministers to support him, but Anglican Jacob Duché (at that time a Revolutionary) and Presbyterian Francis Alison were content with a mere acknowledgement of divine providence. Only the German Reformed minister Caspar Weyberg, whose English was not good, agreed with Muhlenberg. He next went to the newspapers, arguing that "an Episcopal church, a Presbyterian meeting-house, a Roman Catholic church, a mosque, a synagogue, a heathen temple have now in Pennsylvania all equal privileges! Will it not be an asylum for all fugitive Jesuits [the order had recently been expelled from Spain and Portugal] and outcasts of Europe.... If blasphemers of Christ and the Holy Blessed Trinity, despisers of the revelation and the holy bible may hold public office.... Wo unto the city! Wo unto the land!" Muhlenberg's anxieties resonated with his fellow Pennsylvanians.

Scarcely three months after the Declaration of Independence, the state's constitution marked a significant triumph for intolerance.[23]

Catholics were one focus of Muhlenberg and the Pennsylvania Constitutionalists' ire: as Owen Stanwood notes in the preceding chapter, colonial Americans' hatred of the religion of two nations they had been fighting for nearly a century, Spain and France, only began to dissipate when those two nations came to the aid of the Revolutionary cause. Similarly, the Pennsylvania radicals listened to Muhlenberg's entreaty that "Jews, Turks, Spinozists, Deists [and] perverted naturalists [were] ruling over a 'Christian people.'" That keeping Jews out of power was also important to those who approved the Constitution appears from the fact that in 1783, when they petitioned to have the test oath removed on the grounds their behavior "has always tallied with the great design of the Revolution," they were refused.[24]

Pennsylvania radicals did not confine their prejudices to paper. David Franks, charged by the British government during the occupation of Philadelphia in 1777 and 1778 with supplying British troops, was also employed by Congress to feed and clothe British prisoners of war (each side took care of its own through agents who were allowed access to enemy lines). Franks ran short of money from the British and used his own, but finally lost patience and cut off the supplies. Meanwhile he was twice charged with treason, first against the federal government and then against Pennsylvania, although he was acquitted both times. Franks and two Quakers, who were executed, were the only Philadelphians charged with high treason who were not obviously loyalists, and whose trials were strongly condemned by the opponents of the 1776 constitution. This evidence suggests they, among the increasing numbers who considered the new state government tyrannical, had been singled out for religious reasons. The flimsy evidence against Franks consisted of two letters he wrote to his brother Moses informing him of the high price of provisions in Pennsylvania (hardly a secret) and expressing joy that their mutual friend William Hamilton had also been acquitted of treason. Franks's formal acquittal did not make any difference to his opponents, who used the threat of mob action to force him to leave town in 1780. Although he could have lived comfortably in London for the rest of his life, he returned in 1786 when the political climate changed. He died in the yellow fever epidemic of 1793. The Jewish congregation refused to allow his burial in their cemetery, although he had been a faithful and contributing Jew all his life, because he had married an Anglican and raised his children in that faith.[25]

At least David Franks was not the victim of violence. Other American

Jews of the Revolutionary era were less fortunate. As James Rivington's *New York Gazette* reported on December 2, 1780, "Mr. Isaac Hart, of Newport, R. I., formerly an eminent merchant and ever a loyal subject, was inhumanly fired upon and bayoneted, wounded in fifteen parts of his body, and beat with their [a crowd's] muskets in the most shocking manner in the very act of imploring quarter, and died of his wounds a few hours after." While loyalists and patriots murdered each other sometimes, the brutality that accompanied Hart's death suggests anti-Semitism may have been involved, perhaps making him the only Jew in early America to die at least in part for his faith.[26]

During the Revolution, anti-Semitism not only appeared against particular Jews, but also against Jews in general. The Jews' patriotism was questioned in newspapers published in Pennsylvania, South Carolina, and Georgia. Despite the fact that Jews supported the Revolution almost to a person in these states, former loyalists and members of marginal groups sought to deflect hostile attitudes away from themselves and toward Jews. For the first time, Jews (or those who spoke in their name) answered in the public prints challenges to their patriotism and insisted they should receive equal rights in the new republic. Haym Salomon was one of the Jews' most inveterate spokesmen. He was invaluable to the patriot cause because of his ability to transfer and convert currencies from Europe to America. He also worked closely with Superintendent of Finance Robert Morris in the successful effort to stabilize Revolutionary currency and supply the army late in the war. To be sure, Salomon may not have written the piece himself replying to the anti-Semitic Miers Fisher, but Salomon allowed the piece to appear under his name, which thereby suggests the prestige his efforts to help the Revolution had attained. According to Salomon, as a loyalist and a Quaker, Fisher's allegiance to the new republic was doubly suspect, but he sought to divert attention from his own failings to Salomon's faith. Although Fisher's letter does not survive, Salomon's reply provides a good sense of this public indictment: "I should make an apology for introducing a character, fetid and infamous, like yours, to general notice and attention. Your conspicuous *Toryism* and *disaffection* long since buried you in the silent grave of popular oblivion. . . . You not only endeavored to injure me by your unwarrantable expressions, but every other person of the same *religious* persuasion I hold, and which the laws of the country, and the glorious toleration and *liberty of conscience*, have allowed me to indulge and adopt. . . . The attack on the *Jews* seemed wanton, and could only have been premeditated by such a base and degenerate mind as yours." Salomon took pride in being both a Jew and a broker, since "we have in general been early on uniform, decisive whigs, and were second to none in our patriotism and attachment to our country." To Fisher's charges that "the Jews were the authors of high and unusual interest," Salomon suggested that he "turn your own batteries upon yourself: It was neither Jews or Christians that founded the practice, but *Quakers—Quakers* worse than *heathens, pagans or idolaters,*" men "'tho not Jews in *faith*, are Jews in *traffic*, men ablaze with avarice *who neither fear God nor regard men.*"[27] This broad attack on Quakerism was certainly no ecumenical declaration by Salomon, but it was a measure of the substantive religious liberty that American Jews now enjoyed.

In Georgia, an anti-Semitic "Citizen" even sought to turn the Jews' patriotism against them by blaming them for becoming involved in the Revolution to increase their own importance in public affairs. "Had the Jews in this state but conducted themselves with common modesty and decorum," he would have been willing to permit them "to enjoy by *courtesy* some things which it would be impossible to conceded of *right* in a Christian country." But Georgia's Jews were "eternally obtruding themselves as volunteers upon every public occasion, one day assuming the lead of an election, the next asking to direct the police of the town, and the third daring to pass as jurors upon the life and death of a freeman." In short, Jews were condemned for being too active in the Revolution—a natural outcome of their prominence in the colony's affairs from the beginning. Most notably, Mordecai Sheftall had been the leader of the Savannah Parochial Committee, the city's equivalent of the Sons of Liberty, that had spearheaded the Revolution in this heavily divided, reluctant state. Levi Sheftall, Mordecai's brother (who perhaps was trying to clear his own name, as he had worked as a spy for both sides and was accused by the state of treason), responded as a "Real Citizen": pointing to his brother's role in the war, he asked "what the Jew particularly alluded to . . . has done that he should not also be entitled to the rights of citizenship." As for the "Citizen," Sheftall pointed out that he had begged pardon of the British and had become the "destroyer of the rights and privileges of a whole set of people" to mask the fact that he himself was a "base deserter of his country's cause."[28]

In Charleston, South Carolina, an anti-Semite remarked on the arrival of refugees from Savannah, recently seized by the British: "upon inspection of their faces and enquiry I found them to be of the tribe of Israel," and at once concluded that they had first taken "every advantage in trade during the times admitted of in the State of Georgia," but "as soon as it was attacked, fled here for an asylum, with their ill-got wealth, dastardly turning their backs upon the country when in danger." "A real AMERICAN, and True-Hearted Israelite" responded that the family in question consisted entirely of women. Consisting of Abigail Minis (who ran her tavern and commercial ventures until she died aged ninety-three in 1794) and her four unmarried daughters, they had happily arrived at an asylum where a tyrannical enemy was not at their or their dear offspring's heels." Abraham Minis, Abigail's son, served in the Continental Army and loaned $10,000 to the cause.[29]

These attacks against the Jews were only partially successful. America was not going to be a Christian republic and Jews would not be prohibited from voting or holding office. With the exception of Maryland, New Hampshire, and North Carolina, none of the new state constitutions made any mention of Christianity as a requirement to vote or hold public office. But at the same time, there was an almost unconscious acceptance of Christian culture, if not Christian religion, by the people and government. Jews still had to fight Sabbath legislation in nearly every state, and vestiges remain even today, such as laws against Sunday liquor sales. For instance, when Thomas Jefferson's "Bill for Establishing Religious Freedom" was finally passed by the Virginia State legislature after being introduced by James Madison in 1785, it also passed, at Madison's request, his "Bill for Punishing Disturbers of Religious Worship and Sabbath Breakers," which included the provision that "If any person on Sunday shall himself be found laboring at his own or any other trade or calling, or shall employ his apprentices, servants or slaves in labor, or other business, except it be in the ordinary household offices of daily necessity, or other work of necessity or charity, he shall forfeit the sum of ten shillings for every such offence." Jewish businessmen who could in conscience only legally open their stores five days a week had to compete with Christians who could remain open for six. In 1816, for instance, Abraham Wolf of Philadelphia was convicted for working on the Sabbath despite his defense that he faithfully kept his own Sabbath. In 1793 in the same city, the stalwart revolutionary and prominent merchant Jonas Phillips had been fined ten pounds, the equivalent of about two months' wages for a laborer, for refusing to be sworn in as a witness on a Saturday.[30]

At the United States Constitutional Convention in Philadelphia, the Jews of Philadelphia petitioned the convention that no religious requirements for citizenship, voting, or officeholding be written into the document in the manner of the Pennsylvania Constitution of 1776. In the eloquent document penned by Jonas Phillips, "for my self, my children and posterity, and for the benefit of all the Israelites through the thirteen United States of America," he stressed both that "all men have a natural and unalienable right to worship almighty God according to the dictates of their own conscience and understanding," and that the Jews "have been true and faithful whigs, and during the late contest with England they have been foremost in aiding and assisting the states with their lives and fortunes, they have supported the cause, have bravely fought and bled for liberty which they can not Enjoy," that is, the liberty to vote and hold office. Phillips concluded by pronouncing a blessing on the new nation: "May the people of this states rise up as a great and young lion. . . . May God extend peace unto the United States—May they get up to the highest prosperity—May God extend peace to them and their seed after them so long as the sun and moon endureth—and may the almighty God of our father Abraham Isaac and Jacob endow this noble assembly with wisdom judgment and unanimity in their councils, and may they have the Satisfaction to see that their present toil and labor for the welfare of the United States may be approved of through all the world."[31]

Phillips must have been pleasantly surprised to discover that the new instrument would impose no disabilities on Jews. On the other hand, there was no positive insistence that states enfranchise Jews: as with African Americans, whether they could vote or hold office or not depended on the states. The Jews therefore had to win their case in each state, which, with three exceptions, they were able to do.

Republican Jews

George Washington himself endorsed Jewish rights and praised the Jewish contribution to the Revolution. In doing so, he showed that not only toleration, but also an appreciation of religious pluralism and cultural diversity was possible in the late eighteenth century. Upon assuming the presidency, Washington received numerous letters from smaller religious groups—Roman Catholics, Moravians, Quakers, and Jews—applauding his election and praising the fact that their contributions to the Revolution were appreciated and their religious practices were not only tolerated but welcomed. He responded individually and seriously to each group, and had his responses published in the *Gazette of the United States*, using his office to champion toleration. Washington went even further in responding to the Jews and Free Masons of

Newport when Rhode Island belatedly joined the union in the 1790. The remark for which he is famous, "behold a government which to bigotry gives no sanction, to persecution no assistance," was in fact the product of the Newport Jews, and he repeated it in his reply. The Free Masons—a disproportional number of whom were Jews in the Revolutionary era—chose the Jew Moses Seixas and the Gentile Henry Sherburne to pen their address to their "brother" George Washington. Washington—who never referred to Jesus or the Christian religion, but only to Providence or a Supreme Being—implicitly rebuked those who insisted that the United States was a Christian or Protestant republic: "All possess alike liberty of conscience and immunities of citizenship. It is now no more that toleration is spoken of, as if it was by the indulgence of one class of people, that another enjoyed the exercise of their inherent natural rights." Instead of a common culture, there were only "classes" of people within a nation.[32]

But like the harmony that welcomed Washington to the presidency, the attacks on Jews resumed when Alexander Hamilton announced his plans to pay the interest on the national and state debts in specie and found the Bank of the United States. The *New York Journal* complained:

> Tax on tax young Belcour cries
> More imposts, and a new excise.
> A public debt's a public blessing
> Which tis of course a crime to lessen.
> Each day a fresh report he broaches
> That Spies and Jews may ride in coaches.
> Soldiers and Farmers, don't despair
> Untax'd as yet are Earth and Air.

The anti-Federalist populists who had linked Jews with the upper-class revolutionaries, by virtue of the prominent merchants among them, used the fact that a handful of Jews would join thousands of Gentiles in benefiting from the new policies as a reason to oppose them.

Virulent political anti-Semitism in the 1790s reflects the partisanship of the decade. Originally, almost all Jews supported the Federalists. But in 1791, revolutionary France gave Jews full citizenship. Consequently, almost all American Jews became Jeffersonian Republicans, the party that sympathized with the new French republic, at a moment (1793) when the French Revolution became the most heated political issue in the United States. Because nearly all Jews, along with immigrants who came mostly from England, Ireland, and France, supported the French Revolution, the Federalists turned against them. The Federalists had embraced toleration at the time of the Constitutional Convention, but by the late 1790s their vision of the republic's religious culture had become narrowly Protestant. Each party focused on a different Jewish scapegoat: for the anti-Federalists the Jews were wealthy war profiteers, for the Federalists they were leaders of the immigrants and lower classes who were seeking "some means of knocking down a Government, to Emerge from Dirt to Gold."[33]

Federalist newspapers became the principal vehicle to express anti-Semitism. Ironically their editors, John Fenno and William Cobbett, fit the prototype of the wandering Jew. Poor printers who moved from place to place, they sought economic betterment through publications whose morality and accuracy they did not question. Fenno's *Gazette of the United States* denounced the Jews in no uncertain terms, and neither Washington, nor Vice President Adams, nor Secretary of the Treasury Hamilton did anything to stop this despite their own favorable sentiments toward Jews. Much of Fenno's anger fell upon Israel Israel, vice president of the Philadelphia Democratic Society founded in 1793, who, despite his name had been baptized by a Lutheran minister, and later attended Episcopalian and then Unitarian-Universalist services. As if to emphasize with irony the anti-Semitic remarks he had endured, Israel began his last will and testament: "In the name of the Everlasting God the Father the Saviour of All Men through the Atonement of Jesus Christ the Lord, I ISRAEL ISRAEL," with his name in capital letters. Fenno ignored the fact that Israel was a Revolutionary war hero, and had remained as one of the directors of public relief in Philadelphia during the yellow fever epidemic of 1793, in which a tenth of the population lost their lives and those who could afford it (such as Washington and his cabinet) generally left for healthier climes. Fenno suggested that Israel lead his various "un-American" followers on a new exodus: that "would be a second going out of the Children of Israel, or rather of *Israel Israel*: and rather than they should not go, I will engage that the quiet citizens will be more willing than the Egyptians were of old to lend them, if not *jewels*, such other articles as may be useful in a new country." The italicized words suggest Fenno was dubbing Israel Israel a Jew and associating their biblical exile not so much with suffering under Egyptians but rather an intergenerational lust for wealth. Given such rhetoric, it is hardly surprising that Israel and Fenno came to blows in the streets of Philadelphia in 1795.[34]

That Israel Israel could lose his Jewish religion without losing his Jewish ethnicity also appeared in the treatment of his son, John Israel, who had only one Jewish grandparent, and became the leading Democratic-Republican printer in western Pennsylvania. When he began publishing the *Herald* (later the *Tree*) *of Liberty* at the age of twenty-two in 1798, his Federalists opponents circulated a broadside attacking him, his father, and the leading Republican newspaper in Philadelphia, the *Aurora*, along with one of the most prominent republicans, Hugh Henry Brackenridge, of western Pennsylvania:

Have you heard	of the New Press?
Echo:	of the Jew Press?
What, is it published	and by a Jew?
Echo:	and by a Hugh
Of the Aurora	another edition
Echo:	a mother of sedition?
Jacobinism imaginary is	or Is real
Echo:	Israel.

Citizens who wanted the Jews to convert still attacked them for being Jews when they did. John Israel, for his part, replied by making fun of his opponent's name: John Scull became "Numb" Scull.[35]

For the most part, however, publicly displayed anti-Semitism died out in the early republic between 1800 and the 1820s, at least outside of predominantly Federalist, Anglo-Saxon Protestant New England, largely due to the Jeffersonians' overwhelming victory over the Federalists in 1800. Mainly confined to marginal lower and middle classes and social groups prior to the Revolution, elite nineteenth-century anti-Semitism was now most conspicuous in New England. The most conservative and elitist region of the nation had embraced anti-Semitism because the Jews had joined their opponents. The descendants of these mainly Federalist men would found societies to Christianize the Jews, keep them out of elite Boston society, and impose a quota system on Ivy League colleges into the twentieth century.[36] But in general political anti-Semitism was counterproductive. When the western Pennsylvania *Fayette Gazette* attacked John Israel as "the Israelite" hoping "to prove the Jew a fool," Pittsburgh Federalists met to "take this public opportunity of declaiming our abhorrence of the vile calumnies, falsehoods, and slanders" associated with anti-Semitism.[37]

That religious toleration could flourish in a country with anti-Semitic prejudices is attributable to the nation's philosophical belief in freedom of conscience, pluralism, and the fact that Jews were simply too small a minority to be a major concern—there were only about 3,000 Jews in the country in 1790 and 15,000 by 1820.[38] Christopher Grenda is correct that toleration, indeed pluralism, became a major (although not the only) element of the nation's political culture. The lack of a hegemonic religious majority, combined with a complicated hierarchy of likes and dislikes among various ethnic and religious groups, proved James Madison correct when he argued in Federalist No. 10: "A religious sect may degenerate into a political faction in a part of the Confederacy; but the variety of sects dispersed over the entire face of it must secure the national councils against any danger from that source." Furthermore, there were far more serious threats for the colonies and new nation to worry about than the Jews: "Papists," such as French and Spaniards with whom the colonies were frequently at war; Native Americans; Methodists and Baptists, who threatened the elite Anglican and Presbyterian churches; Germans and Scots-Irish in the middle colonies before the Revolution; and Irish immigrants in the early republic. By the mid-nineteenth century, the North and the South had become the principal threats, loyally supported by the Jews of each region.

Conclusion: Leading Statesmen, Proto-Zionism, and the Jews in the Early Nineteenth Century

While not an important item of public debate, attitudes toward Jews in the early nineteenth century foreshadowed the ways in which Americans would long continue to regard them. For instance, John Adams, who greatly admired the Jews, and his son John Quincy and friend Thomas Jefferson, who did not, all wanted the Jews to establish a nation in Palestine. But their reasons were as different as their opinions of the Jewish people.

John Adams remarked scathingly on the French philosopher Voltaire's anti-Semitism: "How is it possible [that he] should represent the Hebrews in such a contemptible light? They are the most glorious nation that ever inhabited this Earth. The Romans and their Empire were but a Bauble in comparison of the Jews. They have given religion to three quarters of the Globe and have influenced the affairs of Mankind more, and more happily, than any other Nation ancient or modern." Adams praised the fact that the United States "has done much. I wish it may do more, and annul every narrow idea in Religion, Government and Commerce." He also became the first American president to endorse a Jewish state. In 1819, acknowledging receipt of Manuel Mordecai Noah's *Travels in England, France Spain and the Barbary States,* Adams wished that Noah had not traveled alone, and that he "had been at the head of a hundred thousand Israelites . . . marching with them into Judea & making a conquest of that country & restoring your nation to the dominion of it."

Adams, to be sure, regarded the restoration of the Jewish nation as a prelude to their Christianization. He added to his reply to Noah: "Once restored to an independent government & no longer persecuted they [the Jews] would soon wear away some of the asperities and peculiarities of their character & possibly in time become liberal Unitarian Christians for your Jehovah is our Jehovah & your God of Abraham Isaac and Jacob is our God." Adams should not be considered anti-Semitic because he thought Judaism had some "asperities" and "peculiarities." Given his scathing critiques of nations, religions, political parties, and personalities throughout his life, the Jews came off very well indeed. He simply thought that everyone, properly enlightened, would (like himself) become a Unitarian Christian.[39]

Although he passed his intellect, appearance, and blunt honesty to his son John Quincy Adams, the elder statesman was unable to convey his appreciation of the Jews. Whereas he had worked with them at the highest levels of government during the Revolution, John Quincy's first experience of Jewish communities (there were none in Massachusetts) was in Europe in the 1790s, where a Dutch Jewish moneylender tried to shortchange him. When he visited Frankfurt, he commented that "the word filth conveys an ideal of spotless purity in comparison with Jewish nastiness." The younger Adams, too, was a Zionist, but largely because he thought that the rest of the world would be better off untroubled by the Jews. His anti-Semitism foreshadowed that of many nineteenth-century Americans, confronted beginning in the mid-1820s with large numbers of unassimilated and impoverished Jewish immigrants.[40]

Thomas Jefferson was more in agreement with John Quincy than John. In theory, he believed that Jews deserved the same rights as all Americans. During the Virginia constitutional convention of 1776 he argued that "neither Pagan nor Mohamedan nor Jew ought to be excluded from the civil rights of the Commonwealth because of his religion." Jefferson appointed Jews to public office upon election to the presidency in 1801, and in 1818 wrote to Jewish leader Mordecai Manuel Noah supporting his opposition to reading the King James Protestant Bible in public schools as a form of "persecution and oppression," a "cruel addition to the wrongs" Jews had endured: "Your sect by its sufferings has furnished a remarkable proof of the universal spirit of religious intolerance inherent in every sect, disclaimed by all while feeble, and practiced by all when in power." He insisted that "religious freedom is the most effectual antidote against religious dissension" and hoped that Jews "will be seen taking their seats on the benches of science as preparatory to their doing the same at the board of government."[41]

Yet Jefferson, who agreed with Adams in opposing all forms of religious revelation and believed the Creator only made himself visible to humanity through the natural world and human reason, differed from Adams in that he could say nothing good about the Jewish religion. "Repulsive and antisocial as respecting other nations," their idea of God "degrading and injurious," their ethics "often irreconcilable with the sound dictates of religion and morality," the rationalist Jefferson had no problem denying his personal experiences with Jews in favor of traditional anti-Semitic stereotypes. He knew that Jews such as Haym Salomon, David Salisbury Franks, and Mordecai Sheftall of Georgia had played important roles in the American Revolution, risking their "lives, fortunes, and sacred honor" every bit as much as the signers of the Declaration of Independence.[42] Gershom Mendes Seixas—hazzan (reader) and de facto rabbi of the Jewish congregation in New York and trustee of Columbia College from 1784 to 1816—was the only clergyman in the nation to publish a sermon that did not praise John Adams's undeclared war with France in 1798 when the president proclaimed a day of fasting and humiliation.[43] Yet Jefferson nevertheless regarded Jews as selfish and stated that their own character, rather than Gentile prejudice, was the reason they had been frequently isolated within Christian societies.

In early America, traditional prejudices against Jews were sometimes overcome and often transformed as popular, revolutionary, and national politics evolved: Jews acquired the right to vote and hold public office in nearly every state by the 1820s. Yet at the same time, anti-Semites regarded Jews as more dangerous even as their numbers failed to increase very much until large numbers of German Jews began to arrive in the 1820s. Jews in the colonial period were considered mercenary, obnoxious, immoral, conniving, yet no real danger. With the Revolution, anti-Semites considered them blemishes on a Christian republic. But only in Federalist propaganda of the 1790s did they become a real threat to the republic's survival: as the 1793 Federalist cartoon "A Peep into the Anti-Federal Club" demonstrated, the supposedly

Jewish Israel Israel was leading a motley crew of African Americans, Frenchmen, Germans, Scots-Irish, and intellectuals in a conspiracy to destroy the state.

The chapters by Christopher Grasso and Owen Stanwood in this volume, dealing with Deists and Roman Catholics, respectively, offer compatible interpretations. Before the Revolution, Deism was rarely admitted and Catholicism, while a hostile international power, had few adherents in the colonies outside Maryland, where they were disfranchised and politically impotent. Whether they belonged in a republican example to a despotic world was simply not an issue. But as Deists and Catholics became more numerous in the late eighteenth and early nineteenth centuries, their role in what many considered a Protestant (they would usually say "Christian") republic became an important issue—much as did that of the Jews. Unlike Jews, however, Deists and Catholics were militant proselytizers of their faiths. They did not hesitate to meet what historian Ray Allen Billington has called "the Protestant Crusade" with equal fervor of their own. Thus, the Jews found themselves caught up in the paradox that with the expansion of the press and extension of political life, voices of intolerance in the United States were more frequently heard as formal religious liberty became legally institutionalized.

Yet although they did not try to convert Protestants and remained numerically tiny until the late nineteenth century, Jews were, at times, considered equally dangerous: they could threaten the republic, not because of their numbers or through physical force, but because they could (mis)lead other gullible ethnic groups, who were also not "real" Americans, through their corrupted intelligence. Jews received the backhanded compliment that despite their small numbers, their superior, albeit evil, intelligence could mislead others who were stereotyped as stupid. As appreciation for the Jews' patriotism brought them full civil and political equality, anti-Semitism also became stronger in a psychological sense. But the real danger was not to the republic, as the anti-Semites claimed (and still do), but to the ability of the Jews to practice their religion and their customs with the general appreciation George Washington insisted was the test of America's devotion to its own principles. The defeat of the Federalists ended any real possibility that Jews would be excluded from the American polity. But when a similar vein of political anti-Semitism emerged in Europe, in which demagogues branded Jews as a "stateless" people disloyal to the nation-state, it threatened the very survival of Judaism on earth.

PART IV

The Persistence of Tolerance
and Intolerance in the New Nation

Chapter 11

The "Catholic Spirit Prevailing in Our Country"

America's Moderate Religious Revolution

CHRIS BENEKE

A revolution in religious culture and politics began in Britain's North American mainland colonies during the 1770s.[1] This movement toward religious liberty, nonsectarianism, and public civility was never undone. There would be no retreat, no Thermidorian Reaction. New laws almost always expanded, and almost never contracted, the range of religious liberties granted to religious groups.[2] While it is true that a handful of states took several decades to grant full political rights to non-Protestants, the progressive character of religious liberty during this period is incontrovertible. Unlike earlier periods of reform in America and Europe, when radical policy shifts and confessional instability often made interreligious peace accord a transient thing, the Revolutionary era inaugurated a durable, if at times strained, period of egalitarian coexistence. The United States' new, moderately ecumenical regime survived both a massive influx of Catholic emigrants to a Protestant country and the rise of highly unconventional and powerful religious communities. In fact, rather than being the great exception to the early American tradition of religious tolerance as some historians have argued and even more have implied, early outsider groups such as Roman Catholics and Jews benefited at least as much as other groups.[3] Describing the novelty of the circumstances facing American Catholics in 1784, the future bishop John Carroll wrote: "in these

United States our religious system has undergone a revolution, if possible, more extraordinary than our political one."[4]

The tolerance that prevailed by the 1780s made almost all previous tolerationist regimes in the Western world, as well as in colonial North America, look halting and limited. In the late eighteenth and early nineteenth centuries, European states were just getting around to making or expanding policies of toleration. Some of these same states had long traditions of informal coexistence between different religious groups, but almost always on the condition of legal inequality. Until the French Revolutionaries pulled the Catholic Church up by its roots, exclusionary establishments were universal. Toleration meant that religious minorities were "dissenters," as they had long been in much of British North America. By contrast, religious liberty in the new United States entailed a high-level commitment to the principle of religious equality. The American Revolution in religious liberty was also distinguished by its durability. Changed social customs and formal legal arrangements proved crucial in this regard, as did the relative absence of anticlericalism and secularism. Yet it was the ineluctable force of widely accepted principles, particularly religious liberty and nonsectarianism—the consistency they demanded, the equity they extended, and the portability they provided—that made it an enduring phenomenon.[5]

The American Revolution in religious liberty began, inauspiciously, in early spring 1772. On March 26 of that year a piece of legislation sponsored in the House of Burgesses splashed prominently across the front page of William Rind's *Virginia Gazette*. "*A Bill for extending the Benefit of the several Acts of Toleration to his Majesty's Protestant Subjects, in this Colony, dissenting from the Church of England*" opened with the declaration that all Protestant *dissenters* in the colony would "have and enjoy the full and free Exercise of their Religion, without Molestation or Danger of incurring any Penalty whatsoever." It seemed generous enough. But this legislative munificence was followed by provisions forbidding dissenters from congregating at night, locking their doors, or worshiping alongside slaves. The penalties imposed on those who extended their faith to African slaves were even more severe.[6] The bill never passed. Nor did any general toleration bill ever make it through the House of Burgesses. There were simply too many objections. There was also too little time. For this provincial institution was about to fall victim to imperial politics. And with the demise of the old regime, pleas for toleration were giving way to assertions of religious equality. To evangelical dissenters and moderate Anglican believers alike, toleration was no longer a sufficient remedy.

The pace of change accelerated during the next few years. By the time Virginia's constitution was adopted in June 1776, a rhetorical shift as abrupt as any in American history had taken place. George Mason's proposal that the state provide "the fullest toleration in the exercise of religion" would have seemed magnanimous a few years earlier. Yet to a twenty-five-year-old representative named James Madison, even the fullest toleration implied that there was only one legitimate form of religious faith and that dissent from it was a regrettable mistake. Madison proposed to replace the phrase "fullest toleration" with the "free exercise of religion." In the end, the Virginia Bill of Rights provided that religion could "be directed only by reason and conviction . . . and therefore all men are equally entitled to the free exercise of religion, according to the dictates of conscience." Although the Church of England continued to enjoy a favored status in Virginian life for the next several years, its establishment—together with the toleration that the church purported to extend to dissenters—had effectively ended. Dissent from Anglicanism would no longer be defined as a crime and the exemptions granted to acknowledged "dissenters" would be renewed annually. By 1786, there would be nothing to exempt Presbyterians, Baptists, and Quakers from. They would no longer be dissenters.[7]

Virginia stood at the vanguard of a broader contemporary movement away from both persecution and toleration. Into the eighteenth century, general proscriptions on movement, speech, assembly, and writing restricted the circulation of religious ideas and the supply of public respect in the majority of colonies. Itinerant ministers could be jailed, church buildings could be restricted or prohibited, and dissenting worship could be made both cumbersome and degrading. Official recognition and public visibility were privileges that only established churches enjoyed. In addition to their substantial advantage in creating and controlling the physical spaces of worship, the established churches sometimes possessed a monopoly on political officeholding. Toleration alleviated the most oppressive elements of these church-state establishments. At a minimum, it suspended criminal penalties for dissenters. Often it did more, permitting groups to exercise many of their faith tenets and enjoy at least some political privileges. Beginning in the late 1720s, for instance, Congregationalist governments in Massachusetts and Connecticut allowed dissenters to direct tax monies to their own churches. In other colonies, property restrictions on dissenting groups were eased and agreements forged to allow dissenting groups to build church communities in designated areas. In short, toleration offered dissenting faiths a restricted, yet welcomed freedom from the most debilitating forms of religious oppression.

By the Revolutionary period America's dissenters and their liberal allies were pushing for the end of establishments altogether—and with them, the end of toleration. The legal system called "toleration" accommodated the "pretended scruples" of believers who could not bear to attend meetings of the established churches or take up arms against a common enemy. What it could not do was relieve dissenters of the inconveniences, the inequities, and the countless indignities that went along with a tolerated status. Toleration had essentially protected a private right to believe and worship, and was often used synonymously with "liberty of conscience" and "the right of private judgment." Maryland's 1649 Act Concerning Religion, which made unprecedented provisions for Roman Catholic believers within the British Empire, declared that all of their religious practices were "to be done as privately as may be" and that Roman Catholics were "to be silent upon all occasions of discourse concerning matters of Religion."[8] Rhode Island's more liberal charter granted religious liberty to the colony's inhabitants (for their "private opinions") on the condition that they behaved "themselves peaceablie and quietlie"—demonstrating that the absence of a traditional religious establishment was no guarantee that anything more than rights to believe freely and worship privately would be protected.[9]

Amid the heated sectarian rhetoric that accompanied the decline of exclusive religious establishments in the 1760s and 1770s, the "right of private judgment" and "liberty of conscience" never came under indictment. Instead, like favorite old tools, they fell into disuse as dissenters took more comprehensive and more egalitarian instruments of religious freedom in hand. The same could not be said for the complimentary language of "toleration" and the legal regimes that provided it. Beginning with the imperial crisis of the 1760s a more inclusive understanding of religious autonomy was consciously substituted for toleration; it was generally called "religious liberty," or the "free exercise of religion," and it incorporated both private and public rights. To be sure, "toleration" survived as an ideal in expressions such as "universal toleration and liberty of conscience" and as a synonym for forbearance, while the practice of toleration continued as long as the remnants of established religion.[10] Yet there was a discernible shift from toleration to religious liberty during the late eighteenth century. Humiliating as they may have been for the religious minorities that lived under them, the conditions of colonial toleration—especially the interdenominational interaction that established patterns of coexistence—provided a crucial foundation for the much more robust regime of religious liberty that emerged during the Revolutionary era. The conditions of colonial toleration also established a legal baseline for religious dissent that could not be easily violated. And while we should not confuse chronological sequence for causation, it is significant that toleration always preceded, and never succeeded, religious liberty in the late eighteenth century.

Like other revolutions, the American Revolution condensed time. Changes that might have taken decades in the absence of a major political crisis now took years or even months. To one degree or another, every state followed the direction that Virginia took in 1776. Georgia's constitution guaranteed "[a]ll persons whatever the free exercise of . . . religion." Massachusetts' provided that "no subject shall be hurt, molested, or restrained, in his person, liberty, or estate, for worshipping GOD in the manner and season most agreeable to the dictates of his own conscience." New York's constitution declared that "the free exercise and enjoyment of religious profession and worship, without discrimination or preference, shall forever hereafter be allowed, within this state, to all mankind" as long as the civil laws were not violated.[11] The word "toleration" did not make an appearance in any of the new state constitutions. Of course, traces of the established churches, and the toleration that restrained them, still abounded. Johan Neem has recently demonstrated the resilience of the Congregationalist establishment in Massachusetts that John Adams famously called "mild and equitable." Still, the rhetorical force of religious liberty made it harder to sustain the legal disparities that had once been an integral part of New England religious culture. That did not mean, as recent work by Neem and Shelby Balik has made clear, that local officials were unable to maintain discriminatory practices in their villages and towns. It did mean that these legal and social artifacts of an intolerant past would be contested, and far more difficult to explain.[12]

Some might dismiss the claim as unfounded triumphalism, but there was an undeniably progressive quality to this revolution in religious liberty. Compared to what came just a few years later, the rights granted to worshipers in the 1770s were relatively limited in what they allowed and more prescriptive in what they required for official recognition, tax support, and full political participation. For example, South Carolina's 1778 constitution required belief in one God, a future state of rewards and punishments, a profession that the Christian religion is the true religion, and an affirmation of the

Old and New Testament as divine inspiration from those churches applying for incorporation. The 1790 Constitution required none of these things; it simply guaranteed the "free exercise and enjoyment of religious profession and worship, without discrimination or preference." The constitutions that were rewritten in the 1780s and 1790s made considerably more generous provisions for religious liberty and political participation. Religious tests for office were among the most momentous victims of these Whiggish reforms. The inertia of existing laws carried the day in those places that did not engage in another round of revision in the 1780s and 1790s. States that framed and revised their fundamental laws earlier, such as Massachusetts, tended to maintain old privileges.[13]

The move to enshrine religious freedom at the founding reflected the structure of the inequalities and persecution that preceded it. It included provisions for mundane instruments of worship such as the right of all churches to hold property directly, hire and fire clergy, build respectable edifices, and accept contributions from their members. These were central components of a cognate principle, one the First Amendment designated "the free exercise" of religion. On the spectrum of rights granted in this period, religious freedoms were about as inclusive as the great common law liberties (such as the right to trial by jury) and far more inclusive than suffrage, which was not extended to white women or most African Americans. One of the extraordinary things about the American Revolution in religious liberty was that it did not just provide for a universal right of individual judgment, or the rights of groups in specified areas, but instead protected the rights of nearly all religious groups no matter what their particular circumstances. Grants of corporate status to almost any church that applied epitomized this new approach to religious difference. As the historians Frank Lambert and Mark McGarvie have demonstrated, churches in many states now enjoyed the benefits of private corporations. This meant that full legal privileges and access to open worship was granted to many groups once denied even a semblance of public recognition.[14]

As extensive as the religious provisions of the early state constitutions were, the 1787 U.S. Constitution had nothing to say about sacred matters except this: religious tests for federal office were forbidden. On this point, the consensus within Independence Hall was formidable. After working for two months in tight quarters with Episcopalians, Presbyterians, Congregationalists, Quakers, Catholics, Methodists, Lutherans, and Dutch Reformed—as well as a sizable number of unconventional believers who could be best described as deists or Christian deists—the imposition of a religious test would have been an unexpected development. Religious diversity, especially when the cumulative diversity of all thirteen states is taken into account, helps explain the ease with which the no-religious-test provision passed. The framers had a trans-state perspective that many of their constituents would only gradually acquire.

Article VI incited a notably parochial reaction across the states. It encountered stiff opposition in a number of city newspapers and state constitutional conventions, where opponents played up the possibility of foreign domination and the growing plague of infidelity. The prohibition on religious tests raised the unsettling prospect that political power would end up in the hands of religious minorities, and the apocalyptic prospect that it would end up in the hands of anti-republican infidels. In the end, however, such sentiments did not prevail. The Constitution was ratified with Article VI intact. The prohibition on religious tests represented a significant expansion in the scope of religious liberty. This was no mere right to worship privately and quietly. It was, instead, a freedom to exercise the highest powers of government no matter what one's faith. An unofficial electoral ban on alleged atheists persisted, the presidency remained the preserve of more-or-less orthodox Protestants (Abraham Lincoln excepted), and Catholics and Jews often (though not always) found themselves at an electoral disadvantage. Yet a monumental change in the religious culture had occurred. Initially condemned as an instrument of infidelity, the prohibition of religious tests, and the more encompassing doctrine of "nonsectarianism" that it implied, emerged as one of the reigning orthodoxies of nineteenth-century Protestantism, a touchstone for public policies with any conceivable religious implications.

The move to nonsectarianism involved a seemingly minor but nonetheless important departure from a related principle that scholars sometimes call "nonpreferentialism." Today, the terms "nonsectarianism" and "nonpreferentialism" tend to be used interchangeably because both can be contrasted with exclusive church establishments and because both were plainly connected in the minds of those who framed early national religious legislation. But whereas the late eighteenth-century injunctions against religious preference entailed that no one group would enjoy special legal privileges, the emergent principle of nonsectarianism entailed that government could take no cognizance of religious differences. In other words, nonsectarianism is akin to our concept of nondiscrimination (and, more confusingly, to the broader sense in which modern commentators sometimes employ the term "nonpreferentialism").[15] During the Revolutionary and Founding eras, every state disavowed preferentialism, or the subordination of one or more sects by another. Nonpreferentialism was the Revolutionary-era alternative to an exclusive establishment. Its tight grip on the nation's ideological imagination lasted into the late 1780s. Virginia's ratifying convention, for instance, recommended that the U.S. Constitution be amended to provide that "no particular religious sect or society ought to be favored or established by law in preference to others."[16] Early drafts of the First Amendment also included nonpreferentialist language (e.g., "Congress shall make no law establishing one religious society in preference to others, or to infringe on the rights of conscience").[17]

The shift toward the principle of nonsectarianism and away from nonpreferentialism must have begun sometime during or after 1788 because the outrage against the federal religious test ban was far from inconsequential. By the 1790s, however, individual states dropped many of their religious requirements for officeholding. Meanwhile, from 1786 onward, nonpreferential establishments were being discarded for systems of government that excluded religious establishments altogether. The absence of nonpreferentialist language in the First Amendment, together with the persistence of Article VI's provision against religious tests, marked a watershed in church-state history. While nonpreferentialism sufficed as an instrument for attacking repressive and exclusive establishments of religion, the case against nonpreferential (or "multiple") establishments themselves required a broader, more ecumenical, and more egalitarian understanding of religion that nonsectarianism could accommodate.

The nonsectarian case against both religious establishments and religious tests required something else: a vigorous distinction between civic and religious identities. Our interminable debates about whether the founders' intended to separate church and state or not have obscured this other significant new form of separation. Some of the more radical founders, such as Benjamin Rush and Thomas Jefferson, went so far as to deny that erroneous opinions posed any harm to the larger polity. They also denied civil authorities the right to meddle with religious principles merely on a suspicion of their "ill tendency." While most of their contemporaries declined to go that far, the state and federal leaders nonetheless made a vaguely Christian manifestation of faith—rather than any particular affiliation or doctrine—a pillar of republican government. As George Washington observed in a 1790 letter to the Universal Church in Philadelphia: "However different are the sentiments of citizens on religious doctrines," he wrote, "they generally concur in one thing; for their political professions and practices are almost universally friendly to the order and happiness of our civil institutions."[18] The severing of church and civic identity meant that minority spiritual beliefs and practices, even Catholic beliefs and practices, were now acceptable in a way that suspected anti-republican international entanglements were not.[19] The connection being forged between "religion" (broadly conceived but, again, often understood as the "Christian religion"), morality, and republican government protected a variety of religious believers from bigotry and discrimination. The new demands of nationalism and republican citizenship might suggest that one form of oppression had simply given way to another—or that Americans had simply found a new way to privilege civil order over religious conformity. Yet sedition had always been forbidden, and laws against dissenting speech, assembly, and print had never been so lenient as they were under the new state constitutions.

Another distinguishing characteristic of the American Revolution in religious liberty was the relative restraint of its anticlericalism. About half of the original state constitutions forbade clergymen from serving in public office. The other half, along with the U.S. Constitution, did not.[20] There were occasional echoes of Enlightenment hostility toward "priestcraft" and "orthodoxy," and evangelical critiques of elite ministries continued. Yet once powerful churches with questionable patriotic credentials, such as the Quakers and Anglicans, were never subject to the violence, the financial ruin, or even the disgrace that we might have expected from the larger population. The subdued character of the new nation's assault on the established religious order was crucial to both the long-term viability of the republican experiment and the revolution in religious liberty. It ensured that the clerical class could reconcile itself with the Revolution without risking humiliation or insincerity. Also helpful was the fact that there was no overt effort to substitute the religious symbols of traditional Christianity with those of civic republicanism, no gratuitous displacement of the sacred with the secular. Conventional Christianity and true republicanism were generally understood as mutually reinforcing phenomenon. In this as in other ways, the American Revolution in religious liberty generally came in peace, rather than with a sword.

Orthodox clergymen did complain of rampant rationalism, and even atheism, in the country. There was, however, at least as much evidence of two other developments with which infidelity was sometimes conflated, namely religious civility and ecumenism. Consider a striking and neglected material fact about the early republic: the widespread interdenominational support for church-building efforts. From New York City to Charleston, eastern Pennsylvania to Kentucky, and in many small towns in between, Protestants assisted other Protestants, as well as Catholics and Jews, while Catholics and Jews returned the favor.[21] If the privacy of dissenting opinions and worship was a distinguishing mark of a system of toleration, the active support for the church-building efforts of other denominations marked the ascendance of something that would have been inconceivable decades earlier. The growing refinement and homogeneity in church and synagogue architecture undoubtedly made the presence of dissenting church buildings easier to countenance. They were (particularly those with steeples and elegant facades) valuable additions to a town's physical landscape and to the general cause of social order. Whatever the economic and social incentives, however, interdenominational support for synagogue and church building provides a useful index of change in the religious culture. We need only recall the ban on Catholic church building in many parts of colonial America and longstanding restrictions on the buildings that Protestant dissenters could construct. Established churches had once been the chief public spaces in towns. Because of their role as symbols of cultural status and political power, church buildings themselves had been a prime source of sectarian angst and interdenominational conflict in several towns during the eighteenth century.[22] The assistance that different kinds of believers lent each other during and after the Founding era may be partly explained by economic self-interest and simple curiosity; it cannot be explained by latent bigotry or discrimination.

If believers could help build their neighbors' churches, they could also bring themselves to sit in one another's pews and to pray together in public. Benjamin Franklin was a famously promiscuous (and famously infrequent) church attendee. But he was not the only one. In fact, Franklin's ecumenical worship practices were symptomatic of a larger trend in the late colonial world. The diary kept by a contemporary, Mary Cooper of Oyster Bay, New York, records numerous visits to Anglican, Baptist, Quaker, and New Light churches. Sometimes Cooper attended two different churches in the same day in the years leading up to the Revolutionary war.[23] As historian Derek H. Davis observes, the largely Protestant delegates of the Continental Congress attended several different places of worship—including Catholic Mass—as a group during their time in Philadelphia.[24] Similar gestures were offered within the halls of the first Continental Congress itself. When one of the delegates proposed that a chaplain be designated to lead the assembled men in prayer, there were objections, based partly on the "diversity of sentiments represented in Congress." But the stern Massachusetts Congregationalist Samuel Adams declared in favor of hearing the prayers of an Anglican rector: "I am no bigot. I can hear a prayer from a man of piety and virtue, who is at the same time a friend of his country."[25] The public esteem that such interdenominational visiting and praying conferred on different faiths—in addition to the legitimacy that it lent to the principles of ecumenism and religious civility themselves—was unprecedented.

Post-Revolutionary religious civility was more than just a neighborly phenomenon. In fact, the most admired man in the new nation, George Washington, may have also been its most conspicuously ecumenical. Countless pages have been devoted to the substance of the first president's faith. Scholars have demonstrated that the nominally Anglican Washington was not an orthodox Christian: he refused to kneel in prayer, left church services before Communion, and almost never referred to Jesus Christ. However, there is no doubt that Washington believed in a guiding providence and the necessity of religion to morality. He is probably best described as a Christian deist.[26] The point of most inquiries into Washington's religious life is to demonstrate either that the nation was, or was not, Christian at its founding and, by extension, to make a larger statement about the separation of church and state. If we instead consider Washington's cultural style, we can learn something about the emerging pattern of tolerance in the new nation. In particular, the practiced restraint Washington exhibited throughout his life was especially evident in his approach to religious affairs and religious tolerance. John Adams once said of George Washington that he "possessed the Gift of Silence."[27] At least as much as nonsectarianism and ecumenism, late eighteenth-century tolerance meant restraint and civility. It meant a determination not to take certain kinds of actions—not to insult, not to offend, not to persecute, not to tyrannize over a minority group—a willful withholding of judgment and a complete swearing off of religious compulsion. These qualities Washington embodied.

In his emphasis on civil religious language, Washington followed the injunctions of the Freemasons, an organization he joined as an aspiring young man. The Masons, who rose to prominence during the mid-eighteenth century, were renowned for their commitment to religious tolerance and the policy of *not* talking about the particular points of their different faiths. In other words, they were distinguished by not addressing what both seventeenth-century irenicists called "indifferent" matters. "Freedom of Opinion thus indulged, but its points never discussed," was, according to Charles Brockwell, "the happy influence under which the unity of this truly *Ancient and Honourable Society* has been preserved, from time immemorial."[28] Accordingly, with American troops prepared to embark upon the invasion of French Canada, Washington penned the following advice to their commander, Benedict Arnold: "as Contempt of the Religion of a Country by ridiculing any of its Ceremonies or affronting its Ministers or Votaries has ever been deeply resented, you are to be particularly careful to restrain every Officer and Soldier from such Imprudence and Folly and to punish every Instance of it." "On the other hand," the general wrote, "as far as lays in your power, you are to protect and support the free Exercise of the Religion of the Country and the undisturbed Enjoyment of the rights of Conscience in religious Matters, with your utmost Influence and Authority."[29] Judgments upon other faiths restrained, but individual religious judgment protected. Here, in short, was the compromise toward which Washington and the new nation were tending.

But Washington was not always silent, and what he did say was equally significant for the nation's traditions of public religious expression and religious tolerance. For Washington, public statements and ritual acts were themselves opportunities for the exercise of civility. In his First Inaugural Address, he observed that "it would be peculiarly improper to omit, in this first official act, my fervent supplications to that Almighty Being who rules over the universe." Not long after stepping into the presidency, Washington wrote supportive letters to groups with long histories of persecution such as the Jews of Newport, the Quakers of Philadelphia, the Baptists of Virginia, and the Catholics of America. Washington assured them, in a way that no head of state had ever done, that they would enjoy not just toleration, but religious liberty, in the new nation. Replying to a letter from the Hebrew congregation in Newport, Rhode Island, Washington wrote: "It is now no more that toleration is spoken of," he wrote, "as if it was by the indulgence of one class of people, that another enjoyed the exercise of their inherent natural rights." Repeating the Newport Congregation's own words, he continued: "For happily the Government of the United States, which gives to bigotry no sanction, to persecution no assistance, requires only that they who live under its protection should demean themselves as good citizens, in giving it on all occasions their effectual support."[30]

The division of civic and religious identities, the rejection of mere toleration as an indignity imposed upon dissenters, and the affirmation of inalienable religious rights evident in this letter were all central to the revolution in religious culture that Washington did so much to shape and sustain. There was more here than an expansion of individual freedom, more than an alteration in the legal environment. As Washington's fellow Virginian, Governor Patrick Henry, wrote in a 1776 letter that made its way into the *Virginia Gazette*: "I am happy to find a catholic spirit prevailing in our country, and that those religious distinctions which formerly produced some heats are now forgotten."[31] The fate of the Revolutionary cause, just one month after the passage of the Declaration of Independence and amid the British invasion of New York, was obviously on Henry's mind. Yet Henry also expressed an increasingly common sentiment, embedded in the last line of the Virginia Declaration of Rights, which enjoined the "mutual duty of all to practise [sic] Christian forbearance, love, and charity toward each other." Of course, saying that civility prevailed did not actually make it so, and late eighteenth-century Americans exercised their right to be completely uncivil toward one another. Into the late eighteenth century, evangelicals tussled with their nonevangelical brethren in terms that were barely fit to print. Upstart churches, particularly those that relied upon itinerant ministers, continued to suffer legal slights and public indignities into the next century.[32] And, as John Sensbach describes in this volume, African-American believers continued to endure the manifold indignities of slavery, segregation, and inequality. But none of these forms of incivility was new. By contrast, the "catholic spirit" that Henry noticed was a novel and vital complement to the legal revolution taking place at the same time. Without it the other changes might have been fleeting.

What Patrick Henry would not have fully appreciated in 1776 was how dramatically the prevailing "catholic spirit" and the accompanying constitutional changes would fundamentally alter the experience of American Catholics, as well as other religious minorities. One of the ironies of this particular revolution's success was that some of the prime beneficiaries, namely Catholics and Jews, were not in its vanguard. They could not be. So ingrained was inherited prejudice toward them that repeated outspoken appeals for religious rights by Catholics and Jews might have provoked a severe counterreaction by hostile Protestants. Although both stood the most to gain from alterations in existing religious laws, Catholics and Jews played secondary roles as diverse groups of Protestants worked out the agreements that comprised the revolution in religious liberty. Nonetheless, Roman Catholics make for an especially revealing case study of how radically American religious culture shifted during the late eighteenth century, and how even the most unlikely of religious outsiders were able to accommodate themselves to these changes. The point bears emphasizing: there was accommodation from both sides. A broadening ecumenism among Protestants was reciprocated by the new nation's first generation of Roman Catholics, especially their first bishop, Father John Carroll. Father Carroll helped American Catholics reconcile themselves to the separation of religious and civic identity, the nonsectarian civility, and the religious liberties that simultaneously expanded the rights enjoyed by individual Catholics and challenged the core tenets of Roman Catholicism.

None of this could have been predicted. The ferocity of anti-Romish sentiment through the Seven Years' War (1756–63) makes it possible to imagine that an independent nation emerging from a colonial union would have been explicitly Protestant and systematically intolerant. Colonial American laws were riddled with anti-Catholicism, and its culture defined by it. Upon the defeat of the Catholic Jacobites in 1745, the great evangelical revivalist and Protestant ecumenist George Whitefield recoiled at the thought that "whole swarms of monks, Dominicans and friars, like so many locusts, [would] have overspread and plagued the nation [had the outcome been different]."[33] Whitefield was not alone either in his Protestant ecumenism or his virulent anti-Catholicism. In 1753, another renowned libertarian and Protestant ecumenist, William Livingston of New York, wrote: "I should always for political Reasons, exclude *Papists* from the common and equal Benefits of Society."[34] The vast majority of the forbearance, cooperation, and recognition extended during the Revolutionary era applied only to Protestants. Catholics were barred from voting and from officeholding in many colonies. Catholic priests were barred altogether from New York and Virginia.[35] As the imperial crisis began to unfold in the 1760s and early 1770s, it looked as though anti-Catholic bigotries would place an indelible stamp on the Revolutionary movement. The Quebec Act of 1774 elicited a predictable outcry from colonial Americans schooled to believe that any compromise to the Catholic powers on their periphery amounted to a deal with the anti-Christ. Not long after, South Carolina's Committee of Public Safety "ordered the disarming of Catholics, Negroes, and Indians."[36] Associations of tyranny and "Popery" were rife and objections to the extension of equal, republican rights to Catholics were numerous. As Derek H. Davis notes, several Continental Congress delegates protested against the employment of Catholic chaplains in the Continental Army.[37]

But a Catholic army chaplain was hired (and *only* one, it appears), new liberties were extended to Catholics, and antipopery rhetoric noticeably diminished.[38] There was no anti-Catholic pogrom amid the violence of the Revolution, and Protestants and Catholics served loyally together in the patriot armies. At first only a handful of new states made religious provisions for Roman Catholics. But within a relatively brief time all of them did. Charles Carroll, a Catholic senator from Maryland, served on the small committee appointed to work out the final language of the First Amendment, which provided federal protection for the free exercise of faith, regardless of religious affiliation. The improbable transformation of these intensely anti-Catholic and predominantly Protestant colonies into a nation defined by religious liberty still begs for a complete explanation. The treaties formed with a Catholic power, France, against a Protestant power, England, obviously played an important role in changing American Protestant approaches to American Catholics.[39] Owen Stanwood's chapter in this volume highlights some of the conceptual gymnastics that were necessary for Revolutionary Americans to reconcile themselves to their alliance with the French. Whatever the causes behind them, the considerations of expediency that made this marriage of necessity possible, as well as the improved treatment of Roman Catholics in subsequent years, illustrate the extent to which Revolutionary Americans were learning to parse out the different dimensions (namely the religious and the civic) of a believer's identity and to extend the principle of religious liberty in previously unimagined ways.

Of course, it was easier to change laws and official language than to alter ingrained popular prejudice. Historian Charles Hanson notes that when the Massachusetts constitutional convention "adopted language requiring that governors and other civil officers declare their belief in 'the Christian religion,' the objection this elicited from voters was not that it was unfair to Jews and atheists but that it was overly indulgent of Catholics."[40] As late as 1787, the Associate Reformed Synod of Philadelphia could say of the Catholic Church that "God has described her as antichristian."[41] Untold numbers of Protestants referred to Catholics as "Papists" and to their church as "slavish." Catholics sometimes returned the favor by characterizing Protestants as hopelessly misguided "sectaries" who could never attain anything approaching truth. Yet by the 1780s, Roman Catholics were generally fitting into the pattern of ecumenism and coexistence already established between Protestant denominations prior to the American Revolution. In the states with the most Catholics, Maryland and Pennsylvania, the old anti-Catholic statutes were eliminated. Elsewhere, Catholics were now accorded the basic privileges of citizenship, such as the right to serve in the militia, to hold public office, and to incorporate their churches.

By the end of the Founding era, Roman Catholics were also benefiting from the public recognition and everyday civility previously reserved for members of Protestant churches. Bishop John Carroll's 1791 visit to Boston, the capital of colonial Congregationalism and antipopery sentiment, was a noteworthy example of this transformation. There, Carroll "preached before the Governor, [and] pronounced the blessing at the annual election" of the Ancient and Honorable Artillery Company.[42] Upon his departure, Boston's *Herald of Freedom* referred to Carroll as a "benevolent Christian" and raved: "as a preacher, his talents were admitted—as a companion, his society was sought—as a man, he was esteemed, revered, and honoured."[43] Carroll perceived a change himself. He wrote to his friend Charles Plowden of the surprising "great civilities" extended to him during his visit.[44] The same civility was extended to Carroll in Maryland where, in 1785, the state assembly had proudly noted that plans for a new public college had been "drawn up by three clergymen of known abilities and different religious persuasions"—a prominent Catholic (Carroll), a prominent Episcopalian, and a prominent Presbyterian.[45] Carroll's own Georgetown College in Washington, D.C., was built and maintained without incident a few years later. Local Protestants were comfortable enough with this Jesuit-run institution to send their sons to be educated in its classrooms and to borrow books from its library. Presidents gave speeches on campus and local newspapers sang it hymns of praise.[46]

This ecumenical turn in Protestant-Catholic relations was not confined to Carroll's immediate world. Recent scholarship on the frontier West, as well as the antebellum North and the antebellum South, suggests a much more cooperative and amicable relationship between Protestants and Catholics than previously imagined.[47] The French-born Father Stephen Theodore Badin was ordained by John Carroll (the first priest to be ordained in the United States) before moving to Kentucky in 1793. There, in this frontier state, Badin found the environment notably congenial to his work. "In this part of America," he later observed, "entire liberty of conscience and religion are enjoyed." Badin emphasized that "respect" was paid to the public performance of Catholic ceremonies: "We march in procession around our cemeteries; we erect crosses on them; we preach in the hotels and other public places, and even in Protestant churches, for want of chapels, and all the sects come in crowds. During the Mass they behave in a respectful and attentive manner—some of them even bring us their children to baptize, and entrust the education of their daughters to our religious [*sic*]—and sometimes we are greatly astonished to defend our belief."[48] This sort of ecumenical civility was not merely a frontier phenomena. Andrew Stern has made a particularly compelling case for Protestant-Catholic cooperation in the antebellum South as well, which he attributes to the willingness on the part of Catholics to support slavery.[49] The fact that something comparable was occurring in the north and west suggests that an enlarged sense of civic identity—including, but not limited to, support for slavery in the south—may have made such cooperation possible.

There was plenty of reciprocity on the part of the Roman Catholic leadership. Catholics generally, and John Carroll especially, made the concessions that were necessary for such cooperation to occur. Carroll undoubtedly eased Georgetown University's acceptance into the wider community by declaring that the school, like other institutions of higher learning at the time, would not impose religious tests on candidates for admission.[50] A proposal for the academy made plain that it would "be open to Students of *Every Religious Profession*." In addition, matriculants would be allowed to attend their own places of worship.[51] Carroll also refused publicly to apply the term "heretics," and avoided the term "sectaries" when referring to the Protestant believers whom Catholics had once treated as vulgar trespassers on sacred principles. Historian Patrick Carey notes Carroll's own "distinction between what he called '*theological* or religious intolerance, which is essential to true religion, and *civil* intolerance.'" The former was legitimate; the latter was not. In other words, it was perfectly acceptable to "assert and believe that the Catholic Church was the only true church without ever imposing this belief upon others through political or civil measures."[52] The most significant concession made by American Catholics may have been their unwavering support for full religious liberty. As historians Peter Clarke and James Lowell Underwood observe, John England of Charleston "chose as the motto for his newspaper the religious clause of the First Amendment," which "appeared on the masthead of every issue of the *United States Catholic Miscellany* as a weekly proclamation of England's affirmation of a free church and a free state."[53]

As foreign as they had been to traditional Roman Catholic thought, religious liberty and a nonsectarian state may have been easier for American Catholics to accept than the social integration that threatened to erode the distinctive qualities of their church. John Carroll's acquiescence to religiously integrated education met some resistance from his coreligionists.[54] And he possessed reservations of his own, especially with regard to religious intermarriage.[55] But when it came to their official policies and public rhetoric, Carroll and his generation of American Catholic leaders subordinated their anxieties about theological dilution, interreligious mixing, and Protestant-inspired egalitarianism to their support for America's republican form of government and the protections it provided. An early indication of the direction Carroll was moving the church was his 1784 letter to a friend in Rome, arguing against the appointment of a Superior for the United States by the Vatican's Congregation of Propaganda. It would, he argued, inspire "jealousy in our Governments." "We cannot expect, & in my opinion ought not to wish," he added, "that they would tolerate any other" jurisdiction, other than that which was "purely spiritual."[56] Only a bishop appointed by the American clergy would be acceptable to his fellow Americans.[57] As repellent as these new republican norms might have been to Catholic conventions, they could not be slighted if American Catholics were to live freely and amicably with their mostly Protestant neighbors.

None of these changes guaranteed a future free of religious violence, bigotry, and discrimination. Popular anti-Catholicism reemerged with a vengeance in the 1830s. Yet it did so only after several decades of peaceful everyday relations, public civility, and legal progress. Toward the end of John England's time, the integration of Roman Catholics into the larger polity was less a matter of anxious speculation than a received fact. "In all our wide domain," he wrote in 1831, "the Catholics of these newly acquired regions and the Protestants of the old British colonies became blended together; they dwell in the same streets, they board in the same house, they preside on the same bench, they serve on the same juries, they have defended their common country in the same ranks, their blood has been commingled in peace and in war. The Catholic clergy, as well as the Catholic laity, are under the eye of Protestant observation."[58] England served as a living illustration of the larger changes that had occurred. In 1826 he was invited to speak before the U.S. Congress where he delivered a mild and erudite address on the distinguishing characteristics of his faith. There, England also assured the assembled representatives that he "would not allow to the Pope, or to any bishop of our church, outside this Union, the smallest interference with the humblest vote at our most insignificant balloting box." He added that the U.S. Constitution had provided that churches and civil government would remain "distinct and separate."[59] Responding to a Protestant critic of the church a few years later

(1831), England took a similarly assimilative approach. Here, the question that Bishop John England took up was not whether Protestants and Catholics could coexist within the same polity, but whether Catholicism could "coexist" with "the enlightened freedom of the republic." England's answer was an emphatic yes: "They have coexisted, they do coexist, they will continue to coexist; they may therefore coexist, they can therefore coexist, let them coexist."[60]

Brief Know-Nothing ballot successes in the mid-1850s and anti-Catholic riots in Philadelphia in 1843–1844 testify to the possibility of decidedly less tolerant turn in American politics. Writing to a Catholic friend in 1854, Archbishop Francis Patrick Kenrick even professed to fear for his life: "For a year past I have felt that we ought to be prepared for martyrdom, but latterly [sic] I flattered myself that the danger was nearly past. . . . We must pray for one another that we may be saved."[61] By the 1850s a more confident and more conservative Catholic Church was increasingly skeptical that the coexistence, about which Bishop England had written so confidently, was possible. Still, one has to marvel at the fact that the Catholic population grew ninefold between 1830 and 1860—at the same time that Catholic doctrine took a distinctly anti-republican turn—and yet the interreligious peace held.[62] Leading Protestants generally did no worse than accuse the Roman Catholic Church of violating broadly shared commitments to republican government, religious liberty, and nonsectarian schooling. Likewise, lay Catholics tended to be indicted for their unfortunate tendency to be Irish, as much as their loyalty to an ostensibly regressive church. Protestants had little use for Catholicism as a theological abstraction or as an international political engine. Catholic citizens were another matter; Irish Catholics were still another. The tangle of anti-Romanism, anti-Catholicism, and anti-Irish xenophobia is not easily sorted out. For its part, the American Roman Catholic Church never gave up on republican government, religious liberty, and some forms of nonsectarianism, despite its marked conservative turn. And for all of the bombastic rhetoric, abusive language, and threats of violence, the religious liberties guaranteed by the founders were never threatened and the pattern of interdenominational cooperation did not cease.

To suggest that religious conditions for minority faiths never worsened, and almost always improved, during the first years of independence is to commit the sin that historians call "Whiggism." Recent histories of early modern Europe have pointed to the shifting sands of legal toleration and the early modern prevalence of coexistence (practical or nonprincipled forms of tolerance) to debunk linear narratives of toleration. If persecution was intermittent and interreligious cooperation widely practiced, then the "rise of toleration" looks less like an objective account of legal and political changes and more like the product of a vain search for improvement in history. This nonlinear, non-Whiggish model works well for early modern Europe, and perhaps even colonial America. It works considerably less well for Revolutionary and Founding era America, where libertarian principles with transregional appeal repeatedly triumphed over local prejudices and discriminatory laws. Shared commitments to vague concepts such as religious liberty and ideals such as nonsectarian government policy could not be confined to a particular time and place. The late eighteenth century saw the institutionalization, formalization, and universalization of norms that had previously resided in the abstractions of Enlightenment thought, the charters of Pennsylvania and Rhode Island, and the egalitarian fellowship of evangelical revivals. The Revolutionary era marked the beginning of a durable, if flawed, religious peace that survived the mass arrival of Catholic emigrants to a largely Protestant country, as well as the rise of radically innovative religious communities such as the Shakers and the Mormons.

The case can be made that a deeply entrenched, unofficial Christian establishment still dominated U.S. culture and politics well past the Founding era. Indeed, orthodox Protestants succeeded in maintaining the age-old prohibitions on blasphemy and Sabbath-breaking, while encouraging Bible reading in the schools (all of which seemed compatible with the increasingly conservative principle of nonsectarianism).[63] Nor was post-Revolutionary culture especially kind to open skeptics and known nonbelievers, as Christopher Grasso argues in the next chapter.[64] But there is no denying the extent of the rights and opportunities enjoyed by religious minorities at the dawn of the nineteenth century. Despite occasional outbreaks of violence against them, upstart groups and churches kept appearing on the landscape, worshiping publicly, and drawing proselytes. Moreover, there is evidence that public officials in the new nation actively defended the principle of religious liberty against mobs that sometimes harassed religious minorities.[65] Older, better established groups fared still better. By 1840, Jews "enjoyed full religious and political equality" in all but five states (there were no official restrictions on their faith at the federal level).[66] Nor did these longer-established faiths have to give up what made them distinctive in order to live among the Protestant majority. American Catholic leaders of Carroll and England's generation altered their ecclesiastical and social policies, as well their external relations with other denominations, to better conform to the conditions of a religiously diverse republic. Yet the liturgical and doctrinal core of faiths such as Catholicism and Judaism was maintained.[67] Inside their churches and synagogues, there was no mistaking them for evangelical Protestants.[68]

The free African Americans who were denied so many other rights and sources of dignity in the early republic, and yet managed to establish their own churches and denominations in the early nineteenth century, could also testify to the change that had occurred. Religious liberty was of obvious benefit to those African Americans who successfully escaped the clutches of slavery. Especially after the American Revolution, free African Americans enjoyed a more vigorous and autonomous religious life than their enslaved counterparts, even though their worship was initially confined to predominantly white churches that condemned them to second-class treatment. Like other fundamental private and procedural rights officially accorded to every citizen regardless of race (for example, the right to due process and trial by jury), the provision of basic religious liberties secured a modicum of autonomy for free African American communities and the individuals who lived in them. In the three decades following the framing of the Constitution, when African Americans were denied the vote in Pennsylvania, Richard Allen and his fellow black Philadelphia Methodists established their own church, and then their own denomination. While the irrelevance of the First Amendment to enslaved African Americans was clear, so was its value to free blacks.

The emergence of religious liberty and civility was more than an accident of circumstances, or the byproduct of prejudice aimed at marginal groups. It was indisputably better to be a religious minority in the United States in 1780 than in colonial America in 1750; better in 1800 than 1780; and better still in 1850 than 1800. It was also, as the experience of African Americans suggests, better to be an ethnic minority because of religious liberty. Moreover, the sweeping libertarian changes of the Founding period emerged from shared traditions of enlightened ecumenism, evangelical fellowship, and Protestant-inspired autonomy that would not be easy victims of future contingencies. Toleration helped to establish the trust, and religious diversity the experiential foundation, on which more expansive rights to worship and more substantive gestures of interdenominational respect became both possible and necessary. In other words, when we consider the emergence of religious liberty and the end of religious establishments, it is very hard to deny that something ordinarily considered "progress" occurred, and that it was enduring.

Chapter 12

The Boundaries of Toleration and Tolerance
Religious Infidelity in the Early American Republic

CHRISTOPHER GRASSO

In 1798, a pamphlet by a member of a Newburgh, New York, deistical club responded to an attack printed in a local paper. The newspaper essayist's denunciation of deism had begged two questions, the pamphleteer wrote: first, "is the gospel or any principle of religion incorporated in our federal or state constitutions," and, second, "are deism and patriotism irreconcilable?" These questions, debated through the first half century of American independence, probed the boundaries of legal toleration and social tolerance. The Newburgh deist answered no to both. Citizens, he argued, were "doubly shielded" in the United States by laws guaranteeing religious liberty and by a spirit of independent opinion and mutual forbearance of differences, a spirit essential in a republican society. Another adversary, however, contended that propagating deism was a crime akin to treason. Accused by their opponents of having blasphemously mocked Christianity by once baptizing a cat and giving communion to a dog, the Newburgh deists seem to have disbanded by 1805. A Christian crusader named Abner Cunningham remembered his "infidel" Newburgh neighbors to warn a new generation of religious skeptics and freethinkers in the 1830s about God's vengeance, claiming that within five years of the sacramental mockery, "some were shot; some hung; some drowned; two destroyed themselves by intemperance, one of whom was eaten by dogs, and the other by hogs; one committed suicide; one fell from his house, and was killed; one was struck with an axe, and bled to death." Debauchery and villainy had proceeded from their anti-Christian principles, this pious writer claimed, and they got what they deserved. The Newburgh deists were gone, Cunningham suggested, but the issues they raised were not.[1]

In the early American republic, questions about religious toleration (a constitutional and legal matter) and tolerance (a reference to cultural attitudes and social practices) were often directly connected to the problems posed by citizens who stood outside Christianity. These outsiders were not pagans or Muslims, whom Christians usually considered in the abstract, or Jews, who were a small percentage of the population and a special case theologically, but deists, skeptics, and freethinkers. Deists believed in a Creator and in morals derived from nature, but not in the divinity of either the Bible or Jesus; religious skeptics and freethinkers—or "free enquirers"—doubted or denied most or all of Christianity's claims about God, man, and salvation. All were called "infidels" by Christians. Infidelity and toleration are relative terms defined by subordination to governmental power and cultural authority. A confessional state, one that has privileged and empowered a particular religious group, may deign to "tolerate" dissenters; believers in a hegemonic religious faith denigrate those who disbelieve or oppose it as "infidels." The Newburgh deist joined others—including some enlightened Christians—who called not for mere toleration but for religious liberty, and who hoped for less bigotry and more tolerance. In the early years of the new nation, the constitutional argument made little headway and the cultural one made less.

The American Revolution had prompted a rethinking of religious liberty as Christian patriots, mobilizing opposition to Britain, had to forge ideological bonds across what had often been bitter sectarian divisions among Congregationalists, Presbyterians, Baptists, and Anglicans. Stepping outside British constitutional rights to argue from a state of nature further broadened the philosophical basis of American citizenship. Framers of the new state constitutions struggled to guarantee liberty of conscience in religious matters while perpetuating a Christian culture. The new federal Constitution, with its First Amendment guaranteeing that the national government would neither establish religion nor interfere with its free exercise, left these issues to the states. For many Americans, however, the French Revolution, which produced a state that was for a time hostile to Christianity and fond of the guillotine, demonstrated that religious liberty was an idea that could be pushed too far or dangerously misconstrued. The American reaction to the astonishing events in France dovetailed with the formation of a deeply partisan national politics in the 1790s, culminating in 1800 with the bitterly fought election of a reputed deist, Thomas Jefferson.

These national and international political concerns also helped shape a cultural politics of patriotism, and of neighborliness and religious identity, even in small villages like Newburgh. A coalition of Federalist political operators and Christian polemicists effectively demonized radical religious views like those held by the Newburgh deists, but they ultimately failed to pin the devil's horns on Jeffersonian republicanism. They were thwarted, in part, by members of rapidly growing evangelical groups such as the Baptists and the Methodists who supported the Virginian's policies despite the rumors of deism. The socioeconomic transformations wrought by new markets and new modes of industrial production after 1815, however, sparked a new generation of social and religious radicalism. From the mid-1820s to about 1840, reformers such as Robert Owen, Frances Wright, and Abner Kneeland touted nonreligious or anti-Christian social philosophies; these were the new infidels, dangerously rousing the working classes, who prompted Abner Cunningham to summon the ghosts of Newburgh and who once again tested the limits of religious freedom in America.[2]

In the republic's first half-century state constitutions dropped colonial provisions that established Christian churches and supported them with tax dollars. For some commentators, this development seems to move the nation, for better or worse, from mere toleration (a Christian state deigning to grant rights to dissenters) toward complete religious liberty (a secular state with citizens free to express themselves on religious matters however they wished). Yet even by 1840, the Newburgh deist's first question—"is the gospel or any principle of religion incorporated in our federal or state constitutions?—remained open. Statutory and common law continued to privilege Christianity and curtail the rights of so-called infidels. Nor did an ethic of tolerance come to dominate public opinion. The idea that a deist, skeptic, or freethinker could be a virtuous neighbor and a patriotic American citizen remained nearly as controversial by the middle of the nineteenth century as it had been at the end of the eighteenth.

Tracking the use of the term "toleration" helps bring those limits—and the place of the "infidel" in American society—into focus. Sometimes writers used "toleration" and "liberty of conscience" almost interchangeably. In a famous 1783 election sermon assessing the state of the nation, Yale President Ezra Stiles spoke hopefully of "American Ideas of toleration and religious liberty" spreading to Europe. But he was also concerned about a contagion of European deism spreading in the United States. Not many Americans, he admitted, had openly embraced deism, yet the early 1780s could nonetheless be called a "period of deism and skeptical indifferentism in religion" because of a general sentiment against even "the most liberal" establishment of Christianity. Americans were beginning to argue that government ought to have no more to do with religion beyond "keep[ing] the civil peace among contending sects." Some even suggested that religious convictions were irrelevant to an assessment of a candidate's fitness for office, or, even worse, that deists or men indifferent to religion were actually the most suited for government because they would not favor their own denominations. The proper "American Ideas of toleration and religious liberty," therefore, for Stiles meant no preference to any particular Protestant sect but still included government patronage of the "principles of our common Christianity." A decade later, Connecticut jurist Zephaniah Swift celebrated that "the right of private judgment in matters of religion is completely recognized, and the full exercise of diversity of opinion is found to be consistent with the peace and good order of government." Writing like Stiles from a state where tax money would continue to support Protestant churches until 1818, Swift's language shifted ambiguously back and forth between discussing inalienable natural rights and the equal rights of Christians only. He did not see any contradiction in claiming that his state upheld a complete liberty of conscience and yet continued to outlaw deism along with atheism because "to prohibit the open, public, and explicit denial of the popular religion of a country, is a necessary measure to preserve the tranquility of a government."[3]

Some who continued to talk about toleration still tended to think about religious freedom less in terms of an individual's rights of conscience than of parity among Christian sects. A debate about Catholicism involving John Carroll (later the bishop of Baltimore) in the mid-1780s did so. In the 1790s an article entitled "Toleration" assumed that having all Christian sects on an equal footing would secure the rights of conscience to individuals, but the Catholic convert John Thayer argued that this sort of toleration-as-parity would end up producing more religious skepticism and unbelief. In a 1799 tract, Mason Locke Weems was one of the few writers to include deists among the "band of brothers" created by the "universal toleration" or nonpreferential treatment of religious groups. A writer in 1820 supporting the Massachusetts constitution's tax support of Protestant churches perpetuated a tradition of construing toleration much more narrowly. Neither state support of Protestantism nor a requirement that officeholders be Christians, the writer argued, violated the notion of toleration. These provisions merely balanced the individual's reasonable liberties with the rights and duties of a Christian society to worship God as it should.[4]

For other commentators, however, religious liberty had to be reimagined for a revolutionary age. Some of these writers acknowledged that toleration had to mean something new and began using the phrase "*universal* toleration" as a synonym for a capacious religious freedom. Others, though, made a sharp distinction between toleration and the rights of conscience. English Dissenter Richard Price argued in 1784 that the ideal of liberty of conscience emerging from the American Revolution meant much more than toleration: "Not only all *Christians*, but all *men* of all religions ought to be considered by a State as equally intitled to its protection as far as they demean themselves honestly and peaceably." Three years before his blistering deistical attack upon Christianity in *The Age of Reason*, Thomas Paine in *The Rights of Man* (1791) applauded the announcement that "The French constitution hath abolished or renounced Toleration, and Intolerance also, and hath established Universal Right of Conscience. Toleration is not the opposite of Intolerance, but is the Counterfeit of it. Both are despotisms. The one assumes to itself the right of with-holding Liberty of Conscience, and the other of granting it." In the mid-1790s, Democratic-Republicans at patriotic events answered Federalist toasts to toleration by raising their glasses to "Universal Freedom of Religion, and no Toleration." Freedom of religious belief and expression was a pre-political right, not a gift bestowed by the state; religious opinion and practice were matters of private judgment, not to be meddled with by a state legitimating some religious groups and not others.[5]

Religious liberals and radicals writing from abroad and republican drinking clubs were not the only ones to make this distinction between toleration and liberty. In his 1790 letter to the Hebrew congregation in Newport, Rhode Island, George Washington wrote that "All possess a like liberty of conscience, and immunities of citizenship. It is now no more that toleration is spoken of, as if it was by the indulgence of one class of people, that another enjoyed the exercise of their inherent natural rights." William Linn, a minister of the Dutch Reformed Church in New York City, argued that the idea of toleration was a remnant from an age of "ignorance and superstition": "Let the word be forever blotted from the vocabulary of Christians." William Findley, a Pennsylvania Presbyterian, answering another Pennsylvania Presbyterian's 1803 criticism of the irreligious character of state and federal constitutions, argued that toleration made sense only in conjunction with a political establishment of religion; neither Pennsylvania nor the United

States, thankfully, tried to interfere with an individual's rights of conscience, he wrote. Findley conceded that this meant that even the kind of deist who did not believe in an immortal soul—though not an atheist—could hold political office. His opponent, Samuel B. Wylie, warned that the state and federal constitutions threw the door open to atheists too. A Massachusetts Presbyterian in an 1812 fast sermon plagiarized Paine on toleration, merely substituting the U.S. Constitution for the French. In 1821, an article in an evangelical magazine noted that despite its continued use in discussions of religious freedom, "the word *Toleration,* is not suited to the present state of the American Churches" because it implied the political establishment of religion. A year before Massachusetts became the last state to drop its support of Protestant churches in 1833, an article in the *Christian Watchman* supporting complete religious liberty quoted from a dictionary to show that toleration, in the strict sense of the word, only existed where government usurped the inalienable right of people to adopt their own religious opinions and forms of worship. "Infidels, and boasting free-thinkers will [also] contend for this liberty of thinking and judging for themselves," the author admitted. But although God could hold them accountable, government should not.[6]

This notion horrified other Christians. It was precisely the perspective that Jefferson had articulated in *Notes on the State of Virginia* (1788) when he famously noted that "it does me no injury for my neighbour to say there are twenty gods, or no god. It neither picks my pocket nor breaks my leg." Federalists trying to exploit religion for political ends went back to this proof text again and again in the election of 1800. It purportedly revealed Jefferson's deism for all who had eyes to see, and since deism was but a step away from atheism, the argument went, America might very well repeat the horrors of revolutionary France if Jefferson ascended to the presidency. Even after Jefferson's inauguration failed to usher in the apocalypse, critics warned of dangers brewing. For the Presbyterian Samuel Wylie in 1803, the election of a deist by a Christian people was "shameful": "Is it to be expected that the man, who is not a brother in the profession of the religion of Jesus, but an obstinate *Infidel,* will make his administration bend to the interests of Immanuel, whose existence he denies, whose religion he mocks, and whose kingdom he believes to be fictitious!" Yet for Wylie, Jefferson's victory was just a sign of a deeper rot. A government that did not protect Christ's church was anti-Christian; a state that did not acknowledge its power emanating from God was atheistic; a constitution that made no distinction between Christians and deists, atheists, Muslims, and Egyptians worshiping crocodiles "gives a legal security and establishment to gross heresy, blasphemy, and idolatry, under the notion of liberty of conscience." The United States did have an established religion, Wylie insisted, just not one that drew from God's Word. Instead, the Constitution established a free-for-all of individual conscience.[7]

Constitutional protections, though, were sometimes not enough to shield infidels from injustices perpetrated under the cloak of the law. David Denniston was a leader of the Newburgh deists in the late eighteenth century. He joined radical politics and religion in the Republican newspaper he took over in 1796 (*The Newburgh Packet*), and helped bring the deist lecturer Elihu Palmer to town. In March 1800, he moved to New York City with $3,000 from his father, bought a newspaper (renamed *The American Citizen*), and with his partner James Cheetham supported Jefferson for the Clintonian faction of New York Republicans (De Witt Clinton was Denniston's cousin), and famously excoriated Aaron Burr. He kept his politics and his deism somewhat more separate on this bigger stage than he had in Newburgh, though he was an active member of a deistical society that gathered around Palmer in the city, too. The partisan press thrived on character assassination, and while Denniston avoided duels he did not avoid expensive libel suits. Nearly bankrupt, he returned to Newburgh by late spring 1803, started editing another newspaper, *The Rights of Man*, and almost immediately began feuding with a rival Republican paper, Dennis Coles's *Recorder of the Times*. On July 16, he took Coles to court, suing him for $480 for breach of agreement. Before taking the oath to testify, Denniston was asked by Judge George Gardner if he believed in a Supreme Being and a future state of rewards and punishments. The plaintiff reportedly answered yes to the first question and quipped that he did not know anything about the second, but protested that the questions were inappropriate and unconstitutional. The judge nevertheless refused to have Denniston sworn in, and dismissed the case.[8]

Denniston, the notorious deist, had been denied access to the courts because of his religious beliefs. The appeal was heard by the Orange County Court of Common Pleas on September 6 before three judges (including Gardner) and two assistant justices. Coles's attorneys argued from precedent in British common law. They also apparently blamed deism for the blood in the streets of France, equated deism and atheism, and warned that Christianity in America was being threatened by civil procedures that took the notion of liberty of conscience too far. Denniston's lawyers attacked on several fronts. They referred the court to Sir William Blackstone's *Commentaries on the Laws of England* (1765–69), which showed how even Muslims and Hindus could be sworn in as witnesses, but then quickly declared that the common law argument was nonetheless moot because those portions of the British common law connected to an establishment of religion had been abrogated by the New York constitution. They contended that the question rested on American law and institutions, pointing to the inalienable rights enshrined in the Declaration of Independence, the religious freedom protected by the First Amendment to the U.S. Constitution, and even the Virginia Act for Establishing Religious Freedom (1786), which was authored, they reminded the court, by the man who now led the nation despite being bitterly attacked for his own religious beliefs by the enemies of government. A New York statute gave them a bit more trouble: it allowed that potential witnesses who (like the Quakers) had scruples against taking an oath could be sworn in by mere affirmation or declaration as long as they believed in a Supreme Being and a future state of rewards and punishments. This statute seemed to open the door to the kinds of questions Judge Gardner had asked about Denniston's beliefs, but the attorneys insisted that it only reaffirmed the principle that witnesses could not be quizzed about their beliefs unless they first refused to take the standard oath. A final decision in the case was postponed until the next session, but observers thought the justices seemed to be leaning three to two against Denniston. The plaintiff, age thirty-six, died suddenly three months later, before the wheels of justice could produce a final verdict.[9]

During the 1830s, in the second wave of intense panic over religious infidelity, these questions about oaths and witnesses were debated again. A twenty-four-page magazine article in 1836, "Qualifications of Witnesses: Ought Any Man to be Excluded from Bearing Witness, on the Ground of Religious Belief?" responded to a fractious debate in the Massachusetts legislature the previous winter and made an argument in many ways resembling that of Denniston's lawyers. The author, who signed as "J.A.B." and was said to be a Suffolk County attorney, acknowledged at the outset that "the question is completely enveloped and surrounded by the irritated nervous system of popular prejudice." He reviewed the history of British common law, noting that at one time only members of the established church were permitted to testify. This rule was gradually liberalized to allow Jews, Muslims, and pagans to provide evidence in court even as Christian dissenters continued to be disqualified. The intent of the law was not to enable a court to discover the truth "but to prevent heresy and dissent from the established creed." This practice, "which originated in papal intolerance, and was nurtured in the bigoted bosom of a national church," had left its mark on American jurisprudence. In most American states by the 1830s, the rule was that witnesses had to believe in a Supreme Being and that sin was punished either in this world or the next—the latter constituting a liberalization of the requirement back in Denniston's day for a belief in eternal hellfire, a modification that allowed Universalists to testify. In Massachusetts the application of this rule to potential witnesses was left up to individual judges rather than being governed by statute. J.A.B. insisted that not a year went by in the state without a case where witnesses were disqualified because of their infidel religious opinions. While claiming to uphold the constitution by showing no preference for one form of Christianity over another, courts thus privileged one class of citizens, took away the inalienable rights of another class, and subverted justice by excluding testimony. The rule was "false, unsound, unjust and hostile to the free spirit of our national and state constitutions."[10]

But J.A.B.'s argument differed from the Denniston defense in three revealing ways. First, the author of "Qualifications of Witnesses" had more positive things to say about infidels. Denniston's lawyers had insisted that their client's religious opinions were a private matter and that his moral character should be judged by his actions only. J.A.B. made a blanket declaration that infidels could be "men of sound minds, of exemplary lives, and of spotless reputation." He showed sympathy for "the frank and honest skeptic, whose doubts, perhaps, are the results of partially completed and candid inquiry," and respect for deists such as David Hume and Edward Gibbon who, theological issues aside, were unsurpassed as historians and scholars. Second, instead of denying that deism was synonymous with atheism and leaving the prohibition of atheists unchallenged, J.A.B. specifically included atheists behind the shield of constitutional protection. As citizens before the law, he wrote, "Jew, Greek, Catholic, atheist, pagan and Christian, stand on the same footing." In contrast to standard pulpit rhetoric, he denied that atheism made a person more inclined to lie. By the 1830s, many identifiable infidels had progressed beyond deism to frankly espouse naturalistic pantheism or atheistic materialism. J.A.B.'s position, though, may have been less a response to this development than the logical implication of his own naturalistic ethics. Truth was not sacred because of God's commandment, he argued; it existed in the nature of things. Human nature and the constitution of society instilled an appreciation for truth over falsehood in every person—atheist, deist, and Christian alike. "Were it possible for just such a world as this of ours to come into being, without God's agency, the inhabitants thereof would be as firmly bound to speak the truth as we are." Most people were inclined to tell the truth unless their material interests were involved; in any event, their honesty or dishonesty, whatever their beliefs about spiritual matters, were motivated more by earthly considerations. A third distinguishing character of this defense of religious liberty was that it came not from an advocate hired to defend a friend of Thomas Paine's but from a Baptist writing in a Baptist journal called *The Christian Review* and invoking "the great father of toleration," Roger Williams. The bill that J.A.B. supported was defeated, however, because opponents portrayed it as an attack on Christianity.[11]

Blasphemy statures were another legal snare for infidels. Three cases illustrate how blasphemy prosecution could define and stigmatize infidelity both in the courtroom and in the court of public opinion. The first sketches the sort of legal argument that could make a defendant's appeal to constitutional rights irrelevant. In November 1818, Robert C. Murray was indicted at the Philadelphia Mayor's Court. Friends gathered at the Rialto tavern to protest what they considered to be the persecution of a man merely for expressing religious opinions similar to those "of *Franklin* and *Jefferson*, two of the greatest and best men." But in court the prosecutor quickly convinced a jury that the case had nothing to do with religious persecution. Two witnesses testified that the defendant had been heard "at various times and places" saying "That *Christ was a bastard—his mother a w— —and the Bible a pack of lies.*" An unrepealed act of 1700 made it a crime to "willfully, premeditatedly, and despitefully, blaspheme, or speak loosely and profanely of *Almighty God, Christ Jesus, the Holy Spirit or Scriptures of Truth.*" Defense counsel presented evidence of Murray's good character and argued against the Pennsylvania constitutionality of the act, pointing to sections on religious liberty and free speech. But, as the prosecution argued and the court explained in greater length at sentencing, Murray was free to express whatever religious opinions he wished as long as he used "decent language." "While one man exercises his rights, let him not offend against the rights of others." Not only did Murray use obscene language, he appeared to do so with malicious intent, accosting people in the streets as they made their way to church. He seemed intent on trying "to destroy the happiness of another, by depriving him in his confidence in revealed religion, and rendering him prey to doubt and despair." Government had a duty to protect a citizen's peace of mind from wanton attack just as it protected private property. Murray needed to "be taught that respect even to the prejudices of others on so important a topic as that of religion, is due to the humblest individual in society." Although the court adopted a Christian perspective when the judge warned Murray that he would ultimately have to face the truth of revealed religion, the conviction was based on the argument that he had used what a later generation would call hate speech, maliciously and in public, that threatened to disturb the peace, and the religious content of those words seemed almost as beside the point as Murray's deism.[12]

The legal logic in a much more famous case, *The People of New York v. Ruggles* (1811), resembled that of the Murray case, but the broader arguments by Chief Justice James Kent articulated assumptions that would continue to bolster Christian hegemony and help position deists, skeptics, and freethinkers as pariahs. Ruggles, too, called Jesus a bastard and Mary a whore. Lacking a statute, the prosecution contended that Ruggles could be convicted under common law. The defense countered that the New York constitution's provisions separating church and state and protecting religious liberty had abrogated those portions of British common law relating to religious establishment—like the precedents shielding the notion of Jesus's divinity from attack. Kent reiterated a lower court jury's conclusion that Ruggles's utterance did not arise from a dispute among learned men but was simply obscene language proclaimed loudly in public with malicious intent, wicked words that were an offense against public peace and safety. Such a verbal assault was not covered by constitutional protections of free speech and religion; it was considered an attack not on an established church but on civil society. Kent, however, unlike the Philadelphia Mayor's Court, did not merely say that the blasphemer's words attacked a neighbor's mental private property—attacked beliefs that, whether truths or just "prejudices," were important to the neighbor's pursuit of happiness. Such words for Kent also struck "at the root of moral obligation and weaken the security of social ties." Christianity deserved special protection, and not only because it was the religion of the majority and therefore defined the community's cultural norms, including those norms determining what words might give so much offense as to disturb the public peace and lead to violence. Christianity was special because it was the essential foundation of a morally refined society, and because it was true. (Kent also declared that one could maliciously insult Jesus but not Mohammed because the former spoke the truth and the latter was an "imposter.") The chief justice argued that Christianity was part of the common law that New York had incorporated. Other states (Pennsylvania in 1824 and Delaware in 1837) would make similar affirmations. And although common law arguments would not be decisive in blasphemy trials or other church and state cases, the assertion by one of America's leading jurists that "we are a Christian people and the morality of the country is deeply ingrafted upon christianity" affirmed that courts could maintain Christianity's privileged position in American society no matter what constitutions seemed to say about religious establishments and the rights of conscience.[13]

The most widely publicized blasphemy prosecution in the nineteenth century was the case of Abner Kneeland, a freethinking editor and lecturer in Boston during the 1830s. Kneeland was a former Baptist and then Universalist minister who had renounced Christianity in 1829. He soon became associated with freethought reformers Frances Wright and Robert Dale Owen. Wright, born in Scotland in 1795, became a sensation in the United States when she began writing and lecturing against the evils of slavery, capitalism, and organized religion, and calling for radical education reform and the rights of women. Owen, the son of Scottish industrialist and utopian socialist Robert Owen, worked with his father to remake society through an experimental community at New Harmony, Indiana, and with Wright at one that existed briefly at Nashoba, Tennessee. Like his father, the younger Owen engaged in public debates with Christians on the evidences of Christianity. With Wright, Robert Dale Owen established and edited *The New Harmony and Nashoba Gazette*, a freethought paper they renamed *The Free Enquirer* and then moved to New York City in 1829. The newspaper's stance on religion was succinctly summarized by a testimonial from a loyal reader in 1829: "I am now a sceptic. . . . I live for this world, because I know nothing of any other. I doubt all revelations from heaven, because they appear to me improbable and inconsistent. . . . I desire to see men's wishes bounded by what they can see and know; for I am convinced that they would thus become more contented, more practically benevolent, and more permanently happy, than any dreams of futurity can make them." Kneeland's *Boston Investigator* and Society of Free Enquirers in that city were closely allied with the work Owen and Wright were doing in New York (similar societies sprouted up in Philadelphia, Baltimore, and Wilmington). Kneeland too combined anticlericalism and reform politics, and tried to support (or co-opt) the political stirrings of the urban working class. He lectured twice weekly before an audience of as many as two thousand people by the mid-1830s; his newspaper was sold by 243 agents and circulated to 2,500 subscribers in twenty-seven states and territories by the end the decade. The Boston Free Enquirers also sponsored dances and published cheap new editions of skeptical books. Prosecuting Kneeland for blasphemy was an attack on the broader phenomenon of organized freethought.[14]

On December 20, 1833, less than six weeks after the people of Massachusetts had voted by a ten to one margin to finally end the state's legal establishment of Protestantism, lawyer and temperance advocate Lucius M. Sargent forwarded a copy of Kneeland's *Boston Investigator* to the county attorney's office, with a note urging that Kneeland be indicted by a grand jury for blasphemy. The prosecution was based not on common law but on a 1782 statute. So began a series of four well-publicized trials and a final appeal that would eventually lead to Kneeland's sixty-day jail sentence in summer 1838. The trials brought up several issues, including charges that the Free Enquirers were spreading information about birth control and dangerous ideas about racial and sexual equality; that their cheap dances encouraged illicit sex; that the use of the word "testicle" in connection with a discussion of the immaculate conception was obscene; and that a comparison of God hearing prayers to President Jackson being besieged by petitions was blasphemous. The prosecution, however, came to focus upon a single sentence of Kneeland's: "Universalists believe in a god which I do not," he had written. Kneeland argued that he was speaking about the Universalist's particular conception of God, and not all conceptions of God. He explained that he was a pantheist, not an atheist, so he did actually believe in God, at least as he defined the term (as a synonym for an unintelligent, material nature). But, he taunted Boston's theologically liberal Unitarians and conservative Calvinist Trinitarians, whose understanding of God, and whose reading of the Bible, was the 1782 blasphemy statute supposed to protect? Even if he had been trying to articulate a general disbelief in God, disbelief—which he described as a probable and provisional judgment based on the best currently available evidence—was not the same as the outright denial mentioned in the statute. At any rate, Kneeland contended, the law was an unconstitutional infringement of his right to free religious expression. On this last point, the prosecution successfully countered that the state constitution protected religious, and not irreligious, expression. In summer 1838, Kneeland watched the construction of the Bunker Hill Monument from the window of his jail cell and cast himself as a martyr for liberty.[15]

Christians were divided over the Kneeland prosecution. Unitarians themselves had been called infidels by the guardians of Calvinist orthodoxy. But in a long review of the published closing arguments for the defense and the prosecution, the Unitarians' leading journal ignored all one hundred thirty pages of the former and endorsed the latter in the name of preserving social order. Universalists, too, had often been denounced by their more theologically conservative Christian brethren as being on the slippery slope toward deism and atheism. Perhaps because they felt the sting of religious prejudice more than upper-class Unitarians, Universalists in *The Evangelical Magazine and Gospel Advocate* condemned the prosecution as "an extremely imprudent, impolitic, foolish, and even cruel act." The anticlerical *Reformer and Christian* and the *Catholic Telegraph* also denounced the decision. The reformist *Spirit of the Age* and the evangelical *Religious Intelligencer* applauded Kneeland's imprisonment, while the Methodist *Zion's Herald* approved of the decision but wished the freethinker's offense had been considered a misdemeanor rather than a crime requiring jail time.[16]

Listing fifty-eight secular and religious newspapers from around the country that opposed the decision, Kneeland claimed that the prosecution had not won its case before the tribunal of public opinion. He was probably right. This hardly meant, though, that by the 1830s a majority would indulge a diversity of opinions on religious questions that had stretched to include deism, skepticism, and freethought. Americans continued to write, as they had heard for decades, about the incapacity of the infidel to be a good citizen. As one magazine article put it, infidels were enemies to themselves, their families, society, and God. Their principles unbalanced their minds, severed the bonds of domestic affection, polluted their communities, threatened American freedom, and manifested malignant hatred toward their Creator. A writer argued in the *Baltimore Monument* in 1836 that even if the skeptics and freethinkers were right and could demonstrate that Christianity was a mere myth, Christians, like patriots who say "Our country right or wrong," would "take for our motto—*Religion right or wrong*, for we would rather have an unreal fabrication—a charm—a delusion, than a sad, distressing, unfortunate reality." Attacking an infidel whose doctrines endangered the state, wrote another essayist in 1839, was no different from opposing a mad monarchist who was trying to pull down republican institutions. But it was unwise to call upon laws, courts, and the strong arm of the civil magistrate. Why make martyrs who would draw sympathy from too many with their cries of persecution when "public sentiment" and "universal odium" could better "furnish an adequate cure"? This was a shift in strategy, not a signal that a broader commitment to social tolerance had been embraced.[17]

How, then, ought a Christian deal with a freethinking neighbor or with a religious skeptic who broadcast his opinions in the public prints? With the speed of communications in the 1830s, an article in the *Southern Literary Messenger* explained, dangerous opinions spread rapidly through the whole society. But in the free institutions of a republic, the power to combat those opinions was dispersed rather than concentrated at the center. Therefore, the author continued, every citizen needed to battle against licentiousness. Opinions differed over how citizens should wage that battle. A Universalist pondering the Kneeland case noted how phrenologists claimed that there were particular parts of the brain for reverence and the appreciation of the marvelous, so perhaps these religious portions of an infidel's brain had become diseased even though other faculties remained unimpaired. Other writers spoke more generally about infidelity resulting from a disease of the mind or from an undeveloped moral nature, and of religious skepticism being produced when doubting became a reflex habit and then hardened into a psychological weakness. Such conceptions of infidelity as infirmity rather than willful depravity suggested that Christians should pity rather than despise. Other commentators normalized the diversity of religious opinion. The author of "Are Great Minds Prone to Skepticism?" argued in 1835 that religious skepticism was a natural phase as a person moved from childhood credulity through the doubts produced by rational inquiry before arriving at a mature and reasonable faith. In his autobiographical novel, Orestes Brownson described how outmoded religious ideas and practices in the early decades of the nineteenth century were causing many thoughtful people to stall in that middle phase. Calls for tolerance and compassion rooted in such points of view, however, were overwhelmed by repetitions of the venerable Christian argument that infidels were merely sinners rationalizing their wickedness. While some Christian apologists offered to publicly debate the freethinkers, others argued that the "degraded, drunken, beastly kind of infidelity abroad in the land" deserved only contempt.[18]

In the 1820s and 1830s Christians were anxious because the problem of infidelity seemed much larger than what might be indicated by the numbers of people attending lectures by Frances Wright or reading Abner Kneeland's *Boston Investigator*. In the 1780s, Ezra Stiles had worried that for every outspoken deist such as Ethan Allen there were many—but how many?—harboring secret doubts about Christianity, just as Stiles himself had concealed his own inclinations toward deism and skepticism as a younger man. Similarly, an observer in 1829 believed that "the number of decided infidels, is probably much more limited than that of a sort of skeptics who are content to remain suspended in doubt whether the Christian revelation is true or false," but who for the time being continued to respect Christianity as the custom of the country and an amiable superstition. A decade later, the *Christian Secretary* prepared a series of articles attacking skepticism and infidelity because the editors had come to the same conclusion. Calvinist biblical scholar Moses Stuart suspected that there was not a small number among the upper classes who would abandon the Bible if doing so became socially respectable; Catholic convert Gardner Jones claimed that at least a third of the professing Protestants in New York City in the mid-1830s were privately "decided infidels." A twenty-four-page essay in *The Spirit of the Pilgrims* focused not on outspoken freethinkers or closeted skeptics but the way that doubt could hollow out Christianity from within without believers being fully aware of what was happening. Newfangled ideas encouraged Christians to doubt one traditional doctrine, qualify a second, and throw out a third, until believers "have been gradually and unconsciously drawn away from their old belief. . . . They begin with doubting; they next give up, and are finally in danger of ending in the disbelief of almost everything but that they are themselves very exemplary believers." Self-proclaimed deists, skeptics, and freethinkers were so threatening because they gave voice to the doubts Christians had about their own faith, or about the fidelity of the fellow in the next pew.[19]

America's spirit of religious intolerance also had its critics. In 1839, an astute college student pondered the power of public opinion in a republic. Public opinion was perhaps the only control over society under such a government, but it could unfortunately operate with little regard to truth or justice: "public opinion is a tyrant, as remorseless in its decrees, and as able to exact obedience to them, as the haughtiest despot the world has ever borne with. If then, this power be directed against any particular set of men or any particular set of opinions, those men and those opinions are placed under the yoke of proscription." He saw how the religious sentiments of the majority "are so closely inwoven with the frame-work of our minds by the magic effects of association . . . they have become with us so like a part of our mental constitution, that any attempt to root them out, seems like doing an act of violence to the laws, which govern our being." The author, however, was not criticizing intolerance toward deists, skeptics, and freethinkers, but the ingrained Protestant prejudices toward Catholics.[20]

Protestant writers frequently cast Catholicism and infidelity as two extremes. Invoking what might be called a Goldilocks epistemology, they insisted that skeptics doubted too much, credulous Catholics doubted too little, and Protestants were just right, the golden mean of a rational faith. The sociopolitical correlate to this spectrum placed infidels with the forces of anarchy and Catholics with slavish submission to tyranny, whereas only Protestantism could sustain the ordered liberty without licentiousness that was the lifeblood of a republic. An article in the *United States Catholic Miscellany* in September 1834, argued that American Catholics suffered far more persecution than the nation's deists, skeptics, atheists, or Jews. The essay was published a month after a mob had destroyed the Ursuline Convent in Charlestown, Massachusetts. The author raged about the constant calumnies flowing from Protestant pulpits and presses, which had "succeeded . . . in kindling the public odium, in exciting savage rage, and in driving the vulgar rabble to outrages and atrocities." Protestants of every sect, but especially the disciples of Calvin, constantly insisted "that liberty of opinion and freedom in judging is the unalienable right of every man" and yet they denied that liberty to others. In a country that theoretically guaranteed religious freedom, they threatened "to reduce American liberty to an empty name." Protestant bigotry and prejudice, the Catholic writer argued, after a lapse of three centuries had suddenly "grown to an enormous extent." As the small freethought movement began to fade and as a flood of Catholic immigrants entered eastern port cities, anxious American Protestants would police the borders of toleration and tolerance with a different threat in mind.[21]

Notes

INTRODUCTION

1. Jon Butler, "Jack-in-the-Box Faith: The Religion Problem in Modern American History," *Journal of American History* 90, no. 4 (March 2004): 1357–78.

2. According to a June 2009 report by Robert Townshend, those identifying themselves as religious historians constitute the most common field of specialization identified by American Historical Association members. See http://blog.historians.org/news/823/aha-membership-grows-modestly-as-history-of-religion-surpasses-culture.

3. What Charles L. Cohen wrote more than a decade ago still holds: "Historians have rehearsed some intellectually powerful themes—the founding of a pluralistic religious order and the growth of toleration, to name two—but how to assess their significance relative to each other and to other phenomena has not been made clear." See Cohen, "The Post-Puritan Paradigm of Early American Religious History," *William & Mary Quarterly* 54, no. 4 (October 1997): 722.

4. On the neglect of the law by religious historians, and for a discussion of what religious scholars might contribute to church-state scholarship, see Sarah Barringer Gordon, "Review Essay: Where the Action Is—Law, Religion, and the Scholarly Divide," *Religion and American Culture* 18, no. 2 (Summer 2008): 249–71. On recent trends in the historical study of American religion, see Catherine L. Albanese, W. Clark Gilpin, Leigh E. Schmidt, and Thomas A. Tweed, "How the Graduate Study of Religion Has Changed in the Past Decade," *Religion and American Culture* 17, no. 1 (Winter 2007): 1–25; David D. Hall, "The Place of Experience," *Religion and American Culture* 13, no. 2 (Summer 2003): 241–50; David Hackett, *Religion and American Culture: A Reader* (New York: Routledge, 1995); Robert A. Orsi, *Between Heaven and Earth: The Religious Worlds People Make and the Scholars Who Study Them* (Princeton, N.J.: Princeton University Press, 2005); and Thomas A. Tweed, ed., *Retelling U.S. Religious History* (Berkeley: University of California Press, 1997). For a recent example of how the history of church and state may be woven into social and cultural history, and vice versa, see Monica Najar, *Evangelizing the South: A Social History of Church and State in Early America* (New York: Oxford University Press, 2008).

5. For leading works of church-state history, see Thomas E. Buckley, *Church and State in Revolutionary Virginia, 1776–1787* (Charlottesville: University Press of Virginia,

1977); Robert L. Cord, *Separation of Church and State: Historical Fact and Current Fiction* (New York: Lambeth Press, 1982); Thomas J. Curry, *The First Freedoms: Church and State in America to the Passage of the First Amendment* (New York: Oxford University Press, 1986); Derek H. Davis, *Religion and the Continental Congress, 1774–1789: Contributions to Original Intent* (New York: Oxford University Press, 2000); Daniel L. Dreisbach, *Thomas Jefferson and the Wall of Separation Between Church and State* (New York: New York University Press, 2002); Leonard W. Levy, *The Establishment Clause: Religion and the First Amendment*, 2nd rev. ed. (Chapel Hill: University of North Carolina Press, 1994); Michael J. Malbin, *Religion and Politics: The Intentions of the Authors of the First Amendment* (Washington, D.C.: American Enterprise Institute for Public Policy Research, 1978); Michael W. McConnell, "The Origins and Historical Understanding of Free Exercise of Religion," *Harvard Law Review* 103 (May 1990): 1409–517; Mark D. McGarvie, *One Nation Under Law: America's Early National Struggles to Separate Church and State* (DeKalb: Northern Illinois University Press, 2004); William G. McLoughlin, *New England Dissent, 1630–1833: The Baptists and the Separation of Church and State*, 2 vols. (Cambridge, Mass.: Harvard University Press, 1971); Vincent Philip Muñoz, *God and the Founders: Madison, Washington, and Jefferson* (Cambridge: Cambridge University Press, 2009); and Leo Pfeffer, *Church, State, and Freedom* (Boston: Beacon Press, 1967).

6. Moreover, as Monica Najar suggests, neither "church" nor "state" were static concepts in early America. The term "church," she points out, "seems at odds with the various self-styled 'religious societies' of the late eighteenth century and 'state' represents a rather grandiose term for the nascent governmental bodies" then taking shape. Najar, *Evangelizing the South*, 5.

7. For the argument that diversity is the field's operating paradigm, see Cohen, "The Post-Puritan Paradigm of Early American Religious History."

8. John England, "The Republic in Danger," in *The Works of the Right Rev. John England: First Bishop of Charleston*, Volume IV, Part III (Baltimore: J. Murphy & Co., 1849), 45.

9. Jon Butler, *Becoming America: The Revolution Before 1776* (Cambridge, Mass.: Harvard University Press, 2000), 189.

10. Jon Butler, *Awash in a Sea of Faith: Christianizing the American People*, Studies in Cultural History (Cambridge, Mass.: Harvard University Press, 1990); and David D. Hall, *Worlds of Wonder, Days of Judgment: Popular Religious Belief in Early New England* (New York: Alfred A. Knopf, 1989).

11. Carla Pestana, *Protestant Empire: Religion and the Making of the British Atlantic World* (Philadelphia: University of Pennsylvania Press, 2009), 6.

12. William M. Offutt, "The Atlantic Rules: The Legalistic Turn in Colonial British America," in Elizabeth Mancke and Carole Shammas, eds., *The Creation of the British Atlantic World* (Baltimore: Johns Hopkins University Press, 2005), 160–81.

13. As the New York publicist and politician William Livingston wrote in 1753: "Nothing can be more unmannerly, as well as unchristian, than for any Protestant Minister, within his Majesty's Dominions, to stigmatize and vilify, a numerous Body of People,

protected by the same Laws, and incorporated under the same Constitution with himself." See Livingston, "Vindication of the Moravians," in Milton M. Klein, ed., *The Independent Reflector* (Cambridge, Mass.: The Belknap Press of Harvard University Press, 1963), 92. Livingston also said that it was common for the clergy to harass such people ("Vindication of the Moravians," 93).

14. William Tennent, *Mr. Tennent's Speech on the Dissenting Petition* (Charleston, 1777), 15–16.

15. See Christopher Grenda, "Thinking Historically About Diversity: Religion, the Enlightenment, and the Construction of Civic Culture in Early America," *Journal of Church and State* 48, no. 3 (2006): 567; and Evan Radcliffe, "Revolutionary Writing, Moral Philosophy, and Universal Benevolence in the Eighteenth Century," *Journal of the History of Ideas* 54 (April 1993): 221–40.

16. Alexandra Walsham, *Charitable Hatred: Tolerance and Intolerance in England, 1500–1700* (Manchester University Press, 2006), especially chapter 2.

17. In this, as in other ways, the Virginia Statute for Establishing Religious Freedom echoed Madison's formulation in the famous "Memorial and Remonstrance" (written in the same context and by the man who ushered the Statute for Religious Freedom to passage) that "Before any man can be considered as a member of Civil Society, he must be considered as a subject of the Governour of the Universe."

18. Willem Frijhoff, *Embodied Belief: Ten Essays on Religious Culture in Dutch History* (Hilversum, 2002); Benjamin J. Kaplan, *Divided by Faith: Religious Conflict and the Practice of Toleration in Early Modern Europe* (Cambridge, Mass,: Belknap Press, 2007); and Walsham, *Charitable Hatred*. See also James E. Bradley, "Toleration and Movements of Christian Reunion, 1660–1789," in Stewart Brown, ed., *Enlightenment, Reawakening, and Revolution, 1660–1815*, vol. 7, Cambridge History of Christianity (New York: Cambridge University Press, 2006).

19. Frijhoff, "The Threshold of Toleration: Interconfessional Conviviality in Holland During the Early Modern Period," in *Embodied Belief*, 40.

20. Kaplan, *Divided by Faith*; Frijhoff tends to locate coexistence in the liminal spaces between private and public spheres, where members of different groups interacted. The historian Benjamin Kaplan instead stresses the significance of everyday segregation that allowed peaceful relations to flourish in places such as the early modern Netherlands. In addition, Kaplan has recently observed that "personal relations could, in practice, be smooth and even amicable without any lessening of people's ideological commitment to the enmities that were an essential part of so much Christian piety in the confessional age." See Kaplan, "Integration vs. Segregation: Religiously Mixed Marriage and the 'Verzuiling' Model of Dutch Society," in Benjamin Kaplan, Bob Moore, and Judith Pollmann, eds., *Catholic Communities in Protestant States Britain and the Netherlands c. 1570–1720* (Manchester: Manchester University Press, 2009), 50.

21. See especially James R. Stoner, "Catholic Politics and Religious Liberty in America: The Carrolls of Maryland," in Daniel L. Dreisbach, Mark D. Hall, and Jeffrey H. Morrison, eds., *The Founders on God and Government* (Lanham, Md.: Rowman and Littlefield, 2004), 253–54.

22. For critical comments on coexistence studies as they apply to Europe, see John Coffey, "Milton, Locke, and The New History of Toleration," *Modern Intellectual History* 5, no. 3 (November 2008): 630–31; and J. H. Elliott, "A Question of Coexistence," *New York Review of Books* 56, no. 13 (August 13, 2009): 39.

23. For the most prominent argument that one confessional regime replaced another, see J. C. D. Clark, *The Language of Liberty, 1660–1832: Political Discourse and Social Dynamics in the Anglo-American World* (Cambridge: Cambridge University Press, 1994).

24. For a brief discussion of how this might be accomplished, see Walsham, *Charitable Hatred*, 29. For an exemplary study along these lines, see Mark Häberlein, *The Practice of Pluralism: Congregational Life and Religious Diversity in Lancaster, Pennsylvania, 1730–1820* (University Park: Pennsylvania State University Press, 2009).

25. Eric Schlereth, "A Tale of Two Deists: John Fitch, Elihu Palmer, and the Boundary of Tolerable Religious Expression in Early National Philadelphia," *Pennsylvania Magazine of History and Biography* 132, no. 1 (October 2008): 5–31.

26. On the expanding limits of what constituted prejudice in early national America, see J. M. Opal, "The Labors of Liberality: Christian Benevolence and National Prejudice in the American Founding," *Journal of American History* 94, no. 4 (March 2008): 1082–107.

27. Historians are less sure about contemporary church attendance rates. For a powerful refutation of the thesis that late eighteenth-century America was characterized by religious indifference, see James H. Hutson's "The Christian Nation Question" in Hutson, *Forgotten Features of the Founding: The Recovery of Religious Themes in the Early American Republic* (Lanham, Md.: Lexington Books, 2003). Hutson's critique of the indifference thesis derives partly from Patricia U. Bonomi and Peter R. Eisenstadt, "Church Adherence in the Eighteenth-Century British American Colonies," *William & Mary Quarterly*, 3rd series, 39 (April 1982): 245–86.

28. For a recent and extreme version of this interpretation by a popular writer, see Allen, *Moral Minority: Our Skeptical Founding Fathers* (Chicago: Ivan R. Dee, 2006).

29. For an unusual argument on behalf of liberty of conscience for children, see John Leland, *The Rights of Conscience Inalienable, and Therefore Religious Opinions Not Cognizable by Law, or, The High-Flying Churchman, Stript of His Legal Robe, Appears a Yaho*, (New London: T. Green & Son, 1791), 8.

30. Susan Juster, *Disorderly Women: Sexual Politics and Evangelicalism in Revolutionary New England* (Ithaca, N.Y.: Cornell University Press, 1994); Catherine A. Brekus, "The Revolution in the Churches: Women's Religious Activism in the Early American Republic," in James H. Hutson, ed., *Religion in the New Republic: Faith in the Founding of America* (Lanham, Md.: Rowman and Littlefield, 2000), 115–36. Christine Leigh Heyrman, *Southern Cross: The Beginnings of the Bible Belt* (New York: Alfred A. Knopf, 1997), esp. 141, 163–89.

31. William Warner, *At Peace with All Their Neighbors: Catholics and Catholicism in the National Capital, 1787–1860* (Washington, D.C.: Georgetown University Press, 1994), 41.

32. Jon Butler, *The Huguenots in America: A Refugee People in New World Society* (Cambridge, Mass.: Harvard University Press, 1983), esp. 81–82; Anne C. Rose, *Beloved Strangers: Interfaith Families in Nineteenth-Century America* (Cambridge, Mass.: Harvard University Press, 2001).

33. Michael Walzer writes that people "properly called tolerant . . . make room for men and women whose beliefs they don't adopt, whose practices they decline to imitate; they coexist with an otherness that, however much they approve of its presence in the world, is still something different from what they know, something alien and strange." See Walzer, *On Toleration* (New Haven, Conn.: Yale University Press, 1997), 11.

34. "Toleration is not the *opposite* of intoleration, but is the *counterfeit* of it. Both are despotisms. The one assumes to itself the right of withholding liberty of conscience, and the other of granting it" (Thomas Paine, *The Rights of Man*). Noah Hobart's 1828 dictionary defined the transitive verb "tolerate" as "To suffer or to be done without prohibition or hinderance [*sic*]; to allow or permit negatively, by not preventing; not to restrain; as, to *tolerate* opinions or practices. The protestant religion is *tolerated* in France, and the Roman Catholic in Great Britain."

35. John Witte, Jr., provides a helpful exposition of the contemporary meaning of "liberty of conscience" and the "free exercise of religion" in *Religion and the American Constitutional Experiment*, 2nd ed. (Boulder, Colo.: Westview, 2000), 41–46.

CHAPTER I. FAITH, REASON, AND ENLIGHTENMENT

1. Ralph Wallis, *Rome for Good News, Or, Good News from Rome: In a Dialogue Between a Seminary Priest, and a Supposed Protestant, at large* (London, n.d.), 11.

2. David Hume, *Essays: Moral, Political, and Literary* (1741), ed. Eugene F. Miller (Indianapolis: Liberty Fund, 1985), 74, Essay X, "Of Superstition and Enthusiasm."

3. The basic framework of this scholarly dispute is established by the following two works: Barry Alan Shain, *The Myth of American Individualism: The Protestant Origins of American Political Thought* (Princeton, N.J.: Princeton University Press, 1994); Michael P. Zuckert, *The Natural Rights Republic: Studies in the Foundation of the American Political Tradition* (Notre Dame: University of Notre Dame Press, 1996). Other works presenting an emerging individualism in the late eighteenth century include Isaac Kramnick, *Republicanism and Bourgeois Radicalism: Political Ideology in Late Eighteenth-Century England and America* (Ithaca, N.Y.: Cornell University Press, 1990); Michael Lienesch, *New Order of the Ages: Time, the Constitution, and the Making of Modern Political Thought* (Princeton, N.J.: Princeton University Press, 1988); Drew R. McCoy, *The Elusive Republic: Political Economy in Jeffersonian America* (Chapel Hill: University of North Carolina Press, 1980). For a different perspective, consider Robert H. Wiebe, *The Opening of American Society: From the Adoption of the Constitution to the Eve of Disunion* (New York: Knopf, 1984).

4. William G. McLoughlin, *New England Dissent, 1630–1833: The Baptists and the Separation of Church and State*, 2 vols. (Cambridge, Mass.: Harvard University Press,

1971); McLoughlin, ed., *Isaac Backus on Church, State, and Calvinism: Pamphlets, 1754–1789* (Cambridge, Mass.: Harvard University Press, 1968).

5. B. R. White, *The English Baptists of the Seventeenth Century* (London: Baptist Historical Society, 1983).

6. Thomas Helwys, *A short Declaration of the Mistery of Iniquity* (1612), "To the Reader": "wee have with all humble bouldness spoken unto our lord the King, our defence for this is, that wee are taught of God especially to make supplications, praiers, intercessions . . . and we are taught that the gracious God of heaven (by whom the King reignes) would, that the King should be saved and come to the knoweledg of the truth."

7. Ibid., preface entitled "the principal matters handled in the Booke."

8. Ibid., 40. Also see 58.

9. Ibid., 41–42, continues: "will our lord the King notwithstanding all that Christ hath done for him, in giving him such a kingdome, with such great dignity and power therein, will the King notwithstanding, enter upon Christs kingdome, and appoint (or by his power suffer to be appointed) Lawes, Lords, Law makers over or in this kingdome of Christ. . . . Far be it then from the hart of our lord the King, to give his earthly power to anie to rule as lords over the kingdome and heritage of Christ, which he hath reserved to himself, to rule and governe onely by his word and spirit, where no earthly power may be admitted, in that it is no earthly kingdome." Similarly, 49: "the K[ing] must needs grant that as he is an earthly king he can have no power to rule in this spiritual kingdome of Christ, nor can compel anie to be subjects thereof."

10. Ibid., 24: "Temporal Lords have the power over mens bodies, so must spiritual Lords have the power over mens spirits, but there is onely one spiritual Lord, which is the Father of spirits." Similarly, 43, "neither hath our lord the King by that sword of justice power over his subjects consciences. . . . For an earthly sword is ordeyned of God onely for an earthly power: and a spirituall sword for a spirituall power: and Offences against the earthly power must be punished with the earthly sword, and offences against the spirituall power with the spirituall sword., and with this sword . . . to cast downe holds, casting downe the ymaginations, & every high thing that is exalted against the knowledge of God, and bringing into captivity every thought to the obedience of Christ. 2. Cor. 10.4, 5."

11. Ibid., 28. Also see 46–47, "not with [the] sword of justice, but by the foolishness of preaching, for that is the meanes whereby God hath appointed to save them that believe 1 Cor. 1.21 and 27." See 44: "he shall sinne against God in entering upon the kingdome of Christ . . . who doth not will nor require to have people commanded and compelled by an earthly sword or power"; Christ's "sword is his word, which is lively and mighty in operation, and sharper then anie two edged sword Heb. 4.12 and therefore needs not the helpe of anie Kings sword."

12. Ibid., 53. "Turks" meant Muslims.

13. Ibid., referring to "them of the Romish religion": "if they be true & faithful subjects to the King . . . wee do freely professe, that our lord the King hath no more power over their consciences then ours, and that is none at all."

14. Ibid., 46.

15. Similarly, see John Smyth's Baptist Confession of Faith, Article 84 in William L. Lumpkin, ed., *Baptist Confessions of Faith* (Philadelphia: Judson Press, 1959), 140: "That the magistrate is not by virtue of his office to meddle with religion, or matters of conscience, to force or compel men to this or that form of religion, or doctrine: but to leave Christian religion free, to every man's conscience, and to handle only civil transgressions (Rom. xiii), injuries and wrongs of man against man, in murder, adultery, theft, etc., for Christ only is the king, and lawgiver of the church and conscience (James iv. 12)."

16. John Murton shared Helwys's understanding of religious toleration. John Murton, *Persecution for Religion Judg'd and Condemn'd* in *Tracts on Liberty of Conscience and Persecution, 1614–1661*, ed. Edward Bean Underhill (London: J. Haddon, 1846) reprint ed. (Elibron Classics Replica Edition, 2005). Murton's pamphlet was published in 1620. Underhill's volume reproduces the 1662 edition. Murton affixed *2 Corinthians 10.4* to the title page of *Persecution for Religion Judg'd and Condemn'd* (86). He emphasized that the earthly sword of kings only applies to the outward things of "his subjects' bodies and goods" (110): "the sword of the magistrate, and all afflictions proceeding therefrom, are only upon the outward man" (113); "God hath given to magistrates . . . a worldly sword, their punishments can extend no further than the outward man" (121); "my soul, wherewith I am to worship God, that belongeth to another King, *whose kingdom is not of this world*; whose people must come willingly; whose weapons *are not carnal, but spiritual.*" (108). Murton concluded that the New Testament requires religious toleration: "it is to fight against God to compel any, contrary to their consciences, to perform any service unto him, in that there are so many places of scripture commanding the contrary. The whole New Testament throughout, in all the doctrines and practices of Christ and his disciples, teach no such thing as compelling men by persecutions and afflictions to obey the gospel, but the direct contrary" (120). Like Helwys, Murton also included Catholics (114).

17. Leonard Busher, *Religions Peace: or A Plea for Liberty of Conscience* in *Tracts on Liberty of Conscience and Persecution, 1614–1661*, 3 (title page). Busher's *Plea* was originally published in 1614. Underhill's volume reproduces the 1646 edition. For commentary, see H. Leon McBeth, *English Baptist Literature on Religious Liberty to 1689* (New York: Arno Press, 1980), chap. 1; McBeth, ed., *A Sourcebook for Baptist Heritage* (Nashville: Broadman Press, 1990), 72: Busher "issued *Religion's Peace: or A Plea for Liberty of Conscience* in 1614, and though it may have been published in Amsterdam, the book was widely circulated in England"; W. K. Jordon, *The Development of Religious Toleration in England*, 4 vols. (Cambridge, Mass.: Harvard University Press, 1932–40), vol. 2, 258–314.

18. Busher, *Religions Peace*, 33.

19. Ibid., 16: "*For the word of God is lively, and mighty in operation, and sharper than any two-edged sword . . . and is a discerner of the thoughts and intents of the heart.* Seeing, then, the one true religion of the gospel is thus gotten, and thus defended and maintained—namely, by the word preached only; let it please your majesty and parliament to

be intreated to revoke and repeal those antichristian, Romish, and cruel laws, that force all in our land, both prince and people, to receive that religion wherein the king or queen were born, or that which is established by the law of man."

20. Ibid., 70–71.

21. Ibid., 20. Similarly, 47: "And so long as persecutions continue, you cannot try the spirits of the *many false prophets that are gone out into the world*, as the holy apostle doth lovingly advise and admonish you. But like the papists, [you] must be tied only to the spirits of your lordly bishops and their ministers, who will have all, both king, prince, and people, to receive their spirits, and therefore will not have any others to preach and print within the land, lest their lying doctrine and lordly discipline be discovered and disclaimed. And instead of disputing and writing by the word and Spirit of Christ against their adversaries, they will cruelly persecute and fight against them by fire and sword."

22. For the utility of toleration, see ibid., 38, hoping that bishops would end persecution "for the salvation of their own souls, the peace both of prince and people, and the safety of the king and state"; 42, arguing that "permission of conscience is a great and sure band and benefit to the king and state."

23. Ibid., 51.

24. [William Walwyn], *Toleration Justified and Persecution Condemned* (1646), in *The English Levellers*, ed. Andrew Sharp, reprint ed. (Cambridge: Cambridge University Press, 2002), 27–28. Similarly, see [William Walwyn], *The Compassionate Samaritane* (1644), in *Tracts on Liberty in the Puritan Revolution 1638–1647*, ed. William Haller, 3 vols. (New York: Columbia University Press, 1933), vol. 3, 71–72, referring to two types of weapons and denouncing persecutors who "fight with weapons which you (doe or at least should) know not to be the weapons of truth." Also, see ibid., 94, referring to intellectual combat in an "open field": clerics "need not avoyde the combate with any sort of men of what opinion soever. Truth was not used to feare, or to seeke shifts or stratagems for its advancement! I should rather thinke that they who are assured of her should desire that all mens mouthes should be open, that so errour may discover its foulness, and truth become more glorious by a victorious conquest after a fight in open field."

25. [Richard Overton], *The Araignement of Mr. Persecution. Presented to the Consideration of the House of Commons, and to all the Common People of England* (1645) in *Tracts on Liberty in the Puritan Revolution*, vol. 3, 214, 220, 234–35.

26. Ibid., 232. Similarly, see 221, desiring to "live peaceable & quietly one by another; bearing one with another, and so of all Religions."

27. *An Agreement of the free People of England, tendered as a Peace-Offering to this distressed nation, by Lieutenant-Colonel John Lilburne, Master William Walwyn, Master Thomas Prince, and Master Richard Overton, Prisoners in the Tower of London, 1 May 1649* in *English Levellers*, 173, explaining the right of worship: "That we do not empower or entrust our said Representatives to continue in force or to make any laws, oaths or covenants, whereby to compel by penalties or otherwise any person to anything in or about matters of faith, religion, or God's worship; or to restrain any person from the profession of his faith or exercise of religion according to his conscience—nothing having caused

more distractions and heart-burnings in all ages than persecution and molestation for matters of conscience in and about religion."

28. Ibid., 175, advocating the ending of religious taxation or tithes: "That it shall not be in their [i.e., "our said Representatives"] power to continue the grievance of tithes longer than to the end of the next Representative; in which time, they shall provide to give reasonable satisfaction to all impropriators; neither shall they force, by penalties or otherwise, any person to pay towards the maintenance of any ministers, who out of conscience cannot submit thereto."

29. Ibid., 176.

30. Michael Watts, *The Dissenters: From the Reformation to the French Revolution* (Oxford: Clarendon Press, 1978), 142–63. For the fate of the Episcopal Church of England in the 1650s, see John Spurr, *The Restoration Church of England, 1646–1689* (New Haven, Conn.: Yale University Press, 1991), 1–28.

31. John Clark, *Ill Newes from New-England: or A Narrative of New-Englands Persecution. Wherein is Declared that while old England is becoming New, New-England is become Old* (London, 1652), 65, 13–14.

32. Ibid., 72: "this outward forcing of men in matters of conscience towards God to believe as others believe, and to practise and worship as others do, cannot stand with the Peace, Liberty, Prosperity, and safety of a Place, Commonwealth, or nation."

33. Ibid., 76. Parentheses deleted. Also see 73–74: "So long as there is an outward force or power to be had to maintain and uphold the carnall interests and advantages of some upon religious accounts, and to persecute others, . . . What hopes are hereby begotten and nourished in some? What jealousies, suspicions and fears in others? What revengfull desires in most? Yea, what plottings and contrivings in all . . . to gain that power and sword to their party, either to crush, suppress, or cause the other to conform, or at the least and best to save themselves from being crushed, suppressed, or forced to conformity? . . . [F]or if there were neither fear on one hand, nor hope on the other, that this sword should be drawn forth to maintain the carnall interests of some, which they enjoy upon religious pretences, and to suppress the understandings and consciences of others . . . so that men of all sects and religions, which now are various, were become hopeless of any other help to support themselves and their way, or to draw others thereto, than what by the word of God they can attain unto, how soon would these tumults cease, the enmity in point of Religion be slain, and all things in peace?"

34. Walwyn offered a similar, though less extensive, analysis. See [Walwyn], *Toleration Justified and Persecution Condemned*, in *The English Levellers*, 22: "the state is not equal in its protection but allows one sort of men to trample upon another. From hence must necessarily arise heart-burnings, which, as they have ever been so they will ever be perpetuated to posterity, unless the state wisely prevent them by taking away the distinction that foments them—namely the particular indulgence to one party and neglect of the other—by a just and equal toleration"; Similarly, [Walwyn], *The Compassionate Samaritane* in *Tracts on Liberty in the Puritan Revolution*, 67: "'tis the principall interest of the Commonwealth, that Authority should have equall respect, and afford protection to all peaceable good men alike, notwithstanding their difference of opinion."

35. Roger Williams, *The Bloody Tenent Yet More Bloody: By Mr. Cottons endevour to wash it white in the Blood of the LAMBE* (1652), in *The Complete Writings of Roger Williams*, 7 vols. (New York: Russell and Russell, 1963), vol. 4, 365: "Civill places of Trust and Credit need not to be Monopolized into the hands of Church-Members (who sometimes are not fitted for them) and all others deprived and despoiled of their naturall & Civill Rights and Liberties."

36. Ibid., vol. 4, 200. Edwin S. Gaustad, *Liberty of Conscience: Roger Williams in America*, reprint ed. (Valley Forge, Pa.: Judson Press, 1999); Timothy L. Hall, *Separating Church and State: Roger Williams and Religious Liberty* (Chicago: University of Illinois Press, 1998); Edmund S. Morgan, *Roger Williams: The Church and the State* (New York: Harcourt, Brace & World, 1967).

37. Ibid., vol. 4, 137. Also see vol. 4, 29, 42–43, 75–80, 131, 149, 154, 190, 198, 276–77, 322; Roger Williams, *The Bloody Tenent, of Persecution, for cause of Conscience* (1644) in *Complete Writings*, vol. 3, 200, 316ff.

38. John F. Wilson, "Religion Under the State Constitutions, 1776–1800," *Journal of Church and State* 32 (autumn 1990): 764, referring to Rhode Island: "at the time of Roger Williams, in 1665, a law provided that no religious tests for office or voting were allowed, which made it the most tolerant state in the colonies, and possibly in the Western World." Rhode Island later adopted a Protestant requirement for public office in 1719 in *Rhode Island Laws, Statutes* (Newport, 1769), 7. For the dating of this law, see Thomas J. Curry, *The First Freedoms: Church and State in America to the Passage of the First Amendment* (New York: Oxford University Press, 1986), 245, n46.

39. Sir Peter Pett, *A Discourse concerning Liberty of Conscience* (1661), 3–4. Andrew R. Murphy, *Conscience and Community: Revisiting Toleration and Religious Dissent in Early Modern England and America* (University Park: Pennsylvania State University Press, 2001), 146, notes how "Authors gave far more attention to prudential and straightforwardly political arguments for toleration in the latter half of the seventeenth century."

40. Pett, *Discourse*, title page, 15. Pett's work was thus a discourse suggesting the political resolution of religious contention, not a pamphlet demanding redress of grievances or making contentious claims. In fact, Pett criticized English writers for having written too many pamphlets and made too many claims: "in nothing more then about Liberty of Conscience querulous persons have shewn a childishness in their complaints"; "so shall I likewise avoid the error of those who cry out for want of Liberty" (2–3).

41. Ibid., 5, explaining "the freedom that is now fit to be given to the severall Protestant parties."

42. Ibid., 23, 32, 63–64.

43. See the drafts of the "Fundamental Constitution" and "Frame of Government" of Pennsylvania in *The Papers of William Penn. Volume Two, 1680–1684*, ed. Richard S. Dunn and Mary Maples Dunn (Philadelphia: University of Pennsylvania Press, 1982), 137–238. See 224, Article XXXIV, which stated a Christian restriction on access to public office. J. William Frost, *A Perfect Freedom: Religious Liberty in Pennsylvania* (University

Park: Pennsylvania State University Press, 1993), 18: "In Pennsylvania, there would be no legal church establishment, no tithes or forced maintenance of any minister."

44. William Penn, *Good ADVICE to the Church of England, Roman-Catholick, and Protestant Dissenter: In which it is endeavored to be made appear, that it is their Duty, Principle, and Interest, to abolish the Penal LAWS and TESTS* (1687), in *Political Writings of William Penn*, 331, 343, 373–74.

45. William Penn, *The Great CASE of Liberty of Conscience once more briefly Debated and Defended, by the Authority of Reason, Scripture, and Antiquity: Which may serve the Place of a General Reply to such late Discourses; as have Oppos'd Toleration* (1670), in *The Political Writings of William Penn*, ed. Andrew R. Murphy (Indianapolis: Liberty Fund, 2002), 86–87; William Penn, *An Address to Protestants of All Perswasions More Especially the Magistracy and Clergy, for the Promotion of Virtue and Charity* (1679), in *Political Writings of William Penn*, 263: "The Kingdoms of this World, stand in outward, Bodily and Civil Matters, and here the Laws and Power of Men reach and are effectual. But the Kingdom of the Church of Christ, that is chosen out of the World, stands not in Bodily Exercise (which the Apostle says profits little) nor in Times nor Places, but in Faith, and that Worship which Christ tels us is in *Spirit and Truth*. To this no worldly Compulsion can bring or force Men."

46. William Penn, *England's Present Interest Considered, with Honour to the Prince, and Safety to the People* (1675) in *Political Writings of William Penn*, 22, 55.

47. William Penn, *One Project for the Good of England, That is, Our Civil Union is our Civil Safety, Humbly Dedicated to the Great Council, The Parliament of England* (1679), in *Political Writings of William Penn*, 125.

48. William Penn, *A Perswasive to Moderation to Church-Dissenters, in Prudence and Conscience: Humbly submitted to the KING and His Great Council* (1686), in *Political Writings of William Penn*, 321; Penn, *Good ADVICE to the Church of England, Roman-Catholick, and Protestant Dissenter*, in *Political Writings of William Penn*, 339.

49. Richard M. Golden, ed., *The Huguenot Connection: The Edict of Nantes, Its Revocation, and Early French Migration to South Carolina* (Boston: Kluwer Academic, 1988); Elisabeth Labrousse, *Bayle*, trans. Denys Potts (New York: Oxford University Press, 1983); B. R. Kreiser, "The Political Ideas of the Huguenot Diaspora (Bayle and Jurieu)," in *Church, State, and Society Under the Bourbon Kings of France*, ed. Richard M. Golden (Lawrence, Kan.: Coronado Press, 1982), 222–83.

50. Locke wrote the *Letter* in Latin in 1685. It was subsequently published as *Epistola de Tolerantia* and then translated into English. See John Locke, *A Letter concerning Toleration* (London, 1689), ed. James H. Tully (Indianapolis: Hackett Publishing, 1983).

51. The 1687 Latin title of *Nature and Qualification of Religion* was *De habitu religionis christianae ad vitam civilem*, "On the Attitude of the Christian Religion toward Civil Life." The English translation appeared a few years later and is reproduced in Samuel Pufendorf, *Of the Nature and Qualification of Religion in Reference to Civil Society* (1698), ed. Simone Zurbuchen (Indianapolis: Liberty Fund, 2002). John Marshall, *John Locke,*

Toleration and Early Enlightenment Culture: Religious Intolerance and Arguments for Religious Toleration in Early Modern and "Early Enlightenment" Europe (Cambridge: Cambridge University Press, 2006), 17, notes how the "1680s constituted one of the most religiously repressive decades in European history," including the severe persecution of French Huguenots and English Catholics.

52. Samuel Pufendorf, *On Duty of Man and Citizen According to Natural Law* (1673), ed. James Tully, trans. Michael Silverthorne (Cambridge: Cambridge University Press, 1991), 20 (Author's Preface): "Human Judicature regards only the external Actions of Man, but can no way reach the Inward Thoughts of the Mind." Also see 229 (Bk. II, Chap. VIII, §10): "The Act of the Mind within itself, which are merely internal . . . are all exempted from the Stroke of human Punishments." Pierre Bayle, *A Philosophical Commentary on These Words of the Gospel, Luke 14:23, "Compel Them to come in, That My House may be Full"* (1708), ed. John Kilcullen and Chandran Kukathas (Indianapolis: Liberty Fund, 2005), 350 (Part III, Chap. XXV): "it does not follow that Princes have the same right over mens Opinions as their Actions; because Opinions are not prejudicial, as sometimes Actions are, to the Prosperity, Power, and Quiet of the State"; 301 (Part III, Chap. VII) and 203, 207 (Part II, Chap. VI): one must "distinguish betwixt that Right with which Princes are invested, of punishing with the Sword those who exercise violence against their Neighbor, and who destroy the publick Security" and religious error for which "Princes have not receiv'd the Sword, to punish Irreverences of this kind."

53. Pufendorf, *Of the Nature and Qualification of Religion*, 11–12 (prefatory paragraph preceding §1), suggests it should be "look'd upon as a Matter of the greatest Consequence . . . to know exactly, what bounds ought to be prescribed to the Priestly Order . . . as likewise to determine, how far the Power of Sovereigns extends." Locke, *Letter concerning Toleration*, 26: "[I] esteem it above all things necessary to distinguish exactly the Business of Civil Government from that of Religion, and to settle the just Bounds that lie between the one and the other."

54. Pufendorf, *Of the Nature and Qualification of Religion*, 68 (§32), 65 (§31): "Churches and Commonwealths are erected for different Ends: so the Offices belonging to both are altogether of a different Nature." "The common security is the main End of every Government" and "the end of the Christian Religion [is] . . . obtaining salvation." Locke, *Letter*, 26, 28: "The Commonwealth seems to me to be a Society of Men constituted only for the procuring, preserving, and advancing of their own Civil Interests." "A Church then I take to be a voluntary Society of Men, joining together of their own accord, in order to the publick worshipping of God, in such a manner as they judge acceptable to him, and effectual to the Salvation of their Souls."

55. For Pufendorf in this context, see Michael J. Seidler, "Pufendorf and the Politics of Recognition," in *Natural Law and Civil Sovereignty: Moral Right and State Authority in Early Modern Political Thought*, ed. Ian Hunter and David Saunders (New York: Palgrave, 2002), 235–52.

56. Pufendorf, *Of the Nature and Qualification of Religion*, 106–7 (§49–50), explains, regarding dissenters, "If any one should undertake to contradict this Publick Form" of

religion "he may lawfully be banished . . . for . . . the Publick safety"; 20 (§7), denying the public expression of atheism, but suggesting toleration of private atheism: "[But] if these are kept within the compass of Peoples Thoughts, without breaking out into publick or outward Action, they are not punishable by the Law, neither can any Humane Power take Cognizance of what is contained only, and hidden in the Heart." Also see Samuel Pufendorf, *The Whole Duty of Man, According to the Law of Nature* (1691), ed. Ian Hunter and David Saunders (Indianapolis: Liberty Fund, 2003), 71 (Bk. I, Chap. V).

57. Pufendorf, *Of the Nature and Qualification of Religion*, 106–7 (§49–50). Detlef Döring, "Samuel von Pufendorf and Toleration," in *Beyond the Persecuting Society: Religious Toleration Before the Enlightenment*, ed. John Christian Laursen and Cary J. Nederman (Philadelphia: University of Pennsylvania Press, 1998), 192, describes Pufendorf's toleration as dependent upon "calculations of political utility."

58. Regarding Catholics, Pufendorf expressed the standard Protestant concern that Catholic loyalty to a foreign power undermined Catholic loyalty to the state. Yet the fact that the Peace of Westphalia recognized the Catholic confession, along with the Lutheran and Calvinist confessions, as tolerated in many parts of the German territories precluded Pufendorf from explicitly endorsing a policy of intolerance toward Catholics. See Pufendorf, *Of the Nature and Qualification of Religion*, 78 (§35), 93 (§41), 113 (§52); Pufendorf, *Whole Duty of Man*, 71–72 (Bk. I, Chap. V).

59. Historians emphasizing differences between Bayle and Locke include Sally Jenkinson, "Two Concepts of Tolerance: Or Why Bayle Is Not Locke," *Journal of Political Philosophy* 4 (1996): 302–22; Raymond Klibansky, "Preface," in John Locke, *Epistola de Tolerantia/A Letter on Toleration*, ed. Raymond Klibansky, trans. J. W. Gough (Oxford: Clarendon Press, 1968). For similarities, see John Kilcullen, *Sincerity and Truth* (Oxford: Oxford University Press, 1988), 96.

60. David Wootton, "Pierre Bayle, Libertine?" in *Studies in Seventeenth-Century European Philosophy*, ed. M. A. Stewart (New York: Oxford University Press, 1997), emphasizes the skeptical nature of Bayle's thought, contrary to revisionist readings. John Christian Laursen, "Baylean Liberalism: Tolerance Requires Nontolerance," in *Beyond the Persecuting Society*, 198, suggests there "is no single path of argument toward Bayle's sort of liberalism. There is no single theory of toleration." Similarly, see Walter Rex, *Essays on Pierre Bayle and Religious Controversy* (The Hague: Martinus Nijhoff, 1965), 173–74.

61. Bayle, *Philosophical Commentary*, 265 (Part II, Chap. X), continuing, "it follows; that all our Belief, whether Orthodox or Heterodox, is finally resolv'd into this, that we feel it, and it seems to us that this or that is true." Also see 262 (Part II, Chap. X): "Man has no characteristick Mark to discern the Persuasion of the Truth from the Persuasion of a Lye. So that it's requiring an Impossibility, to require this Discernment at his hands. When he has done all he can, the Objects he examines shall only appear to him some false and others true."

62. Ibid., 261–62 (Part II, Chap. X); 251 (Part II, Chap. X). The lack of objective criteria concerned religious belief, not moral actions. See 264 (Part II, Chap. X); 275 (Part II, Chap. X); 538 (Part IV or Supplement, Chap. XXIV).

63. Ibid., 233–34 (Part II, Chap. IX): "the Rights of an erroneous Conscience attended with sincerity, are exactly the same as those of an Orthodox Conscience"; "an Action done in Consequence of a false Persuasion, is as good as if done in consequence of a true and firm Persuasion"; 264 (Part II, Chap. X): "It's enough if he sincerely and honestly consults the Lights which God has afforded him; and if, following its Discoverys, he embraces that Persuasion which to him seems most reasonable, and most conformable to the Will of God. This renders him Orthodox in the sight of God, tho thro a defect, which he cannot rectify, his Judgments may not be always a faithful Representation of the real natures of Things." Bayle used the example of a woman falsely judging an imposter to be "her true and lawful Husband." Such a woman was not guilty of immorality, Bayle argued, because her judgment, however erroneous, was sincerely held. Hers was what Bayle called "an Ignorance involuntary and void of Malice" (241, Part II, Chap. IX).

64. Ibid., 352–53 (Part III, Chap. XXV).

65. Ibid., 133 (Part I, Chap. X); 89 (Part I, Chap. IV). Also see 148 (Part II, Chap. I); 231 (Part II, Chap. VIII), explains that "each Church believing it self the only true"; 262 (Part III, Chap. X): "a Papist is as fully satisfy'd of the Truth of his Religion, a Turk of his, and a Jew of his, as we are of ours"; 279 (Part II, Chap. XI), "each believing it self the only true and pure Religion."

66. For Bayles's criticisms of penal laws in religion, see ibid., 76–79 (Part I, Chap. II); 105–10, 118 (Part I, Chap. VI); 189–90 (Part II, Chap. IV); 252 (Part II, Chap. X); 295–300 (Part III, Chaps. IV–V); 340 (Part III, Chap. XX); 369 (Part III, Chap. XXXIII); 389 (Part III, Chap. XL).

67. Locke, *Letter*, 32.

68. John Locke, *Two Tracts on Government* (1660–1662), in *Locke: Political Essays*, ed. Mark Goldie (Cambridge: Cambridge University Press, 1997), 13.

69. As evident in the above endnote, Locke argued for the involuntary nature of the understanding in *Two Tracts on Government* (1660–62), wherein he defended outward religious uniformity. He argued that although persons do not choose their own beliefs, they do choose their actions and can conform their behavior to laws for uniformity, despite what they believed inwardly. By 1667, Locke abandoned the idea of outward conformity.

70. John Locke, "An Essay on Toleration" (1667) in *Political Essays*, 137.

71. Richard Vernon, *The Career of Toleration: John Locke, Jonas Proast, and After* (Buffalo: Mcgill-Queen's University Press, 1997), 31–48, sharply distinguishes "consent" and the involuntary nature of the understanding, and argues that the former was the basis of the *Letter*. Yet consent or inalienability was inherently tied to the understanding's nature and the only time Locke referred to consent in the *Letter* was in the paragraph immediately preceding his discussion of "the nature of the Understanding." See Locke, *Letter*, 26–27.

72. Locke, *Letter*, 43.

73. Locke, *Letter*, 46, continues: "to believe this or that to be true, does not depend upon our Will." Although Bayle and Walwyn also suggested the involuntary nature of the

understanding in passing, neither made it a central feature of their work or logic. See Bayle, *Philosophical Commentary*, 117 (Part I, Chap. VI): "it's necessary, in order to make us affirm what we formerly deny'd, that the matter be render'd true with regard to us, which depends on a certain Proportion between the Objects and our Facultys, and is a Circumstance not always in our own power"; "no one believes things but when they appear to him true, and that their appearing true depends not on the human Mind, any more than their appearing black or white depends on it"; 208 (Part II, Chap. VI): "we are not Masters of our own Ideas." [Walwyn], *Compassionate Samaritane* in *Tracts on Liberty in the Puritan Revolution*, 67–68: "what judgment soever a man is, he cannot chuse but be of that judgement"; "man is by his own reason necessitated to be of that mind he is, now where there is a necessity there ought to be no punishment, for punishment is the recompence of voluntary actions, therefore no man ought to be punished for his judgment."

74. For Locke's intended audience, see John Marshall, *John Locke: Resistance, Religion and Responsibility* (Cambridge: Cambridge University Press, 1994), 357ff, emphasizing that Locke had European events and a European audience in mind; Richard Ashcraft, *Revolutionary Politics and Locke's Two Treatises of Government* (Princeton, N.J.: Princeton University Press, 1986), 457ff, arguing that Locke addressed the *Letter* to the English context. Marshall's argument is more convincing.

75. Locke, *Letter*, 27. Also see John Locke, *An Essay concerning Human Understanding*, ed. Peter H. Nidditch (Oxford: Clarendon Press, 1979), 650–51 (IV.xiii.2): "Just thus is it with our Understanding, all that is voluntary in our Knowledge, is the employing, or with-holding any of our Faculties from this or that sort of Objects, and a more, or less accurate survey of them: But they being employed, our Will hath no Power to determine the Knowledge of the Mind one way or other."

76. Bayle, *Philosophical Commentary*, 252 (Part II, Chap. X); 295 (Part III, Chap. IV); 300 (Part III, Chap. V). Also see 340 (Part III, Chap. XX): "shou'd a Prince punish Disobediences of this nature [religious dissent] by Confiscation, Fines, or by a general Change in the Settlements and Freeholds within his Dominions, he'd be a most unjust Tyrant"; "a Prince who punishes a Disobedience to such Laws [for religious worship] by Confiscations, Prisons, Banishment, makes a tyrannical use of the Power lodg'd in him."

77. Locke, *Letter*, 46, 43.

78. Attempts to link Locke to the no-establishment clause of the First Amendment to the U.S. Constitution are thoroughly unconvincing. Consider Gordon J. Schochet, "John Locke and Religious Toleration," in *The Revolution of 1688–1689: Changing Perspectives*, ed. Lois G. Schwoerer (Cambridge: Cambridge University Press, 1992), 148, 163–64, suggesting that "Locke was implicitly calling for nothing less than the separation of the Anglican Church from the English state" and arguing that Locke's advocacy for the "utter separation of church and state" was "picked up later" in America and formed the basis for "the religious freedoms guaranteed by the First Amendment to the United States Constitution." Schochet's view is untenable not only with respect to his suggestion of far-reaching implications, but also in terms of his particular interpretation of Locke's text. In

fact, Schochet seems to recognize the lack of textual support for his view when he describes Locke as "implicitly" calling for separation. In other words, according to Schochet, "Locke was certainly not direct in calling for this separation." Rather, in Schochet's own words, the notion of ending the Anglican establishment "was far more radical an argument than Locke wanted overtly to make." Indeed, Locke made no such argument at all.

79. Locke, *Letter*, 49–51. John Marshall, *John Locke, Toleration and Early Enlightenment Culture*, 12, 37, 68off, suggests that "in the mid- and later 1680s Locke was struggling to find a way to extend toleration to at least some lay Catholics, while holding many Catholics intolerable" (12).

80. Bayle advocated intolerance of atheists in *Philosophical Commentary*, 242–43 (Part II, Chap. IX) and yet suggested toleration for atheists in Pierre Bayle, *Letter on the Comet* (1682) and *Diverse Thoughts on the Comet* (1683). See Zagorin, *How the Idea of Religious Toleration Came to the West*, 271; Laursen, "Baylean Liberalism: Tolerance Requires Nontolerance," 201. On Catholics, Bayle advocated legal protection of their persons and estates, the private exercise of their religion, and the education of their children in their religion. Yet he excluded Catholics from public office. See Bayle, *Philosophical Commentary*, 191–92 (Part II, Chap. V), 47–48 (Preliminary Discourse).

81. Locke, *Letter*, 54. For Bayle, see Bayle, *Philosophical Commentary*, 262 (Part III, Chap. X).

82. John Marshall, "John Locke and Latitudinarianism," in *Philosophy, Science, and Religion in England, 1640–1700*, ed. Richard Kroll, Richard Ashcraft, and Perez Zagorin (Cambridge: Cambridge University Press, 1992), 254: "Locke was baptized into the Church of England in 1632. In many different writings into the 1690s he identified himself as a member of the Church of England. . . . He died and was buried in Anglican communion in 1704, having received the Sacrament at home in his final months." Marshall's point here is part of a larger debate concerning the political-religious ideology of Locke's writings. Marshall contends that despite important disagreements between Locke and latitudinarians, Locke maintained important and determinative ties with Anglican latitudinarianism. Marshall, *John Locke: Resistance, Religion and Responsibility*, 291, describes "Locke's anxious eclectic combination of elements of extremely Latitudinarian Anglicanism . . . and of Independent thought." Also see W. M. Spellman, *Latitudinarians and the Church of England, 1660–1700* (Athens: University of Georgia Press, 1993). In contrast, Richard Ashcraft more closely associates Locke with an ideology of religious dissent in Ashcraft, "Latitudinarianism and Toleration: Historical Myth versus Political History," in *Philosophy, Science, and Religion*, 165, 176.

83. For Locke's remarks, see *infra* note 79. The official title of the so-called Act of Toleration was "An Act for Exempting Their Majesties Protestant Subjects, Dissenting from the Church of England, from the Penalties of certain Laws." For the text of the act, see Peter Ole Grell, Jonathan Israel, and Nicholas Tyacke, eds., *From Persecution to Toleration: The Glorious Revolution and Religion in England* (New York: Oxford University Press, 1991), appendix ii. For commentary, see J. C. D. Clark, *English Society, 1660–1832: Religion, Ideology, and Politics During the Ancien Regime*, 2nd ed. (Cambridge: Cambridge Univer-

sity Press, 2000), 81: "With more hope than realism, it was nicknamed the Toleration Act: the word 'toleration' appeared neither in its title nor its text."

84. John Locke to Philip van Limbroch, 6 June 1689, in *The Correspondence of John Locke*, ed. E. S. de Beer, 8 vols. (Oxford: Clarendon Press, 1976), vol. 3, 633: "No doubt you will have heard before this that Toleration has now at last been established by law in our country. Not perhaps so wide in scope as might be wished for by you and those like you who are true Christians and free from ambition or envy. Still, it is something to have progressed so far. I hope that with these beginnings the foundations have been laid of that liberty and peace in which the church of Christ is one day to be established. None is entirely debarred from his own form of worship or made liable to penalties except the Romans, provided only that he is willing to take the oath of allegiance and to renounce transubstantiation and certain dogmas of the Roman Church."

85. Church membership as a prerequisite for public office was part of the Test Act of 1673.

86. Sandra Rennie, "Virginia's Baptist Persecution, 1765–1778," *Journal of Religious History* 12 (1982): 48–61.

87. In the 1720s and 1730s, the legislatures in Massachusetts and Connecticut granted Baptists, Anglicans, and Quakers exemption from religious taxes to support the Congregational establishment. The laws required members of these groups to acquire and present dissenting certificates to tax collectors authenticating their membership in their respective churches. See Leonard W. Levy, *The Establishment Clause: Religion and the First Amendment*, rev. 2nd ed. (Chapel Hill: University of North Carolina Press, 1994), 22; Curry, *First Freedoms*, 89, 111; William G. McLoughlin, *New England Dissent, 1630–1833: The Baptists and the Separation of Church and State*, 2 vols. (Cambridge, Mass.: Harvard. University Press, 1971), vol. 1, 482.

88. For an example of what is meant by "understood in Protestant terms," consider the "Revisal of Laws" that Thomas Jefferson authored and James Madison introduced into the Virginia Assembly in fall 1785. The "Revisal" included five bills, numbered 82 through 86, one of which was the "Bill for Establishing Religious Freedom." Another was a "Bill for Appointing Days of Public Fasting and Thanksgiving," which the Assembly did not enact. Yet another, introduced in the Assembly by Madison on October 31, 1785, was a "Bill for Punishing Disturbers of Religious Worship and Sabbath Breakers." This bill, which the Assembly did enact, prohibited labor on the Christian Sabbath and established a system of fines for violations. See Daniel Dreisbach, "Religion and Legal Reforms in Revolutionary Virginia: A Reexamination of Jefferson's Views on Religious Freedom and Church-State Separation," in *Religion and Political Culture in Jefferson's Virginia*, ed. Garrett W. Sheldon and Daniel L. Dreisbach (New York: Rowman & Littlefield, 2000), 189–218; Dreisbach, "A New Perspective on Jefferson's Views on Church-State Relations: The Virginia Statute for Establishing Religious Freedom in Its Legislative Context," *American Journal of Legal History* 35 (1991): 172–204; Dreisbach, "Thomas Jefferson and Bills Number 82–86 of the Revision of the Laws of Virginia, 1776–1786: New Light on the Jeffersonian Model of Church-State Relations," *North Carolina Law Review* 69 (1990):

159–211; Dreisbach, *Real Threat and Mere Shadow: Religious Liberty and the First Amendment* (Westchester, Ill.: Crossway Books, 1987), 120.

89. Douglas J. Den Uyl, "Forward," in Anthony Ashley Copper, Third Early of Shaftesbury, *Characteristicks of Men, Manners, Opinions, Times*, 3 vols. (Indianapolis: Liberty Fund, 2001), vii. This Liberty Fund edition reproduces the 1732 edition of *Characteristicks*.

90. Although Shaftesbury established an important foundation for eighteenth-century moral sense theory, his particular moral-sense philosophy was not the natural empirical version of Francis Hutcheson and David Fordyce. Hutcheson focused on the mind's sensation or reception of affective motives and feelings whereas Shaftesbury viewed the moral senses as actively creative, establishing order and harmony within the human constitution by, in effect, replicating the mind of God. See Stephen Darwall, *The British Moralists and The Internal "Ought": 1640–1740* (New York: Cambridge University Press, 1995), 187–89.

91. Shaftesbury, "Miscellaneous Reflections," in *Characteristicks*, vol. 3, 65–66, 69.

92. Shaftesbury, "A Letter Concerning Enthusiasm," in *Characterssticks*, vol. 1, 11.

93. Shaftesbury even characterized émigré members of the Huguenot Diaspora in England (French Protestants severely persecuted in France) as enthusiasts properly subject to cultural ridicule. See Shaftesbury, "A Letter Concerning Enthusiasm," in *Characterssticks*, vol. 1, 17–18. On eighteenth-century letters, see David S. Shields, *Civil Tongues & Polite Letters in British America* (Chapel Hill: University of North Carolina Press, 1997).

94. Shaftesbury, "A Letter Concerning Enthusiasm," in *Characterssticks*, vol. 1, 12, also decries on the next page "how preposterously we go about to cure Enthusiasm."

95. Ibid., vol. 1, 18.

96. Shaftesbury, "Miscellaneous Reflections," in *Characteristicks*, vol. 3, 69.

97. John Trenchard and Thomas Gordon, *Cato's Letters: Or, Essays on Liberty, Civil and Religious, And other Important Subjects*, ed. Ronald Hamowry, 4 vols. (Indianapolis: Liberty Fund, 1995), vol. 2, 405–42, Lets. 59–63 (natural rights and limited government); vol. 1, 110–17, Let. 15 (free speech); vol. 2, 471–83, Let. 67, vol. 3, 626–31, Let. 87, vol. 3, 643–48, Let. 90 (free trade). Bernard Bailyn, ed., *Pamphlets of the American Revolution* (Cambridge, Mass.: Belknap Press, 1965), 30: "Trenchard and Gordon ranked in the minds of Americans with the treatises of Locke as the most authoritative statement of the nature of political liberty."

98. Particularly see *New York Weekly Journal*, 4 February 1733 and 10 December 1733. For the publication of *Cato's Letters* in other British-American newspapers, see Milton M. Klein's "Introduction" to William Livingston, William Smith, Jr., and William Morin Scott, *Independent Reflector or Weekly Essays on Sundry Important Subjects More particularly adapted to the Province of New York*, ed. Milton M. Klein (Cambridge, Mass.: Belknap Press, 1963), 22. For statistics on the appearance of *Cato's Letters* in British-American libraries, see David Lundberg and Henry May, "The Enlightened Reader in America," *American Quarterly* 28, no. 2 (summer 1976): 263ff.

99. Michael Warner, *The Letters of the Republic: Publication and the Publish Sphere*

in Eighteenth-Century America (Cambridge, Mass.: Harvard University Press, 1990), 49ff; Bernard Bailyn, *The Ideological Origins of the American Revolution* (Cambridge, Mass.: Belknap Press), 43; Klein, "Introduction," in *Independent Reflector*, 21–22. John Adams to Thomas Jefferson, 19 April 1817, in *The Adams-Jefferson Letters: The Complete Correspondence Between Thomas Jefferson and Abigail and John Adams*, 2nd ed., ed. Lester J. Cappon (Chapel Hill: University of North Carolina Press, 1987), 510, refers to "a new Edition of 'The Independent Whig'" printed in Connecticut as late as 1817.

100. Trenchard and Gordon, *Cato's Letters*, vol. 2, 428, Let. 62; vol. 4, 775, Let. 110. For contemporary criticism of "Cato's" position, see John Jackson, *A Defense of Human Liberty, In answer to the Principal Arguments which have been alledged against it; And particularly to Cato's Letters on that Subject* (London, 1725), 99: "The whole of Cato's Reasoning is not more than this, namely, that external Reasons, Causes and Accidents of various sorts, which are out of our Power, necessarily affects Men's Understandings, and occasion various and different Judgments of Things, and even of the same Things at different Times to be form'd in their Minds, all which they cannot help, because they must judge (whether right or wrong) according to the Evidence they have of them."

101. John Trenchard and Thomas Gordon, *The Independent Whig* (Philadelphia, 1724), xiv.

102. Trenchard and Gordon, *Cato's Letters*, vol. 2, 462–71, Let. 66.

103. Ibid., vol. 2, 414, Let. 60.

104. Such empirical assumptions concerning the development of human character help explain why John Locke's *Some Thoughts Concerning Education*, originally published in 1693, was reprinted more than twenty times by 1760.

105. For Trenchard and Gordon's advocacy of a religious establishment, see Trenchard and Gordon, *Independent Whig*, 49: "Every State," they explained in paraphrasing Thomas Erastus in approval, has "the same Authority of modeling their Ecclesiastical as Civil Government," namely the authority "to appoint particular Persons to officiate for the rest." In recognizing that some might disagree with the state's ecclesiastical government, Trenchard and Gordon acknowledged the existence of both dissenting and national churches: "What by the Gospel Liberty is the Right of every one [reading the Scriptures and leading public Prayers] as shall be unanswerably made out hereafter is by the Consent of Voluntary and National Churches the Duty and Business of particular Persons, who are set aside and paid for that Purpose" (16).

106. Ibid., 15, 20. It was in this sense of the cultural formation of virtuous habits that Trenchard and Gordon sought "to inculcate the plain Precepts of Faith and Morality" or "to promote useful Knowledge, true Vertue, and sound Religion."

107. Ibid., 39–40.

108. Trenchard and Gordon, *Cato's Letters*, vol. 3, 591, Let. 81.

109. Ibid., vol. 2, 414, Let. 60.

110. Ibid.

111. Some leaders in early colonial New Jersey tried to combine religious toleration with state provisions for public worship. This combination characterized John Berkley

and G. Carteret, *The Concession and Agreement of the Lords Proprietors of the Province of New Caesarea, or New Jersey* (1664) and *A Declaration of the True Intent and Meaning of Us the Lords Proprietors, and Explanation of there Concessions Made to the Adventurers and Planters of New Caesarea or New Jersey* (1672), in Aaron Leaming and Jacob Spicer, *The Grants, Concessions, and Original Constitutions of the Province of New Jersey* (W. Bradford, 1758). However, state provisions for public worship were never effectively implemented. See Douglas G. Jacobsen, *An Unprov'd Experiment: Religious Pluralism in Colonial New Jersey* (Brooklyn, N.Y.: Carlson Publishing, 1991), 28–29: "The colonial assembly never created the machinery of a religious establishment. This type of independent behavior is paradigmatic of what later became a general pattern. The proprietors, and later the Crown, discovered that the practice of religion in New Jersey followed its own path . . . [and] grew in an ad hoc manner."

112. Julian P. Boyd, ed., *Fundamental Laws and Constitutions of New Jersey 1664–1694* (Princeton, N.J.: D. Van Nostrand, 1964), 120, 141–42; John E. Pomfret, *Colonial New Jersey: A History* (New York: Scribner, 1973), 71–91.

113. For Dickinson's use of "natural Right" and "civil Rights," see Jonathan Dickinson, *The Vanity of Human Institutions in the Worship of God* (New York: J. Peter Zenger, 1736), 11; Dickinson, *The Reasonableness of Nonconformity to the Church of England* (Boston: S. Kneeland & T. Green, 1738), 65–66.

114. Jonathan Dickinson, *The Scripture-Bishop Vindicated* (Boston: S. Kneeland & T. Green, 1733), 29.

115. Dickinson, *Vanity of Human Institutions*, 29.

116. Dickinson, *Reasonableness of Nonconformity*, 22. Dickinson maintained later in this piece that "if the People are to chuse [their religious persuasion], then every Body has full Liberty in this Case by divine Appointment; and ought to be left at full Liberty, without any Church Censure, without any Inconvenience to his religious or civil Rights, without any unkind Treatment; or any Injury to his civil or sacred Communion, to his Honours, Reputation, or any other valuable Interests whatsoever. Which is the Thing I contend for" (65–66).

117. Jonathan Dickinson, *A Defence of a Sermon Preached at Newark . . . Intitled, the Vanity of Human Institutions in the Worship of God* (New York: J. Peter Zenger, 1737), 95–96. Dickinson, *Reasonableness of Nonconformity*, 66, similarly speaks in the first-person plural; "We are deny'd," Dickinson complained, "all Privileges in the State."

118. See the chapter in this volume by Ned Landsman.

119. Dickinson's traditional orthodoxy was evident throughout his corpus. As just one example, consider his stated belief in "the Doctrines of original Sin, of our Justification by the imputed Righteousness of Christ, of the Efficacy of the Sovereign free Grace of God, and of the Perseverance of the Saints." See Dickinson, *Vanity of Human Institutions*, v.

120. Klein, "Introduction," in *Independent Reflector*, 23.

121. William Livingston to Noah Welles, 18 February 1749, describes "a Design of publishing weekly Essays as soon as possible upon the plan of The Spectator," quoted in Klein, "Introduction," in *Independent Reflector*, 13.

122. Charter of the College of New York, 9–11, in Lowe Library, Columbia University.

123. See "Protest of Mr. William Livingston," in Minutes of the Meetings of Lottery Trustees, May 1754, in Box 1, Miscellaneous Collection, Rare Book and Manuscript Library, Columbia University.

124. Following England's Act of Toleration, royal governors in New York were instructed "to permit a liberty of Conscience to all Persons (except Papists)." See Hugh Hastings and Edwin S. Corwin, eds., *Ecclesiastical Records of the State of New York*, 7 vols. (Albany, N.Y.: J. B. Lyon, 1901–16), vol. 2, 1012–13. Subsequently, the New York legislature passed the Ministry Act of 1693 which mandated the collection taxes for the salaries of "good sufficient Protestant" ministers. The act and other similar legislation, however, only applied to the "four lower counties" of New York, Richmond, Queens, and Westchester. See ibid., vol. 2, 1073–79; E. B. O'Callaghan and B. Fernow, eds., *Documents Relative to the Colonial History of the State of New York*, 15 vols. (Albany, N.Y.: Weed, Parsons & Co., 1853–87), vol. 1, 328–31. Although this legislation was not specifically intended to privilege the Church of England, the policies of subsequent royal governors helped direct much of the tax money in the four lower counties to England's Church. Other towns throughout the Province used tax money to support a variety of Protestant churches. See Hastings and Corwin, eds., *Ecclesiastical Records*, vol. 2, 1136–65; John W. Pratt, *Religion, Politics, and Diversity: The Church-State Theme in New York History* (Ithaca, N.Y.: Cornell University Press, 1967), 44–67; Curry, *First Freedoms*, 64, describes "New York's system whereby each town selected a minister and taxed its inhabitants for his support."

125. Levy, *Establishment Clause*, 12, describes New York's local religious taxation to support local churches as a "system of multiple establishments."

126. Livingston, *Independent Reflector*, 195 (12 April 1753), 190 (1 April 1753).

127. Ibid., 179 (29 March 1753), explains how "the established Tenets must either be implicitly received, or a perpetual religious War necessarily maintained." Also see 178: "unless its [the College's] Constitution and Government, be such as will admit of all protestant Denominations, upon a perfect Parity as to Privileges, it will itself be greatly prejudiced, and prove a Nursery of Animosity, Dissention and Disorder."

128. Livingston, *Independent Reflector*, 309 and 311 (2 August 1753). Livingston's Enlightenment epistemology was most apparent when addressing legal penalties. See ibid., 313–14 (9 August 1753), which uses the logic of empiricism to confirm the inefficacy of legal penalties or exterior force on the human understanding. "The Understanding, upon surveying a Set of Ideas that form a proposition, must either determine, that it be true or false; or the Judgment must be suspended for want of clearer Light and Information." "Whence it evidently follows that if the Legislators interfere in Matters of Opinion, they are guilty of the greatest Tyranny and Oppression, and instead of advancing and protecting the Rights of Mankind, enslave the Consciences of their fellow Creatures."

129. For similar hyperbole, see Livingston's comments in "Watch-Tower," *New-York Mercury*, 24 March 1755: "A religious Tyrant . . . pains your Body for the Health of your Soul: and breaks your Head, to illuminate your Mind."

130. John Seed, "Gentlemen Dissenters: The Social and Political Meanings of Rational Dissent in the 1770s and 1780s," *Historical Journal* 28, no. 2 (1985): 301, describing late eighteenth-century rational religion as "the dismantling of much of the theological superstructure of orthodox Christianity: the divinity of Christ . . . and original sin . . . were abandoned as irrational superstitions."

131. James Bugh, *Crito, or Essays on Various Subjects*, 2 vols. (London, 1766–67), vol. 2, 118–19. For recent commentary on Burgh, see Daniel L. Dreisbach, "'Sowing Useful Truths and Principles': The Danbury Baptists, Thomas Jefferson, and the 'Wall of Separation,'" *Journal of Church and State* 39 (1997): 486–90; Dreisbach, *Thomas Jefferson and the Wall of Separation Between Church and State* (New York: New York University Press, 2002), 79–82; Philip Hamburger, *Separation of Church and State* (Cambridge, Mass.: Harvard University Press, 2002), 55–58.

132. Isaac Kramnick, *Republicanism and Bourgeois Radicalism: Political Ideology in Late Eighteenth-Century England and America* (Ithaca, N.Y.: Cornell University Press, 1990), 44, argues that rational dissenters pursued "the complete separation of church and state." Kramnick's conclusion here is related to Isaac Kramnick and R. Laurence Moore, *The Godless Constitution: The Case Against Religious Correctness* (New York: W. W. Norton, 1997), 12–13, which suggests that there are only two alternatives or "two distinct traditions" in American history, "the party of the godless Constitution and of godless politics" on the one hand and "the party of religious correctness" on the other.

133. Richard Price, *The Evidence for a Future Period of Improvement in the State of Mankind* (1787), in *Richard Price: Political Writings*, ed. D. O. Thomas (Cambridge: Cambridge University Press, 1991), 161. Also see 165, suggesting "separating religion from civil policy."

134. Henri Laboucheix, *Richard Price as Moral Philosopher and Political Theorist*, trans. Sylvia and David Raphael (Oxford: The Voltaire Foundation, 1982), 119.

135. Hamburger, *Separation of Church and State*, 1–109.

136. Price, *Discourse on the Love of our Country* in *Political Writings*, 191.

137. Information on publication is in Bernard Peach, ed., *Richard Price and the Ethical Foundations of the American Revolution* (Durham, N.C.: Duke University Press, 1979), preface. For American readership, consider James Stewart, *A Letter to the Rev. Dr. Price* (London, 1776), 50, where a critic of Price complains how Price's works "go by Dozens and Scores to the different [American] Provinces, where they will be read with great Avidity, by all American Insurgents"; Arthur Lee to Richard Price, 20 April 1777, in "Letters to and from Richard Price (1767–1790)," *Proceedings of the Massachusetts Historical Society*, 2nd ser., 17 (1903): 308, comments to Price on *Additional Observations*: "I beg you will accept my thanks for the favour of your pamphlet, than which I never in my life read any thing with more satisfaction"; John Winthrop to Richard Price, 10 April 1775, in ibid., 283, where Winthrop, the Harvard professor of mathematics and natural philosophy, informs Price how "all America is greatly indebted to you for the sympathetic concern you express for their distresses, and for your exertions in their behalf."

138. See Peach, ed., *Richard Price and the Ethical Foundations of the American Revolution*, preface.

139. Richard Price, *General Introduction and Supplement to the Two Tracts on Civil Liberty* (1778), in *Richard Price and the Ethical Foundations of the American Revolution*, 53–54. The notion that Price viewed religious taxation as valid if distributed without sectarian privilege was confirmed by Price's colleague Samuel Kenrick. According to Kenrick, he, Kenrick, read the American Constitutions, "those of Massachusetts bay, and the rest—where I find literally verified the principles of government laid down by Dr. Price." Unlike Price's remarks, which he made in 1778 and thus referred to the Massachusetts system of religious taxation inherited from the colonial period, Kenrick's remarks concerned the tax system in the Massachusetts Constitution of 1780. He made his remarks in a private correspondence quoted in Martin Fitzpatrick, "The Enlightenment, Politics and Providence: Some Scottish and English Comparisons," in *Enlightenment and Religion: Rational Dissent in Eighteenth-Century Britain*, ed. Knud Haakonssen (Cambridge: Cambridge University Press, 1996), 82. The difference between the pre- and post-1780 systems of religious taxation was that the state Constitution of 1780 authorized local towns, not the state legislature, to make public provisions for the support of churches. This local authorization differed from an earlier constitutional draft which empowered the state legislature to make such provisions directly. See John Adams, "The Report of a Constitution, or Form of Government, for the Commonwealth of Massachusetts" (1779), in *The Works of John Adams*, ed. Charles Francis Adams, 10 vols. (Boston: Little and Brown, 1850–56), vol. 4, 221–22. Also see John Witte, Jr., "'A Most Mild and Equitable Establishment of Religion': John Adams and the Massachusetts Experiment," in *Religion and the New Republic: Faith in the Founding of America*, ed. James H. Hutson (New York: Rowman & Littlefield, 2000), 14.

140. Colin Bonwick, "English Dissenters and the American Revolution," in *Contrast and Connection: Bicentennial Essays in Anglo-American History*, ed. H. C. Allen and Roger Thompson (Athens: Ohio University Press, 1976), 88–89, 99, suggests that the rational dissenters "were firmly persuaded that the new relationship between church and state which was emerging across the Atlantic had much of pertinence to their own situation as victims of religious discrimination at home"; as Americans traveled "the path to a total separation of Church from state," they "amassed a corpus of empirical evidence which became available for use in English battles"; Peter N. Miller, *Defining the Common Good: Empire, Religion and Philosophy in Eighteenth-Century Britain* (New York: Cambridge University Press, 1994), 300, perhaps intentionally more ambiguous or cautious in his use of language, describes Price and his rational colleagues as "advocating a separation of the civil and spiritual powers."

141. Another gradation—nonsectarianism—is discussed by Chris Beneke in his contribution to this volume.

142. Thomas Jefferson to Richard Price, 7 August 1785, in *The Papers of Thomas Jefferson*, ed. Julian P. Boyd, 28 vols. to date (Princeton, N.J.: Princeton University Press, 1950–), vol. 8, 356, praises Price's *Observations* and determining that "the bulk of the people will approve it."

143. Richard Price, *Observations on the Importance of the American Revolution and the*

Means of making it a Benefit to the World (1784), in *Richard Price and the Ethical Foundations of the American Revolution*, 194–95. Price continued: "Thanks be to God, the new American States are at present [1784] strangers to such establishments [where a predominant sect enjoys exclusive advantages]." In 1784, the new American states included several states with policies of religious taxation technically on a sectarian equal basis.

144. Joseph Priestley, *Essay on the First Principles of Government* (1771), in *Joseph Priestley: Political Writings*, ed. Peter N. Miller (Cambridge: Cambridge University Press, 1993), 88–89.

145. Adams, "Report," in *Works*, vol. 4, 221–22. For commentary, see Charles H. Lippy, "The 1780 Massachusetts Constitution: Religious Establishment or Civil Religion?" *Journal of Church and State* 20 (1978): 534–35, explaining that "providing public support for religious institutions was seen as a way to promote political stability and social cohesion by guaranteeing that individuals would receive instruction in moral principles, rooted in the common religious sensibilities of the people, which would make them good citizens."

146. [Anonymous], "On the Importance and Necessity of Religion to Civil Society," in *Virginia Gazette and Weekly Advertiser*, 6 and 13 August 1785.

147. Daniel L. Dreisbach, "Church-State Debate in the Virginia Legislature: From the Declaration of Rights to the Statute for Establishing Religious Freedom," in *Religion and Political Culture in Jefferson's Virginia*, ed. Garrett W. Sheldon and Daniel L. Dreisbach (New York: Rowman & Littlefield, 2000), 137–43; William Lee Miller, *The First Liberty: Religion and the American Republic* (New York: Alfred A. Knopf, 1986), 27; Thomas E. Buckley, *Church and State in Revolutionary Virginia, 1776–1787* (Charlottesville: University Press of Virginia, 1977), 91ff; Marvin K. Singleton, "Colonial Virginia as First Amendment Matrix: Henry, Madison, and Assessment Establishment," *Journal of Church and State* 8 (autumn 1966): 344–64.

148. The text of the Assessment Bill of 1784 is in Buckley, *Church and State in Revolutionary Virginia*, 185–89.

149. Isaac Backus, *An Appeal to the Public for Religious Liberty, Against the Oppressions of the present Day* (Boston, 1773), in *Political Sermons of the American Founding Era, 1703–1805*, ed. Ellis Sandoz (Indianapolis: Liberty Fund, 1991), 336.

150. Isaac Backus, *An Appeal to the People of the Massachusetts State, Against Arbitrary Power* (Boston, 1780), 4.

151. "The Petition of Sundry Inhabitants of Prince Edward County," 11 October 1776, in *Virginia Magazine of History and Biography* 18 (1910): 41.

152. "The Memorial of the Presbytery of Hanover," 24 October 1776, in James H. Smylie, "Jefferson's Statute for Religious Freedom: The Hanover Presbytery Memorials, 1776–86," *American Presbyterians Journal of Presbyterian History* 63 (1985): 361–63.

153. "The Memorial of the Presbytery of Hanover," 3 June 1777, in Smylie, "Hanover Presbytery Memorials," 363–64.

154. "The Memorial of the Ministers and Lay Representatives of the Presbyterian Church in Virginia, assembled in Convention," 2 November 1785, in Smylie, "Hanover

Presbytery Memorials," 372. Briefly, in the context of what appeared to be an inevitable victory for the general assessment bill of 1784, the Hanover Presbytery suggested its support for such a bill from the secular welfare perspective: the bill being "absolutely necessary to the existence and welfare of every . . . society." See 12 November 1784, in Smylie, Hanover Presbytery Memorials, 369. Also see Buckley, *Church and State*, 95–96. The extent of negative reaction among the Presbyterian laity for this flirtation with general assessment from its leadership is evident in the fact that the memorial of 1785 cited here, unlike earlier documents, included the voice of lay representatives within the denomination.

155. "The Remonstrants and Petition of the Committee of several Baptist Associations in Virginia assembled in Powhatan County," 3 November 1785. On the Baptists' experience, see Sandra Rennie, "Virginia's Baptist Persecution, 1765–1778," *Journal of Religious History* 12 (1982): 48–61.

156. Neal Riemer, "Madison: A Founder's Vision of Religious Liberty and Public Life," in *Religion, Public Life, and the American Polity*, ed. Luis Lugo (Knoxville: University of Tennessee Press, 1994), 37–50; Walter Berns, "Religion and the Founding Principle," in *Moral Foundations of the American Republic*, ed. Robert H. Horowitz (Charlottesville: University Press of Virginia, 1986), 162; Irving Brant, *James Madison: Father of the Constitution, 1787–1800* (Indianapolis: Bobbs-Merrill, 1950), 271–72. As Madison grew older, he did indeed endorse more of a separationist discourse. See James Madison to Robert Walsh, 2 March 1819, in *Writings of James Madison*, ed. Gaillard Hunt, 9 vols. (New York: G. P. Putnam, 1900–1910), vol. 8, 432, suggesting that "the number, the industry, and the morality of the Priesthood, & the devotion of the people have been manifestly increased by the total separation of church and state." This passage raises an interesting question for historians, namely the practice of indiscriminately referring to Madison's writings without distinguishing between the different contexts of the Revolutionary period on the one hand and the period after Madison's presidency on the other. For examples of this non-contextual approach, see Frank Lambert, *The Founding Fathers and the Place of Religion in America* (Princeton, N.J.: Princeton University Press, 2003), 4, presenting Madison's later writings, namely the famous "Detached Memoranda," as paradigmatic of Madison's thought; Ralph Ketcham, "James Madison and Religion—A New Hypothesis," *Journal of the Presbyterian Historical Society* 38 (June 1960): 78; Levy, *Establishment Clause*, 112–45.

157. Stephen D. Smith, *Getting over Equality: A Critical Diagnosis of Religious Freedom in America* (New York: New York University Press, 2001), 16.

158. Regarding eighteenth-century attempts to redefine religious duty in the softer terms of benevolence, social virtue, and the public good, consider Madison's college professor John Witherspoon, who caricatured such refined endeavors in criticism: "And what an obvious beauty has moral virtue gained from the delicate and skillful hands that have lately been employed in dressing her ladyship! She was once stiff and rigid, like ice or cold iron; now she is yielding as water, and, like iron hot from the furnace, can easily be beaten into what shape you please"; "Conscience . . . is of all things the most stiff and inflexible

and cannot by any art be molded into another shape than that which it naturally bears, whereas the whole principles of moderation are most gentle and ductile, and may be applied . . . [so] that all the particular rules of conduct are to be suspended when they seem to interfere with the general good." See John Witherspoon, *Ecclesiastical Characteristics or, The Arcana of Church Policy* (1753), in *The Selected Writings of John Witherspoon*, ed. Thomas Miller (Carbondale: Southern Illinois University Press, 1990), 89–90, 99–100.

159. James Madison, "Memorial and Remonstrance Against Religious Assessments," §1, in *James Madison on Religious Liberty*, ed. Robert Alley (Buffalo, N.Y.: Prometheus Books, 1985), 56.

160. Goochland County Petition, 2 November 1785. The popularity of this petition is highlighted by the fact that while its pages numbered 19, only four were written text. The other 15 pages were composed entirely of signatures. For commentary, see Buckley, *Church and State*, 149, explaining that the "chief significance of this petition rests in it commitment to the advancement of Christianity."

161. Madison, "Memorial and Remonstrance," §12 in *James Madison on Religious Liberty*, 59.

162. Thomas Jefferson, "A Bill for Establishing Religious Freedom," in *The Papers of Thomas Jefferson*, ed. Julian P. Boyd, 28 vols. to date (Princeton, N.J.: Princeton University Press, 1950–), vol. 2, 545–46, or "A Bill," in *Jefferson: Political Writings*, ed. Joyce Appleby and Terence Ball (New York: Cambridge University Press, 1999), 390–91, which denounces single establishment taxation: "to compel a man to furnish contributions of money for the propagation of opinions which he disbelieves and abhors, is sinful and tyrannical"; which deplores multi-establishment taxation: "that even the forcing him to support this or that teacher of his own religious persuasion, is depriving him of the comfortable liberty of giving his contributions to the particular pastor whose morals he would make his pattern."

163. Ibid., which denounces religious tests for public office: "proscribing any citizen as unworthy the public confidence by laying upon him an incapacity of being called to offices of trust or emolument, unless he profess or renounce this or that religious opinion, is depriving him injudiciously of . . . a natural right."

164. Alley, ed., *James Madison on Religious Liberty*, 16, advocates "the historic line from Madison and Jefferson through the [First] Amendment to the modern Supreme Court decisions on church and state."

165. Lenni Brenner, ed., *Jefferson and Madison on the Separation of Church and State: Writings on Religion and Secularism* (Fort Lee, N.J.: Barricade Books, 2004); Derek H. Davis, *Religion and the Continental Congress 1774–1789: Contributions to Original Intent* (New York: Oxford University Press, 2000); Leonard Levy, *The Establishment Clause: Religion and the First Amendment*, 2nd ed. (Chapel Hill: University of North Carolina Press, 1994); Thomas J. Curry, *The First Freedoms: Church and State in America to the Passage of the First Amendment* (New York: Oxford University Press, 1986); Robert S. Alley, ed., *James Madison on Religious Liberty* (Buffalo, N.Y.: Prometheus Books, 1985).

166. James Madison, *Federalist* 51 (1788), in *The Federalist*, ed. Jacob E. Cooke (Mid-

dletown, Conn.: Wesleyan University Press, 1961), 351–52. For antecedents to such thinking, consider John Clark's thoughts in the text above as well as Pett, *Discourse*, 21–22: "If there are but two parties in a Nation that differ from one another in Religion, 'tis not unlikely but that a civil War may arise on the account of Religion, though the one doth tolerate the other; because either of them that thinks its share in the chief Magistrates favour least, may for that reason attempt a forcible suppression of the other: But any such War can hardly be where the parties differing in Religion are many; For they are not likely to know the exact strength of one another, and their several animosities will keep them from joining together against any one that doth not invade their liberty in generall."

167. Isaac Kramnick and R. Laurence Moore, *The Godless Constitution: A Moral Defense of the Secular State* (New York: W. W. Norton, 2005).

CHAPTER 2. AMALEK AND THE RHETORIC OF EXTERMINATION

Note to epigraph: The earliest biography invoking this utterance as part of Jackson's deathbed pronouncements appears to be John Stillwell Jenkins, *The Life of General Andrew Jackson* (Albany, N.Y.: Derby, 1847), 186–87. I thank Chris Beneke and Christopher Grenda for their careful reading and helpful comments on an initial draft of this chapter.

1. William Graham Sumner, *Andrew Jackson* (Boston: Houghton Mifflin, 1899 [o.p. 1882]), 460.

2. Perry Miller, "The Garden of Eden and the Deacon's Meadow," *American Heritage* 7 (December 1955): 54. See also Abraham I. Katsch, *The Biblical Heritage of American Democracy* (New York: KTAV, 1977), and especially chapter 7, "The Influence of the Hebrew Bible on the Literature of England and America" (pp. 139–64). On the widespread influence of the Bible in America, see Nathan O. Hatch and Mark A. Noll, eds., *The Bible in America: Essays in Cultural History* (New York: Oxford University Press, 1982); James Turner Johnson, ed., *The Bible in American Law, Politics, and Political Rhetoric* (Philadelphia: Fortress Press, 1985); Ernest R. Sandeen, ed., *The Bible and Social Reform* (Philadelphia: Fortress Press, 1982).

3. "L'ensemble de croyances fondamentales qui n'ont même pas besoin de s'affirmer sous la forme d'un dogme explicite et conscient de lui-même" (Pierre Bourdieu, *Méditations pascaliennes* [Paris: Seuil, 1997], 26).

4. Exodus 17:8, 14; Numbers 24:20; Deuteronomy 25:17–19.

5. 1 Samuel 15:2–3.

6. On this aspect of the Amalekite story as an example of the "ban" (hērem, the destruction of all life in Old Testament holy war) see Susan Niditch, *War in the Hebrew Bible: A Study in the Ethics of Violence* (New York: Oxford University Press, 1993). See also Roland H. Bainton, *Christian Attitudes Toward War and Peace: A Historical Survey and Critical Evaluation* (New York: Abingdon, 1960), 151ff, 168 ff.

7. Judges 18:14.

8. Deuteronomy 25:17–19.

9. David Brion Davis, "Some Ideological Functions of Prejudice in Ante-Bellum America," *American Quarterly* 15 (1963): 116.

10. "Samuel Butler," in *Cambridge History of English and American Literature*, ed. A. W. Ward, A. R. Waller, W. P. Trent, J. Erskine, S. P. Sherman, and C. Van Doren, vol. 8 of 18 vols. (Cambridge: Cambridge University Press, 1907–22), VII.II.15.

11. Thomas Taylor, *An Everlasting Record of the Utter Ruine of Romish Amalek* (London, 1624), 5, 7, 13.

12. Ibid., 18, 20–22, 24–25.

13. John Geree, *Iudah's Ioy at the Oath* (London, 1641), sig. C4v. On the protestation oath see David Cressy, "The Protestation Protested, 1641 and 1642," *Historical Journal* 45 (2002): 251–79.

14. John Flavel, *Tydings from Rome, or England's alarm* (London, 1667), 18.

15. Ibid, 18, 19, 15

16. Arthur F. Marotti, *Religious Ideology and Cultural Fantasy: Catholic and Anti-Catholic Discourses in Early Modern England* (Notre Dame: University of Notre Dame Press, 2005), 44.

17. Andrew Marvell, *An Account of the Growth of Popery, and Arbitrary Government in England* (London, 1678 [o.p. 1677]), 5, 11.

18. Andrew Marvell, *A Seasonable Argument . . . for a New Parliament* (Amsterdam, 1677), title page.

19. Jonathan Scott, *England's Troubles: Seventeenth-Century English Political Instability in European Context* (Cambridge: Cambridge University Press, 2000). See also Scott, "England's Troubles: Exhuming the Popish Plot," in *The Politics of Religion in Restoration England*, ed. Tim Harris, Paul Seaward, and Mark Goldie (Oxford: Blackwell, 1990). In Marotti's terms, the blending of religious and political fears "made anti-catholic discourse a fixture of the political rhetoric of the period" (*Religious Ideology and Cultural Fantasy*, 160).

20. Marvell, *An Account of the Growth of Popery, and Arbitrary Government in England*, 11. On Marvell and other anti-Catholic conspiracy theorists see Marotti, *Religious Ideology and Cultural Fantasy*, 131–201.

21. Scott, "England's Troubles: Exhuming the Popish Plot," 108–9; Andrew Marvell, *The rehearsal transpos'd; or, Animadversions upon a late book* (London, 1672), 33.

22. Scott, "England's Troubles," raises the issue of Protestant digestion of Catholic suffering.

23. *A True History of the Horrid Conspiracy to Assassinate his Sacred Majesty, King William* (London, 1626), no author, printed for John Salusbury; J. S., *A True History of All the Memorable Transactions that Have Happen'd in England, Scotland, Ireland, Flanders, &c.* (London, 1696); Sir Richard Blackmore, *A True and Impartial History of the Conspiracy Against the Person and Government of King William III* (London, 1723), 4, 5, 13.

24. William Perse, *A Sermon Preached at Malton in Yorkshire. June 27th. 1706. Being the day of publick thanksgiving* (York, 1706), 1, 25, 21, 18, 23.

25. George Whitefield, *Britain's Mercies, and Britain's Duties* (London, 1746), 14–15.

26. "Histories and Historians of Oliver Cromwell," *United States Democratic Review* 26 (January 1850): 34; "Oliver Cromwell," *American Whig Review* 3 (April 1846): 411. Both articles are reviews of Thomas Carlyle, *Letters and Speeches of Oliver Cromwell* (New York: Wiley and Putnam, 1845).

27. John Greenleaf Whittier, *Old Portraits and Modern Sketches* (Boston, 1850), 294.

28. John Winthrop, *A Modell of Christian Charity* (1630), *Collections of the Massachusetts Historical Society*, 3rd ser., 7 (1838): 46. Useful background is in Susan Niditch, *War in the Hebrew Bible: A Study in the Ethics of Violence* (New York: Oxford, 1993).

29. Jonathan Edwards, *A History of the Work of Redemption* (New York, 1786), 95. The project was based on a series of sermons that he preached in 1739.

30. Charles G. Finney, "Attributes of Love," *Lectures on Systematic Theology* (London, 1851), XX.15.

31. Alexander Campbell, *Popular Lectures and Addresses* (Philadelphia, 1863), 334, 335.

32. Mary White Rowlandson, *The Sovereignty and Goodness of God . . . being a narrative of the captivity and restauration of Mrs. Mary Rowlandson*, originally published in 1682. Cited material is from Carla Munford, ed., *Early American Writings* (New York: Oxford University Press, 2002), 325.

33. Cotton Mather, *A Discourse Delivered unto Some Part of the Forces Engaged in a Just War of New England* (Boston, 1689), title page, 37, 28.

34. Christopher S. Grenda, "Reason, Faith, and Enlightenment: The Cultural Sources of Toleration in Early America," this volume.

35. Alden T. Vaughan, *Roots of American Racism: Essays on the Colonial Experience* (New York: Oxford University Press, 1995), 44–49; Karen Ordahl Kupperman, *Indians and English: Facing Off in Early America* (Ithaca, N.Y.: Cornell University Press, 2000), 27–30, 31.

36. Sabine MacCormack, "Limits of Understanding: Perceptions of Greco-Roman and Amerindian Paganism in Early Modern Europe," in *America in European Consciousness, 1493–1750*, ed. Karen Ordahl Kupperman (Chapel Hill: University of North Carolina Press, 1995), 96. 98, 106, 80; Luca Condignola, "The Holy See and the Conversion of the Indians in French and British North America, 1486–1760," in Kupperman, 196 (emphasis mine); Bobé, *Mémoire sur la découverte de la Mer de l'Quest* (1718), 53, 72–75, quoted in Cornelius J. Jaenen, "'Les Sauvages Ameriquains': Persistence into the Eighteenth Century of Traditional French Concepts and Constructs for Understanding Indians," *Ethnohistory* 29 (1982): 52.

37. Alden T. Vaughan thinks that the ten tribes model "encouraged colonists to 'uplift' rather than enslave or exterminate" the Indians. I argue that it provided the means by which to see Indians as religious kindred and thus to deploy against them the full rhetoric of Amalekite enmity. Menasseh ben Israel, quoted in Vaughan, *Roots of American Racism*, 49; John White, *The Planter's Plea* (London, 1760); Robert Wauchope, *Lost Tribes and Sunken Continents: Myth and Method in the Study of American Indians* (Chicago: University of Chicago Press, 1962), 3. A useful discussion of Hugo Grotius's statement of the theory, *De Origine Gentium Americanarum dissertatio* (Amsterdam, 1642), including

important Spanish precedents and critical opposition to the theory, is in Joan-Pau Rubiés, "Hugo Grotius's Dissertation on the Origin of the American Peoples and the Use of Comparative Methods," *Journal of the History of Ideas* 52 (1991): 221–44.

38. Quoted in Vaughan, *Roots of American Racism*, 51.

39. Cotton Mather, *The Mystery of Israel's Salvation Opened* (London, 1669), 96. Mather seems to have had second thoughts about the theory at a later time, judging by the tone of his remarks about Eliot's embrace of the theory of Indians as the ten tribes (*Magnalia Christia Americana*, bk 3: 192–93). Discussion of Williams, Penn, Sewall, and others is in Vaughan, 50ff and 274 n58, 63, 67; Jonathan Edwards, *A History of the Work of Redemption*, transcribed and ed. John F. Wilson (New Haven, Conn.: Yale University Press, 1989), 155–56; Gerald R. McDermott, "Jonathan Edwards and the American Indians: The Devil Sucks Their Blood," *New England Quarterly* 72 (1999): 539–57.

40. Charles Crawford, esq., *Essay upon the Propagation of the Gospel* (Philadelphia, 1799); James Adair, *Adair's History of the American Indians*, ed. Samuel Cole Williams (Johnson City, Tenn.: Watauga Press, 1930); William Apess, "The Indians: The Ten Lost Tribes," an appendix to *The Increase of the Kingdom of Christ* (1831), in *On Our Own Ground: The Complete Writings of William Apess, a Pequot*, ed. Barry O'Connell (Amherst: University of Massachusetts Press, 1991).

41. Vaughan, *Roots of American Racism*, 52–53.

42. David S. Lovejoy, "Satanizing the American Indians," *New England Quarterly* 67 (1994): 604; Richard W. Pointer, "Native Freedom? Indians and Religious Tolerance in Early America," in this volume.

43. "Report of Commissioner of Indian Affairs," *North American Review* 99 (October 1864): 449.

44. Cited in John Gorham Palfrey, *History of New England*, vol. 2 (Boston, 1860), 225.

45. Thomas Symmes, *Historical Memoirs of the Late Fight at Piggwacket, with a sermon occasion'd by the fall of the brave Capt John Lovewell* (Boston, 1725), i (also paginated as "Front Matter 1").

46. Ibid., p. 1. Symmes theorized, in jeremiad-like tones, that God was not yet ready to deliver Indians into the hands of the English. Thomas S. Kidd has proposed that the publication of such accounts was abetted by the maturing cosmopolitanism of New England, which supplied to authors "an interest in figures such as Indian fighters and brave heroes of the sea" (175). Thomas S. Kidd, "'The Devil and Father Ralle': The Narration of Father Rale's War in Provincial Massachusetts," *Historical Journal of Massachusetts* 30 (2002): 159–80.

47. Cited by Frederick D. Huntington in *Celebration of the Two Hundredth Anniversary of the Settlement of Hadley, Massachusetts* (Northampton, 1859), 31.

48. Robert L. Dabney, *A Defence of Virginia, and through her, of the South* (New York, 1867), 33.

49. Robert L. Dabney, "True Courage: A Discourse Commemorative of Lieut. General Thomas J. Jackson" (Richmond, Va., 1863), 15.

50. "History, as Expounded by the Supreme Court," *Putnam's Monthly Magazine of American Literature, Science, and Art* 9 (1857): 543; George Bancroft, *History of the United States*, vol. 3 of 10 vols. (Boston, 1837–74), 408; F. A. Walker, "The Indian Question," *North American Review* 116 (1873): 330; Edward Eggleston, *Century Illustrated Magazine* 26 (1883): 717; *The Living Age* 111 (1871): 462; Frederick D. Huntington, in Celebration of the two hundredth anniversary of the settlement of Hadley, Massachusetts (Northampton, 1859), 31.

51. Roy Harvey Pearce, *Savagism and Civilization: A Study of the Indian and the American Mind* (Berkeley: University of California Press, 1988). Originally published as *The Savages of America* (1953).

52. Richard Slotkin, *Regeneration Through Violence: The Mythology of the American Frontier, 1600–1860* (Middletown, Conn.: Wesleyan University Press, 1973); Jill Lepore, *The Name of War: King Philip's War and the Origins of American Identity* (New York: Alfred A. Knopf, 1998).

53. James West Davidson, *The Logic of Millennial Thought: Eighteenth-Century New England* (New Haven, Conn.: Yale University Press, 1977).

54. Nathan Stone, *Two Discourses Delivered at Southborough. October 9, 1760. Occasioned by the entire reduction of Canada* (Boston: S. Kneeland, 1761), 2. *The Christian Monitor: A Religious Periodical Work* (Boston, 1809), n.p..

55. "Extermination," *Times and Seasons* 5 (1844): 624. The publication is Mormon and republished the *Boston Investigator* story.

CHAPTER 3. THE EPISCOPATE, THE BRITISH UNION,
AND THE FAILURE OF RELIGIOUS SETTLEMENT

1. Carl Bridenbaugh, *Mitre and Sceptre: Transatlantic Faiths, Ideas, Personalities, and Politics 1689–1775* (New York: Oxford University Press, 1962), xix.

2. Horatio Walpole to the Bishop of London, 29 May 1750, printed in Arthur Lyon Cross, *The Anglican Episcopate and the American Colonies* (Cambridge, Mass.: Harvard University Press, 1902), 324–30.

3. Alison Gilbert Olson, *Making the Empire Work: London and American Interest Groups 1690–1790* (Cambridge, Mass.: Harvard University Press, 1992).

4. American Whig, XII, printed in *A Collection of Tracts From the Late Newpapers, &c. Containing Particularly* THE AMERICAN WHIG, A WHIP *for the* AMERICAN WHIG, With Some Other Pieces, On the Subject of the Residence of Protestant Bishops in the American Colonies, and in answer to the Writers who opposed it, &c. 2 vols. (New York: John Holt, 1768), 177.

5. See especially Donald F. M. Gerardi, "The Episcopate Controversy Reconsidered: Religious Vocation and Anglican Perceptions of Authority in Mid-Eighteenth-Century America," *Perspectives in American History* 3 (1987): 81–114.

6. Susan Juster's essay in this volume confirms the lack of consistency even in enforcing local religious settlements in North America.

7. On centralizing authority within the British state see John Brewer, *The Sinews of Power: War, Money and the English State 1688–1783* (New York: Alfred A. Knopf, 1989). On political and social convergence between Britain and its colonies, see numerous works by Jack P. Greene, including *Pursuits of Happiness: The Social Development of Early Modern British Colonies and the Formation of American Culture* (Chapel Hill: University of North Carolina Press, 1988); although in *Peripheries and Center: Constitutional Development in the Extended Polities of the British Empire and the United States, 1607–1788* (New York: W. W. Norton, 1986) and *Negotiated Authorities: Essays in Colonial Political and Constitutional History* (Charlottesville: University Press of Virginia, 1994) he has also emphasized the extent to which constitutional authority in the early modern empire was negotiated rather than imposed. Work on the Anglicization of American society begins with John M. Murrin, "Anglicizing an American Colony: The Transformation of Provincial Massachusetts" (Ph.D. diss., Yale University, 1966). A contrasting view positing the proliferation of dissent as the obstacle to unified imperial authority is J. C. D. Clark, *The Language of Liberty 1660–1832: Political Discourse and Social Dynamics in the Anglo-American World* (Cambridge: Cambridge University Press, 1994).

8. Ned C. Landsman, "The Legacy of British Union for the North American Colonies: Provincial Elites and the Problem of Imperial Union," in *A Union for Empire: Political Thought and The Union of 1707*, ed. John Robertson (New York: Cambridge University Press, 1995), 297–317. I am currently working on a book-length manuscript on the union and the North American colonies.

9. *A Narrative of a New and Unusual American Imprisonment of Two Presbyterian Ministers and Prosecution of Mr. Francis Makemie* (New York, 1707), available in a modern reprint in *The Life and Writings of Francis Makemie*, ed. Boyd S. Schlenther (Philadelphia, 1971), 189–244. Cornbury's version, in a letter to the Lords of Trade, dated incorrectly as 14 October 1706, does not agree that he ever questioned the application of the Toleration to the colonies; E. B. O'Callaghan (comp.), *Documents Relating to the Colonial History of the State of New York*, 15 vols. (Albany, N.Y., 1856–87), vol. 4, 1186–87. For a revisionist account of Cornbury's career, including his support for toleration, see especially Patricia U. Bonomi, *The Lord Cornbury Scandal: The Politics of Reputation in British America* (Chapel Hill: University of North Carolina Press, 2000).

10. Makemie, *Narrative*, 211.

11. Cotton Mather to Samuel Penhallow, 8 July1707, printed in *Diary of Cotton Mather*, 2 vols. (New York: Frederick Ungar, n.d.), vol. 1, 509. Jonathan Clark has also noted the significance of the case for the privileges dissenters were able to claim in North America, but Clark attributes that to Makemie's initial assertion of his right under the toleration and not the more far-reaching claims expressed later; see *Language of Liberty*, 6.

12. On the union settlement, see especially *Union for Empire*, ed. John Robertson, and Christopher A. Whately, *The Scots and the Union* (Edinburgh: Edinburgh University Press, 2006).

13. Taken from *The Treaty of Union of Scotland and England 1707*, ed. George S. Pryde (Westport, Conn.: Greenwood Press, 1950), 103–7.

14. John Robertson, "An Elusive Sovereignty: The Course of the Union Debate in Scotland 1698–1707," in *Union for Empire*, 198–227.

15. A useful summary of ecclesiastical developments in the Church of Scotland can be found in Andrew L. Drummond and James Bulloch, *The Scottish Church 1688–1843* (Edinburgh: Saint Andrew Press, 1973).

16. On the balancing of denominations in the mid-Atlantic, see especially Evan Haefeli, "The Creation of American Religious Pluralism: Churches, Colonialism, and Conquest in the Mid-Atlantic 1628–1688," (Ph.D. diss., Princeton University, 2000).

17. On Cornbury see Bonomi, *The Lord Cornbury Scandal*; on the situation in New York generally see Richard W. Pointer, *Protestant Pluralism and the New York Experience: A Study of Eighteenth-Century Diversity* (Bloomington: Indiana University Press, 1988), and "Colonel Morris to John Chamberlayne, Esq.," 20 February 1711, and "Statement Respecting the Church of Jamaica," n.d., in O'Callaghan, *Documents*, vol. 5, 318–24, 328.

18. On Bray, see H. P. Thompson, *Thomas Bray* (London: SPCK, 1954), and "Rev. Thomas Bray: His Life and Selected Works Relating to Maryland," ed. Bernard Steiner, *Maryland Historical Society Publications* 37 (Baltimore: J. Murphy Co., 1901).

19. Commissioner Johnston to the Secretary of the S.P.G., 5 July 1710, printed in Charles A. Briggs, *American Presbyterianism* (New York, 1885), lxix–lxx.

20. Cross, *Anglican Episcopate*, 93–95.

21. "Case of the Presbyterian Congregation at New York, 1724," Church of Scotland Ms., Scottish Record Office, Edinburgh; and *The Case of the Scotch Presbyterians of the City of New York* (New York, 1773).

22. "Case of the Presbyterian Congregation at New York, 1724," and *Case of the Scotch Presbyterians of the City of New York*.

23. *Minutes of the Presbyterian Church in America 1706–1788*, ed. Guy S. Klett (Philadelphia: Presbyterian Historical Society, 1976); the incomplete state of the records makes an exact count of ministers and congregations at any particular point impossible.

24. The most recent treatment is Patrick Griffin, *The People with No Name: Ireland's Ulster Scots, America's Scots Irish, and the Creation of a British Atlantic World, 1689–1764* (Princeton, N.J.: Princeton University Press, 2001).

25. James Anderson to the Right Reverend Mr. John Stirling, Principal of the College of Glasgow, August 1716, and 8 August 1717, printed in Charles A. Briggs, *American Presbyterianism* (New York, 1885), lxix–lxxvi. In both New York and Carolina, there appear to have been tensions between Scots and English Presbyterians about how aggressively to press their newfound liberties. Commissary Johnston in South Carolina claimed to have the support of an English Presbyterian minister there, a Mr. Taylour, who he described as a "person of a very peaceable temper," while in New York Anderson left the congregation in what may have been an ethnic dispute. See Briggs, *American Presbyterianism*, lxix–lxx, and "Case of the Presbyterian Congregation at New York," 43–58.

26. "Commission to the Bishop of London for Exercising Jurisdiction in the American Colonies," in *Documents Relative to the Colonial History of the State of New-York*, ed. John Remeyn Brodhead, 10 vols. (Albany, N.Y.1856–58), vol. 5, 849–54; Cross, *Anglican Episcopate*, 67–69.

27. In William Stevens Perry, *Historical Collections Relating to the American Colonial Church*, 5 vols. (Hartford, Conn., 1870–78), vol. 3, 180ff.

28. Bridenbaugh, *Mitre and Sceptre*, 68–77, presents the events from the Congregational point of view.

29. Johnson, *A Letter from a Minister of the Church of England to His dissenting Parishioners* (New York: John Peter Zenger, 1733); and *A Second Letter from a Minister of the Church of England To His Dissenting Parishioners* (Boston: n.p., 1734), printed in *Samuel Johnson, President of King's College. His Career and Writings*, ed. Herbert and Carol Schneider, 4 vols. (New York: Columbia University Press, 1929), vol. 3, 17–130, esp. 28–29, 41.

30. James Wetmore to Bishop Gibson, 1 November 1728, *The Fulham Papers in the Lambeth Palace Library: American Colonial Section Calendar and Indexes*, comp. William Wilson Manross (Oxford: Clarendon Press, 1965), 87; Wetmore, *A Letter From a Minister of the Church of England to his Dissenting Parishioners* (New York: John Peter Zenger [1730]), 18–19.

31. James Wetmore to the Rev. Mr. Beach, in John Beach, *A Calm and Dispassionate Vindication of the Professors of the Church of England, Against the Abusive Misrepresentations and fallacious Argumentations of Mr. Noah Hobart* (Boston: J. Draper, 1749), Appendix, 53–66.

32. James Wetmore, *A Vindication of the Professors of the Church of England in Connecticut* (Boston: Rogers and Fowle, 1747), 29.

33. Hobart, *A Serious Address to the Members of the Episcopal Separation in New-England* (Boston: J. Bushell and J. Green, 1748).

34. Ibid., 9–15.

35. Hobart, *Serious Address*, 9, 10, 13, 35, 64–65; Hobart, *Second Address to the Members of the Episcopal Separation in New-England* (Boston: D. Fowle), 1751.

36. Hobart, *Serious Address*, 35.

37. Thomas Bradbury Chandler, *An Appeal to the Public, in Behalf of the Church of England in America* (New York, 1767). There are numerous discussions of the controversy; see especially Cross, *Anglican Episcopate*; Bridenbaugh, *Mitre and Sceptre*, chap. 8; Gerardi, "Episcopate Controversy"; and Nancy L. Rhoden, *Revolutionary Anglicanism: The Colonial Church of England Clergy During the American Revolution* (New York: New York University Press, 1999), chap. 3.

38. "Clergy of New Jersey and New York to Bishop Terrick," 2 October 1765, cited in *Fulham Papers*, 85; and Chandler, *Appeal to the Public*.

39. Chandler, *Appeal to the Public*; the quotations are from 77, 117.

40. Ibid., 113–14.

41. Chandler, *Appeal to the Public*, 110.

42. Chandler, *Appeal to the Public*, 107–8.

43. Charles Chauncy, *The Appeal to the Public Answered, In Behalf of the Non-Episcopal Churches in America* (Boston, 1768), 111, 180.

44. Chauncy, *Appeal to the Public Answered*.

45. *The Centinel: Warnings of a Revolution*, ed. Elizabeth I. Nybakken (Newark: University of Delaware Press, 1980), 87, 89, 92, 126.

46. Ibid., 85, 87, 151.

47. *The Centinel: Warnings of a Revolution*, ed. Elizabeth I. Nybakken (Newark: University of Delaware Press, 1980), 89.

48. Rhoden, *Revolutionary Anglicanism*, chaps. 2–3; Cross, *Anglican Episcopate*, chap. 10; Patrick Rouse, Jr., *James Blair of Virginia* (Chapel Hill: University of North Carolina Press, 1971); P. G. Scott, "James Blair and the Scottish Church: A New Source," *William and Mary Quarterly*, 3rd ser., 33 (1976): 300–308; and John Frederick Woolverton, *Colonial Anglicanism in North America* (Detroit: Wayne State University Press, 1982), chap. 5.

49. A work that highlights the spiritual rather than ecclesiastical roots of religious liberty in early America in the wake of evangelical influences is Chris Beneke, *Beyond Toleration: The Religious Origins of American Pluralism* (New York: Oxford University Press, 2006).

50. On the whole New Light or pro-revival Congregationalists and Presbyterians were less active than their Old Light counterparts against the bishop, and less concerned with ecclesiastical matters generally, but those who addressed it consistently opposed the Episcopate.

51. Pointer, *Protestant Pluralism and the New York Experience*, 62–65; Ezra Stiles, *A Discourse on the Christian Union* (Boston, 1761).

52. *Centinel*, no. VIII, p. 128. Thomas J. Curry writes of the two meanings of religious "establishment" in *The First Freedoms: Church and State in America to the Passage of the First Amendment* (New York: Oxford University Press, 1986), 116–17.

53. *The Independent Reflector, or Weekly Essays on Sundry Important Subjects More particularly adapted to the Province of New-York*, ed. Milton M. Klein (Cambridge, Mass.: Belknap Press, 1963), no. XVIII, 178–83; Elisha Williams, *The Essential Rights and Liberties of Protestants* (Boston, 1744); Curry, *First Freedoms*, chap. 5.

54. See *Independent Reflector*, esp. nos. XVII–XXII, XXXVI–XXIX, XLIV, and XLIX–LI. The principle responses appeared in *The New-York Mercury*, followed in 1753 by discussions in *The Occasional Reverberator* and subsequent contributions on both sides in the *Mercury*.

55. *New-York Mercury*, 30 July 1753; *Independent Reflector*, no. XLIV. See also Makemie, *A Narrative of a New and Unusual American Imprisonment, of Two Presbyterian Ministers* (New York, 1755), printed by Hugh Gaine, who published Livingston's "Watch-Tower" and other essays.

56. [Benjamin Nicoll], *A Brief Vindication of the Proceedings of the Trustees Relating to the College. Containing a Sufficient Answer to the Late Famous Protest, With Its Twenty Unanswered Reasons* (New York, 1754), 4, 11.

57. *Independent Reflector*, 180–81, 188, 182–83, 193.

58. Rhoden, *Revolutionary Anglicanism*.

59. Ibid., and also see Frederick V. Mills, *Bishops by Ballot: An Eighteenth-Century Ecclesiastical Revolution* (New York, 1978); Curry, *First Freedoms*, chap. 8; Beneke, *Beyond Toleration*, chap. 5.

60. On the multiple sources of toleration in early America, see the essay by Christopher S. Grenda in this volume.

CHAPTER 4. PRACTICING TOLERATION IN DUTCH NEW NETHERLAND

1. Willem Frijhoff, "The Threshold of Toleration: Interconfessional Conviviality in Holland During the Early Modern Period," in *Embodied Belief: Ten Essays on Religious Culture in Dutch History* (Hilversum, Verloren, 2002), 39–65; and Willem Frijhoff, "Dimensions de la coexistence confessionelle," in *The Emergence of Tolerance in the Dutch Republic,* ed. C. Berkvens-Stevelinck, J. Israel, and G. H. M. Posthumus Meyjes (Leiden: Brill, 1997), 213–37. Benjamin J. Kaplan, *Divided by Faith: Religious Conflict and the Practice of Toleration in Early Modern Europe* (Cambridge, Mass.: Belknap Press of Harvard University Press,2007); Benjamin J. Kaplan, "'Dutch' Religious Tolerance: Celebration and Revision," in *Calvinism and Religious Toleration in the Dutch Golden Age,* ed. R. Po-Chia Hsia and Henk van Nierop (Cambridge: Cambridge University Press, 2002), 8–26.

2. Benjamin J. Kaplan, "Fictions of Privacy: House Chapels and the Spatial Accommodation of Religious Dissent in Early Modern Europe," *American Historical Review* 107 (2002): 1031–64.

3. Stuyvesant is cast in a negative light in Frederick Zwierlein, *Religion in New Netherland* (Rochester, N.Y., 1910) and Frederick J. Zwierlein, "New Netherland Intolerance," *Catholic Historical Review* 4 (1918): 186–216. Revisionist studies include George L. Smith, *Religion and Trade in New Netherland: Dutch Origins and American Development* (Ithaca, N.Y.: Cornell University Press,1973); Jaap Jacobs, "Between Repression and Approval: Connivance and Toleration in the Dutch Republic and New Netherland," *De Halve Maen* 71 (fall 1998): 51–58; and Jaap Jacobs, *New Netherland: A Dutch Colony in Seventeenth-Century America* (Leiden: Brill, 2005).

See also Firth Haring Fabend, "Church and State, Hand in Hand: Compassionate Calvinism in New Netherland," *De Halve Maen* 75 (spring 2002): 3–8. On the ways in which colonial authorities in Dutch America continually negotiated for power, see Mark Meuwese, "The Murder of Jacob Rabe: Contesting Dutch Colonial Authority in the Borderlands of Northeastern Brazil," in *New World Orders: Violence, Sanction and Authority in the Colonial Americas,* ed. John Smolenski and Thomas J. Humphrey (Philadelphia: University of Pennsylvania Press, 2005), 133–56; 317–23; and Wim Klooster, "Other Netherlands Beyond the Sea: Dutch America Between Metropolitan Control and Divergence, 1600–1796," in *Negotiated Empires: Centers and Peripheries in the Americas, 1500–1820,* ed. Christine Daniels and Michael V. Kennedy (New York: Routledge, 2002), 171–91.

4. On Stuyvesant's early years, see Jaap Jacobs, "Like Father, Like Son? The Early Years of Petrus Stuyvesant," in *Revisiting New Netherland: Perspectives on Early Dutch America,* ed. Joyce D. Goodfriend (Leiden; Brill, 2005), 205–42.

5. *New Netherland Documents. Council Minutes, 1655–1656,* trans. and ed. Charles T. Gehring (Syracuse, N.Y.: Syracuse University Press, 1995), 133.

6. Joyce D. Goodfriend, "The Struggle over the Sabbath in Petrus Stuyvesant's New

Amsterdam," in *Power and the City in the Netherlandic World,* ed. Wayne Te Brake and Wim Klooster (Leiden: Brill, 2006), 205–24.

7. Harry J. Kreider, *The Beginnings of Lutheranism in New York* (New York, 1949), 7.

8. Kreider, *The Beginnings of Lutheranism in New York*, 3, 8.

9. "Letter from the Lutherans in New Netherland to the Consistory at Amsterdam," October 4, 1653, Arnold J. H. van Laer, trans., *The Lutheran Church in New York, 1649–1772* (New York, 1946), 16.

10. On the Lutherans in Beverwijck (Albany), see Janny Venema, *A Dutch Village on the American Frontier, 1652–1664* (Albany: State University of New York Press, 2003), 102–3.

11. "Petition of the Revs. Megapolensis and Drisius to the Burgomasters, Etc. Against Tolerating the Lutherans," July 6, 1657, Edward T. Corwin, ed., *Ecclesiastical Records of the State of New York* (hereafter *Ecc. Rec.*), 7 vols. (Albany, 1901–16), vol. 1, 387–88.

12. Revs. Megapolensis and Drisius to the Classis of Amsterdam, October 6, 1653, *Ecc. Rec.*, vol. 1, 317–18.

13. "Letter from the Lutherans in New Netherland to the Consistory at Amsterdam," October 4, 1653, van Laer, *The Lutheran Church in New York, 1649–1772*, 16.

14. "Letter from Johannes E. Gutwasser to the Amsterdam Consistory," August [14], 1657, van Laer, *The Lutheran Church in New York, 1649–1772*, 25.

15. "Letter from the Lutherans in New Netherland to the Consistory at Amsterdam," October 4, 1653, van Laer, *The Lutheran Church in New York, 1649–1772*, 16.

16. Ibid.

17. Revs. Megapolensis and Drisius to the Classis of Amsterdam, October 6, 1653, *Ecc. Rec.*, vol. 1, 317.

18. Directors to Stuyvesant, March 12, 1654, *Ecc. Rec.*, vol. 1, 324.

19. "Letter from the Consistory at Amsterdam to the Lutherans at the Manhatans," June 14, 1656, van Laer, *The Lutheran Church in New York, 1649–1772*, 254.

20. Gehring, *New Netherland Documents. Council Minutes, 1655–1656*, 209–10.

21. "Petition of the Lutherans to the Governor [*sic*] and Council, to be permitted to Enjoy their own Public Worship," October 24, 1656, *Ecc. Rec.*, vol. 1, 359. The law imposed stiff penalties on "all those who, being unqualified, assume, either Sundays or other days, any office whether of preacher, reader, or singer, in such meetings" and on "everyone, whether man or woman, married or unmarried, who is found in such meetings" (*Council Minutes 1655–1656*, 209).

22. "Directors to Stuyvesant," June 14, 1656, *Ecc. Rec.*, vol. 1, 352.

23. On connivance, see Smith, *Religion and Trade in New Netherland*.

24. "Petition of the Revs. Megapolensis and Drisus to the Burgomasters . . . Against tolerating the Lutherans," July 6, 1657, *Ecc. Rec.* vol. 1, 387.

25. "Report of the Mayor and Aldermen of New Amsterdam upon the Petition of the Ministers against Allowing Lutheran services, July 14, 1657," *Ecc. Rec.*, vol. 1, 389.

26. "Letter from Johannes E. Gutwasser to the Amsterdam Consistory," September

8, 1657, Van Laer, *The Lutheran Church in New York, 1649–1772*, 27. See also "Letter from Johannes E. Gutwasser to the Amsterdam Consistory," August [14], 1657, Van Laer, *The Lutheran Church in New York, 1649–1772*, 24.

27. "Revs. J. Megapolensis and S. Drisius to Classis of Amsterdam," New Amsterdam, September 10, 1659, *Ecc. Rec.*, vol. 1, 449.

28. On the changes in the formula of baptism see Directors in Amsterdam to the Director-General and Council, May 20, 1658, *Correspondence 1654–1658*, trans. and ed. Charles T. Gehring (Syracuse, N.Y., Syracuse University Press, 2003), 174–75.

29. "Letter from Hendrick Bosch to the Consistory at Amsterdam," August 19, 1663, Van Laer, *The Lutheran Church in New York, 1649–1772*, 47–48.

30. "Letter from the Lutherans at New York to the Amsterdam Consistory," December 8/18, 1664, Van Laer, *The Lutheran Church in New York, 1649–1772*, 50.

31. "Letter from the Lutherans at New York to the Amsterdam Consistory," December 8/18, 1664, Van Laer, *The Lutheran Church in New York, 1649–1772*, 50. The Lutherans were granted religious freedom in December 1664. Harry Julius Kreider, *Lutheranism in Colonial New York* (New York: Arno Press, 1972; originally published 1942), 22.

32. For background on the Jewish migrants from Brazil, see Arnold Wiznitzer, "The Exodus from Brazil and Arrival in New Amsterdam of the Jewish Pilgrim Fathers, 1654," in, *The Jewish Experience in America: Selected Studies from the Publications of the American Jewish Historical Society*, ed. Abraham J. Karp, 5 vols. (New York, KTAV, 1969), vol. 1, 19–36; Egon Wolff and Frieda Wolff, "The Problem of the First Jewish Settlers in New Amsterdam, 1654," *Studia Rosenthaliana* 15 (1981): 169–77; and Leo Hershkowitz, "New Amsterdam's Twenty-Three Jews—Myth or Realities?" in *Hebrew and the Bible in America: The First Two Centuries*, ed. Shalom Goldman (Hanover, N.H.: University Press of New England, 1993). On New Amsterdam's Jews, more generally, see David De Sola Pool and Tamar De Sola Pool, *An Old Faith in the New World: Portrait of Shearith Israel 1654–1954* (New York: Columbia University Press, 1955); Jacob R. Marcus, *The Colonial American Jew, 1492–1776*, 3 vols. (Detroit: Wayne State University Press, 1970); and Eli Faber, *A Time for Planting: The First Migration 1654–1820* (Baltimore: Johns Hopkins University Press, 1992).

33. Samuel Oppenheim, *The Early History of the Jews in New York, 1654–1664. Some New Matter on the Subject* (New York, 1909) [*Publications of the American Jewish Historical Society*, no. 19 (1909)], 4–5.

34. John Megapolensis to the Classis of Amsterdam, March 18, 1655, *Ecc. Rec.* vol. 1, 335.

35. *The Records of New Amsterdam from 1653 to 1674*, ed. Berthold Fernow, 7 vols. (New York, 1897), vol. 1, 291.

36. Oppenheim, *The Early History of the Jews in New York, 1654–1664*, 11, 8.

37. Ibid., 33. (This is a revised translation of a document in New York Colonial Manuscripts., vol. 12, 39. New York State Archives, Albany.) *Records of New Amsterdam*, vol. 2, 262, plus see Oppenheim's discussion in *The Early History of the Jews in New York, 1654–1664*, 34.

38. *Records of New Amsterdam*, vol. 7, 154.

39. *Council Minutes, 1655–1656*, 149–51.

40. Ibid., 261–62.

41. "Deposition of Asser Levi regarding the ownership of a brandy cask which an Indian took from the island opposite the fort," *Early Records of the City and County of Albany and Colony of Rensselaerswyck*, vol. 4, trans. Jonathan Pearson, rev. and ed. A. J. F. van Laer (Albany, N.Y., 1919), 71.

42. *Fort Orange Court Minutes 1652–1660*. trans. and ed. Charles T. Gehring (Syracuse, N.Y.: Syracuse University Press, 1990), 402–403, 407,409, 438, 439, 443, 489. In none of these court appearances was Levy identified as a Jew.

43. *Council Minutes, 1655–1656*, 166, 179.

44. Directors to Stuyvesant, June 14, 1656, *Correspondence 1654–1658*, 93.

45. In 1662, Asser Levy bought a house and lot from Barent Gerritsen. Later that year he sold them to Joghim Wesselsen Bakker. In 1663, he purchased a lot from Wessel Evertsen. He still owned this property in 1667. I owe these references to Adriana van Zwieten. See also Leon Huhner, "Asser Levy: A Noted Jewish Burgher of New Amsterdam," in *The Jewish Experience in America*, ed. Karp, vol. 1, 58–59, for conveyances to Asser Levy, citing *Valentine's Manual*, 1865, 691, 701. In 1661, Asser Levy had hired a house that was to be built for Wessel (Eversen) the Fisher. *Records of New Amsterdam*, vol. 3, 293.

46. *Records of New Amsterdam*, vol. 1, 371.

47. *Council Minutes, 1655–1656*, 261–62. On the legal rights of Jews in Amsterdam, see Arend H. Huusen, "The Legal Position of the Jews in the Dutch Republic c. 1590–1796," in *Dutch Jewry: Its History and Secular Culture (1500–2000)*, ed. Jonathan Israel and Reinier Salverda (Leiden: Brill, 2002), 25–41.

48. *Records of New Amsterdam*, vol. 7, 154.

49. Oppenheim, *The Early History of the Jews in New York, 1654–1664*, 36.

50. *Council Minutes, 1655–1656*, 81.

51. *Council Minutes, 1655–1656*, 128. In the 1655 subscription for the city's defenses, Levy and Barsimson each were taxed fl. 6 compared to their coreligionists tax of fl. 100.

52. *Records of New Amsterdam*, vol. 2, 113, 125, 132, 140–41; *Calendar of Dutch Manuscripts*, vol. 1 of *Calendar of Historical Manuscripts in the Office of the Secretary of State, Albany, New York*, ed. E. B. O'Callaghan, 2 vols. (Albany, N.Y., 1865–66), 180. See also Samuel Oppenheim, "More About Jacob Barsimson, the First Jewish Settler in New York," in *The Jewish Experience in America*, ed. Karp, vol. 1, 42–43, where the full text of the appeal is reproduced.

53. *Laws & Writs of Appeal 1647–1663*, trans. and ed. Charles T. Gehring (Syracuse, N.Y., Syracuse University Press, 1991), 109–10. Wessels, having been ordered to pay Barsimson "one hogshead of tobacco and some loose baskets, amounting to the quantity of 400 lb. at 7 stivers a pound," disputed Barsimson's claim that he had left these items in Wessels's cellar. The outcome of this case is unknown due to missing records.

54. *Records of New Amsterdam*, vol. 2, 2–3; 8–9.

55. *Records of New Amsterdam*, vol. 2, 396, 397. Barsimson was scheduled to appear in court as a defendant in two cases, "Adriaen Keyser, pltf. V/s Jacob Barsomon, a Jew, deft" and "Storm Alberzen, pltf.. V/s Jacob Barsimon, a Jew, deft."

56. *Records of New Amsterdam*, vol. 7, 258–59; 261.

57. *New York Historical Manuscripts: Dutch*; vol. 3, *Register of the Provincial Secretary, 1648–1660*, trans. Arnold J. F. van Laer, ed. Kenneth Scott and Kenn Stryker-Rodda (Baltimore: Genealogical Publishing Company, 1974), 437–38. Among those who leased real property in New Amsterdam to Jews were Rutger Jacobsen, Harmen Douwessen, and Pietertje Jans and her husband Claes Jansen Ruiter (Oppenheim, *The Early History of the Jews in New York, 1654–1664*, 74–75, 76, 89).

58. *New York Historical Manuscripts Dutch. The Register of Salomon Lachaire Notary Public of New Amsterdam 1661–1662*, trans. E. B. O'Callaghan, ed. Kenneth Scott and Kenn Stryker-Rodda (Baltimore: Genealogical Publishing Company, 1978), 142, 157, 198.

59. *Records of New Amsterdam*, vol. 1, 291. The record continues, "The charge having been read before deft., who not understanding the same. It was ordered that copy thereof be given deft. To answer it by next Court day." Whether this severe punishment was carried out is unclear.

60. *Laws & Writs of Appeal 1647–1663*, 50–51.

61. Oppenheim, *The Early History of the Jews in New York, 1654–1664*, 4.

62. *Ecc. Rec.*, vol. 1, 335. Antipathy toward Jews did not automatically translate into hostile action. Reformed church officers, whether grudgingly or not, acted on humanitarian grounds in relieving the distress of the impoverished Brazilian Jews. Dominie Megapolensis himself had been willing to listen to the plight of the individuals concerned. "They came several times to my house weeping and bemoaning their misery."

63. *Register of Salomon Lachaire*, 77.

64. *Records of New Amsterdam*, vol. 2, 416, 417, 419, 424.

65. Bontemantel Papers, New York Public Library. Printed in Oppenheim, *The Early History of the Jews in New York, 1654–1664*, 21. In February 1656, Stuyvesant and his council did act favorably on a petition from New Amsterdam's Jews "that they be permitted to purchase a burial place or that a place might be indicated, granted and allowed them." *Council Minutes, 1655–56*, 229.

66. Directors to Stuyvesant, June 14, 1656, *Correspondence 1654–1658*, 93. On March 13, 1656, the directors had informed Stuyvesant that they had not given New Netherland's Jews "a claim to the privilege of exercising their religion in a synagogue or at a gathering" (Directors to the Director-General and Council of New Netherland, March 13, 1656, *Correspondence 1654–1658*, 83).

67. I. S. Emmanuel, "New Light on Early American Jewry," *American Jewish Archives* 7 (1955): 17, 56.

68. The government acceded to this request (*Council Minutes, 1655–1656*, 68, 229).

69. Minutes of the Executive Boards of the Burgomasters of New Amsterdam in *Minutes of the Orphanmasters Court of New Amsterdam 1655–1663*, trans. and ed. Berthold Fernow (New York, 1907), 165.

70. On Asser Levy, see Huhner, "Asser Levy," Leo Hershkowitz, "Asser Levy and the Inventories of Early New York Jews," *American Jewish Historical Quarterly* 80 (1990): 21–55, and Noah L. Gelfand, "Jews in New Netherland: An Atlantic Perspective," in *Explorers, Fortunes and Love Letters: A Window on New Netherland* ed. Martha Dickinson Shattuck (Albany, N.Y.: Mount Ida Press, 2009), 44–45.

71. *Records of New Amsterdam*, vol. 5, 176–77, 183, 188, 191–92.

72. On the recognition of the Jews as "separate autonomous 'nations' " in the seventeenth-century Netherlands, see Huusen, "The Legal Position of the Jews in the Dutch Republic," 34.

73. *Ecc. Rec.*, vol. 1, 335.

74. For the case of a Mennonist, the Dutch counterpart of an English Baptist, in New Amsterdam's Reformed congregation, see *Ecc. Rec.*, vol. 1, 486–87. 513–14, 555.

75. *Ecc. Rec.*, vol. 1, 300.

76. On the Mennonists in Gravesend, see J. Megapolensis and S. Drisius to the Classis of Amsterdam, August 5, 1657, *Ecc. Rec.*, vol. 1, 396.

77. J. Megapolensis and S. Drisius to the Classis of Amsterdam, August 5, 1657, in *Narratives of New Netherland 1609–1664*, ed. J. Franklin Jameson (New York, 1909), 397. Wickenden was a Particular Baptist (Philip F. Gura, *A Glimpse of Sion's Glory: Puritan Radicalism in New England, 1620–1660* [Middletown, Conn.: Wesleyan University Press, 1984], 105–6).

78. *Calendar of Dutch Manuscripts*, 177.

79. Humphrey Norton, *New England's Ensigne* (London, 1659), 15.

80. *Ecc. Rec.*, vol. 1, 400.

81. Ibid., vol. 1, 410.

82. Ibid., vol. 1, 399.

83. Ibid., vol. 1, 400.

84. Ibid., vol. 1, 400.

85. *Records of New Amsterdam*, vol. 2, 347.

86. Norton, *New England's Ensigne*, 15. Norton may have magnified the sufferings of his coreligionists. The Dutch ministers reported tersely that "After being examined in prison, they [Weatherhead and Waugh] were sent away" (*Ecc. Rec.*, vol. 1, 410).

87. *Ecc. Rec.*, vol. 1, 410.

88. Francis Howgill, *The Popish Inquisition Newly Erected in New-England* (London, 1659), 9.

89. Revs. Johannes Megapolensis and Samuel Drisius to the Classis of Amsterdam, Manhattans, October 22, 1657, *Ecc. Rec.*, vol. 1, 410.

90. George Bishop, *New-England Judged by the Spirit of the Lord* (London, 1703), 218. See also Jacobs, *New Netherland*, 307.

91. On the Flushing Remonstrance, see R. Ward Harrington, "Speaking Scripture: The Flushing Remonstrance of 1657," *Quaker History* 82 (1993): 105–9, and David William Voorhees, "The 1657 Flushing Remonstrance in Historical Perspective," de *Halve Maen* 82 (spring 2008): 11–14. The Flushing Remonstrance has been enshrined as a landmark

document in the movement toward freedom of religion in the state of New York. The 350th anniversary of the Flushing Remonstrance in 2007 occasioned a round of remembrance and reflection. See Dennis Maika, "Commemoration and Context: The Flushing Remonstrance Then and Now," *New York History* 89 (2008): 29–42; Russell Shorto, "The Importance of Flushing," *New York Archives* 7 (2008): 8–10; and Kenneth T. Jackson, "A Colony with a Conscience," *New York Times*, op-ed page, December 27, 2007. The quotation from the Remonstrance is in Shorto, "The Importance of Flushing."

92. *Ecc. Rec.*, vol. 1, 415.

93. *Records of New Amsterdam*, vol. 2, 347.

94. On the history of the Quakers in New Netherland and early New York see Rufus M. Jones, *The Quakers in the American Colonies* (New York: W. W. Norton, 1966; originally published 1911); Arthur Worrall, *Quakers in the Colonial Northeast* (Hanover, N.H.: University Press of New England, 1980); and Mildred Murphy DeRiggi, "Quakerism on Long Island: The First Fifty Years 1657–1707" (Ph.D. diss., State University of New York at Stony Brook, 1994). See also Natalie A. Naylor, ed., *"The People Called Quakers": Records of Long Island Friends 1671–1703* (Interlaken, N.Y.: Empire State Books, 2001).

95. Revs. J. Megapolensis and S. Drisius to the Classis of Amsterdam, New Amsterdam, September 24, 1658, *Ecc. Rec.*, vol. 1, 433.

96. Council Minutes, August 24, 1662, *Ecc. Rec.*, vol. 1, 526–27.

97. Ordinance of the Director General and Council of New Netherland Against Conventicles. Passed September 21, 1662. *Laws and Ordinances of New Netherland 1638–1674*, ed. E. B. O'Callaghan (Albany, N.Y., 1868), 428–29. On October 5, 1662, Micah Spicer and her son Samuel were found guilty of harboring Quakers and distributing seditious and seducing pamphlets to propagate their heresy (*Calendar of Dutch Manuscripts*, 240).

98. John Underhill to John Winthrop, Jr., April 12, 1656, quoted in Herbert F. Ricard, ed., *Journal of John Bowne 1650–1694* (New Orleans: Polyanthos, 1975), 60, n. 55.

99. *Journal of John Bowne*, 20–21.

100. *Journal of John Bowne 1650–1694*, 64–65, Note 87.

101. Ordinance of the Director General and Council of New Netherland prohibiting the bringing of Quakers and other Strollers into New Netherland, Passed May 17, 1663, *Laws and Ordinances of New Netherland*, 439–40.

102. *Journal of John Bowne*, 20–24. Bowne's account book shows accounts between Bowne and Govert Loockermans in 1662 (*Journal of John Bowne*, 63, n. 77).

103. *The Register of Salomon Lachaire*, 209. Lachaire translated documents for other imprisoned English Quakers as well. For the reference to widow Wessels, see *Journal of John Bowne*, 24.

104. *Journal of John Bowne*, 22–24.

105. *Journal of John Bowne*, 23–24. For Bowne's involvement in the book trade under English rule, see Gerald D. McDonald, "William Bradford's Book Trade and John Bowne, Long Island Quaker, as His Book Agent, 1686–1691," in *Essays Honoring Lawrence C. Wroth* (Portland, Me.: Anthoensen Press, 1951), 209–22.

106. *Journal of John Bowne,* 70–71, n. 124.

107. On Quakers in seventeenth-century Amsterdam, see William I. Hull, *The Rise of Quakerism in Amsterdam 1655–1665* [Swarthmore, Pa.], 1938, and J. Z. Kannegieter, *Geschiedenis van de Vroegere Quakergemeenschap te Amsterdam:1656 tot begin negentiende eeuw* (Amsterdam: Scheltema and Holkema, 1971).

108. "Novum Belgium, by Father Isaac Jogues, 1646," in *Narratives of New Netherland,* 260.

109. *Ecc. Rec.,* vol. 1, 544.

110. Goodfriend, "The Struggle over the Sabbath in Petrus Stuyvesant's New Amsterdam."

111. Letter from the Directors to Stuyvesant, December 22, 1659, *Ecc. Rec.,* vol. 1, 460.

112. Directors to Stuyvesant, April 16, 1663, *Ecc. Rec.,* vol. 1, 530.

CHAPTER 5. HERETICS, BLASPHEMERS, AND SABBATH BREAKERS

1. Council of Trade and Plantations to Lord Dartmouth, Whitehall, 19 December 1710, Colonial Office Papers, National Archives, London (hereafter CO) 5/721, no. 10; see also "Petition of Ann Pauley to the Queen," 14 November 1710; CO 5/717, no. 19.

2. Governor Hart to Lord Townshend, 30 July 1715, CO 5/720, no. 21.

3. Foster, "New England and the Challenge of Heresy, 1630 to 1660: The Puritan Crisis in Transatlantic Perspective," *William and Mary Quarterly,* 3rd ser., 38 (1981): 624–60; Michael P. Winship, *Making Heretics: Militant Protestantism and Free Grace in Massachusetts, 1636–1641* (Princeton, N.J.: Princeton University Press, 2002); Louise A. Breen, *Transgressing the Bounds: Subversive Enterprises Among the Puritan Elite in Massachusetts, 1630–1692* (New York: Oxford University Press, 2001).

4. Susanna Linsley provided invaluable research assistance for this chapter, as well as critical summaries of the patterns revealed by the provincial records. Our thanks to the University of Michigan's Rackham School of Graduate Studies for generously providing a summer of financial support under their faculty-student Research Partnership program.

5. These ten sets of court records yield 101 cases of prosecution for religious crimes. An additional twenty cases can be found in the papers of the Colonial Office at the National Archives, London.

6. *Records of the Colony and Plantation of New Haven, from 1638 to 1649,* ed. Charles J. Hoadley (Hartford, 1847), 21, 130.

7. The question of women's veils was a controversial one, pitting Williams against John Cotton; Cotton eventually prevailed, and the law was repealed. *Winthrop's Journal, "History of New England,"* vol. 1, *1630–1649,* ed. James Kendall Hosmer (New York, 1908), 120.

8. *The Reformation of the Ecclesiastical Laws of England, 1552,* trans. and ed. John C. Spalding (vol. 19, Sixteenth Century Essays & Studies, 1992), 64–79; "An Ordinance for the punishing of Blasphemies and Heresies, with the several penalties therein expressed,"

1648, in C. H. Firth and R. S. Rait, eds., *Acts and Ordinances of the Interregnum, 1642–1660*, 2 vols. (London, 1911), vol. 1, 1133–36. In 1697, the law against heretics was revised to give magistrates a choice of penalties to impose: imprisonment, pillorying, whipping, boring the tongue "with a red hot iron," or mock execution—"provided that not more than two of the afore-mentioned punishments shall be inflicted for one and the same fact." "An Act Against Atheisme and Blasphemie," in *Acts and Resolves, Public and Private, of the Province of Massachusetts Bay* (Boston, 1869), vol. 1, 297.

9. Objections against the Massachusetts Charter, 20 July 1677, CO 1/41, no. 35.

10. *Archives of Maryland. Proceedings and Acts of the General Assembly of Maryland, January 1637/8-September 1664*, ed. William Hand Browne (Baltimore, 1883), 96, 341.

11. *The Public Records of the Colony of Connecticut May 1678–June 1689*, ed. J. Hammond Trumbull (Hartford: Case, Lockwood & Co., 1859), 202–3; *The Public Records of the Colony of Connecticut from October 1706 to October 1716*, ed. Charles Hoadly (Hartford, 1870), 51–52, 129, 436; *The Public Records of the Colony of Connecticut, From May, 1717 to October 1725*, ed. Charles Hoadly (Hartford, 1872), 248, 277–78.

12. *Archives of Maryland*, 71–72.

13. Ibid., 244–49.

14. See his essay in this volume.

15. *Documents Relating to the Colonial History of the State of New Jersey, Journal of the Governor and Council, 1682–1714* (Trenton, 1890), 36–37.

16. The question of whether to consider the Indians who died in the thousands in colonial wars as victims of religious violence is addressed in "What's 'Sacred' About Violence in Early America? Killing, and Dying, in the Name of God in the New World," *Common-place: The Interactive Journal of Early American Life* 6, no. 1 (October 2005, available online at http://www.common-place.org).

17. The Quaker sufferings were narrated in loving detail by a spate of pamphlets published in London in the 1650s and 1660s, the most exhaustive of which were George Bishop's *New England Judged, Not by Man's, but the Spirit of the Lord: And the Summe sealed up of New-England's Persecutions* (London, 1661); and Edward Burrough's *A Declaration of the Sad and Great Persecution and Martyrdom of the People of God called Quakers in New-England, for the Worshipping of God. Whereof 22 have been Banished upon pain of Death. 03 have been MARTYRED. 03 have had their Right Ears cut. 01 hath been burned in the Hand with the letter H. 31 Persons have received 650 Stripes. 01 was beat while his Body was like a jelly. Several were beat with Pitched Ropes . . . One now lyeth in Iron-fetters, condemned to dye* (London, 1660).

18. Francis Howgill, *The Popish Inquisition Newly Erected in New-England, whereby Their Church is manifested to be a Daughter of Mysterie Babylon, which did drink the blood of the Saints, who bears the express Image of her Mother* (London, 1659), 13, 26–28.

19. *Records of Massachusetts Colony*, vol. 4, part 2, p. 2.

20. *County Court Records of Accomack-Northampton, Virginia, 1632–1640*, ed. Susie Ames (Washington, D.C., 1954), 128–29; *Criminal Proceedings of Colonial Virginia: [Record of] Fines, Examination of Criminals, Trials of Slaves, etc., from March 1710 to 1754*, ed. Peter Charles Hoffer (Athens: University of Georgia Press, 1984), 72–73.

21. *Records of the Particular Court of Connecticut 1639–1663* (Hartford: Connecticut Historical Society, 1928), 54–55.

22. Because some cases contained multiple charges, the total here (147) is greater than the total number of cases (121) identified in note 5.

23. Mary Beth Norton, *Founding Mothers and Fathers: Gendered Power and the Forming of American Society* (New York, Alfred A. Knopf, 1996); Robert St. George, "'Heated Speech' and Literacy in Seventeenth-Century New England," in *Seventeenth-Century New England : A Conference held by the Colonial Society of Massachusetts*, ed. David D. Hall and David Grayson Allen (Boston: Colonial Society of Massachusetts, 1984); John March, *Actions for slaunder, or, A methodicall collection under certain grounds and heads of what words are actionable in the law and what not [electronic resource]: a treatise of very great use and consequence to all men, especially in these times wherein actions for slaunder are more common and do much more abound then in times past* (London, 1647).

24. The case of Atkinson Williamson, an Anglican minister who in 1683 christened a bear while intoxicated, was a sore spot for the SPG missionaries who struggled to earn the respect of the Carolina Presbyterians; SPG Records, vol. 4, Mr. Stevens to Secretary, Goose Creek S.C., 3 February 1707/8; and Mr. Smith to Mr. Robt Stevens, 16 January 1707/8.

25. Ashley Montague, *The Anatomy of Swearing* (New York: Macmillan, 1967).

26. David Lawton, *Blasphemy* (New York: Harvester Wheatsheaf, 1993), 10.

27. *Archives of Maryland*, May 1638, 35–39.

28. *Records of the Colony and Plantation of New Haven, from 1638 to 1649*, ed. Charles J. Hoadley (Hartford, 1857), 4 May 1647, 308.

29. Lt. Governor Stede to Lords of Trade and Plantations, 19 March 1687, CO 31/4, pp. 24–28.

30. *Records of Court of Assistants of the Colony of the Massachusetts Bay (1630–1692)*, ed. John Noble (Boston, 1901), vol. 3 (1642–73), 35–37.

31. *Records of the Colony and Plantation of New Haven, from 1638 to 1649*, ed. Charles J. Hoadley (Hartford, 1857), 293.

32. Leonard W. Levy, *Treason Against God: A History of the Offense of Blasphemy* (New York: Schocken Books, 1981).

33. Lawton, *Blasphemy*, 6.

34. *Reformation of the Ecclesiastical Laws of England*, 82.

35. Levy, *Treason Against God*, 313.

36. Lawton, *Blasphemy*, 4; "An Act for the better preventing of prophane Swearing and Cursing," *Acts and Ordinances of the Interregnum*, vol. 2, 394–96. The expiatory nature of Puritan prosecutions for speech crimes has been noted before, particularly in the context of securing gendered linguistic codes; see Jane Kamensky, *Governing the Tongue: The Politics of Speech in Early New England* (New York: Oxford University Press, 1997).

37. *Records of the Colony of New Plymouth in New England. Court Orders, Vol. III, 1651–1661*, ed. Nathaniel B. Shurtleff (Boston, 1855), 111–12.

38. *Records of The Colony of New Haven from May, 1653 to the Union together with the New Haven Code of 1656*, ed. Charles J. Hoadley (Hartford, 1858), 364.

39. Abstract of the Sentences given by his Excellency Sir Richard Dutton . . . Governor of Barbados . . . 16–27 August 1681; CO 1/47, no 49. Eccles was prosecuted under the 1680 "Act to prevent the people called Quakers from bringing negroes to their meetings."

40. Petition of John Rogers to Governor and Company of Connecticut, enclosed in Letter from Charles Congreve to Mr. Popple, 4 December 1704; CO 5/1262, nos. 92, 92i.

41. Records of Court of Assistants, Mass., 5 July 1671, p. 211.

42. *Archives of Maryland*, 203–4.

43. *Records of The Colony of New Haven from May, 1653 to the Union together with the New Haven Code of 1656*, ed. Charles J. Hoadley (Hartford, 1858), 242–47.

44. *Record of the Court of Assistants of the Colony of Massachusetts (1630–1692)*, ed. John Noble (Boston, 1901), 253–54.

45. Ibid., 201.

46. *Archives of Maryland*, 1651, 333.

47. *Records of the Colony and Plantation of New Haven, from 1638 to 1649*, ed. Charles J. Hoadley (Hartford, 1857), 262.

48. Minutes of Council of Maryland, 21 September 1696, CO 5/741, pp. 148–59; Copy of Proclamation, Enclosed in Governor Nicholson to Council of Trade and Plantations, James City, Virginia, 27 February 1699, CO 5/1309, no. 75iv.

49. *Records of New Haven*, p. 292.

50. For a discussion of colonial iconoclasm, see Susan Juster, "Iconoclasm Without Icons? The Destruction of Sacred Objects in Colonial North America," in *Empires of God: Religious Encounters in the Early Modern Atlantic World*, ed. Susan Juster and Linda Gregerson (Philadelphia: University of Pennsylvania Press, 2010).

51. Charles Vesey's Petition, 1714, Volume 9, No. 6, New York Papers, p. 191; Society for the Propagation of the Gospel in Foreign Parts, Letter Books, Series "A", 1702–1737 (hereafter SPG Records). The desecration of Trinity Church was reported in the *Boston News-Letter*, March 22–29, 1714, and picked up by the press in London; "A Proclamation," *Daily Courant*, 22 May 1714.

52. C.D., *New England's Faction Discovered; Or, A Brief and True Account of their Persecution of the Church of England* (London, 1690), 259. While Cotton Mather dismissed the charge, arguing that "All the mischief done is the breaking of a few Quarels of glass by idle Boys," the historian Charles Andrews concludes that the charge of desecration "had a basis in fact" (Charles M. Andrews, ed., *Narratives of the Insurrections, 1675–1690* [New York, 1915], 259).

53. Thomas Maule, *New-England Persecutors Mauled with their own Weapons. Giving some account of the bloody laws made at Boston against the Kings subjects that dissented from their way of worship* (New York, 1697), 51.

54. SPG Records, vol. 3, no. CLXXXIV, p. 529.

55. SPG Records, vol. 9, no. 13, 20 April 1714, p. 116.

56. *The Carolina Backcountry on the Eve of the Revolution: The Journal and Other Writings of Charles Woodmason, Anglican Itinerant*, ed. Richard J. Hooker (Chapel Hill: University of North Carolina Press for the Omohundro Institute of Early American History and Culture, 1953), 46 n. 40.

57. *Records of New Haven*, 28; *Records of the Particular Court of Connecticut 1639–1663* (Hartford, 1928), 71; *Colonial Justice in Western Massachusetts (1639–1702). The Pynchon Court Record: An Original Judge's Diary of the Administration of Justice in the Springfield Courts in the Massachusetts Bay Colony*, ed. Joseph H. Smith (Cambridge, Mass.: Harvard University Press, 1961), 224, 275–76.

58. *Records of the Court of Assistants of the Colony of the Massachusetts Bay (1630–1692)*, ed. John Noble (Boston, 1901), vol. 1, 127.

59. *Records of the Court of Assistants*, vol. 3 (1642–73), 213–14.

60. *Records of the Court of Assistants*, vol. 2 (1630–44), 16.

61. Church Wardens &c of St. Marys Church at Burlington, 24 March 1714, SPG Records, vol. 9; Mr. Bass to the Secretary, Burlington, N.J., 2 September 1709, SPG Records, vol. 5.

62. Mr. James Adams to Secretary, Virginia, 4 October 1709, SPG Records, vol. 5.

63. Butler, *Awash in a Sea of Faith: Christianizing the American People* (Cambridge, Mass.: Harvard University Press, 1990).

64. SPG Records, vol. 5, Mr. Talbot to the Secretary, Burlington, 30 June 1709.

65. Beneke, *Beyond Toleration*, 5.

CHAPTER 6. PERSECUTING QUAKERS?

Note to epigraph: Thomas Budd, *A True Copy of three judgments . . . against George Keith and his friends* (Philadelphia, 1693).

1. I use the terms "toleration" and "liberty of conscience" interchangeably in this chapter, unless otherwise noted. While such usage does not necessarily describe the historical progression from nonpunishment to broader conceptions of liberty, it is faithful to Penn's own usage, which never called for disestablishment in the English context. See my *Conscience and Community*, chap. 5.

2. Quotations, respectively: E. Digby Baltzell, *Puritan Boston and Quaker Philadelphia: Two Protestant Ethics and the Spirit of Class Authority and Leadership* (Boston: Beacon, 1979), 143; and Henry F. May, *The Enlightenment in America* (Oxford: Oxford University Press, 1976), 80.

3. See Chapter 5.

4. Thomas J. Curry, *The First Freedoms: Church and State in America to the Passage of the First Amendment* (New York: Oxford University Press, 1986); Edwin S. Gaustad, *A Religious History of America*, new rev. ed. (San Francisco: Harper, 1990); Winthrop S. Hudson, *Religion in America*, 4th ed. (New York: Macmillan, 1987). The quotation from Bronner is taken from *William Penn's "Holy Experiment": The Founding of Pennsylvania, 1681–1701* (Philadelphia: Temple University Press, 1962), 152.

Only a few scholars have entered into the theological, social, and political dimensions of the schism, and those approaches have shed light on the ways in which Keith rallied to his side many Pennsylvanians who had long felt excluded by the Quaker elite that ruled in the proprietor's absence. J. William Frost emphasized the theological disagreements between Keith and his Quaker opponents over the bodily resurrection of Jesus, and Jon Butler identified the core of the schism as a conflict over ministerial authority during the colony's early years. By contrast, Gary Nash viewed the schism and the legal proceedings through the lens of political and economic factionalism. Most people in Pennsylvania, he argued, lacked Keith's university education and likely did not understand, let alone endorse, his theological positions, which after all were conservative and even exclusionary in nature. Nash contends that the Keithian movement "provided a popular means of expressing opposition to an upper layer of Quakers whose political domination was becoming brittle and overbearing." This opposition movement had a distinctly political-economic tint to it: "A whole stratum of lesser merchants, shopkeepers, and master artisans—upward moving individuals, not a few of whom would enter the circle of mercantile leadership in the next decade—found that Keith's program provided a means of challenging the Lloydian 'greats,' who were resented for their narrow control of provincial life." After all, opposition to Keith was concentrated in the organized centers of power in Pennsylvania: the Council, the courts, and the Public Friends. See Gary Nash, *Quakers and Politics*, 154, 160; J. William Frost, "Unlikely Controversialists: Caleb Pusey and George Keith," *Quaker History* 64 (1975): 16–36; and Jon Butler, "'Gospel Order Improved': The Keithian Schism and the Exercise of Ministerial Authority in Pennsylvania," *William and Mary Quarterly* 31 (1974): 431–52.

5. This transformation is documented in Rosemary Moore, *The Light in Their Consciences: Early Quakers in Britain, 1646–1666* (University Park: Pennsylvania State University Press, 2000); the quotation is taken from pp. 214–15.

6. Melvin B. Endy, Jr., *William Penn and Early Quakerism* (Princeton, N.J.: Princeton University Press, 1973), 326; and H. Larry Ingle, *First Among Friends: George Fox and the Creation of Quakerism* (New York: Oxford University Press, 1994), 244.

7. When citing Penn's writings I shall refer to the following three volumes: *The Political Writings of William Penn*, ed. Andrew R. Murphy (Indianapolis: Liberty Fund, 2002); *A Collection of the Works of William Penn*, 2 vols. (London, 1726); and *The Papers of William Penn*, ed. Richard S. Dunn, Mary Maples Dunn, Edwin B. Bronner, and David Fraser, 5 vols. (Philadelphia: University of Pennsylvania Press, 1981–87). These three volumes will be abbreviated (respectively) *Political Writings*; *Works*, vol. number, page; and *PWP*, vol. number, page.

This quotation is from *The Great Case of Liberty of Conscience* (1670), *Political Writings*, 79 (*Works*, vol. 1, 445).

8. *Political Writings*, 385–86 (*Works*, vol. 2, 771); "Petition to Parliament," 1680, *PWP* vol. 2, 52.

9. *A Letter from a Gentleman in the Country . . . upon the Penal Laws and Tests* (London, 1687), 8.

10. Locke, *Letter Concerning Toleration*, ed. James Tully (Indianapolis: Hackett, [1689] 1983), 27.

11. "To Lord Arlington," 1669, in *Works*, vol. 1, 153; *Great Case of Liberty of Conscience* (1670), in *Political Writings*, 81 (*Works*, vol. 1, 444, 452).

12. See, e.g., Penn's *The Reasonableness of Toleration* (London, 1687).
13. *Great Case of Liberty of Conscience* (1670), *Political Writings*, 82 (*Works*, vol. 1, 445).
14. Quotations, respectively: *An Address to Protestants of All Persuasions* (1679), *Political Writings*, 157 (*Works*, vol. 1, 750); and *Great Case of Liberty of Conscience* (1670), *Political Writings*, 87 (*Works*, vol. 1, 447–48).
15. *Great Case of Liberty of Conscience* (1670), in *Political Writings*, 88; *An Address to Protestants* (1679), in *Political Writings*, 261. The Scriptural reference to Christ's kingdom is found in John 18:36.
16. "To the Prince Elector Palatinate of Heidelberg," 25 June 1677, in *Works*, vol. 1, 75.
17. *Good Advice to the Church of England* (1687), in *Political Writings*, 373.
18. See Frederick B. Tolles, *Meeting House and Counting House: The Quaker Merchants of Colonial Philadelphia, 1682–1763* (Chapel Hill: University of North Carolina Press, 1948).
19. *Great Case, Political Writings*, 79–119.
20. "To James Harrison," 25 August 1681, *PWP*, 2:108.
21. Frost, "Religious Liberty in Early Pennsylvania," *Pennsylvania Magazine of History and Biography* 105 (1981): 449.
22. Bronner, "The Failure of the 'Holy Experiment' in Pennsylvania," *Pennsylvania History* 21 (1954): 95.
23. *A Letter from William Penn, Proprietary and Governour of Pennsylvania in America, to the Committee of the Free Society of Traders of that Province* (1683), *Works*, vol. 2, 699–706; and *A brief account of the province of Pennsilvania in America* (London, 1681).
24. See Sally Schwartz, *"A Mixed Multitude": The Struggle for Toleration in Colonial Pennsylvania* (New York: New York University Press, 1987).
25. Pastorius, "Letter from Pennsylvania," October 10, 1691, in *Narratives of Early Pennsylvania, West New Jersey, and Delaware*, ed. Albert Cook Myers (New York, 1912), 436.
26. *The Humble Remonstrance of His Majesty's Most Loyal Subjects of His Majesty's Province of Pennsylvania*, 26 May 1694 (Huntington Library manuscript EL 9596), p. 1; see also "The Anglican Petition," c. 1695–96, in *PWP*, vol. 3, 444.
27. Baltzell, *Puritan Boston and Quaker Philadelphia*, 136. The only adequate biography is Ethyn Williams Kirby, *George Keith, 1638–1716* (New York: D. Appleton-Century and Company, 1942). The biographical details in this section are taken from chapters 4–6 of Kirby's biography.
28. Keith's critique is advanced in a number of works, including *The Presbyterian and Independent visible churches in New-England* (Philadelphia, 1689), and *A refutation of three opposers of truth [Pardon Tillinghast, B. Keech, and Cotton Mather]* (Philadelphia, 1690). Mather's reply to Keith was published as *The principles of the Protestant religion maintained, and churches of New-England . . . against all the calumnies of one George Keith, a Quaker. . .* (Boston, 1690), to which Keith responded with *The pretended antidote proved*

poyson (Philadelphia, 1690). Keith also replied to Mather in *A Serious Appeal to All the More Sober, Impartial & Judicious People in New-England* . . . (Philadelphia, 1692), and defended Rhode Island Quakers from New England Congregationalists in *The Chrisitan faith of the people of God, called in scorn, Quakers, in Rhode-Island* (Philadelphia, 1692).

29. Frost, *The Keithian Schism in Early Pennsylvania* (Norwood, Pa., 1980), vi.

30. Keith, *The true Christ owned* (London?, 1679), 74.

31. Keith, *A plain short catechism*, Epistle, 28–29.

32. *A plain and short catechism*, 9, 11.

33. Butler, "'Gospel Order Improved,'" 437, 444.

34. Kirby, *George Keith*, 55–56.

35. Frederick B. Tolles describes Lloyd as "the patriarch and progenitor of the Philadelphia Quaker aristocracy" (*Meeting House and Counting House*, 120).

36. Outside of Philadelphia, the sense of many of the regular meetings was Keithian: and Joseph C. Martindale, M.D., in his *History of the Townships of Byberry and Moreland*, asserts that, at one time which he does not clearly indicate, Keith's followers had the ascendency in sixteen out of thirty-two Meetings." See Charles P. Keith, *Chronicles of Pennsylvania*, 2 vols. (Philadelphia: Patterson and White, 1917), vol. 1, 220.

37. See Samuel Hazard, *The Register of Pennsylvania* (Philadelphia, 1830–31), 303.

38. See James Green, "The Book Trades in the Middle Colonies, 1680–1720," in *A History of the Book in America. Volume One: The Colonial Book in the Transatlantic World*, ed. Hugh Amory and David D. Hall (New York: Cambridge University Press, 1998).

39. *Some reasons and causes*, 7–9.

40. *Appeal*, 1–2. 6, 7, 8.

41. Condemnations of Keithians by the Philadelphia Quarterly Meetings are found in the 1692 Yearly Meeting minutes (Quaker Collection at Haverford College, Reel 7X, pp. 28, 31, 32); the Bucks County Quarterly Meeting's critique is located in the Historical Society of Pennsylvania's Etting Collection (Early Quakers), p. 79. Condemnations of the Keithian separation also came from Meetings in Barbados (Swarthmore College Quaker Collection, Keithian Controversy MSS, 1692 7 mo 12) and Treadhaven, Maryland (Swarthmore, Keithian Controversy MSS, 1692 8 mo 4).

42. Keith, *Some Reasons and Causes of the Late Separation that hath come to pass at Philadelphia* (Philadelphia, 1692); Keith, *An Appeal from the Twenty-Eight Judges to the Spirit of Truth and True Judgment* (Philadelphia, 1692).

43. Kirby, *George Keith*, 82.

44. Nash, *Quakers and Politics*, 152–53.

45. For a more extended account of the details of the schism see Charles P. Keith, *Chronicles of Pennsylvania from the English Revolution to the Peace of Aix-la-Chapelle, 1688–1748* (Philadelphia: Patterson and White, 1917), chap. 8. Jon Butler addresses some of the schism's after effects on Pennsylvania society in "Into Pennsylvania's Spiritual Abyss: The Rise and Fall of the Later Keithians, 1693–1703," *Pennsylvania Magazine of History and Biography* 101 (1977): 151–70.

46. See Kevin Kelly, *Dictator or Guide? A Study in Seventeenth-Century English Prot-*

estant Moral Thought (London: G. Chapman, 1967); and Timothy C. Potts, "Conscience," in *The Cambridge History of Later Moral Philosophy*, ed. Norman Kretzmann, Anthony Kenny, and Jan Pinborg (Cambridge: Cambridge University Press, 1982), 687–704.

47. It is important to clarify here that these discussions of conscience were confined to belief and doctrinal issues, and presumed a "natural" faculty—often traced back to Aquinas's *synderesis*—that provided guidance for basic moral behavior. Penn, for example, argued that there could be "no pretense of conscience to be drunk, to whore, to be voluptuous, to game, swear, curse, blaspheme, and profane. . . . These are sins against nature; and against government, as well as against the written word of God. They lay the ax to the root of human society" (*An Address to Protestants of all Persuasions*, Works, vol. 1, 733).

48. See my *Conscience and Community*, 110–14, 226–33.

49. See my *Conscience and Community*, 49–51 and 226–33.

50. Cotton, *A Reply to Mr. Williams his Examination* (London, 1647); in volume 2 of *The Complete Writings of Roger Williams*, ed. Samuel L. Caldwell (New York: Russell and Russell, 1963), 26.

51. Williams, *The Bloudy Tenent of Persecution*, (London, 1644); in volume 1 of *The Complete Writings of Roger Williams*, ed. Samuel L. Caldwell (New York: Russell and Russell, 1963), 41, 63, Walwyn, *The Compassionate Samaritane* (London, 1644), 43.

52. *Records of the Governor and Company of the Massachusetts-Bay in New England, 1628–1686*, ed. Nathaniel B. Shurtleff, M.D. (Boston, 1853–54), 2:211.

53. Jennings, *The State of the Case* (London, 1694), 45–46.

54. Keith, *A further discovery*, 40–41.

55. Barclay, *Apology*, Proposition 14. Barclay goes on to cite William Ames approvingly: "Hence Ames *de Cas Cons* 'The conscience, although erring, doth evermore bind, so as that he sinneth who doth contrary to his conscience, because he doth contrary to the will of God, although not materially and truly yet formally and interpretatively'" (*Apology*, Proposition 14).

56. *PWP*, 283. Jane Calvert also points out how Keith grounded his criticisms of Pennsylvania's public life in Quaker orthodoxy; see her *Quaker Constitutionalism and the Political Thought of John Dickinson* (Cambridge: Cambridge University Press, 2009), 124–27.

57. Calvert, *Quaker Constitutionalism*, 124.

58. *A further discovery*, 39–40; also 41–42.

59. Samuel Jennings, *The State of the Case*, 45.

60. Caleb Pusey, *Satan's harbinger encountered* (Philadelphia, 1697), 58; Samuel Jennings, *The State of the Case* (London, 1694), 45–46.

61. Thomas Budd, *A true copy*, 12.

62. *New England's Spirit of Persecution transmitted to Pennsylvania* (Philadelphia, 1693), 28.

63. Ibid., 34.

64. *New England's Spirit of Persecution*, 4.

65. "No strain in the Quaker personality was more visible to his enemies than that of his antiauthoritarianism," Gary Nash has observed; "the Quaker was constantly in the business of setting himself in defiance of authority." See Nash, *Quakers and Politics: Pennsylvania, 1681–1726* (Princeton, N.J.: Princeton University Press, 1968), 168–69.

66. Keith, *A seasonable information and caveat . . .* (London, 1694), 27.

67. *The Anti-Christs and Sadducees Detected* (London, 1696), 3.

68. "To Robert Turner," 29 November 1692, in *PWP*, vol. 3, 354.

69. See also *A testimony and Caution* (Philadelphia, 1693), 8.

70. For a discussion of the ways in which substantive goals (toleration) existed in tension with procedural issues (extralegal royal declarations rather than parliamentary legislation) in James's campaign for toleration, see my *Conscience and Community*, chap. 4.

71. "To Friends in Pennsylvania," 11 December 1693, *PWP*, vol. 3, 383.

72. "To the Provincial Council," 24 November 1694, *PWP*, vol. 3, 405.

73. Daniel Leeds, *News of a Trumpet Sounding in the Wilderness* (New York, 1697), 93. See also Francis Bugg, *News from Pennsylvania* (London, 1703).

74. "From Thomas Holme," 25 November 1686, *PWP*, vol. 3, 131.

75. See my *Conscience and Community*, 226–33.

76. Keith and Thomas Budd, *False judgments reprehended* (Philadelphia, 1692), 6. (Williams to John Winthrop, 24 October 1636? *Correspondence of Roger Williams*, vol. 1, 68.

77. Butler, "Into Pennsylvania's Spiritual Abyss"; Frost, *The Keithian Schism*, i, xx.

78. Butler, *Becoming America: The Revolution Before 1776* (Cambridge, Mass.: Harvard University Press, 2001), 103.

79. *One wonder more, added to the seven wonders of the world [microform] Verified in the person of Mr. George Keith, once a Presbyterian, afterwards about thirty years a Quaker, then a noun substantive at Turner's-Hall, and now an itinerant preacher (upon his good behaviour) in the Church of England: and all without variation (as himself says) in fundamentals*. By a Protestant Dissenter (London, 1701?).

CHAPTER 7. NATIVE FREEDOM?

1. John Brown, *On Religious Liberty: A Sermon preached at St. Paul's Cathedral* (Philadelphia: Andrew Stewart, 1763), iii, iv.

2. Ibid., iv–vi.

3. Ibid., iv, v, vii, x.

4. Ibid., iv, ix, x. On Anglo-American transatlantic thought on religious liberty in the pre-Revolutionary era, see Chris Beneke, *Beyond Toleration: The Religious Origins of American Pluralism* (New York: Oxford University Press, 2006), 79–155.

5. Perez Zagorin, *How the Idea of Religious Toleration Came to the West* (Princeton, N.J.: Princeton University Press, 2003), 16, 43–45 (quotation on 16).

6. Ibid., 88–89, 142–47, 237–38, 248; Ole Peter Grell and Roy Porter, "Toleration

in Enlightenment Europe," in *Toleration in Enlightenment Europe*, ed. Ole Peter Grell and Roy Porter (Cambridge: Cambridge University Press, 2000), 1–8.

7. Stuart B. Schwartz, *All Can Be Saved: Religious Tolerance and Salvation in the Iberian Atlantic World* (New Haven, Conn.: Yale University Press, 2008), 38, 43–69, 121–25.

8. For the Williams-Cotton clash and for Williams's views on liberty of conscience more generally, see Edwin S. Gaustad, *Liberty of Conscience: Roger Williams in America* (Grand Rapids, Mich.: Eerdmans, 1991), 28–30, 78–80, 98–101 (quotation on 78) and Edmund Morgan, *Roger Williams: The Church and the State* (New York: Harcourt, Brace, and World, 1967), 135–41.

9. James Axtell, *The European and the Indian: Essays in the Ethnohistory of Colonial America* (New York: Oxford University Press, 1981), 307–10; David S. Lovejoy, "Satanizing the American Indian," *New England Quarterly* 67 (1994): 603–21; Richard Godbeer, *The Devil's Dominion: Magic and Religion in Early New England* (Cambridge: Cambridge University Press, 1992), 189–93; Alden T. Vaughan, *Roots of American Racism: Essays on the Colonial Experience* (New York and Oxford: Oxford University Press, 1995), 34–54; and Kathleen Brown, "Native Americans and Early Modern Conceptions of Race," in *Empire and Others: British Encounters with Indigenous Peoples, 1600–1850*, ed. Martin Daunton and Rick Halpern (Philadelphia: University of Pennsylvania Press, 1999), 88.

10. Jonathan Edwards, *Original Sin*, ed. Clyde Holbrook, vol. 3 of *The Works of Jonathan Edwards* (New Haven, Conn.: Yale University Press, 1970), 151. Gerald R. McDermott, *Jonathan Edwards Confronts the Gods: Christian Theology, Enlightenment Religion, and Non-Christian Faiths* (New York and Oxford: Oxford University Press, 2000), 6, 10, 12, 194–206, discusses Edwards's views on Native American religion.

11. James Axtell, *Natives and Newcomers: The Cultural Origins of North America* (New York: Oxford University Press, 2000), 164–65; Beneke, *Beyond Toleration*, 11; Michael D. McNally, "The Practice of Native American Christianity," *Church History* 69 (2000): 834–59; James H. Merrell, *The Indians' New World: Catawbas and Their Neighbors from European Contact Through the Era of Removal* (New York: W. W. Norton, 1991), 165; James Axtell, ed., *The Indian Peoples of Eastern America: A Documentary History of the Sexes* (New York: Oxford University Press, 1981), xviii–xxi; Helen C. Rountree, "Powhatan Priests and English Rectors: World Views and Congregations in Conflict," *American Indian Quarterly* 16 (1992): 485–500.

12. Colin G. Calloway, *New Worlds for All: Indians, Europeans, and the Remaking of Early America* (Baltimore: Johns Hopkins University Press, 1997), 26–33; Catherine L. Albanese, *A Republic of Mind and Spirit: A Cultural History of American Metaphysical Religion* (New Haven, Conn.: Yale University Press, 2007), 115–16; Douglas L. Winiarski, "Native American Popular Religion in New England's Old Colony, 1670–1770," *Religion and American Culture* 15 (2005): 162–66; Daniel A. Scalberg, "The French-Amerindian Religious Encounter in Seventeenth and Early Eighteenth-Century New France," *French Colonial History* 1 (2002): 101–12; James Axtell, *The Invasion Within: The Contest of Cultures in Colonial North America* (New York: Oxford University Press, 1985), 302–27.

13. Winiarski, "Native American Popular Religion," 147–86. Joel W. Martin, *The Land Looks After Us: A History of Native American Religion* (New York: Oxford University Press, 2001), provides an introductory overview of Native American religion.

14. Milo M. Quaife, ed., *John Long's Voyages and Travels in the Years 1768–1788* (Chicago: R. R. Donnelly, 1922), 174–75.

15. On Indian religious reformers in this era, see Gregory Evans Dowd, *A Spirited Resistance: The North American Indian Struggle for Unity, 1745–1815* (Baltimore: Johns Hopkins University Press, 1992), 23–46. Brainerd's account of this incident is in Jonathan Edwards, *The Life of David Brainerd*, ed. Norman Pettit, vol. 7 of *The Works of Jonathan Edwards* (New Haven, Conn.: Yale University Press, 1985), 329–30. Sandra M. Gustafson, *Eloquence is Power: Oratory and Performance in Early America* (Chapel Hill: University of North Carolina Press, 2000), 88–89, proposes that Brainerd's choice not to condemn the faith of the Indian reformer may indicate some type of recognition of the legitimacy of Native religion.

16. I borrow, with a twist, the phrase "well as they are" from James P. Ronda, "'We Are Well as We Are': An Indian Critique of Seventeenth-Century Christian Missions," *William and Mary Quarterly*, 3rd ser., 34 (1977): 66–82. Schwartz, *All Can Be Saved*, has found surprising amounts of religious tolerance and even religious relativism on the question of spiritual salvation among early modern Spaniards and Portuguese on both sides of the Atlantic, especially among common people rather than intellectual elites. He suggests, on 244–48, that England and its colonies may have evidenced similar patterns. In contrast, Dominique Deslandres argues that it was "impossible" for French Catholic missionaries to embrace or entertain as valuable any element of Native religion: "the faith of the [Indian] Other remains to him impossible, unthinkable, incorrect, intolerable" ("The Impossible Acculturation: French Missionaries and Cultural Exchanges in the Seventeenth Century," in *Ethnographies and Exchanges: Native Americans, Moravians, and Catholics in Early North America*, ed. A. G. Roeber (University Park: Pennsylvania State University Press, 2008), 67–76 (quotation on 68).

17. Beneke, *Beyond Toleration*, 3–12, 157–201. For this project, I have reviewed actions taken by colonial legislatures in the English mainland colonies from New Hampshire to Georgia. A more comprehensive review of English imperial statutes or laws enacted within local communities that might have touched upon Indian religious rights was beyond the scope of this project. To my knowledge, no such review has ever been conducted. For an historical overview of Indians in relation to U.S. law, see N. Bruce Duthu, *American Indians and the Law* (New York: Penguin, 2008).

18. Vaughan, *Roots of American Racism*, 19–21; Richard W. Pointer, *Encounters of the Spirit: Native Americans and European Colonial Religion* (Bloomington: Indiana University Press, 2007), 93, 161–66, 190–95.

19. Rachel Wheeler, *To Live Upon Hope: Mohicans and Missionaries in the Eighteenth-Century Northeast* (Ithaca, N.Y.: Cornell University Press, 2008), 32–50, *passim*, provides an excellent account of how those processes played out in the eighteenth century among Mohican Indians in western Massachusetts and eastern New York.

20. On the need for greater historical study of anti-Catholicism in the colonial South, see Jon F. Sensbach, "Religion and the Early South in an Age of Atlantic Empire," *Journal of Southern History* 73 (2007): 631–32; on anti-Catholicism in the northern colonies toward Catholic Indians evangelized by French Jesuits, see Thomas S. Kidd, *The Protestant Interest: New England After Puritanism* (New Haven, Conn.: Yale University Press, 2004), 42–48, 93–114; Cotton Mather, *A Letter, about the present state of Christianity, among the Christianized Indians of New-England* (Boston: T. Green, 1705), 11; on captivity narratives, see Alden T. Vaughan and Edward W. Clark, eds., *Puritans Among the Indians: Accounts of Captivity and Redemption, 1676–1724* (Cambridge, Mass.: Belknap Press of Harvard University Press, 1981), and John Demos, *The Unredeemed Captive: A Family Story from Early America* (New York: Alfred Knopf, 1994); Theodorus Frielinghuysen, *A Sermon Preached on occasion of the late treaty held in Albany* (New York: J. Parker and W. Weyman, 1754), 13–14.

21. Merrell, *Indians' New World*, 59, 95–96, 99; Jean O'Brien, "'They Are So Frequently Shifting Their Places of Residence': Land and the Construction of Social Place in Colonial Massachusetts," in *Empire and Others*, ed. Daunton and Halpern, 206, 212; Yasuhide Kawashima, *Puritan Justice and the Indian: White Man's Law in Massachusetts, 1630–1763* (Middletown, Conn.: Wesleyan University Press, 1986), 21–41. Kawashima developed his threefold categorization of Indians on the basis of their status from the standpoint of colonial courts in Massachusetts. As with any rubric, his has its limitations, especially as I apply it more broadly to the experience of Natives in relation to religious freedom. Not all groups of Indians fit neatly into one of the three classifications employed here. For that reason, it is best to think of the categories as existing along a continuum with overlapping points, rather than as three entirely distinct subsets.

22. Kawashima, *Puritan Justice*, 21–28; James H. Merrell, "'The Customes of Our Countrey': Indians and Colonists in Early America," in *Strangers Within the Realm: Cultural Margins of the First British Empire*, ed. Bernard Bailyn and Philip D. Morgan (Chapel Hill: University of North Carolina Press, 1991), 119–21, 147–48. For brief discussions of colonial treaties with Indians, see Sharon O'Brien, "Indian Treaties as International Agreements: Development of the European Nation State and International Law," and Jack Campisi, "Colonial and Early Treaties, 1775–1829," in *Treaties with American Indians: An Encyclopedia of Rights, Conflicts, and Sovereignty*, ed. Donald L. Fixico (Santa Barbara, Calif.: ABC Clio, 2008), vol. 1, 49–55, 69–73.

23. Dowd, *Spirited Resistance*, 16–21.

24. Daniel R. Mandell, *Behind the Frontier: Indians in Eighteenth-Century Eastern Massachusetts* (Lincoln: University of Nebraska Press, 1996), 1–7 (quotation on 7); Kawashima, *Puritan Justice*, 28–35.

25. Merrell, *Indians' New World*, 97–99.

26. "Fundamental Constitutions of Carolina," in *Early American Indian Documents: Treaties and Laws, 1607–1789*, ed. Alden T. Vaughan and Deborah A. Rosen (Bethesda, Md.: University Publications of America, 1998–2004), vol. 16, 10; James Lowell Underwood, "The Dawn of Religious Freedom in South Carolina: The Journey from Limited

Tolerance to Constitutional Right," in *The Dawn of Religious Freedom in South Carolina*, ed. James Lowell Underwood and W. Lewis Burke (Columbia: University of South Carolina Press, 2006), 2–4.

27. Merrell, *Indians' New World*, 90–100 (quotation on 99–100 from Richard Ludlam).

28. Vaughan and Rosen, eds., *Early American Indian Documents*, vol. 15, 16, 18, 40–41, 47–48, 136, vol. 17, 531–32. Volumes 15, 16, and 17 of this documentary set print colonial laws from all the mainland British colonies relating to Indians. My conclusions are based on a review of those laws. For another approach, a range of secondary sources might be consulted. For example, a preliminary sense of Pennsylvania's policies may be gleaned from Sally Schwartz, *"A Mixed Multitude": The Struggle for Toleration in Colonial Pennsylvania* (New York: New York University Press, 1987), 5–12, 17, 30–33, 63–64, 104, 255–56; Amy C. Schutt, *Peoples of the River Valleys: The Odyssey of the Delaware Indians* (Philadelphia: University of Pennsylvania Press, 2007), 62–123; and Steven Craig Harper, *Promised Land: Penn's Holy Experiment, the Walking Purchase, and the Dispossession of Delawares, 1600–1763* (Bethlehem, Pa.: Lehigh University Press, 2006), 72–101.

29. Jenny Hale Pulsipher, *Subjects unto the Same King: Indians, English, and the Contest for Authority in Colonial New England* (Philadelphia: University of Pennsylvania Press, 2005), 3–6, 27–28 (quotation on 3); Richard Cogley, *John Eliot's Mission to the Indians Before King Philip's War* (Cambridge, Mass.: Harvard University Press, 1999), 30–41.

30. *Records of the Governor and Company of the Massachusetts Bay in New England*, ed. Nathaniel Shurtleff (Boston: William White, 1853–54), vol. 3, 98.

31. Cogley, *Eliot's Mission*, 41–43, 276 n. 31, 276 n. 35, 316 n. 45 (quotation on 42), counters the more pessimistic assessments of the impact of these laws put forward by Francis Jennings and others.

32. The best example of one of these codes is the so-called Musketaquid Code of 1646, printed in Thomas Shepard, *The Clear Sun-shine of the Gospel Breaking Forth upon the Indians in New-England*, in *The Eliot Tracts*, ed. Michael Clark (Westport, Conn.: Praeger, 2000), 115–16. Powwows or shamans were Native leaders thought to possess spiritual powers capable of curing the ill, predicting the future, or placing benevolent or malevolent spells on others. Cogley, *Eliot's Mission*, 41, 52, 58, 64, discusses the praying town codes.

33. Axtell, ed., *Indian Peoples of Eastern America*, 32, 55–69, 199–227, documents the sacred nature of these practices within Native communities.

34. Ann Marie Plane, *Colonial Intimacies: Indian Marriage in Early New England* (Ithaca, N.Y.: Cornell University Press, 2000), 74–77; Jean M. O'Brien, *Dispossession by Degrees: Indian Land and Identity in Natick, Massachusetts, 1650–1790* (Cambridge: Cambridge University Press, 1997), 49–50; Elise M. Brenner, "To Pray or to Be Prey: That Is the Question; Strategies for Cultural Autonomy of Massachusetts Praying Town Indians," *Ethnohistory* 27 (1980): 141–48; Cogley, *Eliot's Mission*, 176, 224–31, 242; David J. Silverman, *Faith and Boundaries: Colonists, Christianity, and Community Among the Wampanoag*

Indians of Martha's Vineyard, 1600–1871 (New York: Cambridge University Press, 2005), 63; Winiarski, "Native American Popular Religion," 154–55. The Massachusetts General Court created the post of Indian Superintendent in 1658 to oversee activities in the praying towns, including their judicial proceedings. Daniel Gookin filled that role from 1661 until his death in 1687 but had little time to devote to it. For his views on controlling Native behavior, see Daniel Gookin, *Historical Collections of the Indians in New England*, ed. Jeffrey H. Fiske (n.p., Towtaid, 1970), 20–21, 59–63, 85–86. An interesting comparison with French Catholic efforts to control Native behavior at roughly the same time may be made by consulting Christopher J. Bilodeau, "Policing Wabanaki Missions in the Seventeenth Century," in *Ethnographies and Exchanges*, ed. Roeber, 97–114.

35. Silverman, *Faith and Boundaries*, 105, 113–15, 118–20, 186–87, 200–201, 278; Mandell, *Behind the Frontier*, 1–6, 24–25, 35, 49–62, 68–69, 104–10, 178–80; William S. Simmons, *Spirit of the New England Tribes: Indian History and Folklore, 1620–1984* (Hanover, N.H.: University Press of New England, 1986), 73–92, 118–24, 174–78; O'Brien, *Dispossession by Degrees*, 60–61, 68–70, 119–23, 207–9.

36. Wheeler, *To Live Upon Hope*, 67–73, 94–95, 229–31 (quotation on 229).

37. See the sources listed in endnote 35. Historians remain divided over how and why racism became a powerful force within early America. For one recent discussion focused on the Middle Atlantic colonies, see Peter Silver, *Our Savage Neighbors: How Indian War Transformed Early America* (New York: Norton, 2008).

38. Kawashima, *Puritan Justice*, 35–36; Silverman, *Faith and Boundaries*, 204–22; O'Brien, *Dispossession by Degrees*, 204–9; Mandell, *Behind the Frontier*, 28–29, 118, 177–78; John A. Sainsbury, "Indian Labor in Early Rhode Island," in *New England Encounters*, ed. Vaughan, 268, 274–75.

39. Douglas L. Winiarski, "A Question of Plain Dealing: Josiah Cotton, Native Christians, and the Quest for Security in Eighteenth-Century Plymouth County," *New England Quarterly* 77(2004): 371, 377, 392, 396–408; Winiarski, "Native American Popular Religion," 153, 155–56.

40. Winiarski, "A Question of Plain Dealing," 386, asserts that "not a single Native American was admitted to full communion in any English parish" in southeastern Massachusetts before 1740. Other treatments of Indian Christians in eighteenth-century New England, including their experiences in the Great Awakening, may be found in Silverman, *Faith and Boundaries*; Mandell, *Behind the Frontier*; Winiarski, "Native American Popular Religion"; Wheeler, *To Live Upon Hope*; William S. Simmons, "The Great Awakening and Indian Conversion in Southern New England," in *Papers of the Tenth Algonquian Conference*, ed. William Cowan (Ottawa: Carleton University Press, 1979); and Thomas S. Kidd, *The Great Awakening: The Roots of Evangelical Christianity in Colonial America* (New Haven, Conn.: Yale University Press, 2007), 189–212.

41. Frank Klingberg, "The Noble Savage as Seen by the Missionaries of the Society for the Propagation of the Gospel in Colonial New York, 1702–1750," *Historical Magazine of the Protestant Episcopal Church* 8 (1939): 150–58; Field Horne, ed., *The Diary of Mary Cooper: Life on a Long Island Farm, 1768–1773* (Oyster Bay, N.Y.: Oyster Bay Historical Society, 1981), x, 18, 20, 23; Wheeler, *To Live Upon Hope*, 93–94.

42. Winiarski, "Native American Popular Religion," 147–86 (quotation on 154).

43. As quoted in Klingberg, "Noble Savage," 158 n. 41.

44. On the continuation of Massachusetts' efforts to regulate Indian behavior and belief through law in the eighteenth century, see Cotton Mather, *The Hatchets, to Hew Down the Tree of Sin* (Boston: B. Green, 1705), 1–15, and Mandell, *Behind the Frontier*, 71, 104–10, 143–58. Alongside Massachusetts, Connecticut and Plymouth were the two colonies that took the most legislative action to control Indian ways. In the seventeenth century, both colonies passed several laws aimed at regulating Indian Sabbath behavior. In 1727, Connecticut enacted a statute that required masters and mistresses to teach their Indian children servants how to read and to catechize them in the Christian faith. Vaughan and Rosen, eds., *Early American Indian Documents*, vol. 17, 17, 35, 57, 271, 284, 294–95, 352. David Bushnell, "The Treatment of the Indians in Plymouth Colony," in *New England Encounters: Indians and Euroamericans, ca. 1600–1850*, ed. Alden Vaughan (Boston: Northeastern University Press, 1999), 68–76, discusses laws aimed at Indians within Plymouth, including Sabbath-keeping laws, as well as other means used to govern area Natives.

45. Hannah Adams, *An Alphabetical Compendium of the Various Sects* (Boston: Edes & Sons, 1784), lv–lxx; Beneke, *Beyond Toleration*, 157–58; Albanese, *Republic of Mind and Spirit*, 373. My depiction of the tolerant nature of Adams's views borrows from the definition of tolerance provided by Schwartz, *"A Mixed Multitude,"* 9.

46. Jon Butler, *Awash in a Sea of Faith: Christianizing the American People* (Cambridge, Mass.: Harvard University Press, 1990), 225–56; Silver, *Our Savage Neighbors*, 261–301; Silverman, *Faith and Boundaries*, 93; Beneke, *Beyond Toleration*, 197–98. Religious prejudice against Indians may be seen as feeding into and off of racism toward Indians. I am indebted to Douglas Winiarski for some of the ideas of this paragraph.

CHAPTER 8. SLAVES TO INTOLERANCE

1. Hunter Dickinson Farish, ed., *Journal and Letters of Philip Vickers Fithian: A Plantation Tutor of the Old Dominion, 1773–1774* (Charlottesville: University Press of Virginia, 1957), 140, 151–52. Further description of Daddy Gumby is found on 134–35.

2. Ibid., 38.

3. Sidney Kaplan and Emma Nogrady Kaplan, *The Black Presence in the Era of the American Revolution*, 2nd ed. (Amherst: University of Massachusetts Press, 1989), 13; Ira Berlin, *Many Thousands Gone: The First Two Centuries of Slavery in North America* (Cambridge, Mass.: Harvard University Press, 1998), 139.

4. Herman Bennett, *Africans in Colonial Mexico: Absolutism, Christianity, and Afro-Creole Consciousness* (Bloomington: University of Indiana Press, 2003), 35–46; Stuart B. Schwartz, *All Can Be Saved: Religious Tolerance and Salvation in the Iberian Atlantic World* (New Haven, Conn.: Yale University Press, 2008).

5. On African Catholicism in Africa and America, see John K. Thornton, *Africa and Africans in the Making of the Atlantic World 1400–1680*, 2nd ed. (New York: Cambridge

University Press, 1998); Thornton, "The Development of an African Catholic Church in the Kingdom of Kongo, 1491–1750," *Journal of African History* 25 (1984): 147–67; Linda M. Heywood, ed., *Central Africans and Cultural Transformation in the American Diaspora* (New York: Cambridge University Press, 2001); James H. Sweet, *Recreating Africa: Culture, Kinship, and Religion in the African-Portuguese World, 1441–1750* (Chapel Hill: University of North Carolina Press, 2003); Emily Clark, *Masterless Mistresses: The New Orleans Ursulines and the Development of a New World Society, 1727–1834* (Chapel Hill: University of North Carolina Press, 2007).

6. David Brion Davis, *In the Image of God: Religion, Moral Values, and Our Heritage of Slavery* (New Haven, Conn.: Yale University Press, 2001), 136.

7. The extensive literature on slave laws in colonial America includes Bradley Nicholson, "Legal Borrowing and the Origins of Slave Law in the British Colonies," *American Journal of Legal History* 38 (1994): 38–54; Thomas D. Morris, *Southern Slavery and the Law, 1619–1860* (Chapel Hill: University of North Carolina Press, 1995); A. Leon Higginbotham, *In the Matter of Color: Race and the American Legal Process. Vol. 1: The Colonial Period* (New York: Oxford University Press, 1978); Willam M. Wiecek, "The Statutory Law of Slavery and Race in the Thirteen Mainland Colonies of British America," *William and Mary Quarterly*, 3rd ser., 34 (1977): 258–80; Alan Watson, *Slave Law in the Americas* (Athens: University of Georgia Press, 1989); Jonathan A. Bush, "Free to Enslave: The Foundations of Colonial American Slave Law," *Yale Journal of Law and the Humanities* 5 (1993): 417–70; Barry Gaspar, "'Rigid and Inclement': Origins of the Jamaica Slave Laws of the Seventeenth Century," in *The Many Legalities of Early America*, ed. Christopher L. Tomlins and Bruce H. Mann (Chapel Hill: University of North Carolina Press, 2001), 78–96.

8. For a succinct discussion of the legal connections between baptism and slavery in early Virginia, see Anthony S. Parent, *Foul Means: The Formation of a Slave Society in Virginia, 1660–1740* (Chapel Hill: University of North Carolina Press, 2003), 113–15.

9. Ibid., 238.

10. Forrest G. Wood, *The Arrogance of Faith: Christianity and Race in America from the Colonial Era to the Twentieth Century* (Boston, 1990), 116–17.

11. Winthrop D. Jordan, *White Over Black: American Attitudes Toward the Negro, 1550–1812* (Chapel Hill: University of North Carolina Press, 1968), 184; Wood, *Arrogance of Faith*, 117.

12. Wood, *Arrogance of Faith*, 117–18. On the rise of West Indian slave codes see Richard S. Dunn, *Sugar and Slaves: The Rise of the Planter Class in the English West Indies, 1624–1713* (Chapel Hill: University of North Carolina Press, 1972), 239–50; Larry Gragg, *Englishmen Transplanted: The English Colonization of Barbados, 1627–1660* (New York: Oxford University Press 2003); Elsa Goveia, *The West Indian Slave Laws of the 18th Century* (Bridgetown, Barbados: Caribbean Universities Press, 1970); Gaspar, "'Rigid and Inclement,'" 90–95.

13. Wood, *Arrogance of Faith*, 116–17; Cornelis Ch. Goslinga, *The Dutch in the Caribbean and on the Wild Coast, 1580–1680* (Gainesville: University Press of Florida, 1971),

Joyce D. Goodfriend, "Burghers and Blacks: The Evolution of a Slave Society at New Amsterdam," *New York History* 59 (1978): 126–29; Berlin, *Many Thousands Gone*, 51–52.

14. Christian Georg Andreas Oldendorp, *History of the Mission of the Evangelical Brethren on the Caribbean Islands of St. Thomas, St. Croix, and St. John* (1777), ed. and trans. Arnold R. Highfield and Vladimir Barac (Ann Arbor: University of Michigan Press, 1987), 322. See also Jon F. Sensbach, *Rebecca's Revival: Creating Black Christianity in the Atlantic World* (Cambridge, Mass.: Harvard University Press, 2005), 37, 52.

15. Jack P. Greene, ed., *The Diary of Landon Carter of Sabine Hall, 1752–1778*, 2 vols. (Charlottesville: Univesity of Virginia Press, 1965), vol. 2, 1148–49.

16. Alan Gallay, *The Indian Slave Trade: The Rise of the English Empire in the American South, 1670–1717* (New Haven, Conn.: Yale University Press, 2002), 45, 369, n. 15. On the rise of religious toleration in the Anglo-Atlantic world in the late seventeenth century, see John Coffey, *Persecution and Toleration in Protestant England, 1558–1689* (New York: Longman, 2000); Alexander Walsham, *Charitable Hatred: Tolerance and Intolerance in England, 1500–1700* (Manchester: Manchester University Press, 2006); Chris Beneke, *Beyond Toleration: The Religious Origins of American Pluralism* (New York: Oxford University Press, 2006); Andrew R. Murphy, *Conscience and Community: Revisiting Toleration and Religious Dissent in Early Modern England and America* (University Park: Pennsylvania State University Press, 2003); Sally Schwartz, *A Mixed Multitude: The Struggle for Toleration in Colonial Pennsylvania* (New York: New York University Press, 1989); and Owen Stanwood, "The Protestant Moment: Antipopery, the Revolution of 1688–89, and the Making of an Anglo-American Empire," *Journal of British Studies* 46 (July 2007): 481–508.

17. Morgan Godwyn, *The Negro's & Indians Advocate, Suing for their Admission into the Church* . . . (London, 1680), 13.

18. Cotton Mather, *Small Offers towards the Tabernacle in the Wilderness* (Boston, 1689), quoted in Jordan, *White Over Black*, 58.

19. Cotton Mather, *The Negro Christianized* (Boston, 1706), and Samuel Sewall, *The Selling of Joseph* (Boston, 1700), quoted in David Brion Davis, *The Problem of Slavery in Western Culture* (New York: Oxford University Press, 1967), 344.

20. Godwyn, *The Negro's and Indians Advocate*, quoted in Sylvia Frey and Betty Wood, *Come Shouting to Zion: African American Protestantism in the American South and British Caribbean to 1830* (Chapel Hill: University of North Carolina Press, 1998), 47.

21. Peter Kalm, *Travels into North America*, trans. John Reinhold Forster (1772; Barre, Mass.: Imprint Society, 1972), 201.

22. Berlin, *Many Thousands Gone*, 126–29.

23. Thomas N. Ingersoll, "'Releese us out of this Cruell Bondegg': An Appeal from Virginia in 1723," *William and Mary Quarterly*, 3rd ser., 51 (1994): 777–82, quotations on 781–82.

24. Parent, *Foul Means*, 252 (quotation), 254, 258 (second quotation).

25. Ibid., 159–62, 262. See also John C. Van Horne, "Impediments to the Christianization and Education of Blacks in Colonial America: The Case of the Associates of Dr. Bray," *Historical Magazine of the Protestant Episcopal Church* 50 (1982): 263–89; and Mi-

chael Anesko, "So Discreet a Zeal: Slavery and the Anglican Church in Virginia, 1680–1730," *Virginia Magazine of History and Biography* 93 (1985): 247–78.

26. Kalm, *Travels into North America*, 201. On the rise of evangelical preaching among enslaved populations in Protestant America, see Wood and Frey, *Come Shouting to Zion*; Albert S. Raboteau, *Slave Religion: The "Invisible Institution" in the Antebellum South* (New York: Oxford University Press, 1978); Mechal Sobel, *Trabelin' On: The Slave Journey to an Afro-Baptist Faith*, 2nd ed. (Princeton, N.J.: Princeton University Press, 1988), Margaret Washington Creel, *A "Peculiar People": Slave Religion and Community-Culture Among the Gullahs* (New York: New York University Press, 1988).

27. Harvey H. Jackson, "Hugh Bryan and the Evangelical Movement in Colonial South Carolina," *William and Mary Quarterly*, 3rd ser., 43 (1986): 594–614; Alan Gallay, *The Formation of a Planter Elite: Jonathan Bryan and the Southern Colonial Frontier* (Athens: University of Georgia Press, 1989), 38–47; and Frey and Wood, *Come Shouting to Zion*, 91–95.

28. Sensbach, *Rebecca's Revival*.

29. Samuel Davies, *Religion and Patriotism the Constituents of a Good Soldier* (1755); Davies, *The State of Religion Among the Protestant Dissenters in Virginia* (1751); Davies, *Letters from the Rev. Samuel Davies, Shewing the State of Religion in Virginia, particularly among the Negroes* (1757), quoted in Randolph Ferguson Scully, *Religion and the Making of Nat Turner's Virginia: Baptist Community and Conflict, 1740–1840* (Charlottesville: University of Virginia Press, 2008), 44–47. On the Presbyterian revivals in Virginia, see also Rhys Isaac, *The Transformation of Virginia, 1740–1790* (Chapel Hill: University of North Carolina Press, 1982); and Michael Greenberg, "Revival, Reform, Revolution: Samuel Davies and the Great Awakening in Virginia," *Marxist Perspectives* (summer 1980): 102–19.

30. Erik R. Seeman, "'Justise Must Take Plase': Three African Americans Speak of Religion in Eighteenth-Century New England," *William and Mary Quarterly*, 3rd ser., 56 (1999): 399–402, 411–13. Many scholars have explored the African American appropriation of Christian belief and practice into a distinctive theology of prophetic redemption. See, for example, James Cone, *A Black Theology of Liberation* (New York: Orbis, 1970); Howard Thurman, *Jesus and the Disinherited* (Nashville: Abingdon Press, 1949); Gayraud S. Wilmore, *Black Religion and Black Radicalism: An Interpretation of the Religious History of African Americans*, 3rd ed. (New York: Orbis Books, 1998); Henry H. Mitchell, *Black Church Beginnings: The Long-Hidden Realities of the First Years* (Grand Rapids, Mich.: Eerdmans, 2004); Theophus H. Smith, *Conjuring Culture: Biblical Formation of Black America* (New York: Oxford University Press, 1995).

31. Jon Butler, *Awash in a Sea of Faith: Christianizing the American People* (Cambridge, Mass.: Harvard University Press, 1990); Butler, *New World Faiths: Religion in Colonial America* (New York: Oxford University Press, 2008), 100; Sylvester A. Johnson, "Colonialism, Biblical World-Making, and Temporalities in Olaudah Equiano's *Interesting Narrative*," *Church History* 77 (December 2008): 1003–24; Richard Price, *Alabi's World* (Baltimore: Johns Hopkins University Press, 1990), 67–68, 297, n. 15.

32. Raboteau, *Slave Religion*, 131.

33. The biracial world of the eighteenth-century evangelicals is explored in Raboteau, *Slave Religion*; Frey and Wood, *Come Shouting to Zion*; Mechal Sobel, *The World They Made Together: Black and White Values in Eighteenth-Century Virginia* (Princeton, N.J.: Princeton University Press, 1987); Creel, *A "Peculiar People"*; Jon F. Sensbach, *A Separate Canaan: The Making of an Afro-Moravian World in North Carolina, 1763–1840* (Chapel Hill: University of North Carolina Press, 1998); John B. Boles, ed., *Masters and Slaves in the House of the Lord: Race and Religion in the American South, 1740–1870* (Lexington: University of Kentucky Press, 1988); and Scully, *Religion and the Making of Nat Turner's Virginia*.

34. Alan Gallay, "The Origins of Slaveholders' Paternalism: George Whitefield, the Bryan Family, and the Great Awakening in the South," *Journal of Southern History* 53 (1987): 369–94; Eugene Genovese, *Roll, Jordan, Roll: The World the Slaves Made* (New York: Pantheon, 1974); Charles F. Irons, *The Origins of Proslavery Christianity: White and Black Evangelicals in Colonial and Antebellum Virginia* (Chapel Hill: University of North Carolina Press, 2008).

35. Quoted in Frey and Wood, *Come Shouting to Zion*, 114. See also Sylvia R. Frey, *Water from the Rock: Black Resistance in a Revolutionary Age* (Princeton, N.J.: Princeton University Press, 1992); and Douglas R. Egerton, *Death or Liberty: African Americans and Revolutionary America* (New York: Oxford University Press, 2009).

36. Beneke, *Beyond Toleration*, 131–32.

37. See Merrill D. Peterson and Robert C. Vaughan, eds., *The Virginia Statute for Religious Freedom: Its Evolution and Consequences in American History* (Cambridge: Cambridge University Press, 1988).

38. John Leland, *The Virginia Chronicle* (Norfolk, 1790), quoted in Beneke, *Beyond Toleration*, 132.

39. Raboteau, *Slave Religion*, chap. 4; Milton C. Sernett, *Black Religion and American Evangelicalism: White Protestants, Plantation Missions, and the Flowering of Negro Christianity, 1787–1865* (Metuchen, N.J.: Scarecrow Press, 1975); Janet Duitsman Cornelius, *Slave Missions and the Black Church in the Antebellum South* (Columbia: University of South Carolina Press, 1999).

40. Frey, *Water from the Rock*, chap. 8; Sensbach, *A Separate Canaan*, chap. 6; Frey and Wood, *Come Shouting to Zion*, chap. 6.

41. Carol George, *Segregated Sabbaths: Richard Allen and the Emergence of Independent Black Churches, 1769–1840* (New York: Oxford University Press, 1973); Gary Nash, *Forging Freedom: The Forging of Philadelphia's Black Community, 1720–1840* (Cambridge, Mass.: Harvard University Press, 1991); Richard Newman, *Freedom's Prophet: Bishop Richard Allen, the AME Church, and the Black Founding Fathers* (New York: New York University Press, 2008).

42. For comparisons with other cultural outsiders, see the chapters by William Pencak, Richard Pointer, and Chris Beneke in this volume.

43. Langston Hughes, "Refugee in America," in *Selected Poems of Langston Hughes* (New York: Vintage, 1959), 290.

CHAPTER 9. CATHOLICS, PROTESTANTS, AND THE CLASH OF CIVILIZATIONS

1. *A Letter to the Inhabitants of the Province of Quebec* (Philadelphia, 1774), 47; Worthington Chauncy Ford, ed., *Journals of the Continental Congress* (Washington, 1904–37), vol. 1, 88; *Providence Gazette*, October 27, 1774, quoted in Francis D. Cogliano, *No King, No Popery: Anti-Catholicism in Revolutionary New England* (Westport, Conn.: Greenwood Press, 1995), 48, 64.

2. Some of the few attempts include Thomas More Brown, "The Image of the Beast: Anti-Papal Rhetoric in Colonial America," in *Conspiracy: Fear of Subversion in American History*, ed. Richard O. Curry and Thomas More Brown (New York: Holt, Rinehart, and Winston, 1972), 1–20; Mary Augustina Ray, *American Opinion of Roman Catholicism in the Eighteenth Century* (New York, 1936); Gayle Kathleen Pluta Brown, "'A Controversy Not Merely Religious': The Anti-Catholic Tradition in Colonial New England" (Ph.D. diss., University of Iowa, 1990); Joseph J. Casino, "Anti-Popery in Colonial Pennsylvania," *Pennsylvania Magazine of History and Biography* 105 (1981): 279–309; Jason K. Duncan, *Citizens or Papists? The Politics of Anti-Catholicism in New York, 1685–1821* (New York: Fordham University Press, 2005).

3. See, for example, Peter Lake, "Anti-Popery: The Structure of a Prejudice," in *Conflict in Early Stuart England: Studies in Religion and Politics, 1603–1642*, ed. Richard Cust and Ann Hughes (London: Longman, 1989), 72–106; Anthony Milton, *Catholic and Reformed: The Roman and Protestant Churches in English Protestant Thought, 1600–1640* (Cambridge: Cambridge University Press, 1995); Milton, "A Qualified Intolerance: The Limits and Ambiguities of Early Stuart Anti-Catholicism," in *Catholicism and Anti-Catholicism in Early Modern English Texts*, ed. Arthur F. Marotti (New York: St. Martin's Press, 1999), 85–115; Michael Questier, "Practical Antipapistry During the Reign of Elizabeth I," *Journal of British Studies* 36 (1997): 371–96; Mark Goldie, "Priestcraft and the Birth of Whiggism," in *Political Discourse in Early Modern Britain*, ed. Nicholas T. Phillipson and Quentin Skinner (Cambridge: Cambridge University Press, 1992), 209–31; Tim Harris, *London Crowds in the Reign of Charles II: Propaganda and Politics from the Restoration Until the Exclusion Crisis* (Cambridge: Cambridge University Press, 1987).

4. Ian K. Steele, "Exploding Colonial American History: Amerindian, Atlantic, and Global Perspectives," *Reviews in American History* 26 (1998): 70–95. Since that time this move toward the backcountry has continued, driven by a number of groundbreaking books, including Daniel K. Richter, *Facing East from Indian Country: A Native History of Early America* (Cambridge, Mass.: Harvard University Press, 2001); James F. Brooks, *Captives and Cousins: Slavery, Kinship, and Community in the Southwest Borderlands* (Chapel Hill: University of North Carolina Press, 2002); Allan Greer, *Mohawk Saint: Catherine Tekakwitha and the Jesuits* (New York: Oxford University Press, 2005), and Alan Taylor, *The Divided Ground: Indians, Settlers, and the Northern Borderland of the American Revolution* (New York: Alfred A. Knopf, 2006). For an overview see Eric Hinderaker and Peter C. Mancall, *At the Edge of Empire: The Backcountry in British North America* (Baltimore: Johns Hopkins University Press, 2003).

5. See also John Corrigan's and Richard Pointer's chapters in this volume.

6. This contradiction may help to explain how Americans could move so quickly from demonization of Catholics to relative acceptance in the early republic, as Chris Beneke's chapter in this volume argues.

7. For an overview of these Huguenot colonization schemes see Frank Lestringant, "Geneva and America in the Renaissance: The Dream of a Huguenot Refuge, 1555–1600," trans. Ann Blair, *Sixteenth-Century Journal* 26 (1995): 285–95. On Spanish Florida see Eugene Lyon, *The Enterprise of Florida: Pedro Menéndez de Avilés and the Spanish Conquest of 1565–1568* (Gainesville: University Press of Florida, 1976).

8. Frank Lesringant, "Une Saint-Barthélemy américaine: L'agonie de la Floride huguenote (septembre-octobre 1565), d'après les sources espagnoles et françaises," in *L'expérience huguenote au Nouveau Monde (XVIe siècle)* (Geneva, 1996), 229–42; A. M. Brookes and Annie Averette, eds., *The Unwritten History of Old St. Augustine* (St. Augustine, 1909), 14–19; Francisco Lopez de Mendoza Grajales, "The Founding of St. Augustine," *Old South Leaflets*, no. 89 (New York, n.d.).

9. For Ribault, see Karen Ordahl Kupperman, *The Jamestown Project* (Cambridge, Mass.: Harvard University Press, 2006), 45–47. Ribault's *The Whole and True Discoverye of Terra Florida* . . . was published in London in 1563.

10. The best indication of how the "black legend" of Spanish cruelty affected colonial projects comes from the Dutch side: Benjamin Schmidt, *Innocence Abroad: The Dutch Imagination and the New World* (Cambridge: Cambridge University Press, 2004), 123–84. See also William Maltby, *The Black Legend in England: The Development of Anti-Spanish Sentiment, 1558–1660* (Durham, N.C.: Duke University Press, 1971).

11. "A discourse how hir Majestie may annoy the king of Spayne," 6 November 1577, in David Beers Quinn, ed., *The Voyages and Colonising Enterprises of Sir Humphrey Gilbert* (London, 1940), vol. 1, 170–71.

12. Richard Hakluyt, "Discourse of Western Planting, 1584," in *The Original Writings and Correspondence of the Two Richard Hakluyts,* ed. E. G. R. Taylor (London: Hakluyt Society, 1935), vol. 2, 216, 239, 258. On Hakluyt's religious vision see David Harris Sacks, "Discourses of Western Planting: Richard Hakluyt and the Making of the Atlantic World," in *The Atlantic World and Virginia, 1550–1624,* ed. Peter Mancall (Chapel Hill: University of North Carolina Press, 2007), 410–53.

13. Quoted in Kupperman, *Jamestown Project,* 51; Kupperman, *Roanoke: The Abandoned Colony,* 2nd ed. (Lanham, Md.: Rowman and Littlefield, 2007), 87–88; J. Leitch Wright, Jr., *Anglo-Spanish Rivalry in North America* (Athens: University of Georgia Press, 1971), 28–29. On Drake's efforts to appeal to Indians see also Edmund S. Morgan, *American Slavery, American Freedom: The Ordeal of Colonial Virginia* (New York: W. W. Norton, 1975), 9–14.

14. William Crashaw, *A Sermon Preached in London Before the right honourable the Lord Lawarre* (London, 1610); Douglas Bradburn, "The Eschatological Origins of the English Empire," in *Early Modern Virginia: New Essays on the Old Dominion,* ed. Bradburn and John Coombs (Charlottesville: University Press of Virginia, forthcoming).

15. The uses of antipopery during England's Civil War years are well covered in Lake, "Anti-Popery," as well as in Robin Clifton, "The Popular Fear of Catholics During the English Revolution," *Past and Present*, no. 52 (1971): 23–55. For the colonies during this time see Carla Gardina Pestana, *The English Atlantic in an Age of Revolution, 1640–1661* (Cambridge, Mass.: Harvard University Press, 2004). As Pestana and Karen Kupperman have underscored, much of the anti-Catholic colonizing push at this time focused on the West Indies rather than the mainland.

16. See especially John D. Krugler, *English and Catholic: The Lords Baltimore in the Seventeenth Century* (Baltimore: Johns Hopkins University Press, 2004).

17. *Virginia and Maryland, or the Lord Baltamore's printed Case, uncased and answered* (London, 1655), in *Narratives of Early Maryland, 1633–1684*, ed. Clayton Coleman Hall (New York, 1910), 200; Leonard Strong, *Babylon's Fall in Maryland* (London, 1655), in *Narratives of Early Maryland*, ed. Hall, 236, 242.

18. "Complaint from Heaven with a Huy and crye and a petition out of Virginia and Maryland, 1676," in *Archives of Maryland*, ed. W. H. Browne et al. (Baltimore and Annapolis, 1883–), vol. 5, 134–35, 147–48. For the regional context see Michael Graham, "Popish Plots: Protestant Fears in Early Colonial Maryland, 1676–1689," *Catholic Historical Review* 79 (1993): 197–216.

19. J. F. Bosher, "The Franco-Catholic Danger," *History* 79 (1994): 5–30; Andrew Marvell, *An Account of the Growth of Popery, and Arbitrary Government in England* (Amsterdam, 1677), in *The Complete Prose Works of Andrew Marvell*, ed. Alexander B. Grosart (London, 1875), vol. 4, 248; J. P. Kenyon, *The Popish Plot* (London: Penguin, 1972); Jonathan Scott, "England's Troubles: Exhuming the Popish Plot," in *The Politics of Religion in Restoration England*, ed. Tim Harris, Paul Seaward, and Mark Goldie (Oxford: Clarendon Press, 1990), 107–31.

20. Edward Randolph, "The Present State of New England," in *Edward Randolph: Including his Letters and Official Papers . . . 1676–1703*, ed. Robert N. Toppan and Alfred T. S. Goodrick (Boston, 1898–1909), vol. 2, 243; Bartlett Burleigh James and J. Franklin Jameson, eds., *Journal of Jasper Danckaerts, 1679–1680* (New York, 1913), 44, 65, 79. The only work that examines the crisis during this period beyond any single region is Stephen Saunders Webb, *1676: The End of American Independence* (New York: Alfred A. Knopf, 1984).

21. Edward Randolph, "A Short Narrative of the late Transactions and Rebellion in the Province of New-Hampshier, in New England," *Randolph Letters*, vol. 3, 261. The political dispute was most marked in New England; on that context see Richard R. Johnson, *Adjustment to Empire: The New England Colonies, 1675–1715* (New Brunswick, N.J.: Rutgers University Press, 1981).

22. The best work on the context in Britain is Tim Harris, *Revolution: The Great Crisis of the British Monarchy, 1685–1715* (London: Allen Lane, 2006).

23. Francis Nicholson to [William Blathwayt], [October] 1688, Blathwayt Papers, vol. 15, folder 1, Colonial Williamsburg. The best account of Andros and his Indian policies, as opposed to the colonial reaction to them, is Mary Lou Lustig, *The Imperial Execu-*

tive in America: Sir Edmund Andros, 1637–1714 (Madison, N.J.: Fairleigh Dickinson University Press, 2002).

24. Many of the published and unpublished sources from the period are collected in W. H. Whitmore, ed., *The Andros Tracts: Being a Collection of Pamphlets and Official Papers of the Andros Government and the Establishment of the Second Charter of Massachusetts* (New York, 1868–74).

25. Testimonies of Joseph Graves, Mary Graves, and John Rutter, 3 January 1689, in James Phinney Baxter, ed., *Documentary History of the State of Maine* (Portland, 1869–1916), vol. 4, 446–47. For a fuller account see Owen Stanwood, "The Protestant Moment: Antipopery, the Revolution of 1688–89, and the Making of an Anglo-American Empire," *Journal of British Studies* 46 (2007): 481–508; David Lovejoy, *The Glorious Revolution in America* (New York: Harper and Row, 1972).

26. On Leisler's antipopery see David William Voorhees, "The 'fervent Zeale' of Jacob Leisler," *William and Mary Quarterly*, 3rd ser., 51 (1994): 447–72; and John M. Murrin, "The Menacing Shadow of Louis XIV and the Rage of Jacob Leisler: The Constitutional Ordeal of Seventeenth-Century New York," in *New York and the Union: Contributions to the American Constitutional Experience*, ed. Stephen L. Schechter and Richard B. Bernstein (Albany, N.Y.: New York State Commission on the Bicentennial of the Constitution, 1990), 29–71.

27. Declaration of Silvanus Davis [1690], *Documentary History of the State of Maine*, vol. 5, 146–47.

28. Alden T. Vaughan and Edward W. Clark, eds., *Puritans Among the Indians: Accounts of Captivity and Redemption, 1676–1724* (Cambridge, Mass.: Harvard University Press, 1981), 153–54, 161–64. See also Ann M. Little, *Abraham in Arms: War and Gender in Colonial New England* (Philadelphia: University of Pennsylvania Press, 2007).

29. Nathaniel Bouton, ed., *Documents and Records Relating to the Province of New-Hampshire* (Concord, 1867–73), vol. 2, 318–19; Court Records, 7: 6–7, Massachusetts Archives, Boston; *The Answer Of the House of Representatives, to His Excellency the Earl of Bellomont's Speech* (Boston, 1699), CO 5/860/65.iii, The National Archives, Kew.

30. On the Anglicization of the colonies see especially John M. Murrin, "Anglicizing an American Colony: The Transformation of Provincial Massachusetts" (Ph.D. diss., Yale University, 1966); T. H. Breen, "An Empire of Goods: The Anglicization of Colonial America, 1690–1776," *Journal of British Studies* 25 (1986): 467–99. On political and religious culture see Brendan McConville, *The King's Three Faces: The Rise and Fall of Royal America, 1689–1776* (Chapel Hill: University of North Carolina Press, 2006). The development of provincial nationalism coincided with an anti-French surge of nationalism in Britain itself, on which see especially Linda Colley, *Britons: Forging the Nation, 1707–1837* (New Haven, Conn.: Yale University Press, 1992).

31. Benjamin Wadsworth, *King William Lamented in America: Or, a Sermon occasion'd by the very Sorrowful tidings, of the Death of William III* (Boston, 1702), 9.

32. Benjamin Colman, *A Brief Enquiry* (Boston, 1716), 31–32, quoted in Thomas S. Kidd, *The Protestant Interest: New England After Puritanism* (New Haven, Conn.: Yale

University Press, 2004), 37; Ray, *American Opinion of Roman Catholicism*, 82; Geoffrey Plank, *Rebellion and Savagery: The Jacobite Rising of 1745 and the British Empire* (Philadelphia: University of Pennsylvania Press, 2006), 77–100.

33. McConville, *The King's Three Faces*, 56–63; McConville, "Pope's Day Revisited, 'Popular' Culture Reconsidered," *Explorations in Early American Culture* 4 (2000): 258–80; Alfred F. Young, "English Plebeian Culture and Eighteenth-Century Radicalism," in *The Origins of Anglo-American Radicalism*, ed. Margaret Jacob and James Jacob (London: Allen and Unwin, 1984), 185–212.

34. Cotton Mather, *Shaking Dispensations. An Essay Upon the Mighty Shakes which The Hand of Heaven, hath given, and is giving, to the World* (Boston, 1715), 3, 27, 46.

35. Jon Butler, *The Huguenots in America: Refugee People in New World Society* (Cambridge, Mass.: Harvard University Press, 1983); Philip Otterness, *Becoming German: The 1709 Palatine Migration to New York* (Ithaca, N.Y.: Cornell University Press, 2004); A. G. Roeber, "'The Origin of Whatever Is Not English Among Us': The Dutch-Speaking and German-Speaking Peoples of Colonial British America," in *Strangers within the Realm: Cultural Margins of the First British Empire*, ed. Bernard Bailyn and Philip D. Morgan (Chapel Hill: University of North Carolina Press, 1991), 220–83; John Bonner, *The Town of Boston in New-England* (Boston, 1722).

36. Alan Gallay, *The Indian Slave Trade: The Rise of the English Empire in the American South, 1670–1717* (New Haven, Conn.: Yale University Press, 2002), 127–54; Jane Landers, *Black Society in Spanish Florida* (Urbana: University of Illinois Press, 1999), 21–35.

37. Landers, *Black Society in Spanish Florida*, 37; Mark M. Smith, ed., *Stono: Documenting and Interpreting a Southern Slave Revolt* (Columbia: University of South Carolina Press, 2005), 3–4, 14; John K. Thornton, "The African Dimensions of the Stono Rebellion," *American Historical Review* 96 (1991): 1101–13.

38. Thomas J. Davis, *A Rumor of Revolt: The "Great Negro Plot" in Colonial New York* (New York: Free Press, 1985), 160; Daniel Horsmanden, *The New York Conspiracy*, ed. Thomas J. Davis (Boston: Beacon Press, 1971), 341.

39. Horsmanden, *New York Conspiracy*, 342–43, 369.

40. Cotton Mather, *Frontiers Well Defended* (Boston, 1707), 46, 50. My understanding of the conflict in the region owes much to the work of Christopher J. Bilodeau, "The Economy of War: Violence, Religion, and the Wabanaki Indians in the Maine Borderlands" (Ph.D. diss., Cornell University, 2006).

41. John G. Reid et al., *The "Conquest" of Acadia, 1710: Imperial, Colonial, and Aboriginal Constructions* (Toronto: University of Toronto Press, 2004); Geoffrey Plank, *An Unsettled Conquest: The British Campaign Against the Peoples of Acadia* (Philadelphia: University of Pennsylvania Press, 2001); quotation from Peter N. Doll, *Revolution, Religion, and National Identity: Imperial Anglicanism in British North America, 1745–1795* (Madison, N.J.: Fairleigh Dickinson University Press, 2000), 49.

42. John Mack Faragher, *A Great and Noble Scheme: The Tragic Story of the Expulsion of the Acadians from Their American Homeland* (New Haven, Conn.: Yale University Press, 2005), quotations on 242–43. See also Christopher Hodson, "Refugees: Acadians and the Social History of Empire, 1755–1785" (Ph.D. diss., Northwestern University, 2004).

43. Jonathan Mayhew, *Two Discourses Delivered October 25th, 1759. Being the Day appointed by Authority to be observed as A Day of Public Thanksgiving, for the Success of His Majesty's Arms, More particularly in the Reduction of Quebec, the Capital of Canada* (Boston, 1759), 47, appendix.

44. Bernard Bailyn, *Voyagers to the West: A Passage in the Peopling of America on the Eve of the American Revolution* (New York: Alfred A. Knopf, 1986), 451–61; A. M. Brookes and Annie Averette, eds., *The Unwritten History of Old St. Augustine* (St. Augustine, 1909), 192–95.

45. Philip Lawson, *The Imperial Challenge: Quebec and Britain in the Age of the American Revolution* (Montreal: McGill-Queen's University Press, 1994); Gustave Lanctot, *Canada and the American Revolution, 1774–1783* (Cambridge, Mass., Harvard University Press, 1967).

46. *The Other Side of the Question: or, a Defence of the Liberties of North-America* (New York, 1774), 23–24; Ford, ed., *Journals of the Continental Congress*, vol. 1, 83, 88.

47. *Address to the Soldiers* (Boston?, 1775?).

48. Quoted in Cogliano, *No King, No Popery*, 74. See also Charles P. Hanson, *Necessary Virtue: The Pragmatic Origins of Religious Liberty in New England* (Charlottesville: University Press of Virginia, 1999).

49. On the place of Catholics in Revolutionary America see Chris Beneke's chapter in this volume.

CHAPTER 10. ANTI-SEMITISM, TOLERATION, AND APPRECIATION

1. Twenty-three, not twenty-four, Jews arrived from Brazil. Leo Hershkowitz has shown that Asser Levy, long considered one of the refugees, had arrived previously from the Netherlands, along with at least two other merchants: see his "Dutch Notarial Records Pertaining to Asser Levy, 1659–1692," *American Jewish History* 91 (2003): 471–83, and "By Chance or Choice: Jews in New Amsterdam 1654," *American Jewish Archives* 57 (2005): 1–13.

2. Jonathan Israel, *Empires and Entrepots: The Dutch, the Spanish Monarchy, and the Jews, 1585–1713* (London: Hambledon Press, 1990), 422, 425, 431; Herbert J. Bloom, *The Economic Activities of the Jews of Amsterdam in the Seventeenth Century* (Williamsport, Pa.: Bayard Press, 1937), 124–44.

3. James Homer Williams, "'Abominable Religion' and Dutch (In)tolerance: The Jews and Petrus Stuyvesant," *Halve Maen* 71 (1998): 85–91; Morris U. Schappes, ed., *A Documentary History of the Jews of the United States, 1654–1875*, 3rd ed. (New York: Schocken, 1971), 1–2, 565.

4. Johannes Megapolensis to the Classis of Amsterdam, March 18, 1655, in J. Franklin Jameson, ed., *Narratives of New Netherland, 1624–1664* (New York: Scribner's, 1909), 391–92.

5. Schappes, ed., *Documentary History*, 4–5.

6. Ibid.

7. "Form of Association Proposed to the Inhabitants," Jacob Leisler Papers, Fales Library and Special Collections, New York University, available at http://pages.nyu.edu/~dwvi/jun-1689-.html; thanks to Hermann Wellenreuther for this reference; Jacob Melyan Letterbook (c. 1692), American Antiquarian Society, Worcester, Massachusetts; "Mr. Atwood's Memorial Memorial Concerning New York, His Posts There, and in Neighboring Provinces," Miscellaneous Manuscripts, New-York Historical Society. Thanks to Evan Haefeli for the last two references. John M. Murrin, "English Rights as Ethnic Aggression: The English Conquest, the Charter of Liberties of 1683, and Leisler's Rebellion in New York," in *Authority and Resistance in Early New York*, ed. William Pencak and Conrad E. Wright (New York: New-York Historical Society, 1988), 50–83.

8. Jonathan Israel, *European Jewry in the Age of Mercantilism, 1550–1750*, rev. ed. (Oxford: Clarendon Press, 1989), 127–31; David de Sola Pool and Tamar de Sola Pool, *An Old Faith in the New World: Portrait of Shearith Israel, 1654–1954* (New York: Columbia University Press, 1955), 34–35.

9. Max Kohler, "Civil Status of the Jews in Colonial New York," *Publications of the American Jewish Historical Society* 6 (1897): 84–99.

10. Henry P. Johnstone, ed., *The Correspondence and Public Papers of John Jay*, vol. 1 (New York: Putnam's Sons, 1890), 102–20.

11. B. H. Levy, "The Early History of Georgia Jews," 166–75, in *Forty Years of Diversity: Essays on Colonial Georgia*, ed. Harvey H. Jackson and Phinizy Spalding (Athens: University of Georgia Press, 1984); Malcolm H. Stern, "New Light on the Jewish Settlement of Savannah," *Publications of the American Jewish Historical Society* 52 (1963): 173; Robert Jutte, "Contacts by the Bedside: Jewish Physicians and Their Christian Patients," in *In and Out of the Ghetto: Jewish-Gentile Relations in Late Medieval and Early Modern Germany*, ed. Ronnie Po-Chia Hsia and Harmut Lehmann (Cambridge: Cambridge University Press, 1995), 137–50.

12. Mills Lane, ed., *General Oglethorpe's Georgia, Colonial Letters, 1733–1743* (Savannah: Beehive Press, 1975), 516, also 521, 541.

13. John C. English, "John Wesley and His 'Jewish Parishioners'": Jewish-Christian Relationships in Savannah, Georgia, 1736–1737," *Methodist History* 36 (1998): 200–227; George Fenwick Jones, "A Letter by Pastor Johann Martin Boltzius about Bethesda and Marital Irregularities in Savannah," *Georgia Historical Quarterly* 84 (2000): 292; Stern, "New Light on the Jewish Settlement," 186.

14. Joseph R. Rosenblum, *A Biographical Dictionary of Early Ameircan Jews* (Lexington: University of Kentucky Press, 1960), 138; James William Hagy, *This Happy Land: The Jews of Colonial and Ante-bellum Charleston* (Tuscaloosa: University of Alabama Press, 1993), 35–36: "Bicentennial Celebration of the Jews of Charleston, 1750–1950," Eleanor Halsey Papers, South Carolina Historical Society, Charleston.

15. The best discussion of the contractors is Mark Abbott Stern, *David Franks: Colonial Merchant* (University Park: Pennsylvania State University Press, 2010); meanwhile, see *Letter Book of John Watts, 1762–1765*, Collections of the New-York Historical Society 61 (1917), and Sylvester K. Stevens, Donald H. Kent, and Louis Waddell, eds., *The Papers*

of Henry Bouquet (6 vols. to date, Harrisburg: Pennsylvania Historical and Museum Commission, 1951–1978), vols. 4–6.

16. David Brener, *The Jews of Lancaster, Pennsylvania* (Lancaster: Private publication, 1979), 8–11.

17. Stanley F. Chyet, *Lopez of Newport: Colonial American Merchant Prince* (Detroit: Wayne State University Press, 1970), 34–41; David S. Lovejoy, *Rhode Island Politics and the American Revolution, 1760–1776* (Providence: Brown University Press, 1958), 5–50, 76, 204.

18. Matthis Bush to Barnard Gratz, November 7, 1766, Gratz Papers, ser. 1, vol. 9, Historical Society of Pennsylvania, copy at AJA; *Pennsylvania Gazette*, July 19, 1772; Jacob Rader Marcus, *American Jewry: Documents, Eighteenth Century* (Cincinnati: Hebrew Union College Press, 1959), 399–401.

19. Edwin Wolf 2nd and Maxwell Whiteman, *History of the Jews of Philadelphia from Colonial Times to the Age of Jackson* (Philadelphia: American Jewish Publications Society, 1956), 54, quoting Jacob Henry to Barnard Gratz, January 7, 1771, McAlister Collection, Historical Society of Pennsylvania; Solomon Breibart, "Two Jewish Congregations in Charleston, South Carolina Before 1791: A New Conclusion," *American Jewish History* 69 (1980): 360–63; Hagy, *This Happy Land*, 14, 60–68; Kahal Kadosh Beth Elohim Papers, memorial of January 27, 1775, box 1, folder 54, American Jewish Archives; Naphtali Phillips, "Unwritten History [of Shearith Israel]," *American Jewish Archives* 6 (1954): 82–95; "Minute Book of Shearith Israel," *Publications of the American Jewish Historical Society* 2 (1911): 82–85, 91, 103–5; "Deleted Minutes of Shearith Israel," pages keyed to pp. 73, 94, 99, 100, 114–17 in published minutes, AJA; *Josephson v. Simpson, Hays v. Seixas, and Simpson v. Hays*, New York file, Lawsuits Involving Jews, 1769–72, from John Tabor Kemp Papers, New-York Historical Society, copy at AJA.

20. Abraham Levy file, newspaper articles published in the *Independent Gazetteer* and *Chronicle of Freedom*, October 10, 22, 24, 30, and November 11, 1782, AJA.

21. This is one of the principal theses of my book, *Jews and Gentiles in Early America, 1654–1800* (Ann Arbor: University of Michigan Press, 2005).

22. Wolf and Whiteman, *Jews of Philadelphia*, 81; *Philadelphia Evening Post*, September 26, 1776; Owen S. Ireland, *Religion, Ethnicity, and Politics: Ratifying the Constitution in Pennsylvania* (University Park: Pennsylvania State University Press, 1995), has been instrumental in calling attention to the undemocratic, authoritarian features of the Pennsylvania Constitutionalists/anti-Federalists.

23. *The Journals of Henry Melchior Muhlenberg*, trans. Theodore G. Tappert and Jon W. Doberstein, 3 vols. (Philadelphia: Muhlenberg Press, 1945), vol. 2, 737–43; "Letter of Henry Melchior Muhlenberg, October 1, 1776," *Pennsylvania Magazine of History and Biography* 22 (1898): 129–31.

24. "Letter of Henry Melchior Muhlenberg, October 1, 1776," *Pennsylvania Magazine of History and Biography* 22 (1898): 129–31; "Petition for Equal Rights," reprinted in Schappes, ed., *Documentary History*, 65; Dutch philosopher Baruch Spinoza (1632–77) was a Jew excommunicated from the Amsterdam congregation for his philosophical writings denying God's existence except as an aspect of nature.

25. See Stern, David Franks, which also includes information on his daughter; also see Cecil Roth, "Some Jewish Loyalists in the American War for Independence," in *The Jewish Experience in America, vol. 1, The Colonial Period,* ed. Abraham Karp (Waltham, Mass.: American Jewish Publication Society, 1969), 307–8; *Pennsylvania Gazette,* January 12, 1780, and November 1, 1780; Rebecca Franks to Anne Harrison, February 26, 1778, *American Jewish Archives* 27 (1975): 142–44; Becky (Franks) Johnson to Williamina Bond Cadwallader, February 19, 1784, "Dear Mrs. Cad: A Revolutionary War Letter of Rebecca Franks," Mark Stern, *American Jewish Archives* 57 (2005): 15–24.

26. *New York Gazette,* December 2, 1780.

27. *Independent Gazetteer,* March 13 and 20, 1784.

28. "A Real Citizen," box 23, no. 13, Sheftall Papers, University of Georgia, Special Collections, Athens, Georgia; *Georgia Gazette,* January 13, 1785, reprinted in Max Kohler, "Phrases of Religious Liberty in America with Particular Reference to the Jews," *Publications of the American Jewish Historical Society* 13 (1905): 29–31.

29. "Abigail Minis, Matriarch," typescript at the Georgia Historical Society, Savannah; also there, see Minis to "Dear Sir" in Charleston, January 4, 1789, no. 1515, and will of Abigail Minis, March 28, 1793, no. 568, Minis Collection; Schappes, ed., *Documentary History,* 53–54.

30. Frederic Cople Jaher, "American Jews in the Revolutionary and Early National Period," in Stephen H. Norwood and Eunice G. Pollack, eds., *Encyclopedia of American Jewish History,* 2 vols. (Santa Barbara, Calif.: ABC-CLIO, 2008), 18–19, 22; Julian P. Boyd, ed., *Papers of Thomas Jefferson, Vol. 2* (Princeton, N.J.: Princeton University Press, 1950), 655; John Samuel, "Some Cases in Pennsylvania Where Rights Claimed by Jews are Affected," *Publications of the American Jewish Historical Society* 5 (1897): 35–37.

31. Max Farrand, ed., *The Records of the Federal Convention of 1787,* 3 vols. (New Haven, Conn.: Yale University Press, 1911), vol. 3, 78–79.

32. Schappes, ed., *Documentary History,* 77–84; Morris Gutstein, *The Story of the Jews of Newport* (New York: Bloch, 1936), 204–6; for Washington's religion, see James Thomas Flexner, *George Washington and the New Nation* (Boston: Little, Brown, 1970), 184.

33. *Pennsylvania Gazette,* February 17 and March 17, 1790; *New York Journal,* April 26 and May 1, 1790; Cartoon, "A Peep into the Anti-Federal Club" (New York, 1793), copy in Pencak, *Jews and Gentiles,* illustration following p. 154. For Federalists changing attitudes toward immigrants and diversity see Marilyn Baseler, *Asylum for Mankind, 1607–1808* (Ithaca, N.Y.: Cornell University Press, 1988), chaps. 4–8.

34. For Israel, see John Alexander, *Render Them Submissive: Responses to Poverty in Philadelphia, 1760–1800* (Amherst: University of Massachusetts Press, 1980), 37–42; Ronald Schulz, *The Republic of Labor: Philadelphia Artisans and the Politics of Class, 1720–1830* (New York: Oxford University Press, 1993), 145–51; *Gazette of the United States,* October 9 and 12, 1797; Letter of John Fenno, October 26, 1795, Chicago Historical Society, copies at Special Collections, Paterno Library, Pennsylvania State University, for the fight; Israel Israel file, AJA; Will of Israel Israel, Ellet Papers, Historical Society of Pennsylvania.

35. Carl E. Prince, "John Israel: Printer and Politician on the Pennsylvania Frontier," *Pennsylvania Magazine of History and Biography* 91 (1967): 46–55; *Tree of Liberty*, July 26, August 16, August 23, August 30, and October 25, 1800.

36. Lorman Ratner, "Conversion of the Jews and Pre-Civil War Reform," *American Quarterly* 13 (1961): 43–54; Leonard Dinnerstein, *Anti-Semitism in America* (New York: Oxford University Press, 1995), 86–89.

37. *Tree of Liberty*, August 28 and September 18, 1802, and May 26, 1805.

38. For Jewish population, see Jonathan Saran, *American Judaism* (New Haven, Conn.: Yale University Press, 2004), 375.

39. John Adams to Mordecai Noah, March 15, 1819, Adams Papers (microfilm), reel 123, Massachusetts Historical Society, Boston, reprinted in Mordecai Manuel Noah, *Discourse on the Restoration of the Jews* (New York: Harper Brothers, 1845), available in Mordecai Noah, *Selected Writings,* ed. Michael Schuldiner and Daniel J. Kleinfeld (Westport, Conn..: Greenwood Press, 1999), 127–28; also Adams, *Works,* ed. Charles F. Adams, 10 vols. (Boston: Little, Brown, 1850–56), vol. 9, 609. For Voltaire, see Adam Sutcliffe, "Myth, Origins, Identity: Voltaire, the Jews, and the Enlightenment Notion of Toleration," *Eighteenth Century* 41 (1998): 107–26.

40. Noah, *Discourse*, 128; Frederic Cople Jaher, *A Scapegoat in the New Wilderness: The Origins and Rise of Anti-Semitism in America* (Cambridge, Mass.: Harvard University Press, 1994), 135–36.

41. Thomas Jefferson to Mordecai Manuel Noah, May 28, 1818, Jefferson Manuscripts, Library of Congress, Washington, D.C.

42. Thomas Jefferson to Benjamin Rush, "Syllabus of an Estimate of the Merit of the Doctrines of Jesus Christ, Compared with Those of Others," April 21, 1803, in *Writings of Thomas Jefferson,* 9 vols., ed. Paul Leicester Ford (New York: Putnam's Sons, 1892–99), vol. 8, 226.

43. Schappes, ed., *Documentary History*, 89–92; 589–91; Jacob Rader Marcus, *The Handsome Young Priest in the Black Gown: The Personal World of Gershom Seixas* (Cincinnati: Hebrew Union College Press, 1970), 33.

CHAPTER 11. THE "CATHOLIC SPIRIT PREVAILING IN OUR COUNTRY"

A shorter version of this chapter appeared as "America's Whiggish Religious Revolution: An Instance in the Progress of History," *Historically Speaking* (Summer 2009): 31–35. I wish to thank the editors of *Historically Speaking,* Donald A. Yerxa and Joseph S. Lucas, for permission to include portions of that essay here.

1. The quotation in the chapter title comes from an open letter: "Patrick Henry to Baptist Association meeting in Louisa County, August 13, 1776," that appeared in the *Virginia Gazette*, August 24, 1776 [Dixon and Hunter].

2. For the best illustration of this trend, see John K. Wilson, "Religion Under the State Constitutions, 1776–1800," *Journal of Church and State* 32 (1990): 753–73.

3. For the claim that anti-Catholicism was essential to the creation of liberal democ-

racy in the United States, see Elizabeth Fenton, "Catholic Canadians, Religious Pluralism, and National Unity in the Early U.S. Republic," *Early American Literature* 41, no. 1 (January 2006): 31. For examples of more empirically oriented works that emphasize anti-Catholicism in the early republic, see Michael S. Carter, "'Under the Benign Sun of Toleration': Mathew Carey, the Douai Bible, and Catholic Print Culture, 1789–1791," *Journal of the Early Republic* 27 (fall 2007): esp. 442–43; and Jason K. Duncan, *Citizens or Papists? The Politics of Anti-Catholicism in New York, 1685–1821* (New York: Fordham University Press, 2005). For anti-Whiggish interpretations of the history of toleration, especially as it applies to sixteenth- and seventeenth-century Europe, see Benjamin J. Kaplan, *Divided by Faith: Religious Conflict and the Practice of Toleration in Early Modern Europe* (Cambridge, Mass.: Belknap Press, 2007); Alexandra Walsham, *Charitable Hatred: Tolerance and Intolerance in England, 1500–1700* (Manchester: Manchester University Press, 2006); and Jeremy Waldron and Melissa S. Williams, "Introduction," in *Toleration and Its Limits: NOMOS XLVIII*, ed. Melissa Williams and Jeremy Waldron (New York: New York University Press, 2008), 3.

4. Carroll's letter is reprinted in Guilday, *The Life and Times of John Carroll: Archbishop of Baltimore (1735–1815)* (Westminster, Md.: Newman Press, 1954), 172–73. The quotation appears on p. 172.

5. For a lucid account of what revolutions owe to ideas, see Jonathan Israel, *Enlightenment Contested: Philosophy, Modernity, and the Emancipation of Man, 1670–1752* (Oxford: Oxford University Press, 2006), 4–5. The notion that toleration gave way, in a mostly linear way, to religious liberty is an old one, developed influentially in Sidney E. Mead, *The Lively Experiment: The Shaping of Christianity in America* (New York: Harper & Row, 1976).

6. *Virginia Gazette*, March 26, 1772 [Rind].

7. For a discussion of the emergence of the ideal of religious equality, see Rhys Isaac, *The Transformation of Virginia, 1740–1790* (Chapel Hill: University of North Carolina Press, 1992), 279–82; William L. Miller, *The First Liberty: Religion and the American Public* (New York: Alfred A. Knopf, 1986), 3–16; Irving Brant, "Madison: On Separation of Church and State," *William and Mary Quarterly*, 3rd ser., 8, James Madison, 1751–1836: Bicentennial Number (January 1951): 5–6. The best account of events in Virginia during the Founding era can be found in Thomas E. Buckley, *Church and State in Revolutionary Virginia, 1776–1787* (Charlottesville: University Press of Virginia, 1977). The developments that occurred in 1776 are discussed on pp. 17–37.

8. "Instructions to the Colonists by Lord Baltimore" (1633), in *Narratives of Early Maryland, 1633–1689*, ed. Clayton C. Hall (New York: Charles Scribner's Sons, 1940), 16.

9. John Russell Bartlett, ed., *Records of the Colony of Rhode Island and Providence Plantations, in New England*, 10 vols. (Providence, 1856–64), vol. 2, 5.

10. Samuel Williams, *A Discourse on the Love of Our Country* (Salem, 1775), 16.

11. Quotations from all state constitutions in this paragraph taken from Edwin S. Gaustad, *Faith of Our Fathers: Religion and the New Nation* (San Francisco: Harper & Row, 1987), Appendix A–B.

12. Shelby M. Balik, "Equal Right and Equal Privilege: Separating Church and State in Vermont," *Journal of Church and State* 50, no. 1 (winter 2008): 23–48; Johan N. Neem, "The Elusive Common Good: Religion and Civil Society in Massachusetts, 1780–1833," *Journal of the Early Republic* 24, no. 3 (fall 2004): 381–417.

13. For a comprehensive explication of these changes see John K. Wilson, "Religion Under the State Constitutions, 1776–1800," *Journal of Church and State*, 32, no. 4 (1990): 753–73.

14. Frank Lambert, *The Founding Fathers and the Place of Religion in America* (Princeton, N.J.: Princeton University Press, 2003); and Mark D. McGarvie, *One Nation Under Law: America's Early National Struggles to Separate Church and State* (DeKalb: Northern Illinois University Press, 2004).

15. Vincent Philip Muñoz adeptly discusses the "noncognizance" principle in "James Madison's Principle of Religious Liberty," *American Political Science Review* 97, no. 1 (February 2003): 23.

16. As quoted in Derek H. Davis, *Religion and the Continental Congress, 1774–1789: Contributions to Original Intent* (New York: Oxford University Press, 2000), 30.

17. These sentiments extended beyond the ratifying conventions. The Presbyterian United Synod of Philadelphia made alterations to the Westminster Confession (May 28, 1787), indicating that "it is the duty of civil magistrates to protect the Church of our common Lord, without giving the preference to any denomination of Christians above the rest, in such a manner that all ecclesiastical persons whatever shall enjoy the full, free, and unquestioned liberty of discharging every part of their sacred functions without violence or danger." Quoted in Philip Schaff, *Church and State in the United States: The American Idea of Religious Liberty and Its Practical Effects with Official Documents* (New York: Charles Scribner's Sons, 1888), 50.

18. George Washington, "To the Convention of the Universal Church Lately Assembled in Philadelphia," in *The Writings of George Washington*, ed. Jared Sparks, 12 vols. (Boston, 1834–37), vol. 12, 193.

19. The Shakers, whose rapid growth in the northern United States in the late eighteenth and early nineteenth centuries caused a great deal of consternation among contemporaries, are especially notable in this regard. Yet, significantly, as Adam Jortner points out, "anti-Shaker writings, in addition to raising biblical or religious objections, spent many pages worrying about the effect of centralized religious authority on liberty. To critics, loyalty mattered more than blasphemy. The proper response to theological innovation, it seemed, was political attack" ("The Political Threat of a Female Christ: Ann Lee, Morality, and Religious Freedom in the United States, 1780–1819," *Early American Studies: An Interdisciplinary Journal* 7, no. 1 [April 30, 2009]: 180–81). See also Chris Beneke, *Beyond Toleration: The Religious Origins of American Pluralism* (New York: Oxford University Press, 2006), 190–91.

20. Wilson, "Religion Under the State Constitutions, 1776–1800," 770, table 1.

21. John Dichtl, *Frontiers of Faith: Bringing Catholicism to the West in the Early Republic* (Lexington: University Press of Kentucky, 2008), esp. 96; Jonathan D. Sarna, *Juda-

ism in America: A History (New Haven, Conn.: Yale University Press, 2004), 40; Joseph Agonito, "Ecumenical Stirrings: Catholic-Protestant Religions During the Episcopacy of John Carroll," *Church History* 45, no. 3 (September 1976): 362; on Benjamin Franklin's ecumenical church contributions, see David L. Holmes, *The Faiths of the Founding Fathers* (New York: Oxford University Press, 2006), 56.

22. As late as 1777, William Tennent gestured toward the larger significance of church building when he contrasted the unfair treatment meted out by the existing law, which "builds superb churches for the one" while "it leaves the others to build their own churches." See William Tennent, "Writings of the Reverend William Tennent, 1740–1777," ed. Newton B. Jones, *South Carolina Historical Magazine* 61, no. 4 (1960): 199.

23. Field Horne, ed., *The Diary of Mary Cooper: Life on a Long Island Farm, 1768–1773* (Oyster Bay, N.Y.: Oyster Bay Historical Society, 1981). On the use of Protestant buildings by Roman Catholics for Mass, see Agonito, "Ecumenical Stirrings," 360–61.

24. Davis, *Religion and the Continental Congress*, 68.

25. Delegates quoted in Davis, *Religion and the Continental Congress*, 74.

26. For a good account of Christian deism among the founders, see Holmes, *Faiths of the Founding Fathers*.

27. John Adams to Benjamin Rush, November 11, 1807, *Old Family Letters: Copied from the Originals for Alexander Biddle*, Series A (Philadelphia: J. B. Lippincott, 1892), 170.

28. Brockwell, *Brotherly Love Recommended* (Boston, 1750), 13–14.

29. Cited in Boller, "George Washington and Religious Freedom," *William and Mary Quarterly*, 3rd ser., 17, no. 4 (October 1960): 51.

30. Washington to the Hebrew Congregation in Newport, Rhode Island, August 18, 1790, in *The Papers of George Washington: Presidential Series*, ed. Dorothy Twohig, 9 vols. (Charlottesville: University Press of Virginia, 1996), vol. 6, 286, n. 285.

31. *Virginia Gazette*, August 24, 1776 [Dixon and Hunter].

32. For examples, see Shelby M. Balik, "Equal Right and Equal Privilege," 39–40; and Eric Baldwin, "'The Devil Begins to Roar': Opposition to Early Methodists in New England," *Church History* 75, no. 1 (March 2006): 94–119.

33. Whitefield, quoted in Mary Augustina Ray, *American Opinion of Roman Catholicism in the Eighteenth Century* (New York: Octagon Books, 1974), 82.

34. William Livingston, *The Independent Reflector*, ed. Milton M. Klein (Cambridge, Mass.: Belknap Press of Harvard University Press, 1963), 183.

35. Davis, *Religion and the Continental Congress*, 153.

36. Peter Clarke and James Lowell Underwood, "Bishop John England and the Compatibility of the Catholic Church and American Democracy," in *The Dawn of Religious Freedom in South Carolina*, ed. Underwood and W. Lewis Burke (Columbia: University of South Carolina Press, 2006), 190.

37. Davis, *Religion and the Continental Congress*, 153.

38. See Charles H. Metzger, "Chaplains in the American Revolution," *Catholic Historical Review* 31 (April 1945): 35–36. For more on Roman Catholics in the American Revolution, see Maura Jane Farrelly, "Papist Patriots: Catholic Identity and Revolutionary Ideology in Maryland" (Ph.D. diss., Emory University, 2002).

39. Cite Charles P. Hanson, *Necessary Virtue: The Pragmatic Origins of Religious Liberty in New England* (Charlottesville: University Press of Virginia, 1998).

40. Hanson, *Necessary Virtue*, 192.

41. *A Draught of an Overture, Prepared and Published By a Committee of the Associate Reformed Synod* (Philadelphia, 1787), 118.

42. Oscar Handlin, *Boston's Immigrants: 1790–1880* (Cambridge, Mass.: Belknap Press of Harvard University Press, 1979), 180.

43. *Herald of Freedom*, June 24, 1791.

44. Carroll to Charles Plowden, June 11, 1791, in *The John Carroll Papers*, ed. Thomas O'Brien Hanley, 2 vols. (Notre Dame: University of Notre Dame Press, 1976), vol. 1, 505.

45. *Maryland Gazette*, September 29, 1785.

46. William Warner, *At Peace with All Their Neighbors: Catholics and Catholicism in the National Capital, 1787–1860* (Washington, D.C.: Georgetown University Press, 1994), esp. 16–30.

47. See especially Margaret C. DePalma, *Dialogue on the Frontier: Catholic and Protestant Relations, 1793–1883* (Kent, Ohio: Kent State University Press, 2004); and Dichtl, *Frontiers of Faith*; see also Margaret Abruzzo, "Apologetics of Harmony: Mathew Carey and the Rhetoric of Religious Liberty," *Pennsylvania Magazine of History and Biography* 134, no. 1 (January 2010): 5–30; Agonito, "Ecumenical Stirrings"; Andrew Stern, "Southern Harmony: Catholic-Protestant Relations in the Antebellum South," *Religion and American Culture: A Journal of Interpretation* 17, no. 2 (summer 2007): 165–90; Chris Beneke, "'Mingle with Us': Religious Integration in Eighteenth- and Nineteenth-Century American Education," *American Educational History Journal* 33, no. 1 (June 2006): 29–37.

48. Stephen Theodore Badin, "Origin and Progress of the Missions of Kentucky," *Catholic World* 21 (September 1875): 830–31.

49. Randall M. Miller, "Catholics in a Protestant World: The Old South Example," in *Varieties of Southern Religious Experience*, ed. Samuel S. Hill (Baton Rouge: Louisiana State University Press, 1988), esp. 121–27; Randall M. Miller, "Catholic Religion, Irish Ethnicity, and the Civil War," in *Religion and the American Civil War*, ed. Harry S. Stout and Charles Reagan Wilson (New York: Oxford University Press, 1998), 261–96; Stern, "Southern Harmony."

50. Emmett Curran, *The Bicentennial History of Georgetown University*, vol. 1, *From Academy to University, 1789–1889* (Washington, D.C.: Georgetown University Press, 1993), esp. 26.

51. Guilday, *The Life and Times of John Carroll: Archbishop of Baltimore (1735–1815)* (Westminster, Md.: Newman Press, 1954), 458.

52. Patrick Carey, ed., *American Catholic Religious Thought* (New York: Paulist Press, 1987), 9.

53. Clarke and Underwood, "Bishop John England," 188.

54. See Agonito, "Ecumenical Stirrings," 365–66.

55. William Warner details a long tradition of Catholic intermarriage in Maryland; see *At Peace with All Their Neighbors*, 41–42.

56. "John Carroll to Ferdinand Farmer [Dec. 1784]," in *The John Carroll Papers*, ed. Hanley, vol. 1, 156.

57. Ibid., vol. 1, 157.

58. John England, "The Republic in Danger," in *The Works of the Right Rev. John England: First Bishop of Charleston*, vol. 4, part 3 (J. Murphy & Company, 1849), 33.

59. John England, "Address Before Congress," in *The Works of the Right Reverend John England, First Bishop of Charleston*, ed. Sebastian G. Messmer, 7 vols. (Cleveland: Arthur H. Clark, 1908), vol. 7, 32.

60. England, "The Republic in Danger," 42.

61. Francis Patrick Kenrick to John Patrick Spaulding, August 17, 1855, 34 J24, Associated Archives at St. Mary's Seminary and University.

62. Jay Dolan, *In Search of American Catholicism: A History of Religion and Culture in Tension* (New York: Oxford University Press, 2002), 58.

63. Tracy Fessenden, *Culture and Redemption: Religion, the Secular, and American Literature* (Princeton, N.J.: Princeton University Press, 2007), 61; and David Sehat, "The American Moral Establishment: Religion and Liberalism in the Nineteenth Century" (Ph.D. diss., University of North Carolina–Chapel Hill, 2007).

64. Although by 1829, Eric R. Schlereth observes, that it was "common to cast a skeptical eye on a range of subjects, from politics to religion, and one could even announce one's atheism and the reasons for this position in 'mixed society' or on the streets of ordinary American towns like Utica without automatically inciting personal opprobrium or legal censure" ("Fits of Political Religion: Stalking Infidelity and the Politics of Moral Reform in Antebellum America," *Early American Studies: An Interdisciplinary Journal* 5, no. 2 [2007]: 321).

65. Historian Paul Gilje notes that public officials in early national New York City demonstrated little patience for religious mobbing: "regardless of the religious orientation of the churches threatened by mobs, the magistrates acted to defend the principle of religious freedom and to demonstrate the reinvigorated desire to maintain public order" (*The Road to Mobocracy: Popular Disorder in New York City, 1763–1834* [Chapel Hill: Published for the Institute of Early American History and Culture by the University of North Carolina Press, 1987], 209–11). Similar protections were offered to Catholics during Philadelphia's school wars of the early 1840s. See Vincent P. Lannie and Bernard C. Diethorn, "For the Honor and Glory of God: The Philadelphia Bible Riots of 1840," *History of Education Quarterly* 8 (spring 1968): 44–106.

66. Stanley F. Cheyt, "The Political Rights of the Jews in the United States: 1776–1840," *American Jewish Archives* 10 (1958): 66–67.

67. For the accommodations made by Jews, see Richard and Belinda Gergel, "'A Bright Era Now Dawns upon Us': Jewish Economic Opportunities, Religious Freedom, and Political Rights in Colonial and Antebellum South Carolina," in *The Dawn of Religious Freedom in South Carolina*, ed. Underwood and Burke, 77; and Jonathan D. Sarna, "The Impact of the American Revolution on American Jews," *Modern Judaism* 1 (1981): 155.

68. Though, as Ryan K. Smith details, a surprising number of Protestant churches took on the trappings of Catholic churches after the 1820s. See Smith, *Gothic Arches, Latin Crosses: Anti-Catholicism and American Church Designs in the Nineteenth Century* (Chapel Hill: University of North Carolina Press, 2006).

CHAPTER 12. THE BOUNDARIES OF TOLERATION AND TOLERANCE

1. *General Remarks, on the Proceedings Lately Had in the Adjacent Country, Relative to Infidelity* (Newburgh, N.Y.: David Denniston, 1798), quotations on 21, 10, 45. John Wood, *A Full Exposition of the Clintonian Faction, and the Society of the Colombian Illuminati* (Newark, N.J.: for the author, 1802), compares deism to treason (30); Wood focuses on an allied group in New York City, but David Denniston and Elihu Palmer were leaders of both that and the Newburgh club (later called the "Druids"). See also "A True Declaration of the Character and Principles of the Infidels in Orange County, and Especially those of Newburgh" by "A Countryman," (Newburgh, N.Y.) *Recorder of the Times*, August 3, 1803, which condemned what the author saw as the seeds of an anti-Christian political party, ready to "draw the sword" for power. "From the Palladium. Illuminism," *New-York Evening Post* (October 6, 1802) related the story about the cat baptism and dog communion, later resurrected in "Decline of Infidelity," *Newburgh (N.Y.) Witness*, reprinted in the *Hampshire Gazette* (February 5, 1823), Abner Cunningham, *Practical Infidelity Portrayed and the Judgments of God Made Manifest* (New York: Daniel Cooledge, 1836), 43–47, discussed the bizarre deaths. See also John Johnston, *The Autobiography and Ministerial Life of the Rev. John Johnston* (New York: M. W. Dodd, 1856), 81–93 and appendix B, and E. M. Ruttenber, *History of the Town of Newburgh* (Newburgh, N.Y.: E. M. Ruttenber, 1859), 87–90, 98. The standard account of the group is in G. Adolf Koch, *Republican Religion: The American Revolution and the Cult of Reason* (New York: Henry Holt, 1933), 114–29.

2. For recent studies of late eighteenth-century deism and early nineteenth-century skepticism and freethought, see Christopher Grasso, "Deist Monster: On Religious Common Sense in the Wake of the American Revolution," *Journal of American History* 95, no. 1 (June 2008): 43–68, and Christopher Grasso, "Skepticism and American Faith: Infidels and Converts in the Early Nineteenth Century," *Journal of the Early Republic* 22, no. 3 (fall 2002): 465–508. See also Herbert M. Morais, *Deism in Eighteenth-Century America* (New York: Columbia University Press, 1934); Albert Post, *Popular Freethought in America, 1825–1850* (New York: Columbia University Press, 1943); Martin E. Marty, *The Infidel: Freethought and American Religion* (Cleveland: World Publishing Company, 1961); Henry F. May, *The Enlightenment in America* (New York: Oxford University Press, 1976), 153–362; Marshall G. Brown and Gordon Stein, *Freethought in the United States: A Descriptive Bibliography* (Westport, Conn.: Greenwood Press, 1978); Kerry S. Walters, *Rational Infidels: The American Deists* (Durango, Colo.: Longwood Academic, 1992).

3. Ezra Stiles, *The United States Elevated to Glory and Honor* (New Haven, Conn.: Thomas and Samuel Green, 1783), 52–53, 72, 70, 74; [Zephaniah Swift,] *The Correspondent*

(Windham, Conn.: John Byrne, 1793), 137; Zephaniah Swift, *A System of Laws of the State of Connecticut* (Windham, Conn., 1795–96), vol. 1, 323. This paragraph has been adapted from Grasso, "Deist Monster." For a study of seventeenth-century toleration and liberty of conscience see Andrew R. Murphy, *Conscience and Community: Revisiting Toleration and Religious Dissent in Early Modern England and America* (University Park: Pennsylvania State University Press, 2001).

    4. [John Carroll,] *An Address to the Roman Catholics of the United States of America*, (Annapolis, Md.: Frederick Green, [1784]); [Charles Henry Wharton,] *A Reply to An Address to the Roman Catholics of the United States of America* (Philadelphia: Charles Cist, 1785); "Toleration," *Philadelphia Gazette* (October 14, 1797); John Thayer, *Controversy between the Reverend John Thayer, Catholic Missionary, of Boston, and the Reverend George Leslie, Pastor of a Church, in Washington, New-Hampshire* (George-Town, [D.C.]: Alexander Doyle, 1791) Mason Locke Weems, *The Philanthropist; or, A Good Twenty-Five Cents Worth of Love Powder, for the Honest Adamites and Jeffersonians* (Charleston, S.C., 1799), 26; "On Provision by Law for the Support of Christian Institutions," *Christian Disciple and Theological Review* (September 1, 1820): 368–72.

    5. For "universal toleration" or "toleration, complete and perfect" as religious liberty, broadly construed, see Americanus, "Mr. Jefferson," *National Magazine* (September 1, 1800): 226–335, and "Philadelphia, Sept. 9," *Carolina Gazette* (September 25, 1800). Richard Price, *Observations on the Importance of the American Revolution, and the Means of Making it a Benefit to the World* (London, 1784; rpt. Boston: Powars and Willis, [1784]), 30; Thomas Paine, *The Rights of Man, Part One* (London, 1791; rpt. Philadelphia: Samuel Harrison Smith, 1791), 47; these passages from Price and Paine were excerpted in newspapers; see, for example, "Rights of Man," (Charleston, S.C.) *City Gazette* (June 28, 1791) and "Extract from 'Observation on the Importance of the American Revolution' by Richard Price," *Republican Spy* (April 23, 1804). On toasting cf. [July Forth Toasts in King's County,] *Greenleaf's New York Journal* (July 15, 1795) and "George-town, February 24" [President's Birthday Toasts,] (Baltimore, Md.) *Federal Gazette* (February 27, 1796) (quotation); see also "Revolution Dinner. Crown and Anchor," *New-York Packet* (September 15, 1791).

    6. "The President's Answer. To the Hebrew Congregation, in Newport, Rhode Island," (Boston, Mass.) *Herald of Freedom* (September 7, 1790); William Linn, *Discourses on the Signs of the Times* (New York: Thomas Greenleaf, 1794), 44; William Findley, *Observations on The Two Sons of Oil* (Pittsburgh: Patterson and Hopkins, 1812), responding to Samuel B. Wylie, *The Two Sons of Oil; or, The Faithful Witness for Magistracy and Ministry* (Greensburg, Pa.: Snowden and M'Corkle, 1803); "Liberty—No. XLIX, Extract from a Sermon Delivered Aug. 20, 1812, by John Giles," (Philadelphia) *Herald of Gospel Liberty* (March 5, 1813); "Toleration—Liberality," *Evangelical and Literary Magazine and Missionary Chronicle* (February 1821): 89–93, quotation on 89; "Religious Toleration," *Christian Watchman* (November 16, 1832): 182.

    7. Thomas Jefferson, *Notes on the State of Virginia* (Philadelphia, 1788), 169; Wylie, *Two Sons of Oil*, 15, 40–41, quotation on 40. For a sampling of the debate about Jefferson

and religion, see "Philadelphia, Sept. 9," *Carolina Gazette* (September 25, 1800); *A Vindication of the Religion of Mr. Jefferson and a Statement of his Services in the Cause of Religious Liberty. By a Friend to Real Religion* (Baltimore, Md.: W. Pechin, [1800]); [John M. Mason,] *The Voice of Warning, to Christians, on the Ensuing Election of a President of the United States* (New York: G. F. Hopkins, 1800); [DeWitt Clinton,] *A Vindication of Thomas Jefferson* (New York: David Denniston, 1800); "From the Bee. Advice to Federalists," (Boston.) *Constitutional Telegraph* (February 21, 1801); "From the Boston Chronicle," (Trenton, N.J.) *True American* (May 4, 1801). On Jefferson and religion, see Edwind S. Gaustad, *Sworn on the Altar of God: A Religious Biography of Thomas Jefferson* (Grand Rapids, Mich.: William B. Eerdmans, 1996). For another call for the United States to declare itself a Christian nation and restrict the rights of deists and other infidels see "Indifference to Religion in the Administration of a Government a Great National Sin: Taggart's Fast Sermons," *Utica Christian Magazine* (December 1, 1813): 229–36, (January 1, 1814): 267–71, (February 1, 1814): 310–14.

8. On Denniston and Palmer at Newburgh, see "Theistical Society," *Philadelphia Gazette* (September 21, 1802); on a libel suit that cost Denniston $500, see "Mr. David Denniston," *National Intelligencer* (August 18, 1802) and *Connecticut Journal* (August 19, 1802), the latter describing a large crowd of spectators at the trial and citing the New York *Evening Post* as its source; on Cheetham's denial that he is actively promoting deism, see *New-York Herald* (September 15, 1802) and *Evening Post* (September 20, 1802); on Denniston's more limited denial of the promotion of deism, see *New-York Herald* (September 22, 1802) and *Evening Post* (September 28, 1802); on the link between the Newburgh and New York City deist societies, see "From the Palladuim. Illuminism," *Evening Post* (October 6, 1802); on the dissolution of the Cheetham-Denniston partnership, see *American Citizen* (April 4, 1803); on Denniston's difficult financial situation, as revealed in testimony in another libel suit, see *Evening Post* (May 11, 1803); on criticism of Denniston and his plans to move back to Newburgh, see "Extract of a Letter from a Gentleman in Orange County, March 10, to His Friend in This City," *Evening Post* (March 24, 1803); for notice and criticism of Denniston's new paper, see "Rights of Man," *Evening Post* (June 14, 1803); on *Denniston v. Coles* and Gardner's decision, see *Evening Post* (July 22, 1803), an account reprinted in many papers. The Denniston-Coles feud was played out in the *Rights of Man* and the *Recorder of the Times* from the end of June through September 1804, and then somewhat less regularly through an issue of the *Recorder* published a day after Denniston's death (December 14, 1803). Although he is mentioned in passing in several studies, there is no scholarship focused on Denniston; on his partner James Cheetham see Steven C. Smith, "'The Art of Printing Shall Endure': Journalism, Community, and Identity in New York City, 1800–1810" (M.A. thesis, University of Missouri–Columbia, 2007), chap. 2.

9. On the *Denniston v. Coles* appeal, see *Recorder of the Times* (September 14, 1803); the fullest account of the arguments was published in the *Rights of Man* and reprinted as "From the Newburgh Rights of Man. Orange County Common Pleas," *American Citizen* (September 23, September 27, and October 14, 1803). This account summarizes the argu-

ment from one of Denniston's lawyers (W. Ross), apparently using Ross's notes; the arguments from Coles's attorneys are inferred from Ross's response.

10. J.A.B., "Qualification of Witnesses. Ought Any Man to be Excluded from Bearing Witness, on the Ground of Religious Belief?" *Christian Review* (December 1, 1836): 479–502, quotations on 479, 489, 482. "Qualification of Witnesses," *Trumpet and Universalist Magazine* (January 28, 1837): 126, praised the essay and speculated that it was written by a member of the Suffolk bar.

11. J.A.B., "Qualification of Witnesses," quotations on 490, 485, 486, 488. For another argument against the exclusion of atheists see "Review of New Publications: Bates's Christian Politics," *Christian Observer* (August 1806): 482–93 and (October 1806): 621–35.

12. "Law Case," *Religious Remembrancer* (November 21, 1818): 51–52.

13. "The People Against Ruggles: Judgment Affirmed," *Christian Visitant* (November 18, 1815), 193–95. On blasphemy cases and the common law, see Stuart Banner, "When Christianity was Part of the Common Law," *Law and History Review* 16, no. 1 (1998): 27–62, and Sarah Barringer Gordon, "Blasphemy and the Law of Religious Liberty in Nineteenth-Century America," *American Quarterly* 52, no. 4 (2000): 682–719. Banner persuasively argues that the common law argument made little difference to the legal logic deciding the cases but he fails to see the political power of such discussions outside the courtroom. Gordon exaggerates in the other direction, however, when she claims that blasphemy jurisprudence "elevated legists into enforcers of Christian doctrine" became "a proven mechanism for the management of religious dissent" and vanquished deists and freethinkers (702, 707, 699).

14. "Communications. Prossimo," *Free Enquirer* (December 3, 1828). On Robert Dale Owen see *Robert Dale Owen, a Biography* (Cambridge, Mass.: Harvard University Press, 1940), and on Frances Wright see Celia Morris, *Fanny Wright: Rebel in America* (Urbana: University of Illinois Press, 1984). On Kneeland, see Grasso, "Skepticism and American Faith," from which this paragraph has been drawn. See also Roderick S. French, "The Trials of Abner Kneeland: A Study in the Rejection of Democratic Secular Humanism" (Ph.D. diss., George Washington University, 1971); Roderick S. French, "Liberation from Man and God in Boston: Abner Kneeland's Free-Thought Campaign, 1830–1839," *American Quarterly* 32 (1980): 202–21; Robert E. Burkholder, "Emerson, Kneeland, and the Divinity School Address," *American Literature* 58 (March 1986): 1–14. "An Act Against Blasphemy," *Acts and Laws, Passed by the Great and General Court or Assembly of the Commonwealth of Massachusetts* (Boston: Benjamin Edes, 1782), 150, reads in part: "That if any Person shall willfully blaspheme the Holy Name of GOD, by denying, cursing, or contumeliously reproaching GOD, his Creation, Government, or final Judging of the World, or by cursing or reproaching JESUS CHRIST, or the HOLY GHOST, or by cursing, or contumeliously reproaching the Holy Word of GOD, that it, the canonical Scriptures contained in the Books of the Old and New Testaments, or by exposing them, or any part of them, to contempt and ridicule . . . every person so offending, shall be punished by Imprisonment not exceeding Twelve Months" (the act passed July 3, 1782).

15. Pamphlets and court documents related to the case (totaling nearly 600 pages)

have been reprinted in Leonard Levy, ed., *Blasphemy in Massachusetts: Freedom of Conscience and the Abner Kneeland Case* (New York, De Capo Press, 1973). Kneeland's objectionable sentence, originally in a letter to the editor of a Universalist newspaper, is in Kneeland, *An Introduction to the Defense*, in *Blasphemy in Massachusetts*, ed. Levy, 37.

16. "ART. III.—1. Report of the Arguments of the Attorney of the Commonwealth at The trial of Abner Kneeland for Blasphemy . . . (1834), and A Speech delivered before the Municipal Court of the City of Boston, in Defense of Abner Kneeland, on an Indictment for Blasphemy in January Term, 1834. By Andrew Dunlap. Boston, 1834," *Christian Examiner and General Review* (September 1834): 23–43; "Blasphemy—Atheism—Prosecution," *Evangelical Magazine and Gospel Advocate* (April 19, 1834): 125; "Prosecution for Opinions," *Reformer and Christian* (March 1834): 127; "Rights of Conscience," *Catholic Telegraph* (December 10, 1835): 12; "Boston," *Spirit of the Age and Journal of Humanity* (March 6, 1834): 1; "When We Are Strong Enough," *Religious Intelligencer* (December 13, 1834): 456; "Conviction of Abner Kneeland," *Zion's Herald* (November 18, 1835): 182.

17. Kneeland, *A Review of the Trial*, in *Blasphemy in Massachusetts*, ed. Levy, 585; A.A.L., "Marble for the Monument," *Baltimore Monument* (November 26, 1836): 58; Rev. Dr. Beasley, "The Student's Diary: Dedication to the Free-Thinkers," *American Museum of Literature and the Arts* (January 1839): 50–59, quotations on 53–54.

18. "The Influence of Morals on the Happiness of Man, and the Stability of Social Institutions," *Southern Literary Messenger* (March 1838): 145–61; "Blasphemy—Atheism—Prosecution," *Evangelical Magazine and Gospel Advocate* (April 19, 1834): 125–26 (diseased brain); "Are Great Minds Prone to Skepticism?" *New-England Magazine* (August 1835): 87–96; [Orestes Brownson,] *Charles Elwood, or the Infidel Converted* (Boston, 1840); "Tom Paine-ism," *Christian Secretary* (May 6, 1837): 68 (quotation). On infidelity as a disease of the mind see "Rennell on Scepticism, No. 2," *Religious and Literary Repository* (March 25, 1820): 85–88; on infidelity as the result of an undeveloped moral nature see "ART. I.—Review of the Argument in Support of Natural Religion. A Dudleian Lecture, delivered in the Chapel of the University in Cambridge, May 13, 1835. By John Brazer," *Christian Examiner and General Review* (November 1835): 137–62; on doubt as a reflex mental habit, see "Credulity and Incredulity," *Evangelical and Gospel Advocate* (May 5, 1832): 139–40; on calls for pity or kindness see "Review of Duties of Christians Toward Deists," *Christian Disciple and Theological Review* (May 1, 1821): 202–9, and C. S., "Skepticism," *Evangelical Magazine and Gospel Advocate* (June 8, 1833): 180–81.

19. "Infidelity," *Christian Register* (July 18, 1829): 114; "Scepticism and Infidelity," *Christian Secretary* (October 4, 1839): 2–3; M. Stuart, "Article I. The Evidences of the Genuineness of the Gospels, by Andrews Norton," *American Biblical Repository* (April 1838): 265–343; Gardner Jones, "Infidelity—Its Consequences!" *Catholic Telegraph* (June 27, 1834): 244–46; "Natural History of Enthusiasm," *Spirit of the Pilgrims* (May 1830): 256–79, quotation on 277.

20. "Toleration—Its Nature and Influence," *The Yale Literary Magazine. Conducted by the Students of Yale University* (February 1839): 183–91, quotations on 185, 187.

21. "Article 1," *United States Catholic Miscellany* (September 13, 1834): 86.

Contributors

Chris Beneke is Associate Professor of History and Director of the Valente Center for Arts and Sciences at Bentley University. He is the author of *Beyond Toleration: The Religious Origins of American Pluralism* (Oxford, 2006) and is working on a history of educational integration in nineteenth-century America.

John Corrigan is the Lucius Moody Bristol Distinguished Professor of Religion and Professor of History at Florida State University. He is editor of the *Chicago History of American Religion* book series at the University of Chicago Press and co-editor of the journal *Church History*. His recent books include: *Religious Intolerance in America: A Documentary History*, ed. with Lynn Neal; *Religion in American History*, ed. with Amanda Porterfield; and, *Religion in America* (8th ed.), with Winthrop Hudson; and *The Spatial Humanities* (co-edited).

Joyce D. Goodfriend, Professor of History at the University of Denver, is the author of *Before the Melting Pot: Society and Culture in Colonial New York City, 1664–1730* (Princeton, 1992) and editor of *Revisiting New Netherland: Perspectives on Early Dutch America* (Leiden, 2005).

Christopher Grasso is the editor of the *William and Mary Quarterly* and is a Professor of History at the College of William and Mary. His publications include "Deist Monster: On Religious Common Sense in the Wake of the American Revolution," *Journal of American History* 95, 1 (June 2008), 43–68, and "Skepticism and American Faith: Infidels and Converts in the Early Nineteenth Century," *Journal of the Early Republic* 22, 3 (Fall 2002), 465–508.

Christopher S. Grenda is Associate Professor of History at Bronx Community College of the City University of New York. His publications include

"Religious Culture and Natural Rights: Understanding the 'Paradox' of Early America," *Journal of Law and Religion* 22, 2 (2007): 353–96; "Thinking Historically about Diversity: Religion, the Enlightenment, and the Construction of Civic Culture in Early America," *Journal of Church and State* 48, 3 (2006): 567–600; "Revealing Liberalism in Early America: Rethinking Religious Liberty and Liberal Values," *Journal of Church and State* 45, 1 (2003): 131–63.

Susan Juster is Professor of History and Associate Dean for Social Sciences, College of Literature, Science, and the Arts, University of Michigan. She is the author most recently of *Doomsayers: Anglo-American Prophecy in the Age of Revolution* (University of Pennsylvania Press, 2003), and is currently working on a cultural history of religious violence in British North America in the seventeenth and eighteenth centuries.

Ned Landsman is Professor of History at the State University of New York at Stony Brook and author of the forthcoming *Crossroads of Empire: Middle Colonies in the Making of a British Atlantic*, which will be published with the Johns Hopkins University Press. He is also working on a study of the significance of the British Union of 1707 for the North American Colonies.

Andrew R. Murphy is Associate Professor of Political Science at Rutgers University, New Brunswick. He is the author of *Prodigal Nation: Moral Decline and Divine Punishment from New England to 9/11* (Oxford, 2009); and *Conscience and Community: Revisiting Toleration and Religious Dissent in Early Modern England and America* (Penn State, 2001). In addition, he has edited and provided an introduction to *The Political Writings of William Penn* (Liberty Fund, 2002); and co-edited *Religion, Politics, and American Identity: New Directions, New Controversies* (Lexington, 2006); and *Literature, Culture, Tolerance* (Peter Lang, 2009). He is currently at work on a book exploring the life, political career, and political thought of William Penn; and on editing the *Blackwell Companion to Religion and Violence* (forthcoming, 2011).

William Pencak, Professor of History and Jewish Studies at Penn State University, is the author of *Jews and Gentiles in Early America: 1654–1800* (University of Michigan Press, 2005) which was the runner-up for the National Book Award in American Jewish History for that year.

Richard W. Pointer is Professor of History at Westmont College where he holds the Fletcher Jones Foundation Chair in the Social Sciences. He is the author most recently of *Encounters of the Spirit: Native Americans and European Colonial Religion* (Indiana University Press, 2007).

Jon Sensbach is Professor of History at the University of Florida. He is the author most recently of *Rebecca's Revival: Creating Black Christianity in the Atlantic World* (Harvard, 2005) and is working on a study of religious exchanges in the early American South.

Owen Stanwood is Assistant Professor of History at Boston College. He is completing a study titled *For God and Empire: The Glorious Revolution and the Making of British America*, which will be published by the University of Pennsylvania Press.

Index

Acadia, 220, 236
de Acosta, José, 65
Act Concerning Religion (Maryland, 1649), 268
Act of Toleration (England, 1689), 79–80, 123, 204, 318n83
Act of Uniformity (England, 1662), 58, 80, 85
Act of Union (England and Scotland, 1707), 78, 80
Adair, James, 67
Adams, Hannah, 192
Adams, James, 140
Adams, John, 257, 259, 269, 275
Adams, John Quincy, 259–260
Adams, Samuel, 275
Addison, Joseph, 43
African Americans, 2, 4, 14–15, 197–199, 204–206, 210–212, 217; evangelicals and, 208–209; indignities heaped upon, 277; limitations on, 214; religious liberty for, 14, 18, 285; segregation and, 215–216; toleration for, 206–207; violence against, 142. *See also* African American Christianity; African Americans; slavery
African religions, 206, 211
Africans, 5, 174, 196–204, 211, 235
Aikenhead, Thomas, 135
Aines, Katherine, 135
Alison, Francis, 92–93, 250
Allen, Ethan, 300
Allen, Richard, 216, 285
Amalekites, Biblical story of, 12, 54–65, 68–72; Catholics as Amalekites, 56–62, 70–72; Native Americans as Amalekites, 64–65, 68–71
American Episcopal Church, 96
American Indians. *See* Native Americans

American Presbyterian Church, 83–84
American Revolution, 3, 37, 50–51, 269; anti-Catholicism and, 239–240; anti-Semitism and, 252–254; expansion of religious liberty and, 265–266, 270; Jews and, 241–242, 244, 249–250, 252–253, 255, 261; Protestant-Catholic relations during, 279; Quebec Act and, 238–239; religious liberty and, 25–26, 51, 287; restrained anticlericalism of, 273; slavery and, 197
Amsterdam, 27, 119–121, 243; Jews in, 105–106, 108, 111–112, 244; Lutherans in, 103–105. *See also* Netherlands
Anderson, James, 84
Andros, Edmund, 139, 228–229
Anglican Church. *See* Church of England
antiauthoritarianism, 354n65
anti-Catholicism, 15–16, 171, 216, 219–222, 224–226, 229–237, 239–240, 278; Amalekite story and, 56–62, 70–72; American Revolution and, 239–240; Glorious Revolution and, 229; Gunpowder plot and, 224; as ideological glue, 231–234; Native Americans and, 64; in New France, 236; in Pennsylvania, 283; post-Revolutionary decline in, 279–282; Puritans and, 225; Quebec Act and, 239; reemergence of, 282–283; toleration and, 233; violence and, 237. *See also* Catholics
anticlericalism, 160–161, 266, 273, 297
anti-Federalists, 242, 256–257
antipopery. *See* anti-Catholicism
anti-Semitism, 15, 241–242, 252–254, 262; American Revolution and, 249–250; of early U.S. presidents, 259–261; Federalism and, 257; in Georgia, 246; in New Amsterdam, 105–107, 110; in New York, 243–245;

390 *Index*

anti-Semitism (*continued*)
  political, 242; in Rhode Island, 248; stereotypes and, 248; toleration and, 258–259. *See also* Jews
Apess, William, 67
Appleton, Samuel, 69
Arnold, Benedict, 276
atheism, 33, 36, 271, 273, 279; linked to deism, 289, 294
attendance, 17, 306n28
Atwood, William, 244
Augsburg Confession (1530), 100, 104
de Aviles, Pedro Menéndez, 221–222

Backus, Isaac, 48
Bacon's Rebellion (1676), 226, 227
Bale, John, 223
Baltimore, Lord, 162
Bancroft, George, 53
baptism of slaves, 199–210
Baptists, 27, 212–213; American Revolution and, 287; geographical location of, 5; Keithian schism and, 165; in Massachusetts, 45; New Light, 210, 337n50, 212n1; in New Netherland, 112–113; persecution of, 124; racial segregation and, 215; religious taxes and, 319n87; support of Jefferson, 288; toleration of, 204, 267; Washington and, 276
Barbados, 200–201
Barclay, Robert, 157–159
Barsimson, Jacob, 108–109
Barton, Thomas, 247
Bartow, John, 139
Bassaker, Peter, 130
Bayle, Pierre, 33–36
Beneke, Chris, 3, 9, 16, 385; chapter by, 1–20, 265–285
Berkeley, William, 226
Bible, the, 53–55, 56
Bill for Establishing Religious Freedom (Virginia, 1786). *See* Virginia Statute for Religious Freedom (1786)
Billington, Ray Allen, 262
Bill of Rights (U.S. Constitution), 214. *See also* First Amendment
biracial ritual practices, 212, 215
Bishop, George, 115
Blackmore, Richard, 61
Blackstone, William, 292
Blackwell, John, 162

Blair, James, 82–83, 92, 207
blasphemy, 5, 16–17, 123, 125–126, 133–138, 141–142, 186, 284; prosecution for, 131, 295–300. *See also* profanity; religious crime
Boltzius, Johann, 246
Bonner, John, 234
Bosch, Hendrick, 104
Boston Free Enquirers, 297–298
Bowne, John, 117–118, 120
Bradford, William, 152–153, 155, 160
Bradstreet, Anne, 67
Brainerd, David, 68, 177–178
Bray, Thomas, 83
Brazil, 199, 211, 222; Jews from, 105, 111, 243–244, 342n62, 370n1
Brekus, Catherine, 18
Brewster, Margaret, 130
Bridenbaugh, Carl, 76
Bromfield, William, 139
Bronner, Edwin, 144
Brown, John, 169–172
Brownston, Orestes, 300
Bryan, George, 92
Bryan, Hugh, 208–209
Bryan, Jonathan, 213
Buade, Louis, 230
Budd, Thomas, 153, 155, 160
Burgh, James, 44
Burr, Aaron, 292
Bush, Mathias, 248
Busher, Leonard, 27–29, 36
Butler, Jon, 1, 151, 165, 211, 219, 349n4

Calvert, Cecil, 225
Calvert, Charles, 226
Calvert, George, 225–226
Calvert, Jane, 158
Calvinists, 5, 11, 100–101, 222; in England, 30; in New Netherland, 98, 119, 121, 243; Quakers and, 118; Stuyvesant as, 99, 101, 103, 105, 112, 114; Unitarians and, 298
Campbell, Alexander, 63
Canada, 192, 218, 220, 228–229, 238–239, 276; Jews in, 247
Carey, Patrick, 281
Caribbean, 200, 203, 208–210
Caribbean islands, 224–225
Carolina, 82, 183–185, 204, 222. *See also* North Carolina; South Carolina
Carroll, John, 265, 280–282, 284, 289

Carter, Landon, 204
Carter, Robert, 195
de las Casas, Bartolomé, 65, 173, 223
Catholics, 4–5, 218–240, 262; in Africa, 235; as Amalekites, 56–62, 70–72; in Canada, 218, 238–239; Catholic-Protestant struggle and, 15–16; coexistence and, 8; contrasted with infidels, 301–302; disenfranchisement of, 251; electoral disadvantage of, 271; in Europe, 124; expansion of religious liberty and, 277–282, 284–285; in France, 227; French Revolution and, 266; as heretics, 173; as immigrants, 265; intermarriage and, 18–19; intolerance of, 36, 72; liberty of conscience for, 162; in Maryland, 268; Native Americans and, 170, 179–181; in New Spain, 221–226; Penn and, 147; persecution of, 127, 302; prejudice against, 4, 15; purported disloyalty of, 315n58; Quebec Act and, 239; repression of, 229; slavery and, 198–199; toleration of, 28, 265–266, 289; violence against, 216; Washington and, 255. *See also* anti-Catholicism; Protestant-Catholic relations
Chandler, Thomas Bradbury, 89–92, 95
Charles II, 130, 227
Chauncy, Charles, 91–93, 96
Cheetham, James, 292
Christian Indians, 187–190, 229
church-building, 274, 377n22
Church of England, 75–77, 80–96, 267, 273; in America, 82–87, 89, 91–92, 96; American Revolution and, 287; attacks on, 138–139; church-state relations and, 81–82, 87–92; English-Scottish union and, 84–86; intermarriage and, 19; Keithian schism and, 165; as national religion, 90; in Pennsylvania, 149; religious taxes and, 319n87; slavery and, 205; in southern colonies, 4–5; toleration and, 80
Church of Ireland, 91
Church of Scotland, 76, 80–86, 93–94, 96; Act of Union and, 78
church-state relations, 2–3, 52, 272–273; Church of England and, 81–82, 87–92; colleges and, 94; denominational privilege and, 44–45; in early America, 304n6, 325n140; in Massachusetts, 185–186; Quakerism and, 158; toleration and, 267
church vandalism, 37, 138–139

civil rights, 36, 41, 148, 231, 322n116
Clark, John, 30–31, 36
Clarke, Peter, 281
Cobbett, William, 257
Cock, Lacy, 160
Cody, Edward J., 164
coexistence, 8–11, 13, 265–266, 269, 283–284, 305n20; in New Netherland, 99, 112, 118, 121–122; Protestant-Catholic relations and, 279
Cogley, Richard, 186
Cohen, Jacob, 111
Cole, Dennis, 292
de Coligny, Gaspard, 221
College of New York, 43
Colman, Benjamin, 232
common law, 134, 200–202, 231, 238, 292–293, 296–298, 383n13
Condignola, Luca, 66
Congregationalist church, 4, 77, 83–84, 86–87, 269; American Revolution and, 287; geographical location of, 5; Great Awakening and, 93; intermarriage and, 19; religious taxes and, 319n87; toleration and, 267
Connecticut: Congregationalist establishments in, 77, 86; denominational dominance in, 4–5; Native Americans in, 360n44; religious crime in, 124, 126–127; toleration in, 37, 267
conscience. *See* liberty of conscience
contempt of church, 37, 138–141
Conversos, 173
Coode, John, 137, 229
Cook, Arthur, 151
Cooper, Anthony Ashley, 38
Cooper, Mary, 274
Coote, Richard, 230–231
Copeland, John, 130
Cornbury, Lord, 79–80, 82
corporal punishment, 36–37, 43–44; for blasphemy, 134–135; for heresy, 345n8; of Quakers, 346n17; for religious crime, 125–131, 137, 140–141
Corrigan, Jon, 3, 12, 26, 174, 385; chapter by, 53–72
Cotton, John, 156, 174, 186
Cotton, Josian, 190
Craay, Teunis, 107
Crabb, Goody, 136–137
Crabb, Richard, 136
Cranfield, Edward, 228

Crawford, Charles, 67
Creoles, 206–207
crime. *See* religious crime
Cromwell, Oliver, 30, 61–62
cultural diversity, 255
cultural history, 1–2
Cunningham, Abner, 286–289
Curacao, 202
Curry, Thomas, 144
Cutler, Timothy, 86

Dabney, Lewis, 69
D'Acosta, Joseph, 108–110
Danckaerts, Jasper, 227
Dandrada, Salvador, 107–108, 111
Davidson, James West, 72
Davies, Samuel, 209–210, 212, 213
Davis, David Brion, 56
Davis, Derek H., 274, 278
Davis, James, 130
Davis, Silvanus, 230
Declaration of Independence (1776), 277, 293
Defoe, Daniel, 81
deism, 178, 251, 262, 286–289, 299–300; of Jefferson, 291–292; prejudice against, 288, 292–293; synonymous with atheism, 294
Delancey, Oliver, 247
De la Sina, Abram, 110
Delaware, 296
de Lucena, Abraham, 111
Denniston, David, 292–294, 380n1
denominational equality, 45–46, 47. *See also* religious equality
denominational privilege, 44–45
Dewey, Thomas, 130
Dickenson, James, 152
Dickie, Adam, 207
Dickinson, Jonathan, 41–42, 92
disestablishment, 48, 50, 96–97, 216, 349n1
dissent, 11, 76, 124, 140, 145, 157–164, 266–269; in Carolina, 184; in England, 147, 149; limitations on, 3–4; in Pennsylvania, 13–14, 147–149; protection for, 19, 204, 206, 214, 273; punishments for, 5, 8, 16, 26–28, 37, 125; toleration of, 198, 234, 274, 276, 287–288
Drake, Sir Francis, 224
Drisius, Dominie, 113–114, 116
Duché, Jacob, 250
Dustan, Hannah, 230

Dutch Reformed Church, 82, 93, 101, 202–203, 243, 270
Dutch West India Company, 102–103, 105, 112, 120, 202; Jews and, 243–244
Dyer, Mary, 129

Eccles, Solomon, 135
ecclesiastical dependence, 88
ecclesiastical equality, 84, 88, 91. *See also* religious equality
ecumenism, 233–234, 274–275, 285; Protestant-Catholic relations and, 278, 280–281
Edwards, Jonathan, 62, 66
Eggleston, Edward, 53
Eliot, John, 66, 186
emancipation, 213
enfranchisement, 248; of Jews, 249–250, 255
England: conflict with Spain, 223–224; toleration in, 77, 306n24; union with Scotland, 78–87
England, John, 281–283, 284
English Toleration Act (1689), 3, 36, 79–80
Enlightenment, the, 6, 33, 54, 323n128; Enlightenment reasoning for toleration, 24, 26, 32, 36–37, 39, 43, 46–47, 50, 51
Episcopalians, 31–32, 81–82, 87, 91, 94, 96; racial segregation and, 215–216; Scottish, 77, 80–81, 92. *See also* Church of England
Episcopate controversy, 78–79, 93, 95–96
equality. *See* religious equality
evangelical church, 48, 212–213, 277, 284–285, 288; black evangelicals, 197; Great Awakening and, 11, 93; sexual egalitarianism and, 18; slavery and, 208–210, 215

Fawkes, Guy, 58, 233
Feake, Tobias, 116
Federalists, 242, 257–258, 261–262
Fenno, John, 257
Findley, William, 290–291
Finney, Charles Grandison, 63
First Amendment (U.S. Constitution), 3, 142, 270–272, 279, 287, 293; Locke and, 317n78; slavery and, 214, 285
Fisher, Miers, 252–253
Fithian, Philip Vickers, 195–196
Flavel, John, 58
Fletcher, Governor, 155, 162
Florida, 220, 221–223, 234
Flushing Remonstrance, 116, 343n82

Foster, Stephen, 124
Fox, George, 158–159
Foxe, John, 223
France, 60, 220, 223, 226–227, 229–230, 287; American Revolution and, 239–240, 251, 279; Indians as allies to, 64, 180; Jews in, 256–257; religious persecution in, 33; Seven Years' War and, 237
Franklin, Benjamin, 274
Franks, David, 247, 251, 261
Franks, Jacob, 247
Franks, Moses, 247
freedom of worship. *See* religious freedom
Freemasons, 255–256, 275
freethought, 8, 16–17, 299–302; prejudice against, 288; toleration of, 287
Frelinghuysen, Theodore, 180
French and Indian War, 72
French Revolution, 256–257, 266, 287, 292
Frijhoff, Willem, 8
Frost, J. William, 149, 165, 349n4

Garretson, Freeborn, 212
Gatchell, Joseph, 137
Gaustad, Edwin S., 144
genocide, 55–57, 70, 211
Georgetown College, 280–281
Georgia: denominational dominance in, 4–5; immigration to, 234; Jews in, 245–246, 253–254; religious freedom in, 269
Geree, John, 58
Gerry, Eldridge, 239–240
Gibbon, Edward, 294
Gibson, Edward, 206
"Glorious" Revolution (England, 1688–1689), 220, 229, 231–232
Godwyn, Morgan, 205
Goodfriend, Joyce, 4–5, 8, 13, 243, 245, 385; chapter by, 98–122
Gookin, Daniel, 358n34
Gordon, Thomas, 39–40, 43
Gove, Edward, 228
Grasso, Christopher, 3, 8, 25, 385; chapter by, 16–17, 286–302
Gratz, Barnard, 248
"Great Awakening," 11, 93, 179, 190; for Native Americans, 183
Grenda, Christopher S., 12, 16, 259, 385–386; chapters by, 1–20, 23–52
Grimston, Thomas, 130

Gunpowder Plot, 58, 224
Gutwasser, Rev. Johannes, 103

Habersham, James, 213
Hakluyt, Richard, 223–224
Hale, Matthew, 134
Haliday, Thomas, 139
Hall, John, 131
Hallett, William, 113
Hamilton, Alexander, 256–257
Hamilton, William, 251
Handsome Lake, 193
Hanson, Charles, 279
Harrison, James, 149
Helwys, Thomas, 27–29
Henricques, Jacob Cohen, 106, 108
Henry, Patrick, 277
Henry, William, 247
heresy, 34, 124–127, 138, 172–173; executions for, 129; Keith accused of, 151–152, 164; prosecution for, 131, 141; punishment for, 345n8; Quakerism as, 114, 116, 344n97. *See also* religious crime
Heyrman, Christine Leigh, 18
Hindus, 293
Hobart, Noah, 87–88
Hodgson, Robert, 114–115, 117
Holder, Christopher, 130
Holme, John, 160
Holme, Thomas, 163
Hood, Nathan, 189–190
Hooten, Elizabeth, 130
Hughes, Langston, 217
Huguenots, French, 221–222, 225, 226, 228, 233, 320n93; intermarriage and, 18
Hume, David, 24, 294
Huntington, Frederick D., 53
Hutchinson, Anne, 145, 157, 164
Hutchinson, Thomas, 248

immigrants, 175, 242, 249, 257, 302; hostility against, 216, 219, 259; Jews as, 106, 108, 110–112, 260; to New Netherland, 100–101, 119; religious plurality and, 5
imperialism, 75–76
Indians. *See* Native Americans
indifference, 17, 141, 289, 306n28
individual Indians, 182–183, 189–191
infidelity, 271, 273, 287–288, 294; contrasted with Catholicism, 301–302; criticism of, 299–302; prosecution for, 295

interdenominational cooperation, 283, 285
interdenominational mixing, 6, 9–11
intermarriage, 18
inter-religious interaction, 10–11, 269
intolerance, 16, 19–20, 262; Amalekites and, 55; contrasted with toleration, 290; criticism of, 301; in the eighteenth century, 36–37; in Massachusetts, 156–157; narratives of, 8; in New Netherland, 99–100; religious argumentation and, 26; in the seventeenth century, 26–27; story of Amalek and, 72; toward black Christianity, 205; vs. civil intolerance, 281. *See also* tolerance; toleration
Irish Rebellion (1641), 225
Iroquois League, 228
Israel, Israel, 257–258
Israel, John, 258
Israel, Menasseh ben, 66

Jackson, Andrew, 53, 70
Jacobites, 61, 96, 232, 278
Jamaica, 201–203
James II, 147, 162, 228–229, 243
Jarratt, Devereux, 212
Jefferson, Thomas, 48, 50–51, 242; anti-Semitism of, 261; bills introduced by, 50, 319n88; church-state relations and, 272; Jews and, 259–260; on religious liberty, 7–9, 214, 254; reputed deism of, 287–288, 291–292
Jennings, Samuel, 153, 155, 157, 159, 160
Jersey College, 93
Jesuits, 227, 235
Jews, 241–262; as Amalekites, 71; in the American Revolution, 249–250, 252–253; blasphemy laws and, 136; in the British Empire, 247; discrimination against, 279; disenfranchisement of, 250; early nineteenth century attitudes toward, 259–261; electoral disadvantage of, 271; expansion of religious liberty and, 277, 284–285; fear of, 62; Federalism and, 256–258; intermarriage and, 18; intolerance of, 216; intra-Jewish conflict, 24; legal status of, 293; minority status of, 259; Native Americans and, 247; Native Americans as, 65–67; in the Netherlands, 119; in New Netherland, 13, 99, 105–112, 118, 120–122, 342n62; in New York, 243–245; patriotism of, 241–242; prejudice against, 15; Quakers and, 253; Sabbath legislation and, 254; in Spain, 173; stereotypes of, 242, 248, 261–262; toleration of, 28, 265–266, 287; G. Washington and, 255–256, 276. *See also* anti-Semitism
Jogues, Isaac, 119
Johnson, Samuel, 41, 86
Johnson, Sylvester, 211
Jones, Absalom, 216
Jones, Gardner, 301
Jordan, Winthrop, 201
Juster, Susan, 3, 4–5, 13, 18, 26, 159, 246, 386; chapter by, 123–142

Kalm, Peter, 206, 208
Kaplan, Benjamin, 8
Keith, George, 13–14, 150–155; anti-clericalism of, 160–161; trial of, 153–155, 157–160; as victim of persecution, 163–164
Keithian schism, 143–145, 148–149, 151–155, 157, 161, 163–165, 349n4; as religious persecution, 163
Kenrick, Francis Patrick, 283
Kent, James, 296
Kentucky, 280
King, George, 134
King, William, 137
King Philip's War, 182, 188, 193, 227
King William's War, 230
Kneeland, Abner, 288, 297–300
Know-Nothing Party, 283
Kupperman, Karen, 65

Lachaire, Salomon, 117
Lachaire, Simon, 109–110
Lambert, Frank, 270
Landsman, Ned, 12–13, 386; chapter by, 75–97
Lane, Ralph, 224
Laud, William, 225
de Laudonnière, René Goulaine, 222
Lawton, David, 134
Leddra, William, 129
Leisler, Jacob, 244–245
Leland, John, 215
Le Loutre, Jean, 236
de León, Cieza, 65
Leonard, Joseph, 139
Lepore, Jill, 71
Levellers, 29–30, 36
Levy, Asser, 107–110, 112, 341n45, 370n1
Levy, Leonard, 134

Levy, Levy Andrew, 247
Lewis, William, 132–133
liberty of conscience, 19–20, 25, 129, 155–159, 163, 259, 268; for Catholics, 162; contrasted with toleration, 288–290, 349n1; in court of law, 164; in France, 290; inflexibility of, 327n158; Native Americans and, 174; in New Netherland, 101; in Pennsylvania, 154; Protestantism and, 59; slavery and, 198, 216–217; in U.S. Constitution, 292; Washington on, 290. *See also* religious freedom; religious liberty
Linn, William, 290
Livingston, William, 42–44, 94–95, 278
Lloyd, Thomas, 151, 153, 157–158, 160, 352n35
Locke, John, 33–36, 148, 184, 317n78, 318n82, 319n84
Long, John, 68, 176–178
Loockermans, Govert, 117
Lopez, Aaron, 248
Lost Tribes of Israel, 65–67, 71, 331n37
Louisiana, 220
Louis XIV, 226–227
Lovejoy, David, 67
Lovewell, John, 69
Lucena, Moses, 109
de Lucena, Abraham, 108
Lumbrozo, Jacob, 136
Lutherans, 5, 119; in New Netherland, 13, 99, 100–105, 112, 118, 121–122, 243
Luyckersen, Maryn, 109

McComb, John, 153
MacCormack, Sabine, 65
McGarvie, Mark, 270
McLoughlin, William, 26
McLure, David, 247
Madison, James, 48–49, 52, 254, 259, 267, 319n88
Maine, 228
Makemie, Francis, 79, 83–85, 88, 153
Marotti, Arthur F., 59
Marshall, John, 47
Marvell, Andrew, 59–60, 227
Maryland, 8, 254; Catholics in, 225–226; Church of England in, 82–83; denominational dominance in, 4–5; religious crime in, 123, 124, 126–129; slavery in, 200; toleration in, 18, 268
Mason, George, 267
Massachusetts: Congregationalist establishments in, 77, 86; denominational dominance in, 4–5; denominational equality in, 45; intolerance in, 156–157; multi-establishment in, 46–47; Native Americans in, 185–186, 191, 228, 360n44; persecution of Quakers in, 130; religious crime in, 124, 126–127; religious freedom in, 269; slavery in, 197, 205; state support of churches in, 291, 298; toleration in, 37, 267, 289–290
Matanzas massacre, 222–223
Mather, Cotton, 64, 80, 150, 230; anti-Catholicism of, 233, 236; on Native Americans, 66–67, 180; on slavery, 205
Maule, Thomas, 139
Mayhew, Jonathan, 237
Megapolensis, Johannes, 103–104, 113–114, 116, 342n62; anti-Semitism of, 105, 110, 243–244
Melyan, Jacob, 244
Mennonists, 113
Methodists, 6, 209, 259, 299; geographical location of, 5; racial segregation and, 215–216, 285; slavery and, 212–213; support of Jefferson by, 288
Miller, Perry, 54
Miller, William, 193
Minis, Abigail, 254
Minis, Abraham, 254
Minis, Philip, 246
missionaries, 64–67, 173, 199, 230–231, 236; Native Americans and, 170, 174, 177, 179, 182, 185, 187; persecution of, 114–115, 124; slavery and, 200, 203, 209, 214
Mitchell, William, 137
Mohican tribe, 188
Moody, Deborah, 113
Moravians, 209, 212, 215, 255
Mormons, 62, 64, 68, 284; as Amalekites, 70–72
Morris, Robert, 252
Morsicos, 173
Muhlenberg, Henry Melchior, 250–251
multi-establishment, 43, 46–48, 328n162
Murphy, Andrew R., 4–5, 386; chapter by, 143–165
Murray, Robert C., 295–296
Murrin, John, 245
Murton, John, 27, 309n16
Muslims, 173, 287, 293
mutual toleration, 38, 40

Narragansett tribe, 68
Nash, Gary, 154, 349n4
nationalism, 230, 232, 273, 368n30
Native Americans, 2–3, 14–15, 169–194; as Amalekites, 12, 65, 68–71; animosity toward, 192–193; anti-Catholicism and, 64, 234, 239; as Catholics, 179–181, 221; as Christians, 187–190; colonial wars against, 64–65; depopulation of, 179; efforts to evangelize, 170; freedom of worship for, 185–186; healing practices of, 175, 358n32; "heathenism" of, 172, 174, 178–180; as individual Indians, 182–183, 189–191; Jews and, 247; missionaries and, 67, 230–231; as "Papist Indians," 170, 179, 236; as "Plantation Indians," 183–185, 187–189, 191; regulation of behavior of, 360n44; relation to English authority, 182–183; religious beliefs of, 4, 68, 174–179, 182–183, 192–193; religious laws and, 185–187; religious liberty and, 18, 171–172, 192, 194; Spanish cruelty toward, 223; as Ten Lost Tribes, 65–67, 71, 331n37; toleration and, 172–174, 180–181, 193, 204; as "Tribal Indians," 182–183; violence against, 216; wars with American colonists, 228–230
natural rights, 9, 25, 39, 40–41, 214–215, 289; Washington on, 256, 276, 290
Neem, Johan, 269
Neff, Mary, 230
Neolin, 183
Netherlands, the, 98–99, 107, 119, 148, 202–203, 224, 226
New Amsterdam, 243–244; Jews in, 105–112; Lutherans in, 100–105; Quakers in, 112–118. *See also* New Netherland; New York
New England. *See* Connecticut; Massachusetts; New Hampshire; Rhode Island
New England Confederation, 68
New France, 15, 199, 230, 236–240. *See also* Canada; Quebec
New Hampshire, 4–5, 124, 228, 254
New Harmony, 297
New Jersey, 41; Church of England in, 77, 83; Presbyterians in, 95; religious crime in, 124, 128; toleration in, 37
New Jersey College, 95
New Light Baptists, 210, 212, 337n50
New Netherland, 13, 99–100; coexistence in, 8; Jews in, 106, 243; liberty of conscience in, 101; Lutherans in, 102; slavery in, 202–203; toleration and, 121–122. *See also* New Amsterdam; New York
New Smyrna, 238
New Spain, 15, 199, 221–226. *See also* Florida
New York: anti-Catholicism in, 229, 278; Church of England in, 77, 82, 83; church vandalism in, 138–139; common law in, 296; immigration to, 234; Jesuits in, 227; Jews in, 241, 243–245; Lutherans in, 104; Native Americans in, 185; Presbyterians in, 335n25; religious crime in, 124; religious freedom in, 269; slavery in, 203; toleration in, 204. *See also* New Netherland
Nicoll, Benjamin, 95
Noah, Manuel Mordecai, 260
nonconformity, 4–5, 125, 173; as religious crime, 126–127, 129; toleration for, 12, 173
nonpreferentialism, 271–272, 289
nonsectarianism, 16, 271–272, 281, 284
North Carolina, 4–5, 124, 254. *See also* Carolina
Norton, Humphrey, 113, 130
Nova Scotia, 236–237

Oates, Titus, 60, 227
Oglethorpe, James, 235, 245–246
Oldenthorp, Christian, 203
Old Testament, 12, 53–55, 61–63, 71–72, 126
Oliver, Andrew, 248
Oliver, Peter, 248
original intent, 2
Ottolenghe, Joseph, 213
Overton, Richard, 29
Owen, Robert Dale, 288, 297

pagans, 174–175, 197, 201, 293–294; Christainizing of, 67, 203; Native Americans as, 179–180, 186, 188, 191, 193; toleration of, 28–29, 184, 260, 287
Paine, Thomas, 290
Palatine migrants, 234
Palestine, 259–260
Palmer, Elihu, 292, 380n1
Party-Colleges, 94–95
Pastorius, Francis Daniel, 149
Pawquash, 137
Pearce, Roy Harvey, 71
Pencak, William, 3, 15, 386; chapter by, 241–262
Penn, William, 13–14, 32–33, 143–149, 161–162; founding of Pennsylvania by, 148–149;

Keith and, 157; liberty of conscience and, 157–158; on Native Americans, 66; Quakerism of, 144; religious toleration and, 147–148
Pennsylvania, 13–14, 161–163, 204; anti-Catholicism in, 283; common law of, 296; denominational equality in, 45; founding of, 149; Jews in, 248–249, 250–251; liberty of conscience in, 154; Presbyterians in, 335n25; Quakerism in, 144; religious crime in, 124, 295; religious laws in, 4; spiritual freedom in, 77; toleration in, 18, 37, 143–145
Pennsylvania Constitution of 1776, 250–251, 254–255
The People of New York v. Ruggles (1811), 296
Perse, William, 61
persecution, 3, 7, 19, 37, 142, 146–147, 155–157, 270; of Anglicans, 77; of Baptists, 124; biblical reasoning for, 4–12, 309n16; by Catholics, 218, 224; of Catholics, 127, 238, 302, 313n51; of heretics, 172; Keithian schism and, 159, 163–164; post-Revolutionary decline in, 276, 284; private worship and, 13; Protestant-Catholic relations and, 60, 170; of Quakers, 114–115, 124, 129–130, 135–137, 163, 346n17; ridicule as substitute for, 38; of Roger Williams, 163–164; state-sanctioned, 26; toleration and, 28, 30, 39–40. *See also* violence
Pestana, Carla Gardina, 5
Pett, Peter, 32
Phillips, Jonas, 254–255
philo-Semitism, 247
Plantation Indians, 183–185, 187–189, 191
plantation missions, 215
Plowden, Charles, 280
Plumstead, 247
plurality, 34
Pointer, Richard W., 3, 14, 18, 68, 386–387; chapter by, 169–194
Polhemus, J.T., 120
political anti-Semitism, 242, 249–250, 256, 258
political order, 159
Pope's Day rituals, 219, 233
Popish Plot, 148
popish plot literature, 61
Portugal, 173, 199, 224; religious tolerance of, 356n16
powwowing, 187
praying towns, 186–188

Presbyterians, 81, 83–85, 87, 335n25; American Revolution and, 287; colleges and, 93–95; geographical location of, 5; Great Awakening and, 93; intermarriage and, 19; racial segregation and, 215; slavery and, 209, 212; toleration and, 267
Price, Richard, 44–45, 211, 290, 325n139
Priestley, Joseph, 44, 46
profanity, 124–125, 127, 131–133. *See also* blasphemy; religious crime
property restrictions, 5, 267
Protestant-Catholic relations, 15–16, 37, 56, 60, 170, 218–221, 223–224, 301–302; after Seven Years' War, 238–240; during American Revolution, 279; Catholic "disloyalty" and, 315n58; ecumenism and, 278, 280–281; in Europe, 224, 227; Glorious Revolution and, 231–232; toleration and, 173, 178. *See also* anti-Catholicism; Catholics; Protestantism
Protestantism, 131, 225, 271, 302; anti-Catholicism and, 219–220, 232–233, 302; coexistence and, 8–9; geographical location of, 5; intermarriage and, 18–19; liberty of conscience and, 59, 155; in Massachusetts, 289, 298; Native Americans and, 188–189; Quakerism as, 150; religious liberty and, 6; toleration and, 147
Protestant revivals, 208
Public Friends, 151–152, 159–161
public office, religious tests for, 17, 27, 36, 39–40, 254, 319n85; arguments against, 30–31; Dickinson on, 42; U.S. Constitution and, 270–272
public opinion, 27, 30, 301
public practice, 7
Pufendorf, Samuel, 33, 36
Puritans, 64, 86, 100, 176, 186, 225; in England, 56–57, 62, 132; Jews and, 67; Mather as, 66; Native Americans and, 69–70; Quakers and, 114, 130, 136, 150, 158, 163; religious crime and, 123–124, 126–127, 131, 134

Quakers, 273; anti-authoritarianism of, 354n65; disenfranchisement of, 250–251; effect of Keithian schism on, 163–165; geographical location of, 5; Jews and, 253; Keith as, 150–151; Keithian Schism and, 143–145, 151–155; legal status of, 293; liberty of conscience and, 155, 158–159; in the

Quakers (*continued*)
Netherlands, 119; in New Netherland, 13, 99, 112–118, 243; Penn as, 143–144; in Pennsylvania, 13–14, 149–150; persecution of, 114–115, 124, 129–130, 135–137, 346n17; as privileged group in Pennsylvania, 161–162; religious taxes and, 319n87; slavery and, 205; sympathy for Catholics of, 221; toleration of, 204, 267; Washington and, 255, 276
Quebec, 218, 238–239
Quebec Act (1774), 218, 238–239, 278
Queen Anne's War, 180

rational dissenters, 44–46
rationalism, 273
Read, Phillip, 136
religious authority, 131, 151, 159, 182, 376n19
religious civility, 273, 275
religious crime, 4–5, 13–14, 123–142; categories of, 125; contempt of church as, 138–141; executions for, 129–130, 135; Native Americans and, 185–187; penalties for, 35–36, 127–128, 130–131; prosecution of, 131, 159, 295–300; sacrilegious speech as, 132–138. *See also* blasphemy; church vandalism; corporal punishment; heresy; Sabbath breaking
religious diversity, 1–2, 11, 56, 78, 170, 219, 234, 271; on Long Island, 118; in Pennsylvania, 149, 165; in port cities, 17–18; religious freedom and, 192, 285
religious equality, 16, 171, 189; denominational equality as, 45–46, 47; ecclesiastical equality as, 84, 88, 91; for Jews, 284; slavery and, 206, 212–213, 266
religious freedom, 18, 20, 142, 184, 216–217, 261, 270, 302, 379n65; Brown on, 169, 171; contrasted with toleration, 268, 289–291; Jefferson's Virginia Statute on, 3, 7, 50, 214, 254, 293, 305n17, 319n88; limits of, 228; Locke and, 317n78; Native Americans and, 178, 181, 192, 194; religious diversity and, 192; slavery and, 14–15, 216–217. *See also* liberty of conscience; religious liberty
religious historians, 303n2
religious inequality, 6, 44
religious laws. *See* religious crime
religious liberty, 6–8, 19–20, 40, 169, 284; for African Americans, 285; American Revolution and, 25–26, 51; Catholicism and, 281; coexistence and, 9–10; contrasted with toleration, 30, 268–269, 276–277, 288–291; debate over, 37; expansion of, 265–266, 269–271, 277–282; French Revolution and, 287; intolerance and, 262; Native Americans and, 171–172, 185–186; for racial minorities, 18; in Rhode Island, 268; sectarianism and, 51–52; theories of, 36; toleration and, 267; women and, 18–19. *See also* liberty of conscience; religious freedom
religious taxation, 36, 37, 39–40; arguments against, 28, 30, 48, 311n28; Church of England and, 91; criticism of, 31; exemptions from, 319n87; Livingston on, 43; in Massachusetts, 45, 48; Price on, 325n139; Priestley on, 46; punishments for nonpayment of, 5; single *vs.* multi-establishment, 328n162; in Virginia, 47–51
republicanism, 2, 142, 197, 272–273, 282–283, 286, 288
Rhode Island, 31, 256; Jews in, 248; religious crime in, 4, 124; religious liberty in, 268; toleration in, 37
Ribault, Jean, 222–223
Ribiero, Nunes, 245
Rind, William, 266
Robinson, William, 129
Rogers, John, 135
Roman Catholics. *See* Catholics
Rouse, John, 130
Rowlandson, Mary White, 63–64
Rush, Benjamin, 272
Russell, John, 140

Sabbath laws, 4, 5, 125, 127–128, 131, 138, 140–141, 284; Jews and, 254; Native Americans and, 18, 360n44
sacred reasoning for toleration, 12, 28, 31, 46, 51, 128
sacrilegious speech, 131–138. *See also* blasphemy; heresy
St. Augustine, Florida, 222–224, 234–35
Salomon, Haym, 252–253, 261
Salvador, Francis, 246
Salzburgers, 234
Sargent, Lucius M., 298
Sawser, Benjamin, 133–134
science of politics, 31
Scotland, 77, 96, 150; union with England, 78–87. *See also* Church of Scotland
Scott, Jonathan, 59
Scott, Thomas, 59

Seabury, Samuel, 96
secular reasoning for toleration, 24, 32–33, 36, 39, 43, 46, 51, 128
sedition, 158, 163, 273; heresy as, 126, 138
segregation, 212, 215–216, 277, 305n20
Seixas, Gershom Mendes, 261
Seixas, Moses, 256
Sensbach, Jon, 3, 14, 18, 277, 387; chapter by, 195–217
"separate" churches, 6
Seven Years' War (1756–1763), 169, 237, 278
Sewall, Samuel, 66, 205
sexual egalitarianism, 18
Shabash, 188
Shaftesbury, Earl of, 38, 40, 320
Shakers, 284, 376n19
Sheftall, Levi, 253
Sheftall, Mordecai, 253, 261
Sherburne, Henry, 256
Silvester, Nathaniel, 135
Simon, Joseph, 247
skepticism, 8, 16–17, 288, 299–302; toleration of, 287
slander, 125, 131, 133, 159
slave codes, 200–202
slavery, 3, 14–15, 196–217; African religions and, 211; anti-Catholicism and, 234; baptism and, 199–210; biblical justification for, 54; Catholics and, 221; evangelical church and, 208–209; religious liberty and, 285; slaves as Christians, 196–217, 266; toleration and, 198
Slotkin, Richard, 71
Sloughter, Henry, 245
Sluyter, Peter, 227
Smith, Adam, 219
Smith, Arthur, 137–138
Smith, Joseph, 193
Smith, William, 93
Smyth, John, 27
social thought, 26
Society for Promoting Christian Knowledge (SPCK), 83
Society for the Propagation of the Gospel (SPG), 83, 185
South Carolina, 234; anti-Catholicism in, 278; denominational dominance in, 4–5; interdenominational mixing in, 6; Jews in, 246, 253–254; religious liberty in, 269; slavery in, 201, 209. See also Carolina
Spain, 173, 199, 251; conflict with England, 223–224; domination of the Americas by, 222–224; religious toleration of, 356n16. See also New Spain
spiritual equality, 212–213
Stamp Act, 91
Stanwood, Owen, 25, 278, 387; chapter by, 15–16, 218–240
Steele, Richard, 43
Steenwyck, Cornelis, 117–118, 120
Stern, Andrew, 281
Stevenson, Marmaduke, 129
Stiles, Ezra, 93, 288–289, 300
Stockdale, William, 151
Stone, Nathan, 72
Strong, Leonard, 225
Stuart, Moses, 301
Stuyvesant, Petrus, 13, 99–121; anti-Semitism of, 110, 112; Baptists and, 113; intolerance of, 99, 119–121, 243–244; Lutherans and, 101–104; Quakers and, 114–118
suffrage, 241, 270
Sumner, William Graham, 53
Swarton, Hannah, 230
Swift, Zephaniah, 289
Symmes, Thomas, 69

Talbot, John, 141
taxation. See religious taxation
Taylor, Thomas, 57
Tennent, William, 6
Tenskwatawa, 193
Terry, Samuel, 139
Test Act (1673), 319n85
Thayer, John, 289
Theodore, Steven, 280
Thirty Years' War (1618–1648), 26, 32–33, 60
Thornhill, Thomas, 133
Thorowgood, Thomas, 66
tolerance, 287. See also toleration
toleration, 3–4, 12, 19–20, 265–268, 285, 287; of African religion, 206; Amalekites and, 55; anti-Catholicism and, 219, 233; anti-Semitism and, 258–259; Bayle on, 34, 36; of black Christianity, 206–207; Busher on, 29; of Catholics, 225, 302; Church of England and, 77; civility and, 275; coexistence and, 8–10; in colonial America, 124; contrasted with intolerance, 290; contrasted with religious liberty, 30, 268–269, 276–277, 288–291; Cooper on, 38; in early modern England, 306n24; economic advantage

400 *Index*

toleration (*continued*)
 of, 244; in Europe, 266; in France, 290; Helwys on, 27–29; indifference and, 17; of infidels, 300; of Jews, 241, 243–246, 259; liberty of conscience and, 349n1; Livingston on, 42–43; Locke on, 35–36, 319n84; Murton on, 309n16; narratives of, 284; Native Americans and, 68, 172–174, 176, 180–181, 193, 204; in the Netherlands, 98–99, 119; in New Netherland, 100, 120–122; Penn on, 32–33, 147–148; post-revolutionary rise in, 11; Protestant-Catholic relations and, 173, 178; public discussion of, 23–24; Pufendorf on, 33; for Quakers, 115–116; reasoning processes for, 24–25; religious equality and, 266–267; sectarianism and, 51–52; Shaftesbury on, 38; slavery and, 14–15, 198, 216–217; Spanish and, 356n16; Trenchard and Gordon on, 39–40; universal, 289–290; Washington as champion of, 255, 275–276
Tolerationists, 156
town and parish studies, 10–11
Townsend, Henry, 115
traders, 175–176
Treaty of Paris, 238
Treaty of Utrecht (1713), 236
Trenchard, John, 39–40, 43
Trent, William, 247
Tribal Indians, 182–183
Trinity Church, 94, 138, 140
Turnbull, Andrew, 238
two kingdoms doctrine, 27, 33, 41, 49
two swords doctrine, 27, 29, 31

Underwood, James Lowell, 281
Union of Utrecht (1579), 101
Unitarians, 260, 298–299
United States Constitution, 270–271, 273, 287; liberty of conscience and, 292. *See also* First Amendment (U.S. Constitution)
Universalists, 294, 299–300
universal toleration, 268, 289–290
Ursuline Convent, 302
Ury, John, 235

van Hooghte, Frans Jans, 110
Van Tienhoven, Cornelis, 110
Vaughan, Alden T., 65, 66
de la Vega, Garcilaso, 65

violence, 17, 236; Amalekites and, 55–56; anti-Catholicism and, 60, 237; against Catholics, 216; against Jews, 251–252; against Native Americans, 65, 193, 216; in New Spain, 221–222; post-Revolutionary, 284; against Quakers, 115–115, 129–130; religious crime and, 134; Sabbath-breaking and, 138. *See also* corporal punishment; persecution
Virginia, 47–51, 224–225; anti-Catholicism in, 278; Church of England in, 82–83, 92; denominational dominance in, 4–5; Native Americans in, 185; religious crime in, 124; religious freedom in, 267; slavery in, 196–197, 200–201, 206–209
Virginia Bill of Rights, 267
Virginia Declaration of Rights, 277
Virginia Statute for Religious Freedom (1786), 3, 7, 50–51, 254, 293, 305n17, 319n88; slavery and, 214

Wabanaki tribe, 180
Wallis, Ralph, 24
Walpole, Horatio, 76
Walsham, Alexandra, 8
Walwyn, William, 29, 156
Wardel, Lydia, 130
Warner, William, 18
War of the Spanish Succession, 234
Washington, George, 47, 242, 255–256, 262, 275–277, 290
Watts, John, 247
Waugh, Dorothy, 114
Weatherhead, Mary, 113–114
Weems, Mason Locke, 289
Wesley, John, 246
Wessels, Warnaer, 109
Westminster Confession (1787), 376n17
Wetmore, James, 41, 86–88, 191
Weyberg, Caspar, 250
White, Ellen Gould, 63
Whitefield, George, 61, 208, 213, 232, 278
Whittier, John Greenleaf, 62
Wickenden, William, 113
Wightman, Edward, 129
Willard, Samuel, 150
Williams, Roger, 30–31, 36, 127, 156, 163–164, 174; on Native Americans, 66–67
Williams, Zebadiah, 140
Williamson, Atkinson, 347n24
Wilson, Deborah, 130

Wilson, Thomas, 152
Winningham, Francis, 126
Winthrop, John, 62
witchcraft, 138, 178
Witherspoon, John, 327n158
Wolf, Abraham, 254
women: religious liberty and, 18–19

Woodmason, Charles, 139
Wright, Frances, 288, 297, 300
Wylie, Samuel B., 291

xenophobia, 283. *See also* immigrants

Zionism, 259–260

www.ingramcontent.com/pod-product-compliance
Lightning Source LLC
Chambersburg PA
CBHW051204300426
44116CB00006B/434